IRISH SECRETS

IRISH SECRETS

GERMAN ESPIONAGE
in IRELAND

1939–1945

Mark M. Hull

Saint Louis University, Missouri

IRISH ACADEMIC PRESS
DUBLIN • PORTLAND, OR

First published in 2003 in by
IRISH ACADEMIC PRESS
44 Northumberland Road, Dublin 4, Ireland

and in the United States of America by
IRISH ACADEMIC PRESS
c/o ISBS, 5824 N.E. Hassalo Street, Portland
Oregon 97213-3644

Website: www.iap.ie

British Library Cataloguing in Publication Data

A catalogue record of this book is available from the
British Library

ISBN 0-7165-2756-1

Library of Congress Cataloging-in-Publication Data

A catalog record of this book is available from the
Library of Congress

Typeset by Variorum Publishing Limited, Lancaster and Rugby, UK

Printed by MPG Books Ltd, Bodmin, Cornwall

Contents

Tables

Photographs

Appendices

Foreword

Presenting the reader with a great wealth and variety of information, this fascinating book examines the claimed, the suspected and the actual activities of members of German intelligence services during the Second World War in Ireland, a nation that remained neutral despite its status as a member of the British Commonwealth.

The myth of an extensive and secret German–Irish brotherhood of German spies in Ireland working against the Allied Powers, which was all the more dangerous because its activities were not suppressed with sufficient vigour, survived long after the war had ended. The idea of this secret brotherhood was spread by people who simply took it at face value, but also by some who were motivated by malicious intent, such as the famous British novelist Nicholas Monsarrat who boldly claimed in his best-selling novel *The Cruel Sea* that 'Irish neutrality, on which she placed a generous interpretation, permitted the Germans to maintain in Dublin an espionage centre, a window into Britain, which operated throughout the war and did incalculable harm to the Allied cause'. There was a growing anger in the Western democracies that little Ireland had the audacity to remain neutral in this worldwide struggle, even refusing to let the Allies use its navy ports (only recently turned over by the English in 1938) to combat German submarines. It was this very anger that induced persons and institutions, including some that should have known better, to keep the evil myth of German–Irish cooperation alive.

This resentment is clearly reflected in the note presented to the Irish government by the American envoy in Dublin, David Gray, on 21 February 1944. Like a lightning bolt coming out of a blue sky, and in unusually harsh terms, the note demanded the expulsion of the German and Japanese diplomats still accredited in Ireland. The explanation given in this document was as rude as it was false: it stated that Ireland's neutrality favoured the Axis powers unilaterally, because the geographic location of the island enabled them to engage in highly organized espionage activities directed against the United States. Since the border between Northern and Southern Ireland was hard to protect, Axis agents would be able to take military information vital for England and the US to Southern Ireland virtually unimpeded, and were able to transmit it from there back to Germany in a number of ways. Even though the Allies claimed that they did not doubt the good intentions of the

Irish regarding the termination of these spy activities, they felt that they could not at all be certain whether, and to what extent, the Irish government had been successful in this endeavour.

What made this American message particularly insulting was its deliberate disregard of a fact well known in Washington, i.e. that the Irish and British secret services had been discreetly cooperating in unmasking German spies since the beginning of the war; that all couriers sent by Germany had long since been put under lock and key; and that there had been no chance for clandestine radio traffic between Ireland and Germany for quite some time now.

It is not surprising, then, that the tone of Eamon de Valera's reply of 7 March 1944 – after curtly refusing to comply with the American demand – reveals a certain sense of irritation. The Prime Minister wrote:

> From the beginning of the war, by the establishment of strong observation and defence forces, by a wide and rigorous censorship of the Press and of communications, by an extensive anti-espionage organization, and by every other means in our power, we have endeavoured to prevent any leakage through Ireland. ... American officials have had an opportunity of seeing the measures which have been taken – they have indeed made favourable comments on their effectiveness. ... The transmitter in the German Embassy, Dublin, had not been used for a long time and for some months had been in the custody of the Irish government. The total number of person held in Irish prisons under suspicion of espionage was ten foreigners and two Irish nationals. These are the facts and it is doubtful if any other country can show such a record of care and successful vigilance.

Indeed, these were the facts, and when the Second World War in Europe ended a year later with the unconditional surrender of the Wehrmacht on 8 May 1945, the Irish counter-espionage organizations – the military intelligence service G2, commanded first by Colonel Liam Archer and then by Colonel Dan Bryan, as well as the police special branch – had a right to be proud of their successes in frustrating German espionage activities in Ireland.

In this book, composed with extraordinary care and abundantly supported by secret documents from previously inaccessible military archives, Mark M. Hull does not limit his scope to a mere tracing of the sometimes tragically comedic escapades in Ireland of 'suspected espionage agents', as Prime Minister de Valera called them. Taking a much broader perspective, he offers the reader a spellbinding and thoroughly detailed view of all aspects of a merciless 'war within a war'. Even the seemingly 'small' example of Ireland shows quite clearly why the mighty war machine of the National Socialist Third Reich was ultimately bound to fail against the forces of democracy and freedom.

ENNO STEPHAN
Varel, Germany
September 2002

Acknowledgements

With the completion of this work, it is now time to pay part of my debt to some of the people who have been instrumental in its creation. Without overwhelming generosity from so many sources, not a word of this project would have been written.

First, and specifically, I would like to thank Commandant Peter Young of the Irish Military Archives. Peter died in 1999, before he ever read a word of this manuscript, but his intelligence, thoughtful guidance and friendship made it all possible. His subtle understanding of both the personalities and the material helped a foreigner through the labyrinth of Irish documents to the point where there was light at the end of the tunnel. He was a good officer and a good man, and will be sorely missed by an entire generation of researchers.

In several instances, people who began as possible sources of information have become good friends – who have additionally provided valuable information! Herr Enno Stephan, whose pioneering work in the field of German intelligence operations in Ireland opened up a new historical chapter, has been helpful in more ways than I could have possibly expected. Where Peter Young guided me through Irish sources, Herr Stephan did the same for the German material. His thorough and insightful understanding of the period and the people are a model for any historian, and his friendship and support have been invaluable. Both he and his charming wife Mercedes deserve my deepest gratitude. Likewise, Dr David O'Donoghue has been an intelligent sounding board through the laborious process of research and writing, and one who has unselfishly shared both his time and material.

My parents, LTC (ret.) Donald R. Hull and Jane Hull deserve special thanks. Their support made the work possible.

A number of others have also given valuable assistance on a personal and professional basis: Professor Christopher Andrew (Corpus Christi College, Cambridge), Christina Bohl, James and Maggie Cellan-Jones, Elizabeth Clissmann, Tom Desmond (NLI), Professor Dr Reinhard R. Doerries (Universität Erlangen-Nürnberg), LTC (ret.) John Duggan, Olivia Fitzpatrick, Douglas Gageby, Dieter Gärtner, Michael Ginns, OBE (Jersey), Dr Peter Grupp (Politische Archive des Auswärtigen Amtes), Corinna Jaspers, Professor Eunan O'Halpin (TCD), Jean Sheridan Healy,

Professor J. J. Lee (UCC), Jan van Loon, Michael Mac Evilly, Dr Alf MacLochlainn, Dr Fearghal McGarry (TCD), Donal O'Donovan, Dr Donal Ó Drisceoil, Dr Mervyn O'Driscoll (UCC), LTC (ret.) Phillip Robinson, Professor Dr Jürgen Rohwer (formerly of the Bibliothek für Zeitgeschichte), Laura Schacht, Michael Schütz, Penny Steinbach (University of Texas), Francis Stuart (d. February 2000) and Josias Prinz zu Waldeck und Pyrmont.

Special gratitude to Linda – for believing.

The staff at the Irish Military Archives (Commandant Victor Laing, PO Paul Brennan, Pte. Brendan Mahony and Pte. Alan Manning) have endured endless hours of my presence and, in violation of all common sense, never made me feel anything but welcome.

Professor Dermot Keogh (UCC), my dissertation adviser at University College, Cork, merits grateful recognition for suggesting the topic in the first place and his comments en route.

Note on translation

To avoid confusion and distraction, German language text and terms have been kept to a minimum, but in some cases are unavoidable for reasons of accuracy. With common terms (e.g. *Reich, Führer*) there has been no attempt to Anglicize them. German military rank poses a special problem for most English-speaking civilians and to lessen this problem, I have translated the initial usage, but retained the original German for all other occurrences. A complete table of equivalent officer ranks appears in Appendix II.

Most of the original German documents required translation. Original spelling has been retained although, as of 1996, the German language has undergone a controversial change with a standardized and revised spelling that is now officially common to Germany, Austria and Switzerland. I'm comfortable being a linguistic dinosaur and have remained loyal to the older system. Names of cities are given according to the German spelling (e.g. Nürnberg instead of Nuremberg).

In one instance alone, I have deviated from the proper translation. The German term *Auswärtiges Amt* should properly be translated as 'Foreign Office' or 'Foreign Department'. To avoid confusion with the British Foreign Office, which is also referred to in the text, the German term has been rendered as 'Foreign Ministry'.

Abbreviations

Alst	Abwehrleitstelle (Abwehr sub-post)
Ast	Abwehrstelle (Abwehr post)
AO	Auslandsorganisation (NSDAP overseas section)
BA	Bundesarchiv
BdU	Befehlshaber der Unterseeboote (Commander of submarines)
BIH	MI5's Irish security section
BND	Bundesnachrichtendienst (West German intelligence)
COMSEC	Communications security
C3	Garda Síochána special branch
DNB	Deutsche Nachrichten Büro (German Press Agency)
DCU	Dublin City University
FHO	Foreign Armies East (OKH intelligence section)
FHW	Foreign Armies West (OKH intelligence section)
G2	Irish Army intelligence
GC&CS	Government Code and Cypher School
HUMINT	Human intelligence
Ia	Operations staff section (German)
Ic	Intelligence staff section (German)
IMA	Irish Military Archives, Dublin
KO	Kriegsorganisation (Abwehr post in neutral countries)
Kr.Tb.	Kriegstagebuch (staff journal)
LDF	Local Defense Force
LTC	Lieutenant Colonel
NSDAP	Nationalsocialistiche Deutsche Arbeiterpartei
MI5	British Intelligence (domestic)
MI6	British Intelligence (foreign)
NAI	National Archives of Ireland
NLI	National Library of Ireland
OKH	High Command of the Army (German)
OKL	High Command of the Air Force (German)
OKM	High Command of the Navy (German)
OKW	High Command of the Armed Forces (German)
OPSEC	Operational security
PRO	Public Record Office, London
RSHA	Reichssicherheitshauptamt (Reich main security office)

RSS	Radio Security Service (British)
RTO	Radio-telegraph operator
SA	Sturmabteilung
SD	Sicherheitsdienst (security service)
SIGINT	Signals intelligence
SIPO	Sicherheitspolizei (SS security police)
Skl	Seekriegsleitung (German naval operations)
SLB3	MI5 unit responsible for apprehending 'renegades'
SS	Schutzstaffel (protection detail)
SIS	Supplementary Intelligence Service (Irish)
III b	German Intelligence (First World War)
TCD	Trinity College, Dublin
TO&E	Table of Organization and Equipment
UCC	University College, Cork
UCD	University College, Dublin
USNA	United States National Archives, Washington, DC, and College Park, MD

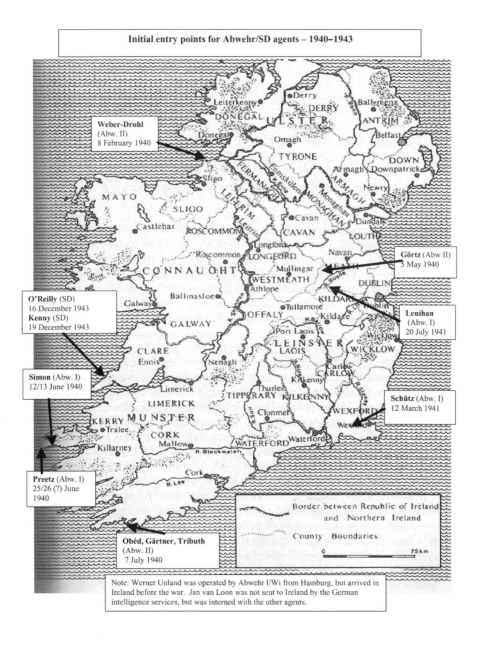

Initial entry points for Abwehr/SD agents – 1940–1943

Weber-Drohl
(Abw. II)
8 February 1940

Görtz (Abw II)
5 May 1940

O'Reilly (SD)
16 December 1943
Kenny (SD)
19 December 1943

Lenihan
(Abw. I)
20 July 1941

Simon (Abw. I)
12/13 June 1940

Schütz (Abw. I)
12 March 1941

Preetz (Abw. I)
25/26 (?) June
1940

Obéd, Gärtner, Tributh
(Abw. II)
7 July 1940

Border between Republic of Ireland
and Northern Ireland

County Boundaries

0   75km

Note: Werner Unland was operated by Abwehr I/Wi from Hamburg, but arrived in
Ireland before the war. Jan van Loon was not sent to Ireland by the German
intelligence services, but was interned with the other agents.

Introduction

German intelligence first expressed a modicum of interest in Ireland, though largely of a temporary and transitory nature, during the years leading up to the First World War. German assistance to malleable nationalist groups within Ireland was seen as an alternative way of attacking global British supremacy and forcing Britain to divert troops and attention that might be otherwise directed against genuine strategic German interests. German planning consistently discouraged any idea of a military adventure in Ireland which required the presence of sizeable numbers of personnel, because, as one pre-war German staff officer observed, 'foreign landings in Ireland had a habit of going wrong'. With the exception of a handful of spies sent by IIIb (German military intelligence), Karl Hans Lody and Corporal Robert Dowling being the most notable, the Kaiser's Reich had little to do with the island other than providing minimal support to a poor idea gone bad – Sir Roger Casement's attempt to form an 'Irish Brigade' from among British POWs – and attempting to supply the Irish Republican Brotherhood (IRB) with surplus rifles and ammunition to coincide with the planned Easter Rising.[1] When this latter plan fell apart in 1916, the Germans became understandably wary of again getting involved with Irish nationalists.

Nevertheless, when war came again in 1939, that is exactly what the Germans did, disregarding in the process all they should have theoretically learned in the earlier excursions during World War One. Ireland was appreciated for its special geographic position and varying relationship with England, something German intelligence mistakenly thought it could exploit for a strategic advantage. From the mid-1930s until at least 1941, Ireland was the target of a modest effort by the German intelligence service, the Abwehr. Agents were sent, reports were collected and Ireland was included in the greater geopolitical plan of the Third Reich. If all went well in the struggle against England, Ireland would be yet another associate member of the Greater German Reich. But things did not go well. Events quickly moved beyond the point where Ireland was significant, and ultimately – as in the First World War – the island no longer played a part in the calculations of a Germany in the midst of losing another world war.

Since the end of that conflict more than fifty years ago, only a few historians have worked on the subject of German espionage in Ireland.

Noted German journalist Enno Stephan was the first. When *Geheimauftrag Irland* ('Secret Mission – Ireland') appeared in 1961 (later translated in 1963 as *Spies in Ireland*), it described a history which had not, up to that time, appeared in print. As the major archival sources were not then open, Stephan conducted oral interviews with the major participants, both Irish and German, and had exclusive access to the Abwehr II journal. A primary source was former Sonderführer Kurt Haller, who intimately knew the story of Irish operations from his work with the Abwehr and the Foreign Ministry and who was anxious to get the facts on the record before his death. Stephan was also able to interview James O'Donovan, Kapitän zur See a. D. Herbert Wichmann (Hamburg Abwehr), former agents Günther Schütz and Jan van Loon and many of the people connected to Hermann Görtz, including his family. Most of the people Stephan interviewed have since died, making his contribution to this field even more significant. Particularly for one working in the era before many key documents were released, his work was remarkable. In preparing this work, I have had (with the author's permission) exclusive access to the original, unpublished manuscript of Stephan's work, which contains significant material not found in the printed versions.

Other than Stephan, the only German historian to work in the area of German–Irish relations during wartime is Horst Dickel, whose little-known (at least to non-German academicians) 1983 book *Die deutsche Aussenpolitik und die irische Frage von 1932 bis 1944* (German Foreign Policy and the Irish Question from 1932 to 1944) is exceptionally well-researched, thorough and readable. It does, however, only deal with the subject of espionage as an adjunct to the larger political questions, and its exclusive availability in German has precluded the use of this work by monolingual historians.

Carolle J. Carter revisited the topic in 1977 when she published *The Shamrock and the Swastika*. She took advantage of the available files in the German Foreign Office Archive and likewise took the opportunity to conduct interviews with many participants, including Colonel Dan Bryan of Irish Army Intelligence and Dr Richard Hayes, the amateur code-breaker who was more adept than many professional cryptographers. Carter's narrative had several flaws: she mistranslated some of the German documents, allowed easily correctable errors to sneak into the manuscript and, in some cases, relied to her detriment on interviews with participants whose memory was unreliable. Carter seemed unfamiliar with the terminology and methods of military intelligence, though she did have one principal advantage in that her work was partially supervised by Professor Charles Burdick (San José State University), a recognized authority on the Second World War period. Despite its flaws, Carter's work is valuable, if for no other reason than she was able to get important people on the record, even if that record is less than perfect. Due to potential legal difficulties involving the peculiar Irish libel laws, her book was never marketed in Ireland.

Several other published works have touched on the topic of wartime espionage in Ireland, including John Duggan's *Neutral Ireland and the Third Reich* and Robert Fisk's excellent work, *In Time of War: Ireland, Ulster and the Price of Neutrality 1939–1945*. Duggan's work, essentially a revised version of his D.Litt. thesis on wartime German Minister Eduard Hempel, is notable for unearthing several items and provides a good though selective examination of the German Foreign Ministry documentation. Other aspects of the book are more speculative and at the time it was written, only limited Irish sources were available. Like Carter, Duggan had the foresight to interview several of the participants and he did much to flesh out certain aspects of the German–Irish wartime relationship. Robert Fisk's book (*In Time of War*) is very thorough and superbly written, but principally deals with the larger questions of Ireland in the war years and is not particularly devoted to the secondary aspects of military intelligence or espionage, although Fisk does handle these areas with finesse. Recently, Professor Eunan O'Halpin released *Defending Ireland*, an excellent examination of Irish intelligence policy, but which is not specifically directed at German intelligence activities. To the list must also be added *Hitler's Irish Voices* by Dr David O'Donoghue, an important and well-written look at Germany's radio propaganda broadcast service to Ireland. This too, borders on several tangents of German espionage, but only to the degree to which they are connected to radio propaganda activities. However, O'Donoghue's thorough research into the pre-war Dublin Nazi Party is a necessary starting point for understanding Abwehr operations in Ireland.

Part of the difficulty in separating the wheat from the chaff in the area of German intelligence operations is the sheer volume of misinformation that appears in print. Many books about wartime espionage operations refer to the missions connected to Ireland, and though some are excellent, many are riddled with errors. To cite but two examples, Lauran Paine's *German Military Intelligence in World War II* and David Johnson's *Germany's Spies and Saboteurs* are so replete with factual mistakes that it is difficult to say anything positive about them.[2] *The Jackboot in Ireland* by Seán O'Callaghan[3] also falls into this category, with the added novelty that its author invents situations and dialogue for which there is no historical provenance. The cardinal academic sin of correctable error is frequently due to authors not checking the original documentation or sources, but relying on earlier, spurious, or anecdotal accounts of events.

Thankfully, recent years have proven fruitful for serious researchers of espionage and military history. Document archives that were largely or completely closed are now being opened. The Irish Military Archives in Dublin are perhaps the greatest repository for original material on the subject of German espionage in Ireland, followed closely by the Public

Record Office (PRO) in London. Due to the slow release of British security service (MI5) files, there is the distinct possibility that much more information is extant but not yet available. Even with the new climate of archival *glasnost*, there are some notable exceptions; files pertaining to MI6 are not scheduled for release in the foreseeable future.

Other significant pieces of the puzzle exist in the *Bundesarchiv* system (Militärarchiv/Freiburg, Bundesarchiv/Berlin and the Political Archive of the Foreign Office/Berlin), the Irish National Archives and the United States National Archives II at College Park, Maryland. Sadly for the historian, most of the Abwehr files were destroyed during the war and the sections that remain are of a more general nature, and shed little light on individual case management in any of the operations in Ireland. However, at all of these archival locations many original intelligence-related files are available to the serious researcher, allowing many earlier historical misconceptions to be finally addressed. Many of these files have never before been examined by the public, while others that were available have been grossly understudied and underutilized by earlier researchers.

As the written sources have become available, witnesses have diminished. Of the eleven agents interned during the war, only two remain alive. Both have been interviewed for this work. I have also spoken with other individuals who were witnesses to the events described. In some instances, their memories enhance and clarify the documentary record; in other cases, the opposite is true. Memory is elastic and can be unreliable. It is hoped the combination of live and written sources, and rigorous examination of earlier works, will allow for the complete story to be told, within the limits of the scope of this book. By their very nature, the military intelligence services are in the business of preserving secrets. In some cases, questions are raised where no certain answer exists. It is also true that information is sometimes accidentally or deliberately distorted, compounding the historian's confusion, and adding to an already impressive list of repeated errors and historical truisms which are, in fact, absolutely false. I have tried to distinguish fact from fiction to the best of my ability.

This work is not a political, economic or social examination of wartime Ireland. It is not specifically concerned with the diplomatic situation between Germany and Ireland, and is not a study of the Irish military, or even of Irish military intelligence.[4] It is intended only as an examination of German foreign intelligence activities in wartime Ireland, though this topic necessarily impinges on other areas. Irish activities are analysed and discussed only as they relate to the German perception of events, and include Irish citizens abroad who assisted the German espionage effort in Ireland in one way or another. However, there are several unexplored but related areas that are beyond the limits of this thesis but would make for original studies by other historians. These would include an examination of the archival records in Italy, Japan and Spain to determine the extent and substance of military intelligence information from Ireland that was passed by diplomats back to their home countries. Any such studies will be considerably enhanced once the files on these legations are released by the Irish Military Archives.[5]

The book generally follows a chronological course through the events described. Chapter 1 (Background to the German Intelligence Service) examines the history, organization, personnel and methods of the Abwehr, Germany's main intelligence gathering agency. The section also focuses on inherent weaknesses in the German intelligence system, as well as looking at the tools of the espionage trade, with a specific emphasis on those related to Irish operations. Chapter 2 (Germany and Ireland, 1933–39) explores the political and diplomatic ties between the Third Reich and Ireland, the growth and influence of fascism and Nazi groups in Ireland, and the characters and organizations which eventually attracted the attention of German Intelligence, the IRA and the Blueshirts. This section also considers the development of the pivotal intelligence exchange between MI5 and Irish Military Intelligence (G2) and the early participation of Irish who knowingly helped Hitler. In the third chapter, German pre-war intelligence contact with dissident groups is thoroughly examined and reveals new information about the connections between noted Irish personalities and emissaries of Hitler's Germany. German contacts with the Irish, which go back as far as 1937, are treated in detail and analysed as part of the overall German intelligence plan. Chapters 4–7 concern German agent activities in Ireland, both those personnel who were in place before the invasion of Poland as well as those who arrived more surreptitiously from 1940 to 1943. This also includes the identification of previously unknown agents and collaborators, an accurate picture of Abwehr and SD intentions, the machinations of the German Foreign Office in respect to intelligence activities in Ireland and a detailed description of Irish and British counter-intelligence in the war with Germany. Chapter 8 looks at the role of the Irish in Germany as they fit into the larger picture of espionage operations. The gamut of personalities from Francis Stuart to Charles Bewley is examined (based on new documentary sources and interviews) to determine the significance of their collaboration with the German war effort and their contribution towards intelligence operations in Ireland. The case of German agents in custody – and their continuing threat to the security of the Irish state – is the subject of Chapter 9. Newly released documents provide a window into the world of espionage behind bars, and an insight into the level of Anglo-Irish security cooperation.

The story of Germany's espionage effort in neutral Ireland is rich with detail and covers a wide variety of characters and issues: numerous villains, a couple of heroes, betrayal and deceit, politics, sex, violence, comedy, intrigue, ignorance and insight. The subject is sometimes uproariously funny and, at other moments, quite sad. All of it, though, is part of the common Irish and German historical landscape and describes events that are all too real. Had the situation gone even slightly the other way, the events that occurred in Ireland between 1939 and 1945 could have been critical on a global scale. And yet, German involvement in Ireland remains one of the least well-known scenarios of the Second World War – until now.

1
Background to the German Intelligence Service

INTRODUCTION TO MILITARY INTELLIGENCE

Military intelligence has a double function, at the same time both offensive and defensive. When used properly, it can alter the outcome of events, spread confusion and discontent, affect public morale and destroy the political and military decision-making process. Defensively, it should provide commanders with the kind of strategic information to gauge enemy intentions and capabilities properly in the form of accurate, first-hand information from the enemy camp. In the eternal battle for the possession of the most accurate and up-to-date information, it is usually the side that makes the most effective use of intelligence information that prevails. In the case of Ultra, the top-secret decoding of Germany's most secure and sensitive Enigma communications system, the intelligence breakthrough of the Allies was quite possibly the deciding factor in the Second World War. Success in obtaining and evaluating intelligence data directly translates to victory on the battlefield.

The essence of military intelligence is the gathering of sufficient accurate data to form an intelligence estimate, which is at once a situation report and a forecast. The purpose of the estimate is to give an accurate picture of enemy strengths, weaknesses, foreseeable technical and tactical developments, and an estimation of all possible courses of action open to an enemy commander. Among a myriad of other things, the intelligence estimate factors in weather, terrain, nationality, history and even the personal lives of the enemy commanders. When performed correctly with proper resources and personnel, it allows a friendly commander almost literally to get inside the head of his opponent and misdirect the enemy decision-making process to his advantage. The process of intelligence-gathering has always accompanied warfare, a millennium before Joshua's spies wormed their way into Jericho: 2,500 years ago, the great Chinese strategist Sun Tzu noted that 'only the wise ruler and the wise general who will use the highest intelligence of the arm for purposes of spying, and thereby they achieve great results. Spies are a most important element in war because upon them depends an army's ability to move.'[1] This relationship, between espionage and combat operations, is at the heart of the military intelligence system; one cannot be considered without reference to the other. Systematic intelligence processing increased exponentially with the growth of professional staff planning, largely an offshoot of the Napoleonic Wars (1804–15). Modern military headquarters always have a staff intelligence section, usually designated as an 'S-2' in battalion or brigade level units, 'G-2' in divisional, corps, army or army group units, and 'J-2' at the supreme level of command.

Generally speaking, military staff sections do not operate agents. Their work is to process the active intelligence reports produced by others. With a complicated hierarchical structure, specialized aspects of intelligence-gathering are performed by separate agencies. In theory, all of these should work in harmony. In the United States, for example, active foreign intelligence operations are conducted by the Central Intelligence Agency; communications/signal intelligence is gathered by the National Security Agency; domestic intelligence and counter-intelligence is the responsibility of the Federal Bureau of Investigation. This process allows for intelligence information to be disseminated at a both strategic and tactical level, based on the respective needs of the particular organization and level of command. At one end, it gives a national leader and his military and political staff the necessary information to make informed strategic decisions; at the other, it lets a platoon leader know about the weapon systems likely to be encountered on the enemy tanks that are 1,000 metres distant. In either scenario, the crucial factor is accurate intelligence. Every major nation realizes that the systematic production of intelligence is vital to the defence of the state. Historically, Germany was no exception.

ADMIRAL WILHELM CANARIS AND THE ABWEHR

Formal intelligence acquisition in the German state dates to the birth of the Prussian Great General Staff under Helmuth Graf von Moltke, which incorporated academic lessons from Carl von Clausewitz, and the practical experience of the Franco-Prussian war.[2] During the First World War, the German foreign intelligence service (designated as III b) was directed by Oberst (Colonel) Walther Nicolai, who was succeeded in the uncertain post-Versailles Treaty period by Oberst Friedrich Gempp, who was later followed by Kapitän zur See Conrad Patzig.[3] The term 'Abwehr' made its first appearance in 1920, and the intelligence branch was administratively placed under the Reichswehr Ministry in 1922.[4] Differences with the new National Socialist government after 1933 led to Patzig's resignation and he was followed by Kapitän zur See (soon to be Admiral) Canaris.

When Admiral Wilhelm Franz Canaris took over command of the German Intelligence Service, the Abwehr, on 1 January 1935, he faced a difficult task. His mission was nothing less than creating a worldwide espionage network and intelligence-gathering agency for a nation faced with the prospect of a European war within the foreseeable future.[5]

Born in 1887, Canaris was a career naval officer of the Kriegsmarine (Navy), who had been involved in espionage activities since the First World War. In the intervening period between the two global conflicts, with the political implosion in German politics, it seemed that he was preparing to retire gracefully on the eve of Hitler's ascension to power. Canaris had the reputation of being intelligent, thoughtful, and secretive – but he was certainly not a supporter of Hitler and the National Socialist Party. He additionally had several friendships that he could use to his advantage, most notably a long-standing relationship with General Francisco Franco. It was also true that his position as spy-master in Nazi Germany gave him access to secrets on almost everyone of importance – perhaps a necessary hole card in a system where the life expectancy was shorter than average. Canaris also operated from a motive that is generally rare in an intelligence chief: morality. Despite his role as the director of German Intelligence abroad, he was increasingly concerned about the moral tone of the new regime – a concern that would develop as events took on a more ominous character.

It must be stressed that the Abwehr was an intelligence *gathering* agency; and dealt with raw intelligence reports from field agents and other sources. The Chief of the Abwehr reported directly to the German High Command. Intelligence summaries and intelligence dissemination were the prerogative of the Operations Branch (as distinct from an intelligence branch, something that did not exist in the German command structure) of the Oberkommando der Wehrmacht (OKW or High Command of the Armed Forces) and, through it, to the intelligence-evaluation sections of the Heer (Army), the Kriegsmarine (Navy) and the Luftwaffe (Air Force).[6] In technical intelligence language, the Abwehr dealt exclusively with HUMINT (human intelligence sources) and relied on agent reports to fulfil its intelligence-gathering function.[7]

The Abwehr was subdivided into three main sections.[8] The Central Division (also called Department Z – *die Zentrale*) acted as the controlling brain for the other three sections, as well as handling personnel and financial matters, including the payment of agents. Throughout Canaris's tenure, it was directed by Generalmajor Hans Oster, Canaris's closest subordinate, who was deeply involved in the anti-Hitler conspiracy. The Foreign Branch (later the Foreign Intelligence Group) was the second subdivision of the Abwehr and had several functions: liaison with the OKW and the general staffs of the services, coordination with the Foreign Ministry on military matters, evaluation of captured documents and evaluation of foreign press and radio broadcasts. This liaison with the services and the OKW was vital, since this was the appropriate channel to request the Abwehr support for a particular mission. While the Central and Foreign branches were important, the striking power of German military intelligence was contained in the three sections, Abwehr I, II, and III, somewhat deceptively called 'counter-intelligence' branches. They can more properly be described as 'intelligence gathering' sections.[9]

Abwehr I was responsible for foreign intelligence collection – the heart of the intelligence business; Abwehr II, the sabotage division, directed the covert contact and exploitation of discontented minority groups in foreign countries for intelligence purposes; Abwehr III, the counter-intelligence division, was responsible for counter-intelligence operations in German industry, planting false information, penetration of foreign intelligence services and investigating acts of sabotage on German soil. Each section had specialized subdivisions. For example, Abwehr I was broken down into I-Wi (economic intelligence), I-H (army intelligence), I-L (air intelligence), I-M (naval intelligence) and I-T/lw (technical air intelligence). Abwehr liaisons were also established with the Army, Navy and Luftwaffe high commands, and would pass on specific intelligence requests to the operational sections of the Abwehr.[10]

Abwehr headquarters was located at 76/78 Tirpitzufer, Berlin, near the Army High Command headquarters. However, the main operational power of the Abwehr lay in yet a further administrative subdivision.

The Abwehr placed a local station in each military district (Wehrkreis) in Germany, called an Abwehrstelle or Ast. Following the TO&E model of Abwehr headquarters, each Ast was usually subdivided into sections for espionage (I), sabotage (II) and counter-intelligence (III).[11] Typically, each Ast would be commanded by a senior Army or naval officer and would be answerable to Abwehr headquarters in Berlin. Operations carried out by the Asts would be done in concert with the overall strategic plan developed by Admiral Canaris, who in turn would be given his intelligence priorities directly from the OKW and, after 1941, from Adolf Hitler. In practice, however, the Ast was given considerable latitude in mission planning and execution, something that had a negative effect on systematic intelligence gathering.

In addition to running operations as directed from Berlin, the local Ast would recruit potential candidates for espionage missions. The Abwehr additionally employed freelance recruiters who vetted candidates from a variety of sources, many of them questionable. In most cases, the agents who formed the striking power of the Abwehr were not 'intelligence officers' – which implies a military officer with a speciality in intelligence, but rather recruited civilians, who might or might not have any permanent connection to the Abwehr or the German military. This increased the available pool of agents, but had consequences in situations where professional training and military experience would have produced more desired results. On the whole, from the recruiters to the upper echelons of the Berlin headquarters, the emphasis seemed to be on quantity of agents and missions, rather than quality.[12]

In neutral countries, the Abwehr frequently disguised its organization by attaching its personnel to the German embassy or to trade missions. Such postings were referred to as *Kriegsorganisationen* (war organizations) or KOs.[13] In neutral but friendly Spain, the Abwehr had both an Ast and a KO; Ireland had neither. In friendly countries of interest and occupied countries or in Germany itself, the intelligence service would normally organize *Abwehrleitstellen* (Abwehr sub-stations) or *Alsts* and *Abwehrnebenstellen* (Abwehr adjoining posts) or *Nests*. The Alst or Nest would fall under the jurisdiction of the geographically appropriate Ast, which in turn would be supervised by the Central Division in Berlin.

Chief among Canaris's concerns was the fact that his organization, still in an embryonic stage, was in no way ready for a major military conflict. Part of the difficulty stemmed from a lack of transitional experience between covert operations in the First World War and those of Canaris's Abwehr. Successfully placing intelligence-gathering assets (spies) in foreign countries normally takes decades; Canaris had less than five years before the outbreak of a global war. After targeting the country of interest, the ideal situation would be to place 'sleepers' – persons who blend in with the citizens of the country, get jobs, raise families and are otherwise indistinguishable from anyone else. If intelligence planning goes according to a moderate timetable, foreign intelligence, military and government services would be penetrated and agents recruited using a host of different techniques.[14] To make a reasonable intelligence estimate, such as that required by the planners of the OKW Operations branch, the intelligence-gathering service (Abwehr, in this case), would need intimate local knowledge of the target country, highly placed contacts in private industry, government, the military and the private sector, accurate topographical information and military and political capability assessments. Unfortunately for the Abwehr, when war broke out in 1939, they had almost none of these. Once war had been declared, they never again had an opportunity to repair the oversight.

DIE SCHWARZE KAPELLE

Another set of problems for Hitler and the OKW, though unknown to them at the time, was that the chief operational and administrative personnel at the Abwehr were quietly working against the government they were supposed to be serving. While Canaris outwardly seemed to be the model of intelligence-gathering efficiency, evidence indicates that he quietly opposed Hitler's policies from the start of the war. Canaris, his chief deputy, Generalmajor Hans Oster, and the chiefs of Abwehr sections I, II, and III were all heavily involved in what was called the Schwarze Kapelle (the Black Orchestra) – the organized (or disorganized) plot to overthrow Hitler and the Nazi regime.[15] The Schwarze Kapelle is distinct from the Rote Kapelle, another unsuccessful, largely Communist opposition movement. Clearly, the intelligence-gathering process is severely compromised when the people responsible for estimating enemy intentions and collecting foreign intelligence are intentionally working against their own government. At the very least, it would have the effect of compromising the results – in this case, the outcome of the Second World War.

This is perhaps most clearly reflected in a quote from Canaris himself on 3 September 1939, the day England and France declared war on Germany: 'The Abwehr must do nothing that would prolong this war by a day.'[16] Testifying at the Nürnberg Trials, the head of Abwehr II, Generalmajor Erwin von Lahousen, stated that 'Canaris was a pure intellect, an interesting, highly individual and complicated personality, who hated violence as such and therefore hated and abominated war, Hitler, his system and particularly his methods'.[17] Lahousen also mentioned Canaris's initial mission statement on the outbreak of the war: that there should be an express 'failure to carry out enterprises whose execution can be avoided anyway'.[18] The course of Abwehr intelligence operations in Ireland from 1939 to 1943 reflects this cross-purpose confusion which emanated from the very heart of the German intelligence community.

There are some indications that Canaris hoped to work against the Nazi establishment by assisting the British Intelligence Service, MI5. This was done by a number of means, both obvious and covert. As early as November 1939, sensitive German technical and military data began finding their way to the British.[19] Though outwardly efficiently pursuing his intelligence mission, Canaris was seemingly stacking the deck in favour of the Allies. According to General Ulrich Liss, head of the Fremde Heere West (FHW – Foreign Armies West),

> I saw Canaris frequently during the Case Yellow [invasion of the Low Countries] and the intelligence planning for Sealion [the invasion of Britain]. ... I came to the conclusion that his offensive intelligence operations against the French, Norway, Belgium and the Low Countries were all models of efficiency. But the same could not be said of his Sealion operations. I thought then that, while he appeared to be efficient, he was not doing his job against England with conviction. *We never got the intelligence from England that we needed to make the correct estimates of England's strengths and dispositions on the ground* [Italics added].[20]

If Canaris was actively sabotaging the Third Reich's intelligence apparatus, it was largely for nothing. Any overtures of cooperation received were disregarded by MI5, who took the view that there were no 'good Germans' in the Nazi military or political system. There is considerable debate on the exact nature and extent of Canaris's activities. The wartime head of MI6, Sir Stewart Menzies, observed that 'Canaris was never a British agent in the accepted sense of that term. ... Canaris never betrayed his country's secrets to me or to anyone else on the British side, although his men did. On the other hand, he did give me assistance.'[21] Ironically, Canaris's nephew was an SS-Standartenführer (Colonel). In his post-war interrogation, Constantine Canaris noted that his uncle 'was working against Hitler since the beginning of the war; he intended to do all he could to stir up trouble against him and undermine his influence'.[22]

ORGANIZATIONAL WEAKNESSES

Another limiting factor of the German intelligence service was simply bad management. Canaris had a devoted following among his people, but he failed to identify a specific agenda of intelligence priorities. It proved the old dictum that military intelligence requires more than merely being intelligent. He would react as needed, but central control was largely absent, leaving the day-to-day running of the intelligence service to the commanders of the various Asts (Abwehr posts) and KOs (Abwehr in neutral countries). In post-war interrogations, it emerged that even the commanders of major Asts – such as Hamburg – had very little idea about individual agent missions, other than a very general understanding of their task. By and large, the officers in charge of operating agents in foreign countries had no background in intelligence work themselves, and conducted their affairs accordingly.

Also lacking was a sense of continuity from the First World War, meaning that practical experience gained from that conflict was lost and lessons had to be relearned, if they were ever learned at all. From an analysis of the missions to Ireland, this lack of expertise in the German intelligence community becomes apparent. This inevitably had a negative effect on the types of personnel chosen for overseas assignments. Not having a trained pool of agents, the Abwehr decided to opt for expediency and used a mixture of civilian and military personnel to carry out the missions. Almost to a man, the civilian agents sent to Ireland were unfit for serious employment, and lacked both training and experience. While the military personnel were usually of a higher calibre, they were so poorly briefed as to have no meaningful chance of achieving their mission objectives. In this latter category, two enlisted soldiers (Gärtner and Tributh) were only in Ireland as a transit point to an equally ill-defined mission in England.

The picture of German intelligence becomes even more confusing due to the fact that the Abwehr was only one of several agencies in the German state that gathered intelligence information. In addition to the Abwehr and the SD (the Sicherheitsdienst or Security Service, see below) – the only two organizations which operated agents – each major section of the government had at least one intelligence unit. These included the Postal Ministry, the Economics Ministry, the Foreign Ministry (Department Inf III), the Propaganda Ministry (the DNB), and the Forschungsamt (a wire surveillance service that worked directly for Hermann Göring outside military control). To this list must be added the Fichte-Bund, a semi-private propaganda enterprise that maintained a list of contacts.

Military intelligence was also acquired and evaluated by several distinct agencies within the armed forces. The Luftwaffe had two of these, the Technical Intelligence section and the Fifth section of the Luftwaffe General Staff, called Foreign Air Forces (evaluation of air intelligence). The German Navy, not to be outdone by the air force, had two agencies, the 2/Skl (called the B-Dienst) and the 3/Skl (Foreign Navies – evaluation of naval intelligence). The German Army, generally considered the most important of the three services, had two main sections for intelligence analysis: the Third Branch of the Army General Staff (Foreign Armies West) and the Twelfth Branch (Foreign Armies East). To this may be added the Cipher Branch of the OKW. While it might seem that the specialization would work to Germany's advantage, in practice the only element that these disparate agencies shared was a singular unwillingness to share information with each other. Information was a precious commodity, especially in a 'dog eat dog' system where political and practical survival often depended on stealing a march on competing intelligence agencies.[23]

To give an example, SIGINT information was collected and analysed by no fewer than nine separate agencies, to include the Forschungstelle (Postal Ministry), Pers Z (Foreign Ministry), the OKW Cipher Branch, the Radio and Observation post of RSHA VI, and the individual radio intelligence units of the armed services.[24] In terms of the Abwehr, the most serious competition came from the SS – and it was a battle that would eventually result in the total defeat of German Military Intelligence by its voracious Nazi rival.

THE SD

In addition to Canaris's own agenda against his Nazi masters and numerous organizational difficulties, there was another limiting factor to Abwehr success against Britain – and, by extension, Ireland. The intelligence process works the worst when needless confusion or administrative duplication accompanies it. While this situation is in many ways typical of some aspects of Hitler's Germany, the design of the intelligence-gathering apparatus contributed to the problem. The Nazi Party had its own intelligence organization, which generally ran counter to the intelligence directives and priorities of the Abwehr. This competing intelligence service, the Sicherheitsdienst (Security Service) or SD, was part of the larger structure of the Nazi Party/SS security system collectively under the administrative umbrella of the Reichssicherheitshauptamt (Reich Main Security Office) or RSHA.[25]

The SS intelligence service and the other tentacles of the SS state were under the command of Reichsführer SS and Chief of the German Police Heinrich Himmler. While the SS was the province of Heinrich Himmler, his chief deputy and chief of the RSHA was Reinhard Heydrich, the initial head of the SD from its foundation in 1932.[26] When Heydrich was promoted to RSHA chief, he divided the security functions among several different, and sometimes competing agencies. The SD, Sipo (Sicherheitspolizei – Security Police), and later the Einsatzgruppen (mobile extermination squads) were directly answerable to Heydrich. The dreaded Gestapo (Geheime Staatspolizei – Secret State Police) and the Kripo (Kriminalpolizei – Criminal Police) were subordinate to the Security Police.

Heydrich defined the SD charter in July 1937, although it was later to be expanded. Initially, the organization was responsible for matters of art, party and state, the constitution and administration, and foreign lands. Officially, the SD was an investigative security agency only, with no powers of arrest; threats to state security were to be turned over to the Gestapo for 'executive treatment' (*exekutivmäßig*). The SD was divided into two sections, Domestic Intelligence (under Otto Ohlendorf) and Foreign Intelligence (under SS-Brigadeführer Walter Schellenberg).[27]

Originally charged with internal security for the Nazi party, the SD rapidly expanded its role to include areas that should logically have been under the direction of the Abwehr.[28] For example, reports from the overseas branches of the Nazi Party, the Auslandsorganizationen or AO, went directly to the SD and not to the Abwehr, as did political and economic intelligence in the Reich. This was critical, since it deprived the Abwehr of local sources and, sometimes, agents in favour of the SD.[29] Following a tense meeting between Heydrich and Canaris in May 1942, the SD assumed complete control of counter-espionage activities within the Reich, an area which had formerly been under the jurisdiction of Abwehr III. After Heydrich's assassination, the SD's role was even further expanded when Hitler gave it the responsibility for acquiring technical intelligence information overseas.[30] On the ultimate dissolution of the Abwehr following the 20 July 1944 attempt against Hitler, the SD absorbed much of what was left of the Abwehr and became the single German intelligence-collection agency.[31]

The SD-sponsored intelligence initiatives included at least two missions to wartime Ireland.

THE BRANDENBURG REGIMENT

A singular advantage that the Abwehr possessed over the rival SD was the existence of the Brandenburg unit. Originally conceived in 1938–9 by

Hauptmann Dr von Hippel of Abwehr II, this unique group was a prototype for unconventional warfare units and it originated many of the tactics and innovations later employed by the SAS, Spetsnaz (Soviet/ Russian special forces), and the US Special Forces. For security reasons it was initially designated with the benign title of 'Bau-Lehrkompanie z.b.V 800' (Special Duty Construction Demonstration Company 800). In reality, it was an elite unit of commandos financed and supervised by the Abwehr.[32]

The Brandenburg unit, later to expand from company to divisional strength within a three-year period, also pioneered many of the techniques used in espionage. Intelligence, initiative and physical fitness were minimum qualifications for those who were admitted to the unit, plus the ability to speak the languages of Germany's enemies fluently. In addition, the Brandenburg unit was to provide additional training to those assigned to espionage, but who might not otherwise meet the strict criteria for permanent duty.[33] Training for unit personnel and temporarily attached officers would include instruction in airborne techniques, radio set-up and transmission procedure, weapons and sabotage training. Contrary to the Abwehr's intentions, the tactical employment of the Brandenburgers was a story of misspent resources – rather than limited to small-unit special operations, they were frequently committed as infantry in roles for which they were not designed. Though the unit achieved deserved recognition fighting in such diverse places as North Africa, Russia and in the Battle of the Bulge, their essential capabilities were never used in ways designed to maximize success in the field.[34] Much of this was due to the German (and British) tendency to designate units as 'elite' – which, more often than not, was a licence to misapply the particular troops in situations where their special skills were not of use.[35]

The Brandenburg unit increased from company strength in 1939 to divisional strength by 1942, an expansion that only further complicated an already difficult operational situation. It was merged in December 1944 with the Grossdeutschland Division to form the Grossdeutschland Korps.

AGENT BASIC TRAINING

For the agents that the Germans sent abroad, the degree of training varied widely, depending on the exact nature of the mission and the individual capabilities of the personnel assigned. Typically, the Hamburg Ast at nearby Hamburg-Wohldorf would supervise basic training for the agents or *Vertrauensmänner* (V-men), under the supervision of Abwehr I and II. Like the main office at the Tirpitzufer, Berlin, the Hamburg Ast was subdivided into several specialized component parts: Department I (*Erkundigung* or reconnaissance); Department WI (*Wirtschaft* – economic intelligence); Department LU (Luftwaffe – aerial intelligence); and Department MA (*Marine* – naval intelligence).[36] Sabotage training was conducted at the facility at Berlin-Tegel, which also housed the extensive network of Abwehr laboratories. At this laboratory, Abwehr technicians could produce everything from an exploding thermos to forged documents and banknotes.

Kapitän zur See Herbert Wichmann commanded the Hamburg Ast and had several associated sections that provided the specific training required by agents for their various missions. Oberstleutnant (Lieutenant Colonel) Werner Trautmann oversaw communications training for new agents, Oberst Nikolaus Ritter supervised the training cycles in section I-L (aviation intelligence training), and there was an additional section, I-G, which was devoted to ciphers and invisible inks.[37] The Hamburg Ast lacked an Abwehr II section and agents employed by that branch were usually recruited and controlled by other Asts. Hamburg did, though, provide training to Abwehr II personnel. Agent training could take as little as a few weeks to many months, depending on the complexity of the assignment.[38]

RADIO TRAINING AND PROCEDURE

In the period between the First and Second World Wars, technology had taken several leaps forward. Wireless or radio communication had been possible for many years, but the full military development and application of that technology did not occur until the mid-1930s. Where previously agents had been required to send messages in writing or by word of mouth, radio made it possible to communicate by relatively secure means over vast distances. With the use of repeater stations, which passed (and sometimes enhanced) the original signal, there were no theoretical limits to the effective range between transmitter and receiver. Communications training emphasized several aspects of sending and receiving. The standard agent transmitter, called an *Agenten-Funk* or *Afu* (or *Klamotten* – 'trash' in Abwehr-speak) was surprisingly powerful for its size. The standard model, usually a separate transmitter, receiver and Morse key, would fit comfortably in an attaché case along with the portable aerial and repair tools. It operated on a relatively small bandwidth, but a trained operator would normally have no significant difficulty with reception or transmission.

The student-agents practised reception techniques in the communications centre in Hamburg-Wohldorf, with the transmitters set up in an open area some distance away.[39] The receiving station consisted of twenty-four radio receivers, divided into separate stations for overseas and European traffic. The Abwehr transmitter station – quite distinct from the students' practice transmitters – was made up of twenty-two transmitter sets, mostly the 400-watt variety.[40] Students were expected to learn the basics of the Morse code and, hopefully, attain a sending rate of 100 letters per minute. The operators at the receiving stations in Germany would be able to recognize the sender by the style of transmission – his 'fist' – as a security measure designed to detect if a sender was being duplicated or had fallen under enemy control.[41] Students received extensive instruction in the construction of radio transmitters and receivers, so that replacement sets could be manufactured, if necessary, and minor repairs could be performed.

Operators in the field were given specific times and frequencies for the transmission of coded messages. Generally, there would be a main day frequency and one for night-time use, with the frequency being monitored for approximately one hour and ten minutes for each scheduled contact. Depending on which of two transmitters were issued, either a crystal or battery-powered model, the agent would be given normal and back-up frequencies. Should the reception be poor or impossible, new frequencies could be requested through Abwehr control. In the abbreviated international Morse system favoured by the Abwehr, the initials 'QSW' referred to a frequency change. Each operator was given an identification code, which was changed on a regular basis.[42]

Though this identification of German agents by a three-letter group posed a recurring problem for Irish Intelligence during the Second World War, Dr Richard Hayes, Director of the National Library and amateur code expert, finally solved the riddle. Over several months in late 1940, G2 (Irish Army Intelligence intercepted numerous radio calls intended for a station in Ireland. The call letters for the receiving station varied: LMR, REE and LMZ. It was suspected that these referred to different stations, but the signals were broadcast on the same bandwidth. Dr Hayes finally determined that they were actually a type of anagram that identified agent Wilhelm 'Willy' Preetz.

WILHELM PREETZ	LMR
WILHELM PREETZ	REE
WILHELM PREETZ	LMZ[43]

CODE ABBREVIATIONS

The reasons for encoding the transmissions are obvious. Any transmitted signal can be picked up by anyone with a suitable receiver, friend or foe. Though there are numerous choices of frequency, depending on the power and band of the transmitter, none are secure by themselves. Because messages from distant agents could not be transmitted 'in the clear,' (i.e. uncoded) the student-agents would also have to become familiar with various encoding techniques and radio abbreviations. The most simple of these abbreviated texts, called the *Betriebsabkur* or operational abbreviations, were taken almost directly from the international Morse abbreviations and were a selection of shorthand words in German and English:

AR	*Schlusselzeichen* (key sign)
AS	*Warten* (wait)
ALL	*Rufzeichen rufen* (call sign)
DR	*Liebe* (love)
ES	*Und* (and)
GB	Good bye
GE	Good evening
GM	*Guten Morgen* (good morning)
GN	*Gute Nacht* (good night)
GRS	*Langsamer Senden* (transmit more slowly)
GRU	*Haben Sie etwas für mich?* (Do you have anything for me?)
GRU	*Ich habe nichts für Sie* (I have nothing for you)
..	Minute oder Minuten
NW	*Jetzt! Achtung! Ich emfange keine sendung* (Now! Attention! I am not receiving your transmission)
OB	*Alter Knabe* (Old boy)
TKS	*Danke* (Thanks)[44]

More secure means of transmission were available, such as the Enigma rotary cipher machine or the Lorenz teletype. In practice, these systems were never employed for operational espionage missions, but were reserved for field and garrison use with active (and more conventional) military units, where the physical security of the devices was less of a concern.

SECRET INKS

Radio communication was vulnerable to mechanical breakdowns, weather, positioning error, interruption from civilian and other military radio traffic and human error. Despite any temporary difficulties, it was vital that the message got through, even if by a slower method. A popular alternative means of transmitting messages was by use of secret inks. The oldest form of this was by using lemon juice, but by the time of the Second World War, the Abwehr had made some significant technological improvements. Using the chemical compound called Pyramidon (which was also sold commercially as a headache tablet under the same name), agents received clothing with the chemical impregnated into the cotton shoulder pads.[45] The chemical was dissolvable in alcohol (or water) and the agent would then use a toothpick with cotton wrapped around it to write the message.[46] Once in Abwehr hands, a seemingly innocuous letter would be treated with reagent chemicals to reveal the hidden message. On later occasions, the agents themselves were issued the reagent chemicals to enable the Abwehr to communicate with them by the same means.[47] Secret inks operate on a universal principle: they can usually be made from any fluid, usually organic, that has a high carbon content and will char easily. Department

I-G was the Abwehr section responsible for developing secret writing, headed by Captain Albert Müller, who also oversaw the production and duplication of forged documents.[48]

For the letters containing secret ink messages, the agents were provided with the address of at least one mail-drop in a neutral country, usually Portugal or Spain. While ordinary citizens might live at the addresses, an Abwehroffizier assigned to the local embassy, KO or Abwehrstelle collected the mail. Frequently agents awaiting assignment overseas would be detailed to monitor incoming correspondence from active agents and informants and to act as case or control agents.[49]

If secret ink was not available, agents were also trained to use coded phrases that could be inserted unnoticed into normal-looking correspondence. For example:

Congratulations on birth of a son – *radio in order*
Congratulations on birth of a daughter – *light damage, can be repaired*
Congratulations on birth of a child – *radio kaput*
Yours truly – *impossible to transmit* [50]

CODING SYSTEMS

The German military in the Second World War used three distinct levels of communications security (COMSEC) for high-priority messages. This was largely due to the changing nature of warfare and the indispensability of radio for command and control of the various units. German forces had an advantage early in the war due to their far-sighted decision to install radios in the command tracks of the Panzer divisions. This allowed for almost instantaneous communication and control of a battle, and was a means of passing along items of military intelligence from visual reconnaissance. Radio communication was also essential in the other branches of service, from coordinating U-boat attacks on Allied shipping to ensuring that Luftwaffe close support aircraft were in constant contact with their ground controllers. Land-line communication, whether by telephone or telegraph, was obviously prone to disruption and interception, but radio communication was more mobile, more reliable, and could reach anywhere on the globe with the appropriate equipment. The disadvantages of radio are equally apparent: radio signals do not distinguish between friend and foe; they can be and are received simultaneously by both friendly forces and the enemy.[51] To ensure that military radio traffic communicates the message in an exact and secure manner necessitates some form of cipher or code. The Germans thought they had the perfect solution.

In the Third Reich, the highest-priority military signals were those which passed between Hitler and his senior commanders. For such messages, the Germans used the Lorenz SZ40 encryption machine, which consisted of a series of electrically-controlled rotors and plug connections which encrypted the clear text before it was transmitted via radio to the receiver. With the creation of Colossus, the world's first programmable computer, experts at the British Government Code and Cypher School (GC&CS), Bletchley Park, managed to break the secret of the Lorenz and were reading German command messages in their entirety by 1943.[52]

The famous Enigma machine provided the second level of security for German forces. Working on the same basic principle as the Lorenz SZ40, Enigma machines were distributed to all regimental and higher headquarters, providing, in theory, an unbreakable security net for all command radio traffic. Over several years' work, the GC&CS managed to break the Enigma in 1940, and kept designing calculating machines ('bombes') to keep up with the changes in the design and transmission protocol throughout the Second World War.[53] The breaking of Enigma represented the ultimate intelligence coup – it put the British inside the German command structure and provided early warning of their situation, plans and intentions on a tactical and strategic level. It is difficult to overestimate the impact that this SIGINT breakthrough had on Allied success in the Second World War.

The Germans were content with Lorenz and Enigma security during the war, never guessing that their secrets were being revealed. For agents in the field, however, far away from any semblance of a regimental headquarters, the flagship security systems were not appropriate. It was considered too risky to equip a secret agent with an Enigma, so alternative means had to be used that would allow for relative, but not perfect, security between agents and Abwehr headquarters.

For standard radio transmissions, both to and from the agent overseas, it was essential that the messages be encrypted using systems that were thought to be secure. There were a number of variations that were taught to German agents during the course of the war. As hostilities continued, new and improved methods were introduced, often with mixed results. The earliest were based on hand-encoding systems that dated back to the First World War or a Vigenere cipher that was even older than that. These were usually either a double-transposition system or, after 1940, based on a modification of the 'Double Playfair' code, with elements added from the German ADFGVX cipher system. Essentially, the idea of Playfair was to construct a rectangle of twenty-five letters ('j' was omitted, being transmitted as 'ii'). Using a key word selected at random, but known to both parties, the letters would be substituted. For example, if the key word was 'secret,' *a* would be transmitted as *s*, *b* transmitted as *e*, etc.[54] There were several considerations however. First, the success of this method depended on the secrecy of the key word; it was not supposed to be anything personal to the agent, which might lead to discovery if the agent was caught and identified.[55] Second, this method, and the others employed by the Abwehr, depended on the care and skill of the agent to encode and decode the messages correctly. An inexperienced or sloppy operator/receiver might make a minor but critical mistake, or at least risk detection by requiring the message to be retransmitted due to his enciphering/deciphering error. Part of the problem with this system is that its workings were widely understood and had been explained in the pre-war (1931) treatise *The American Black Chamber* by Herbert Yardley. This proved to be a fatal flaw as it applied to German codes used in Ireland in the Second World War.

By far the most successful method of sending messages over a non-secure radio (the Enigma system was considered secure) was by use of the book code. Dating at least from the Napoleonic period, it was a relatively reliable means of covert communication.[56] For this method, messages were usually transmitted in groups of five letters and the sender would notify the receiver what particular page of the agreed book was to be used for the day's transmissions.[57] The letter *k* equalled zero and *x* was a dummy letter. To notify the sender that page 143 was to be used, the operator would send *x-a-d-c-x*. The group containing the page number was always the third of the message, the first two groups being meaningless decoys. The main message was then put in a grid, with the keyword (the first word on the page) written above. For example, in Table 2, certain spaces are blocked out, according to the number assigned the letter in the keyword. In the example, i is the ninth letter of the alphabet, so the ninth space (counting from the left) is blocked out; r is the seventeenth letter (omitting k) so seventeen spaces from the first blacked-out space would be another one, as we can see in Table 2. If the intended message was 'US FIFTH DIVISION ARRIVED IN BELFAST,' it would be inserted into the table as shown in Table 3. The enciphered message would then be transmitted in groups by reading down the first column under the key word beginning with the letter of the alphabet closest to *a*. In this case, this would be transmitted as *f-i-r-t-h/i-v-e-u-f/i-a-i-a-u/d-o-e-l-i/v-r-n-s-t/s-i-b-s-n/d-f.*[58]

An alternative method, one used by Wilhelm Preetz at various times, was also based on the book or keyword cipher, but with an additional degree of

Table 1

I	R	E	L	A	N	D

Table 2

I	R	E	L	A	N	D
	■					
				■		

Table 3

I	R	E	L	A	N	D
U	S	F	I	F	T	H
D	■	I	V	I	S	I
O	N	A	R	R	I	V
E	D	I	N	■	B	E
L	F	A	S	T		

difficulty. The key to the cipher was the first un-indented twenty-six letters on the designated page in the key book (usually a novel). Supposing that the key phrase was 'it took years for him to realize' and that the intended message was again 'US Fifth Division arrived at Belfast yesterday – heavy tanks and machine guns,' the grid would be as shown in Table 4. Rather than merely transmitting the columns in sequence, the agent would then assign a number to each letter in the key group based on the position of that number in the alphabet, even though it would almost necessarily mean an incomplete alphabet since it would be unlikely that any given phrase in the book would contain all 26 letters. In the group used above, letters *a* would be assigned a *1*, letters *e* a *2* (since there are no *b*s, *c*s or *d*s in that group) and so on – see Table 5. The letters are then transmitted in groups of five, beginning with the first column marked *1* (reading left to right). In our example, the first group would be *i-e-h-v-y*, etc.[59]

Though the book code was more secure than some other systems, it was still possible to extrapolate the keyword by using mathematics. The beauty of the book code was that it obviated the need to send updated keys to the agent in the field, usually a major weakness of coding systems. As long as the agent

Table 4

I	t	t	o	o	k	y	e	a	r	s	f	o	r	h	i	m	t	o	r	e	a	l	i	z	e	
u	s	f	i	f	t	h	d	i	v	i	s	i	o	n	a	r	r	i	v	e	d	a	t	b	e	
l	f	a	s	t	l	a	t	e	y	e	s	t	e	r	d	a	y	h	e	a	v	y	t	a	n	
k	s	a	n	d	m	a	c	h	i	n	e	g	u	n	s											

Table 5

5	12	12	9	9	6	13	2	1	10	11	3	9	10	4	5	8	12	9	10	2	1	7	5	14	2
I	t	t	o	o	k	y	e	a	r	s	f	o	r	h	i	m	t	o	r	e	a	l	i	z	e

and his controller had the same book, the keywords were self-sustaining. By contrast, the theoretically more secure Enigma system required a massive paper distribution every month, in order to make sure all machine operators received their new rotor and plug board settings. In most cases, an agent's mission would have been completed before the book became unusable, and in such a case, the agent would have been given the title of an alternative novel before leaving his base.

THE GÖRTZ SYSTEM

In yet another variation of the same system, used by both Hermann Görtz and John O'Reilly, the transmitted messages were entirely numerical. This was another variation of the 'Double-Playfair' and the German ADFGVX cipher, but was more sophisticated again.[60] The system required the use of two grid squares. For the first square, it was necessary to start with the keyword, say 'THE NORWEGIAN COAST.'[61] It was also important that the keyword contained an even number of letters, preferably 16 to 20. Next, all repeated letters had to be eliminated: THE NORWGIACS. The remaining letters were added in alphabetical order, omitting 'J' – B, D, F, K, L, M, P, Q, U, V, X, Y, Z – and placed in the 5×5 numbered square shown in Table 6. A number can now express every letter. For example, 'k' would be represented as '41.' The next step would be to create another grid using the original key word (and numbering system for the keyword used in the previous example) and encode the message into numbers – see Table 7. The message would again be transmitted according to the numerical sequence of the letters in the key word group: 13, 22, 2/1, 15, 52/ and so on. As an even more complex variation, the numbers could be transferred back to letters (using the 5×5 grid) and then sent as letter combinations in five-letter groups.[62]

Microdots

German technology was also advanced to the degree that agents sent to Ireland from 1941 onwards were to be equipped with the latest innovation in concealed information – the microdot. Essentially, this process – the exact reverse of normal photo enlargement – made it possible for a page of closely typed text to be reduced in size until it was literally a dot. As such, it was routinely inserted in otherwise innocent-looking typed material, such as a newspaper. Depending on the care taken by the technicians at Abwehr headquarters, it would be impossible with the naked eye to distinguish the dot over a normal letter 'i' from one containing highly sensitive secret material. The advantages were obvious: agents would not have to rely exclusively on memory and would not have to undergo the normal risks of having compromising documents on their person if stopped and questioned. In the case of Günther Schütz, for example, his entire mission portfolio was

Table 6

	1	2	3	4	5
1	t	h	e	n	o
2	r	w	g	i	a
3	c	s	b	d	f
4	k	l	m	p	q
5	u	v	x	y	z

Table 7

t	h	e	n	o	r	w	e	g	i	a	n	c	o	a	s	t
15	7	4	9	11	13	17	5	6	8	1	10	3	12	2	14	16
1	1	1	2	1	3	2	5	4	3	1	2	2	1	2	4	3
1	2	5	1	4	3	2	2	4	5	3	1	1	1	2	1	1

contained in the microdots of two newspaper cuttings. Under the 'o' in the word 'Aspro' in one of these cuttings, he had access to his list of Irish contacts, recognition words and the address of a new mail drop for Werner Unland. Dots in other parts of the cuttings contained his transmission times, frequencies, encoding procedures, weather reporting guide and operational abbreviations.[63]

Relying on the apparent invulnerability of the microdot system, Schütz's Abwehr controllers also included his list of intelligence priorities in Northern Ireland, the ultimate destination of agent and transmitter. According to this target list, the Abwehr had a wide range of interests: the location and capacity of corn and oil supplies, margarine and soap factories, sugar and oil refineries, carbide works, shipyard activity, condition of harbours (specifically Liverpool), the extent and nature of transatlantic shipping traffic, bomb damage from German raids, foodstuffs sent from Ireland to England, morale and whatever Army, Navy or Royal Air Force information he happened upon. Though his primary mission seems to have been weather reporting, Schütz was instructed to operate as a general-purpose agent, presumably with the idea that the subsequent insertion of other Abwehr operatives might be difficult and he would have to carry on alone.[64]

In some instances, but not those involving operations in Ireland, agents would be trained to create their own microdots and pass the information back to Germany by that means.[65]

Disc cipher

While not issued to all agents, the disc cipher wheel was carried by John F. O'Reilly when he landed in County Clare in 1943 and was also used by Abwehr agent Robert Petter, who was landed in Scotland in 1940.[66] The advantage of the cipher disc is that it is a simpler and, therefore, more reliable method for correctly enciphering coded messages. The disadvantage is that by examining a combination of letter frequency and distribution, an experienced code-breaker can still decipher the message.

The disc (also known as an autoclave) can be used in two distinct ways. In the simplest method, it can encipher a message using what is called a 'Caesar shift.' The outer ring of letters is the plain alphabet and the inner ring represents the cipher alphabet. For a Caesar shift of one, for example, the 'A' on the inner ring is aligned with the 'B' on the outer ring and thus the message is encoded. Technically, this results in a combination substitution/ transposition cipher. The second method, which is slightly more secure, requires a keyword known to both sender and receiver. As an illustration, let us suppose that the keyword is 'MARK' and the message we want to encipher is 'attack.' We would align the outer 'A' above the inner 'M', noting the first letter of the message 'a' on the outer ring and writing down the corresponding letter on the inner ring. For the second letter of the message, the 'A' on the outer ring would be set above the next letter of the keyword, 'A,' and the same procedure followed until the message is complete. The result is a polyalphabetic cipher that is more difficult to break than the Caesar shift.[67]

O'Reilly's list of 400 numerical combinations was also thought to have added an extra dimension of complexity to the disc cipher in that a completed message would then be again enciphered using the numerals as a base for generating another cipher. O'Reilly was singularly uncooperative when asked to explain the relationship of the disc cipher and the numerical list. O'Reilly's cipher disc was found with his other espionage gear, but he did not have the opportunity to send a message using this system.

2
Germany and Ireland, 1933–39

IRELAND AND GERMAN INTELLIGENCE PLANNING

Ireland was important to German intelligence as the result of geographic
accident. Unlike Sweden (iron ore) or Romania (oil), Ireland had no natural
resources that were of benefit to the German Reich. Geographically,
however, Ireland presented a real value – but only in terms of the German
effort against England. As part of a strategic initiative against the British,
Ireland occupied the position of an Atlantic gateway and was conveniently
located on the far side of the British Isles. Control of Ireland – or at least
the neutralization of Ireland against British use, would mean the de facto
control of the Atlantic re-supply line on which England depended. German
naval and air power was largely insufficient completely to disrupt the main
convoy routes from the United States, most of which passed by Ireland or
went directly into British-controlled Northern Ireland.[1] If Ireland could
be turned into a German ally, all the better – but German purposes would be
achieved if Ireland remained uncommitted but friendly towards the German
Reich and denied the use of its harbours and territory to the Western Allies.
German policy towards Ireland eventually coalesced around the idea that
Irish neutrality was the best position, at least in the short term, as far as the
interests of the Third Reich were concerned. With this goal in mind, de
Valera's wartime policy in Ireland was acceptable to the Germans, if not
ideal. The philosophy that 'half a loaf is better than none' seemed to prevail
in the German Foreign Ministry.

In most cases, German understanding of the Irish political and military
situation was rudimentary, making it necessary for the Abwehr and the
Wehrmacht to rely on 'experts' to fill in the numerous gaps in their
knowledge.[2] This sliding scale of expertise ran the gamut from those really
in a position to know to individuals whose main area of concentration was in
fairy folklore and the Irish language as it was spoken in the Middle Ages.
Several Germans had important positions in pre-war Irish society and they
were counted on to make some sense out of the Hibernian chaos. The
Abwehr and the Foreign Ministry depended on the impressions of the
German Minister in Dublin, but also employed outside expertise on a
regular basis.

German strategic interest in Ireland was obvious, but German intentions for Ireland were more opaque. The political and military situation changed rapidly and the Reich's plans for Ireland likewise ebbed and flowed. Hitler is quoted as saying that possession of Ireland would mean victory for Germany.[3] At best, it represented a momentary fancy. Hitler did not express any lasting interest in Ireland for either military or political purposes, and the various German enterprises involved in the Irish adventure were generally those created by lesser lights in the Nazi firmament. Ultimately, German victory was possible only if British military power could be decisively defeated in the air and on the high seas. Germany's failure to accomplish this using conventional means by the middle of 1941 eliminated their chances for the decisive global victory they sought. German adventures in Ireland *in connection with* a successful offensive against England might have had decisive results, even if Ireland was only used as a secondary or diversionary theatre of operations.

THE GERMAN PRESENCE IN IRELAND

By 1939, there were fewer than 200 known German aliens in Ireland, but their numerical inferiority camouflaged both their political impact and their potential utility in intelligence-gathering.[4] In addition to the German nationals themselves, there were 54 Austrians (whose country was an integral part of the Reich after the March 1938 *Anschluss*) and over 100 nationals from Hitler's 'Pact of Steel' ally, Italy. Though the overwhelming majority of these citizens lived their lives without any connection to the Abwehr or to the Nazi Party, those that were more active posed a clear threat to the Irish state and were a potential asset to German intelligence. Both Irish Military Intelligence (G2) and the Irish Police (Garda) closely monitored aliens of all descriptions. Comprehensive surveillance (visual, postal and electronic) ensured that most obvious security threats were contained before a problem materialized.

German interest in Ireland before the advent of National Socialism was largely scholarly. In the period before the Gaelic Revival and the 'rediscovery' of the Irish language, German scholars (most particularly Franz Bopp, Heinrich Zimmer and Kuno Meyer) authored pioneering works in the field of Celtic languages. German engineers also worked in the fields of electrical power (the Electricity Supply Board and the Shannon Hydro-electric Scheme), forestry and turf production.

The Auslandsorganisation

As probably the largest single organized German group in Ireland, the Auslandsorganisation (AO) provided a logical starting point from which to gather intelligence information, recruit local informants and generally keep an eye on the host country. Founded in 1931, and directed by Ernst-Wilhelm Bohle, this overseas affiliate of the NSDAP (Nazi Party) had several functions that would seemingly merge well into the intelligence-gathering process, at least in theory. Its task was to promote trade links between Germany and the host country, to monitor political developments and suggest useful resources for espionage and to maintain a watchful eye on German nationals living outside the Reich. It was also to provide political and ideological instruction, facilitate travel to the Reich by deserving Party members and to make arrangements for sister-city status between Germany and the host country.[5] By 1939, the worldwide AO membership reached over 50,000 and Bohle was rewarded with a position as State Secretary in the Auswärtiges Amt (Foreign Ministry).[6]

The AO was organized into country groups (Landesgruppen), districts (Kreise), local groups (Ortsgruppen) and bases (Stützpunkte).[7] On the odd occasion, AO service could even be dangerous; the AO leader in Switzerland, Wilhelm Gustloff, was shot dead in 1936 and a grateful Führer agreed to the renaming of a passenger liner in his honour.[8]

Though the actual Nazi Party membership in Ireland was only about 30, the number belied the influence that this group could muster at any one time. Influential Nazi Party members (who also belonged to the AO) included Dr Adolf Mahr, director of the National Museum; Colonel Fritz Brase, head of the Irish Army School of Music and Dr Friedrich Herkner, professor of sculpture at the National College of Art.[9] In addition to being a relatively senior Irish civil servant, Dr Mahr had the distinction of being head of the AO (Ortsgruppenleiter) in Ireland until July 1939.[10] His influence in Party circles was such that he engineered the political destruction of one minister to Dublin (Dr Georg von Dehn in 1934) and politically damaged the chargé d'affaires (Ernst Schrötter) in 1936.[11] Mahr was in regular contact with Dr Eduard Hempel (German Minister to Ireland, 1937–45), and was of such importance in the German community that he was invited as a guest to the coronation of King George VI in 1937.[12] Though the AO was politically active, there is no indication of any direct contact between the AO and the IRA, except that maintained through the person of Helmut Clissmann.

While the AO membership did unquestionably provide sources of information for both the Foreign Ministry and the SD, its actual value to the Abwehr was negligible. Bohle established a liaison with the Abwehr in 1937, but as a clear indication of favouritism the chief of his personnel department, Erich Schnaus, was tasked to work with the Nazi Party intelligence service, the SD.[13] The AO provided monthly reports of the local situation to Bohle – which were then transmitted to the SD and senior figures in the Nazi chain of command.[14] According to one senior Abwehr officer, there was 'never any coordination permitted between the Abwehr and the AO'.[15]

In practice, the AO served as a visible lightning-rod for Irish Military Intelligence and most of its activities and personnel were under constant surveillance. Rather than keep a discreet profile, some members of the German community, and the AO in particular, were rather strident about their political beliefs and national pride. The favourite Dublin watering-holes frequented by Mahr and the others were the Red Bank Restaurant in d'Olier Street and the Gresham Hotel in O'Connell Street. On occasion, the Nazi faithful would meet for weekends at the Kilmacurragh Park Hotel in County Wicklow – an establishment operated by German nationals Karl and Kurt Budina. German guests at these gatherings included Helmut Clissmann and Dr Hempel.

As an example of the public lives led by Ireland's Nazi community, their Christmas celebration in 1937 was typical. Under a decoration of swastika flags and Irish tricolours and the watchful eyes of their Führer's large portrait, the party faithful gathered in the Gresham Hotel for an evening of singing, drinking and being entertained by a children's play. At the apex of the celebration, the German Minister Dr Hempel requested that all 'rise and salute the Führer and Reich Chancellor', and with right arms raised in the Nazi salute the gathering sang *Deutschland über Alles*, the *Horst Wessel Lied* (the Nazi Party anthem) and *The Soldier's Song*, hardly the type of covert group that the Abwehr would have preferred to see in the forefront of its intelligence-gathering and support network in Ireland.[16]

The Italian fascists also maintained a political organization in Dublin, though on a considerably reduced scale compared to the AO. Called the 'Fascio di Dublino Michele D'Angelo', it was tied to the Fasci Italiani all'Estero (the Italian fascist overseas organization), Mussolini's counterpart to the Auslandsorganization. The erstwhile Duce in Ireland was Count Eduardo Tomacelli, who taught Italian at Trinity College. Like its Nazi counterpart, Irish intelligence and the Garda closely monitored the Italian fascist organization.[17]

When Mahr returned to Germany in 1939, he was employed by the Foreign Ministry in the section dealing with Irish issues, and was responsible for suggesting the establishment of a propaganda radio station directed at an Irish-speaking audience – the genesis of the Irland-Redaktion.[18] By 1944, he was the director of section Ru-9, the Foreign Ministry's desk dealing with political broadcasting to the US, Britain and Ireland.[19]

Mahr's own Nazi pedigree was beyond question. In 1944 he attended a joint SS, Foreign Ministry and Propaganda Ministry meeting on the subject of the 'Jewish Question'. The purpose of the meeting was to devise an effective strategy for disseminating anti-Semitic material overseas. Mahr was described in the minutes as 'handling the foreign anti-Jewish action on the radio'. He recommended the dissemination of anti-Semitic 'warning material' via radio broadcasts to foreign countries and the compilation of a list of 'Jewish inspired high-grade freemasons, journalists, writers, and economists'. Mahr also advocated the publication of a handbook (in French and English) for diplomats on 'Jewish World Politics'.[20]

THE GERMAN ACADEMIC EXCHANGE SERVICE

In addition to the rather obvious ties between Germans in Ireland and the Reich, such as those promoted by the AO, more subtle exchanges of personnel and information also took place. One of the major characters in this covert pre-war connection was Helmut Clissmann.[21] Previously a student at Trinity College, Dublin, he had returned to Ireland as the representative of the Deutscher Akademischer Austauschdienst – the German Academic Exchange Service, which brought German students and scholars to Ireland for one-year study exchange programmes.[22] It was not coincidental that many of these students and scholars, such as Joseph "Jupp" Hoven and Dr Hans Hartmann, were later involved in espionage activities. To a degree, Clissmann operated under the direction of Adolf Mahr. While there was some attempt at recruiting Irish citizens into the net of German espionage, it was largely ineffectual. Part of this failure must be attributed to the lack of time necessary to build an efficient framework, rather than a personal failure on Clissmann's or Hoven's part.[23]

In what was seemingly a cultural mission with at least propaganda overtones, Clissmann proposed in March 1939 to the Irish Secretary of Education that winners of the German Prize Scheme for Secondary Schools be awarded an annual travelling scholarship, which would be jointly sponsored by the German Foreign Ministry and the Academic Exchange Service. The student scoring the highest in the German component of the Leaving Certificate examination would be given an all-expenses-paid trip to Nazi Germany. In addition to cultural sights, the winner would spend one to two weeks in a State Youth Camp – presumably operated by the Hitler-Jugend (Hitler Youth) or the Bund Deutscher Mädel (League of German Girls).[24] De Valera ultimately decided to reject Clissmann's offer, though not from fears of political indoctrination: 'In the present position of the Catholic Church in Germany, the Government should not take the responsibility of sponsoring a scheme for sending Catholic children to German Youth Camps.'[25] The idea that a non-Catholic might come first in the German section of the Leaving Certificate was apparently too remote to merit consideration.

Ironically, Clissmann had earlier been viewed as being too left-wing. As a student, he had been member of the Young Prussian League and at one point, Peadar O'Donnell mistakenly referred to Clissmann as a Communist in a newspaper article. Clissmann did manage to get back into the good graces of the official German community, but not without some degree of effort.[26] According to Clissmann himself, he unsuccessfully attempted to attract the attention of Abwehr II to Ireland in 1938, only to be told that covert involvement between Germany and Ireland was 'forbidden' and must await a more appropriate time in the future.[27] Despite this prohibition from Abwehr II, Clissmann maintained and encouraged contact with senior IRA personnel.

On 11 September 1939, Clissmann departed from Ireland with many of the other German nationals aboard the mail boat *Cambria*. He continued working for the German Academic Exchange Service in Copenhagen until called up for active service in July 1940. Because of his educational and linguistic skills, he was posted to the Brandenburg Regiment and later assigned military and political missions relating to Ireland.[28]

THE GERMAN LEGATION

While the German legations stationed in other areas of the world would naturally act as centres for intelligence-gathering activity and analysis, the minister posted to Ireland, Dr Eduard Hempel, would prove to be something of a disappointment to German intelligence, selected members of the Foreign Ministry, the SD and the German war effort as a whole. Hempel was a career diplomat, cultured, careful and, in a word, diplomatic. He did not have the inclination or the training to actively run or assist intelligence operations in a meaningful way. Carolle Carter describes Hempel as 'a shrewd and sensible diplomat of the old school'.[29] His mission was to 'keep Ireland neutral until the "balloon went up in the West"'.[30] In this respect, he succeeded in encouraging Ireland to maintain a balanced position between the warring states, though one which was inevitably going to lean towards the Allies.

Some of Hempel's other qualities, however, proved to be more frustrating. He had a marked tendency to not make any decisions on the spot if he could pass on the problem for a decision by someone in Berlin.[31] Hempel also showed an unusual acumen when it came to protecting his own position. On numerous occasions, he would defer otherwise necessary action if the result might be embarrassing to him personally or politically. This coin, too, has two sides. While he was not aggressively active, Hempel was careful not to make any egregious mistakes. More forceful and reckless action by a less cautious diplomat could have easily resulted in the expulsion of the legation staff and the closure of the one reasonably secure centre of German information in Ireland. This was particularly true during the 1943–4 period, when de Valera was under increased pressure to deport the Axis diplomats, and had only Hempel's overt good conduct as a counter-argument.

From his initial posting in Ireland in 1937 until his mission terminated in 1945, Hempel endeavoured to fulfill his diplomatic brief to the letter – without the added complications of intelligence work if he could possibly avoid it. Part of the reason for this lack of interest in intelligence gathering can be traced back to the personnel assigned to the German Legation; the embassy was notoriously short-staffed.[32] A wartime attempt to augment the staff with military (and presumably qualified intelligence) personnel was stopped cold by de Valera and the Secretary for the Department of External Affairs. Hempel's deputy was the legation counsellor, Henning Thomsen. Like Hempel, Thomsen was a recent convert to the Nazi Party – probably for occupational security – and was the closest thing the Dublin legation had to an intelligence officer.[33] Thomsen was suspected by some of being a member of the SD. Though most major embassies were equipped with an Abwehroffizier, usually in the form of the once-ubiquitous 'passport control officer', the German legation in Dublin did not have one assigned – an operational oversight that was to present complications as the need for professional intelligence-gathering and analysis became critical.[34] Other than Thomsen, the legation staff consisted of Robert Wenzel, Wilhelm Müller, Herr Kochner, Johannes Bruckhaus (who kept the books) and two female secretaries, Hilda Mallie, née Six, and Edeltrude Freidinger.[35] None of the supporting staff are believed to have been involved in intelligence-gathering activities, with the sole exception of the press attaché, Dr Carlheinz Petersen.[36] Hempel also employed a number of German nationals as part of his personal domestic staff, Freifrau (Baroness) Elizabeth von Offenberg (lady's companion), Karl Schneider (butler) and Gerhard Günther (tutor).[37]

The German Legation, situated at 58 Northumberland Road, Dublin, was also equipped with a short-wave transmitter, which functioned as a back-up to the normal transmission of coded messages via telegraph. At the outbreak of war, all telegraph communications were routed through Britain, causing Hempel to rely more and more on his own transmitter, for fear that the British would break the diplomatic cipher of messages that passed directly through their hands. Unbeknown to Hempel, the British were not the only ones interested in the German Legation from a security standpoint. Irish Intelligence tapped his phone line, read his mail and carried out round-the-clock visual surveillance on all persons seen entering and leaving the legation. Similar surveillance was carried out on the Italian, Japanese, Spanish and US Legations.[38]

Prior to the outbreak of hostilities, the German Legation was a secondary source of intelligence data – and indeed, even once the hostilities began, Hempel and his staff seemed incapable of reporting anything other than information that was available in the local Dublin or British newspapers.[39] Hempel also had a tendency to panic – in one instance, he was apparently in fear for his life over the possibility of a British invasion in 1940. Hempel had plans to move his family into Dublin from the suburb of Dún Laoghaire where he lived, to disperse his staff to neutral embassies and to burn all his confidential papers. Only a series of telegrams from the German Foreign Ministry managed to calm him and return the situation to normal.[40]

Though the German Legation was the major asset for Axis intelligence-gathering, at least in theory, the Italian Legation at Northumberland Road was also a potential nerve centre for espionage operations. The Italian secret service (Servizio Informazioni Militare or SIM) was not known to have operated agents in wartime Ireland, but both it and another fascist intelligence service, the Sezione Prelevamento (Special Collection Service) would have collated reports sent to Rome from the Italian Legation.[41] The German and Italian legations cooperated to some extent on press and diplomatic matters, although the cultured Dr Hempel enjoyed far more diplomatic respect in Irish circles than did his Italian counterpart, Vincenzo Berardis.[42]

PETERSEN AND THE DEUTSCHE NACHRICHTEN BÜRO (DNB)

In the Third Reich, press reporting also served the interests of national propaganda and German stories from and about Ireland were not exceptions. The first German press representative in Ireland was actually a news agent named Mrs Lia Clarke, who had been appointed in 1936. Clarke, a native of Austria, was appointed on the recommendation of Dr Mahr and she was thought to have the correct ideological attachment to Nazi Germany. Her mission was to act as an Irish adviser for the German press and to 'furnish them with any material which would assist their anti-British press policy'. Her appointment, though, was short-lived. The decision was made in late 1938 to give the assignment to a regular member of the Deutsche Nachrichtenbüro (DNB), Dr Carlheinz Petersen. As a consolation prize, Clarke was made the representative of the Graf Reischach Dienst, a competing news service.[43] Clarke did not abandon her pro-Nazi bias: she was later involved with the Irish Friends of Germany.

As the official representative of the DNB, Petersen was posted to the German Legation in Northumberland Road.[44] He was gradually to devote more and more time to acting as the legation's public relations officer and eventually Hempel made him the press attaché, paying him a salary of fifty marks a month for duties outside those required by the DNB. He also oversaw the publication of *Weekly Review of the German News Agency*, counterpart to *Agenzia Stefani – News from Italy*. The German publication was mailed to a list of 3,000 subscribers (the names having been supplied by Fianna Fáil TD Dan Breen), which included government ministers, members of the Dáil, Irish Army officers and civil servants. Despite pressure from the British, and later the American Minister, the Irish government refused to suppress Petersen's newsletter.[45] Petersen enjoyed being one of the most sought-after dinner companions of Dublin diplomatic society – as well as having a reputation for being a drunk.[46] Petersen's indiscretions with alcohol led to his arrest in 1939 and he was almost charged with fighting an Irish Army officer and a Garda while under the influence. Hempel planned to send Petersen back on the plane that was scheduled to bring new personnel to Ireland, but the flight was cancelled and Petersen was forced to stay for the duration.[47] Petersen was often the contact man for persons wishing to give confidential information to the German Legation – a habit that earned him perpetual surveillance from Irish Army Intelligence and the Garda.[48] Petersen also acted as the espionage go-between for Joseph Andrews and Charles McGuinness, and was prepared to do the same for agent Günther Schütz.[49]

On the whole, Hempel did not provide anything useful for German military intelligence officials, but he did attempt to answer direct inquiries which were addressed to him from Berlin, as well as to pass along intelligence information which was brought from outside sources, usually adding his own evaluation of its trustworthiness. After a request to find out about the strength of the Irish Army, Hempel duly reported both their pre-war strength and the force additions since 1939 – all information culled from the pre-war *Irish Times*. He never succeeded in establishing an independent intelligence contact, much to the frustration of officers in the Foreign Ministry, who were more adventurous.[50]

CHARLES BEWLEY AND THE IRISH LEGATION IN BERLIN

Charles Bewley, the Irish Minister in Berlin from 1933 to 1939, posed a continuing wartime security and public relations problem for the Irish state and was a potential asset to the German intelligence community. From a Quaker background (though he converted to Catholicism), Bewley had been the Irish representative in Berlin from 1921/2, but his developing anti-Semitism proved a hindrance to his further utility in that post and he was replaced.[51] He was later appointed as Irish Minister to the Vatican. Once in Berlin, Bewley set about toeing the Nazi line as it pertained to the Jews, and his reports to Dublin about the worsening situation in Germany during the 1930s stressed that the Jews themselves were responsible for whatever unpleasantness they were experiencing.[52] Bewley did not attempt to contain his blatant pro-Nazi, anti-Semitic bias and his reports became little more than extensive paeans of praise for Hitler and the National Socialist system.[53] However, his resignation in August 1939 was not precipitated by official repudiation of his extreme views, but rather his acrimonious attitude towards the Department of External Affairs and what Bewley viewed as the pro-British direction of Irish foreign policy.[54]

After a brief sojourn back to Ireland, Bewley returned to Berlin in September 1939, following Britain's and France's declaration of war against Germany. In a posthumous autobiography, *Memoirs of a Wild Goose*, Bewley stated that he moved to Italy in January 1940, where he earned a living as a freelance journalist, and as an occasional expert commentator for the German Foreign Ministry, including a 'lengthy' report on the military value of the IRA to the German war machine.[55] Again according to his official account, he returned to Berlin on two occasions during the war, but stayed apart from the fighting. He also claimed that he refused Ribbentrop's offer of a position in the Foreign Ministry.[56] In fact, his activities were a little more nefarious than his sanitized version would suggest.

IRISH SECURITY AND IRISH MILITARY INTELLIGENCE

Both German and Italian aliens and diplomats were the subject of extensive pre-war surveillance by the main institutions of Irish security, G2 and the Garda Special Branch. As an integral part of the Irish Army, G2 – the staff intelligence designation in division or higher units – was not blessed with an overabundance of manpower either before or during the war. Ireland's use of the staff military intelligence section for domestic counter-intelligence work is perhaps unique. Britain's counter-intelligence agency, MI5, though an abbreviated form of 'Military Intelligence' is actually quite separate from the military intelligence section in the command TO&E (Table of Organization and Equipment); Ireland had no such distinction – G2 performed both tasks.

There were two wartime chiefs of Irish Intelligence: Colonel Liam Archer (until mid-1941) and Colonel Dan Bryan. Both had been active in the War of Independence and the Civil War. Bryan, in particular, had concerned himself with the strategic aspects of Irish security since 1936, when he authored the paper *Fundamental Factors Affecting Irish Defence Policy*, which examined Ireland in relation to Britain and provided the genesis of a security policy that would bear fruit three years later. Telephone and mail censorship issues in wartime had been examined since 1925–6.

> Many of the security problems which it dealt with during the emergency, together with the kinds of measures necessary to address them, had been anticipated and studied professionally, even when political, financial, staff and policy constraints prevented any action on them. Combined with the fact that its two most senior officers had extensive intelligence experience from the War of Independence and the Civil War, this meant that G2 was reasonably placed to handle the various jobs given to it between 1939 and 1945.[57]

Irish Intelligence adopted the mission of coordinating all aspects of state security, including those areas that are outside traditional areas of strategic or tactical interest. The pre-war G2 chief, Colonel Liam Archer, maintained files on all suspect persons and organizations without regard to whether the threat was domestic or foreign. Indeed, in the years leading up to World War Two, the main threat to security was clearly the subversive activity of the IRA, not German or Italian Intelligence.

During the war, G2 was also able to supplement its mission with personnel who were not officially responsible to G2 or even the Irish Army, but rather were a 'secret adjunct' to Local Defence Force (LDF). This auxiliary cadre, called the Supplemental Intelligence Service (SIS), was described as 'a network of carefully chosen persons of special ability' who assisted the regular military intelligence officers in the Southern Command area after June 1940. The SIS personnel were known only by code numbers for communications, and 'were given clear and detailed instructions on what to look out for and on how to report. Essentially, the mission of the SIS was limited to the fields of combat intelligence, counter-intelligence and "stay-behind" reporting in the event of invasion.'[58]

It is a testament to its dedication that G2 was able to fulfil its mission given the lack of personnel resources. Even at the height of the war, no more than about forty soldiers (officers and enlisted) were detailed for this work, divided between Southern, Western, Eastern and Curragh Commands, plus the headquarters at Parkgate Street, Dublin.[59] G2 necessarily maintained a liaison with the Garda, particularly the Aliens Section and Special Branch, to carry out the surveillance and interviews required. When the danger of continental war increased in the late 1930s, both G2 and the Garda focused increased attention on the activities of the vociferous Auslandsorganization and its leader, Dr Adolf Mahr.

As it happened, Irish concern over the presence of a thriving Nazi movement in Dublin led to one of the first cooperative intelligence interchanges between the Irish and British governments. On 31 August 1938, Secretary of External Affairs Joseph Walshe contacted the British Dominions office 'on the question of a liaison on counter espionage matters'.[60] Walshe subsequently told Guy Liddell of MI5 that 'the Eire Government was anxious about the NSDAP Group in Dublin' and that they felt it 'virtually infringed on their sovereign rights'. Liddell reciprocated by providing 'a copy of our memorandum on the NSDAP' together with another outlining recent British experience in investigating German espionage activities.[61] A meeting in London in October 1938 between Colonel Liam Archer of Irish Intelligence and MI5 marked the inauguration of the 'Dublin Link'.[62] As the espionage war became livelier, this start of Anglo-Irish intelligence dialogue was the first step on a road that would prove beneficial to the security of both countries. While cooperation was blooming concerning the Axis threat, Irish intelligence officers were perhaps more concerned with events even closer to home.

THE IRISH REPUBLICAN ARMY

Coinciding with the rise of Nazi Germany in the early 1930s, the Irish Republican Army had undergone a metamorphosis. Since the end of the Irish Civil War in 1923, the IRA leadership had changed considerably, with many of the earlier, more traditional leaders being converted to mainstream political activity with less reliance on violence. In particular, with the formation of Fianna Fáil in 1926, Republican sentiment, though still a factor in the issue of reunification between the Irish Free State (Saorstát Éireann) and the six counties of British-controlled Northern Ireland, was largely marginalized as a political force. Following the somewhat uncertain political landscape of the 1920s, the movement was largely in disorder, with a characteristic tendency towards factionalization. The most serious of these rifts was the formation of the Republican Congress under Frank Ryan, Peadar O'Donnell and George Gilmore, which effectively separated the extreme leftist membership from the core IRA.[63]

In practical terms, the IRA had difficulty rising above the image of loosely organized gunmen, more willing to fire the random shot than effectively to organize a system directed towards their goals.[64] Another difficulty facing the movement was the amalgamation of quite diverse groups under the IRA banner. Though it was thought that the political goals would be sufficient to maintain an organizational focus, this turned out not to be the case. In its philosophy, the IRA was socialist and it contained a high percentage of individuals who were of like mind. It also attracted a number of women – from the moderately glamorous Maud Gonne to the dowdy but determined Mary McSwiney and Helena Moloney.[65] While not a group that would be traditionally targeted by German Intelligence, the Republican women were to play an integral part in the outcome of various Abwehr and Foreign Ministry schemes.

A political foil to the IRA in the early 1930s was the rise of the Blueshirt movement under General Eoin O'Duffy.[66] A veteran of the War of Independence and later fighting on the side of Free State forces in the Civil War, O'Duffy is one of the most controversial figures in modern Irish history. After the victory of the Free State army over the IRA, O'Duffy, as a supporter of William T. Cosgrave, was appointed as Garda commissioner. His fortunes changed when de Valera came to power in 1932. O'Duffy was dismissed in 1933.

O'Duffy arguably had proto-fascist tendencies before this period, but his decision in July 1933 to join the Army Comrades Association (ACA) brought these inclinations into the open. On the surface, this was merely a fraternal society designed to promote camaraderie between old veterans, but in actuality it was a right-wing answer to what was seen as IRA dominance of fringe opposition politics. The ACA quickly became transformed into the 'National Guard' and their true nature was apparent when they adopted the blue shirt as their uniform – a direct link to the blackshirts of Benito Mussolini and Sir Oswald Mosley, and the brown-shirted SA (Sturmabteilung – Storm Troopers) in Nazi Germany.[67] The National Guard flag was a St Patrick's cross on a blue field. The party was based on the 'Führerprinzip' with General O'Duffy at the top of the hierarchical pyramid. The 'Blueshirts' (as they came to be called) were also avowedly Roman Catholic – no heretical religions were welcome – anti-Communist and committed to the reunification of Ireland.[68] This cross-sectional appeal was designed to bolster the Blueshirts' political popularity. They further allied themselves with the plight of small farmers; Blueshirt thugs made frequent appearances at forced livestock and land sales to disrupt the proceedings. The political significance of the party soon became apparent; in September 1933 Cumann na nGael (Cosgrave), the Young Ireland Association (Blueshirts) and the Centre Party (Frank MacDermot and James Dillon) merged to form the United Ireland Party, Fine Gael. William T. Cosgrave became the party leader in the Dáil.

O'Duffy's popularity reached its zenith in August 1933, when it was expected that he would turn an announced march in Dublin into a *coup d'état* in the fashion of Mussolini's march on Rome. The Minister for Justice banned the planned assembly on St Stephen's Green. Though tensions ran high in expectation of what was to follow, O'Duffy did not have the confidence to take the next step and cancelled both the march and the ceremony.[69] The Dáil passed a bill banning uniforms (specifically directed against wearing the blue shirt) in March 1934; O'Duffy resigned the presidency of Fine Gael on 22 September 1934, as well as his party membership. Later that year, he attended the International Fascist Congress in Montreux, Switzerland.[70] Blueshirt and IRA violence continued for some time, as did O'Duffy's involvement with the factions of the movement, but it was largely a spent force. The Blueshirts were a more natural ally of Nazi Germany than the IRA, but by the time that Germany became moderately interested in Ireland, there was no longer a Blueshirt movement with which to collaborate.

By 1936, O'Duffy was looking for a vehicle that would return him to political and popular prominence. He declared that he wanted to lead an Irish Brigade to Spain adding, 'If only two Irishmen go to Spain, I shall be one of them'.[71] The Spanish Civil war had erupted in July 1936 and the publicly anti-Communist Nationalist forces under Franco seemed to be ideologically tailored to win support among the church and population in Ireland ('The Spanish Nationalists were fighting for God and the Republic for communism').[72]. The fact that Franco was a fascist was deemed incidental. Volunteers from across the globe streamed into Spain to fight for both belligerents.[73] Finally collecting about 700 motley volunteers, O'Duffy left for Spain in November to fight for Franco.[74] Designated the 'Bandera Irlandesa del Terico', it was destined to see little combat and, on the whole, did nothing to bolster the reputation of either Irish or Spanish Nationalist military prowess.[75] The bulk of the brigade returned in June 1937. It had suffered a few deaths from friendly fire, and at least two had died from sickness.[76] By contrast, the Irish volunteers to the Republican cause, including its organizer Frank Ryan, generally fought well as members of the

International Brigade.[77] Ryan was captured by Italian 'volunteer' troops in 1938 and sent to languish in Burgos Prison under a death sentence. [78]

The public profile of the IRA rose somewhat in response to the growth of the Blueshirt movement under Eoin O'Duffy, but by the mid-1930s, the IRA leadership was in a quandary as to what direction to take in order to realize its political goals.[79] From 1936 onwards, the IRA was seeking new channels to outside assistance. Still organized by brigades, the organization had units both north and south of the Northern Ireland/Irish Free State border. The Dublin, Cork and Belfast units were traditionally the most active. Sources for IRA recruitment came both from cities and towns, but the tradition of sons following fathers was still an important determining factor; tradition, more than ideology, played the key role.

Several of the leaders from the War of Independence and the Civil War were still active in one way or another, but the leadership was ageing and no new and viable candidates had stepped forth. Seán Russell and Jim O'Donovan were still there from the War of Independence period (1919–21), but Russell was an ageing warrior and O'Donovan had retired to less hazardous work for the Electricity Supply Board. Moss Twomey had been chief of staff in the ten years leading up to 1936, but he had become prematurely old with the responsibility as an underground guerrilla chief. Even after the Republican Congress split in 1936, the IRA continued to factionalize further; the 1938 army convention divided over Russell's planned bombing campaign in England, polarizing the membership into partisanship for either Tom Barry or Seán Russell.[80] A further dilution of strength was not what the IRA needed at this particular time. The IRA was officially a banned organization from 1936 and subject to the full legal pressure that the Fianna Fáil government could bring to bear.[81] Many key IRA leaders were jailed and the movement was deprived of its usual sources of support.

SEÁN RUSSELL AND THE BOMBING CAMPAIGN

Born in Dublin in 1890, Russell was, in many ways, the stereotypical IRA man. He had been prominent in the organization as director of munitions during the War of Independence. Russell journeyed to America in 1936, and while meeting with the Clann na Gael leader in the United States, Joseph McGarrity, is thought to have initially created the idea of the bombing campaign against England. Upon his return to Ireland, anticipating a political shift in the IRA that would propel him to the upper leadership, he was surprised to find himself brought before an IRA court martial and convicted of misappropriating funds and held liable for the loss of twelve Thompson sub-machine guns in County Kildare. This was both a political and disciplinary measure by MacBride and Barry. While temporarily stranded in the political wilderness, Russell, prompted by McGarrity, pushed ahead with his bombing campaign directly against targets in England, drafting James O'Donovan to do the actual planning. Matters came to a head at the April 1938 army convention in Dublin, where the membership elected to approve Russell's plan over that of Barry.[82] Barry resigned as chief of staff and Russell, who was banned from attending the convention, was selected *in absentia*.

The bombing campaign opened on 16 January 1939 with seven separate explosions on electrical lines and power stations, followed in subsequent months by attacks on the Grand Canal, the Birmingham Navigation Canal, the Willesden Railway Bridge and an especially vicious attack in Coventry. Militarily, the attacks failed to impair the British to any significant degree. Most notably, the campaign was also symptomatic of the long-established IRA pattern of incompetently executed operations, carried out by personnel who were of questionable capability. In one instance, the police arrested Joseph Kelly, who just happened to be carrying a copy of O'Donovan's S-Plan. Police searches of suspects also uncovered documents that proved the IRA link, along with coded messages and decryption keys – all seized in the same raid. One of the IRA local bomb-making factories blew up when a less-than-stellar volunteer dropped a lit cigarette 'onto a potassium-sprinkled floor'.[83]

The Germans, too, had difficulty interpreting the IRA bombing campaign and it caused some problems with later attitudes towards the IRA. This is partially explained by Hitler's own admiration for England and his assertion that England and Germany were natural allies, not competitors, on the European stage. This political (and racial) attitude had the effect of compromising German military intelligence even further, officially restricting deep-cover penetration operations in England from 1935 to 1937, meaning that the Abwehr would have an even smaller resource base for future covert activities.

The official German position towards the IRA changed as the situation demanded. In an editorial of 23 June 1936, the *Völkischer Beobachter* praised de Valera for his handling of the 'sogenannten [so-called] IRA', while still referring to him as 'Ireland's dictator'. By 1939, the attitude had changed, and semi-official German publications (all subject to strict censorship) began referring to the IRA in more understanding terms. This coincided with the growing political and military hostility between Germany and England, which had the effect of jump-starting Abwehr operations in previously inviolate England and Ireland. On 27 January 1939, the same paper reported more favourably on the national aims of the IRA (no longer referred to as 'so-called'). Referring to British arrests of suspected persons, the *Völkisher Beobachter* editorialized that 'Die bomben in London, Birmingham und Manchester waren die Antwort der IRA auf diesen willkürakt' (The bombs in London, Birmingham and Manchester were the IRA answer to this arbitrary act.). An editorial in the *Frankfurter*

Zeitung from 24 January 1939 sympathized with the Irish people in their 'fight for freedom' against the British and praised the Irish 'spirit of rebellion'. In a testimonial of understanding which might have come directly from the pen of the IRA itself, the paper commented that 'the passionate activity, which now claims undivided attention, is perhaps only the last phase of a war in which Ireland successfully rebels against England'.[84] In total, there were approximately a hundred completed or attempted acts of sabotage during the S-plan campaign, which lasted until February 1940.[85] Innocent lives were lost and some property was damaged, but the resulting flurry of legislation from both the Irish and British parliaments turned the bombing campaign into a counter-productive and foolish exercise for the IRA leadership, and one which ultimately delivered a blow from which the IRA would not recover. It also meant that the IRA was less able to help Germany once war began.

The English response was the Prevention of Violence Bill in July 1939, which gave the police and security forces much wider latitude in dealing with internal threats. Many suspected Irish nationals were deported or fled, depriving the IRA of the support system necessary to its campaign. Ireland's even more strict emergency legislation followed the IRA attack on the Magazine Fort in Phoenix Park, Dublin, on 23 December 1939.

Historically, both funding and weapons came from Irish groups in the United States, principally the Clann na Gael. While this pipeline continued to function to some degree, particularly when it came to light automatic weapons – the Thompson sub-machine gun was popular – and a few transmitters, funding for the now illegal group had largely dried up.[86] Many former Irish supporters in the United States were less inclined to support an Irish nationalistic movement once the Free State was achieved and the struggle for national liberation was replaced by traditional democratic processes; the partition issue did not strike the same emotional chord in the US once nationhood was a reality. Contact continued, however, and the same channels that carried materials and money for the Irish Hospitals Sweepstakes between the United States and Ireland also carried weapons and cash intended for the IRA.[87]

The Germans were initially to regard the IRA as an underground band of terrorists, but this attitude changed as chances of an acceptable political settlement with Great Britain worsened. To the eyes and ears of the German intelligence community, the IRA seemed more significant than it was in reality. Openly anti-British and publicly committed to a reunification of Ireland by force, the IRA seemed to be a disaffected nationalist movement with which the Germans could work, provided that the contact was handled in a skilful manner and that the IRA was as professional in action as their name suggested.[88] Minister Hempel did attempt to warn the German government that the IRA was not a feasible partner in grand strategy, but his warnings were largely ignored:

The IRA is hardly strong enough for action with promise of success or involving appreciable damage to England and is probably also lacking in a leader of any stature ... sensible adherents of the radical nationalist movement, correctly sizing up the situation and the dangers, are opposed to coming out into the open at the present time; they also recognize, in agreement with the overwhelming majority of the population, the determination to maintain neutrality. ... Interference on our part would, in their opinion, prematurely endanger the whole nationalist movement, including groups which are not radical because the latter would accuse the IRA of making national interest dependent on Germany.[89]

By contrast, the IRA saw the various German offers of aid and assistance as a meal ticket for their own agenda. The IRA was never principally interested in furthering the cause of global Nazism, but saw it as a means to a united Republican Ireland. The overused phrase 'England's difficulty is Ireland's opportunity' encapsulates the driving philosophy and it is arguably what led the IRA to ruin in its complicity with Nazi Germany. German Intelligence was prevented, by decree from Hitler, from engaging in espionage operations in England (and, by extension, Ireland) until 1937, which seems to have been the date of the earliest German contact with the IRA.[90]

3
Pre-war intelligence contacts

It is difficult to pinpoint when Germany became seriously interested in Ireland for the purposes of espionage. At some point between 1937 and 1939, Ireland and its political resources became a factor in Abwehr planning, though the development of this situation was neither quick nor easy.

British Intelligence, in a classified summary of German activities, pinpointed the earliest contact between the Abwehr and Ireland to an incident involving a German national named Kurt Wheeler Hill. Hill came to Ireland in March 1937 and stayed in Dublin with the German Consular Secretary, Robert Wenzel, a Nazi Party member since 1935. En route to Ireland, Hill gave his English address as 5 Cleveland Terrace, the headquarters of the Nazi AO in Britain.[1] In Ireland, Hill placed a newspaper ad that read: 'German student would exchange German for English conversation.' It was answered by an Irishman (name censored by MI5) who worked as a salesman in a bicycle shop. In August 1937, Hill persuaded the man and his wife to travel to Germany, where he was introduced to Dr Luders of the Hamburg Ast. Following a hearty German welcome, the prospective Irish recruit agreed to help the Abwehr and was asked to set up a secure radio link with Hamburg-Wohldorf, and to find sources of information in the Royal Tank Corps, the RAF and the IRA. Upon return to Ireland, the contact did nothing, but was persuaded to return to Germany in March 1938. At this meeting, the contact learned that messages were exchanged when German ships called into Irish ports, using the first officers as conduits for messages between the Abwehr and the agents. Though the Irish contact reported that he had found suitable sources in the Royal Tank Corps and the RAF, they were in fact imaginary. He then surrendered to the British War Office in London and was used in an early Double-Cross operation.

MI5 wanted to use the Irishman to recommend another to take his place, an MI5 officer. When the SS *Finckenau* arrived in Dublin on 11 May 1938, First Officer Küster sent word that he wanted to meet with the Irish contact. The Irishman passed along his recommendation of the MI5 officer (masquerading as a journalist), and the Germans accepted this. Subsequently, the British passed military disinformation material through the same channel when the SS *Finckenau* returned to Dublin. The MI5 officer was even introduced to Dr Adolf Mahr and other leading members of the AO when he attended a dinner meeting at the Red Bank Restaurant.

According to the MI5 agent's report, other Irish were also involved with the Germans. Several Irish were observed speaking to crew members of the *Finckenau* and the original Irish informant claimed that the brother-in-law of a Garda officer was a German agent in Galway. The SS *Lindenau*, the sister ship of the *Finckenau*, was also believed to be a message conduit between Dublin and Hamburg. Kurt Wheeler Hill remained in the picture; G2's report added that 'he [Hill] urged a woman of partial German origin who was a student of his to associate with the German colony in Dublin'. Because of the recently created 'Dublin link' between MI5 and G2, the case was passed to Irish Intelligence, but no further developments were reported. Information passed to MI5 suggested that Kurt Wheeler Hill became alarmed and left Dublin quickly in early 1939, 'suddenly recalled to Hamburg' – according to Irish Intelligence.[2] A subsequent G2 report noted that Hill was 'stated to be a German agent recruited by [Legation Counsellor Henning] Thomsen'. Hill was not known to have returned to Ireland.[3]

LEON MILL-ARDEN

In subsequent interrogations of suspects and collaborators, Irish Army Intelligence (G2) determined that a French national named Leon Victor Mill-Arden (originally Louis Millardot), with an office in Dublin's O'Connell Street, was among the early contacts. Mill-Arden belonged to the disaffected group of Breton separatists that had been targeted as an ideological resource by German intelligence. His company, Agricultural Products Company, imported seed potatoes and was, according to Mill-Arden, partially 'funded by the SS' (it is clear in the summary that he meant 'Secret Service' or Abwehr, not the Schützstaffel). His name was also found on Görtz's list of potential contacts seized in the Garda raid on Stephen Carroll Held's house in May 1940.

The scope of Mill-Arden's activity is not known, but he admitted to acting on behalf of the Germans and IRA into the early 1940s. His statements to G2 included the admission that he made a trip to Paris in July 1939 to collect a parcel for James O'Donovan, which Mill-Arden thought was cash.[4] He further wrote a business letter on behalf of O'Donovan in 1941 addressed to Spanish attorney Jaime Michel de Champourcin into which O'Donovan inserted a message in invisible ink.[5] This is significant in that it ties together a number of seemingly unrelated threads: Jim O'Donovan – leading IRA member, German Intelligence contact, and author of the S-Plan to bomb England; Mill-Arden, sometime conduit for the German-Irish connection; and Champourcin, the attorney hired by the Irish ambassador to Spain, Leopold Kerney, to help free Frank

Ryan. Champourcin also had the distinction of being a close friend of Francisco Franco and Abwehr chief Admiral Wilhelm Canaris.[6]

SEÁN MACBRIDE AND TOM BARRY

Another German Intelligence resource was Seán MacBride. The son of Maud Gonne MacBride and executed 1916 insurgent John MacBride, Seán MacBride had been especially active in the IRA during the 1920s and 1930s and was Chief of Staff of the IRA in 1936. His family had a history of anti-British activity, and he was a frequent visitor to the home of German minister Eduard Hempel.[7] According to a G2 report, the German proposed a cooperative arrangement in 1938 while Tom Barry was IRA chief of staff. Barry was said to have been a good friend of the German Joseph 'Jupp' Hoven.[8] Hoven, a sometime anthropology student who spent much of 1938 and 1939 in the west of Ireland and Ulster, was actually a German agent. On the outbreak of war, Hoven returned to military service with the Brandenburg Regiment and was assigned various missions for the Abwehr and the Foreign Ministry for the remainder of the war – including the release of Frank Ryan from Burgos Prison in 1940 and the recruitment scheme among Irish prisoners of war. He later saw active service as an intelligence officer (Ic) with the Luftwaffe airborne troops.

According to Irish Army Intelligence files, Barry took a trip to Germany in 1937, accompanied by Hoven.[9] The purpose of the trip was to investigate the cooperation between Germany and the IRA, particularly with respect to German support for guerrilla war and sabotage against England.[10] Barry returned with a proposal for German assistance under the condition that the IRA limit its targets to British military installations in Northern Ireland or England once war was declared between German and England. This plan, proposed by Barry at the army general convention in April 1938, was rejected in favour of the Seán Russell-supported S-Plan ('S' for Sabotage) against civilian targets in England. Barry resigned over the dispute and Russell took effective charge of the IRA as its new chief of staff. Hoven is said to have visited Barry after the trip to Germany and the collapse of the German proposal, and Barry was certainly in contact with Hoven and Helmut Clissmann – both suspected German agents – as late as February 1939. The pair of Germans also met on two occasions with Moss Twomey, former IRA Chief of Staff.[11] In a subsequent interview with Captain Foley from Southern Command G2, Barry admitted that in the 1937–8 period, the Germans were offering to fund the IRA through the Clann na Gael in the United States.[12]

Some early German contacts may have been of scant operational significance. In a background report on German–IRA contacts, G2 alleged that a German named van Gruman, representing the Detering Oil Company, had expressed an interest in official German–IRA collaboration during the 1937–8 time frame. Likewise, an ex-German Army officer named Bismarck, representing the Landskrona Company – which was attempting to sell armoured vehicles to the Irish Army in 1937 – visited Ireland and was interested in the possibility of an alliance between the IRA and the Irish Army, negotiated by Germany.[13]

According to the same G2 report, the German–IRA link was then handed over to Barry's Director of Intelligence, Seán MacBride. Indeed, the report goes on to state that MacBride 'was working for the Germans even more than for the IRA'.[14] Fellow lawyer Con Lehane, intelligence director of the Dublin Brigade IRA, assisted MacBride in this liaison with German Intelligence.[15] Though he was officially 'legitimate' at this point as far as the public was concerned, MacBride was subsequently involved in contacts between the IRA and German intelligence. MacBride's connection to German Intelligence did not end with the Stuart episode (see pp. 66–9). According to coded telegrams sent by Minister Hempel to the Foreign Ministry in Berlin, a man identified as 'M.B.' had been contacted by Abwehr agent Ernst Weber-Drohl soon after his seaborne landing in 1940. Hempel described the mysterious 'M.B.' as being 'very anti-British and reliable, yet retained strong sympathies for France and had contacts with the French Embassy'. At the time, MacBride had a position as a correspondent for a French newspaper.[16] When Günther Schütz escaped from Mountjoy in 1942, he also reportedly contacted 'M.B.'[17] Of course, MacBride's involvement is complicated by the fact that, in 1948, he became the Minister for External Affairs. Information that he actively supported Nazis in Ireland during the war would, if made public, have proven detrimental to his political career and to his subsequent place in Irish history.

During the 'Emergency', MacBride was considered enough of a security threat to have his telephone tapped and his mail intercepted, but for various reasons – most of them political – he did not end the war in the Curragh.[18] MacBride, of course, went on to recognition in a number of ways. As Minister of External Affairs in the Costello inter-party government of 1948–51, he was an important political figure when Ireland proclaimed its formal independence in 1949. Internationally honoured as the winner of the Nobel Peace Prize and Lenin Peace Prize, he was also the UN representative to Namibia.

MacBride's wartime conduct in relation to the Germans is difficult to assess. Without more direct evidence, it would have been impossible to arrest him, let alone convict him of an offence against the state. Certainly, he was brilliant, anti-British, and had a multitude of suspicious contacts. On the evidence of Francis Stuart, his brother-in-law, he was an accessory, if not the principal, behind a contact with German intelligence in 1939–40. More than that, however, cannot be conclusively established. While there was no direct proof of fire, a less politically connected man might have died from smoke inhalation.

CHARLES BERNARD COMPTON PHILLIPS

Charles Bernard Compton Phillips, a 35-year-old Irish solicitor, came to the attention of both G2 and MI5 when he passed through Holyhead, North Wales, in June 1939 wearing a large swastika badge. Examination of his passport revealed that he was a frequent traveller between Ireland and Germany. A postal surveillance report noted the fact that Messrs. Kol and Company of Amsterdam (one of the Abwehr's money-laundering operations) transferred a payment of £10 for Mr Phillips. However, the information from Holyhead and the postal surveillance was not collated in time, and MI5's information was not passed on to G2.[19] Phillips seems to have held the momentary attention of German Intelligence and was active as a German agent in Ireland and Northern Ireland.

Later investigation by G2 revealed that Phillips instigated the contact himself, writing to the German ambassador in London in 1937, offering to sell information, and asking to be put in touch with the German secret service. He heard nothing from the German embassy, but received a letter a few weeks later from a P. van Zuiden in Amsterdam, who enclosed three £5 notes and asked Phillips to meet him in Cologne.[20] Phillips first met with his intelligence controller at the Hotel Hohenzollern in February 1938. Van Zuiden introduced him to a 'Dr Pfeiffer' and the pair of them asked Phillips to visit England and Northern Ireland to report on military preparations, but to cease operations in the event of war between Germany and England.[21] They told the Galway-born solicitor to subscribe to military journals and to send interesting clippings to a Frau Nohl in Hamburg. Phillips was code-named 'Tipperary'.

Phillips was summoned to another meeting in June 1938 and told that he was to locate a man at the coffee stall in Hamburg train station. The contact would be smoking a briar pipe and Phillips was to identify himself by humming 'It's a long way to Tipperary'. The recognition signal worked and Phillips was introduced to his new controller, 'Dr Lutz'. Lutz wanted specific information about 'whether British troops were stationed in Irish ports'.[22] The hand-over of the Treaty Ports would be completed in the following month, a fact apparently unknown to Dr Lutz.[23]

Though Phillips maintained to Irish Intelligence that he made no reports of substance, he met with German Intelligence a third time in March 1939. At this session, he was told that his new task was to observe British military movements and to forward maps of Aldershot, Bristol and Liverpool. His specific target and the time he was to leave on his mission would be communicated by post. The target was indicated by the placement of the stamps on the card. Using the standard 'Hindenburg Kopf' stamps then in circulation, if the target was Northern Ireland, the head on the stamp would be positioned to face north; east if Liverpool was the destination; south if southern England was intended. The cards would be signed 'Rose', and the exact date he was to leave would follow the lines that mentioned the names 'Jack Mauricy' and 'Gordon Higgs'. Upon reaching his target area, Phillips was to locate and send a postcard with a picture of a train if he found a state of alert, or one of a church steeple if all was quiet. To provide a plausible reason for the correspondence to and from Germany, Lutz pretended to have hired Phillips to trace the Aryan ancestry of people living in Germany with Irish antecedents.

For more detailed reports, Phillips was provided with secret ink that was disguised to look like toothpowder. To make his report, he had to mix the powder with an amount of standard black ink and then write the message on the outside of a small envelope. This envelope would then be placed inside a slightly larger envelope and then the entire thing was placed under pressure (an occupied chair was recommended) for at least two hours. When finished, an invisible message would have been transferred to the interior surface of the outer envelope and then a decoy letter could be inserted and the letter mailed to Lutz in Germany.

Part of the problem with Phillips's career in the world of espionage was that, to quote a G2 evaluation, '[Phillips] is regarded as not being mentally stable'.[24] He also seems to have had a noticeable deficit of intelligence. On at least one occasion, 'he received a postcard dated 24.4.39 and went to England in consequence, though the stamp had actually indicated Northern Ireland, as he afterwards realised'. He also did not seem shy about advertising his connections to Germany, including the Nazi pin he habitually wore. At one point, his girlfriend became worried 'and got him to cease decorating his car with a Hamburg flag'.[25]

In June 1939, Phillips had one more meeting with Dr Lutz in Hamburg. As a consequence of this visit, he was sent to Belfast in August and eventually mailed a local map with marked military positions back to Germany. The outbreak of war in September effectively severed any further contact between Phillips and his controller.

Although circumstantial evidence against Phillips had existed since 1939, no action was taken and his case was not investigated. He was again brought to G2's attention in December 1942. In October 1942, Phillips volunteered for service in the Irish Local Defence Force (LDF) and was assigned as a private in the No. 2 Company, 43rd Rifle Battalion. He came to his commander's attention when he asked for a transfer to intelligence and casually remarked that he had been in pre-war contact with German Intelligence.[26] Phillips was subsequently detained and interrogated by G2. They did not, however, see fit to incarcerate him and he was released. Phillips's post-war career was not exemplary; he was sentenced to twelve months' imprisonment in 1947 for receiving stolen property.[27]

PROBLEMS IN THE DUBLIN LINK

The MI5/G2 security arrangement functioned reasonably well, but there were occasional examples where one side or the other was slightly less than candid. In July 1939, MI5 received an indirect report from the Czech Consul in Dublin stating that Hempel and 'three members of the Nazi Party in Dublin' held a personal meeting with the IRA at the Drumbeg Hotel in Inver, County Donegal.[28] General Eoin O'Duffy and Seamus Burke were supposedly responsible for the arrangements, along with Theodor Kordt, the counsellor to the German Embassy in London. MI5 confirmed that Kordt had indeed been in Ireland, and that Hempel had visited Kordt in London on 23 July. They also learned that the Drumbeg Hotel was 'owned by a German named Hammersbach' – his name was, in fact, Wilhelm Hemersbach – and that two officials of the German Legation, Robert Stumpf and Consular Secretary Wenzel, had been staying there.[29] That aside, MI5 considered the cooperation between O'Duffy and the IRA to be improbable and discounted the idea that the IRA would hold a meeting in such a public place.[30]

G2 received similar, if not identical, reports from their own informants. According to an unnamed Garda source, a meeting was held in August 1939 in Louisburgh, County Mayo, between 'Hempel, members of the German colony, General O'Duffy and members of the IRA'.[31] Stories even appeared in the press. The *Birmingham Post* reported the alleged meeting in Inver, citing

> prevailing rumours of 'German Gold' at the back of the IRA are treated with scant courtesy in Eire, where similar rumours, without positive proof, have been common for many years. ... During the past week or two there have been whisperings of a secret meeting in the wilds of Donegal between members of the IRA and certain German officials who hold high place in Eire.[32]

MI5 received another report from the previous source in August 1939, which said that Hempel was in contact with the writer Francis Stuart and Stuart's brother-in-law Seán MacBride about organizing an Irish legion to fight alongside Germany against Britain. MI5 passed the information to G2, telling them that the source was a Czech servant in the German Legation. Somehow, Joseph Walshe, the Secretary of External Affairs, was let into the loop and he immediately tried to downplay the information, saying that the informant was unreliable and 'a villainous type'. According to the MI5 report, 'there is little doubt that Joe Walshe feared that the Czech informant in the German Legation might prove embarrassing to the Eire Government. ... He did his best to discredit the informant in the eyes of the British, and it is believed, later informed the German Minister, who sacked him.'[33] It is unclear why Walshe would be apprised of intelligence sources and methods, but it is even more puzzling that he would take it upon himself to sever the source of the information; whether or not the informant's messages proved to be fully accurate was quite beside the point. G2 seems never to have placed another asset inside the German Legation, though they did conduct visual, electronic and postal surveillance.

OSCAR PFAUS

The distinction of being the most significant Abwehr contact with the Irish Republican Army goes to ardent propagandist turned agent Oscar K. Pfaus. Originally from Illingen in Würtemburg, Pfaus's background prior to his Irish mission reads like a fable – as indeed, much of it probably is. Pfaus certainly went to the United States in the 1920s where he allegedly served a short time in the US Army and an equally short time as a policeman in Chicago.[34] While on army service, Pfaus claimed that he served under the command of General van Horn Mosely while assigned to the US Sixth Corps at Fort Sheridan, Illinois.[35] Despite his nomadic working pattern, Pfaus found the time to become a founder of the German-American Bund. An aberrant newspaper article that appeared in the German-language paper *California Journal* on 26 February 1932 alleged that Pfaus was nominated for the Nobel Peace Prize due to his writings ('famous in all circles of the world') in the cause of peace.[36] Needless to say, the Nobel committee was apparently unaware of Pfaus's good work and he was never short-listed for the coveted award.[37] Pfaus appears to have worked periodically for several German-language papers, most notably the *Weckruf und Beobachter* (*Roll Call and Observer*) in Chicago and the *Sonntagsbote* (*Sunday Messenger*) in Pittsburgh.[38] While in the United States, Pfaus began working for the Deutscher Fichte-Bund, an organization dedicated to distributing Nazi propaganda worldwide.[39]

The announced purpose of the Fichte-Bund, as described on the organization's letterhead, was slightly more circumspect: 'Serving the cause of peace and understanding by giving free information about the New Germany, direct from the source [and] to protect human culture and civilization by disseminating facts about world Bolshevism, its authors and dangers'. Heinrich Kessenmeier founded the Fichte-Bund in 1914 but by 1937 the organization was directed by his son, Dr Theodor Kessenmeier.[40] It even had its own printing press, the Falken Verlag. Kessemeier had direct links with the Abwehr, particularly the Hamburg Ast. While the Abwehr under Canaris certainly did not share the rather virulent racial and political propaganda aims of Kessenmeier, the Fichte-Bund mailing list did provide a useful starting point for recruiting potential German sympathizers in enemy and neutral countries. Pfaus's usefulness sprang from the fact that he spoke excellent English and had contacts in a number of important circles.

Pfaus returned to Germany in December 1938 and promptly began working in the English section of Fichte-Bund headquarters in Hamburg's

Jungfernstieg.[41] Shortly thereafter, he was 'loaned' by Dr Kessenmeier to the Abwehr II officer in Hamburg, Kapitänleutnant Walter Schneidewind. Schneidewind needed an English-speaking operative and Pfaus seemed to fit the bill.[42]

Pfaus was introduced to only one small part of the Abwehr organization, the Abwehrstelle located at Knochenhauerstraße, Hamburg, in the building occupied by the X Army Corps. Here his English ability was tested and he was familiarized with news stories of the IRA bombing campaign in England. His mission was explained to him: to seek out the IRA leadership; make contact; ask if they would be interested in cooperation with Germany; and, if so, to send a liaison man to Germany to discuss specific plans and future co-ordination. Pfaus's mission did not include a military component, and he was not authorized to discuss items of an intelligence nature. In further preparation for his mission, Pfaus travelled to Berlin where he was met by the officer in charge of Office 1 West (Abwehr Headquarters), Hauptmann (Captain) Friedrich Carl Marwede, code-named 'Dr Pfalzgraf.' Marwede introduced Pfaus to his primary source of information about contemporary Ireland, 'Professor' Franz Fromme.

FRANZ FROMME

An early Abwehr candidate as an 'expert' on Ireland, Franz Fromme was involved in many aspects of German Intelligence planning in Ireland. His earliest known contact with the country was in 1932, when he came to research his book, *Irlands Kampf um die Freiheit: Darstellung und Beispiel einer völkischen Bewegung bis in die neueste Zeit* (Ireland's Struggle for Freedom: Description and study of a people's movement in recent times), which was published in Berlin in 1933. In the course of his research, which drew heavily on existing secondary sources, he had spoken to both Caitlín Brugha and Mrs Tom Clarke, and this foray into Irish affairs was sufficient to move him to the top of Germany's list of Irish experts.[43] He would eventually be eclipsed by Dr Adolf Mahr and Professor Dr Ludwig Mühlhausen, but only Fromme would have the direct link to the German Intelligence community, which placed him in a significant position when the issue of espionage was eventually raised.

According to the often unreliable memoirs of Nora O'Mara, Fromme told her that he had been 'in charge' of Sir Roger Casement in the 1915–16 period when the Irishman was attempting to raised Irish volunteers from among British prisoners of war in preparation for the 1916 Easter Rising.[44] At the time, according to O'Mara, Fromme was 'an important executive in the counter-intelligence department of the Ministry of War'. Because of his passion for languages, many of them obscure, he was eventually pressed to work with the discontented minority section of Abwehr II.[45]

Fromme seems to have been something of an eccentric. O'Mara describes him as a 'small, lithe, athletic man, his eyes flashing with humour behind his frameless glasses'.[46] She also noted an unusual tendency: he liked to dance impromptu jigs on tabletops. Fromme was the person responsible for briefing both Oscar Pfaus and Hermann Görtz prior to their missions to Ireland. His preparation for the Pfaus mission was evidently considered successful; he was a witness at Pfaus's wedding in August 1939.[47]

Fromme later returned to Ireland in 1939, after the conclusion of Pfaus's mission. Arriving at Cobh from Hamburg on 12 April, Fromme reported to Irish immigration officers that he was merely visiting Ireland as a tourist and would be staying with his friends, Mr and Mrs M.W. O'Reilly at Roebuck, Clonskeagh, Dublin. Mr O'Reilly was the managing director of the New Ireland Insurance Company. Fromme is supposed to have met his daughter Irene while she was on a singing tour of Germany.[48] Fromme, however, did not stay at his listed address, but rather at the Mayfair Hotel in Lower Baggot Street. Irish Intelligence and the Garda maintained surveillance on him and reported that his only visitor at the Mayfair was Dr Friedrich Herkner of the National College of Art.[49] He also spent time in the Irish-Nazi watering hole, the Red Bank restaurant. Though surveillance was present for the duration of Fromme's visit, its effectiveness leaves something to be desired; given subsequent developments, it appears that Fromme met with Francis Stuart during this period, though this fact is not reported by either the Garda or G2 surveillance team.

LIAM WALSH

After a mere two-hour briefing by Fromme, Pfaus (now code-named '*Stier*' – bull) proceeded to Ireland. His only contact was a Fichte-Bund subscriber by the name of Liam Walsh and it was to Walsh that Pfaus eventually turned for help.[50]

Walsh had an interesting career. Originally serving with the IRA's Third Battalion, Dublin Brigade, during the Irish Civil War, he was imprisoned for embezzling army funds during the Truce period. Despite this, or perhaps because of it, he joined the Irish Army in 1922 with the rank of captain, but was demobilized in 1923 when the Army learned of the earlier theft.

Walsh became a confidant of General Eoin O'Duffy at some point, and followed O'Duffy from the formation of the Fine Gael Party in 1933. O'Duffy obtained employment for him in the Fine Gael offices in Merrion Square, but Walsh, for a second time, was eventually dismissed when there was a discrepancy in the party funds that pointed to embezzlement. He joined O'Duffy, who soon left the Fine Gael Party. In 1936, O'Duffy became associated with Patrick Belton's Irish Christian Front (ICF), which took over much of the political platform advocated by the Blueshirts, and gave unqualified support to Franco's Nationalist forces in the Spanish Civil War. When O'Duffy led his volunteers to Spain in late 1937, he left Walsh in a senior ICF position during his absence. O'Duffy returned sooner than either he or anyone else anticipated and it was discovered that there was £2,300 missing from the ICF while under Walsh's stewardship. Walsh resigned from the ICF and obtained work in the crossword puzzle section of the *Irish Independent*. That, too, was destined to be short-term employment. He was fired from this position when it was alleged that he sold the key to the crossword competition for £50. O'Duffy came through for Walsh yet again and managed to get him a position at the Italian Legation in 1938, using his established pro-fascist connections with the Italian Minister, Vincenzo Berardis.[51]

PFAUS'S ARRIVAL IN IRELAND

Pfaus arrived at the English customs checkpoint at Harwich on 2 February 1939. He later claimed that he was carrying a .45 Smith & Wesson pistol. The passport control officer seemed suspicious, but he was eventually cleared to enter England and on the morning of 3 February, he boarded the *Cambria* in Holyhead for the brief voyage (three-and-a-half hours) to Dún Laoghaire. Upon arrival in Dublin proper, Pfaus checked into O'Neill's Hotel on Lower Gardiner Street. He evidently did not notify Walsh in advance of his visit, but once contacted, Walsh did as requested and introduced the German to General Eoin O'Duffy.

Having never before visited Ireland, Pfaus seemed genuinely surprised to learn that the Blueshirt general was politically and ideologically hostile to the Irish Republican Army, and initially it looked as if Pfaus had chosen the wrong introduction to the Irish underground political scene. O'Duffy, whom Pfaus described as 'overall, not very friendly', openly questioned the wisdom of contacting the IRA at all and did not seem inclined to lend his assistance. The former Blueshirt leader maintained that he had no contact with the nationalist group, but Liam Walsh eventually put Pfaus in touch with a third person who was 'rumoured' to know about them.[52]

The contact was Mrs E. Martin (Bird Avenue, Clonskeagh), who worked for the Hospitals Trust. She, in turn, arranged a meeting between Pfaus and the IRA.[53] While waiting for the rendezvous, most of Pfaus's time in Dublin was spent contacting others who appeared on his Fichte-Bund mailing list. These included Kevin Cahill and Maurice Hickie and a number of people throughout the country, including another follower of O'Duffy, Alex McCabe.[54] Pfaus also acquired an admirer. Joy N. Payne was a young philology student, and Pfaus apparently stayed for a time in her parents' home in Spencer Villas, Glenageary. The elder Paynes were followers of O'Duffy. Joy Payne had it in mind to marry Pfaus, and she continued to write him through a cover address in Switzerland long after he had left Ireland.[55]

Pfaus's contact with the IRA occurred on 13 February, ten days after his arrival in Ireland. He received a message to stand on a corner of O'Connell Street outside an office supply store. At approximately 18.30, Pfaus, armed with his .45, was picked up by Maurice 'Moss' Twomey and driven to a house in Clontarf for his long-anticipated meeting with the IRA command staff.[56] Pfaus described a meeting with several IRA men, including Chief of Staff Seán Russell, Twomey and James O'Donovan. At first, he was unable to establish his bona fides as a German courier (his cover was as a correspondent for the *Deutsche Allgemeine Zeitung*) and was concerned that he might be shot. In his consistently melodramatic description, Pfaus adds 'Mein Leben war damals keinen Penny wert' (At that moment my life was not worth a penny). Pfaus claimed that he encouraged the IRA men to telegraph Dr Kessenmeier in Hamburg to establish his true identity, which they did. While waiting for the answer, Pfaus (improbably) considered shooting his way out of the 'Höhle des Löwen' (lion's den). He actually spent the time drinking tea, smoking cigarettes and playing nervously with his tie. Kessenmeier wired back that Pfaus was in Ireland, alleviating the concerns of the IRA.

Russell asked many questions that Pfaus was unable to answer. His mission was only a preliminary to more substantive contact, and he was not qualified or authorized to take the discussions further. The meeting closed with apparent interest on the part of the IRA and it was decided to initiate further contact between the Republicans and the Abwehr. For the next step, an IRA liaison man to be sent to Germany, it was necessary to agree on a recognition signal. Jim O'Donovan took a £1 note from his pocket, tore it in half, and gave Pfaus one of the torn sections. The selection of the liaison officer had yet to be determined, but the torn bill would serve to identify whoever was chosen.

Irish Intelligence reported that 'on the eve of his departure to Germany from Dublin, Pfaus appeared to be very panicky and burned some documents after he had been handed a letter by an unknown man'.[57] Another contemporary G2 report notes that Pfaus departed Ireland, 'probably owing to nervousness'.[58] However, G2 surveillance had missed the one significant event of Pfaus's visit: the link-up between Germany and the IRA. Pfaus left Ireland on 14 February 1939. The IRA clearly had reason to be pleased: their primary concerns in the struggle against Britain, money and weapons, would potentially be alleviated by the Abwehr, as a contingency for any shortage from the Clann na Gael in the United States. German advice and motives were not things that were immediately important. In any case, the IRA had its own agenda independent from that of Germany.

From his perspective, Pfaus could consider the mission a success. He had made the requested contact for the Abwehr and had added to his list of subscribers for the Fichte-Bund propaganda material, though this would later create security concerns that Pfaus had not anticipated.[59] Almost a year later, Pfaus heard from Joy Payne that Seán Russell had been abducted and murdered by British agents on his return from the United States. Pfaus, by this time detached from any connection with German military intelligence, believed this story, not knowing that at the same moment, Russell was living a short distance away in Berlin.[60]

Though Joy Payne did not know of it, Pfaus had other plans on his return from Ireland. Almost immediately, he married a young lady from Hamburg and his wedding reception in the Hamburg hotel 'Esplanade' was attended by some of Abwehr notables: Hauptmann Marwede, Kapitänleutnant Schneidewind and, as a witness, Franz Fromme.[61] Pfaus would periodically act as a briefing officer for other German agents going to Ireland (Walter Simon, Görtz and Schütz) and later accompanied Hauptmann (later Major) Marwede when he was assigned to work with 'Regiment 1001' – a German unit responsible for the training and employment of the General Andrei Vlasov's Russian KONR (Committee for the Liberation of the Peoples of Russia) forces.

PFAUS'S SUBSEQUENT CONTACT WITH IRELAND

Even after his mission to Ireland, Pfaus stayed in contact with individuals closely connected to Irish affairs, and on at least one occasion tried to infiltrate Irish clergy abroad for purposes of espionage. For the most part, he maintained the Fichte-Bund contact list and, prior to the war, kept an aggressive correspondence schedule with his Irish acquaintances. While the Fichte-Bund was to 'disseminate facts' about the dangers of Bolshevism, Pfaus's version of the truth was more in keeping with a vile form of anti-Semitism. In response to a letter from Mr T. Kelly of 581 North Circular Road Dublin, which asked for an employment recommendation, Pfaus answered:

> I am deeply sorry that you too are a victim of the Jew-British business invasion of Eire. Unemployment, and consequently a lower standard of living are the results of letting the infernal Jew and his British henchmen into Eire. ... I cannot afford to do so directly [make a recommendation] for these Jewish-British liars would yell that we are about to Nazify Ireland![62]

Pfaus believed that he had found a receptive audience in Maud Gonne MacBride and he exchanged several letters with her in the period before the war. He continued to preach his strident anti-Semitic message, but adding elements that he felt sure would resonate with the nationalistic Maud Gonne: 'Of course, the Jews do not exert their influence in a manner which attracts too much attention. They are very quiet at first but only till they have everything in their hands. Then you will know the Jew! ... But I assure you the Jews will never return to Germany.'[63]

Pfaus himself seemed aware that his message might be too blatant and he modified his approach to this reader, adding that 'this Jewish-British agency is against Unification, it is against the Church and, of course, it is against Germany'. He was evidently hoping to ally Germany with everything that was right and proper in the view of a celebrated Irish nationalist, but his approach to Madame MacBride went slightly off the mark. She responded by asking Pfaus for his sources for the 'Jewish-British conspiracy' in Ireland and added that she had not noticed any hard evidence of what he mentioned. While Mrs MacBride was openly pro-German and helped in the flight of Hermann Görtz, evidently there were some lines that even she would not venture across.

Liam Walsh ventured to Germany in July 1939 and consulted with Pfaus, Otto Leiter (a.k.a. Theodor Kessenmeier) and Irish expatriate Dan Reeves, now working for the Fichte-Bund.[64] In his subsequent interrogation by Irish Intelligence, Walsh admitted 'he had undertaken the job of German propaganda agent in Ireland'. According to Pfaus, 'He [Walsh] wanted to help us, but he delayed too long and no further use for him could be found.' Pfaus also said that Walsh really wanted to move to Germany and 'work for Ireland's freedom'.[65]

Walsh adopted the Fichte-Bund philosophy quite quickly. In a letter to Mr Philip Gaffney of New York, he wrote:

> I have your letter of June 8, written me on the advice of our good friend Oscar Pfaus. I am very glad to learn from your letter that you are doing such a good work to help smash the Semitic groups in America ... In the meantime, could you give me some further information as to your requirements; what part the Irish in America are already taking in anti-Semitism, and what further part you think they can take.[66]

He was unaware that Gaffney was actually an undercover member of the Non-Sectarian Anti-Nazi League in New York, that his correspondence with both Pfaus and Walsh was part of an ongoing intelligence operation, and that it was reported to the British Consul in New York and eventually to MI5.[67]

Walsh's activities as a Fichte-Bund left him plenty of spare time. He supplemented his income by distributing Spanish nationalistic propaganda (the publication *Spain*), for which he received money from the Spanish Press Services, London.[68] His principal achievement for the Fichte-Bund seems to have been his assistance in promoting the Celtic Confederation of Occupational Guilds, an organization that he hoped would be the major mouthpiece of German propaganda in Ireland. His speech to this group in August 1939 on the subject of 'Ireland's Attitude Toward International Affairs,' was sufficiently pro-Nazi to warrant written thanks from Dr Hempel of the German Legation.

In addition to Pfaus, Walsh was also in contact with another Fichte-Bund personality, Dan Reeves. Born in County Clare, Reeves deserted his wife to follow his children's former governess, Elfrede Schultz, to Germany. While there, he evidently became involved with Pfaus and the Fichte-Bund, and was classed by Irish Intelligence under the heading 'Class 'E' – Propagandists'. From letters written back to Ireland from his matrimonial sanctuary in Germany, Reeves noted that on one occasion, he 'had a good time with Mr Warnock [William Warnock, the Irish Chargé d'Affaires in Berlin], who said he was a fellow student at Trinity College'. Reeves also made a number of pithy comments about fellow expatriate Francis Stuart: 'He was giving lectures in Berlin University. The poor students must have been bored as hell because he is without doubt the greatest bore that ever existed.'[69] Reeves's specific activities are difficult to ascertain, but his familiar contact with both Pfaus and Walsh make it clear that he was not a benign personality. He was reported in New York in 1943 but there was no further mention of him in official files.[70]

PFAUS'S FURTHER ACTIVITIES

Pfaus's last connection with the Irish occurred in the November 1943, when he travelled to Paris in search of Irish nationals who could provide information on the Allied military build-up in preparation for the invasion of continental Europe. Pfaus found his way to the Chapelle St Joseph (50 Avenue Hoche) because of the Irish and English clergy who still lived there under the German occupation of Paris. He eventually persuaded a Father Kenneth Monaghan from St Joseph's to provide him with safe Irish addresses; Father Monaghan also helped him to find an Irish girl living in Paris who was, to use Pfaus's description, 'starkem Heimweh hatte' (very homesick). Pfaus hoped to get approval from Berlin to send the girl back to Ireland through an official Irish channel (Leopold Kerney in Madrid), and once there she would relay pre-invasion information back to the Abwehr. The plan collapsed before it could get started. Unbelievably Berlin approved the questionable proposal but Pfaus shortly got word from Father Monaghan that the Irish girl had been killed, whether from murder or suicide was never explained.[71] Father Monaghan retired to a cloister in Wales after the war.[72]

JAMES O'DONOVAN

Shortly after Pfaus's departure, Russell decided to send the IRA director of munitions and chemicals, Jim O'Donovan, to Berlin as the Republican envoy to the Abwehr. O'Donovan was a logical choice; he spoke some German and was the most appropriate man in the underground organization to discuss the specific inventory of military items wanted by the IRA

O'Donovan was born in 1896 and originally from Castleview, Roscommon town. He had seen active service in the War of Independence,

as well as fighting for the IRA during the Civil War. His practical
experience with explosives was immediately apparent to anyone who met
him: he was missing two fingers and the tip of another from his right hand,
the result of an experiment that went wrong.[73] According to a later Irish
Intelligence report, he had been in touch with the Germans since 1937,
which would date from the first known IRA contacts between Tom Barry/
Seán MacBride and Jupp Hoven.[74]

At the conclusion of the War of Independence, he held the post of
'director of chemicals'.[75] O'Donovan also had academic credentials that
would appeal to the Germans: an M.Sc. from University College, Dublin, in
chemistry. He briefly taught at the Jesuit-run Clongowes Woods College
in the early 1920s and by 1924, 'retired' from active IRA membership to
take up a legitimate job with the Electricity Supply Board (ESB).[76] Russell,
then the IRA director of munitions, approached O'Donovan in 1937 to
draw up a sabotage plan ('S-Plan') for a bombing campaign against the
English mainland. Though O'Donovan was officially out of the IRA, he
agreed to actively rejoin the organization and began conducting classes for
the younger generation of IRA bombers.

Acting under his new orders from Russell, O'Donovan made three trips
to Germany in 1939. In late February, both Pfaus and the Abwehr were
surprised to learn from a phone call that O'Donovan had arrived and was
staying in the Baseler Hof in Hamburg. An initial meeting was quickly
organized between O'Donovan and Hauptmann Marwede of Abwehr II. Due
to the nature of the proposed connection between the two groups – active
support for sabotage operations by a 'discontented minority' – Abwehr II
was the appropriate section of German military intelligence to oversee
the contact. O'Donovan and Marwede discussed the expected wartime
role of the IRA and its specific requests for arms and ammunition. Even at
this stage, certain differences between the positions of the parties can be
noted. The Germans were adamant that they could not supply immediate
help for the IRA in its (from the German viewpoint) foolishly provocative
English bombing campaign.[77] The Germans were specifically concerned
over difficulties in arming the IRA when and if war actually developed
between Germany and England, and about the IRA's ability to mount
offensive operations in Northern Ireland. The initial meeting lasted just
three days. When O'Donovan returned to Ireland, he carried the German
code name 'V-Held (Agent Hero)'.[78] Little else of substance emerged from
the contact.

After reporting the details of his meeting to the IRA command, who
were optimistically encouraged by the contact, O'Donovan returned to
Germany on 26 April for another series of meetings with Marwede, this
time to discuss radio contact, a courier route for messages and armaments,
and the location of a safe house in London to act as an end-terminal for
the courier route. O'Donovan returned to Ireland on 15 May and tested the

courier route himself.[79] Major changes for the IRA had taken place in his absence: Seán Russell had left for the United States and selected Stephen Hayes as acting chief of staff until his return. The selection was to prove a costly blunder for the IRA and even more expensive for the German hopes of cooperation with a semi-professional nationalistic organization. Russell made the decision to go to America shortly before Jim O'Donovan set off on his second mission to Germany. This was outwardly done to secure increased financial support from the Irish-American community for a continuation of the bombing campaign. Following the meeting in February 1939 with Pfaus, Russell had decided on a novel strategic approach. Against the advice of all the top IRA men, he prepared to embark on a personal propaganda tour of America as a way of increasing the level of financial support sent in by Irish-Americans, principally in the influential Clann na Gael. Leaving the IRA under the questionable leadership of Stephen Hayes, Russell set sail for New York.[80]

Russell's decision to leave Ireland at the height of the bombing campaign is outwardly curious. Prior to the stoppage of direct shipping connections between the United States and Ireland, much of the IRA funding was routed through the same Clann na Gael pipeline as was the Irish Hospital Sweepstakes, a lottery that annually raised as much as £9 million. The Sweepstakes was illegal in the United States but, via the Clann na Gael, ways were found to distribute lottery tickets and collect money. The central administration of the lottery in Ireland was also home to many unreconstructed Republicans and opponents of de Valera. Between the combination of these two forces, there was a concern that money was skimmed off the sweepstakes profits in the United States or Ireland and reserved for the IRA. When direct transatlantic traffic between America and Ireland was suspended at war's outbreak, so too was the flow of cash. Russell went to the United States to correct this problem personally.[81] G2's Colonel Bryan was aware of the links between the IRA, the Clann na Gael and the sweepstakes 'especially as the Clann and its leader Joe McGarrity are practically the Sweep organization in America'.[82] Abwehr clearly had contact with both the IRA and the Clann na Gael, as a joint meeting with these groups followed in August.

MI5 was also monitoring the developing situation between the IRA and the Germans. While they had no hard evidence linking German money or supplies to the bombing campaign, they believed that Carlheinz Petersen had been exploring the idea of German–Irish cooperation in the event of war. 'They were inclined to regard the danger of Germany organizing sabotage with the assistance of the IRA terrorists as a very serious one.' G2 was also investigating the Petersen–IRA connection. 'An attempt was made by Petersen in 1939–40 to contact the IRA for support through Seán O'Brien, school teacher of the Synge St. School. When O'Brien raised the matter at an IRA conference, it was decided not to have anything to do with

Petersen.'[83] MI5 received a report in July that a meeting had taken place on 20 and 25 June between 'Admiral Canaris, head of the Abwehr, a representative of the German War Office, and a responsible member of the IRA who was said to have reported on the bombing campaign in Britain. Canaris was reported to have undertaken to supply him with arms and funds.'[84] This is almost certainly a report of the May 1939 meeting between O'Donovan and the Abwehr – though the MI5 source incorrectly reported the date. From the available information, there is no suggestion that security officials, either Irish or British, had identified O'Donovan as the liaison between the IRA and Germany.

O'Donovan returned to Hamburg and Berlin for a last set of meetings in August 1939. He brought his wife Monty along, partially as cover. They travelled from Harwich to Hamburg with Joseph McGarrity, but the two pretended not to recognize each other though they were, in fact, representing two symbiotic factions in the meeting with Germany: the IRA and the Clann na Gael. O'Donovan's reception into Germany did not turn out quite as he expected. He and Monty were routinely questioned by a German customs official and announced that they had nothing to declare. A cursory search of their luggage revealed that Monty had several cartons of undeclared cigarettes, prompting a strip-search by a female customs officer and a decision by O'Donovan to 'donate' the offending cigarettes to the German Red Cross – prompting an attitude change of epic proportions.[85]

They were met by Oscar Pfaus and he was immediately struck by the change in O'Donovan's attitude. 'He mocked the swastika flag, the brown party uniform, ridiculed the "cadaver-like obedience" of the German Wehrmacht and doubted that such soldiers could be fit for war. Everything about Germany got on his nerves.'[86] The German hosts did everything possible to make amends. They arranged for the O'Donovans to stay at the elegant Russischen Hof and provided small gifts and some money in an effort to calm the angry Irishman.[87] This strategy apparently worked; when the O'Donovans left for Ireland, Mrs O'Donovan gave Pfaus a dedicated copy of *Gone With the Wind* as a thank-you present.

O'Donovan's diary reveals that he was escorted to his sessions with German Intelligence personnel by a Herr Neumeister of the Foreign Ministry.[88] He wrote that he was not introduced to the others in the room by name. The topics under discussion included: 1, the possibility of reviving the English sabotage campaign in the event of war; 2, IRA capabilities in England, Northern Ireland and the Free State; 3, the policies, intentions and probably reactions of the Dublin government to any outbreak of hostilities between Germany and England; 4, the standard of IRA equipment and their exact arms requirements.[89] His conference over, Mr and Mrs O'Donovan boarded a KLM flight bound for Croydon and then back to Ireland. O'Donovan noted in his diary that his hosts had told him that 'There is to be war. Probably in one week.'[90]

The O'Donovans left for home not a moment too soon. A few days later, on 1 September, German air, infantry and armoured forces crossed the Polish border, beginning World War Two. Things were not all joy at Abwehr II headquarters on the Tirpitzufer. They had three moderately successful meetings with Jim O'Donovan, but now realized that they had forgotten to agree on a keyword for enciphered radio transmissions.[91] In the first operational test of the courier route, the Abwehr dispatched a Breton national, Paul Moyse, and his fiancée from Brussels to London with the keyword 'House of Parliaments' – the spelling error acting as positive check to prevent the keyword from being accidentally compromised.[92] Moyse made the journey but was almost arrested when his ship returned via hostile Calais, rather than proceeding as scheduled directly to neutral Ostend.[93] With the keyword delivered, the Abwehr waited for the first transmission from Jim O'Donovan. They would have a long wait; the first transmission was received on 29 October: 'By means of a coded radio signal, contact, which has been broken for weeks, was again established with the IRA. The chief agent asks for the transport of weapons and other equipment. However, he did not say by which means this transport was possible at the moment.'[94] It seems that the coordination between the IRA and the Abwehr was not so precise after all.

In the end, the radio transmitter was to prove useless to Abwehr's plans. The radio itself is contentious. The set was a 100-watt model made by the Gross Radio Company, New York. Carolle Carter states that it was smuggled in by Joseph McGarrity and the Clann na Gael organization from New York, but Irish Intelligence reported (after it physically had the transmitter in hand) that it was purchased by a Margaret Thornton (8 Adelaide Road, Dublin) for £26 5s from Telefunken Ltd, 122 Stephen's Green.[95]

The transmitter was obviously powerful enough for German purposes – it had already made successful radio contact – but the IRA had other ideas for the transmitter. Beginning in November 1939, the IRA started using the machine to make regular – and illegal – broadcasts to the people of Ireland. The content of the broadcasts was mostly political, anti-British, anti-de Valera and, occasionally, anti-Semitic. Like any professional broadcasting system, the IRA announcers clearly identified themselves at the beginning of the transmissions ('This is the Irish Republican Army broadcasting station') and faithfully aired their message on the times and dates announced in advance. Here was the rub: since the Garda knew in advance when the broadcast was going to be made, they had little difficulty triangulating the source using their Marconi FSM detection equipment. The fledgling IRA communications team also made some other minor errors. Rather than using an unoccupied radio band, they usually 'stepped on' existing broadcast stations, meaning that anyone in the vicinity of the transmitter who happened to be listening to that station would immediately sustain damage to their hearing or their radio, or both.[96]

The IRA transmitter was located on 29 December 1939 at Ashgrove House, Highfield Road, Rathgar. Along with the radio, gardaí also found the evidence of coded transmissions to Germany – precious few – which convinced them that the threat of espionage was more than a myth. They also arrested four IRA members.[97] O'Donovan was not linked to the transmitter and he escaped notice until he was arrested and interned in September 1941.

Though the transmitter was seized, O'Donovan continued to monitor and transcribe coded broadcasts from Germany. The existing logs show an almost continuous period of monitoring from January through September 1940. In many cases, the reception was weak or blocked, or there were various staffing and competency problems:

30/12/39	Owing to illness and lack of decision, no reception.
24/1/40	Conditions bad.
14/2/40	Morse receiver did not turn up. Abandoned.
9/3/40	Almost perfect except for what came in like jamming in each of three repeats. However reconstructed blanks ok. 3103. Should have been but was not 5103. IFQ Wrong code word.
13/3/40	Untrained Morse man. Says got RVK and a number, but no message.[98]

In any event, the transmission of information did not live up to anyone's expectations, from either the German or IRA viewpoint.

4
German agent activities, 1939–40

Following the declaration of war in September and the Ashgrove House transmitter raid in late December 1939, several events occurred that had an impact on the eventual direction of German intelligence operations in Ireland. With few tangible results from the celebrated bombing campaign, the IRA was under increasing attack, both at home and abroad. English courts of justice sentenced IRA men Peter Barnes and James Richards to death for the 25 August bomb attack on Coventry, in which five people were killed.

The war and the German blockade around England also reduced the flow of cash, weapons, and ammunition that previously came from America. In an effort to get replacement ammunition, as well as score a propaganda victory for the increasingly unpopular IRA, the organization mounted the daring Magazine Fort Raid on 23 December 1939. The target was the Irish Army arsenal in Phoenix Park, Dublin. The raid itself, which succeeded thanks to lax security by the soldiers of the Seventh Infantry Battalion (their commander was in town during the raid), netted the IRA more than a million rounds of small-calibre ammunition.[1] Most of the ammunition was eventually recovered, but the international publicity given the event had an unfortunate impact on the German audience; it gave the false impression that the IRA was a military force to be reckoned with and served to reinforce erroneous impressions formed from the bombing campaign and the meetings with Jim O'Donovan.[2] From this point, the IRA became an integral part of Abwehr plans for the intelligence war against Great Britain. Some German Intelligence officials believed that the IRA represented a ready-made 'fifth column' behind British lines and one that, with a minimum of support, leadership and encouragement, could supply raw intelligence information and conceivably tie down substantial numbers of British troops.[3] The Abwehr could not have been more wrong.

To the Irish government, which had done little of substance to stop or investigate the IRA bombing campaign as long as it was safely confined to England, the new IRA initiative seemed a genuine threat. In response to the Magazine Fort Raid, the government passed the Emergency Powers Act and added several provisions to the existing Offences Against the State Act. It also ordered a round-up of IRA activists, though this turned out to be legally premature.[4] The Offences Against the State Act and the Emergency

Powers Act were again modified in August 1940 to make several offences punishable by death. These included high treason, receiving or writing down messages which endangered public or national security, kidnapping, possessing arms or munitions, possessing explosives or causing an explosion or being an accessory to these crimes – in short, everything which made the IRA what it was.[5]

The transmitter seizure left the IRA in limbo. There was no further support likely from the United States and without a means of communication even the tenuous prospect of German support was severed. With the assistance of the German Minister and the apparent connivance of the Abwehr and the IRA, Irish writer Francis Stuart arrived in Berlin in January 1940 to restore the IRA–German link. Stuart, born in Australia to a family of County Antrim Protestants, came from what might be euphemistically called a 'dysfunctional family'. His father probably committed suicide and his mother's subsequent return to Ireland eventually brought young Stuart into contact with the people who would ultimately side with Germany and, in the course of doing so, put Francis into situations where he would make some questionable moral choices.

At the age of 17, he married Iseult Gonne, the illegitimate daughter of Maud Gonne and the anti-Semitic French parliamentary deputy Lucien Millevoye. If possible, Iseult's family was even more dysfunctional than that of Francis – her mother, the great inspiration for William Butler Yeats's poetry and the unrequited love of his life, was a larger-than-life figure. Intimately connected to the Easter Rising in 1916, she had earlier married John MacBride, but had lived apart from him almost since the moment of the marriage. Though she gave birth to her son Seán from this momentary union, her interests seemed mainly concerned with society and politics, not with family.[6] Madame MacBride's mental state is also open to question; according to one historian, she deliberately conceived Iseult on the grave of her previously deceased illegitimate son.[7] Stuart was briefly an active member of the IRA and was interned following his capture in Dublin in 1922. He seems to have taken up Irish nationalism as a momentary interest, more from an effort to please his wife and her mother than with any idealistic commitment to the movement.[8]

In Ireland during the late 1930s Stuart became friendly with Helmut Clissmann and his Irish wife, Elizabeth. At the time, Clissmann was running the German Academic Exchange Service and also working for the Deutsche Akadamie (DA), ostensibly facilitating academic exchanges between Ireland and the Third Reich. In reality, Clissmann was forming connections which might later be of benefit to the German Intelligence services and also acting as a point-man for the Irish branch of the Nazi Auslandsorganisation (AO) – the Nazi Party's foreign organization – in pre-war Ireland. Stuart was also friendly with the German Minister to Ireland, Dr Eduard Hempel, largely through the excellent rapport established between Maud Gonne MacBride and the German minister. By late 1938, Stuart was seeking an escape from his marriage and what he viewed as the provincialism of Irish life. Iseult intervened with Clissmann to arrange for Stuart to travel to Germany in April 1939 to give a series of academic lectures in conjunction with the DA. His official host during the visit was Professor Walter F. Schirmer, the senior member of the English faculty with the DA and Berlin University. During the war, Schirmer worked at the Foreign Ministry as deputy head of the section that controlled Germany's foreign-language transmissions.[9] Starting with Berlin, Stuart was given a first-class tour of the Third Reich, and eventually visited München, Hamburg, Bonn and Köln. While Stuart was certainly aware of the official Nazi attitude towards the Jews, as his letters home indicated, he did not let that stand in the way of his open admiration for the 'New Germany'.[10] At the completion of his lecture tour, Stuart was invited to return to Germany for an appointment as a lecturer in English and Irish literature at Berlin University. With no other prospects on the horizon, Stuart accepted the appointment for the following year, 1940. He unsuccessfully attempted to persuade Iseult to join him in Germany in mid-1939, but in the meantime, entertained himself with some of the impressive public spectacles which were part of the public education programme in Nazi Germany.[11]

Stuart returned home to Laragh in July and was waiting on further word from Berlin when war was declared on 3 September. Writing again to Berlin on 21 September, Stuart again stated that he would accept the offered position at Berlin University. He applied for a new passport, but as all continental passenger traffic was now routed through London, he needed a plausible excuse for a visit to mainland Europe.[12] He decided to plead a bogus medical condition after finding a cooperative physician who testified that his non-existent lung condition required treatment in Switzerland.

Stuart's activities were not going unnoticed by Irish Army Intelligence or the Garda. The Stuarts (both Iseult and Francis) had their mail examined from June 1939 on.[13] As early as April 1939, Gardaí were reporting on Dr Hempel's presence at Laragh Castle.[14] Hempel made a visit there while Francis Stuart was still in Germany, accompanied by Maud Gonne MacBride. In what seemed to G2 as a measure designed to maintain security, the maid was dismissed for the day when the party arrived.[15] Maud Gonne, in particular, seems to have had fairly regular contact with Hempel. In a surveillance report dating from July 1941, Garda officers noted that Hempel was a regular visitor to her home, 'Roebuck House', where Seán MacBride and his wife also resided. In one particular instance, the report quoted Francis Stuart's daughter as saying (referring to Hempel), 'that is the man for my Grannie's letters'.[16] The implication was obvious: that both the Stuarts and the MacBrides were involved in illicit communication with Germany.

Though the authorities were concerned that Stuart was trying to return to Germany, they could not prevent him doing so on basis of the information gathered to date. Irish Intelligence was unaware that Stuart was embarking on a mission on behalf of the IRA and the Abwehr which would lead him to the heart of Nazi Germany.

STUART AS IRA COURIER

When Stuart's plans for travelling to Germany were finalized, his brother-in-law, Seán MacBride, summoned Stuart to a secret meeting. Although officially inactive in the IRA, MacBride seems to have been keeping his hand in the game. This meeting followed the seizure of the illegal IRA transmitter on 29 December 1939. Stuart's session with MacBride and O'Donovan took place at O'Donovan's house in Killiney, County Dublin. The recently appointed IRA Chief of Staff Stephen Hayes and two of his bodyguards joined them. Stuart was instructed to take a message to Abwehr headquarters upon his arrival in Berlin and was given half a torn piece of paper as proof of identity. Iseult did her part by sewing the paper into the lining of Stuart's winter coat and he continued his covert preparations for departure.

There seems to have been some problem with the exit, however. A Garda surveillance report in early January reveals an almost comic series of movements by Stuart. On 29 December, he left Laragh with two suitcases and arrived at Maude Gonne's Roebuck House, where Iseult later joined him. The two of them proceeded by car to Hempel's house 'Gortleitragh', Dún Laoghaire. At approximately 1900 hours the same day, Stuart returned to Roebuck House with his suitcases, and Mrs Stuart simultaneously returned to Laragh. Stuart himself returned to Laragh by bus on 2 January.

Stuart eventually reached Holyhead, North Wales, by mailboat and proceeded by train to London, where he would need to acquire his Swiss visa. A small delay in the process was evidently enough to panic Stuart; he removed and destroyed the identifying paper sewn into his coat. He later claimed, unconvincingly, that it was of no matter to him if German Intelligence believed him or not.[17] When he arrived in Berlin in early January, he presented Hempel's letter of introduction to State Secretary Ernst Frhr. von Weizsäcker of the German Foreign Ministry. At this meeting, Stuart made a facetious comment about William 'Lord Haw Haw' Joyce that ultimately – and unintentionally – helped him get a job with German radio.[18]

His mission at Abwehr headquarters was not quite as smooth. When shown into the presence of a nameless officer, Stuart delivered the IRA message, but without his identifying paper, he was not immediately believed. At Stuart's suggestion, the Abwehr then contacted Franz Fromme, who finally vouched for Stuart's identity.[19] According to Stuart, the German officer asked him whether he had come to Germany because he thought they were going to win the war. Stuart answered, 'No, I've come here because a writer has to be on the losing side always.'[20] It would seem doubtful that this answer made any sense to the German Intelligence service. Stuart did have some discussion with the Abwehr on the conditions in Ireland and the fate of the IRA–Abwehr radio link. In the report which appeared in the Abwehr II *Kriegstagebuch* (War Diary) Stuart is identified as the 'Representative of Irish agent V-Held' ('Der Abgesandte des irischen V-Mannes V-Held'). V-Held was Jim O'Donovan. The Germans were not overjoyed to discover that 'contrary to the directions which had been given, the transmitter delivered from the USA was not only being used occasionally for communication with Germany but was also frequently used for internal propaganda purposes'.[21] The Germans should have been able to extrapolate from this episode that the Irish Republican Army might lack the sense of professionalism and purpose that was necessary, but they seem not to have made the connection.[22] At the time, Stuart was not shy about his IRA–Abwehr connection. According to a German student who met Stuart at the university, he 'stressed wherever we went that he had come on a mission of the IRA, though he never explained to which group inside the IRA he belonged'.[23] Stuart would change this attitude in the post-war period when such revelations were no longer helpful to his image.

German espionage operations in Ireland can be broken up into three distinct phases: coordination missions with the IRA preceding the French campaign; military missions directed against Britain for the purposes of gathering technical and weather data; and political missions against Britain undertaken later in the war, when the threat of direct German action against Britain had receded. While the specific objectives could be quite diverse, the general preparation and execution contained similarities that underlie the operational problems in the German intelligence services. The stories of the missions themselves paint a vivid picture both of German plans and capabilities – or a lack thereof – and the integrity of the Irish and British counter-intelligence systems opposing them. German efforts to cultivate a working relationship with the IRA formed the basis for two wartime missions (Weber-Drohl and Görtz) but the Abwehr later chose to rely on support mechanisms exclusive of the IRA. Neither strategy proved viable, and the task of inserting and supporting agents went quickly from one disaster to another.

ERNST WEBER-DROHL

During O'Donovan's meetings with the Germans and in the brief, subsequent radio contact between the IRA and German Intelligence, the plan was for a German Intelligence liaison officer to go to Ireland. Francis

Stuart arrived in Berlin in January 1940, delivering the same request. The liaison mission was seemingly in the works, but the capture of the IRA transmitter – and the dismal prospects for obtaining a replacement – meant that Germany would now have to provide this equipment if the IRA was to continue to act in concert with the agreed scheme. It was technically possible to air-drop a transmitter/receiver, but there were a number of complications, both technical and political. A pinpoint drop over Ireland with the parachute technology then available was a practical impossibility and any pathfinder (to mark a drop zone and signal to approaching aircraft) on the ground would risk immediate detection. A German transmitter falling into the hands of the Garda and G2 would also cause political problems that could, if the news became public, jeopardize Ireland's neutrality – something that would not please the German Foreign Ministry. German contact with the IRA, both in terms of personnel and equipment, would have to be covert.

The Abwehr explored another possibility even before the Ashgrove House transmitter was seized. A letter from the Commander of Submarines (BdU), Operations section to the Abwehr on 2 October 1939 stated that 'The landing of an agent by U-boat will be possible. An appropriate time cannot yet be given. It is requested that the BdU be contacted at the appropriate time.'[24]

Further coordination between the Abwehr and the Navy specifically addressed the issue of landing an agent in Ireland. The German Navy obviously had some reservations about using its prize submarines for this type of non-essential (from the Navy's point of view) mission. Korvettenkapitän Reinicke, of the Naval Operations Staff (1/Skl) explained that only 'in special cases' was it possible to conduct such an operation, and with a proviso attached: the Irish were not to be consulted beforehand about the time and place of the landing. The 1/Skl obviously was not reassured by the IRA's ability to keep secrets and was unwilling to risk a submarine and crew on their good intentions. The Navy further agreed (29 December 1939) to a specific mission proposal to land a single agent on the Irish coast 'for the purpose of strengthening the connection to the Irish Republican Army'.[25]

The exact scheduled date for the mission is uncertain, but the BdU announced in late January 1940 that the mission would have to be postponed because of heavy ice conditions. Once conditions improved, the Navy promised to notify the Abwehr three days before the mission was scheduled to depart. The Abwehr did not have long to wait; on 26 January the BdU gave the warning that the agent's departure was to take place at 09:00 on 28 January.[26] U-37 had been selected to transport the agent to his destination. The Navy kept to its schedule and the agent and submarine departed as planned.[27] A great deal of time and trouble to transport one agent, but this particular man was himself out of the ordinary.

Ernst Weber-Drohl was the agent in question. When he left from Wilhelmshaven in early 1940, he was 61 years old, somewhat arthritic, and had a distinctive body that had been fashioned from a lifetime lifting weights.[28] In addition to these prominent outward features, Weber-Drohl seemed to have an unusual facility with women of all sorts, a feature that actually recommended him for this particular mission. Born near Edelbach, Austria in 1879, Weber-Drohl had worked as a professional wrestler and strong-man in acts in the United States and Ireland, had 'purchased' the title of 'doctor of chiropractic' while in the United States and, most usefully for the Abwehr, had previously worked in Ireland (under the name Atlas the Strong), where he fathered two illegitimate children with an Irish woman.[29] He likewise had an illegitimate daughter in the US.[30] Weber-Drohl was recruited by the Nürnberg Ast because of his obvious familiarity with Ireland and his passable English language skills. His initial mission was limited to the delivery of money and instructions, but after police seized the IRA transmitter, he was assigned additional priorities. Weber-Drohl was equipped with an 'Afu' transmitter, cash and new instructions for the chief Irish agent, Jim O'Donovan. His mission was to make contact with O'Donovan as soon as possible after landing and then try to return to Germany by whatever means possible.

The German Navy was not taking any chances with either Weber-Drohl or the Abwehr missions that were taking up valuable time and naval resources. In a top secret order of 22 January 1940 to the commander to U-37, Korvettenkapitän Werner Hartmann, the BdU was very clear about the nature of the operation. At this time, the Navy (and the Abwehr) was clearly planning on transporting two passengers for the Abwehr mission. The crew was to be told of the mission only once under way and then only that the two were press reporters, operating under the instructions of the High Command. They were further instructed that the death penalty would be applied for any breach of security. Korvettenkapitän Hartmann was given considerable latitude in deciding where to land the agents, given freedom of action to choose the place based on weather and navigational factors. It was specified that the landing be accomplished in an area near a railway line.

The landing was to be attempted in one of three areas: Killala Bay (code-named 'Karl') or Clew Bay ('Caesar'); Dingle Bay ('Dora') or Brandon Bay ('Bruno'); Dungarvan Bay ('Gustav') or the neighboring coast ('Nordpol'). Successful landing was to be transmitted as e.g. 'Karl 25' – meaning a landing at Killala Bay on the 25th of the month. Once the landing area was reached, the agents were to row ashore in a Luftwaffe-issue inflatable rubber boat. Hartmann was specifically told that '*no* crew members are to accompany them to the shore'. The boat was to be destroyed after use. If conditions did not permit the use of the Luftwaffe boat, the commander was authorized to use the dinghy, and that 'loss of the dinghy is non-essential'.[31]

Before Weber-Drohl actually arrived in Ireland via U-37, several things had changed. His accompanying radio-operator dropped out of the project. According to Kurt Haller, the man was one of the best amateur radio operators in Germany, and he was fully trained with the specially constructed transmitter/receiver that the Abwehr intended for the IRA. The supervisors at Abwehr II hoped that the pair would be able to find a remote cottage somewhere in the Irish countryside and be able to broadcast with relative security. Forty-eight hours before the pair was to depart, the radio operator notified Haller that he could not continue on the mission: the company of his 'free-style wrestling' partner was just too odious. Abwehr II decided that such a personality conflict might compromise the mission, and accordingly, Weber-Drohl, with transmitter, was sent on alone.[32] He landed in Killala Bay during the night of 8 and 9 February 1940.[33] The entire operation was completed by 0150 hours on the morning of 9 February.

Hartmann's report was more prosaic; the rubber boat set out and returned immediately because of the conditions. Weber-Drohl apparently capsized and the third officer of the watch (Leutnant zur See Kuhlmann) pulled him out and was then dispatched to take the slightly waterlogged spy to land, though this specifically violated the BdU orders. Officer and boat returned to the submarine.[34]

WEBER-DROHL IN IRELAND

Weber-Drohl made his way inland and eventually reached the house of Jim O'Donovan, a journey of over 100 miles. When he arrived, 'soaked, exhausted, and with swollen knees', according to O'Donovan, Weber-Drohl related how he lost his radio when the boat overturned. The exact means by which he reached O'Donovan's house in Shankill are unknown. In another G2 report, it is reported that upon landing, Weber-Drohl met with IRA Chief Stephen Hayes in the Sligo house owned by Barney O'Donnell.[35] This would imply that Hayes was briefed first and only then was the German sent to O'Donovan, which would explain how he was able to travel unnoticed from his entry point to O'Donovan's house in Killiney. The German agent delivered the cash, and wrote out his instructions (from memory) for O'Donovan. The paper, in indifferent English, was titled the 'Pfalzgraf Section' and conveyed the hopes and intentions that German Intelligence had for the IRA–Abwehr link.

The text asked the IRA to focus on military, as opposed to civilian, targets in its campaign of violence. The message also requested that an agent be dispatched to Germany to coordinate future activities and the shipment of weapons to Ireland. The designated agent should be clear about the plans and political objectives of the IRA, and be prepared to discuss the type of weapons and material needed by the underground army, financial requirements and all other matters. The Irish agent should remain in Germany until the weapons are ready to be shipped and then accompany the equipment back to Ireland.

O'Donovan was instructed not to use the previous London cover address, but was provided with a new one by Weber-Drohl. Once radio communication was possible between Ireland and Germany, transmissions should only be made daily at 0900 hours. To facilitate future messages, O'Donovan was given new code words for the traffic: 'Bullfrog' for Portugal, 'Mackerel' for Ireland, and 'Bulldog' for England – it was anticipated that the new courier route would come to Ireland via neutral Portugal. The re-established radio communication was the responsibility of a second agent soon to arrive in Ireland, a Dr Schmelzer. The message requested that O'Donovan assist Dr Schmelzer with the placement of his transmitter. O'Donovan was asked to procure a few young men who could be taught the code that Schmelzer was bringing. Schmelzer turned out to be none other than Leutnant der Reserve Dr Hermann Görtz. Weber-Drohl gave O'Donovan the sum of $14,450 – keeping $650 to replace the money lost in his boating accident[36] – and signed this missive as 'Dr Drohl'.

Weber-Drohl had completed his mission, or at least part of it. Though the valuable transmitter was lost, he made the promised payment to the IRA and passed along the request for an IRA liaison officer to be sent to Germany. Acting as an Abwehr version of John the Baptist, Weber-Drohl had paved the way for Görtz, who was soon to come on a mission of greater significance.

Ambassador Hempel reported on 27 March 1940 that Weber-Drohl (now the 'Haupt-V-Mann') had given the money to the 'Irish friends', indicating that the German legation had contact with their new 'main agent'. O'Donovan supported Weber-Drohl for several weeks, and the elderly spy eventually took a room in Dublin's Westland Row. He was not to remain free for very long. On 24 April 1940, Gardaí arrested Weber-Drohl for illegal entry in violation of the Aliens Act; he was held pending a hearing before the Dublin District Court.

Under the headline 'German's strange journey to Ireland', the *Irish Times* reported on the continuing Weber-Drohl legal saga. Not suspected of being an important Abwehr agent, Weber-Drohl successfully held himself out to be the poor victim of circumstances. He told the court that he disembarked on the Waterford coast from an Antwerp steamer, and had made his way to land by a small boat. The boat capsized and he had lost many of his prized possessions, including his passport, marriage certificate, pipe and letters; Weber-Drohl wisely omitted any mention of losing his Abwehr transmitter. The sad figure then reached the main street in Waterford and eventually took a bus to Dublin. Why did this pathetic, arthritic refugee come to Ireland? Here Weber-Drohl told the story of a family separated by cruel circumstances – and mixed fact and fiction in equal measure.

The incredulous court heard how, in 1907, the successful weightlifter and strongman met and fell in love with an Irish woman. They had a child, but her family objected to their marriage on religious grounds and Weber-Drohl left for America, intending to send for the mother and son. He sent the woman a letter with £500, so that they could join him in the United States, but heard nothing. Weber-Drohl tearfully told how he wrote to the Dublin police and then, three years later, came to Ireland in search of his lost family. An aunt of the lost woman finally told him that she had died, and that the woman had a second son by Weber-Drohl. Years later, living in Nürnberg, he was encouraged by his wife to try and find his lost children. According to this tale, she gave her husband money and sent him off to Ireland with her blessing. Because of the war, he said, there was no legal way of entering the country, and he had resorted to desperate measures. Weber-Drohl said that he was just starting his search for his children when he was arrested.

The district judge questioned him about the money involved – Weber-Drohl said that his passage cost $200 and that his wife had given her savings to him, $2300 – and added the non sequitur that his wife had a sister who lived in Switzerland. The court heard testimony from Dr Cournihan (23 Westland Row), who stated on the defendant's behalf that Weber-Drohl picked his name out of a medical directory and had written to him for help searching for his children. Cournihan maintained that he was surprised to find Weber-Drohl on his doorstep on 9 February, but had taken the man to a hotel. In retrospect, Cournihan is a suspicious character due in large part to his address, which seemed to be a magnet for German agents in Ireland.

The judge astutely noted that Weber-Drohl's story 'was a difficult one to check and more difficult to believe'. Notwithstanding the improbable set of circumstances, no evidence was then available that the Austrian had been engaged in activity hostile to the state. The judge mentioned that nothing would prevent Weber-Drohl from internment as an alien, but added that 'one could not but have sympathy with the defendant and all he had gone through'. Weber-Drohl, part-time refugee and full-time German agent, was fined £3 and released.[37]

Though he had succeeded in hoodwinking a gullible Irish court, G2 was not impressed with either Weber-Drohl or his sob story about lost children.[38] He was re-arrested on 27 April 1940, just three days after his release from the district court, and held under the Emergency Powers Act. Unfortunately, G2 was not in complete charge of the case. Almost immediately, Weber-Drohl began the first of many hunger strikes, prompting a sympathetic Department of Justice to order his release. The department was concerned that the premature death of another inmate, coming after the hunger strikes by IRA prisoners, would attract unwelcome publicity.

In the meantime, G2 had a chance to investigate other aspects of Weber-Drohl's cover story and, not surprisingly, found that it radically departed from the truth. In particular, they discovered that the facts behind the story of Weber-Drohl's lost children were more poignant than his cut-and-paste version. In a statement to Gardaí, Anne Brady (Woodbine Cottage, North Road, Finglass) was able to fill in a few gaps in the narrative. The mother of Weber-Drohl's children was Pauline Brady, her adopted sister. Pauline was born in 1873 and lived with Weber-Drohl in Dublin. Her first child was born in 1908 and a second arrived in 1909. Weber-Drohl left for Belfast and later the United States, promising to send for Pauline and the children as soon as he was settled. Though he never sent the passage money, Pauline would go daily to the post office in hopes for a letter from America that never came. Eventually, an American friend of Weber-Drohl's said that he had seen his obituary in an American paper. The children, Emil and James, were placed in the Sacred Heart Home in Drumcondra and later moved to St Vincent's Home in Cabra. Pauline Brady eventually married a man named Jones and had a child from that marriage, but died in Grangegorman Mental Hospital in March 1923.

Annie Brady said she received a letter from Germany that purported to be from Weber-Drohl's brother (it was actually from Weber-Drohl himself) in the middle 1920s, but she did not reply. Weber-Drohl's son Emil was in London, but had served in the Irish Army from 1936 to 1938. Mrs Brady said that she wanted no further contact with Weber-Drohl.[39] Minister Hempel reported to the Foreign Ministry that Weber-Drohl had been arrested and interned 'for passport difficulties', but promised to see about getting him quietly released. The combination of hunger strike and gentle diplomatic pressure seems to have worked.[40] Though officially awaiting deportation, he was released from Mountjoy on 4 May, a mere eight days after being arrested.[41] Deportation proceedings were suspended. Hermann Görtz, alias Dr Schmelzer, arrived by parachute the next day.

HERMANN GÖRTZ GOES TO IRELAND

Of all the German agents sent to Ireland in World War Two, Hermann Görtz is the most written about, the most popularly known and certainly the most overrated. He is variously described as a 'master spy' and 'chief agent', but in reality he was neither. He is also variously described as 'Major' or 'Lieutenant-Colonel' Görtz, but, again, he was neither. Using any objective military standard, Görtz should never have been selected for active service and his case is another indicator that something was fundamentally flawed in the Abwehr decision-making process, whether by accident or design. His fame is mostly due to his length of time on the run, the nefarious contacts he made, and his untimely demise, rather than anything he accomplished while as an active agent. Görtz himself disdained the word 'spy', referring to himself as a 'representative of the Supreme Command' – though he could be neatly put into neither category.

Part of the mystique surrounding Görtz springs from the legends that he created in captivity about his own effectiveness. Over-eager historians have multiplied the errors, attributing events to Görtz that never occurred or failing to check independently the reliability of his self-serving statements. The Görtz case was a tragedy, but it was largely a tragedy of Görtz's own making, his inexperience, and an epic case of continuous poor judgement.

Görtz's family background is simple enough. He was born on 15 November 1890 in the Hanseatic town of Lübeck, the fourth of seven children. His father Heinrich Görtz, was a well-known solicitor and judge who provided a comfortable and stimulating environment for young Hermann. By all accounts, Görtz grew up with a sense of refinement and developed a life-long interest in music, literature and art. According to some sources, he had an English governess and his knowledge of that language dates from his earliest childhood. He attended a Lübeck school for ancient languages and later studied English and French at the Realgymnasium. As an adult, Görtz would speak fluent English, but still retained a few common grammatical mistakes and was never able to completely discard his German accent.[42] He may have taken a walking trip to Scotland as a boy as a precursor to many later years spent in English-speaking countries, both voluntarily and involuntarily.

His military training started before the First World War. He enlisted as a reserve soldier in the Fifth Foot Guards Regiment on 1 April 1910, attaining junior non-commissioned officer rank in March 1911, and was promoted to vizefeldwebel (sergeant) in April 1912. Görtz apparently did not envisage a soldier's career, and did not take either of two routes that would have led to a direct commission.[43] He would have learnt the basics of soldiering in the Kaiser's Army, probably as fine a military system as Germany ever produced. Honour and loyalty were watchwords – both to the German Emperor and to the country. Görtz certainly learned these concepts well, though he later applied them to situations never anticipated by the Imperial German Army.

Görtz's career aspirations were to follow in his father's footsteps; he completed the law course at the University of Heidelberg and also studied in Kiel, Edinburgh and Berlin. He passed his qualifying exam (Referendarexamen) in June 1914. By the outbreak of the war, he was a 23-year-old attorney in Lübeck.

GÖRTZ IN THE GREAT WAR

Görtz was recalled to his unit on 4 August 1914 and served with his regiment in both Belgium and Russia, receiving a promotion to leutnant (second lieutenant) and the Iron Cross, Second Class, following infantry patrols at Namur. Transferred to the Eastern front, he participated in the fighting at the Masurian Lakes. He eventually suffered a severe wound in his arm, followed by a respiratory illness. His recovery took several months and after a short stint with his regiment in Kurland, applied to join the Army Air Service. Görtz was trained as a flight observer, graduating from the flight school at Adlershof in September 1915, and was posted to an active service unit from October 1915 until February 1917, flying reconnaissance missions over Russian (Minsk area) territory while assigned to Field Flying Detachment 31 (Feldfliegerabteilung 31).[44]

He became ill again, this time with a cold, and had to retire from active flying, instead transferring to the Observation School at Schwerin-Goeriss. Görtz's military personnel dossier records that he was awarded the pilot's badge (Flugzeugführerabzeichen), but does not list his unit assignments other than to say that he served as an instructor at the photo reconnaissance school at Lockbitz and was later posted to the staff of the Commander of the Air Service on 5 February 1918 as a photo-reconnaissance officer and officer 'for special duties' as a interrogator of captured Allied fliers.[45] Though Görtz was in active service for the entirety of the First World War, he was never again promoted and eventually left the service at the same grade, second lieutenant. He was seemingly transferred again to the Fifth Flieger Abteilung in May 1918 and flew on several long-distance photo-reconnaissance flights[46]. For reasons that are not clear, Görtz went from flying back to being an observer – an operational demotion and one that was not typical in German military aviation without cause.[47]

Part of the problem in piecing together Görtz's background is his frequent tendency to lie about it. Depending on his situation and the intended audience, he frequently made up details, confused events or gave a deliberately distorted picture of what actually occurred. While his service during the early part of the war was quite active, his subsequent transfer to aviation never seems to have amounted to much. According to a later letter to the Luftwaffe, he had only been appointed to interrogation duties in the last months of the war, but 'through an American officer, whom I caused to make statements, but who then escaped from German captivity the enemy received cognizance of the nature of my technique in obtaining evidence. On two American flying officers, who were brought down, I found a warning against me as being a particularly dangerous intelligence officer.'

Görtz stayed in this assignment until the Armistice in November 1918. There were some positive personal events during this period of European carnage; in July 1916, Görtz married Ellen Aschenborn, the daughter of a German vice-admiral, Richard Aschenborn. Ellen and Görtz's sister had once shared an apartment on a visit to England. The couple would eventually have three children, Wiebke, Rolf and Ute. In another early example of the 'Görtz myth', he told his wife that at the time of the Armistice he had a disagreement with Hermann Göring. In this version, Göring wanted to destroy his aircraft rather than surrender them to the

Allies, as required under the Armistice. Görtz argued with the future Reichsmarschall that the aircraft technology would soon be obsolete and that the destruction of the aircraft would only mean a higher reparations bill for Germany.[48] The problem with this story is that it is impossible. Hauptmann Hermann Göring was the last commander of Jagdgeschwader I 'Richthofen', and had flown his aircraft into Aschaffenburg for the surrender. Görtz was stationed in Berlin and then in France, nowhere near the Fokker Triplanes and DVII aircraft of JG1.[49] He seems to have invented the tale for his wife's benefit. In all the self-serving material captured in England, or in the plethora of material written in captivity, there is not one word about such an incident. Undeniably, the First World War was personally difficult for the Görtz family; he had two brothers in the Great War, one killed in action and the other severely wounded.

POST-WAR CAREER

Görtz returned to Lübeck and practised in his father's law firm.[50] He passed his assessor's examination in 1921 and eventually moved to the larger firm of Bergbau AG Lothringen, as a corporate attorney in Bochum and Hannover. The family-owned firm eventually disintegrated and Görtz decided to take a break from active practice and journey to the United States, before returning once again to Hamburg. According to a statement published posthumously, he said that 'My first contact with Irishmen was in the USA where I met an American lawyer engaged in the Irish nationalist movement. Through him I met other Irishmen, some of whom were prominent in the national movement, but the contacts were merely friendly meetings.'[51] Görtz later claimed to be a specialist in international law, dating from his time in the US, but what specific qualifications he had for this assertion are not apparent. His legal career foundered, according to Görtz, because of 'the fact that Jewish lawyers who have emigrated to the principal towns of Europe and America have drawn the international legal business to themselves'.[52]

Görtz and his wife made a trip to Ireland in 1927 and they toured the area around Dublin and Wicklow, their visit coinciding with the funeral of murdered TD and Minister for Justice Kevin O'Higgins. 'I learned something of the hot political passions in the country,' he later noted.[53]

On his return to Germany, Görtz returned to private law practice, but was unable to make a financial success of it in the depression-ravaged country. In what seemed like a wonderful opportunity, a colleague, Dr Heinz Ehlers, asked if he would like to accompany him to England on behalf of an important client. Ehlers, the lead counsel for Siemens & Halske, was suing International Telephone of America at the High Court in London. The case dragged on from 1929 to 1931, and the results were something less than spectacular: Ehlers lost the case, and then defaulted on his oral promise to pay Görtz's expenses. Rather than suing Ehlers to recover his lost income (about 150,000 RM, by Görtz's accounting, he decided to sue Siemens, the proverbial 'deep pocket'. This strategy was misplaced. The German court ruled, correctly, that Görtz did not have privity of contract with Siemens, but only a non-binding association with Ehlers and that Ehlers's legal agency from Siemens did not extend to hiring Görtz.[54] On the edge of bankruptcy, Görtz returned to a private legal practice in Hamburg.

Were this not depressing enough, Görtz also found himself on the losing end of a libel suit filed by Mrs Ehlers. The cause of the action was Görtz's inability to keep quiet concerning the ongoing case against Dr Ehlers. Writing to his university club, and giving an enhanced version of his relationship with Dr Ehlers, Görtz claimed, referring to the non-payment of fees, that 'the whole was a pre-arranged subterfuge on his and his wife's part'. Suit was brought in January 1933 and Görtz, unable to prove the truth of his assertion, was fined 800 Reichsmarks. Görtz attempted several times to get the case reopened, claiming to have discovered new witnesses, but was unsuccessful. He also neglected to pay the fine and was in danger of being jailed for civil contempt. However, a Nazi decree of August 1934 proclaimed a general amnesty, and the fine was remitted. This case later came back to haunt him, when his application to rejoin the Luftwaffe was denied after Görtz failed to mention the incident.[55]

Politically, Görtz was a conservative: he joined Alfred Hugenberg's ultra-conservative Deutsch-Nationale Volkspartei (DNVP – German National People's Party) and, significantly, the Nazi Party in 1929.[56] Görtz, who was always interested in physical fitness, earned the coveted civilian Sports Badge and obtained his private pilot's licence in Kiel. He later joined the Provincial Flying Group III of the Deutsche Luftsport Verband (German Air Sport Club) in 1933.[57] This contrasts sharply with his later claims to have been a member of the 'Black Luftwaffe' or the 'Black Reichswehr'. With his professional legal career going nowhere fast, Görtz applied for readmission to Göring's new Luftwaffe; he was turned down. By 1935, Görtz was 45 years old, practically bankrupt, and with few prospects for the future.

MISSION TO ENGLAND

Görtz solved his own problem, at least in the short-term. Typically, his own version of this has its share of half-truths:

> When the Führer came to power in Germany I was immediately called for military re-training. On this duty I learnt [*sic*] the German official view about the Royal Air Force, which did not correspond with my personal view and

experience. I offered to prove that England was about to build up a great bomber front directed exclusively against Germany. My offer was accepted and thus I became active in the German Military Intelligence and went to England.[58]

Görtz's official personnel file provides an interesting contrast. It shows that he was *not* called up for military training, *not* recalled to active duty and, in essence, was accepted by the Abwehr as a civilian volunteer agent (or spy) for an undercover mission to England. If caught, he was beyond the reach of official help. Görtz's later myth making would not allow for the reality that he was nothing more than an unpaid spy, so his official testament had to be altered accordingly.[59] Even for the Abwehr, this was a dangerous move; Hitler had forbidden espionage activity against England since the beginning of 1935, in keeping with his desire in *Mein Kampf* to form an alliance with both England and Italy.[60] Görtz resigned from the Nazi Party prior to leaving for England in August, so that if anything went wrong, it would not directly discredit Hitler and the National Socialist movement.[61]

Görtz had been campaigning for an espionage mission since at least the autumn of 1934. His letter to the Air Ministry notes that 'I consider that I am particularly suited for the Intelligence service'. Referring to his wartime position as interrogation officer, Görtz closed by saying 'I place myself at your service to take up this work again'.[62] The Air Ministry turned him down – but Görtz simultaneously contacted the Abwehr, looking for work along the same lines.

He had what he thought was a foolproof plan. He would spy on Royal Air Force bases while masquerading as a writer working on a novel, *Bridge over the Grey Sea*. The book was supposed to be about two Anglo-German families, one of whom lived in England and the other in Schleswig-Holstein. His research into family history would provide a plausible reason for travels up and down the English east coast, and the inclusion of a sub-theme on airplanes would explain his interest in British aviation. His book was to be a fiction in more ways than one.

Cover story complete, he moved to the next step of his plan: companionship. He recruited pretty 19-year old Marianne Emig, a stenographer/typist in his floundering law office, as his travelling companion. Though officially describing her as 'my niece' and as his secretary, once in England, their relationship transcended the barriers that such terms might imply. They planned to take Görtz's Zündapp motorcycle (with sidecar) along on the journey. MI5's later investigation suggested that Marianne Emig was not the innocent young thing she pretended to be. She picked up an RAF airman named Kenneth Lewis and began asking him about military aircraft. She successfully persuaded the enamoured Lewis, who worked at the School of Naval Co-operation, to supply her with photos of planes and offered to buy amateur film of new aircraft. Emig asked that Lewis visit her in Germany, and stated that 'financial assistance' could be made available to him. She asked Lewis to write her, and he agreed, stipulating that he should use RAF crested paper with matching envelopes.[63] According to another letter from Görtz to Germany, written in September 1935, he and Emig would 'be here for another week, then our work will be finished ... at present we are writing a big report'. Görtz and Emig left England on 24 October and Görtz accompanied Emig to Hamburg via Ostend. Leaving his belongings behind, Görtz evidently expected to return to England.

Görtz's hope for financial salvation and espionage glory came to a screeching halt on 26 October 1935 when MI5 was informed by the Special Branch of an unusual situation in Kent. Mrs Florence Johnson, owner of 'Havelock', Stanley Road, Broadstairs, notified the police that she had found something of interest in the belongings of one of her tenants. LTC Hinchley-Cooke of MI5 arrived to investigate. Mrs Johnson explained that her German tenant and 'his niece' departed without paying their rent, but had sent a postcard from Ostend explaining that he would return, asking her to take care of his motorcycle and wardrobe trunk in the meantime.[64] Mrs Johnson, who obviously had some curious notions about landlord-tenant rights, opened the trunk, making the find that prompted her to call to the police. The police and MI5 quickly determined that Görtz had some curious notions about security.

Hinchley-Cooke was amazed at what he discovered: a detailed sketch of the RAF base at Manston, an Ordnance Survey map of south-eastern England with RAF airfields marked, a miniature camera, letters and documents, photographs of RAF aircraft, a diary and several notebooks. The diary entries were themselves cause for alarm: 'Aug 29 1935 Mildenhall; Aug 31 Duxford; Sept 1 Mildenhall, Sept 2 Hunstanton; Sept 3 Feltwell; Sept 5 and 6 London; Sept 7 Hatfield; Sept 10 Martlesham; Sept 11 Broadstairs, Ramsgate; Sept 12 Broadstairs; Sept 13 Mildenhall; Sept 19 Broadstairs'. The diarist had apparently made a habit of visiting some of the most sensitive RAF installations in Great Britain. The papers included a six-page application from Görtz to rejoin the Luftwaffe, and a copy of the RAF List – complete with check marks next to the names of several airfields.[65]

Hinchley-Cooke immediately put out an alert to all immigration and customs stations to detain Görtz and Emig, should they attempt to re-enter England.[66] He did not have long to wait: Görtz was arrested on 8 November 1935 when he stepped ashore at Harwich. He was charged on 18 November with violations of the Official Secrets Act of 1911 and 1920. Görtz entered a plea of not guilty and was detained until the start of his trial on 4 March 1936 at the Old Bailey.[67] The trial of the 'Flying Spy' soon attracted newspaper attention; Görtz was the most widely publicized German in England, something that certainly did not please the Abwehr or Hitler.

Much of the Crown case was in the form of in camera testimony, due to
the sensitive nature of the crime and evidence. Görtz took the stand in his
own defence and repeated his cover story about writing a novel. He did not
live up to the expectations of his defence counsel. Görtz backed himself into
a corner during a series of questions about his associations in Germany and
he refused to answer further, adding that 'I would not try to defend myself
here if I thought that in Germany I would be tried for high treason'. With
the accumulated evidence and Görtz's weak alibi, there was very little doubt
of the verdict: guilty, sentenced to four years' imprisonment.[68] In speaking
about the incident, one author observed that it 'proved Görtz to be
incredibly simple-minded for a successful spy, carrying about with him and
eventually leaving behind papers which would damn him beyond
redemption if they fell into enemy hands'. It was Görtz's first serious
mistake; it would not be his last.

The evidence seized at Görtz's bungalow was clearly embarrassing to the
Germans. His own letters detailed his repeated, failed attempts to rejoin
the Luftwaffe, to the point where the German Air Ministry pointedly asked
him to stop writing to them.[69] His professional life was also open to ridicule:
Görtz was desperately attempting to stop administrative proceedings in the
Hanseatic Chamber of Solicitors to drop him from their list of attorneys
licensed to practise.[70] In addition to details about his relationship with his
'niece' Marianne Emig, MI5 was also in possession of a letter Görtz sent to
a Julinka Doerderlein, referring to her as 'my beloved'. The German's
extracurricular romantic life was apparently not unknown to Frau Görtz:
police seized a letter to her with the phrase 'If a few times my power of
resistance failed me, when I did not want it to – let it be'.[71] Ellen Görtz,
however, remained loyal to her husband, though his prior and subsequent
conduct clearly indicated that he did not reciprocate the attitude.

Görtz served his time at Maidstone Prison, where he came into contact
with an unusual assortment of other inmates. According to his later
statement,

> In Maidstone Prison, where I served my sentence, I met an officer of the
> British Army, a native of Dublin. He had a wide knowledge of Irish affairs,
> and from him I learned the story of Easter Week and the later developments
> as seen by a Unionist. Here, also I met members of the IRA sentenced for
> activity in the 'English Campaign,' and from them I learnt the opposite point
> of view.[72]

As in most sections of his posthumous testament, this statement of
fact deviates from the truth. His British Army contact was Norman
Baillie-Stewart, who had been sentenced to prison for espionage in
1933. Baillie-Stewart was released from Maidstone in 1937 and left for
Germany; he had no pre-war connection with Ireland.[73] Görtz's assertion
that he met members of the IRA is also doubtful. Görtz claimed to have met

Irish prisoners of the English Campaign, yet the campaign started in the middle of January 1939 and Görtz was released in February, before any bombing suspects were incarcerated in Maidstone. The actual truth is a little more prosaic; writing to Mrs Iseult Stuart in 1945, he described how 'at the Maidstone Prison I had met IRA men and an Irishman who had strangled his wife because she had sung "God Save the King" when George was crowned. And he was not mad.'[74] However, in an interview with Irish Intelligence, Görtz 'explained that he was not in actual contact with the IRA men at Maidstone. He had a job as gardener – wore a red band on his arm – and had met them occasionally in the course of his gardening activities.'[75] Perhaps the most ironic statement on his imprisonment is from Görtz himself. In his 1939 application to the Reichsschrifttumskammer (Reich Literary Chamber), Görtz had to include a brief biographical statement. He dealt with his time in prison in a masterpiece of literary omission: 'I have often been overseas, especially in England. I was there from 1935 to 1939.'[76]

Görtz was released after serving only three years and was returned to Germany. He had become the most famous German spy in recent memory, largely from his bungling failure, but despite this, his adventures in the world of espionage were just beginning.

THE SPY RETURNS

From his official file, it appears that Görtz was finally called to active duty on 1 August 1939, one month before the start of the Second World War and six months after his release from Maidstone. There is no record of what happened to him in the interval, but he must have been questioned by the Abwehr, and possibly by the Gestapo or SD; he hardly received a hero's welcome and congratulatory handshake. To date, Görtz had accomplished little for the Reich other than generating a mass of unwelcome publicity and holding the German Intelligence community up to international ridicule. It must remain a mystery why he was re-employed by the Abwehr. His first posting was to Flight Training Regiment 21 at Magdeburg, followed by a two-month course at the Supplementary Flight Battalion No. 21 at Jüterborg, and then an assignment from 21 November 1939 to 18 January 1940 to the Command Staff of Air Fleet No. 2. For a junior officer (Görtz was still a reserve second lieutenant) who had not seen active service in twenty-three years, his training was necessarily rudimentary. Görtz was now almost 50 years old and it seems no thought was given to employing him in a conventional military role; he didn't have the experience or training necessary.

Despite his record – and the possible psychological damage caused by an enforced prison sentence – the Abwehr reclaimed Görtz in early 1940. Given the short duration of his first three postings, it is certainly possible

that they retained control of him all along. As of 19 January 1940, Görtz
reported to the Lehr Regiment Brandenburg zbV 800 under the command
of OKW/Abwehr II.[77] A new role had finally been found for the ageing
second lieutenant of reserves: he was to become a secret agent in Ireland.

Never one to be outdone by others, Görtz later took the full credit for
the genesis of his mission to Ireland:

> On my release, I returned to the German Air Force, I suggested to my
> command that it might be possible to make use of the IRA in England for
> intelligence purposes when the now inevitable war broke out. I urged that the
> astonishing fact of their having declared war on England should be taken
> seriously, and pointed to the possibility of starting a revolt in the Six Counties
> – or, as we in Germany generally call it, Ulster. My suggestions, no doubt,
> had some influence.[78]

Whether at the suggestion of its junior officer, or in connection with an
already developed mission plan, Abwehr II decided, that Görtz was the
right man to send – not to England, as Görtz said he suggested – but to
Ireland. His attachment at the Brandenburg training facility at
Brandenburg/Havel gave him the opportunity to see some of the
techniques developed in his absence. Görtz would have presumably
received some parachute training, but most of his efforts were focused on
academic preparation for his intended mission. Görtz was to be
parachuted in uniform (he maintained that this was his own idea: 'I was
going in full uniform to work, not as a spy or agent, but as a military
leader.') and equipped with several items. Under the terms of the *Zehn
Gebote* (ten commandments) for the military conduct of German soldiers –
included in every soldier's paybook – German troops were required to be
uniformed at all times or to display a visible identifying badge.[79] No
exceptions were made for spies/'military leaders' on missions. However,
since Görtz was on a secret mission, it was decided to falsify his
identifying *Soldbuch* (paybook). This may have something to do with the
fact that Görtz, due to his English escapade, was the most famous
Germany spy of the century, and that his name (and face) were well
known to British security officers.

In contrast to later documents issued to German agents, Görtz's material
was of an amateurish nature, without even the pretence of cleverness or any
serious attempt to pass as authentic. He was given the cover-name of
Leutnant der Reserve Heinz Kruse, but mistakenly signed the book as 'Dr
Hermann Kruse'.[80] Most of the necessary information in the book was
omitted – it usually contained dates of unit assignment, an immunization
record, decorations, a dental chart and so on – but, curiously, some false
details were inserted. His date of birth was incorrectly given as 16 August
1890 and his wife was listed as Margarete (nee Werner). Görtz later said
that:

My military papers legitimizing me as an officer of the Luftwaffe were written out by order of the German authorities in a different name. This was done to protect me as far as possible against bad treatment by British authorities if taken prisoner, in view of my record. I had such papers since the outbreak of the war. It is established international law that a military legitimization is not a passport ... the Germany Reich, as a sovereign State, was free to give me any name.[81]

One wonders what effect that this argument by a British POW would have had on a German military tribunal in similar circumstances.

In Görtz's many subsequent statements he consistently held that he was a designated 'representative of the Supreme Command'. By 'Supreme Command' he meant the High Command of the Armed Forces – the OKW. His written statements abound with such references: 'before I had been transferred to the Supreme Command'; 'During the time I was in the Supreme Command'; 'My position was that of an Air Force officer in the Supreme Command, detached by the Supreme Command to the Abwehr of the Supreme Command'. Other than his questionable translation of *Oberkommando* as 'Supreme Command', this is simply an inaccurate statement of fact.[82] Görtz worked for the Abwehr; the Abwehr was a division of the OKW. This did not make Görtz a representative of the OKW any more than a private soldier in the US Army could be said to be a representative of the Joint Chiefs of Staff, but it flattered Görtz's ego to hold himself out as more than he actually was.

Görtz did make an effort to find out more about the Irish situation, and through the offices of Franz Fromme he made contact with two members of the 'Irish colony' in Berlin, Francis Stuart and Nora O'Mara. Francis Stuart later tried to play down his contact with Görtz, but Kurt Haller stressed that the Abwehr was 'most grateful for all his assistance'. Nora O'Mara's Irishness is questionable, but in her memoirs she describes working as a 'secretary' for Görtz before his departure for Ireland. Görtz said later that he made contact with Northern Irish who were living in Italy, calling them the 'Independent Group,' and noting that they were loosely connected to the Breton independence movement, Breiz Ataio. He added that these Irish expatriates distrusted the IRA 'as an organization, and disliked its methods'.[83] Görtz claimed that he received the address of a safe house in Tyrone from this group and the location of another one in County Meath. Görtz gave the impression that he learned of Laragh Castle from the same group, but this is false.[84] It was Francis Stuart who gave him that address, with the caveat that it was for 'emergency' use only.[85]

Görtz later said that he chose a drop zone in County Tyrone after a personal reconnaissance flight over the possible landing areas. This is doubtful, even assuming the Luftwaffe would authorize Görtz to conduct a purely observation flight over Ireland. Most military services operate in a standard fashion: the specific mission details are decided by the operations staff, approved by the commanding officer and executed by the junior officers and men. Görtz was still a junior officer, regardless of his age. His claim that he intended to land in Northern Ireland is probably intended to give credence to the position that he never meant any mischief in the republic, but only ended up there as a matter of unfortunate chance. It remains true, however, that during his eighteen months of freedom in Ireland he never attempted to take the war to the British in Northern Ireland, a fact that casts considerable doubt on his stated intentions. Görtz also took credit for suggesting that Frank Ryan be released from Burgos Prison 'as a friendly gesture towards the national movement in Ireland, although he had fought against our interests in Spain'. He also said that 'special men' were dispatched to the US and Spain to wait for his correspondence from Ireland.[86] Görtz was supposed to be in constant radio contact with the Abwehr and any correspondence could be sent to an already-manned cover address, making it likely that this was yet another part of Görtz's 'legend'.

In actual fact, Görtz's limited military mission was directed at Northern Ireland, operating with resources collected in the south. His objectives were: 1, to establish a secure communications link between Ireland and Germany; 2, to consult with the IRA on the prospect of a reconciliation between the Irish state and the IRA; 3, to direct the military activities of the IRA towards British military targets (specifically naval installations) in Northern Ireland; and 4, to report any incidental items of military importance.[87] He was not authorized to interfere in Irish political matters as such a move could jeopardize Ireland's neutrality policy, a policy that effectively served German strategic interests. Though unsuccessful in the past, the Abwehr was still attempting to direct IRA energies in a more productive direction. This had been the goal of the Tom Barry–Abwehr link in 1937, and was reinforced by Weber-Drohl's mission earlier in 1940. Had Weber-Drohl been more adroit, there would have already been an existing radio link, but now Görtz would have to rectify this problem himself. Weber-Drohl and Görtz were supposed to have worked in concert but this plan, too, had been compromised by events. As far as is known, the only Irish contact names Görtz possessed were those of Jim O'Donovan and Mrs Iseult Stuart.

Görtz was scheduled to depart for Ireland (or Northern Ireland, as he would have it) in later April 1940, but his flight was delayed for a week by poor weather over the drop zone. In the interval, Stephen Held arrived in Germany with the 'Kathleen Plan' – an amateurish IRA outline for the German invasion of Northern Ireland. Görtz was recalled to Berlin to observe Held, but never met or spoke with him. This connection between the two would have unfortunate consequences for both, particularly for Held.

On the evening of 4 May 1940, Görtz was preparing to depart from the Luftwaffe airfield at Fritzlar. As Görtz has been periodically described as a 'romantic figure', it would be inappropriate to continue without one other vignette. In 1959, Enno Stephan interviewed Luftwaffe Hauptmann Wilhelm Kaupert. Kaupert said 'One day I received the order to organize Herr Görtz's flight to Ireland. Görtz was already at the *Schloßhotel* in Kassel-Wilhelmshöhe, together with his wife'. When Stephan later showed the report to Kurt Haller, he was shocked: 'For God's sake, Herr Stephen, don't write that about the wife. It is true, Görtz had a woman with him in the Kassel hotel, but it was not his wife. Ellen Görtz, the widow, should never find that out!' Haller continued that Görtz had many weaknesses and that this particular incident illustrated his disregard for operational security but added: 'We didn't have anyone else but Görtz, and so finally we let him fly to Ireland, against all common sense.'[88]

Before departing for Ireland, Görtz also had one other item of business to attend to. He requested that Admiral Canaris provide him with a cyanide capsule. According to Kurt Haller, Canaris became angry and replied 'We don't work with poison'. Görtz explained that he wanted the option of suicide in case he was captured by the British and forced to reveal the names of his Irish accomplices. Canaris, who should have been wary about Görtz before now, passed on the request to the OKW chief, Generaloberst Wilhelm Keitel, who eventually authorized the poison capsule for Görtz.[89] Görtz, code-named 'Gilka' (the brand name of a Berlin schnapps) was now ready to launch 'Operation Mainau'.[90]

LANDING IN IRELAND

Görtz's flight left Germany at approximately 21:00 on 4 May 1940. The pilot of the He-111 was Oberleutnant Karl Eduard Gartenfeld and though there was extensive cloud cover over England, it was anticipated that the Irish skies would be clear.[91] They were not. Görtz later said that he could have ordered the pilot to return to Germany or jumped. He jumped. Upon his return, Gartenfeld reported that he had been attacked by an RAF night-fighter after the drop and that he had no clear idea whether Görtz jumped into the sea or landed safely.[92]

Görtz jumped from the He-111 in the early hours of 5 May.[93] Wearing his Luftwaffe parade dress uniform and carrying at least $26,000, Görtz also had a standard 'Afu' transmitter, a Belgian Browning 9mm pistol and a 'parachute' knife. The radio was fastened to a separate parachute and dropped slightly after Görtz, to allow for a slower descent.[94] Upon landing, Görtz was to remove his harness, gather the radio, bury both parachutes with his spade (in the pack with the radio) and set about on his way. Görtz jumped from an altitude of about 1,500 metres and his descent took several minutes. Within several minutes of landing, however, nearly everything that could go wrong, had gone wrong.[95]

First, Görtz had no idea where he was. According to his post-war statement, he was supposed to have landed in Northern Ireland or by the (fictional) farm near Trim. His actual location was a complete mystery to him. He was, in reality, just outside Ballivor, County Meath, about as far from anywhere as he could have asked for. Second, he couldn't find the other parachute with the radio. Görtz searched for the next several hours to no avail. Without the shovel contained in the missing package, he also had no effective means of burying his own parachute. At daylight, after hiding his parachute under a bush, Görtz finally made his first contact with the natives.

The subsequent Garda investigation detailed the almost comic character of this initial meeting. The two Irishmen were Andrew Gooney and Christopher Reilly, from Ballivor, County Meath. Reilly appears to have suffered from some type of mental disability and was referred to as 'the half-wit' by Görtz, Gooney and the investigating Garda officers. Gooney testified that 'he saw Reilly the half-wit beating the ditch with a fork and cursing at somebody'. Reilly then yelled at Gooney 'Come out here until you see this old bowsy.' Gooney, 'a small, elderly, poor-looking man', was 'afraid that Reilly was 'in one of his fits'' and did not go near him. Later he saw a man come out of the ditch. The man was Hermann Görtz. According to Gooney, the stranger asked the direction to Wicklow and gave Reilly £1 to quiet him down (this was Görtz's only Irish pound note, given to him by Francis Stuart). Gooney also added that the stranger gave him $100 but he did not take it.[96] Despite his supposedly thorough preparations for the mission, Görtz said later that he was unaware English currency was accepted in Ireland.

Görtz's account states that he was walking in full German uniform during this part of the journey, having decided to make the eighty-mile trek to Mrs Stuart's house at Laragh, County Wicklow. After his encounter with Gooney and Reilly, he also decided to confine the walking to night-time, resting during the day. He reported reaching a tributary of the Boyne near Kinnegad. On the second evening march, he finally arrived at the Boyne itself and decided to swim the river when he noticed a guarded crossing. This proved to be an unfortunate choice: Görtz forgot about the invisible ink, the *G-Tinten*, hidden in his shoulder pads. The river crossing ruined his only supply and, again according to Görtz, 'I had a fainting spell'.[97]

Soon thereafter, Görtz decided to abandon his uniform tunic, which he hid in Ballinkill Bog, Carbery, County Kildare, from where it was later recovered by the police. Görtz decided to retain his Luftwaffe garrison cap ('as a vessel for drinks'), World War One pilot and observer badges, his ribbon bar and the embroidered Luftwaffe eagle from over his right breast pocket. He continued on wearing a sweater, riding boots (which he was, for some unfathomable reason, wearing when he jumped), riding breeches and a black beret. If he was aiming for a look that would draw attention, he made a wise choice. He walked through Newbridge in daylight dressed in this costume, and even stopped at the Garda station at Poulaphouca to ask for directions.[98] Despite whatever other failings he might have had, Görtz was certainly not averse to taking chances. With no food and little sleep, he marched the entire distance undetected and arrived at Mrs Stuart's doorstep at 10:00 on 9 May. She seems not to have expected visitors from Germany.

THE FIRST SAFE HOUSE

Görtz's arrival at Mrs Stuart's, by all subsequent accounts, was a surprise, though Minister Hempel's visit to Laragh on 5 May raises the possibility that there was some forewarning. Almost a month later, Hempel would send telegrams to Berlin claiming to have no knowledge of Görtz's identity or mission. Given his close friendship with both Mrs Stuart and her mother, Maude Gonne MacBride, this is questionable.

According to Görtz's account, Mrs Stuart, once she accepted that he knew her husband, put the exhausted spy in a bed and went along to notify her mother what had happened. Mrs Lily Clements, Francis Stuart's mother, was also at Laragh when Görtz arrived. While Görtz slept, Iseult Stuart and Maude Gonne proceeded to Switzer's in Dublin, where they bought a suit and assorted clothes for Görtz, and are understood to have sent a message at this time to Jim O'Donovan.[99]

Iseult Stuart's relationship to Görtz is interesting. Though the two had never before met, there was obviously some sort of romantic interest. In her diary, she imagined a scene where she married the German, and when Görtz was later captured she noted: 'No voice has ever caressed my ears like one which I may never hear again, no smile has so inveighled [sic] me.'[100] For his part, Görtz maintained contact with Mrs Stuart while on the run, writing letters that suggested they had more than a platonic relationship.[101]

On the evening of 9 May, after Iseult and Mrs MacBride returned, Jim O'Donovan collected Görtz,[102] who did not expect O'Donovan, thought he might be kidnapped and ran into a nearby field until convinced that it was safe.[103] He was taken to O'Donovan's house, 'Florenceville' in Shankill, south County Dublin, where he remained until 11 May. The O'Donovans let him sleep in a loft in the garage and he spent the days in the orchard behind the house.

On 11 May O'Donovan, Stephen Held and Patrick McNeela shifted him to the home of J.J. O'Neill (11 Winston Avenue, Rathmines). The transfer was not without incident; McNeela apparently introduced himself to the frightened German by saying 'Where's the money?'[104] Once in a more secure setting, Görtz reported that he learned more about the Irish political situation talking to Mrs O'Neill, a daughter of Ely O'Carroll. He also gave the IRA the sum of $16,500 during this period, but kept $10,000 for his own use. There seems to be no explanation of how Görtz planned to convert such a large amount of cash into Irish or English money without attracting attention. Görtz stayed with the O'Neills until at least 19 May, when he moved to Stephen Held's house at Templeogue.

THE HELD RAID

In 1890, German national Michael Held journeyed to Ireland where he founded a successful sheet-metal business, Michael Held Ltd. He married an Irish woman, who had a child from her previous marriage, Stephen Carroll. Michael Held adopted the boy, who himself adopted the name Stephen Carroll Held. As a German citizen, Michael Held was interned for the duration of World War One, but returned to his business on his release. Stephen worked with his adopted father before finally emigrating to the United States, where he married. He returned to Ireland in the 1930s to join Michael Held & Son once again, leaving his wife and children in America. Though he had the linguistic advantage of an adoptive German father, Stephan Held never learned the language.

At some point, Held established ties with the Irish Republican Army and because of his adopted ethnic background, Stephen Hayes decided to send him as a representative to German Intelligence headquarters in Hamburg.[105] In his 'confession', Hayes later said that Minister of Agriculture Dr James Ryan approved of the mission, 'as the Government were very anxious to find out Germany's intentions towards the 26 County area'.[106] Though the Weber-Drohl mission had occurred in the time between Pfaus's visit in 1939 and April 1940, there had been no further direct contact between German Intelligence and the IRA since O'Donovan's last flying visit in August 1939. Some coordination must have occurred, because Held was met at his Brussels hotel by a German who 'had been in Dublin and saw Sean Russell in 1938'. Though the dates are slightly wrong, the identity of this person can be none other than Oscar Pfaus. Inexplicably, Pfaus later said that he first learned of the mission with Held's arrival at Pfaus's Hamburg apartment on 20 April 1940 (Hitler's birthday). Pfaus said that he was even more astounded when his visitor announced that he was the representative of the IRA Army Council. With approval from the Hamburg Ast, Held was installed in a room at the Hotel Continental – where the Abwehr lodged its foreign guests. Pfaus returned later with Kurt Haller from the Abwehr II office in Berlin.

They took Held to a house in the Traunsteiner Straße. Their initial reaction was that Held was probably a British plant. Haller recalled: 'He was extremely nervous. He could not sensibly answer my questions and didn't have the half-Pound note that we had already agreed with Jim O'Donovan would be the identification for an eventual IRA courier'.[107] Held's credibility was further questioned because of his name. Jim O'Donovan had been code-named 'agent Held' and then a second Irishman, also claiming to represent the IRA, arrived with the same name.

The Abwehr remained sceptical. They were likewise not reassured when Held produced what he called an 'invasion plan' for Ireland. The plan, correctly described by Haller as *dillettantisch*, was variously referred to as the 'Artus Plan' or 'Plan Kathleen'.[108] Its author was IRA member Liam Gaynor and, in the view of the Germans, it was a perfect example of non-military laymen at work. The plan envisaged a landing in the neighbourhood of Derry (in the manner of Narvik) and a successful conquest of Ulster with assistance from the IRA. The IRA planned a ground offensive beginning in County Leitrim with a front on Lower and Upper Lough Erne which would, somehow, lead to the destruction of all British forces in Northern Ireland.[109] The bait for the Germans was supposed to be the chance of neutralizing the RAF's use of Lough Erne as a tactical base against the U-boat fleet. The plan called for the deployment of 50,000 German troops. The Abwehr officers were not impressed.

After the impromptu briefing on Plan Kathleen, Held requested that a German officer be sent to Ireland to coordinate plans between the IRA and the German High Command. Unknown to Held, he was being observed by the German agent already designated as a liaison between the two organizations, Hermann Görtz.

The drama would be incomplete without another scene involving Oscar Pfaus. According to yet another dramatic recollection from the former agent to Ireland, he went into Held's room, drew his .45 Smith & Wesson automatic and said: 'Held, see here, if even for a moment you fail to tell the truth, then you will never leave this house alive.' Held, now pale, is supposed to have replied: 'By the Holy Mother of God, I swear it to you, I tell you the truth!' Pfaus then pronounced him *echt* (genuine). When later interrogated by G2, Held neglected to mention any scene with Pfaus and his revolver. Held merely said that 'we were taken by a German, a handsome young man who was a doctor, but I cannot recollect his name. He had a deformed foot and wore a thick-soled large boot [Haller].' Held then said he passed on the messages from Hayes and asked about the release of Frank Ryan from Burgos.[110]

Held only remained in Berlin for three days, departing on 23 April.[111] He was pleased with the German response and remembered that the Germans said 'at the end of the war they would look for preferential national treatment to establish a transatlantic airport at Galway'. While this last promise would probably play to a puzzled audience with the IRA Army Council, Held was reassured with the promise that a German liaison officer was going to be sent very soon.

Held had some difficulty with his passport when travelling from Belgium to Germany. In spite of his protestations to the customs officials, his passport was stamped with the German eagle and swastika. This presented a problem because Held, who was not approved for travel to Germany, was going to have to travel back through England en route to Ireland. Pfaus helpfully used some hair lotion to smear the stamp and Held eventually did reach Ireland without incident.[112]

German intelligence did not learn the appropriate lesson from either the Held visit or from Plan Kathleen. It should have realized that the IRA was unsuitable, hopelessly immature, badly disorganized and not a reliable partner for a protracted covert relationship. Without doubt, the IRA was well-intentioned (in a sense) but inept. If the German authorities noticed such troubling clues, they did a fine job of sublimating these thoughts and proceeding with a partnership doomed to disaster. Held himself was firmly on the road to ruin. Though he escaped notice on this visit to the Abwehr in Germany, his association with the Abwehr in Ireland was to prove more consequential.

By the time of Görtz's arrival, Held was already well known to the Abwehr; the German Legation in Dublin, however, had another opinion of him. In 1938, Held had been associated with an Englishman named John David Hamilton, and the two became frequent drunken companions. They were reported to the Garda after being overheard making threats against de Valera – a charge investigated and discounted. The pair then became involved in a scheme to design a parachute safety device for aircraft (apparently revolving around the idea that an airplane in trouble could release a parachute of its own), but the partnership ended in mutual accusations and a brief court case over the patent. Held claimed that he had given the design to Hempel at the German Legation, prompting an embarrassing public denial by the German minister. Writing for G2, Dan Bryan noted in a letter to Garda Chief Superintendent Carroll, 'It is particularly desired to ascertain if Hamilton is a Jew or not, and if so, would he be actuated by a desire to damage the Germans or merely to obtain money.'[113] Anti-Semitism was not unknown in Irish Intelligence, apparently; neither was moralizing in official reports: 'He [Held] is of immoral tendencies and is believed to have been cohabiting with Mrs Elizabeth Hall.'[114]

While at the O'Neills', Görtz first met IRA Chief of Staff Stephen Hayes (17 May) and together the two of them met at Hayes's house (Auburn Villas, Donnybrook) with Liam Gaynor, the author of Plan Kathleen. Görtz had seen a copy of this plan when Held brought it to Germany. His negative initial impression may explain his actions when he met Gaynor, who later told the Garda that Görtz spent the entire time writing postcards and that the German only addressed two questions to him: when was he leaving, and had he ever been to Scotland?[115] Görtz is also believed to have sent word of his safe arrival to Germany, but the postal censors misplaced the postcard before it could be examined by G2.[116] Afterwards, with Hayes, Görtz was told about the IRA strength: '5000 sworn-in members, of whom 1500 [are in] Northern Ireland. Hayes counts on a further 10,000 Northern Irish and 15,000 Southern Irish in the case of an armed revolt in

Northern Ireland.'[117] To say the least, the numbers were grossly exaggerated, but that would not become immediately apparent to Görtz.

Görtz's first impression of Hayes was that he was an 'upright patriot, whose roots are in the people, quiet, almost passive. Not outstanding as a natural leader.' The German also had difficulty understanding Hayes's Wexford accent.[118] Görtz asked Hayes to retrieve his parachute and uniform from the places he had hidden them after landing. IRA teams were dispatched on the assignment, but not with the greatest subtlety. Several people in the area of Ballivor reported to the Garda that men had searched through the fields at night and that they looked 'like detectives'. The IRA search team also gave a variety of explanations for their presence; to one farmer, they said that they were looking for a tablecloth lost in a high wind, while to another, the men reportedly said that they were from the Board of Works.[119] They were successful in recovering the parachute, but did not locate either the still-missing radio or Görtz's uniform tunic.[120] Görtz, who seems not to have realized the ludicrous nature of the idea, was planning to offer a £10 reward for the safe return of his radio, but did not have time to put this plan into effect.[121]

Görtz attempted to get a general consensus about the future of the IRA and the attitude of the Irish people. According to the IRA leadership he consulted, it was thought that only a British invasion of the Irish Free State would galvanize popular support. To allay any fears of a German invasion – as opposed to German logistical and financial support – Görtz told Hayes that there was no intention for a German landing.[122] Hayes again stressed the need for automatic weapons, but Görtz stipulated that these weapons, should they arrive, would not be used in the Free State. Görtz also displayed his lack of mastery of the Irish political situation, as well as his ignorance of the military system in Germany, by pushing for the IRA to be integrated into the Irish Army. He used the argument that a similar situation existed in Germany, but that the SA was then incorporated into the German Army.[123]

Held's house at Templeogue, 'Konstanz', was anything but secure, despite assurances from the IRA.[124] Held lived there with his mistress, Elizabeth Hall, their son and his mother. The presence of a stranger did not go unnoticed for very long. Görtz had another scheduled meeting with Hayes for the evening of 22 May and spent that day preparing notes for the meeting. He was informed about 22:00 that the meeting was cancelled and went for a short walk with Held at about 23:30. On their return, they noticed a car pulling up in front of the garden gate. Fearing the police, Görtz jumped over an adjoining wall and hid, while the officers detained Held. The Gardaí found a virtual treasure-trove of espionage-related material inside the house.

Detectives quickly noticed Görtz's distinctive uniform paraphernalia – his ribbon bar, hat, black tie and Luftwaffe insignia – and the new clothes from Switzer's. They seized a transmitter, his parachute, assorted notes in English, nineteen coded messages and also a locked safe in the upstairs room. Held denied having the keys, but a search revealed that he did. Inside the safe was a box containing $20,000.[125] When questioned, Held maintained that the money and other items belonged to a Heinrich Brandy, the relative of a deceased former lodger. The Garda officers were not convinced and Held was arrested early on the morning of 23 May.

The notes themselves proved interesting. Görtz obviously intended speaking to Hayes about arms drops, since one note read, 'Ventry Harbour as operation base. Fishing motor-boat – where to get – provisions, crew, harbour.'[126] Contemplating the use of Ventry Harbour, suggests that Görtz's planned actions in Ireland were not quite so incidental as he later maintained. Accompanying notes in Görtz's writing confirmed this attitude. Under the heading 'Possibilities of propaganda' Görtz noted: 'Here – directing common opinion, strengthening our forces; b) N.I. – do'. On one of the papers was the notation 'Communication by Leg. through help of L.H. last chance'. Much later, Görtz confirmed that 'Leg.' was the German Legation and 'L.H.' was Laragh House. G2's conclusion was that 'there can be little doubt that the legation must have been aware of Görtz's arrival if for no other reason than the close friendship existing between the Hempels and Mrs Stuart'.[127]

The coded messages, when deciphered much later, also contained some items of note. In one, meant to be transmitted to the OKW, Görtz briefly outlined his actions to date: 'My tactics of first night march were right. 16th May discussed with Chief in suburban house. Dollars to Henry Mad. unknown. Chief sympathetic about getting me transmitter by all means in his power. Russell to remain in Germany. Ryan's release asked for if made public that German government occasioned it. Propaganda plan Ulster discussed.'[128] This shows that the IRA, specifically Hayes, was not anxious about Russell's return to Ireland, but that Ryan (at the time still in Burgos prison) was of interest to both the Germans and the IRA. It is also significant that Ulster is mentioned in connection with propaganda, not sabotage or intelligence-gathering. The reference to 'Henry Mad'. was never clarified.

For his part, Hempel pretended to the German Foreign Ministry that he knew nothing. In a coded telegram to Berlin, he detailed the arrest of Held and the belongings found in the house – all details reported on Irish state radio. Using Held's alibi, Hempel referred to the stranger as 'Brandy' – though Hempel certainly knew his correct name. Hempel continued:

> I warned about Held in telegram No. 181 of April 1. Since he collaborated with the provocateur Hamilton, there is the possibility of English provocation instigated through Hamilton, which might also be aimed at me, in order to destroy Irish neutrality. I consider the following conjecture conceivable and

will use it in so far as it is possible and advisable: The supposed Brandy is a British agent and was sent to the credulous Held, whom the Englishman knows through Hamilton. ... Brandy disappeared after leaving the incriminating material. The English also know about W[eber] D[rohl]. They then set the police on Held. It is an act of vengeance against me and Held.[129]

The Foreign Ministry answered Hempel's message on 1 June, and essentially told him what he already knew:

Inquiries made of the competent authorities have revealed that B[randy] was actually entrusted with special missions directed exclusively against the English and was to make use of personal contacts with the Irish. Any activity directed against the Irish Government was expressly forbidden. From a group of certain Irish personalities subversive plans against the Irish Government were frequently submitted, and probably also to B., but they were always rejected.[130]

Though the situation was clear enough to Hempel, the Foreign Ministry liaison with the Abwehr seems to have broken down. Under Secretary of State Dr Ernst Woermann prepared a memorandum for Foreign Minister Ribbentrop on the situation in Ireland. This internal memorandum is curious in that it continues to refer to Görtz as 'Brandy' though both Hempel and the Abwehr certainly knew his actual name, and while the Abwehr continued to designate him as 'Gilka' or 'K' (from Kruse, the false name in his paybook). According to this document, 'the Abwehr gave Brandy the addresses of Held and Mrs Stuart as confidential agents with whom he could find shelter if necessary'. Woermann counselled that 'reprisals for the arrest of Held are out of the question, because he is an Irish citizen, and furthermore German interest in his case should not be shown'.[131]

LOOSE IN IRELAND

Görtz remained free after the Held raid, but he was alone and without a safe house or enough local knowledge to find one. He still had several thousand dollars and a few English and Irish pounds, but did not dare to stop anywhere to spend them. He likewise had no way of contacting Hayes, O'Donovan or any of his other accomplices; his maps had been seized, he had no idea of Dublin's geography and seems not to have trusted the telephone. Görtz decided to make his way on foot, again, to the only safe refuge he knew: Iseult Stuart's home at Laragh Castle, County Wicklow. Before he could get there, however, the situation had changed dramatically. Iseult Stuart was arrested on 25 May on a charge of harbouring a person unknown who threatened the security of the state. Despite her clear guilt, she was acquitted following a two-day trial on 2 July 1940.[132] By contrast, Held received a five-year sentence for his continuing role in the Görtz affair.

Held and Mrs Stuart were merely the first in a long series of judicial casualties. It soon became apparent that wherever Hermann Görtz went, the police followed.

After arriving at Laragh after his 24-mile walk, Görtz learned from Helena Moloney that Iseult was in custody and he recognized that Laragh Castle was no longer safe. He hid for a while in the gorse bushes behind the house, where the Stuart children brought him food.[133] According to his own report, Görtz also sought food from Iseult's neighbors, a brother and sister named MacMahon. In his report, he inserted a little homily about the MacMahons: 'Irishmen and especially Irishwomen are fundamental enemies of the police, their hospitality is unusually sacred and the political refugee is an everyday sight.' Moloney took Görtz back to Jim O'Donovan's house and the next evening he was again moved, this time to Maeve Kavanagh McDowell's house at 57 Lakefield Grove.[134]

Helena Moloney was the first of several Irishwomen who sheltered and assisted Görtz during his flight from justice. The secretary of the Women Workers' Union and a dedicated socialist, she had numerous ties to the IRA and to sympathetic people who would be willing to assist the German. She was a close friend of the Stuarts (particularly Iseult) and Maude Gonne McBride.[135] Görtz stayed at a number of houses, usually shuttling from one to the other at night. In June 1940, he occupied a room in Mary Coffey's house at 1 Charlmont Avenue, Dún Laoghaire, and a second safe house was rented by Helena Moloney and her friend Maura O'Brien at 'St. Albans', Nerano Road, Dalkey. To ensure a continuous presence, Moloney took up residence at the Dalkey house herself.

THE IRISH FRIENDS OF GERMANY

Unknown to the Abwehr or to Görtz, the months preceding his arrival had been busy ones for potential Irish collaborators with Nazi Germany. Since the hurried departure of most of Dublin's German colony and enforced break-up of the Dublin Auslandsorganisation with its regular series of meetings at the Red Bank Restaurant, there was a definite void in the area of public pro-German political action. This soon changed. Liam Walsh had earlier written to Oscar Pfaus asking what he should do if and when war came. Pfaus gave him no definitive mission, but Walsh took it upon himself to become active in founding the Cumann Náisiúnta ('National Organization'), also known as the Coras na Poblachta, and later as the Irish Friends of Germany. On 14 April 1940, Walsh hosted a sherry party for the pro-Nazi group at his home in Dundrum. Among those attending were former DNB representative Lia Clarke, General Eoin O'Duffy, Seamus Burke (ex-TD from Tipperary), Dr Andrew Cooney (medical advisor to the Hospitals Trust Ltd and former IRA Chief of Staff) and Alex McCabe (founder of the Educational Building Society [EBS] and former Cumann na nGaedheal TD). The Special Branch detectives observing the party also noted that McCabe was 'accompanied by two young girls'.

There was another pro-Nazi gathering at Wynne's Hotel on 15 May, and the same group were in attendance, with the addition of Seamus Hann. Hann was a partner in the firm of Hann and McDonnell and was 'a frequent visitor to the Kilmacurra Park Hotel' run by German brothers – and AO members – Karl and Kurt Budina.[136]

Walsh's home was searched under warrant on 23 May, and the police officers discovered a membership list for the Cumann Náisiúnta that included the name of Francis Stuart.[137] According to the information seized, the next meeting of the Irish Friends of Germany was scheduled for the next evening from 20:00 to 22:30 at the Red Bank Restaurant, but the raid upset the social timetable and the meeting was rescheduled for 31 May. This gathering featured all the 'usual suspects,' with a few new attendees.[138] According to one report, George Griffin regaled the audience (said to be between forty and fifty people) with tales of the 'Jewish stranglehold on Ireland'. 'He gave details of a harrowing nature of various unfortunate people who had fallen into the clutches of the Jews, especially in matters of moneylending and the Hire Purchase of Furniture'. Alex McCabe also spoke to the meeting, expressing his sincere hope that Germany would win the war. G2 believed that 'It is reasonable to conclude that McCabe's sympathies are predominantly pro-German and that he would be disposed to facilitate the German espionage system in so far as it may exist in this country'.[139] Walsh had precious little time to bask in the warm fellowship of his fellow Nazi sympathizers; he was arrested on 25 June.

Walsh's confinement posed an additional burden on the Irish Friends of Germany, because Mrs Walsh petitioned for support money during the period that her husband was confined (June–October 1940). At the next meeting, held on 26 June, it was decided to give Mrs Walsh a weekly stipend of £2 10s. while her husband was incarcerated. However, this simple act proved difficult because, as one IFG member complained, Mrs Walsh 'was a most difficult person to deal with as she was extravagant'.[140] After the announced business, the leaders took questions from the audience. In the course of the discussions, it emerged that the IFG founders were General O'Duffy, Liam Walsh, Séamus Burke and a Mr Callaghan. The subject of the People's National Party platform was mentioned, but discussion was delayed until 'a more appropriate occasion'.

George Griffin, also a founding member of the IFG and the People's National Party (PENAPA), had an important announcement: the German Army was to invade England by 14 July and would be in Ireland by 15 July. To assist them, Griffin wanted to compile a list of loyal Irish nationals upon whom they could rely and who wished to be in a position to render maximum assistance to the German forces.[141]

With the arrest of Walsh and McCabe, the Irish Friends of Germany was placed under the direction of Maurice O'Connor. If the IFG was looking to O'Connor to be a firm hand at the wheel, they were in for a disappointment. Prior to the next meeting on 29 July 1940, O'Connor had a conference with Eoin O'Duffy in which the general urged O'Connor to 'organize as many people as possible together as the military situation might change overnight'. The meeting was held at the Broadway Soda Fountain and Café, 8 O'Connell Street. O'Connor explained to the audience that the IRA had signed an agreement with the Germans, asking for their support. O'Connor also said that Seán Russell had landed in Ireland accompanied by a German officer, and that he (O'Connor) was compiling a list of sympathizers and planned to link up with both German nationals and the IRA.[142] Leaflets printed by the Irish Friends of Germany about this time show that the group had difficulty expressing their particular ideology in a clear manner, in addition to a problem spelling key words such as 'England'.[143]

Walsh was not interned for long, but Mrs Walsh set about notifying the Fichte-Bund chain of command about his circumstances. In almost identical handwritten letters, she wrote to Oscar and Eda Pfaus at their home address, to Pfaus at the Fichte-Bund address in Hamburg and to Otto Leiter (a.k.a. Theodor Kessenmeier). Her 20 June 1940 letter to Oscar Pfaus contained the curiously underlined words 'Realy [sic] truly friendly'. G2 suspected that this might be some sort of anagram, but other than revealing the Irish word for 'new' – *nua* – this proved to be a wasted exercise. Irish Intelligence eventually concluded that 'Mrs Walsh gave the impression of being a rather soft-minded woman who knew little if anything about the various incidents in the husband's activities'. [144]

Walsh's unplanned incarceration meant that he was fired from the Italian Legation, much to the relief of Minister Vincenzo Berardis. Even though he had written to Berardis of his internment, closing with the line 'Accept my loyalty to the cause for which your country is fighting', Walsh was soon singing a different tune. 'If Germany wins the war the Minister [i.e. the Italian Minister] knows it would take some explaining as to why I was dismissed.'[145]

Walsh did not continue to be a significant factor in the story of wartime espionage. As Colonel Bryan noted, 'no doubt his political ardour has been dampened somewhat by the present lack of remuneration.'[146] While there is no direct connection between the various pro-German/anti-Semitic groups and active espionage, they formed a willing net of potential low-grade sympathizers which might have been successfully exploited by German intelligence (whether Abwehr or SD). Dermot Keogh suggests, with some foundation, that these groups 'may have received encouragement, if not financial support from the propaganda wings of the German and Italian legations'.[147] Liam Walsh was certainly connected to the pro-Nazi groups, as well as to the Italian legation and, peripherally, to the Abwehr. G2 also suspected a link between Carlheinz Petersen, the German Legation press attaché, and the Irish Friends of Germany.[148] In the event of an actual German invasion, these cranks would have been a ready, if not altogether valuable, asset to occupying German forces.

This was not the only pro-Axis group to arise from the Irish landscape. Commandant Brendan-Whitmore (who had fought in Dublin during Easter Week and thereafter served in the IRA's North Wexford Brigade, later transitioning to the Irish Army) was actively setting up a similarly minded organization as early as 1939, with many of the same characters who subscribed to the IFG. His group, called the All-Purposes Guild, was decidedly pro-Axis and corporatist in outlook, and boasted among its members such personalities as Liam Walsh, Dr P.O. Suilleabhain, J.N.R. MacNamara, and Claire Clark.[149] Its purpose, with an implied anti-Semitic overtone, was rather broad: 'To recognise England as our most dangerous enemy ... to offer unrelenting opposition of every group, party, organization, sect, or race, the principles or affinities, or practices of which are inimical to the sovereign interests of the historic Irish nation or the Christian religion.'[150]

Privately, the opinions of Irish Intelligence, which kept a watch on Commandant Brendan-Whitmore, were not so charitable: 'vain, superficially somewhat brilliant, and has a "glib" pen, and tongue, which considerably impress the inexperienced'. The All-Purposes Guild went through a nominal metamorphosis, calling itself for a time the Celtic Confederation of Occupational Guilds, before settling on the name Saoirse Gaedheal (Free the Irish People). There were links between this group and the Irish Friends of Germany, and even the Red Cross Society, in that they had members in common. Brendan-Whitmore maintained his contact with the German Minister Dr Hempel, but did not play a known role in the various German espionage efforts.

THE PEOPLE'S NATIONAL PARTY

The People's National Party (PENAPA) did not become active until after the German OKW operations staff disappointed the Irish Friends of Germany and failed to invade either Ireland or England in the autumn of 1940.

PENAPA was the low-wattage brainchild of George Griffin, whose career as an anti-Semitic pro-German activist dated from at least February 1939, when he was suspected of painting the words 'Boycott Jews' on numerous walls in Dublin. He was also suspected, but never convicted, of sending letters to various Jews in Dublin, warning them to 'clear out of the country or they would meet the same fate here as the Jews in Germany'. Griffin and his wife, another sympathetic employee of the Irish Hospitals Sweepstakes Trust, almost single-handedly ran the Irish Rights Protective

Association. Griffin was described by the Garda as 'not a very intelligent person and in fact is inclined to be slightly abnormal'. G2 also connected Griffin to Walsh, believing that he was merely the anti-Semitic front man for the 'International Fascist Movement', allegedly controlled by Walsh from the Italian Legation.[151]

Though Griffin was the leading figure of PENAPA, General Eoin O'Duffy was likewise active.[152] The group also published its own short-lived newspaper, called *Penapa*, which first hit the news-stands in December 1940. Though the editors had submitted the issue to the Irish censors, they published material that was not approved, including a cover which showed a caricature of the 'Eternal Jew' complete with a Star of David watch-chain, sitting atop bags of money representing the Irish economy. The next issue (January 1941) had the same cover and similar contents, including articles on Jewish money-lending, 'The Jewish Nation and Freemasonry' and a poem called 'The Hibernicised Jews'. The Garda seized all 8,000 copies of the issue and Griffin made no further attempts to publish *Penapa*.[153]

However, in 1942 Griffin did try to publish a leaflet from another anti-Semitic group that he had established, the Irish Christian Rights Protection Association. The substance, such as it was, of the leaflet was an attack on the practices of money-lending and hire purchase which were in the control of 'aliens'. The censor ordered the leaflet seized as a threat to the peace and 320 copies were impounded.[154]

A NEW MISSION

The IRA–Abwehr link prior to the summer of 1940 had been relatively insubstantial from the German perspective. Attempts to direct IRA activity in concert with an overall German plan met with failure, particularly since the two previous attempts to establish a radio link fell victim to carelessness and accident. While the IRA continued merrily along with its own agenda, the military priorities of the OKW demanded that Germany again involve itself in Ireland, but without the intervention of the IRA link established by Abwehr II.

The French campaign officially ended on 25 June 1940 and the OKW began gearing up for its next logical target: England. In the east, Germany was still allied with Russia and the only remaining obstacle to total German domination of the European continent was Great Britain. The time to strike was now. British forces had just been thrown off the continent at Dunkirk and had been rebuffed in Norway, and the Empire was committed to defending isolated strategic posts scattered around the globe. Never again would they be stretched so thin and so vulnerable, with their morale so low. Conferences between Hitler and the senior generals of the OKW emphasized that the projected operation against England, code-named *Seelöwe* (Sealion), had an excellent chance of success if it was launched soon.

5
A busy summer: Ireland and Operation Sealion

SEELÖWE AND THE CREDIBLE THREAT

The Abwehr also received the new change of orders. Even before the official end of the French campaign, the war diarist of Abwehr II noted the new mission. 'On the order of the department chief [Canaris], the work of Abwehr II will be directed to the war with Great Britain. For that reason, overseas missions will be prepared.' Abwehr II also ceased all ongoing operations involving Holland, Belgium and France (these countries had been conquered) to direct its resources against the new primary threat.[1]

On 2 July 1940, Hitler issued the preliminary warning order for operations against Britain. More detailed directives followed on 16 July. Prior victories had been achieved against exclusively land powers, but the Germans had no doubt that their combined-arms 'blitzkrieg' tactics would have equal effect against the island nation of Britain. Necessarily, though, certain operational changes would have to be made. Blitzkrieg depended on rapid movement by all elements in the attack, from combat troops to logistical personnel. The scale of the attack necessary to subdue Britain would put severe constraints on the capabilities of the German forces and on the OKW planning staff.

First, because of the obvious geographical factors, the attack against mainland Britain would have to be a combined naval and air-landing operation. Most of the infantry and all the mechanized vehicles and supplies (particularly POL – petroleum, oil and lubricants) would have to be brought in by sea. Landing craft were non-existent in the German naval inventory, so commercial barges would have to be substituted.[2] Of even more concern was the fact that the German armed forces had never before attempted a major amphibious landing and had no data or experience in this very specialized type of warfare.[3]

If combat power was to have any immediate effect, it would have to be delivered quickly and with almost total surprise. This involved airborne operations: compared with the amphibious component, the Germans were the most experienced parachute warriors in the world. Their successful employment in Holland and Belgium demonstrated to the world that airborne forces, acting in concert with conventional infantry, armour and artillery, could spearhead an assault by seizing key installations and sites, securing airfields and bridges and spreading confusion to the enemy command. Complete defence against airborne forces is almost impossible, but even with such obvious advantages, parachute forces have an inbred weakness: their mobility is largely due to a lack of heavy equipment, meaning that paratroopers are not designed to act as regular infantry and are vulnerable if a ground link-up is not achieved quickly.

For a parachute offensive to work, and for air-landing/glider forces to follow in a second wave, air superiority is a minimum requirement. Air superiority indicates that friendly air power controls the skies and air operations can be taken anywhere, at any time, with a minimum risk from enemy aircraft. Effective ground anti-aircraft fire can play a role, but the prime consideration is the elimination of enemy fighter aircraft. Under extreme necessity, an operation can proceed with air parity – an equal match of friendly and enemy air forces, but this is risky because it opens friendly ground troops to potentially catastrophic losses, and ensures that resupply operations will be haphazard, at best.

Both Hitler and the OKW recognized the minimum requirements if Operation Sealion was to have a chance of success. Hitler's initial warning order of 16 July 1940 set out basic minimum conditions necessary before any landing in England could be attempted. He prefaced the order by stating that 'I have decided to prepare a landing operation against England, and if necessary to carry it out'. The pre-conditions were:

1. The Royal Air Force was to be 'beaten down in its morale and in fact, that it can no longer display any appreciable aggressive force in opposition to the German crossing'.
2. The English Channel was to be swept of British mines at the crossing points and the Straits of Dover must be blocked at both ends by German mines.
3. The coastal zone between occupied France and England must be dominated by heavy artillery.
4. The Royal Navy must be sufficiently engaged in the North Sea and the Mediterranean so they cannot intervene in the crossing. English home squadrons must be damaged or destroyed by air and torpedo attacks.

Hitler also asked that the Army, Navy, and Luftwaffe submit plans for any subsidiary actions to take place in connection with Sealion. One of these plans directly concerned Ireland.[4]

This put the responsibility for Sealion's success on the shoulders of the OKM (Großadmiral Erich Raeder) and the OKL (Reichsmarschall Hermann Göring).[5] Göring designated 8 August 1940 as the start of

'Adlertag' (Eagle Day), when the fighters of the Luftwaffe would begin clearing the skies over southern England of the troublesome Spitfires and Hurricanes. The air offensive would be in concert with bombing attacks on RAF bases and other command and control centres. The OKH, meanwhile, had some training to do. The Army and the Navy assembled barges – as opposed to landing craft – at Ostend and began moving them to the projected embarkation ports of Calais, Boulogne and Le Havre. Troops began simulation exercises and the SS and Gestapo did their bit, compiling lists of English people to be arrested (the *Sonderfahndungsliste*) once Sealion was successful.[6] On 1 August, Hitler issued Directive 17 for the 'Conduct of Air and Sea Warfare against England'. According to this order, 'the intensified air war is to be carried out in such a manner that the Luftwaffe can be called upon at any time to support naval operations against advantageous targets of opportunity in sufficient strength. Also, it is to stand by in force for operation *Seelöwe*.'[7]

There were a few other external factors that the Germans had to consider. Though Britain was seemingly on the ropes, help was forthcoming from the 'neutral' United States, in the form of supplies of all kinds and military hardware. The tenuous logistical link between the United States and Britain, the vast Atlantic, would have to become a 'German lake'. This was another task for Grand Admiral Raeder and his commander of submarines, Admiral Karl Dönitz. Their responsibility was to make the US–Britain link incidental by sinking as many merchant vessels as possible, so as to increase military and domestic pressure on Great Britain. Once isolated and demoralized, Britain could, and would be, annihilated.

A second consideration was the weather. As one of the basic items in the staff planning inventory, any experienced commander knows that operational success is often directly attributable to weather conditions. If the weather favours offensive operations, they often succeed; if the weather conditions favour the defence, then, often as not, all the king's horses and all the king's men cannot change what will be a costly exercise for the friendly forces. For the Luftwaffe, good weather meant that airborne, air-landing and close-air-support operations could take place; to the Navy (and to their Army passengers) it indicated that amphibious operations could proceed as planned – probably at high tide – and that naval escort ships could stay on station to supply and support the landings. In particular, Atlantic weather forecasting was critical to projected German operations against England. It is at this point that Ireland stumbles back into the OKW picture. Being by chance located on the extreme western edge of Europe, weather forecasting from Ireland would give the OKL and OKM the necessary 'heads up' for their operations.

Given the historical conclusion to this story, it is difficult to know whether Hitler ever seriously contemplated invading Britain, though the OKW certainly took him at his word and prepared accordingly. Hitler had a notorious soft spot for the English – he was even respectful of them in his *Mein Kampf* diatribes – and always seemed to hold out the hope that Britain would 'see reason' and come to a common understanding with Germany. In this forlorn hope, he seriously misjudged the character of both Winston Churchill and the British people, but he maintained the hope.[8] Even though the outward tone directed against Britain was perfectly bellicose ('Germany is not considering peace. She is concerned exclusively with preparations for the destruction of England'[9]), other mentions of the expected German offensive were more tentative: 'The Führer replied that he could not conceive of anyone in England still seriously believing in victory. If the fight were to continue, it would extend over wide areas and would certainly not be easy.'[10]

In order to assess correctly the importance of German espionage missions in Ireland, it is first necessary to make a basic determination: was Hitler serious about Sealion and if not, were the espionage missions to Ireland merely part of a decoy or diversion plan for something else? In an unpublished OKW directive signed on 28 June, just three days after the end of the French campaign, the OKW indicated that measures against Britain were something other than preparation for an actual landing. The directive to the Abwehr ordered it to engage in operations that would convince the British that 'Germany is preparing war against the British mainland and overseas possessions with all dispatch in the event that Britain desires to continue the fight'.[11] A further indication that the landings were theoretical and aimed at pressuring Britain to sue for peace can be seen in Hitler's simultaneous decision to reduce the size of the German Army from 155 active divisions to 120.

Even after the initial order was given to prepare for Sealion, Hitler's language to his generals suggested that he was not completely confident of a victory: 'A landing by German troops in England is an undertaking whose success appears certain only if all the preparations are made with the most painstaking care. ... The demands the first assault imposes upon the various units are too great to be readily met by commanders who have not occupied themselves for months with these assignments.'[12]

At a military conference at the Berghof on 13 July, Hitler again had doubts about the England operation:

> The Führer is most strongly occupied by the question why England does not yet want to take the road to peace. Just as we do, he sees the solution of this question in the fact that England is still setting her hopes on Russia. Thus he too expects that England will have to be compelled by force to make peace. He does not like to do such a thing, however.[13]

As the summer days dwindled, Hitler seemed almost looking for plausible reasons why he might cancel the promised invasion. On 21 July, already knowing of the Navy's misgivings, he ordered Grand Admiral Raeder to report on his readiness within a week and noted that all planning must be complete by 15 September. Raeder briefed Hitler again on 25 July and argued against Sealion on the grounds that the Luftwaffe was not prepared and that the assembly of barges was causing a disruption in the German civil economy.

If Hitler really wanted an excuse to cancel the operation, he was presented with it on 31 July at a meeting of the OKW chiefs, the OKH and the OKM at the Berghof. The Navy started out and proposed that the entire operation should be postponed until May 1941. They proffered several reasons: after considering the visibility and tides, there were only two optimum periods for launching an invasion against England in 1940: 20–26 August (which would allow insufficient time to complete preparations) and 19–26 September (poor weather predicted). Admiral Raeder again mentioned the economic effect being experienced from the commandeering of civilian barges and fishing boats. The Naval chief also noted that the battleships *Bismarck* and *Tirpitz* would be completed and ready by May 1941, giving the Germans four heavy battleships to ensure that the Führer's directives would be achieved.[14]

On 13 August, Hitler told Raeder that he would await the results from the Luftwaffe air offensive before reaching any final determination. Ironically, Raeder had urged air attacks on British naval bases back in June, but had been rebuffed by Hitler. If the Luftwaffe plan wasn't already weak enough, the OKW issued further directives the same day (13 August) which specified that German forces would not use poison gas; air attacks were forbidden on certain types of shipping in certain areas; and there was, under no circumstances, to be any air attack on London itself. This last policy was amended at the end of August when the British had the temerity to bomb Berlin. The next day, Hitler again muddied the waters by announcing that his plan was to use the bomber attack and the *threat* of invasion to wear down the British.[15]

Despite any private reservations that Hitler might have had, the German propaganda machine did its part by creating the popular mood of expectancy for an invasion of England. The most requested soldier's song on Radio Berlin was 'Wir fahren gegen England' ('we are marching against England'), followed by other equally popular, suitably martial tunes.[16]

The Abwehr was given a multiple mission for Sealion: they were to prepare an intelligence package directly tailored to the needs of the other armed services. The separate sections included forming an estimate of the strength and morale of forces in Great Britain, providing a means of weather prediction and reporting, preparing to conduct sabotage operations against selected targets in advance of the airborne and amphibious landings, and establishing radio links between agents and the Continent before and during the actual landings themselves.[17] Like the tasks given to the Navy and Luftwaffe, the successful completion of the Abwehr's task was essential before any attempt could be made to invade England.

Without an accurate knowledge of the enemy, German planners could only begin to complete their staff estimates and proposals. The staff process itself waited on the Abwehr.

FALL GRÜN

The OKW, however, could prepare some operational studies that were independent of intelligence information from Britain. Coincident with Sealion, another contingency plan which directly affected neutral Ireland was developed. 'Fall Grün' (Case or Plan Green), as it was called, was the full-scale operations plan for the invasion of Ireland in coordination with Sealion. Whether it was the brainchild of the OKW operations staff or the operations section of a subordinate command is not known. Implementing Fall Grün was the responsibility of Generalleutnant Leonhard Kaupitsch, commander of the German Fourth and Seventh Army Corps of Army Group B. The planning for Fall Grün was characteristically thorough, at least at first glance, despite the short time available to complete the preparations. Civilians who seemed to have a keen eye for what types of information were needed by the German military had obviously done much of the groundwork before the war.[18]

The full information package consisted of five separate volumes, each devoted to a particular area of interest.[19] Of particular note in the *Militärgeographische Angaben über Irland* (military-geographical data on Ireland) was a seventy-eight-page booklet on Éire and Northern Ireland. It described the frontier, size, historical background, industry, transport, administrative structure, vegetation, climate and weather. The book also included seventeen pages of thumbnail sketches of 233 cities, towns and villages, and a map that even accurately depicted the Gaeltacht (Irish-speaking) region, complete with a lexicon in Irish with German equivalents. Most Irish charts would be fortunate to be as accurate. In many cases, the Germans modified the existing Ordnance Survey maps, but included details from other map studies of Ireland.[20] Some of the comments, designed to describe Ireland helpfully for invading German troops, were interesting: 'The German Army can count upon rather large quantities of butter, cheese, eggs, meat, oats and potatoes. The rather monotonous native food, however, will not always appeal to our soldiers.'

Separate volumes of photographs (120 illustrations) accompanied this booklet. An annexe contained street maps of twenty-five cities and towns, including street names, hotels, important buildings and petrol stations – including the names and addresses of the garage owners, presumably to wake them if the German Army arrived after closing hours. Another booklet, *Von Mizen Head bis Malin Head*, gave a pocket guide to ninety-eight words in Irish, mostly geographic, many badly translated, and some inexplicably in Scots Gaelic. A second printing of the data in May and October 1941 contained 332 photographs of the Irish countryside and coastline, some obviously tourist photos, and these were used with reference to a highly accurate 1:250,000-scale map. The pamphlet also gave details of spring tides, geological formations and possible routes off projected invasion beaches. In yet another addendum, this one published in 1942 by the OKL, *Kusten-Beschreibung des Irischen Freistaates (Eires)* – coastal description of the Irish Free State (Éire) – high-altitude aerial photographs were printed, some taken from as high as 30,000 feet. Individual houses and trees were clearly visible.[21]

Dr Adolf Mahr, Dr Hans Hartmann, Professor Ludwig Mühlhausen, Dr Jupp Hoven and others could be proud; their pre-war work had reached the higher echelons of the OKW.[22] In many instances, the data seem to pinpoint a source inside the Siemens-Schuckert-Werke, the German company responsible for constructing the Shannon hydroelectric scheme.[23] Despite their contribution, however, there were apparent weaknesses in the data. Every section included a military assessment, but one of limited utility to a field commander. There are several instances where the information, though thoroughly assembled, was simply out of date:

> Irrelevance and inaccuracy are too often encountered in this work and the troop commander would have cause for high blood pressure on several occasions if he conducted his campaign, with sword in one hand and these five Volumes in the other. If he decided to use the Galway-Clifden railway he would not know that the wooden sleepers were long since placed side by side in the construction of many a snug cow byre – a byre incidentally containing shorthorn cattle and not the small black 'Kerry' breed mentioned.[24]

Like Sealion itself, it is difficult to know how seriously the Germans actually contemplated invading Ireland. As late as 3 September 1940, a mere two weeks away from the anticipated start of the invasion, the daily OKW conference made mention of this part of the plan. 'The order on S-day minus ten [ten days before the invasion] must include the putting into force of the deception measures. The Army and Navy still have conflicting attitudes concerning the "green" and "blue" movements.'[25] The operative word is 'deception' – not decoy or diversion. The intent seems obvious: Hitler and the German High command intended Fall Grün to be a credible threat – not an actual operation. Of course the planning would be much the same and tactical conditions could easily change, as could Hitler's intention. While Fall Grün was an impressive looking tiger on paper, its creator never designed it to roar.

WALTER SIMON

At the time when active preparation of Sealion commenced, Canaris could boast that he already had an agent in place in Ireland who had the primary function of addressing some of the vital tactical questions necessary for OKW operations staff. Unfortunately for the Abwehr and the OKW, the agent in question was Walter Simon, and he was interned in Bridewell Jail. Even under the best possible interpretation, Simon did not quite live up to the expectations of his controllers.

Born on 12 December 1881, Simon, like Weber-Drohl before him, was relatively elderly when he was tapped for his Irish mission. Simon had run away from home as a boy to Rotterdam in search of adventure on the high seas. He worked his way up from ordinary seaman to steersman, and finally to captain of his own vessel. In the course of his travels, he picked up English, Spanish in the West Indies and French. Simon happened to be in Australia on the outbreak of the First World War and was interned there for the duration. Upon his release, he returned to the ocean until he first came into contact with the Hamburg Ast in late 1937 during a stopover. He accepted his first espionage mission in late 1937.

Major Nikolaus Ritter of Abwehr I-L (air intelligence collection) in Hamburg commissioned Simon to go to England to investigate metal production works and the rumours of new airfields. Herman Görtz had been sent on a similar mission in 1935. Simon successfully completed two separate similar assignments to England by the end of 1938. His activities did, however, attract the attention of MI5. A letter to a known Abwehr mail drop, the home of a Mrs Duncombe, ordered that she give Simon the enclosed £15. In November, he received £18 from the Abwehr via the front of Kol & Co., Amsterdam.[26] Though he had been stopped by justifiably suspicious customs officials at Harwich, he carried a finished manuscript which, he said, he was trying to publish on behalf of a friend. Though there was nothing outwardly wrong with Simon except for the frequency of his travel, he was placed on the 'watch list' by MI5 due to the other attendant circumstances. He had been compromised.[27]

Impressed with his luck to date, the Abwehr decided to gamble on Simon for a third time, and he was sent to Britain for a third trip shortly before Christmas 1938. Simon himself was more cautious on this trip. He stayed as a seaman's home in Whitechapel, London, and made his espionage excursions while retaining this as his base. For two months, he travelled all over southern England, investigating new airfields. During the course of his travels, he encountered two politically sympathetic Welsh nationalists, who expressed an antipathy towards England. He gave them the sum of £20 and a cover address in Rotterdam where the pair might make further contact with German intelligence. This was the beginning of a small Welsh nationalist espionage and sabotage cell that operated under Abwehr orders during the Second World War.[28] On 5 February, Simon was spotted at Kidbroke in Kent at the site of the RAF barrage balloon unit. He paid a visit the next day to the RAF airdrome in Hendon.[29]

Simon's luck ran out on the evening of 7 February 1939 at an inn in Tonbridge Wells, Kent. Already late when he arrived the previous night, he put off filling in his registration card until the next morning. He was tired, and it was nothing that couldn't wait a few hours. Simon was not sure whether this incident or another recruitment incident in Tunbridge Wells had alerted the police, but the result was the same. Simon was unaware that he had been under surveillance by MI5. When he returned to the inn the next day, the police were waiting. He was arrested and charged with violating the Aliens Registration Act of 1920 by failing to register as such at his hotel.

Simon was taken to Wandsworth Prison where it was obvious that he was suspected of much more than a minor technical violation. His interrogator was no police sergeant, but Lieutenant-Colonel Hinchley-Cooke of MI5.[30] Hinchley-Cooke spoke fluent German, but Simon insisted on speaking in English. When Simon's possessions had been inventoried, it was discovered that he had a General Staff map and a notebook with coded entries. According to Simon, his interrogator offered him tea, sandwiches and cigarettes in an effort to ease the atmosphere. Simon accepted but said nothing of value. Ultimately, the British were able to learn significant information from his possessions alone. They quickly discovered he had the means of sending secret messages: a buff-coloured piece of wax paper used between two sheets of ordinary writing paper as a sort of carbon copy. Sprinkling it with graphite powder revealed the marks on the lower sheet.[31] He was eventually sentenced to two concurrent terms of three months and was deported from Grimsby on 16 July 1939. On his departure, Hinchley-Cooke warned him: 'Don't come back ... you won't be so lucky next time.'[32] Amazingly, the British returned Simon's notebook to him, which had all his secret observations in carefully coded entries. Major Ritter (alias Dr Rantzau) was delighted with the information.[33]

The Germans had reason to be pleased. Their pre-war agents had amassed a great deal of invaluable intelligence data. Much of this was directly translated into their Sealion planning: 'Factories, mines, airfields, ports, harbour defences, military establishments, throughout the British Isles had been surveyed, photographed and filed with meticulous attention to detail.'[34] This data also found its way into an intelligence summary prepared by the RSHA (SS security apparatus) in 1940 in preparation for Sealion. *Informationsheft Grossbritannien*, among a myriad of other detail, included a highly accurate description of MI6 down to its office locations and room numbers. The document identified and explained the function of the Joint Intelligence Committee, a body that was unknown even to the general public in England. It is suspected, but not conclusively established, that the MI5 and MI6 material came from interrogations of Captain Sigismund Best and Major R. Stevens, two MI6 officers kidnapped by the SD on the Dutch-German border at Venlo in November 1939.[35]

Though his cover had been blown by MI5, the Abwehr still had plans for Walter Simon. He reported to the Hamburg Ast in the Knochenhauerstraße in early 1940 for a new assignment. It was not planned to send Simon back to England – his voice, if nothing else, would act as a dead give-away – but he could serve the cause by going to Ireland, instead.[36] Kapitän Wichmann wanted him to relay weather reports by radio, which could then be transmitted to the Kriegsmarine and Luftwaffe. The early-warning data were crucial to their operations. Simon was also asked to observe the movement of British escort vessels in Northern Ireland, information that was critical to the U-boat fleet. He was ordered not to have contact with the IRA under any circumstances.

Simon began a radio training course at Hamburg-Wohldorf and was introduced to the new-generation of Abwehr suitcase transmitter/receivers. He was taught the book-code and was to use lines from Schiller's poem 'Glocke'. He was also given seemingly innocuous messages that could be inserted in correspondence sent to cover addresses in neutral countries, in the event that radio contact was impossible. As a cover, Major Ritter provided him with the papers of a Swedish-born naturalized Australian seaman by the name of Karl Anderson. Simon also received an extremely short briefing from Oscar Pfaus at the Fichte-Bund offices. Almost at the beginning of the meeting, Simon seemed to feel some discomfort with his assignment, exclaiming 'Mensch, das is doch ein gottverdammichtes Himmelfahrtskommando!' (Man, that is a goddamn suicide mission!) Though it seemed innocuous at the time, Pfaus gave Simon some contact names in case of emergency. These included Alex McCabe, Liam Walsh and Charles McGuinness.[37] His Abwehr controllers later said that he was supposed to link up with dormant agent Werner Unland in Dublin. Unland had been told to expect a 'representative of the firm' from Germany.[38]

Simon embarked from Wilhelmshaven at the end of May 1940 aboard U-38, under the command of Kapitänleutnant Heinrich Liebe. Liebe had the same flexibility in choice of landing sites as was earlier given to U-37 on the Weber-Drohl insertion. The crew was to be told only that their passenger was a reporter.[39] They rounded the northern point of Scotland, before running down the Irish western coast. During the voyage, which included a violent storm in Pentland Firth, Simon wore the uniform of a naval officer, so that in the event of capture, he would be treated as a sailor, instead of what he was – a civilian spy – thus facing internment rather than execution.

U-38 arrived in Dingle Bay on the night of 12/13 June 1940. Simon was successfully landed by the submarine's dinghy and he immediately buried the case containing his transmitter, intending to return later once he was safely in Dublin. Once there, he could better decide where to set up his transmitter. Before leaving Germany, the planners at the Hamburg Ast thought that Connemara might provide the most promising location, but to complete his secondary mission, reporting information on British escort vessels, he would have to position himself in the North Channel between Northern Ireland and Scotland. In the event, this was not something that he had to worry about for very long.

Simon walked for several hours along the railway tracks, headed eastward. At one point, uncertain of where he was (he was near Dingle), he asked several workmen when the next train was due. They answered that he would have a long wait; the last train passed through fourteen years previously. At that point, Simon noticed that the railway tracks were rusted and grass was growing between the sleepers. His map, which showed an active railway line, obviously left something to be desired.[40]

Once in Dingle, things took a turn for the worse. At about 07:15 Simon asked Dingle resident Michael Nelligan about the next bus to Tralee, from where he could take a train to Dublin. Mr Nelligan informed him that the 09:00 bus was the next scheduled, but invited Simon back to his pub to wait. By the time Simon had consumed three glasses of whiskey, both his tongue and judgment were loosened. He gave the opinion that the poverty of Ireland would change 'when Hitler comes to this country'. He then made 'derogatory remarks' about Neville Chamberlain and Winston Churchill. Simon told Nelligan that he was heading to Dublin on 'fishing business' and to see a throat specialist. Mercifully, he finally caught the 09:00 bus to Tralee before blowing his cover any further. Once on the bus, he began distributing a bottle of whiskey to the other passengers, saying 'We will have a *deoch an dorais*' (essentially 'one for the road').

By the time Simon arrived at Tralee railway station, he was obviously intoxicated. His accent and behaviour attracted the attention of two plain-clothes detectives, D/Sgts. Colley and Walsh. They struck up a conversation with him on the platform and later on the train. Simon told them that he was coming from Dingle, and before that, from German-occupied Rotterdam. When one of the detectives jokingly asked Simon if he might be looking for someone in the IRA, Simon responded, asking the detectives if they were in the IRA and whether they might know 'Commandant' Alex McCabe and Captain Walsh. The detectives also noticed that Simon was clutching a brown paper bag. At one of the scheduled halts, the detectives called ahead to Dublin and a police reception committee was waiting when Simon arrived at Kingsbridge Station.

Simon seemed to have difficulty keeping his stories straight, and kept telling different versions of how he happened to be in Ireland. The first, apparently also told to the officers on the train, was that he had been visiting his sister-in-law (named Sullivan) in Annascaul, but he had a fight with her in the middle of the night and was making his way home to his wife and children in Dublin. A second version, told when in Dublin police custody, was strikingly different. He was, he said, born in Nottebick,

Sweden, and that in February 1939 he came to live in Rotterdam, having previously resided in Panama. Upset at living in German-occupied Europe, he took $3000 out of the bank and gave the skipper of a Dover fishing cutter (the *Maid Nelly*) £50 to take him to neutral Ireland.[41]

Unbelievably, the Dublin Garda were initially inclined to believe him. Sergeant Gantly of the Dublin Metropolitan Division wrote that according to the information now available 'his account is correct and that he had no motive in arriving in the country beyond that expressed by him of wishing to have peace and quietness'.[42] Sergeant Gantly did not seem perturbed by Simon's conflicting stories, his acquaintance with suspicious Irish nationals, or what a British fishing boat would possibly be doing in German-occupied Holland. Fortunately, 'Anderson's' prints were forwarded to England and on 27 June he was positively identified as Walter Hermann Christian Simon, who had been arrested and deported from England in 1938. The English also sent along Simon's 'mug-shot' for positive visual identification.[43] Despite the conclusive evidence to the contrary, Simon continued to insist that his correct name was Anderson. Upon being shown the photograph of himself, Simon's only comment was 'Yes, that's a very nice picture.'[44]

On 8 July 1940, Simon pleaded guilty before the Special Criminal Court on the charge of illegally landing near Dingle. The prosecution wisely entered a *nolle prosequi* (dismissal) on a second charge of landing at other than an approved airport[45] He was sentenced to three years. The *Dublin Evening Mail* reported the Simon story on 22 June 1940 under the title 'Foreign Seaman in Kerry.' The paper reported on Simon's inconsistent version of events and detailed the property found on him at the time of his arrest. No specific mention was made of any suspicion of espionage activity.[46] In a brief follow-up story after the conviction on 8 July, the paper reported the sentence and that a police officer testified that the same individual had been convicted in England in 1939 under the name Hermann Christian Simon to two three-month terms of imprisonment.[47]

Simon carried with him an unusual assortment of odds and ends. In the brown paper bag the Garda found a substantial amount of cash, both US dollars and British pounds. The final official total was $1910 and £215 15s. 10d. There was some dispute over the amount. In a G2 report from 15 June, it was stated that 'Anderson' had 'a brown paper parcel with 3000 or 4000 dollars'.[48] Simon himself later said 'I had $2000 with me. Four men counted the money, which consisted of a pile of notes of small denominations. The final result was $1910, a loss of $90. When my sentence of penal servitude was changed to internment my money was transferred from police custody to the prison office. There was only $1900, a further loss of $10 compared with the first count. The number of pounds was wrong also.'[49]

Simon also had a 1921 US Navy certificate made out to Karl P.W. Anderson, Australian naturalization papers, a seaman's discharge book, a small magnifying glass and two boxes of 'Promonta Injections', each containing two tubes. In checking their files, the Irish and British discovered some past references to Simon's assumed name. The British authorities located a Swedish seaman, Karl Johan Andersson who had been arrested for 'drunken and quarrelsome habits' in 1936 and was a 'non-desirable alien'.[50]

A later review of Werner Unland's case file – he would not be arrested until 1941 – revealed that a Walter Simon living in pre-war Ireland had been corresponding with a suspicious address in France. This particular Simon seems to have actually been a Jewish refugee from Austria. He arrived in Ireland on 7 July 1938 and his last known address was the Jewish Refugee Society, 43 Bloomfield Avenue, Dublin – probably the last place that Walter Simon the spy would have made his residence.[51]

In a mission which was planned – and possibly executed – simultaneously with Simon's, Abwehr I dispatched another agent with a similar objective. It is not known whether the two were supposed to link up and work together (though that is probable), but the results of the second mission were similar to those of the first: underwhelming.

WILHELM PREETZ

Wilhelm Preetz was born in Bremen on 23 July 1906. Nothing is known of his background before 1922. From 1925 to 1927, he worked as a shipping clerk in Vera Cruz, Mexico, and from 1927 to 1929 was a crewman on the private yacht *Victoria Mary* out of New York, where he met Sarah Josephine Reynolds from Tuam, County Galway. He served on the SS *Karlsruhe* from 1929 to 1932 and then returned to Bremen, where he worked in a telephone exchange and at a watch and clock repair shop. Preetz's prospects looked dim until Hitler's take-over in January 1933. As yet one more opportunistic Nazi, Preetz joined the National Socialist Party on 1 February 1933 and his membership dues were current until he later covertly departed for Ireland. Preetz also joined the SA (Sturmabteilung) – the brown-shirted stormtroopers who paved the way for Nazi election successes and led the early campaign of intimidation against German Jews. A photograph for his Nazi membership card in 1934 shows Preetz in the uniform of an SA Unterführer.[52] He resumed his job as a ship's steward on the North German Lloyd and the Hamburg-South lines in 1935.[53]

Preetz married Sally Reynolds in Bremen in 1935 and travelled to meet her parents in Tuam in 1937 and again in 1938. Since his mission was coincident with Simon's, he probably was picked up by the Bremen Ast (Abwehr post) and sent to basic agent training in late 1939 or early 1940. Typically, the Abwehr did not work with National Socialists and did not want or trust them anywhere near active intelligence work.[54] Preetz, however, had a few personal items that made up for his political 'deficit':

he spoke good English and he happened to be in possession of an Irish passport.

According to the unreliable testimony of his in-laws, Preetz arrived unexpectedly in Tuam on 2 September 1939, just before legal transport on the Germany–England–Ireland route was suspended on 3 September.[55] Preetz had been in Ireland on 5 March, arriving at the port of Galway with a German passport, £40 and a return ticket. Irish immigration did not record his second arrival and it is very possible that he overstayed his legal welcome from the March visit.[56]

At some point following his March arrival, Preetz successfully obtained an Irish passport in the name of Patrick John Mitchell, Eyrecourt, Galway. The passport application was presented to the Garda barracks in Sligo, but the exact mechanism by which an obviously German national miraculously became an Irish citizen is unknown, though it is likely that the Reynolds family was involved. Later G2 investigation on this point determined that his 'uncle-in-law' from Sligo made the arrangements. (The real Patrick John Mitchell emigrated to Australia.) When finally seized by Gardaí in 1940, Preetz's Irish passport was missing pages 7–14, making it impossible to tell the previous use, or to reconstruct the sequence of events with more specificity.[57] The passport incorrectly gives his date of birth as 25 June 1908 and lists his profession as 'Stewart' [sic]. It was stamped by the Department of External Affairs in March 1939.[58]

While in and about Tuam, Preetz resumed several of his old acquaintances. He met again with Joseph Donohue, a grocer's assistant in Tuam. They had known each other since 1934/5 and as Donohue was another individual with no decent prospects, the association with Preetz promised some excitement and adventure. Preetz also established close contact with his extended family – in some cases, too close. Though his wife was living with his parents at Hartung Straße 2, Bremen, Preetz was enjoying an affair with her 19-year-old sister, Annie Reynolds.[59] According to Carolle Carter's research, the affair reportedly progressed to the point where she became pregnant.[60]

Preetz was in the country illegally and the Garda, following passage of the Aliens Registration Act, briefly detained him in November 1939. Preetz decided to take a radical course of action. With the assistance of his ever-helpful in-laws, he travelled to Dublin where he stayed at O'Brien's Hotel and was in constant contact with Sante Staffieri, an Italian national, until around December 1. Preetz's failure to report to the Garda for registration resulted in his name being passed along to the Aliens Office and placed on the alert list. At this time, the Gardaí were not aware of his 'Paddy' Mitchell alias.

According to Staffieri, Preetz stowed away on an outgoing ship on 1 December. Later investigation revealed that only the SS *City of Antwerp* left Dublin at the relevant time; his brother-in-law later said that he left on a

Belgium-bound ship. Staffieri also said that Preetz gave him the Irish 'Patrick Mitchell' passport and it was not returned to him until the following June.[61] The next contact was a message from Preetz to Joseph Donohue in December: 'I am sure anxious to find out about everything. My business partner was also very glad, for right now is the busiest time in the whole year and we did very good so far.'[62]

This was apparently in a jargon code, since Donohue immediately applied for a passport to visit Holland. Acting on information from the Garda, his application was refused.[63] Preetz would have begun his Abwehr training soon thereafter. The exact means by which he arrived in Ireland are unknown, but presumably by U-boat. A telegram in early June 1940 from the Skl/3 to the Abwehr reports that U-38 (which dropped Simon during the night of 12/13 June) would be expected to be outward bound on 5 June and it would report completion of its second special mission ('zweiter Sonderaufgabe'). The log from U-38 blocks out the entire period from 16:00 on 11 June to 00:42 on 13 June 1940 with the notation *Sonderaufgabe* (special mission) – an extraordinarily long time to land one agent. Despite this, the operations order for U-38 only mentions landing 'ein Mann', not two. The answer may be contained in the Skl/1 diary entry that mentions U-26 transporting 'a particularly important man'.[64] By whatever means, Preetz was reported to have landed in the Minard/Dingle area on the night of 25/26 June, though this date is not firmly established.[65] Preetz evidently buried the transmitter suitcase on landing. He stopped overnight in Hanratty's Hotel, Limerick on the night of 27 June and checked into Wynne's Hotel in Dublin on the evening of 29 June.[66] From his subsequent actions, it would seem that he met with his in-laws in Tuam during the period between 27 and 29 June. Donohue joined him in Dublin on 1 July.

Preetz met up with his Italian friend Staffieri on 30 June and Staffieri later testified that he returned the Mitchell passport to Preetz at that time. On 1 July, Staffieri accompanied Preetz to the Provincial Bank in O'Connell Street, where Preetz lodged £100 and put £200 in a savings account. When Donohue arrived later in the day, the pair bought an Austin car and rented rooms at 51 Great George's Street, paying fourteen days in advance. The same day they rented another room at 32 Parkgate Street (the same street as Military Intelligence headquarters and near the Army and Garda HQ) as a live letter drop; another Italian acquaintance, Antonio Forte, lived at this address.[67]

On 2 July, Donohue dropped a blue suitcase at the Parkgate Street address while Preetz took the train back to Limerick, staying once again in Hanratty's Hotel. The next day, he drove to Minard, picked up the buried transmitter and reburied the original rubber case (it was found on 26 July). Preetz and Donohue meet up the following day with Staffieri at the Del Rio Café (owned by another fascist sympathizer, Amadeo del Rio). Donohue took the train to Castlebar while Preetz and Staffieri rented a flat at 32 Westland Row. Not so coincidentally, this was the same address as Dr Cournihan – the man who so gallantly testified for Ernst Weber-Drohl earlier in the year.

Preetz also set up a mail drop with his in-laws in Tuam. Mail addressed to Pat Mitchell c/o Mrs Nicholson, Bishop Street, Tuam was collected by Annie Reynolds and passed on to Preetz by Tommy 'T.J.' Reynolds, his brother-in-law.[68] In one instance, T.J. Reynolds hired a lorry driver named Bernard O'Shaughnessy to take a message to an unnamed man (Preetz or Donohue) at North Wall, Dublin, when he made his regular Tuam–Dublin run.[69]

In Donohue's absence, Preetz continued his association with Staffieri and Del Rio and began seeing Maura Owens, the daughter of his landlady at 51 Great George's Street. On Donohue's return, the social circle was enlarged with the addition of Maureen O'Hanlon (72 Clontarf Road) and Kathleen Ward (7 Blessington Street).[70] Donohue contracted VD from a prostitute at some point during this process, an indication that he and Preetz had other things on their minds than working for *Führer, Volk und Vaterland*.[71] The G2 biographical report on Preetz concluded that the two 'spent a great deal of time in dissipation'. Preetz and Staffieri fell out after an argument at the Phoenix Park races, followed by an incident where Preetz crashed the Austin into a gate while driving back from Portmarnock drunk.[72]

On 19 August, Preetz sold the slightly dented Austin and purchased a brand new grey Chrysler Saloon five-seater from Messrs F.M. Summerfield. Not exactly a low-profile automobile for an undercover German agent, but it complemented Preetz's lifestyle since his arrival in Ireland.

His shenanigans continued. Neighbours at 32 Westland Row complained about the constant noise and activity coming from his flat. Kevin Gogan, who lived in an adjacent apartment, was awakened one morning at 06:45 by 'a girl who came into the room very annoyed at something Mitchell or his friend had done to her. She used very obscene language.'[73] Maureen O'Hanlon and Katherine Ward had their own problems with Preetz. O'Hanlon later told Gardaí about the time she and Ward were driven to a tavern by Preetz, who then surreptitiously poured alcohol in their drinks. Both of them were sick, but returned to the apartment at Westland Row. 'Mitchell went into the bedroom and called for Miss Ward who went into him. She came back about a half-hour later in a distressed condition and had a row with Mitchell.'[74] Preetz's sexually predatory days were fast coming to a close. On 26 August, he and Donohue were arrested outside the apartment as they were getting into the Chrysler.

Preetz had actually been under radio surveillance for some time and the messages to and from his broadcasting station at 32 Westland Row had been intercepted, though not fully deciphered. The volume of radio signals in Dublin made triangulation difficult, but this process was assisted by Preetz's habit of transmitting at regular intervals.[75] On 22 July he sent his first message to Abwehr, saying: 'I have a favourable residence in Dublin. Donohue is with me. He is going one of these days to England.' Preetz didn't seem in a hurry to make contact; he sent this message just slightly over three weeks after he arrived in the city. The transmission also indicates that Donohue was a full partner in the espionage enterprise and that the Abwehr already knew him. It also seems to suggest that a plan had been formed in advance for Donohue to carry out some other part of the mission in England.[76]

The Irish Army intercept crew did make a few notes on the Preetz's technical abilities: he was only able to transmit at about fourteen words per minute, and the German sender had slowed down his transmissions to match Preetz's ability to receive. Preetz also made mistakes in his Morse signalling and often had to retransmit his messages, thus increasing his transmission time and giving the Irish intercept team a second chance to check their copy. They also determined that Preetz usually used the LMR call sign, but that he interchanged this station identification with REE and LMZ. The ultimate conclusion was that he selected his call signs from a variation of the letters in his first name and surname, Wilhelm Preetz.[77]

Upon his arrest, the searching officers found a windfall of espionage material in the flat at 32 Westland Row. In addition to the radio (in a three-compartment locking case with Morse key, headset, transmitter and receiver), they also captured a cipher written in five-letter groups, totalling 174 characters. Preetz had also made enciphering notes on the blotting paper from this desk, apparently when he was working on the text of messages to Germany. The messages, once deciphered, proved disappointing. Most of Preetz's outgoing communications complained of poor reception or local interference with his transmissions, and repeated requests to change his frequency. It never seemed to occur to him that transmitting from the middle of the largest city in Ireland might have a negative impact on the quality of his radio signals. Alternatively, the social life in the country would not measure up to the pace he found in the city.

On 19 August 1940, the Germans sent Preetz the message 'Weather and tactical reports wanted. Shipping traffic between Ireland and England? Is it possible to confirm the massing of troops in Northern Ireland?' From the records of intercepted traffic, it would appear that Preetz was unable or unwilling to provide exact answers to these questions. He had no meteorological instruments, so his only apparent means of giving weather forecasts would be from looking out the window or reading the dated reports in English papers (weather reports were censored from Irish newspapers). In a report by MI5, Preetz is reported to have admitted in interrogation that 'he ascertained barometric pressure and temperature by studying instruments on display in shops.'[78]

Preetz's main encoding system was based on a book code, using a specially constructed book that was found at his apartment. The cover and the first six pages were from the novel *Hole in the Dark* by Frances Hart (Doubleday 1929), but the remainder of the book was composed of pages 7–274 of Katherine Mansfield's *Journal*. The specialists at Berlin-Tegel did a masterful job of re-stitching the book so that the difference would not be immediately visible. The transmission key phrase was selected by combining the date of the month, the numerical month, adding the random number of 23 and turning to the page in the book indicated by the total. Unlike other book codes, Preetz was to select a key phrase from the first letters of the words on the left margin, with indented lines being ignored. The keyword was then inserted into a five-by-five-letter square and the message was enciphered. The complete coded message was then transferred to a ten-by-twenty grid and transmitted by column, based on the numerical values assigned to the letters in the keyword. The letter X was used for zeroes and full stops.[79] There were a few puzzling things to come out of the Preetz messages. In several, he referred to another agent by the name of 'Bates'. Dr Richard Hayes's (the Irish Intelligence cryptanalyst) conclusion was that Bates was an agent known to Preetz who was working in England or another part of Ireland. He was not successfully identified. A further complication was that several transmissions to Ireland had been monitored using the DES call-sign. This did not match up to any known agents. If Dr Hayes's theory about the call-signs being related to the agent's name was correct, then DES referred to an unknown agent.[80]

Preetz's Irish passport was discovered behind some wallpaper in the apartment, but even before that Preetz had given his real name to the arresting officers. Police had been searching for Preetz since his disappearance the previous November and were puzzled by the Mitchell identity.[81]

Preetz and Donohue were interrogated after their arrest, but Preetz refused to give any detailed answers to the questions asked. Dr Hayes, who participated in the initial interrogation sessions, concluded that Preetz had a 'junior clerk mentality' and that 'Donohue is fully implicated in German espionage as far as his limited abilities allow'.[82] Despite an overwhelming accumulation of evidence and protests from G2 chief Colonel Liam Archer, Minister of Justice Gerald Boland decided on 22 November that Donohue was not to be charged or detained further. 'Donohue was liberated because of his connection with some Fianna Fáil clubs in Galway', read one anonymous G2 report.[83]

Despite his fortunate release, Donohue did not prosper. He soon obtained a job working for the Turf Development Board in Robertstown, County Kildare, but decided to leave for England in March 1942. He was arrested by British security officials on 5 October and interned under General (Defence) Regulation 18 B, sent to Brixton Prison and then to an internment camp on the Isle of Man. Donohue blamed G2 and the Garda for alerting the British about his past connections.[84] He was probably correct. In any event, British justice was more than willing to make up for any minor shortfall in the Irish Department of Justice; membership in Fianna Fáil did not carry the same weight in London as it might in Dublin.

THE ITALIAN CONNECTION

The arrest of Preetz and Donohue also prompted raids on their Italian supporters. When the Garda executed search warrants on Staffieri and Forte, and questioned Gerado-Vella and Amadeo del Rio, Italian Minister Vincenzo Berardis complained to Frederick Boland at the Department of External Affairs. The potential for a diplomatic incident was too high, and both G2 and the Garda were instructed to consult with External Affairs beforehand, should further similar action be necessary.[85]

The 'Italian connection' was never a serious threat to Irish security, but Italian nationals were put under tight surveillance. Three of them, Albert Arcari, Antonio Staiano and Ernesto Jaconelli were ultimately deemed to have crossed the line. The problems centred around Albert Arcari. Born in 1900, and former treasurer of the Italian Fascist Party in Leeds, he arrived in Ireland between 2 and 9 September 1939, apparently to avoid internment in England. With his father, he operated a slot-machine business in England and Ireland and used a variety of mailing addresses. He was subject to both mail and visual surveillance by Gardaí. The suspicious activity came to a head when Arcari received by post a January 1943 edition of the *Daily Mail*. Inside was a hand-written note that mentioned the delivery of a transmitter and doubts about whether 'Fritz' would be able to pay for it. The newspaper had been sent from England. Arcari was brought in for questioning and denied all knowledge of the note or who could have sent it or the newspaper.

The Gardaí and G2 were also running a parallel investigation on Arcari, but on a different set of facts. He had been seen meeting a blonde woman near his Monkstown home in circumstances that suggested they might have been passing information. Photographs were taken of the meetings, and Gardaí did a discreet door-to-door inquiry in an attempt to learn the blonde's identity and her relationship to Arcari. By accident, they found out more than they planned. One of the Garda officers knocked on the door of Mr Theodore Teggert. Teggert was surprised to see that the blonde in question was his wife – the young Garda officer was surprised as well. Police subsequently learned that Arcari had known her prior to his 1923 marriage to Louise Jaconelli, but had recently renewed their acquaintance. The proximity of Mrs Teggert was thought to be the reason behind Arcari's suspicious move to Monkstown.

In addition, Arcari's nephew Ernesto Jaconelli, described on his business card as 'Britain's Ace Accordionist', also worked in the slot machine business and, like Arcari, had failed to register with the Garda as an alien.

Antonio Staiano, another pre-war member of the Italian Fascist Party in Leeds, was an associate of both Arcari and Sante Staffieri. Gardaí also picked him up.[86] All three were deported to Northern Ireland in September 1943 and were handed over to MI5 for further questioning.[87] In 1943 Olimpio Nardone and his brother Ernesto (owners of the Roman Café and the Pantheon Café) were put under surveillance because of information that their businesses were possibly being used as 'a clearing house for espionage reports for the Axis legations'. This charge was never substantiated.[88] Eunan O'Halpin accurately sums up the participation of the Italians by writing that 'a congeries of lesser lights – ice cream parlour proprietors, chip shop owners, and the like – became a "serious embarrassment" in 1944 through their secret endeavours to keep the fascist flame alight. They did not, however, do any obvious harm.'[89]

LOBSTER I

As a natural precursor to final staff planning against Britain – even before the air component of the mission had been established, in fact – the Amt Ausland/Abwehr was given the task of providing hard intelligence data regarding the state of Britain's defences, exploring the feasibility of a landing in Ireland and inserting a 'fifth column' which could activate sabotage missions and link up with German invasion forces. While the Görtz mission might be seen as a supporting element of Sealion, this is inaccurate. His mission was planned and executed before the Sealion directive was issued, and before the successful Wehrmacht campaign in France made it remotely feasible for Germany to invade England.

Direct Abwehr support for the English project was code-named 'Lena' and the various aspects of intelligence gathering were farmed out to local Asts, with control of the operation resting with Abwehr headquarters in Berlin. All three operational branches of Abwehr were involved to some degree, but the majority of the manpower was from Abwehr I and II. The operations were complicated enough but the additional factor of a Foreign Ministry liaison made things even more difficult. Nonetheless, the Abwehr fulfilled its mission, at least on the surface, by dispatching to Great Britain and Ireland in the summer and early autumn of 1940 almost twenty agents who were ostensibly in support of the OKW planning staff directives.[90] Whereas the Simon and Preetz missions had actually been planned and executed before Hitler gave the detailed warning order for Sealion on 2 July, the operations executed after this point were directly tied to that plan, regardless of whether Hitler ever intended Sealion to be more than a credible attention-getter to mask his larger plans for an invasion of the Soviet Union.

The most prominent component of Lena, if only for its almost comical ineptitude, was a series of operations broadly code-named *Hummer*

('Lobster') and controlled by Major Klug of Office WN 2 (Abwehr II) in Berlin.[91] Lobster involved sending agents to England by a variety of means, but generally by sea. As part of the larger operation, three agents were dispatched to make their way to Britain via Ireland, where it was supposed that they could more easily travel to British territory. There was some reason for predicting that this might work. Hermann Görtz was still at large, though totally ineffective, and the German legation in Dublin could theoretically provide a safe-haven.

In practice, however, this proved to be a totally incorrect analysis of the situation, largely based on a misreading of the conditions in Ireland. Weber-Drohl had been partially successful, but the other agents sent had been captured without achieving anything of substance. German Intelligence seemed to have no working knowledge of the Irish Army's counter-intelligence capability and was completely oblivious to the fact that their British operations had been compromised even before they started in earnest. As was the case with most espionage missions, faulty analysis was supplemented by poor preparation. The agents selected for the various tasks in Operation Lobster were uniformly under-trained, linguistically ill-equipped to undertake a confidential mission in an English-speaking country and generally not the sort that would have passed muster in any serious and professional attempt to perform an intelligence gathering/sabotage mission.

THE VOYAGE OF THE *SOIZIC*

The Irish involvement in Lobster began on 7 July 1940. At approximately 05:30, an Irish lookout at his post at Toe Head, County Cork, spotted a small boat heading towards Traginono Bay. The lookout called the Castletownshend Garda station to report, but in violation of orders, no one notified the Southern Command Intelligence Officer.[92] On board the craft were three Abwehr agents, Herbert Tributh, Dieter Gärtner and Henry Obéd. The yacht, named the *Soizic*, was under the able command of Christian Nissen, universally known as 'Hein Mück' after a legendary North German sailor. As a successful pre-war sailing champion, Nissen was the perfect choice as pilot on this covert mission. The boat itself had been appropriated by the Germans from its French owner and then hurriedly modified for the mission.[93] The passengers were likewise an unusual lot.

Herbert Tributh was born on 23 May 1910 in what was then German South West Africa, later taken over by the British and renamed South West Africa (now Namibia). In 1932 at the age of 22, he went to Germany and studied German and English at the University of Marburg. Tributh attended Kiel University from 1934 to 1939, but strangely did not obtain his university degree, only a qualification as a gymnastics instructor. Tributh volunteered for service in the German Army in May 1939 – he was eligible to do this as an ethnic German – and at the start of the war he was posted to an infantry unit in Flensburg. Apparently recruited for the Abwehr because of his knowledge of English, he was seconded to Amt Ausland/Abwehr and sent to Brandenburg for a sabotage course.[94]

Dieter Gärtner, likewise an ethnic German, was born in 1919 in Oreteiwa, South West Africa, and went to Germany in 1937 to study medicine at Berlin University. Gärtner quit his medical course the following year to join the Army. At the outbreak of the war, he was attached to an artillery corps at Eger, in the former Sudetenland, as a corporal. At the conclusion of the Polish campaign, Gärtner, like Tributh, was sent on a two-month sabotage course operated by Abwehr II at Brandenburg on the Havel.[95] Gärtner is not known to have had any great familiarity with English prior to his mission. At the time of his mission to Ireland, he had two sisters still in South West Africa and a married sister who lived in Munich.[96]

Of the three agents dispatched on this part of Lobster, the most curious and out of place was certainly Henry Obéd. While the other two were at least ethnic Germans who might have conceivably passed for Irish in a quick visual inspection, Obéd, as an Indian national, could not have been sent to a more inappropriate destination.

A Muslim born in Lucknow, India, in 1895, Obéd left India in 1914 and worked as a ship's steward on the Clan and Prince steamship lines until 1920. He visited the United States and eventually set up a shop in London that catered to Indian seamen. He moved to Hamburg, Germany, in 1922 and started an export business with India, mostly motorcycles, bicycles and gramophones. Obéd married a German national, Carolina Dora Homann and moved to Antwerp, Belgium, in 1925 as European agent for an Indian livestock dealer in birds and zoo animals, one Husein Buxsch.[97] Obéd prospered in Antwerp and had two businesses, the zoo animal export trade and a retail pet store in the city. Business was doing well enough for Obéd to afford two cars and a truck. As part of his business in the zoo animal trade, he made annual trips to India. During one of these trips in 1934 the Deputy District Police Commissioner of Calcutta, Mr Evans, asked him to find out if Indian seamen were bringing small arms from Antwerp to India. During the interval between the 1934 trip and his next visit in 1936, he was approached by a man named Mukerjee, who wanted arms and ammunition for Indian nationalists. As Obéd did not see fit to report this incident to the British, who apparently learned about it nonetheless, Obéd was arrested on his return to Calcutta in 1936. He was charged and tried for abetting terrorists, but was acquitted for lack of evidence. Though Obéd's case was legally discharged, the British cancelled his passport, leaving him stranded in India with no legal means of returning to Antwerp.[98]

Obéd stowed away on the SS *Malauja*, which was en route from Bombay to England. He jumped ship in Marseilles, finally reaching Antwerp. So far as can be determined, Obéd's only contact with Ireland was a letter he wrote before the war to the Dublin Zoo, offering them a polar bear and, ironically, a sea lion. While he certainly had legitimate business interests, the available evidence does indicate that he had at least a sideline as an arms dealer/smuggler and that this brought him into contact with the Germans. Sonderführer Kurt Haller of Office I West at Abwehr II reported making a delivery of six thermite grenades to Obéd in Antwerp in January 1940 – and almost having a grenade explode because of one of Obéd's hyperactive dogs.[99]

The German occupation of Antwerp following the invasion of Holland and Belgium in May 1940 changed Obéd's relationship to his sometime German masters. By directive, the Abwehr closed down its intelligence-gathering functions in those countries and geared up for intelligence operations directed against Britain.[100] When arrested, Obéd denied any earlier contact with German Intelligence, but fashioned a story that mixed fact and fiction to explain how he came to be in Ireland with a German sabotage group. Initially, he claimed to have escaped Antwerp in the company of two Jews and to have given £50 to the captain of a boat in Brest to escape continental Europe.[101] When that story was obviously not accepted, Obéd varied it slightly, maintaining that the German authorities had arrested him when a truck exploded in the neighbourhood of his private zoo. Though released, he was soon approached by three German naval officers and two Army officers, who wanted him to take a 'group' to England. Not given the option to refuse, for fear of his wife's safety, he said that he was then driven to Brest, given £100 by a German officer named Kern, and boarded a boat formerly belonging to a French consular official in Switzerland. According to this version, the boat was captained by a 'German-American' and the members of the party became seasick during the crossing. This story, however, is at odds with Obéd's post-war version told to Indian officials. In that one, he stated that he was approached by Malik Rauf of Berlin Radio's Indian Service and told that 'all Indians must do something for the motherland', and remarked that the 'plight of England is an opportunity for India'. Obéd said that Rauf asked him to go to 'Eire and assist the Irish National Army against Britain, as Germans had good relations with it'.

Essentially, given his knowledge of British customs and language, Obéd was drafted to act as guide to the Abwehr sabotage mission. He did have contact with an Indian national who had lived in Ireland, a Mr Sardar Bahadar Khan.[102] While exact mission details are not known, it may be assumed, given the explosives found in their possession later, that the Tributh/Gärtner party was tasked to perform a series of sabotage operations on English targets. Obéd is not thought to have had any training in the operational details of the mission and would not have an active part to play in the greater Abwehr plan in support of Sealion.

Regardless of Abwehr's initial intention, the mission was compromised almost immediately. After landing on shore, the trio tried unsuccessfully to hide their ten-foot red, white and blue dinghy and, for reasons not immediately clear, remained in the area of Traspaleen Sound, Castletownshend, for almost an hour and a half after landing.[103] It is possible that they buried a wireless transmitter, though the available records do not record a search for additional equipment other than what was visible.[104] Several local residents observed the three around the beach area, but eventually they walked the short distance to the Skibbereen road. After questioning a local boy named Patrick Geany, they were directed to Skibbereen as the quickest means of reaching Dublin. Somewhat ridiculously, one of them, probably Tributh, asked, 'Is this West Cork?' When the boy confirmed their general location, they asked about the location and times of the nearest train. Geany told the incognito agents that there was no train leaving from Skibbereen to Dublin, but that they could catch the bus. According to Geany, one of the Germans responded with a very un-Irish 'The boss is it'.[105]

Arriving late in Skibbereen, the men had missed their bus, but Florence Lynch, the driver of a creamery lorry, gave them a lift to Drimoleague where they finally boarded a bus to Cork. Obéd gave Mr Lynch five shillings as payment. Unfortunately for the spies, Garda Sergeant Patrick Murphy noticed them as they descended from Lynch's truck and asked the driver about the strangers. Lynch could only tell what the men had told him, that they were off a recently arrived boat at Baltimore. Using his initiative, Murphy called the Baltimore Garda station and was told that the boat in question had left the night before. He promptly rang the Union Quay Garda station in Cork and had a police reception committee waiting for the three men when their bus arrived. The police apparently did not have any trouble identifying the trio, no doubt due in large part to the presence of Henry Obéd.[106]

LOBSTERS IN THE TANK

Once in police custody, the pretence quickly came to an end. When their possessions were searched, Garda discovered the following:

- eight incendiary bombs – each was eight ounces. in weight, four to five inches long, and made of cylindrical paper tubes filled with thermite with a high sulphur content;
- four tins of gun cotton (nitro-cellulose) to a total of 102 ounces. Each tin was labelled 'Carres French Peas';
- six No. 8 detonators, concealed in wooden containers disguised as fishing reels;

- six lengths of safety fuse, about two-and-a-half feet each, three lengths each in black leather waist-belts worn by Obéd and Gärtner;
- two reels of insulating tape;
- two cutting pliers;
- currency totalling £829 (Obéd £551, Tributh £135, Gärtner £134).[107]

In addition to the explosives and supplies, Tributh had a paperback copy of E.M. Forster's *A Passage to India* – possibly indicating that it was the source for a 'book-code' to be used with the undiscovered transmitter/receiver – and certainly indicating that the people at Abwehr II had a sense of humour, given Obéd's presence. Obéd also had a French alarm clock, which could be wired for use with timed detonations. In addition, he had a letter written in Hindustani addressed to Sardar Khan and a letter signed S.B. Khan with the words 'Dr Kern' written in Germanic script.[108] Though this would certainly violate operational procedure and basic common sense, Gärtner's luggage contained a role of adhesive tape marked 'Vorwerk prima Qualität' – as well as, for some obscure reason, a bottle of suntan lotion and his bathing suit![109] Though Obéd consistently claimed to be carrying his own money drawn from his Antwerp bank before leaving for Brest, the Irish authorities noted that all the banknotes carried sequential numbers.[110]

Despite the earlier foul-up with notification when the yacht was spotted, the word that three saboteurs had arrived on Irish soil was immediately dispatched. In what remains a curious incident, one Irish government official was dispatched to Cork with quite a different mission. In a report filed on 9 July 1940 – and addressed to the 'Secretary' (presumably secretary to the Minister for External Affairs, Joseph Walshe) – the writer describes his brief as 'to ascertain if a British "plant" or frame-up was involved of such a kind as to embarrass the Government and to prejudice our neutrality'. After his investigation, and the obvious clues that the strangers were sent by Germany, the mysterious author decided that it was 'probably' not a sinister British deception, but 'nothing that was said was sufficient to prove that a British plot could definitely be ruled out'.[111]

When the report of the agents' capture reached the German authorities, the reaction was predictably pragmatic: 'Report through the Foreign Ministry (Minister Hempel) that the personnel from Hummer 1 were arrested by Irish police after landing. ... The decision of the Office Chief [Canaris] is that Ireland is not to be used for further sabotage acts against England, rather these are to be made directly against England.'[112] This ban was observed until it became expedient for the Abwehr to do otherwise.

Interrogated by both the Garda and Irish Intelligence officers, Tributh and Gärtner remained close-mouthed about their mission and training. Obéd seemed the most talkative of the group and he was deliberately isolated by the other internees for a variety of reasons, some of them racial.

Asked about the wisdom of sending agents to neutral Ireland, Tributh inadvertently testified to German inter-service rivalry when he responded that 'my organization would have different views from the German Foreign Ministry'[113] and that he expected to link up with German invasion troops in England. This was practically the last operational detail given by Tributh or Gärtner to their Irish captors. MI5 believed, through their double-agent network, that Tributh and Gärtner were destined for a linkup with Snow – Welsh spy Arthur Owens – in preparation for the Sealion landings.[114]

On 25 July 1940, Obéd, Tributh and Gärtner were convicted of violating article 3, Emergency Powers Order of 1939 and section 5, Emergency Powers Act of 1939 in that they landed in Ireland through an unapproved seaport. They were sentenced to three years' imprisonment. The court also found, almost as an afterthought, that they had likewise violated section 4(1) of the Explosives Substances Act of 1883, in that they had on them incendiary bombs, tins of explosives and detonators. The sentence for this violation was seven years, to run concurrently with the three-year sentence.[115] Tributh and Gärtner pleaded guilty, Obéd not guilty. Upon conviction, Obéd appealed to the Court of Criminal Appeal, but this was refused. Though officially convicted under the criminal law, the prisoners' similarity to normal defendants ended there. All three were eventually transferred to Athlone to join the growing population of German espionage internees.[116]

FRANK RYAN

Though German interest in the Irish arena was strong through the autumn of 1940, while Sealion was still a possibility, a final unrequited Foreign Ministry initiative really spelled the end of German Intelligence operations in Ireland, at least those in direct support of an invasion of England. Despite endless rounds of historical discussion about his motives, Frank Ryan was a player in the German espionage game from 1940 until his death in 1944. His importance has been romanticized out of all proportion since the war, but Ryan figured frequently in the plans of the Foreign Ministry and to a lesser extent the Abwehr.[117]

At one time an acting-brigadier in the International Brigade during the Spanish Civil War, Ryan was captured by the Italian 'volunteer' troops fighting for the Nationalists. He was accused and convicted of murder by a Nationalist court and sentenced to death. He was incarcerated in Burgos Prison in 1938, awaiting execution.

Ryan's presence fighting in Spain was enough of an international embarrassment for the ostensibly neutral Irish government (the official neutrality policy would not be proffered until de Valera's speech to the Dáil on 2 September 1939), but the Irish government was in an even more awkward position when Ryan was condemned to death, though his sentence was later commuted. In October 1938, Ryan was visited in Burgos Prison by the Irish Minister to Spain, Leopold Kerney. Although he did nothing officially to get Ryan released other than an appeal to Franco, Kerney did hire a lawyer with impressive connections.[118] The lawyer, Jaime Michel de Champourcin, was supposed to see what he could do unofficially.[119] Quite a bit, as it turned out.

Champourcin was an interesting choice. Kerney, seemingly by random chance, had selected the one person in all of Spain who just happened to have connections to the German Abwehr – specifically with Admiral Canaris – as well as with the Franco's fascist National government. In the event, it was the Abwehr connections that succeeded where Kerney had failed. Kerney's curious series of connections with the representatives of the German Intelligence services did not end there; he had several incidents still to follow.

Ryan's plight in Spain had attracted a diverse mix of interested parties, especially once war was declared.[120] Helmut Clissmann, an old friend of Ryan from Ireland, and then training with the Brandenburg Regiment, made the suggestion through his commanding officer that perhaps it would be in Germany's best interests to help free Ryan.[121] This proposal was taken up by Canaris, who gave his approval. Both Francisco Franco (Canaris's old friend from the First World War) and Champourcin were to play their parts, as was the Madrid-based Abwehr agent Wolfgang Blaum.[122]

The Abwehr II war diary entry for 12 July 1940 laconically notes that 'KO Spain reports that an agent of Office 1 West [Frank Ryan] whose use is planned for Irish operations, is to be turned over on 14 or 15 July at the Spanish border at Irun-Hendaye.'[123] Ryan was taken to the border by Wolfgang Blaum and handed over to Sonderführer Kurt Haller. After briefly explaining to the concerned Ryan what had happened, the first priority was to get him deloused and into more acceptable civilian clothes. At this point, Ryan was so hard of hearing that Haller had to shout to him in English just to make himself understood. Ryan was immediately taken to the resort town of Biarritz; then Haller, accompanied by Alfred Toepfer, an officer from the Abwehr satellite station (Alst – Abwehr Leitstelle) in Paris, took Ryan to the occupied French capital.[124] Ryan was treated to several days of hospitality, eating in the finest restaurants and staying at an expensive hotel – all courtesy of the German Intelligence service. He was eventually transferred to Berlin where he was reunited with his revolutionary comrade and sometime adversary, former IRA Chief of Staff Seán Russell.

Kerney's conduct did not escape the attention of either Irish Intelligence or the Irish government. Faced with evidence that Kerney had been conspiring with Ryan's sister Eilis to avoid postal censorship and that he had been passing letters to and from Ryan via Elizabeth Clissmann (for whom he also evaded postal censorship and facilitated correspondence with

her family in Ireland), Colonel Bryan sent Captain Joseph Healy to Madrid
to interview the Irish Minister. Healy's pointed questioning of Kerney
revealed that the minister had knowingly acted in concert with German
Intelligence:

> The Minister had a Spanish friend, a lawyer [Champourcin] who had been in
> the National Secret Service, and who was still in contact with the German
> Secret Service ... early in 1940 this Spanish friend suggested to the Minister,
> 'Why not try the Germans? Perhaps they could even get Ryan in a submarine
> to Ireland'. ... [Champourcin] returned very jubilant and said 'Yes, they are
> interested, they have been authorised to do something from Berlin'. ... The
> Minister had no doubt that Frank Ryan went willingly to Germany and was
> apparently anxious to collaborate with the Germans on some basis. ... [Kerney
> believed] it would be inspired by his desire for the return of the Six Counties as
> part of the national territory.[125]

Healy also learned that Kerney 'was given to understand by Ryan while the
latter was in jail in Spain that Ryan knew that Russell had left the States for
occupied Europe. The Minister could not say how Ryan was aware of
Russell's movement.' The answer to this question might lie in the fact that
Kerney approved of a visit by 'a German friend named Winzer or Winzner'
to Ryan while he was in Burgos.[126] Making the logical inference that the
'friend' was actually tied to the Abwehr KO in Spain, Ryan would have
learned of the Reich's arrangements for his former IRA comrade. The
German motive behind Ryan's release was not altruism. As Ryan was to
learn, the Foreign Ministry and the Abwehr had an ambitious plan for him
and Russell in connection with Operation Sealion.

SEÁN RUSSELL

Russell had been in the United States since April 1939, but the planned
American excursion went awry. The aim of the mission to the United States
was to 'show the flag' and to build up Russell in the public mind as the
leader of militant Irish nationalism. He made several public addresses and,
not surprisingly, came to the attention of US security officials.[127] The Secret
Service detained Russell in Detroit during the American visit of King
George VI. The authorities understandably suspected that Russell might
have something unpleasant planned for the royal couple in conjunction with
the opening of the British pavilion at the 1939 World's Fair in New York.
While at liberty in Detroit, Russell and his Clann na Gael host Joseph
McGarrity met with Robert Monteith, one of Casement's accomplices in
1916, and at that time the director of Father Charles Coughlin's Union of
Social Justice. Monteith was also a liaison between the Clann and Harry
Bennett, the head of personnel for Henry Ford, who played an important
role in the American isolationist movement.[128]

Russell was later released on bail, but was anxious to surreptitiously leave the United States before his bail expired on 16 April.[129] Joseph McGarrity had signed as surety for the bond, but Russell had things on his mind other than bond forfeiture.[130] Through the offices of McGarrity, Russell made contact with German agent 'V-Rex', also known as Carl Rekowski, who in turn, managed to get a message to a John McCarthy.[131] McCarthy was a steward on the steamship *George Washington*, which made the transatlantic route from the still-neutral United States to Italy. The message was successfully delivered while the *George Washington* was temporarily berthed in Tampico, Florida, and it called for McCarthy to contact the German consulate in Genoa and to see whether the Germans would facilitate Russell's return to Ireland via Germany. Presumably McCarthy was an IRA associate and had an earlier relationship with 'V-Rex'.[132] He was given half a torn postcard as a recognition signal for the Abwehr.[133]

At this point, the energetic Franz Fromme re-enters the picture. Since his previous connection with the Oscar Pfaus mission, Fromme continued to keep his hand in the espionage game and was sent to Genoa in 1940 as a courier of propaganda leaflets intended for the Breton nationalists supported by Abwehr II. While there, he was given the additional mission of making contact with John McCarthy. McCarthy arrived in Genoa on 24 January and his request for Russell's asylum was received at the German consulate. The consul, in turn, notified the Foreign Ministry, which alerted Abwehr headquarters of the proposition. The Abwehr journal from that date recorded the arrival of McCarthy and the suggestion that Russell ('the Chief of Staff of the Irish movement') travel incognito from New York to Genoa, eventually to be returned to Ireland with German assistance. McCarthy was to return on 27 January – his ship was due in Naples – for an answer.[134]

Despite McCarthy's stated sense of urgency, the date came and went. The next relevant item in the Abwehr diary dates from 30 January and reports that Admiral Canaris approved, in principle, further discussions between Abwehr II and Russell; Russell's presence obviously did not immediately excite the Abwehr chief, but he wanted to keep the channel open. The entry of 12 February mentions a new factor: the Foreign Ministry suspended any further Abwehr contact until it could reach a decision on the matter.

This highlights an interesting trend in the German decision-making process, and one that directly affected the efficiency of German Military Intelligence. From 1940 onwards, the Foreign Ministry (Auswärtiges Amt) came to exercise veto power over operations that would normally have been viewed as exclusively military. This is almost certainly the result of Hitler's 'divide and conquer' policy among the various branches of the German government and military services, and it necessarily sacrificed military priorities to political expediency.

In this instance, the Foreign Ministry was given conflicting advice from the Abwehr and the cautious Dr Hempel in Dublin. In his memorandum on the situation, Under Secretary of State (and SS-Brigadeführer) Ernst Woermann briefly outlined the current situation regarding the IRA and Germany. He accurately summarized that

> The Irish Republican Army (IRA) is a secret military society which fights for the union of Northern Ireland with the Irish Republic and the complete separation of Ireland from the British Empire. This is also the ultimate objective of the present Irish Government. The difference between the government and the IRA lies mainly in the method. The government hopes to attain its objective by legal political means while the IRA tries to achieve success by terrorist means. Most of the members of the present Irish Government formerly belonged also to the IRA. By reason of its militant attitude towards England the IRA is a natural ally of Germany.

Woermann went on to review the contact with McCarthy and the Abwehr's interest in Russell to promote 'acts of sabotage' in Ireland. On the other hand, the Foreign Ministry gave great weight to Hempel's recommendation that the IRA was not yet strong enough to act as a credible threat to Britain and his fear that if collaboration between Germany and Russell was made known, it could be to Britain's benefit. Hempel presumably was also referring to the possibility that his own position would be compromised. The Foreign Ministry ultimately decided that the time had not yet come for Russell's return to Ireland, but that the situation might change in the foreseeable future. It recommended that contact with McCarthy be maintained and that the Abwehr be allowed to continue to act in this regard.[135] It was evident, from this memorandum, that the Foreign Ministry wanted to hijack the Abwehr's option on the proposed Russell operation, and that political soldiering was seemingly more significant than military or intelligence operations. Alternatively, a perceived weakness in the Abwehr's loyalty or competency might mean that the Foreign Ministry thought the operation would be safer in their hands.

The Abwehr recorded this decision in its *Kriegstagebuch* (war diary) entry of 12 February 1940. Accordingly, 'Professor' Franz Fromme was dispatched to Genoa on 19 March 1940 to 'meet with McCarthy, the representative of Irish leader Russell'. McCarthy seems to have made a number of transatlantic voyages during this period. The Abwehr II diary also reports that 'Dolmetscher Fromme' from Abwehr 1 West travelled to Italy with three distinct missions.[136] First, he was to deliver the promised Breton leaflets to the agent stationed there; second, he was to liaise with McCarthy, whose ship was due in two days; third, he was to meet with IRA personnel who were in Rome in connection with the Easter celebrations.[137] Upon Fromme's return on 30 March, he reported that he made contact with McCarthy and laid the foundation for Russell's arrival. Fromme also reported to the Abwehr that he had spoken to his IRA contact in Rome, James O'Donovan's brother Colman, as well as with Bishop O'Rourke.[138] The Abwehr diary further recorded on 21 March 1940 that the 'VAA [*Verbindungsmann zum Auswärtigen Amt* – liaison to the Foreign Ministry] explained that the Foreign Ministry does not intend any interference in Abwehr's handling of the Russell matter, provided that Russell is only given military, not political, tasks'.[139] The Foreign Ministry continued to steer its own course in relation to Russell, with the obvious intention of limiting the Abwehr's authority. Following a meeting with Foreign Minister Joachim von Ribbentrop, Woermann prepared another memorandum on 28 March 1940, which outlined the Foreign Ministry position. Perhaps more importantly, the Foreign Ministry designated a new 'hired-gun' for the Irish question, Dr Edmund Veesenmayer.

DR EDMUND VEESENMAYER

Veesenmayer was born on 12 November 1904 in Bad Kissingen and joined the Nazi party (no. 873780 of 1 February 1932) prior to Hitler's rise to power. He was simultaneously a member of the Allgemeine-SS.[140] The Nazi period was kind to Dr Veesenmayer, and he eventually reached the rank of SS-Brigadeführer (major-general) as well as receiving the Iron Cross, first and second class, without so much as hearing a shot fired in anger.[141] Veesenmayer studied international politics at Munich University, receiving his degree in 1926. He was awarded his doctoral degree in political science in 1928, and taught at the Political-Economics Institute of the Munich Technical College from 1929 to 1933. After the Nazi Party victory in 1933, Veesenmayer was assigned several political-economic missions by the party, mostly in the area of south-east Europe. State Secretary (and SS-Gruppenführer) Wilhelm Keppler brought him into the Foreign Ministry in 1934 and he remained there, without official rank or title, until March 1944.[142]

According to his SS file, Veesenmayer was officially assigned to the 'Central Post for the Economic-Political Organizations of the NSDAP', later transferring to the personal staff of Reichsführer Heinrich Himmler. He was, in fact, an SS officer on detached duty to the Foreign Ministry.[143] Veesenmayer, who has been described as Ribbentrop's '*coup d'état* specialist', was most active in the Balkans, where he successfully engineered the overthrow of hostile regimes in Croatia (1941), Serbia (1941), Slovenia (1943) and Hungary (1944). Veesenmayer was appointed as the German Minister to Hungary in 1944, where he oversaw the deportation of approximately 450,000 Hungarian Jews to the extermination camps.[144]

Veesenmayer was sentenced to twenty years' imprisonment at a subsequent Nürnberg trial, but was released after serving slightly over six. He went into business selling rubber floor-coverings from his home in Darmstadt and died in 1978.

As part of his roving brief with the SS and Foreign Ministry, Veesenmayer was intimately involved in all planned Irish operations from 1940 to 1943, particularly those involving Russell and Frank Ryan. His ultimate intentions for Ireland are debatable. He was undoubtedly a Foreign Ministry/SS 'trouble-shooter', but what did he have in mind for Russell? An IRA rebellion against de Valera's government, the establishment of an Irish 'fifth column' for an impending invasion of Ireland or the promotion of rebellion against the British government in Northern Ireland? Evidence would suggest that Veesenmayer kept his options open, and that no scenario was excluded from his calculations. Kurt Haller, who worked with Veesenmayer as liaison between the Foreign Ministry and the Abwehr, ruled out a few scenarios:

> The Foreign Ministry never had the view towards starting a great action in Ireland. Ireland was a neutral country, whose neutrality was in the interests of the conduct of the war, and not an acute problem. At most, it could have been a secondary theatre of war, if the British isle was the main theatre, and acted to put military pressure on the English in Northern Ireland from the South. For this eventuality, one did not want to close the possibility to find a chance for German and Irish cooperation. More was not expected from the Russell action.[145]

FOREIGN MINISTRY PRIORITIES

Woermann delineated several points that would guide the Foreign Ministry's position in the Russell affair, none of them helpful to German Military Intelligence:

1 Ribbentrop has designated Dr Veesenmayer 'to deal with this matter';
2 Russell is to be brought to Italy through the channel with McCarthy;
3 Veesenmayer is to meet directly with McCarthy and McCarthy is not to be told of the Foreign Ministry plan to use him in Ireland;
4 Abwehr is not to be notified of the planned meeting with McCarthy ('The Foreign Minister then decided that the Intelligence Department should not yet be acquainted with the matter at this stage');
5 Veesenmayer (currently on 'a tour' in the Balkans) is to be notified when McCarthy is returning to Genoa. Veesenmayer will then be called to Berlin and sent to Genoa.[146]

By then, however, Fromme had already met with McCarthy and the Abwehr appears to have stolen a march on the rival Foreign Ministry. Canaris could be proud; he had been quicker than Ribbentrop and had better information. The Abwehr diarist reported on 30 March – two days after von Ribbentrop's pronouncements about keeping Abwehr out of the information loop – that Fromme had returned from Genoa and reported that he met with McCarthy and that Russell was expecting to leave the United States by ship on 6 April, and expected to arrive in Genoa on 16 April.[147]

This scheduled arrival did not take place and the Abwehr recorded on 26 April that Russell had a 'last minute difficulty' in the plan to bring him aboard ship as a blind passenger, but that he would attempt to take the next ship to Italy. By this time, the squabbling Foreign Ministry and Abwehr seem to have arrived at a *modus vivendi* and the foreign liaison officer passed along a telephonic report from Genoa on 1 May that Russell had arrived and had been met by Fromme, who would bring him to Germany. The diary entry for 5 May announces that Russell (described as the 'former adjutant of the IRA leader') had arrived on 1 May and 'travelled to Berlin in the company of Professor Fromme'.[148] After consulting with the Foreign Ministry representative, Veesenmayer, it was decided to take Russell to the safety of a weekend house near Berlin. Franz Fromme was detailed to act as Russell's interpreter.[149] The Foreign Ministry asked the Abwehr to prepare immediately for the possibility that Russell could be used in 'political actions'.[150]

Despite his apparent usefulness, Professor Fromme did not receive a standing ovation from all quarters. When asked in 1977 about Fromme's later mission to coordinate Seán Russell's arrival, Dr Veesenmayer was less than complementary. Veesenmayer described the 'comic ineptitude' of Fromme and went on to say that Fromme was 'neither a politician, a proper professor, a soldier nor an Abwehr man'.[151] Fromme stayed in Abwehr service on odd intervals, eventually travelling to Oflag (Officer internment camp) IX in a failed attempt to recruit Irish-born British officers to serve with the Germans.[152]

Though the Abwehr might have momentary control of Russell, Veesenmayer left no doubt that this was ultimately a Foreign Ministry operation from start to finish. This was apparently not unwelcome at the Abwehr:

> After the Görtz fiasco, he [Lahousen] was to see that no more wild-cat schemes against the UK or Eire were carried out by the over-zealous staff of Referat WN. When Brigadeführer Veesenmayer of the Ausw. Amt appeared on the scene, Canaris handed over the Irish complex with great relief to the Ausw. Amt, the more so since Canaris, and therefore Lahousen, judged the Brigadeführer to be a striking specimen of the gentlemen of the SS, then high on the list of the Admiral's pet aversions.[153]

Almost immediately upon arrival, Russell was launched on his first task in support of the Greater German Reich. Russell was informed of the Görtz mission, and when it was learned that bad weather had postponed Görtz's flight, Haller and Russell were sent to intercept him. The plan was for Russell to brief Görtz on Ireland and to provide him with the names and addresses of suitable contacts. They were apparently unable to raise the Luftwaffe airfield at Kassel-Fritzlar by telephone or radio, so Haller and Russell set out in a speeding car to stop Görtz before his departure. The effort was for nothing; as the car approached Kassel, the He-111, with the elderly Görtz on board, was already winging its way towards Ireland.[154]

RUSSELL AND RYAN

As planned, Russell quickly adjusted to his new routine in Berlin. By 20 May 1940, the Abwehr journal reported that 'training has begun for the Irish leader Russell in the used of sabotage materials. The training is given at the request of Foreign Ministry mission specialist Dr Veesenmayer and in continuing consultation with him.'[155] Even in the post-war period, Veesenmayer continued to hold a high opinion of Russell: 'Er had viel gedacht; wenig gesagt' (he thought much, said little). He also found Russell to be 'straightforward, strait-laced; a traditionalist who wanted only what was good for Ireland'.[156]

Russell's training in the latest German explosive ordnance was held at the Abwehr training school/laboratory in Berlin-Tegel. The laboratory specialized in the design of ordinary objects that actually contained powerful explosive charges. Russell was also exposed to numerous types of delay detonators, some of which could be set up to as many as forty days in advance, as well as the new developments in plastic explosives.[157]

Russell also visited the 'Quenzgut' – the training area for the Brandenburg Regiment, where he observed trainees and instructors working with sabotage materials in a field environment. This was his first exposure to a real military system with modern equipment, quite apart from what he had experienced with the IRA. While in Nazi Germany, Russell lived 'like a monk' and insisted on regularly attending Sunday Mass, accompanied by Feldwebel (Sergeant) Planer, his Austrian 'shadow'. Dr Veesenmayer tried to limit Russell's visibility, and gave strict instructions that the Irishman be denied personal access to anyone but himself, Fromme, Feldwebel Planer, and Sonderführer Haller. Helmut Clissmann and Jupp Hoven, both attached to the Brandenburg Regiment, broke this rule frequently and had many meetings with Russell, whom they knew from their time in Ireland before the war.[158]

Russell and his clique evidently discussed the proposal to recruit Irish volunteers from among captured British Army POWs, an idea that would eventually bear rotten fruit at the Friesack Camp.[159] This idea, combined with the return to Ireland by submarine, seemed to complete the historical analogy between Russell and Sir Roger Casement in 1916. The two adventures also had one other factor in common; both ended in abject failure. Oberst (later Generalmajor) von Lahousen also referred to the

Russell mission as 'a new version of the Casement operation'.[160] This was not intended as a compliment.

While Russell trained, German plans for his employment moved swiftly ahead. In a meeting on 25 May 1940 with Veesenmayer, Lahousen, Hauptmann Marwede and Russell, it was planned that he would land in Ireland by submarine on 6 June, along with two radio operators.[161] Further questions about the transport of his radio equipment and demolitions material needed to be discussed with naval authorities. Though it is not specifically stated, the preparations for Russell's return clearly suggest that he was given a definite sabotage objective. The diary also states that further discussions were to be held to consider the 'plan for Russell's action in Ireland and the effective possibilities against English objectives'. [162]

Two days later, it was decided, after consultation with the naval operations staff (Seekriegsleitung) that a submarine would be ready from 1 June for a ten-day period in order to transport Russell to Ireland. He was supposed to be landed at a pre-arranged spot with his demolition equipment and transmitter in a special case, which could be dropped into the water and later recovered by Russell and his 'IRA people'.[163] Despite the coordination with the Skl about the submarine, Russell's operation was again delayed, probably due to intelligence priorities being focused on the French campaign, which ended on 25 June with a complete victory for the Wehrmacht. Russell's mission is again mooted in the Abwehr journal entry for 12 July 1941. The OKM (Skl) – Naval High Command Operations Staff – agreed, again, to transport two agents to Ireland. In this variation of the plan, Russell was to be accompanied by a Breton agent, who was to be landed slightly in advance of Russell. The Breton picked for this mission was to be none other than Paul Moyse, whose last mission for the Abwehr had been to deliver Jim O'Donovan's keyword to London at the start of the war.[164]

Before this operation could be launched, several events occurred. Frank Ryan was released from Burgos prison and received by the Germans on 15 July. Though not officially anticipated at the time Russell's mission was conceived, this offered a potential windfall for the Germans by sending two agents back into Ireland simultaneously.[165] The second event was more sobering. In a report from Dublin, Hempel informed the Foreign Ministry that the agents from 'Lobster I' – Tributh, Gärtner and Obéd – had been captured by Irish police, along with their demolition material. In consequence, Admiral Canaris ordered that action against Britain would no longer be mounted via Ireland, but directly against England.[166] Clearly, with Foreign Ministry interest in the Russell mission, Abwehr directives aimed at espionage activities in England would not apply to Veesenmayer's pet project in Ireland. Admiral Canaris (as of 3 August) agreed to oversee the transport of Russell to Ireland.[167]

The Abwehr diary further states that Russell was not given a 'concrete mission' by either the Abwehr or the Foreign Ministry: 'The Foreign Ministry gives Russell only the chance to be of use in Ireland's hour.' If the diary is to be believed, the only coordination plan involved a signal to Russell as to when to begin his sabotage activity: a red flower pot in a window of the German Legation in Dublin.[168] Though this is the stated version, it seems most unlikely. Russell had been in intensive (and expensive) training for a period of more than three months; he had participated in high-level planning sessions about his 'mission'; extensive logistical preparation was necessary to return him to Ireland. It is hardly reasonable to assume that a master-manipulator like Dr Edmund Veesenmayer would simply turn Russell loose with almost no guidance or purpose, other than a vague understanding about possible action in the event of direct German operations against England. According to Veesenmayer's later version of events, the idea was 'to give them [Russell and Ryan] a chance to prove themselves and to give them all they wanted then'. His belief was that 'to have any prospect of a successful operation in Ireland the initiative must come from the Irish themselves; it must not be superimposed though perhaps it could, through Irishmen like Russell and Ryan, be guided.'[169]

Ryan, meanwhile, was transported from Paris to Berlin, where he met with Dr Veesenmayer and, briefly, with Seán Russell, on 4 August. During this initial meeting, where the old IRA former adversaries met for the first time in at least five years, Ryan agreed to accompany Russell on his mission to Germany; almost certainly, this is what the Germans had intended all along.[170] It has been suggested that Ryan did not have enough time to learn the mission details from Russell, but this is not borne out by the official chronology. Ryan was not, however, adequately trained by the Abwehr to carry out any mission for which Russell had been selected; Ryan was a passionate advocate for his own causes, but he was not an explosives expert. On the morning of 6 August, Major Frederich Carl Marwede and Sonderführer Haller accompanied Russell and Ryan to the German naval station at Wilhelmshaven, and the pair left the port on 8 August. Russell's code-name was 'Richard 1' and Ryan was 'Richard 2'. The overall mission was dubbed *Taube* ('Dove').[171] This particular dove was to have a life-span of less than one full week

The next official mention of Russell and Ryan comes from the 1/Skl (Naval Command Staff) diary of 14 August 1940: 'U-65 reports the death on board of General Russell, who was to have been landed on the Irish coast. The discharge of the special assignment is therefore abrogated with regret.'[172] The bad news was relayed to Abwehr II, where the diary entry for 15 August reads: 'V-Mann Richard 1 died from uncertain causes on the transport. Richard 2 is coming back with the submarine.'[173]

It is possible to reconstruct the events of the voyage from surviving accounts. Admiral Karl Dönitz, the commander of the submarine fleet

(BdU), though he had reservations about using his valuable combat power as merely transport for Abwehr missions, had assigned an experienced officer for the mission. Korvettenkapitän Hans-Gerrit von Stockhausen was among the best submarine commanders in the fleet. His orders were to transport his passengers to a point somewhere in the area of Ballyferriter, County Kerry, south of Ballydavid Head in the bay near Smerwick Harbour. The landing was scheduled to coincide with the celebration of the Feast of the Assumption (15 August) and it was thought that Russell and Ryan would pass unnoticed among the other pilgrims. They could then travel to Tralee and thence to Dublin.[174]

Shortly after leaving Wilhelmshaven, Russell became ill. He complained of stomach pains, which grew worse with each passing hour. U-65 was not equipped with a doctor, but only a former medical student who had been trained as a combat medic. Russell died on 14 August, with U-65 a short hundred miles from Galway. He was buried at sea, given that the submarine had no facilities for keeping a decomposing body during the summer and Ryan had decided to abort the mission and return to Germany.

Ryan could have elected to continue, but he chose not to. In reality, he was ill equipped to go forward. The submarine still carried the radio and demolition material, but Ryan did not even have the keyword or knowledge of radio procedure to make radio communication possible. With his deafness, it was also impossible for him to receive a full briefing from Russell in the confined spaces of a U-boat, and Russell's illness made any communication a practical impossibility.[175]

U-65 wired for instructions, and was told to continue with its normal patrol route. Due to engine problems, the submarine was forced to cut the patrol short and returned to Lorient two weeks later. Veesenmayer, understandably upset about the mission's failure, instituted an inquiry and interrogated all officers and men aboard U-65, including Ryan. The conclusion was that Russell died from a burst gastric ulcer.[176] Carolle Carter noted that Stockhausen 'was killed in an auto accident in Berlin which, coming so soon after Russell's death, suggested mystery in some circles'.[177] In fact, Stockhausen was killed on 14 January 1943, over two full years after the mission was prematurely terminated.[178] Veesenmayer commissioned a painting of Russell, which was destroyed along with Russell's personal papers when Veesenmayer's office was bombed later in the war. Stories of Russell's death soon attracted a rash of conspiracy theories. Hermann Görtz, by this time hopelessly cut off from anything resembling reality, offered his own opinion:

> Most people know the rumours about the journey of Russell and Ryan on the U-boat and the alleged death of Russell on that journey to Ireland. I was never in a position to know exactly what happened. Nevertheless, I raised the point in my messages to Germany and, unless I was being completely

disregarded by my own command – which I do not for one minute believe – I assert that this journey never took place. Russell was shot by the British Secret Service in St Nazaire.[179]

During his post-war interrogation, even Lahousen was not immune from spreading the odd rumour. Revealing that some people in the Foreign Ministry had spread the malicious story that Canaris eliminated Russell to deliberately scuttle the mission, Lahousen offered that 'I think it is possible that he [Russell] may have been poisoned by his very radical associate, Frank Ryan, who accompanied him until the U-boat's departure. Internal difficulties and political rivalries within the IRA probably played a part in this matter.'[180] Espionage gadfly Nora O'Mara later told John F. O'Reilly that Russell had been murdered by Kurt Haller – something that she still maintains to this day.[181]

The Irish government was likewise confused about Russell's fate. Information on Russell's whereabouts, almost all of it erroneous, was funnelled to G2 on a regular basis:

January 1940	Russell at Sunday mass, St. John's Church, Kilkenny.
February 1940	Russell reported in Germany.
April 1940	Russell and McGarrity reported in Berlin.
May	1940 Russell landed on the west coast of Ireland.
August	1940 Russell parachuted into Kill, County Kildare.
September 1940	Russell travelled from Switzerland to England and then on to Belfast.
November 1940	Russell reported living 5 miles from Dublin.
March 1941	Russell seen on a train, Milltown, County Dublin.[182]

On a visit to Madrid in December 1940, Elizabeth Clissmann, not wishing to reveal German involvement in the attempt to send Russell back to Ireland, told Irish Minister Kerney that he had died in France.[183] In a subsequent letter to Kerney, Frank Ryan admitted that Russell had died in his arms, but deliberately gave no exact details about when and where.[184] Surprisingly, Seán McBride seems to have known the details before anyone else and in October 1940, told Moss Twomey that Russell had been dead since August.[185]

POST-MORTEM ON SEALION

Russell and Ryan were not the last agents sent to pave the way for Sealion. On 3 September 1940, two separate amphibious reconnaissance groups landed near Dymchurch, Kent. The quartet consisted of Dutch volunteers van Kieboom, Pons and Meier, and German agent Waldberg. They were sent by inflatable raft and boat to scout the coast in preparation for the projected invasion. Equipped with an 'Afu' transmitter, they were to pay particular attention to beaches clear of mines and tank traps, coastal areas suitable for glider landings, and then report this information back to the Abwehr. None of them was well trained, all spoke varying degrees of English and all were apprehended within a short time. Waldberg managed to send three short reports back to Germany before he was discovered. Three of them were convicted and executed in December 1940, but Pons was miraculously acquitted by the jury and interned under the 18B provisions.[186]

Ireland was again almost involved in Sealion preparation in September, when former German Academic Exchange Service director turned Brandenburg Regiment NCO Helmut Clissmann was directed to land in Sligo. He was accompanied by Corporal Bruno Rieger as his RTO, and the landing party was ferried to the Irish coast by none other than Christian Nissen, this time in command of the French fishing trawler the *Anni Braz-Bihen*. Clissmann was supposed to use his familial connections to help him reach England, where he was to prepare for the Sealion landings, apparently following the same general plan as that used by Tributh and Gärtner in the earlier attempt. Failing that, he was to make contact with the IRA and Hermann Görtz. As it happened, he was never able to test the mission plan. Unknown to either Clissmann or Nissen, the boat's motor had been sabotaged before leaving Brest and it was impossible to make Ireland in the heavy seas with sails alone.[187] Another operation, *Walfisch* ('Whale') was subsequently planned for November 1940. The amphibious transport was to have been piloted by Nissen (code-named *Hein*), and carry Clissmann (code-named *Lehrer* – teacher) and Corporal Rieger to Wales to establish a liaison with Welsh and Scottish nationalists. Clissmann said later that he would have actually attempted to reach Ireland, a sentiment echoed by Abwehr II chief Lahousen. The mission was ultimately abandoned.[188]

Collectively, the agents sent by the Abwehr accomplished little or nothing. They utterly failed in every aspect of their military missions and made no contribution to the intelligence picture so desperately needed by the OKW for Sealion planning. The lack of actual data did not prevent Canaris from passing along discouraging information. Though he had absolutely no data on which to base his raw intelligence estimate, he advised the OKW that the British had thirty-seven combat-ready divisions with which to defend English soil.[189] The consequences of invading England, he advised, would be costly, if not catastrophic. On 17 September, with the concurrence of the OKW chiefs, Hitler decided to postpone the invasion until further notice.[190]

It is difficult to escape the idea that the failures of Simon, Preetz, Tributh, Gärtner and Obéd – not to mention the more publicized failures of Hermann Görtz – were intentional. The agents themselves certainly did not deliberately throw the missions, but is it conceivable that German

Military Intelligence, by chance, would have consistently picked the worst personnel possible to accomplish a mission of such importance? Canaris was no fool, something about which his friends and even his enemies agreed, and neither were his command officers. The 'send in the clowns' approach is evident; obviously unqualified agents were sent on missions when more experienced and better-trained personnel were standing by. The Brandenburg Regiment, full of authentic, highly trained soldiers, as opposed to civilian agents of marginal quality, was never once employed for the role ideally suited to it.[191] Although some of the agents did receive training at the Brandenburg compound, the key resources and personnel were never assigned the mission they were most capable of achieving. Did Canaris deliberately scuttle Sealion?

Dr Edmund Veesenmayer, formerly the 'Irish specialist' at the Foreign Ministry, thought as much. In his only known post-war interview, he told John Duggan that 'Canaris was a damaging influence on Irish affairs and wanted always "to walk them into it"'. Veesenmayer had no difficulty in labelling Canaris 'a traitor' for the way he handled the agents.[192]

In a final postscript to Sealion planning and to the projected invasion of Ireland as part of the operation, Grand Admiral Erich Raeder briefed Hitler on Ireland in December 1940 – almost two months after the decision to suspend Sealion and while the plans for the invasion of the Soviet Union were already under way. On 27 November, Hitler requested a feasibility study from the Luftwaffe and Navy on the occupation of Ireland.[193] The Navy quickly termed the proposal 'completely hopeless'.[194] By analogy, Raeder's responsive report to the Führer on 3 December was largely the act of shooting a corpse, but he felt it necessary to go on the record and kill any chance that the spectre of *Sealion* would be raised from the dead. He said that an Irish operation was not feasible because 1, Germany did not have naval supremacy; 2, because of Ireland's geographic position, the 'invasion would have to be launched from the coast, which would mean sacrificing the element of surprise'; 3, the terrain afforded no protection; 4, unpredictable weather problems complicated air support; 5, there were no defended anchorage or bases that the Germans could occupy; and 6, even in the unlikely event that the invasion was a success, the peculiar geographic location presented an insoluble problem with establishing supply lines.[195] The Luftwaffe concurred in this assessment. In short, Ireland might have a future role in the political relationship between Germany and England, but using it as an arena for military operations was not a viable option.

Once the decision was made to abandon Sealion – and Fall Grün along with it – there was one final public change that had to take place. In an attempt to correct what could become an embarrassing public relations nightmare, Joseph Goebbels had the *England Lied* withdrawn from the radio playlists by the end of September 1940. If nothing else, the Minister for Propaganda and Public Enlightenment knew when something had served its limited purpose and became obsolete, much like Sealion itself.[196]

THE CONTINUING PROBLEMS OF HERMANN GÖRTZ

During the time that the Ryan and Russell episode played out, Hermann Görtz was still very much on the run, and was constantly shifted from one location to another. Görtz was officially known as 'Mr Richards' while at Mrs Mary Coffey's house, but as her duplicitous statements to the Garda later proved, both she and her large family were aware of her lodger's true identity. Görtz did not immediately make contact with Stephen Hayes, largely out of a growing sense of distrust following the Held raid. Görtz obliquely accused Hayes of informing the police of his whereabouts, but produced no proof of his allegation, lamely concluding that 'there was something dangerously rotten in the organization of the IRA'.

His growing unease with Hayes caused Görtz to make some unauthorized tactical decisions about his mission. While at the Coffey house, he decided to abandon temporarily any thought of working in Northern Ireland or continuing with his intelligence-gathering and liaison mission. 'In order to supply arms [to the IRA] I needed contact. To set up this contact was considerably easier for me in Éire than in Northern Ireland.'[197] Though his brief was to work as a liaison with the IRA, Görtz was determined to do this with as little contact with the IRA as possible.

THE GÖRTZ TRANSMITTER

Görtz also had another problem – he had no means of contacting Germany. His new friends rallied together, but their amateur efforts did not produce much by way of results. Mrs McDowell seems to have organized the radio effort and drafted her nephew, Leon Redmond, to provide a working transmitter. Redmond purchased two sets from Parkinson of Donegal for £17 7s. each. The first set was sent directly to Mrs Coffey, and a James Madigan collected the second set. Mrs Coffey was careful to prepare an alibi, and told Redmond to say, if asked, that the radio was for her personal use. Redmond later received a plate from one of these radios in a parcel from Helena Moloney and mailed the repaired part to Mrs Stuart at Laragh Castle.[198] Redmond added that he was given no instructions as to the power of the radios that he purchased, which helps explain the next series of events.

In October 1940, Michael Kinsella, an engineer at Pye Radio in Dublin, was sent to Kevin Cahill's home (59 Sidney Parade Avenue) to examine one of the sets.[199] After performing his checks, he explained that the particular model was insufficient for transmission for over ten to fifteen miles – and certainly not powerful enough to transmit to the Continent. In November of the same year, Kinsella was again asked to look at a radio, this time at the house of Liam Redmond in Harold's Cross. To his surprise, it was the identical radio he had examined in October, and he gave the same opinion: unsuitable. Redmond asked his advice about setting up an aerial, despite the opinion that the radio would not reach Germany, no matter what aerial configuration was erected. In December 1940, only a month later, Kinsella was once more directed to examine a radio – the same radio – this time at Maeve McDowell's house on Lakefield Grove. He gave, for the third time, the identical opinion, and answered the same question about the aerial.[200] Görtz's transmitter problem lingered until July 1941, when Kinsella finally built him a transmitter that was capable of sending a message to Germany.

While Görtz was desperately trying out his various transmitters at a multitude of sites, he decided to train two part-time Morse operators. He initially used Donald O'Brien and John Dunne, students at Atlantic Wireless College, but since he didn't yet have a functional radio, he was forced to let them go. Görtz was later assigned IRA man Anthony Deery, who proved to be capable.[201] Since he was from Northern Ireland, Görtz had more faith in Deery than he might have had in one of Hayes's local nominees. The various unsuccessful attempts to purchase radios and set up stations started to put a financial strain on Görtz: 'Even though I paid no fixed salaries, my transmitting station cost me, after its erection also, when in operation, not inconsiderable sums. The question whether the expenditure was worthwhile is no simple sum in arithmetic and cannot be answered in the sense of a book balance. ... On the other hand, cash must not be equated to the value of production.'

MARY P. MAINS

Though Görtz's situation seemed desperate, the Abwehr was working to alleviate his financial position. In September 1940, Admiral Canaris directed that two Spanish Falangists (fascists) proceed to London with the address of an IRA safe house and money intended for Hermann Görtz. According to Kurt Haller, the Abwehr KO station chief in Madrid had recruited the two, and they eventually reached their destination in England. However, Görtz never seems to have received his money. The Abwehr must have suspected as much, since they next dispatched a most unlikely agent to Ireland, Miss Mary P. Mains.

In *Spies in Ireland*, Enno Stephan refers to her as 'Mrs Daly' but she was actually Mary Pauline Mains, born in Portrush in 1889. The Mains case is important because it is another link in the chain that tied Irish minister in Spain Leopold Kerney to German Intelligence. By 1940, Mains was living in Madrid and acting as a governess to elderly ladies. The Irish Department of External Affairs was badgered by a series of letters from her extended family in Dublin (Mr and Mrs Doody) as to her whereabouts. As a result of these missives, Kerney took to making regular reports of her location and circumstances. According to a letter from Kerney to her estranged family, she was in Spain originally to collect a legacy that Mains claimed was left to her by a wealthy widow, but there seem to have been legal complications with the settlement. In May 1940, Kerney established contact with Mains care of the *Servicio Domestico* in Madrid.

In July 1940, Mains sent a letter to Peggy Doody which revealed that her contacts in Spain extended beyond those connected with domestic services: 'Can you find out from Basil if the IRA have any representative in Spain? I know someone who is rather interested in this affair and would like to get in touch with them (Spanish), that is if there is no reason to keep it a secret.' The 'someone' was likely from the Abwehr KO in Madrid. 'Basil' was never identified.[202]

Nothing was heard of her for several months, until Kerney sent an urgent message to Boland in November 1940, stating that Mary Mains must get to Ireland on the NYK *Fushimi Maru* because of 'urgent personal reasons, but will have to be in Spain at an early date to pursue to a conclusion a lawsuit in which she is engaged'. Kerney then went on to ask that Boland get permission from the British to allow her to travel and also to aid her in obtaining an exit visa to allow her return to Spain via England. The *Fushimi Maru* was travelling around the world, picking up Japanese civilian nationals who had been stranded by the outbreak of the war. She made a port of call in Lisbon and was then scheduled to arrive in Galway. Due to Kerney's plea for executive treatment, Mains was able to board the ship and was duly taken to Galway. The problem was that she was now acting as an Abwehr courier for the Madrid KO chief, Wolfgang Blaum.

In the Abwehr II war diary, Mains is code-named 'Agent Margarethe' and the diarist noted that 'Irish agent Margarethe will shortly be returning to Spain', seemingly with the assistance of Leopold Kerney.[203] She carried the sum of $10,000 to Görtz, as well as a new supply of secret ink (*G-Tinten*) and a new keyword for radio transmissions. Once her mission was accomplished, she returned to Spain on 29 December, her path cleared by the Irish Department of External Affairs, carrying a situation report from Görtz. The Mains–Kerney connection was not long lost on Irish Intelligence or External Affairs. Both found it difficult to understand how Kerney just happened to give preferential treatment to the one woman who turned out to be an Abwehr courier.

When she landed in Galway on 1 November, a reporter from the *Irish Press* interviewed Mains. She told him that she was from Coleraine, and was 'on holiday in 1939 and could not return because of the war'. This flatly contradicted Kerney's account of her remaining in Spain in pursuit of a testamentary legacy. Kerney's account was also questioned when it was learned that other Irish nationals were stranded in Spain and Portugal at the same time – and had similarly appealed to Kerney for assistance – but that Mains was the only one deemed worthy of his ministerial intervention.

In one instance, the trapped Irish national was an Army officer; Kerney suggested that the officer should write to the Department of Defence to obtain travel permission. When confronted by Boland, Kerney maintained that Mains was either mistaken or misquoted by the *Irish Press* reporter, and that there were no other Irish citizens who wanted to leave – a position that Boland knew to be false. Though Bryan urged it, no action was taken against Leopold Kerney.[204] G2 put out an alert on Mains at the Customs and Passport offices in case she tried to re-enter Ireland.

Mrs Elizabeth Clissmann suggested one possible, though unlikely, explanation for Kerney's actions, other than carelessness or treason. Mrs Clissmann had a long association with Kerney and had several meetings with him during the course of the war, almost exclusively on the subject of Frank Ryan. She also took part in occasional missions on behalf of the Germans, and was informed about Abwehr matters by her husband, Helmut Clissmann. According to Mrs Clissmann, Mary Mains acted as a private courier from Kerney to the Department of External Affairs.[205] Chronologically, this was Kerney's second, seemingly accidental encounter with German Intelligence (the first was during Frank Ryan's 'escape' from Burgos prison); it would not be his last. His meetings with Dr Veesenmayer and Helmut Clissmann would complete the cycle.

Görtz's report to the Abwehr was brief, to judge by the synopsis in the Abwehr II war diary. He told them some of what they already knew: his transmitter had fallen into the hands of the police, though Görtz did not see fit to explain that this was not his original Abwehr radio. He predicted success for the work of the IRA against England, which agreed with numerous reports of successful sabotage already received by Abwehr II. Görtz recounted that he had sent several pleas for the equipment that had been requested by the IRA. Lahousen, the Abwehr II chief, decided to try and get Görtz another working 'Afu' transmitter, realizing that without radio communication the question of sending such supplies to the IRA didn't arise.[206] In short, Görtz had sent a report to his headquarters that failed to inform them of the true situation with regard to the IRA and of his dim prospects for future success. In the long run, the report carried by Mary Mains came to haunt him. From his own lips, the Abwehr heard that the situation was under control and consequently, there would be no reason for him to return to Germany. Even though her work for the Germans was well known, Mary Mains was granted a new Irish passport in 1945, over the strenuous objection of Colonel Dan Bryan.[207]

'MIDSUMMER MADNESS'

From his confused narrative, it seems that Görtz initiated contact with interested Irish politicians and citizens shortly after abandoning this attempt to escape:

> The incident caused me to come more out of my reserve. I began to feel myself safer. I asked my friends no longer to keep my existence secret. I met people who interested me. I met, at a cautious estimate, far more than 500 persons, with whom I had more or less exhaustive discussions. In the last months I often spoke with people, till then unknown, who declared to me that they were glad to speak to the German officer, of whom they had heard so much.[208]

It is difficult to determine the exact identity of these '500 persons'. For understandable reasons, no one in authority was later anxious to admit dealings with an agent from Nazi Germany. The autumn of 1940, however, resulted in what Professor Desmond Williams later called 'Midsummer Madness'. German troops had vanquished France, Norway, Denmark, Holland, Belgium and Luxembourg; German submarines were on the verge of winning the Battle of the Atlantic; Luftwaffe bombers were destroying military and civilian targets in Britain; the invasion of England seemed only a matter of time. The mood certainly brought out the Irish quislings, both in and outside the government. The Secretary of the Department of External Affairs, Joseph Walshe, was telling Minister Hempel that he hoped Germany wouldn't forget Irish national aims when drafting the peace agreement with England, and Major-General Hugo McNeill approached the German minister on the subject of cooperation between the Irish Army and the Wehrmacht.[209] Members of the Dáil, such as Cristóir O'Byrne (a.k.a. Christopher Byrne), have been identified as having visited Görtz, along with the Minister for Agriculture, Dr Jim Ryan, and P.J. Little, Minister for Posts and Telegraphs – if the statements in the 'Hayes confession' are in any way accurate.[210] John Duggan suggests, on very sketchy evidence, that Görtz met with the Minister for Coordination of Defensive Measures, Frank Aiken.[211]

Major-General McNeill's initiative was a serious threat to neutrality – more so than any single aspect of the Görtz affair. McNeill was the co-founder of the Military Academy and former Director of Defence Plans. As one of the senior officers in the Irish Army (he would command the Second Division from 1941 to 1946), his flirtation with the German Legation and Görtz was very dangerous to the Irish neutrality position, and certainly to British security. Hempel reported that McNeill approached Henning Thomsen in December 1940, with the stated aim of telling the Germans that the Irish Army expected a British attack and wanted to know what logistical and material support Germany could provide in such an event. McNeill, according to Hempel's telegrams back to Germany, wanted to interface with a German liaison officer – something the Dublin Legation lacked.[212] Hempel passed along McNeill's request for a list of weapons, but received no immediate answer. Finally tired of waiting on the German Foreign Ministry, McNeill announced that he wanted to be put in touch with the IRA, which was said to be in touch with the OKW (through Görtz), something that Hempel seemed unable to accomplish.

McNeill eventually found his way to Görtz, provoking telegrams of mistrust from Hempel.[213] This step markedly increased the danger. McNeill was involving the Irish Army in collaboration with Nazi Germany, and Görtz was certainly extending his mission guidelines beyond the breaking point. The Abwehr had intended Görtz to incite action in Northern Ireland, not to act as an official German representative to neutral Ireland. Had such contacts existed earlier, they might have played into Veesenmayer's attempts to foment rebellion in Éire, but with the official German focus on plans for the invasion of Russia instead of England, such feelers from the Irish military had lost their relevance.

At the moment, however, Görtz had precious little to show for several months on Irish soil. He had not succeeded in directing, or really attempted to direct, IRA activity to Germany's advantage, and had not managed to pass on a single report of any intelligence value – or even to set up a transmitter to make a situation report. The IRA, too, was beginning to regret his arrival. After the Held raid, Görtz became 'public enemy number one' and the spy-hunt was bound to have disastrous consequences for the IRA's own internal organization. By virtue of his being cut off from communication with the Abwehr, Görtz certainly could not make good on promises of arms and other supplies. He was fast becoming a liability.

Görtz gradually resumed contact with Hayes and met with him about every second week. Hayes did not know about the room at Mrs Coffey's home. Görtz's aggressive travelling schedule eventually led to his meeting Maisie O'Mahony, who became his chauffeur and another romantic interest. Because of her blonde hair, he called her 'Golden Queen' or 'GQ'.[214] O'Mahony was the daughter of well-known anti-Treaty Fianna Fáil TD Sean O'Mahony; while her mother ran a guest house at 32 Gardiners Place. Mrs O'Mahony's home was periodically used as an IRA safe house and Stephen Hayes sometimes stayed there. Maisie had worked for the Irish Hospital Sweepstakes before landing a job in Dr Andrew Cooney's office on the Hospitals Commission. She would later transfer to the Dublin Hospital Bureau (popularly called the 'Bed Bureau'), which was 'controlled and operated by the Hospitals Commission'.[215] The links between Cooney and O'Mahony, and their individual connections to the IRA, the Irish Friends of Germany, and Görtz, were of serious concern to Irish Intelligence.

ANDREW COONEY AND THE 'FIFTH MAN'

Dr Andrew Cooney, Secretary of the Hospitals Commission and medical advisor to the Hospitals Trust Ltd, played a shadowy role in the Görtz case. G2 linked Cooney to the Germans as early as October 1940, when they noted that 'Dr Cooney is now acting as go-between for the IRA and the Germans'. The source of the information is not listed, but the report goes on to link O'Mahony and Cooney through their work at the Hospitals Commission.[216] Cooney was already a suspect for attending the preliminary meeting of the Irish Friends of Germany at Liam Walsh's house in April 1940. To compound the suspicion further, during this period, Cooney was in touch with J.J. Walsh, who had once been W.T. Cosgrave's Postmaster General, and was now avowedly pro-German. Thinking Cooney of like mind, Walsh added his name to the mailing list for the IFG; the list came into G2's possession in July 1941.

The IFG mailing list acted as a convenient roll of subversives for Irish military intelligence. Following the arrest and interrogation of Walsh and Alex McCabe and the forced dismemberment of the Irish Friends of Germany, G2 concluded that 'the Germans require an organisation headed by men of some standing, past or present in the IRA, to work for a complete sell-out to Germany in the event of an invasion of England. To this end, five have been invited to form a new emergency executive of the IRA. Four of the five involved are Maurice Twomey, Padraig MacLogan, Sean MacBride and Con Lehane. The name of the fifth man is not known.'[217] G2 recognized the possibility that Cooney could be the 'fifth man' and as such, would constitute a clear and present danger to the state.[218] However, although G2 lacked hard proof, it took action to remove Cooney as secretary of the Hospitals Commission in September 1941. Maisie O'Mahony, already identified as a security risk for her known assistance to Görtz, did not last much longer. She was arrested on 20 October 1941, and though she was released on 24 January 1942, her employment at the suspect Bed Bureau was terminated.[219] No one was ever directly charged with participating in a conspiracy to aid German forces, but it is possible that the proactive investigation by Irish Intelligence had prevented such an event.

German agent activities, 1941–42

The beginning of 1941 marked a definite change in Görtz's mission to Ireland, though largely one of his own making, rather than being based on directives from the Abwehr in Berlin. For their part, the Abwehr had finally accepted the idea that the IRA was not sufficiently organized to be of any use to German Military Intelligence. From this point forward, the Germans depended on their own or native resources, without the added complication of the Irish Republican Army.

According to his own statement, Görtz was working to effect a truce between the IRA and the government, but was blocked by Stephen Hayes. Görtz wanted the truce so that the IRA might be free to engage in military action in Ulster, but Hayes, according to Görtz, said that the Executive Council had refused such a request. Görtz wrote to Jim O'Donovan in August, asking him to approach 'Mr T' on this subject. 'Mr T' remains unidentified.[1] The German was not exclusively concerned with reconciliation between the IRA and de Valera's government; he was also investigating the possibility of returning home.

Using more of his dwindling funds, he purchased a fishing boat, the *Venture*, and had it outfitted in Fenit, County Kerry. Through Hayes, he managed to assemble an all-IRA crew and the boat was supposed to be captained by Joseph O'Sullivan. Görtz tells a series of contradictory stories about this effort, insisting that James Crofton was assigned the task of taking the boat to France with a coded message from Görtz. Crofton, an IRA agent in the Garda Special Branch, was arrested on 20 February, after a subsequent attempt to escape by sea. The *Venture*'s projected sailing from Fenit came to nothing, because of arguments among the crew as to who was to command the vessel; Hayes had them recalled. During the same period, another of Görtz's willing helpers, Bernard O'Donnell, along with Maisie O'Mahony, travelled to Donegal to investigate the possibility of leaving from there and to examine the suitability of Inishduff island as a site to land radio equipment and supplies. O'Donnell purchased another boat, the *Sunbeam*, and rounded up a crew of locals. For reasons that are not clear, this plan never matured.

For any escape plan to succeed, Görtz would have to establish radio communication with Germany, despite the fact that his mission specifications did not include abandoning his assignment and returning to

Germany. Görtz justifies this, saying that the situation required a personal report and that he would have to return in order to facilitate arms supplies to the IRA. At the time, he was still attempting to use the under-powered radios purchased by Leon Redmond and believed that the German stations might not know he was trying to contact them. Accordingly, through an intermediary, he approached Minister Hempel at the German Legation to send a message to the Abwehr. Hempel, who was certainly frightened about any contact with Görtz, complied, but in an anaemic fashion. His telegram to the Foreign Office on 23 August asked them to notify the OKW to listen for a message from Görtz on the following Saturday and Sunday. The transmitter identification signal was GUSTL and would be sending on the 33.25-metre band. To ensure that Görtz would not again avail himself of the legation as a conduit to the Abwehr, Hempel asked that Görtz ('Dr HK') not be informed that he had passed on the message.[2] Presumably Görtz intended to send a message concerning his escape attempt. Because of his transmitter problems, the Abwehr heard nothing. Görtz himself later observed: 'I had a working transmitter, which however did not get through.'[3]

While the German Legation did not approve of contact with Görtz, it apparently continued to forward messages concerning him to the Abwehr via the Foreign Ministry. As noted in the Abwehr II war diary, Minister Hempel sent a message informing them of Görtz's planned escape in a 'chartered motorboat' to occupied France. Abwehr II responded, asking Hempel to stop the attempt, presuming that he had contact with Görtz, but made arrangements to protect Görtz's ship if and when it reached German waters.[4] When the attempt collapsed, Hempel's intervention was not required.

THE SECOND ESCAPE ATTEMPT

Other than his insidious links to Irish political and military figures, Görtz seems to have forgotten about the aspect of his mission involving Northern Ireland. His first action of 1941 was to attempt another escape from Ireland, again involving the *Venture* in Fenit, County Kerry. The previous year's attempt failed because of internal squabbling among O'Sullivan's IRA crew, and this next attempt was hardly error free. Assured that the boat was ready for sea, Görtz travelled to County Kerry expecting to depart immediately. Görtz later said that he was actually planning to stay and carry out his mission, but was persuaded by Hayes to travel personally to Germany. By this time, Görtz was developing a paranoia about Hayes, a situation not helped when Maisie O'Mahony (who drove for Hayes and Görtz) informed the German that she saw Hayes in the company of what looked like a detective. The detective was James Crofton, an IRA plant in the Garda Detective Branch. Hayes explained that he wanted Crofton to accompany Görtz to occupied France – Crofton was formerly a seaman – and Görtz agreed.

Görtz was becoming increasingly agitated and suspicious. In his later statements, he constantly accuses Hayes of treachery and of attempting to betray him. 'That Hayes had not tried again before this to give me away is not inexplicable. He did not know where I was. He did not dare to ask me. He had told the police that I am often somewhere in Dun Laoghaire. He did not know any more. When I was with him he could not have me arrested without being himself suspected as a traitor.'[5] Görtz later attributed the failure of his Fenit departure to Hayes, and it is clear that he was becoming depressed and despondent:

> All this time, too, I was anxious to return to Germany. I had seen very early that the main purposes of my mission could not succeed and that the German Supreme Command could not hope for anything in the shape of serious military action by the IRA. Clearly my instructions needed to be rewritten if any considerable military diversion was to be created in the Six Counties. All my original plans for landing-grounds, all the money I had hoped to spend quietly, but effectively, on building up equipment for German troops when they should come; the detailed military preparations for an effective descent on enemy territory – all this was useless when I could not find sufficient solid support among the one body in Ireland avowedly out to fight Britain.[6]

Görtz was planning to leave in February and had made all the arrangement he thought necessary. Writing to his supporters, he said: 'The ch[ief = Hayes] has asked me to go home as their representative and come back as soon as possible.' In a separate letter, he noted that

> events have developed in such a way that I have decided to go. ... I shall inform you as soon as possible of my arrival. It cannot be before Saturday next 22 of Febr. at the agreed time and in the agreed way ... if you get the message give word to Bernard [O'Donnell] and the post card to H [Hempel? Hayes?]. All further informations [sic] you will get from my Golden Queen [O'Mahony] verbally.[7]

Helena Moloney did her part in the escape and borrowed three books for Görtz from the Dublin Public Library in Rathmines: *Navigation and Astronomy, Amateurs Afloat* and *Practical Navigation for Yachtsmen*. This proved to be an error. When an overdue book notice was mailed to her on 3 April 1941, postal censors notified G2, who placed Moloney under surveillance.[8] According to Görtz, such books as *Amateurs Afloat* would have been superfluous: 'I myself am a sailor and grew up in a fishing harbour.'[9]

Upon arrival in Fenit, he found that his usual bad luck had accompanied him. 'On the day before our departure a westerly heavy storm damaged the rudder of the boat in the harbour ... suddenly my crew was arrested.' Görtz later alleged, unconvincingly, that Colonel de Buitléar told him, 'We had intended at the beginning to catch you in the open sea; otherwise we just could not get you. But that seemed to us too dangerous – you could perhaps have slipped through. Then we preferred to arrest the crew.'[10] Crofton was arrested by members of the Local Defence Force (LDF) at the home of Michael Moriarty, the original owner of the *Venture*, on 20 February 1940.[11] Görtz managed to avoid capture and returned to Dublin via Cork, with the help of IRA men O'Connor, Sheehy and Daly. He predictably blamed the treachery of Stephen Hayes for the failure of the attempt. He also observed that 'the people in Kerry were fine men, but I could not close my eyes to the obvious treachery on the part of someone. It was plain that I was to be betrayed to the Irish police, or, if by some miracle I should escape and slip out to the open sea, I was to be betrayed to the British.'[12] The refrain of treason and betrayal permeates every account by Görtz of his Irish mission; he never seemed to take into account that the responsibility for failure might be laid at his own door and that incompetence and bad luck, rather than treason, were the culprits.

The Abwehr had again been informed that Görtz intended to try and return home, but the Abwehr II diary of 4 March 1941 notes that his planned departure did not occur and that his companions had been arrested. In a follow-up telegram from Hempel two days later, the minister added a few details, and quickly pointed out that he had no regular contact with Görtz – meaning that he was anxious to disqualify himself as a future conduit for Abwehr messages.[13] Since Görtz did not yet have a working transmitter of his own, and coordination of an air-drop through the German Legation was not feasible, there was no way for the Abwehr to send him materials or extract him from Ireland. He was on his own, and he was about to have unexpected company from Germany.

GÜNTHER SCHÜTZ

Walking along a deserted road in County Wexford on 13 March 1941, Günther Schütz had no sense of danger. Before leaving occupied Europe the previous night, he was assured that conditions in Ireland were different; German agents were already moving around freely; the Irish government was covertly, if not openly, hostile to the British enemy and he should have no difficulty in completing his mission. He noticed two policemen approaching on bicycles and, just to be safe, stepped back into the field from where he had just emerged. But he had been seen. Schütz emerged and began talking to the officers. They asked him his name and he confidently answered 'Hans Marschner, I'm South African.' He showed them his passport that verified his name and nationality. Schütz added that he was a student. Garda Sergeant Fullam asked the man why his passport had no Irish visa stamp, and he replied that he did not need one, since he had been in the country for more than nine months. The curious officers asked Marschner how he happened to be in these parts and he responded that his car had broken down between Dublin and Naas and he was walking home. This had been the pre-arranged cover story before he left Germany and, in his momentary panic, he used it, even though he knew he was nowhere near Naas or Dublin. That simple mistake changed the course of his life.

In the years before he assumed the identity of a South African student, 'Hans Marschner', whose real name was Günther Schütz, had been a German citizen. Born on 17 April 1912 in the Silesian town of Schweidnitz – which was also home to the famous von Richthofen clan – his family owned a prosperous metal manufacturing business. He performed an obligatory stint in the local army reserve unit in Schweidnitz in 1934–5 and later attended a five-week training period with the 2/58 Mounted Artillery Regiment at Oldenburg in 1938. During 1938 and 1939, Schütz attended the German Commercial College at Eaton Rise, Ealing, England, but his stay in Britain was not entirely devoted to academic pursuits.

On a visit home before Christmas 1938, Schütz met an old friend, Hans Walter Krause, who coincidentally worked with the Abwehr in the Knochenhauerstrasse, Hamburg. The next morning, he received a telephone call from 'Dr Scholz', asking him to report to the Hamburg Ast. When he arrived, he was introduced to Hauptmann Dr Friedrich Karl Praetorius, the senior officer in the economic section of Abwehr I in Hamburg.[14] Dr Praetorius did not ask Schütz to be a 'spy' but merely to do his 'patriotic duty' and to keep his eyes open. He was expected to send reports on the English economic and industrial situation to a cover-address in Hamburg. With few other options, Schütz agreed and was sent back to England as a representative of Remy and Company, an Abwehr front. Sonderführer Hans Blum ran the company as a cover, and an arrangement was made with Dr Muntz, the quasi-legitimate director, to provide Schütz the necessary documentation.[15] Coincident with his cover, Schütz was allowed to take more money out of the country than was generally permitted, and told to keep £25 per month to cover his own expenses.

According to a statement later given in captivity, his reports were considered unsatisfactory ('childish and poor in value', according to Praetorius) and an agent named Haberichter from the Abwehr's Referat I West reprimanded him in person.[16] Though Schütz later tried to play down any serious espionage activity while in England, MI5 thought this was only part of the truth. While at Eaton Rise, Ealing, Schütz stayed in a house at 41 Webster Gardens, West London, and befriended a Portuguese man named Pierce.[17] According to Pierce's later confession to MI5, he and Schütz travelled up and down the country taking pictures of factories. Once back in Germany, Schütz wrote to Pierce and suggested that he take over the espionage work. Pierce went to MI5 and with their approval, Pierce (code-named 'Rainbow') met with an Abwehr control officer in

Antwerp. Rainbow was asked to assess bomb damage (presumably from IRA S-Plan attacks), report on internal transportation facilities and complete a questionnaire concerning British air defences. He was provided with a mail address in Antwerp and a suitable cover story as a worker for a Belgian firm in England. Given money and a quantity of secret ink, Rainbow was told that future instructions would come in the mail in the form of microdots placed at the end of the date in the letter. (At this time, microdot technology was new to the British security authorities.) Rainbow made another trip to Antwerp in April 1940 and received new mail addresses and another questionnaire. MI5 section B1(a) successfully operated the Rainbow deception until June 1943.[18]

Schütz returned to Germany in August 1939 and was immediately reactivated for military service. Rather than return to his artillery posting, he was assigned to Abwehrstelle I Wi, Generalkommando Hamburg – the Hamburg branch of German Military Intelligence specializing in economic espionage.[19] As a cover, Schütz was posted to the 'translator company' of Wehrkreis X. His fluent, though accented, English and experience were prized by his intelligence superiors. Though his expertise was in English matters, it was soon planned to send Schütz not to England, but to Ireland. From at least December 1939, he carried out a variety of tasks for Abwehr I/Wi, none of which were related to his planned mission. Schütz visited Belgium, Italy and Switzerland, primarily to collect letters from live-letter drops sent by German agents overseas. He also attempted to persuade an elderly relative of his in Switzerland to agree to be an Abwehr 'post office', but the old lady refused.[20] Letters addressed to such people from agents overseas would normally give the incorrect middle initial, identifying that letter as one to be saved for Abwehr collection.[21]

One of his duties in Brussels was to maintain contact with a sympathetic Guatemalan Consul. These meetings continued, though Schütz was periodically sent to Spain, beginning in June 1940. Another mission during that time period was to act as a controller for Abwehr agent Werner Unland, who wrote to Schütz care of a letter drop at the Majestic Hotel, Barcelona. Unland was to have remained as a live asset in England, but he fled to Ireland on the outbreak of war and was continuing to communicate with Abwehr I, principally to request payment for services rendered.

Schütz was recalled to Hamburg in December 1940 and told about the mission to Ireland. Dr Praetorius explained that his job would be to collect and send weather information (desired by Section I-L – air intelligence), observe British convoy traffic (data needed by Section I-M – naval intelligence) and conduct economic espionage against selected targets in Northern Ireland. In particular, Abwehr I wanted data on the condition of harbours; the location and capacity of plants producing corn oil, margarine, soap and sugar; oil refineries, carbide works, oil lines and storage tanks; shipyard activity; bomb damage assessments of Luftwaffe raids; and the amount of food being sent from Ireland to England.[22] His supervisor at I/ Wi, Dr Praetorius, stated that he was supposed to set up a working wireless transmitting station and perform his intelligence-gathering in partnership with Werner Unland in Dublin.[23] Schütz was likewise supposed to bring money to Johannes Ernstberger in Cork.

He was given the address of the German Legation at 58 Northumberland Road, Dublin, where he could turn for help in the event of an emergency. Communication with Germany would be independent of the German Legation, however, and Schütz was to be trained in the operation of an 'Afu' transmitter, which he would carry with him.

Because of the recent difficulties with inserting agents into Ireland by sea (Simon, Preetz, Tributh, Gärtner and Obéd), it was decided to find a more conventional way of sending Schütz to Ireland. The idea was that he could travel as an ordinary passenger and once there, set out on his mission as an Abwehr agent. As part of the cover plan, he obtained a Paraguayan passport in the name of Alfredo Grabow. When the Abwehr learned that such an identity would not allow him to travel to Ireland via Portugal (the intended route), he was given a second identity card in the name of Judel Rothmensch, a Jewish refugee. The passport originally came from an Abwehr member who worked in the Hamburg passport office. This man provided the passport of a Pole and it was thought that Schütz's photo could merely be replaced on the document. The fate of the passport's original owner is unknown.

At this point, Gaelic scholar and SS officer Ludwig Mühlhausen becomes involved. As a renowned Irish expert, the Abwehr coopted Mühlhausen to take Schütz/Rothmensch to the Irish Legation and see about getting him into Ireland under the category of an asylum-seeking refugee.[24] This might have seemed like a workable plan to the Abwehr, but Ireland had a closed-door policy to Jews and the chances of acceptance were slight, even without the sinister attendant circumstances. The Irish Chargé d'Affaires, William Warnock, was suspicious of the situation; it was beyond the bounds of possibility, even in the best of times, to expect Ludwig Mühlhausen – a Nazi Party member since 1932 – to take a personal interest in the case of a Jewish refugee.

According to Schütz, Warnock said: 'Herr Rothmensch, you don't look very Jewish, as you maintain, and this is also not a Polish passport, as you maintain, but rather a Polish emigrant passport. I'm sorry, but I can't give you the visa.' Warnock later remembered that 'the sight of this man [Mühlhausen], who was temporarily going around in SS uniform, introducing me to a Jew, seemed peculiar'.[25] The Abwehr was back to the starting point; they had a ready agent, but no clever, legitimate means by which to insert him into Ireland.

Schütz finally solved the problem himself. He remembered his friend, Hans Marschner, whose parents were also from Schweidnitz. The

Marschners returned to Germany from South Africa on the death of Hans's mother and he and young Gunther Schütz were childhood friends. They eventually lost touch with each other, but were reunited in London, where Marschner was studying pharmacy and, as we have seen earlier, Schütz attended the German Commercial College in Ealing. Once war came, Marschner was prohibited from service in the German Army because of his South African citizenship. He was ordered to report to the Hamburg Ast and willingly surrendered his passport to Schütz for the mission.[26]

The next stage of the operation was in the hands of the Abwehr document 'wizard', Herr Schlütter. The passport had to be altered to include Schütz's physical features and to reflect a new occupation in agreement with his cover story. Schlütter's specialty was matching existing handwriting samples and then writing in the required details. His skills were considerable; the passport continued to puzzle Irish G2, even once they knew that it had to be a forgery. Though he now had a functional passport, the problem of transportation continued. The dangers of trying to get Schütz to Ireland legitimately were just too great. The decision was made: he would have to parachute in. This route, too, was hardly free of risk. When the Abwehr dropped Hermann Görtz by this method, he lost his transmitter and had to walk at least 70 miles to safety. Schütz and his transmitter would be dropped simultaneously, hopefully reducing the chances of man and equipment becoming separated.

Because his mission's success was linked to regular radio contact, Schütz was taught the basics of radio transmitting and given a new coding system. His primary means of encoding messages would be by using the book code so beloved by the Abwehr. In this particular case, the book was the second edition of the pocket novel, *Just a Girl* by Charles Garvice. Hamburg would retain a copy of the same edition, so that both sender and receiver would literally be on the same page. To encipher a message, Schütz would add the numerical representation for the day and the month and then add his base number, 17, to identify the page used to encode the message. His call sign was changed with each message, being the last bottom word, reading right to left, on the page identified for that day's transmissions. In an emergency, his call sign was GUN – confirming Dr Hayes's belief that the agent's call signs were based on a combination of letters in their real names.[27] Schütz was not a superlative pupil in Morse transmission; he achieved a speed of forty to fifty words per minute (eighty to a hundred was the goal), but was far above the mediocre skill demonstrated earlier by Preetz.[28]

As part of this special mission training, Schütz was taught the basics of meteorology, to estimate wind speed, cloud formations, cloud ceiling and wind direction. To ensure that transmissions were kept to a minimum, he was given lists of operational abbreviations that were to be used in place of sentences and words. Though his economic and military intelligence mission components were important, it was stressed to him that the weather reporting must take priority. Because of the volume of his instructions, and because the mission was of considerable importance, Schütz didn't have to worry about memorizing the details. He was the first agent sent to Ireland with the new microdot system. All his instructions, procedures and contacts were reproduced in a typed format – but in a form that was invisible to the naked eye. To read the microdots, he was to bring along a microscope as part of his baggage.

The mission was of unlimited duration and Schütz was financially provided for any eventuality. He was given £1000 sterling and $3200. The British £5 notes were counterfeit (unknown to Schütz), but the £1 notes and the US dollars were genuine. As part of his task, he was to give £300 to Unland and £100 to Johannes Ernstberger. Schütz later said that the Abwehr wanted him to change the US currency at the German Legation in Dublin, but it is equally possible that he was acting as a courier between the Foreign Office and Dr Hempel.[29] In the event of difficulty, Schütz was told to call on Dr Petersen at the German Legation.[30] In his coded instructions, he was informed that Petersen knew about the mission. The identification sign was a cable from Dr Hempel on 14 January 1941: 'Instructions carried out. The individual concerned will be able to be reached here at any time. What nationality does the correspondent have?'[31] The German Legation would soon be attempting to place as much distance between itself and Schütz as possible – and the Irish government would aid in their duplicity.

JOHANNES 'JUAN' ERNSTBERGER

Juan – or more accurately, Johannes Paul – Ernstberger is an unusual element in the Schütz story. Schütz was supposed to make a payment to him, suggesting that he, like Unland, had a continuing relationship to Abwehr I. However, from the information Schütz was given, Ernstberger had not been in regular contact for a while. Born in Freiburg in 1900, Ernstberger emigrated from England to Ireland on 31 May 1939, followed by his wife, Hedwiga, on 5 July. He found work at the Sunbeam Wolseley plant in Cork and moved into an apartment at 30 Wellington Road, the contact address provided to Schütz. In June 1940, he moved to 'Landscape', Hartlands Avenue, Cork, before relocating again to Harbour Road, Skerries, County Dublin, in 1944. G2 was not aware of Ernstberger's ties to the Abwehr until Schütz was apprehended and his microdot list examined, and consequently G2 did not have ongoing mail and/or telephone surveillance on him. The only revealing letter intercepted after Schütz's arrest was written by the plump Hedwiga Ernstberger in December 1945, well after the end of the war in Europe. Mrs Ernstberger wrote about the dismal situation: 'Our people in the dock, our Hitler dead ... and the jews [sic] on top again'. Had surveillance been initiated at an earlier point, it might well have revealed something more interesting.[32] After the war,

Ernstberger went to work for the Balbriggan Hosiery Company. Following the discovery of the Schütz microdots, G2's Colonel Bryan classified him as an 'A-Category' Nazi sympathizer.[33]

Schütz was supposed to deliver a new set of letter phrases for Ernstberger: 'My dear friend John'; 'How are you'; 'How is Hedwiga'; 'Mrs Ottilla is well'; 'The bearer of this letter is a friend'; 'Compliments of Mother Emma.' Since Schütz had never met Ernstberger, he was to use a series of agreed-upon recognition phrases when first arriving – Schütz: 'Kind regards from Charlotte.' Ernstberger: 'Is she still in Manchester?' Schütz: 'No, she has gone home.'[34]

PREPARATION FOR THE MISSION

Schütz's mission to Ireland was cancelled in July 1940 and he was sent to the Abwehr Leitstelle in Paris (the Hotel Lutetia) in August to prepare for a mission directly against England. At the same time, he recruited a Frenchman named de Buisson to work for Abwehr I-M, though this was later abandoned. He was surprised in September when he received another change of orders: the Irish mission was back on and he would return to his training for that assignment. His new controller at I/Wi was Hauptmann Schauenburg (a.k.a. Miller and Dr Hans Lorentz).[35]

Like many Irish-bound agents before him, Schütz met with Oscar Pfaus at the Fichte-Bund headquarters in Hamburg. Schütz wanted the names of contacts in the Irish Free State. Pfaus passed this request up through channels, but the request came back disapproved. Abwehr headquarters in Berlin refused permission for Schütz to have any contact with the IRA, for any reason.[36] If Schütz had any IRA contact names and addresses, they are not evident from his operational instructions.

However, Schütz did carry the names of other Irish citizens. On a separate piece of paper tucked into his wallet, he had written 'Giollachriost O'Broin, 2 Ballygall Road, Kimmage'. When contacted by a suspicious G2, Mr O'Broin said that he had visited Hamburg in 1937 as part of a group of Irish singers led by a Miss Cadwell. The trip had been organized by the Nazi organization Kraft durch Freude ('strength through joy') and a Mr Hans Blau was the tour guide. Blau was actually an officer at the Abwehr's Hamburg Ast. No other evidence was produced that further implicated Mr O'Broin, but it is unusual that Schütz would be given his name unless the Abwehr had some reason for believing him sympathetic.[37] Schütz also had the names of 'Mr Breacht' and 'Miss Reeves'. Breacht was believed to be the name of an Irish national who had unsuccessfully attempted to contact the German Legation in Dublin, and Miss Reeves was believed to be the sister of Irish renegade Dan Reeves, who was working for the Germans in Hamburg. Schütz later said that this was the name of a young lady, an acquaintance in Germany, but G2 did not believe this, concluding that Dan Reeves was 'unlikely to have brought a sister to Germany, considering that he deserted his wife to follow a German governess there'.[38]

In a less sinister, but no less puzzling reference, the words 'Lamb Bros. Inchicore' were written on part of Schütz's ITA map of Ireland. Sure enough, the Lamb Brothers of Inchicore were real, but a brief investigation could find no link to suspicious activity.[39]

In the event that his radio link failed and he was unable to secure another transmitter, Schütz was to carry *G-Tinten* – the yellowish invisible ink – impregnated into the shoulder pads of his civilian suit coat. He received training in this from Hauptmann Werner von Raffey, the officer responsible for secret inks at the Hamburg Ast.[40]

Accompanied by Sonderführer Huckried from the Hamburg Ast, Schütz travelled to Amsterdam. The first attempt to reach Ireland in the specially modified He-111 went badly, and the aircraft was forced to return to base in the face of severe weather – underscoring the Luftwaffe's need for accurate weather forecasts. After a week's delay, Schütz was again prepared for departure. On the night of 12 March 1941, he was collected from the Amsterdamer Hotel by the chief of the Hamburg air intelligence section, Major Nikolaus Ritter and driven to the airfield.

His pilot on this mission was Oberleutnant Gartenfeld, who had earlier dropped Hermann Görtz. Schütz and his transmitter case were fitted into the bomb bay of the He-111 and the mission departed from the Schipol airfield at 2000 hours.

LANDING IN IRELAND

The flight to Ireland was to take approximately three hours, and there was broken cloud cover over the drop zone. Gartenfeld cut his engines at 3,000 metres and glided noiselessly to an altitude of 2,000 metres before giving Schütz the jump commands, 'Achtung, fertig, los!' Schütz and his case were rigged to a static line on the inside of the aircraft and, on command, he jumped through the open space in the belly of the Heinkel and into the empty sky below. Schütz had never before made a parachute jump, but his first effort was not too bad. He was disoriented after hitting the ground and came to with blood on his face – from a nosebleed. He had been wearing a parachute helmet and overalls when he jumped (he would later claim to have been wearing his uniform tunic). He quickly separated himself from the parachute harness and buried the parachute and helmet.[41]

But before Schütz could even leave the area, he had been spotted. He noticed the figure of a man standing near a house, seemingly looking directly at him. Though he watched him for several minutes, the farmer did nothing and eventually went back inside his house.[42] Schütz now needed to discover where he was. He had two compasses and an ITA map of

Ireland, but neither was of any great use in total darkness. If all had gone well with Oblt Gartenfeld's navigation, he should be in the vicinity of Newbridge, about twenty miles from Dublin. Prior to departure, it had been agreed that if stopped by police, he should say that he was headed from Dublin to Naas, but that his car developed a mechanical problem and that he was merely walking home. Unfortunately for Schütz, Oberleutnant Gartenfeld had been slightly off target – by about 100 kilometres. Rather than landing, as planned, in County Kildare, Schütz was actually in County Wexford, and far from any semblance of a safe house.

Schütz walked for a short while and eventually rested for several hours. He still had no idea of his position, but shortly after daybreak he noticed a sign reading 'New Ross 10 Miles'. All road signs were supposed to have been taken down since the previous January– they might assist belligerent parachutists like Schütz –but this one had been overlooked. Schütz scanned his map of the Kildare area, not seeing any town names that even remotely looked like New Ross. Folding his map away, he happened to glance down and saw New Ross near the bottom of the map, not in Kildare, but in County Wexford.[43] He had landed near the village of Taghmon, between New Ross and Wexford town, and. had a three-day walk ahead of him before reaching the safety of Unland's flat in Merrion Square.

As the morning wore on, Schütz at last began to see other people out on the road. He exchanged greetings with a woman on a bicycle, and asked a boy with a donkey cart for a lift in the direction of Dublin. The boy was going the other way and declined. The woman on the bicycle turned out to be an important individual, but not in the way Schütz might have hoped. She had been on her way to work at the Garda station at Carrickbyrne, and reported seeing the stranger to the duty sergeant.[44] According to her account, the stranger was on the New Ross/Wexford road, heading towards Wexford.

Schütz, who decided to head for Wexford and take a bus or train to Dublin, had meanwhile been taking another break under a hedge by a field bordering the road. When he emerged at approximately 1220 hours, he noticed two men cycling past. One happened to turn and catch a glimpse of the stranger out of the corner of his eye. The two men, Garda Sergeant Fullam and Garda R. Fitzpatrick, who had been alerted by the earlier report, turned their bicycles around and stopped Schütz.

With their suspicions aroused by his statement of walking home to Dublin from Naas, one of the Gardaí drew his attention to Schütz's case. He asked Schütz if he might happen to be in the haberdashery trade. Schütz, not knowing this particular vocabulary word, said that he was. The Gardaí then asked him to open his case and see if he had a button to replace one missing on his tunic. With that request, Schütz knew the game was up. When he opened the case, the Gardaí immediately saw the transmitter, money, microscope, and the German's lunch: salami and a bottle of cognac; Schütz was placed under arrest.

SCHÜTZ IN CUSTODY

Though the Gardaí were not armed and Schütz still had a parachute knife, he made no attempt to resist arrest or to attack the officers. Instead, he accompanied them back to Sean Rochford's pub in Taghmon, the Gardaí walking their bicycles alongside Schütz. The officers kindly bought Schütz sandwiches and Guinness while one of them phoned the Garda station for a car. He freely talked with the Gardaí, admitted being a German and landing by parachute at 2230 the previous evening.[45] On the walk back to Taghmon, Schütz had his first experience of Irish humour. When he asked one of the Gardaí what he thought would happen to him, the officer replied: 'Don't worry, we'll hang you, that's all.' The jest was lost on an already dismayed German agent.[46]

When the other Gardaí arrived by car, Schütz accompanied them to the spot where he had buried his overalls, parachute and steel helmet (near Yoletown) by a stream. He was unable to find the uniform tunic he insisted that he was wearing. A military shovel was later found in the same area, but the tunic never turned up.[47] Schütz was taken by car to the Bridewell jail and transferred, briefly, to Arbour Hill prison on 15 March 1941. When he arrived at the Bridewell, Schütz took the opportunity to use the latrine and disposed of his supply of invisible ink. Since all his possessions were confiscated, he was allowed to buy replacement toilet articles from the money seized when he was arrested. The Gardaí made an inventory of his possessions and eventually notified G2 of Schütz's arrival.[48]

Though Schütz freely admitted to being a German parachutist, he did not provide the Irish interrogators with his correct name. When he first arrived in New Ross, he kept to his story about being Hans Marschner and, according to an Irish Army officer, maintained that he was born in Ludovig, German South West Africa.[49] G2 soon learned the truth, but Schütz maintained the Marschner alias until the end of the war, to the extent that even letters from his family were addressed to Hans Marschner – and his parents accepted mail addressed to them as Herr and Frau Marschner, and signed their letters as such. Schütz correctly identified his rank as Wachtmeister, a grade of sergeant in the mounted artillery; his G2 personal entry file does not reflect that he carried or wore the standard German identity disc.[50]

Once in Dublin, Schütz was subjected to a more professional interrogation, this time by Commandant Eamon de Buitléar and 'Captain Grey' – actually Dr Richard Hayes. Both spoke German, Hayes particularly, and they had many questions for the disoriented German parachutist. Asked about his Hersolt/Wetzlar microscope, Schütz replied that he was an avid amateur botanist. This did not fool the G2 officers who soon discovered the contents of Schütz's microdot instructions. If the microscope was not enough of a clue on its own, the newspaper clippings that he carried were sufficient to arouse doubt. They appeared to be totally innocent: an advertisement for the Green Park Hotel; testimonial letters about the efficacy of Aspro Medicated Tablets; a review of the four latest pamphlets in the 'Oxford Series'.[51] It was inconceivable that a spy on an operational mission would parachute onto potentially hostile territory complete with a glowing recommendation for Aspro tablets.

The interrogators further asked him about IRA contacts and told Schütz about Wilhelm Preetz and Walter Simon, who had also carried transmitters similar to his. As an indication of his lack of mission preparation, this was the first that Schütz had heard of either one of these two earlier agents.[52] After reviewing Schütz's personal effects, the officers asked about the photograph he had in his wallet. He said that it was a picture of his Abwehr supervisor at Hamburg, Dr Lorenz (an alias of Hauptmann Schuenburg at I/Wi). It was in fact, a passport photograph of Werner Unland, with whom the G2 officers were already acquainted. Further confirmation about the relationship between 'Marschner' and Unland came to light when Dan Bryan noticed that a piece of paper Schütz carried, with a lip-stick impressed kiss, was of the same type that Unland had previously sent in messages to Barcelona. The obvious conclusion was that this was supposed to serve as an identification mark between the two spies. It was also the first indication that 'Marschner' was really Unland's pen pal, Günther Schütz.[53] Ironically, one reason that Schütz stayed with the fiction of being Marschner was to avoid implicating Unland. It didn't work; Unland was arrested on 21 April 1941.

Schütz, age 29 at the time of his arrest, had a 17-year-old girlfriend in Bremen, Lisselotte 'Lilo' Henze, and he carried four photographs of her in his transmitter case. One of his first requests was for the Red Cross to notify her that he was safe and unharmed.[54] Unusually, Frederick Boland at the Department of External Affairs was in favour of suppressing all of Schütz's outgoing mail. G2's Colonel Archer pointed out that the other internees were allowed mail privileges, after censorship, and that there was no logical reason for treating Schütz any differently.[55]

His mail was eventually forwarded, but not all of it; sealed letters to his girlfriend and parents were still in his file at the Military Archives, some almost sixty years after the fact. That the German Minister Dr Hempel regarded Schütz with caution is revealed in an otherwise small incident from August 1941. Schütz had written a letter to Hempel asking for the loan of some German book from the legation library. Secretary of External Affairs Joseph Walshe personally took the letter to Hempel. According to Walshe's account, 'Herr Hempel read the letter in my presence and said at once that he would prefer not to have direct communication of any kind with Marschner ... he thought it would be just as well if Marschner was not told that it was he who supplied the books'.[56] Walshe was clearly puzzled by the reaction, but he needn't have been; Hempel seemed to view Schütz – or at least what Schütz knew about him – as dangerous. His future contact with the German agent was not destined to be pleasing for either party.

Though initially reluctant to reveal anything to G2, Schütz overcame his shyness and was soon providing a fairly accurate and thorough picture of life at the Hamburg Ast. He discussed Unland, Pfaus and the key Abwehr personnel connected with his training and employment; however, he falsely maintained that he was merely delivering the transmitter to a German officer who operated in England and that this officer was supposed to report on bomb damage from Luftwaffe attacks. Schütz also said he was supposed to radio Hamburg-Wohldorf on reaching Unland. It is possible that he was supposed to provide a replacement transmitter for Görtz, but this seem unlikely in the face of later, more verifiably truthful statements by Schütz, and the fact that he received intensive weather training for that exact mission. Another, more likely possibility was that he was supposed to work in concert with Görtz in Northern Ireland, although Schütz never raised this point himself in interviews with G2 or in post-war statements. He did, however, attempt to smuggle a message to Görtz from prison, which was supposed to be sent out on Görtz's transmitter. The message was signed 'Rothmensch' – a clear indication that Görtz would have reason to know about the Schütz's discarded alias. Curiously, Schütz had acquired this false name after Görtz left on his mission.[57]

Schütz remained at Arbour Hill for slightly over a month and then was transferred to Sligo jail and finally lodged in Mountjoy Prison. He was interviewed several times during this period, and in post-war interviews he seems to have had the idea that his G2 interrogators in Arbour Hill were playing one German prisoner off against the other; taking what Schütz said and then reporting it to Hermann Görtz in another cell. Schütz used this as the beginning of the deterioration of relations between himself and Görtz. There was only one problem: it never happened. Schütz was transferred from Arbour Hill in April 1941; Görtz was not arrested until November. Schütz himself admits that he never actually saw the other German during this period – 'they made sure that he could not contact me'.[58] This seems to be yet another carefully orchestrated G2 deception plan that had the desired effect and prompted the prisoner to talk.

WERNER UNLAND: THE ABWEHR'S MAN IN DUBLIN

Werner Unland certainly owed his arrest to the landing of Günther Schütz, but he had attracted the attention of the Irish and English authorities much earlier. In a world infatuated with the idea of the 'master spy' Unland remains very much a humbug, his sole contribution to the German intelligence war being the scale of his fraud, and his negligible contribution to the secret war is his only legacy.

Very little is known of Unland's background. He was born in Hamburg on 6 August 1892, and it is believed that he served in the Uhlan (German lancers) regiment during the First World War.[59] He arrived in Britain in 1929 and had a British registration certificate issued on 14 June that year. Prior to his arrival in England, and at a time and place undetermined, Unland met an Englishwoman named Muriel Dugarde in 1928, and they married in September 1930. Mrs Unland had relatives in Hendon, and it was suspected that Unland returned to England to take advantage of this family connection. Mrs Muriel Unland did not work, but had briefly been a child actress at the age of ten and thus had skills that would later prove useful.[60] Her husband was an agent for German textile firms and a trader in hardware, ribbon and cotton twine, but he soon became an agent of a different sort. While on a visit to Germany, Unland was recruited by Hauptmann Dierks of Hamburg Ast section I-M and was controlled by Dr Praetorius of section I/Wi. He was asked to forward any reports of interest on industrial or technical matters in exchange for a monthly payment of £25.[61] On his return to England, Unland became the manager of a notional company called Ferrum Stock Services Ltd, registered with British authorities in 1938.[62]

From an investigation conducted subsequent to Unland's decision to move to Ireland, it was established that Ferrum Ltd was a front, and never engaged in commerce of any kind. The physical address of the business was 14 Cursitor Street, London, but it was actually a room rented from the General Office Agency. Mr E.C. Wheatley, the manager of the General Office Agency, remembered Unland well when he was later questioned by the police. Unland said that he was Swedish, and Wheatley remarked on the lack of business activity from the rented office. In January 1939, Unland visited Hamburg, and on 26 August he received a payment of £40 from Kol & Co., on the orders of P. Straaten – identical to the earlier Abwehr payments made to Walter Simon in 1938.

For reasons that are not entirely clear, the Unlands suddenly left London and arrived in Dublin on 29 August, leaving behind a total of £96 18s.6d. in various debts and one step ahead of a worthless cheque charge.[63] Unland had been to Ireland earlier, having opened an account at the Northern Bank, Grafton Street in July 1939. Unland told Mr Wheatley that he would be out of town for a short time and asked that any mail for him be forwarded to his home at 36 Smithfields, Hendon. In actuality, this was his mother-in-law's address, and it was soon apparent that the Unlands would not be returning to England voluntarily. Upon arrival in Dublin, the couple checked into the Royal Marine Hotel, Dún Laoghaire. They did not stay long at the Royal Marine, and moved to the Gresham Hotel, where they remained until 30 April 1940.[64] The Unlands were conspicuous only by the fact that they would not socialize with any of the other guests and went to extraordinary lengths to keep to themselves.[65] While staying at the

Gresham, Unland attempted to find a new home. They approached Mr Charles Archer about renting a house at 22 Ely Place, Dublin and gave the address of Ferrum Stock Services Ltd as a reference, probably guessing that Mr Archer would not go to the trouble of checking. He did. When Mr Wheatley in London received the letter addressed to Ferrum, he opened it, not having heard from Unland in more than a month and with Unland's back rent yet to be collected. Wheatley realized that Unland was in Dublin and promptly notified the police.

Unland was registered as a German national and his unexplained disappearance at the outbreak of war worried British security officials. Detective Constable Walton arrived at 36 Smithfields, Unland's last address, and happened to stumble upon an elderly lady packing boxes. Inquiring, DC Walton learned that he was talking to Mrs Dugarde, Muriel Unland's mother, that the Unlands had gone away, but the older woman said she did not know their location. This was slightly silly, since she was obviously packing the Unlands' possessions and after admitting she had forwarded mail to them, Mrs Dugarde said that she had several letters yet to post, but that these were at her home at 86 Vivian Avenue. She agreed to allow DC Walton to look at the letters and get the address, but angrily replied that it would not be possible to see him until 5 October. When Walton arrived at Mrs Dugarde's home as arranged, she showed him some mail that had arrived on 4 October, but denied having any other letters. According to DC Walton's report, Mrs Dugarde was 'obviously comfortable about lying to the police'.[66]

With a working address for Unland at the Gresham Hotel, the Metropolitan Police passed the investigation over to the Irish, and the Garda Detective Branch (Special Section) took over the surveillance of Werner and Muriel Unland. The highly effective Detective Sergeant Michael J. Wymes, who was later to become the Garda Commissioner, led this division of the Irish police. Wymes's reports, which were both thorough and sometimes humorous, provide a day-by-day record of Unland's activities before his eventual arrest.

Though Unland looked to be every bit the stereotypical rotund, balding civil-servant, his romantic life, in no way confined to Mrs Unland, would be the envy of many more physically attractive men. In addition to using the premises of the Northern Bank for his more routine monetary transactions, Unland also received personal mail at this address. While much of it consisted of material concerning espionage, he also maintained an active correspondence with a number of women overseas. In a letter received in December 1939 at the Northern Bank, a Mrs Anna Hart of The Hague wrote to Unland that 'what I am missing is my big comfortable bed. I am longing for it and other things too. I hope you do the same.'[67] Not put off by the incidental fact that Unland was married, Mrs Hart later added 'I am only living for the time when we can be together again'.[68] Unland also maintained an equally passionate long-distance relationship with a Fraulein Hildegarde Schlattau.[69]

The Unlands moved to their new address at 46 Merrion Square on 4 April 1940, where they occupied an apartment on the first floor.[70] The Garda searched this address in May, but nothing of interest was discovered. While still at the Gresham Hotel, Unland started his regular correspondence with German Intelligence. Following the outbreak of war and the departure of most of Ireland's German colony on the *Cambria*, there was a lack of adequate supervision for German agents still in the field, which meant that no one in authority could properly investigate whether reports were at all accurate. Unland used this loophole to his short-term advantage. In a real way, he was the German version of Graham Greene's character in *Our Man in Havana*: he succeeded in convincing a remote German Intelligence headquarters that he had a fully functional network established in Ireland. The problem for German Intelligence was that Unland's network was wholly notional and that his skill in deception worked not against Germany's enemies but rather their own war effort. In a broad sense, Unland's messages can be classified into several different categories: whining requests for money, fictional descriptions of his intelligence contacts and attempts to dissuade the Germans from sending to Ireland more agents, who could expose his tissue of deception.

THE MESSAGES

Beginning in November 1939, Unland was addressing mail to the Dansk Import and Export Co., PO Box 106, Copenhagen, Denmark. This was actually an Abwehr LLD (live letter drop) under the guise of a legitimate business. Unknown to Unland, who took only minimal precautions with security, his correspondence was being intercepted and copied by the Garda and later Irish Military Intelligence. His first message read: 'Mr Ryan, the buyer from Harland and Wolff, requires your present prices for a repeat order of the machine tools delivered earlier this year.' Unland's code, referred to in the trade as a 'jargon code', is somewhat difficult to decipher. The outward meaning would seem to suggest that someone in Northern Ireland had earlier received a shipment of arms from Germany, but this is not conclusive.[71] In late November, Unland sent a number of letters to his Danish drop talking about a contract proposal for Lux and Palmolive toilet soap. He repeatedly used the word 'tablets', leading Irish Intelligence to suspect that he was actually referring to ammunition. A December letter to the same address, speaking of orders for 'bacon and butter' is equally ambiguous: 'If there are any orders to fill for your Belgian clients, please let me have the details, as this could be very well attended to from here.' This too could refer to orders for weapons. In his letters to Germany, Unland repeatedly mentions his 'contacts' in Northern Ireland

and states that he will be out for several days on 'buying trips' and meeting the 'clients'. This no doubt pleased the people at Abwehr, but they had no idea that during the time in question, Unland never left his apartment at 46 Merrion Square. In an early assessment of Unland prepared for G2, the Garda concluded that

> It would appear that Unland is an elderly pagan, extremely fond of himself, who adventured in younger days, but came to live in Ireland mainly to save his own skin ... He speaks of 'trips' when it is known from Garda reports that he has not left his rooms, and 'friends' when from the same source it appears that he had no acquaintances whatsoever. He has all the average German's contempt for and impatience with Ireland.[72]

Unland continually had to remind his masters at Abwehr to forward his cheques. In the era before direct bank deposits, Unland depended on these cheques, drawn on a number of banks in different countries, as his only source of income. His usual monthly payment from Abwehr was in the amount of £24 15s.10d. (posted from both London and Sweden) and on at least one further occasion, a £40 payment from Kol & Co. in Amsterdam. In his letter to 'Dansk' in January 1940, Unland mentioned that 'the Technical director, of whose arrival I had been advised with your letter of December 9th 1939, has not turned up so far'. This could conceivably be a reference to Ernst Weber-Drohl, who landed in Ireland in February 1940.[73] Unland continues in this same letter to complain, asking that more attention should be paid to 'remitting my commissions regularly'. Though he complained, Unland continued to string the Abwehr along with tales of espionage success: 'Our clients in Northern Ireland are clamouring for the prices for the repeats for the machine tools. ... I really expect very good and numerous orders as well as important new business.'[74]

Irish Intelligence and Garda officers were puzzled on a few occasions when Unland made bank deposits in cash seemingly without receiving cheques from abroad. It was suspected, but never established, that he might have been paid by a local source, the German Legation at Northumberland Road. Despite what they would later claim – a claim de Valera would later support – the German Legation was involved in the active support of espionage operations in Ireland. While Dr Hempel did this job with very little enthusiasm or competence, he did act as a clearing house for information passed to Germany and for Abwehr communications to the agents through the Foreign Ministry communication channels. Beginning in October 1940, Unland's reports began to refer to the 'US Head Office'. For example, in a letter of 7 October he asked: 'Could you please very kindly arrange for our (US) Head Office to accept my bill for November till January 1941?' In another instance he wrote: 'Will you please see to this [payment] for us and cable the (US) Head Office?' Similarly, 'I can always send copies of my letters to the (US) Head Office'. Irish Intelligence was convinced that 'US Head Office' meant German Legation in Dublin; 'our friends at H Office' was the Abwehrstelle in Hamburg; 'my family' meant the British; and that 'contracts' was jargon code for reports. As an example, Unland wrote on 12 February 1941 to Schütz that 'contracts have been sent direct to the HQ (in the USH) as arranged'. In addition to showing that Unland was very unimaginative when it came to communications security, it points to the participation of the German Legation in his activities.

Unland apparently began to get concerned when in February and March 1940 he began to receive correspondence from his new handler, Anderson. Anderson kept inviting Unland to a meeting on the continent or, alternatively, suggested sending a representative to Ireland. Unland responded: 'Owing to local conditions, I do not feel justified to ask for a further increase in the staff, as suggested by you during January/February and early March.' Unland signed this letter as 'Walsh'. In a series of letters, Unland did his level best to prevent another agent being sent to examine his operation. However, the Abwehr did send 'a representative from the firm' to see Unland – but Walter Simon was arrested before he could make contact.[75]

In June 1940, Unland received a message from 'Schmidt' instructing him to send any future correspondence to Günther Schütz via Barcelona, since 'you cannot communicate with Tafelli.' This was the initial connection between Unland and his Abwehr controller, Schütz.

Unland's movements were closely watched, as were his banking transactions, telephone calls, mail and purchases at local stores. The Garda were puzzled when the Unlands (both Werner and Muriel) began buying large amounts of clear nail polish. The theory was that since this product contains acetone, it might be used for some kind of secret writing, but this was never proven.[76] Unland usually left his apartment only to visit the bank or on shopping trips. He did visit the Ulster Bank on O'Connell Street and went to the floor which contained the offices of M. Devlin and Co. Ltd and the Leipzig Fair, but no connection was ever positively established. Like Görtz before him, Unland apparently could not resist the patriotic appeal and took his dirty clothes to the Swastika Laundry.[77] That both Unlands were involved in pseudo-espionage was beyond doubt; both sent letters to themselves on several occasions to check to see if their mail was under surveillance.[78]

Unland's fate was decided on 13 March 1941 with the arrival in Ireland of Günther Schütz by parachute. In the form of microdot instructions, he carried Unland's name and address, a sample of the paper used by Unland in his letters to Schütz in Barcelona, and Unland's passport photograph in his wallet. According to the instructions, Schütz was supposed to give Unland $300 in six monthly instalments as well as a new recognition code. It is assumed that Schütz was sent on the mission to Ireland specifically because of his earlier contact with Unland and the trust placed in Unland's representations about his Irish network.

Unland was arrested at 1430 hours on 21 April in Clare Street, Dublin, while walking with his wife. She returned to the apartment with two detectives, who executed a search warrant at that time. They seized a briefcase with miscellaneous correspondence, a portable typewriter, papers relating to the Northern Bank account and the book *Secrets of German Espionage* by Bernard Newman, which dealt with codes, ciphers and communications. D/Sgt. Wymes interrogated Mrs Unland, but she did not reveal much. She was described as 'a shrewd type of person who was evidently prepared for questioning, and she was none too candid in her replies to questions'. Muriel said her husband was an agent for textile goods or firms (which conflicted with his account), and admitted sending the letter to her husband addressed to Unland c/o National Tourist bureau. Mrs Unland's purse was searched, revealing a receipt for £170 in jewellery from Messrs West and Co., Grafton Street, and cash in the amount of £60 in English £5 notes and two Irish £5 notes. Several of the Bank of England bills had sequential serial numbers.[79]

Unland himself was rather circumspect when questioned by the Garda. He admitted to writing the Dansk letters and the ones to Schütz – a minor confession since a forensic analysis of the typewriter had already matched his machine to the notes. When questioned about his curious financial transactions, he would only reply that both he and his wife brought money from England, but that neither had any idea how much the other had. Unland's responses to any other questions consisted of only three answers: 'It's a rather sad story for me'; 'I wouldn't be surprised'; and 'Everybody has his duty to do'. He maintained that the letters to Schütz were an attempt to get orders to and from the Dana Shoe Company of Copenhagen (which, he said, had an office in New York), apparently unaware that the Irish had already checked and discovered that there was no Dana Shoe Company.[80] Unland seems to have put little thought into his cover story.

He was eventually transferred to Arbour Hill prison and then to Athlone. It was decided not to intern Mrs Unland, though evidence strongly suggested that she aided and abetted her husband's espionage activities. When Mrs Unland was allowed to visit her husband at Arbour Hill, it was almost as if the two had rehearsed the scene. She seemed puzzled about his arrest and he explained that another person had entered Ireland illegally coincidentally in possession of Unland's passport photograph. Unland told his wife that he had no idea how this had happened and asked Muriel to contact the German Legation, which she did.[81]

Unland later became the spokesman for the other prisoners, which is generally thought to be because of his service in the First World War, which made him the only prisoner with prior, commissioned military experience before the capture of Hermann Görtz. Mrs Unland became a persistent source of complaint to the German Legation, demanding that they pay her a £30 monthly allotment while her husband was interned. After seeking approval from the Foreign Ministry, Dr Hempel agreed, paying Muriel Unland the sum of £30 a month.[82]

THE 'NORTHERN GROUP'

Schütz's arrival and Unland's arrest meant nothing to Hermann Görtz; he was not made aware of these events until after his capture. Görtz's previous attempts to flee had failed, and with any hope of escape temporarily on hold, Görtz was left with no alternative but to return to hiding in Ireland. In his later report to what he thought was the OKW, Görtz said that he decided to 'to work against England with my own organization. For more obvious reasons I shall not write in more detail about its operation, than that the experiment completely succeeded. ... When I was arrested I had just set up my own station for this organization ... until the erection of this station however success was more important than reporting success. To go to Northern Ireland myself was pointless.'[83] In his posthumous statements, he continued to elaborate on this theme of an 'organization' he set up to carry out espionage in Northern Ireland: 'The way was now clear for me to develop my own work in the Six Counties. I kept this absolutely separate from my contacts with the IRA. They knew nothing about it, and I managed to build up in the North an organization independent of, unknown to, and, I might say, undreamed of by my friends in Éire.'[84]

What then is the truth? Did Görtz, unknown to anyone, set up a secret intelligence-gathering and sabotage group in Northern Ireland, or was this Görtz's last fiction from beyond the grave? There are several facts to consider. The commander of G2 from 1941 onward, Colonel Dan Bryan, acknowledged that people had been sent to the North to collect military information, but that they possessed no military knowledge of their own and their reports were of little use and grossly exaggerated.[85] A junior IRA man named Brendan O'Boyle – later accidentally killed attempting to bomb Stormont in 1955 – was said to have mapped Ballymena army base and transmitted the information to Görtz.[86] Robert Fisk conducted an interview with Paddy Devlin in Belfast; Devlin remembered an IRA intelligence officer named Maguire who came to Belfast to collect military information. The local IRA were to list Belfast's ground defences and each IRA battalion logged the gun positions around the city, passing the details to the intelligence officers.[87] Helena Kelly, Maisie O'Mahony's cousin, was arrested in October 1941 with a 'comprehensive report on military forces and installations in Northern Ireland' – presumably based on the information culled from the Belfast IRA. The report, like the Plan Kathleen from 1940, was strictly an amateur intelligence-gathering attempt, and would have been of limited utility to the Abwehr.[88] Görtz's 'organization', such as it was, would appear to have been nothing more than a tiny and militarily inexperienced group attempting to gather information. At the time, separated from Hayes's mainstream IRA leadership, Görtz's organization consisted of little more than the Republican women and his radio operator, Anthony Deery – who lacked a working transmitter until July 1941.[89] Görtz would later note that he wanted to go to work in the North personally, but would have to do so in uniform, and complained that he could not get a proper Luftwaffe uniform made in Ireland.[90] In retrospect, the talk about a sabotage and intelligence group in Northern Ireland seems like a attempt by Görtz to justify his inaction and failure to achieve any of his specific mission objectives, to which neither his meetings with Major-General McNeill or his incidental contact with the Northern IRA related.

Following the failure of the Fenit escape, Görtz engaged in little constructive effort throughout the first half of 1941. His little circle was enlarged with the addition of the O'Farrell sisters, Bridie and Mary, who occasionally offered him a safe refuge and, in the process, developed a respectful adulation for the German officer. He also received financial support from Caitlín Brugha. The O'Farrell sisters, with assistance from Maisie O'Mahony, were involved in the purchase of another boat for Görtz: a blue, rubber, two-seater sailboat with an eight-horsepower engine. O'Mahony, identifying herself as Miss Duffy of Roseville, Cobh (actually the name of another cousin), and Bridie O'Farrell collected the boat. The price was £41 10s., but the boat was returned a few days later by O'Mahony and a man (probably Görtz himself), who said that the engine 'did not give satisfaction'.[91] Görtz was also singularly unlucky when it came to procuring other means of escape: 'I thought of an aircraft. We found out a Gypsy Moth which was almost capable of flight. I had flown this type in England. It seemed possible to get possession of her without using force ... but we found that the magneto was missing.'

Hayes, meanwhile, was still trying to assist Görtz. The IRA chief was simultaneously attempting to print and distribute an 'IRA Bond' as a way of raising money for the bankrupt organization. The bondholder would receive 3.5 per cent interest once 'six months after the Republic starts to function'. In a letter to Jim O'Donovan, Hayes also discusses Görtz: 'His biggest trouble is to get away. Can you help in this? As regards message, I am arranging alternative transmission of his messages, which I am sure will turn out all right. This is apart from his own set.'[92] Presumably Hayes meant the commission to Michael Kinsella to build a suitable transmitter for the German agent. In the same correspondence, Hayes also refers to something surprising – an ongoing liaison between the IRA and the Irish Army, in the person of Major General Hugo McNeill. 'I have had further information re/Hugo. Expect fuller details tomorrow and will send you an outline. I feel very satisfied that we did not jump at his previous offer. Will explain after full report is submitted.' Did Görtz actually manage to

(1) Admiral Wilhelm Canaris. Chief of the Abwehr and an opponent of Hitler (USNA).

(2) Liam Walsh, embezzler and German sympathizer who facilitated German contact with the IRA (IMA).

(3) James O'Donovan, Irish bomb expert and Abwehr liaison (IMA).

(4) Pre-war photograph of Seán Russell (IMA).

(5) Frank Ryan addressing a crowd in pre-war Ireland (Hermann Görtz).

(6) Frank Ryan, a youthful photo of the IRA radical in the 1920s (IMA).

(7) Frank Ryan on the cover of a Republican magazine. When this appeared he was near death in Germany (IMA).

(8) Stephen Held. He made one trip to Germany on behalf of the Abwehr and provided a safehouse for Hermann Görtz (IMA).

(9) Eda Pfaus and O'Donovan (Stephan).

(10) Hermann Görtz's official photograph (IMA).

(11) Marianne Emig, who accompanied Görtz to England in 1935 (IMA).

(12) Marianne Emig and Görtz (IMA).

(13) Görtz mug shot (IMA).

(14) Ernst Weber-Drohl in 1940 (IMA).

(15) Ernst Weber-Drohl in a publicity photo for his strongman act (NLI).

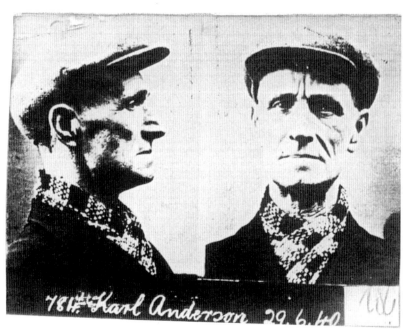

(16) Walter Simon (IMA).

(17) Wilhelm Preetz in his SA uniform, c. 1933 (BA).

(18) Preetz in Irish custody in 1940, note the less optimistic facial expression (IMA).

(19) Oscar Pfaus at the time of his mission to Ireland in 1939 (Stephan).

(20) Henry Obéd at the time of his arrest (IMA).

(21) Dieter Gärtner after his capture in July 1940 (IMA).

(22) Herbert Tributh after the collapse of 'Lobster' (IMA).

(23) Lilo Henze, Schütz's girlfriend; he carried three copies of this photograph to Ireland (IMA).

(24) Passport photograph of Werner Unland; Schütz carried a copy of this to Ireland in order to positively identify the rogue agent (IMA).

finally persuade Hayes to reconcile the IRA with certain elements in the Irish Army?

From the later testimony of Joseph Andrews and James Murtaugh, it would seem that Görtz and McNeill had at least one meeting together. In a statement from 1943, Murtaugh told of a meeting between Görtz, a mystery man, General O'Duffy, 'Charlie' and two Army officers at his home on Finglas Road.[93] Andrews related that a Molly Hyland Lawlor, an old girlfriend of McNeill, who had contacts through IRA man Pearse Paul Kelly, facilitated the liaison between McNeill and Görtz.[94]

ARREST OF STEPHEN HAYES

The Garda made a matter-of-fact report on the surprising events of 8 September: 'At about 12 o'clock yesterday the 8th instant, Hayes arrived at Rathmines Police Station with chains on his legs and a revolver in his hand. He was excited, in bad condition and stated that the IRA was about to shoot him.'[95] The arrest of Stephen Hayes on 30 June 1941 substantially changed the relationship between Görtz and the IRA. Long distrusted by the Belfast and Cork IRA brigades, Hayes had a drinking problem and the series of arrests in 1940 and 1941 led to the suspicion that Hayes had sold out the IRA. Prior to Hayes's arrest, Görtz apparently had some minor contact with some members of the Belfast group, notably Sean McCaughey, and his relationship with that segment improved in the aftermath of the *coup d'état*. McCaughey carried out Hayes's arrest. Hayes was beaten, court-martialled and sentenced to death, in short order, was granted a stay of execution for several months while he wrote out his 'confession' in a Rathmines safe house.[96] The Northern IRA clearly felt that 'proof' of Hayes's treachery would be necessary before taking the final decisive step. Hayes's brother-in-law, Lawrence de Lacy, was also kidnapped and beaten by his former IRA comrades, but eventually managed to escape.[97] A typed version of the confession was distributed by the 'caretaker IRA' in September, in both a longer and a redacted format. It purported to detail Hayes's double-cross of the IRA and his involvement with certain government ministers, principally Dr James Ryan, the Minister for Agriculture, and Thomas Derrig, the Minister for Education. Görtz's name also figured prominently.

It is difficult to assess Görtz's link, if any in the Hayes kidnapping. In his report to the OKW, Görtz later gave himself a prominent role in the affair:

> The IRA leaders, I believe that all three gentlemen were Northern Irishmen, explained to me that countless treacheries within the leadership of the IRA led again and again to Hayes, so that they had decided to arrest and try him. He had already made confessions and was now writing them down. [They asked] whether I had proofs [*sic*] against him ... I was thus asked if I wanted him shot. This question came as a great surprise to me. I asked for a few minutes

to think. They wanted to give the decision on Hayes' life into my hands. ... When the young IRA leaders asked what they should do they gave into my hands not nominally but practically the leadership of the IRA. I needed only to order the death of Hayes and I was their leader.[98]

Görtz's idea that the death of Hayes would lead to his taking over the IRA, is fanciful in the extreme. Like Caesar refusing the kingship of Rome, Görtz claimed that he magnanimously decided against taking over the IRA, but agreed to spare Hayes's life. 'The immediate shooting of Hayes would in fact make the carrying out of my intentions in Germany more difficult. ... I am convinced even to-day, that I could not have decided otherwise, so painful is the remembrance of that hour to me.'

FURTHER ESCAPE ATTEMPTS

Görtz was still determined to leave the country as soon as humanly possible, apparently concerned to get away before the Hayes matter was resolved one way or another. With the assistance of the O'Farrell sisters and Maisie O'Mahony, he purchased another boat, referred to as a 'canoe', equipped with an outboard motor. In July, Helena Moloney rented a hut in Brittas Bay, from where Görtz was planning to launch his escape bid. In the company of Bridget and Mary O'Farrell, their niece Evelyn O'Farrell and Maisie O'Mahony, he spent almost the entire month of August there, in preparation for his departure.[99] Görtz spent most days practising his nautical skills in Brittas Bay. The craft had a fuel radius of 500 kilometres. Because of the lack of electricity in Brittas Bay, Görtz could not bring his new transmitter, but did report his intention to embark through a message to Deery before he left. In the Abwehr II diary, they recorded receiving a distorted message from Görtz that he was leaving on 13 August in an attempt to make for the French coast.[100] The Abwehr could do little but inform the harbour authorities to possibly expect the waterlogged German. In any event, the message to the Abwehr was premature. He made an attempt to reach France, but his motor gave out and he had to make it back Brittas Bay by sail. Bad weather kept Görtz stationary for the remainder of August, but by early September he was prepared to depart again. Unknown to Görtz, the Abwehr was trying to resupply him with cash, and had made arrangements with the Foreign Ministry to have Hempel pay him £500. The Abwehr was supposed to mail the money to a letter-drop in London (Helge J. N. Moe, Spring Street Post Office, Waddington Lane), and it would then make its way to Hempel.[101] This plan was evidently abandoned.[102]

On 2 September, Görtz got as far as the Tuskar Rock lighthouse before his motor flooded and his boat began taking on water. He managed to return to Brittas Bay. He claimed later that a German aircraft had flown directly overhead while he was off the coast and later reappeared when he was again safe at Brittas Bay. Whether this really occurred is unknown, but Görtz's conclusion from the incident is curious: 'Some of my Irish friends pressed me to spread out my German [home-made swastika] flag. Then one of the aircraft would have landed and picked me up.' Görtz said that he did not do so because he did not want to expose the aircrew to danger. This has all the hallmarks of another fantasy; the Germans had not dispatched a plane or even notified the Luftwaffe of Görtz's planned departure which, in any case, they last believed was to be in the middle of August. By the next account of Görtz to appear in the Abwehr II diary, it seems clear that the German Intelligence service had made the decision to cut him loose: 'Agent Gilka reported by wireless that he abandoned his attempt to return from Ireland to France by cutter as his motor broke down. He asked whether an aircraft could be sent to collect him. Otherwise, on 20 September 1941, he would make another attempt to return by motor cutter. As dispatch of an aircraft could not be approved, further attempt by motor cutter was left to Gilka's discretion.'[103] As he had earlier to the IRA, Görtz was fast becoming more trouble than he was worth to the Abwehr.

From the Abwehr perspective, Görtz's messages – now that he could finally transmit them – were incomplete and seemed mainly concerned with his efforts to get home. Abwehr was forced to ask the German Legation for a clear report on the situation inside the IRA. Dr Veesenmayer complained that 'the details reported by Görtz were incomplete and contradictory. There was a general requirement to have clearer information.'[104] Görtz also became aware that complaints were being made about his effectiveness from IRA channels, probably through his mail addresses in Portugal and Spain – addresses that Görtz never seems to have utilized himself. 'These people had even dragged my private life and my friends through the mire. If I had not enjoyed the confidence of my superiors, I would have been dismissed from my duty in disgrace.'[105] Görtz never seems to have learned that his superiors continued to harbour doubts about both his performance and his state of mind.

There is another puzzle to consider when writing of Görtz's radio contact with Germany. Though Görtz speaks of sending messages and getting several responses from Germany during the period he could theoretically transmit – July to November 1941 – the hard evidence for that contact is lacking. British intercepts of Abwehr hand-ciphered messages, as opposed to the Enigma and Lorenz systems, reveal no Görtz messages to the Abwehr in the relevant period of time. Neither is there any traffic between the Abwehr Asts that even mentions Hermann Görtz. The Germans did acknowledge receiving a few messages, but stopped short of saying that they were transmitted by Görtz – they could have easily come through the Foreign Ministry traffic from Dublin to Berlin, assuming that Hempel would agree to send more messages, and he did appear willing to send what information came his way. Görtz was also not beyond telling lies about his activities or his mission, usually attempting to put a veneer on anything that suggested he was anything less than competent or thorough.

CONTACT WITH THE IRISH ARMY

In his report, Görtz said that he was approached by an Irishman with the offer to take him to France in a more powerful motorboat. Presumably this offer came from Charles McGuinness, but Görtz, who had been so desperate to leave, now decided to stay and pursue a new contact with the Irish Army.[106] This latest contact is thought to have been with Major-General McNeill, as the Murtaugh and Andrews testimony revealed. His contact with McNeill did produce a few items of interest:

> When I came into contact with the Irish officers we very quickly discovered that we had the same view on affairs. ... The officers told me they planned to make proposals to the Irish government that it should accept German help. As matters stood, they could not officially approach the German embassy on such a delicate question. The officers asked me what sort of German help might be possible. I replied that I was not in the position to answer that sort of question. However, if they put an aircraft at my disposal, I would be back in about fourteen days with the German High Command's answer. Thereupon, the officers said that an aircraft would be in readiness for me on and after a specified date.[107]

If true, these proposals from a rogue section in the Irish Army raise a number of problems. These negotiations were certainly beyond the scope of Görtz's mission. Indeed, he had been ordered to direct the IRA into military activity in Northern Ireland and specifically warned against interfering in Irish internal affairs, and certainly did not have the necessary authority to act as a roving ambassador for the OKW. For the Irish themselves, serious issues were raised. To invite German assistance, without government sanction, was tantamount to treason. Despite this, and G2's awareness of McNeill's actions, he never faced a court-martial or any other type of judicial sanction; quite the contrary. Why? McNeill commanded the Irish Army Second Division from 1941 to 1946 and retired honourably in the 1950s. The historical record shows that de Valera maintained a neutrality policy that generally favoured the Allies, and the idea of official permission for Irish Army contact with Germany from the Fianna Fáil government would seem ludicrous. The other possibility, and one which has been suggested, is that McNeill acted under Army orders to sound out the Germans – without the knowledge of the government – as a fall-back position in case the war went against the Allies. This hypothesis further suggests that General Michael Costello was conversely directed to be friendly and receptive to the Allied powers.[108]

Such an approach would have the effect of establishing prior relations with the victorious power, no matter which side that happened to be. No documentation exists to explain the mystery, yet there would seem to be few other reasons to clarify why McNeill was never censured for his dealings with Görtz and Hempel.

THE ARREST

As it happened, Görtz was never able to take advantage of his Irish Air Corps taxi. After meeting with the Army, he unsuccessfully attempted to convince the new IRA leader Pearse Paul Kelly of the wisdom of joining forces with reactionary elements in the Army. The IRA were also angered when they learned that Görtz had been pursing another Irish Army meeting through the intermediary of General Eoin O'Duffy. Introduced by Jim O'Donovan, Görtz and O'Duffy met on 1 November. Görtz viewed O'Duffy's Blueshirts as being analogous to the SA 'Storm Troopers' of Nazi Germany but noted that 'his [O'Duffy's] movement lacked the believing storm-man who conquers the street when it is disputed to him, whilst the IRA lacked equipment and leading [*sic*]'. Görtz reported that O'Duffy said that 'he started his Blue Shirt movement unfortunately too early; Ireland was not yet ripe ... he had fought his whole life long for a Christian, free Ireland. This goal could be reached only by means of a military dictatorship.' O'Duffy agreed that the government would never take action and that Görtz should get in touch with the Army, where he would find a more sympathetic welcome. O'Duffy then put Görtz in touch with the Army officers who made the offer of a return flight home.[109]

Görtz claimed that he made arrangements to see a 'high Catholic dignitary' in an attempt to mediate between the Army and the IRA. Görtz's sympathizers later maintained that the person involved was Cardinal MacRory, Archbishop of Armagh and Primate of Ireland.[110] Görtz never had the chance to make this meeting.[111]

After returning from Brittas Bay, he stayed for a time with the O'Farrells and later moved to the house owned by Hugh O'Neill – a Coras na Poblachta supporter and another ex-Hospitals Trust employee. His move was made none too soon: Gardaí served a search warrant on the O'Farrell house at 7 Spencer Villas on 24 September and discovered a $100 bill under a bronze figurine on the mantelpiece. The O'Farrell sisters were arrested, but revealed nothing useful in interrogation. Mary O'Farrell's daughter Doreen was also questioned, being described by Gardaí as 'a feckless individual, not likely to be trusted'. If the detectives needed another piece of evidence to be sure they were on the right trail, when they returned the next day to question the O'Farrells' lodgers, they found an envelope under the front door scraper, marked 'Doc – most important and urgent'. It contained several typed pages of the Hayes confession dealing with Görtz and Agriculture Minister Ryan. A simultaneous raid on the Coffey house uncovered a novel with 'Read 1 Fby 1941' in 'a Germanic script'. In November, Görtz moved to the house of Mr Patrick J. Claffey, at 1 Blackheath Park, Clontarf. Görtz was sheltered here with the assistance of Joseph Andrews, who was connected to Patrick Claffey's son John Joseph.[112] Though warned by Pearse Paul Kelly that the house was unsafe, Görtz returned here after a brief spell away. He had been at this address on 17 September, but left after he heard strange noises outside and became convinced that he was about to be kidnapped by the British Secret Service.[113]

On the evening of 27 November 1941, Gardaí raided the Clontarf house and captured Hermann Görtz. According to one report, the police were actually conducting a raid on an adjacent property when a woman opened the back door to number 1, looked around anxiously, and then closed the door. When the police investigated, they found Görtz sitting in the living room, smoking his pipe.[114] Placed in custody, the German was shouting all the way to the waiting car: 'You are arresting the best friend Ireland has ... your government know [*sic*] why I am here, there is no room for a military attaché – that's why I am here.'[115]

Pearse Kelly was not any luckier. As the de facto IRA chief, he had some contact with Görtz in the previous few months, and had also agreed to accompany Görtz back to Germany to speed up the promised shipments of arms and money to the IRA. He mentioned the trip to Seán MacBride and Maurice 'Moss' Twomey, who strongly disagreed with his planned journey. On the night of 27 November Kelly became concerned that Görtz had returned to the Clontarf address and went over to warn him:

> The house was ablaze with lights when I got there, and although this was unusual enough to have alerted me, I was too annoyed with Görtz to suspect anything, so I rapped impatiently at the door. It was opened a few inches by a woman who said the owner was ill in bed. I asked curtly where was H. and immediately the door was flung open. Two detectives appeared with drawn revolvers, and before I knew what happened I was pulled inside the house.

Kelly was initially mistaken for Anthony Deery, Görtz's radio operator, but the detectives quickly realized their error and placed him under arrest.[116] In *Spies in Ireland*, Enno Stephan raises the possibility that Kelly was the actual target of the raid and that Görtz might have been discovered accidentally.[117] There is no mention in the Görtz files as to how the Special Branch detectives knew to search the house at Blackheath Park.

Görtz was searched and he was found to be unarmed. His possessions included a diary, set of keys, his Luftwaffe *Soldbuch* (in the name of Leutnant der Reserve Kruse) which enclosed a photo of Frank Ryan, his Wehrmacht identity disc, and £25.[118] At Dublin's Arbour Hill Prison, Görtz continued to maintain that his name was Heinz Kruse, though he soon dropped the pretence.[119]

Görtz's possessions did not reveal much in the way of intelligence information, but his diary entries were an indication of his priorities – escape and women:

26 August [1941]	Barometer rising
27 August	The First Attempt
2 September	The Great Attempt
10 September	The Lonely Rider
13 September	Decision No. 1 – Happiness
16 September	The Mystery Man
17 September	The Dream Lady
18 September	Vidi – girlfriend
26 September	**PHILEMON VIA FAIRY**

WEBER-DROHL RETURNS

Even after his miraculous release from custody in 1940, Ernst Weber-Drohl was still engaged in what G2 euphemistically termed 'suspicious activities'. Their postal intercept order netted an interesting item in March 1941. Weber-Drohl mailed an Easter card to his family ('to Mrs Drohl and my daughter Gusti-Weber'), but he addressed it to Signor Luigi Vigani, Lorenzo-Calla-della-Madonetta 5141, Venezia, Italia. Glued to the hidden underside of the card was a newspaper clipping from his previous Irish court appearance.[120]

In May 1941, Jim O'Donovan received a letter from the circus strongman that detailed arrangements for a booking at Dublin's Royal Theatre and Queen's Theatre, but Weber-Drohl needed financial help in order to build the necessary platform for his act. He wondered if O'Donovan would lend him £12 in the meantime. He then mentioned that he was planning a tour of the provinces with his strongman act. At the end of his letter, Weber-Drohl also noted that the Gardaí were still watching him. In this supposition he was quite correct; his room at the Fitzpatrick Hotel (38 Westland Row) was searched under warrant on 23 May. Nothing incriminating was discovered.[121] Weber-Drohl moved to an apartment at 26 Pearse Street in November. At this time, he was in contact with several Italian nationals, some of whom had previous contact with Wilhelm Preetz.[122]

In a second, undated letter to Jim O'Donovan, Weber-Drohl told how the plans for his act had run into a snag. He had the possibility for a four-week engagement at the Royal Theatre and the Queen's Theatre, and then a travelling show to Limerick and Cork. He had engaged a young lady named Mary Flanagan (Aghadreena, Crosskey, County Cavan) as his partner and had already printed the publicity photos for the act. Flanagan unexpectedly came to him and said her mother was sick and that she must return home for a short time. When she did not return or make contact, Weber-Drohl was left stranded: there was not enough time to find a new partner before the opening date. He suspected a 'police intrigue'. Someone, according to Weber-Drohl, had been spreading stories about him to Mary's mother: 'Some dirty Blackguard done that dirty trick and blackmailed me to her mother.'[123] Mary herself wrote a short time later, explaining that she would have returned, but that her mother would not allow it. In an exchange of letters with Mother Flanagan, the older lady said that she had reports that Weber-Drohl had a bad character, and had also read the reports of his April court appearance (illegitimate children and so on). Weber-Drohl asked O'Donovan to visit him at his apartment at 26 Pearse Street, first floor. He ended by saying that if he didn't answer the door, O'Donovan was only to say that he brought the photos.[124]

Characteristically, Weber-Drohl rebounded quickly from this adversity. According to a Garda surveillance report, 'Drohl visited Stradone to see his old partner Miss Flanagan who, however, apparently avoided him. Drohl "picked up" a dame on his way, Miss Nancy Brady ... and is getting her to influence Flanagan to write to him.'[125] A later Garda report added more detail: 'Drohl engaged a Nancy Brady (Drumkirk, Aghadreena, Stradone, Co. Cavan) for a job in his act.' At the time, Miss Brady was 17 years old.[126]

Mrs Flanagan's mother was right to worry about her daughter. Weber-Drohl seems not to have used Miss Brady for the act in Dublin, but instead contracted Mrs Rosaline Parker to do the work. Born in 1920, she had married Richard Parker, who was serving in the Royal Welsh Regiment. Her husband had been captured in North Africa and was an Italian prisoner of war. Her father, Hugh Bracken, was a corporal in the Irish Army, stationed at Portobello Barracks. In her later statement to G2, Mrs Parker was not clear about how she met Weber-Drohl, but in July 1941, he asked her father's permission for her to accompany the German on a trip to Baltinglass, where he was going to check on a theatre booking. Mrs Parker related how they both got drunk and awakened in the same bed, but she did not specifically remember having sex. Upon their return to Dublin, and at Weber-Drohl's urging, she took a room at 18 North William Street, where they met and had sex on a daily basis. Mrs Parker became pregnant in October 1941 and the child, Eithne Teressa Antoinette Bracken was born on 13 May 1942.[127] Her mother (Elizabeth Bracken) pretended that the child was hers, filed a false welfare claim, and even moved into the house on North William Street to maintain the pretence. This incident was first brought to the attention of G2 when Mrs Parker called the Garda detective branch on 4 June 1942 to complain that Weber-Drohl was harassing her.[128] Though of little use to the German espionage effort, Weber-Drohl remained free in Ireland until arrested on 22 January 1942, but the Department of Justice again intervened and he was subsequently freed by the order of S.A. Roche on 31 January.[129]

JOSEPH LENIHAN

Perhaps the strangest – and one of the most ineffective – episodes in the Abwehr's Irish operations occurred in July 1941 with the arrival of Joseph Lenihan. The Lenihan family name is well-known today due to several generations of distinguished political service, but few are aware of Joseph Lenihan's work with German Intelligence. Though Lenihan was not mentioned by Enno Stephan in *Spies In Ireland* (because his name did not occur in the Abwehr II war diary and was inexplicably not mentioned by any of the Abwehr sources that Stephan consulted), he is nonetheless an important part of the German espionage initiative in Ireland and likewise a character in the story of British counter-intelligence.

Born in Ennistymon, County Clare, Lenihan's exact date of birth is not recorded in the surviving documents, but it is known that he attended St Flannan's College in Ennis and that his performance there was impressive enough to earn a university scholarship to study medicine. According to his later statement to G2, he was an 'IRA associate' in 1921–2.[130] Though he did begin studying medicine in 1923, according to his brother Patrick, he 'chucked it up and studied for the Customs examination'. Lenihan passed the Customs exam and worked in that government department until 1931, when he was dismissed for an unspecified act of dishonesty. Not letting his dismissal stop his evident desire to re-enter the Irish civil service, he immediately took the employment clerks' exam, where he was placed second. Unfortunately, the bureaucracy that he wished to join worked against him and his earlier dismissal from the Customs service was revealed. Lenihan left Ireland shortly thereafter and went to America, but returned to Ireland in 1932 or 1933. The return to Ireland did not agree with him; he was convicted in July 1933 for creating a public disturbance and sentenced to fourteen days in jail. This was followed by a conviction in 1935 for forgery, for which he received a sentence of nine months in jail.[131] After he completed his sentence, Lenihan made his way to England and finally onto the island of Jersey, just in time for the German occupation of the island in July 1940.

Lenihan seemed to lack a specific destination, but his fortunes were about to change. He evidently attempted to escape from Jersey in a stolen boat and set sail for England, but the motor flooded and he was washed ashore on the Cotentin peninsula. He later recalled that he was interrogated for four days at Carteret, but was finally approached by two German officers who offered to release him from Gestapo custody and improve his prospects. Lenihan agreed. Taken to Paris, he was lodged until the end of 1940 near German Intelligence headquarters at 22 Avenue de Versailles, where he received tutors in various aspects of espionage. The Paris adventure also included a short spell in prison following a bar fight at Freddy's Bar in the Normandy Hotel.[132] Unusually, neither he nor his mission appear in the operational war diary for Abwehr II, nor are they mentioned in any contemporary German Intelligence documents. In all likelihood, Lenihan was recruited and trained by Abwehr I – the espionage division of German Intelligence.[133] Lenihan maintained that he attended a six-week wireless course in Paris and was also sent to The Hague for additional training, and even a two-day trip to Brussels. His salary was set at 1,000 francs a month – again unusual, in both currency and denomination.

Lenihan's apparent mission was to set up a weather reporting station in Sligo: he would be followed by trained meteorological personnel when the wireless station was up and running. As with the weather-reporting mission assigned to Günther Schütz, this one was also in support of the weather forecasting information needed by the Luftwaffe and the Kriegsmarine. Lenihan was scheduled to have landed in Ireland on 29 January 1941, but the heater in his high-altitude He-111 broke at 30,000 feet and the entire crew was frost-bitten, with the exception of the pilot. Lenihan lost several toes and damaged his hands and remained in the hospital until he was again ready for duty, in May 1941.[134] Further delays again postponed the mission and it was not until 18 July 1941 that he was dropped by parachute over Summerhill, County Meath. Lenihan's mission remained alive for six days. He was equipped with two transmitters, both a battery operated model and one which operated off direct current; £500; several vials of invisible ink and the powdered reagent for reading secret ink messages; a copy of *Pan in the Parlour* by Norman Lindsay; and, most surprisingly, a typed copy of his radio procedures and frequencies.[135] As a back-up, Lenihan was assigned two additional novels with which he could operate his book code: *A Windjammers Half Deck* and, appropriately, *The Loot of the Lazy*. In addition to the usual Abwehr agent accoutrements, Lenihan also had a Morse code device that could be attached to the vacuum tubes of a standard radio so that, he later said, it would convert the radio into an emergency transmitter.

Landing successfully, Lenihan headed off to Dublin and immediately set about contacting his family and friends. Irish Intelligence was not completely in the dark, since Lenihan's camouflage parachute was pulled out of a ditch by a cow and spotted by a Mrs McKay. She and her farmer husband became momentary media sensations. On 19 July, he deposited £370 at the Ulster Bank, Dublin, and bought several items of new clothing. He first located his brother Gerald, who worked in central Dublin. Not having seen his brother for almost three years, Lenihan was free to invent a plausible story about his sudden arrival in Ireland. He decided to claim that he had joined the merchant marine and had been torpedoed off Cadiz en route from Valparaiso, Chile. This unfortunate and imaginary incident helped explain the obvious damage to his hands and feet. Lenihan apparently decided to 'improve' his version of events when he finally located his brother Patrick, who was manager of the General Textiles (GENTEX) plant in Athlone. This time, he admitted to being on the

Channel Islands when they were overrun by German forces, but said he had escaped with the help of a sympathetic German NCO in a motorboat, and then somehow (he didn't try to explain how) he made it to England where he enlisted in the merchant marine until his ship was torpedoed off the Cape Verde Islands. He added that his new-found wealth was the result of back pay due from his maritime misadventure and that he had to report soon to Bristol for a physical, after which he expected to be assigned a new ship.[136]

Though certainly happy to see their long-lost brother, Patrick and Gerald did not believe his story, which sounded like the usual routine of half-truths they had learned to expect from Joseph. The three brothers also met with their sister, Maura, who was now married to a man named Blake.[137] In a unusual development, Gerald Lenihan later reported to G2 that Joseph had a lunchtime meeting with Charles McGuinness on 19 July at the Bailey Restaurant on Duke Street – the same Charles McGuinness who managed to worm his way into many of the mini-dramas involving German espionage, which would suggest that he was on a list of Lenihan's contacts – but this angle was not pursued in the investigation.

Lenihan travelled to Dundalk, where he registered at the Lerne Hotel. He had no plans to stay here, but merely dropped his suitcase (containing a transmitter and his supply of invisible ink and reagent) and proceeded to Goraghwood, Northern Ireland, where he turned himself into the RUC, asking to be taken to a representative of MI5.[138] After being transferred to the RSLO (Regional Security Liaison Officer) Belfast, Lenihan was flown to London the same day, 23 July, taken to Camp 020 and vetted for consideration in the Double-Cross (or XX) programme.

Brilliantly operated by John. C. Masterman, the objectives of Double-Cross were to 'turn' German agents inserted into Britain against their German masters by pretending that the agents were still 'live' and continuing to operate their transmitters. In most cases, the Abwehr was never aware that their agents had fallen under foreign control and continued to receive and pass on fake intelligence information as genuine. Double-Cross was the perfect counter-intelligence tool and it enabled MI5 to send skilfully orchestrated disinformation to the enemy over a period of several years. Additionally, Double-Cross was coordinated with the SIGINT intercepts received through the ULTRA information from the German Enigma rotary code machine and the even more sophisticated Lorenz system.[139] The result was a British-directed plan that completely fooled the German Intelligence service.[140]

Initially, Lenihan, now code-named BASKET, was put to work sending coded letters to his Abwehr cover address, Luis Fernandez de Herida, Plaza de Jesus 3, Madrid.[141] This was possible since Lenihan carried with him a series of phrases that could be inserted into normal correspondence:

Congratulations on the birth of a son
and Always yours truly   **radio in order**

Congratulations on the birth of a daughter *and* Yours very truly	**light damage, can be repaired**
Congratulations on the birth of a child *and* Yours Truly	**radio inoperative**[142]

He was scheduled to report by radio ten days after his landing and MI5 kept this schedule. However, B Division of MI5 eventually decided that Lenihan/BASKET was not a suitable candidate for Double-Cross because if the plan were to function, it would be necessary to actually transmit from Sligo, meaning that G2 would have to be brought into the plan. Given the Irish neutrality position, it was unlikely that G2 would be allowed to cooperate, even if Colonel Bryan had agreed to do so. Transmitting from any other location would raise the possibility that German radio experts could use basic direction finding techniques and discover that Lenihan was not where he said he was.[143]

The standards for Double-Cross were that

1 Capture had to follow almost immediately upon landing [otherwise the agent might have already communicated with Germany];
2 The capture had to be unobserved except by a very few, and those trustworthy people;
3 The spy had to be 'turned around' and convinced he could save his life by working for us;
4 We had to satisfy ourselves that his code was understood and that messages could in fact be sent which would satisfy the Germans that the agent was actually working ... these conditions were not often satisfied, and many apparently promising cases had therefore to be rejected.[144]

The length of time at liberty and the familial contacts (to say nothing of the communication with Charles McGuinness) precluded Lenihan's further operational use by MI5. Though not among the chosen ones for Double-Cross, the evaluation of Cecil Liddell, head of MI5's Irish section (B9), was quite complimentary of the Irish spy: 'Though of rough appearance, he was fairly well educated, intelligent and with a phenomenal memory for facts and faces. He gave more fresh and accurate information about the Abwehr in the Netherlands and Paris than any other single agent.'[145] In another MI5 appraisal, it was concluded that 'the volume of intelligence which he yielded to them [his British interrogators] in defiance of his narrow nationalism was surpassed only by its quality'.[146]

Though many other German agents were executed by the British, Lenihan was not even interned for the duration of the war.[147] In a quirky series of telegrams between MI5's Cecil Liddell and Colonel Dan Bryan, it is clear that Lenihan was allowed relatively unsupervised freedom.[148] This exchange also demonstrates the degree of cooperation between officially neutral Ireland and the United Kingdom, made possible through the Dublin Link. Though cooperation was taking place, the charade of bureaucratic diplomacy was maintained. On 30 January 1943, Liddell (through W.C. Hankison at the office of the British Representative in Éire) wired Dan Bryan (who received the message via the Irish Department of External Affairs) that 'Joseph Lenihan reference [file number] PF 60920B.I.H. of 22.7.42 has applied for permit to spend holiday in Éire. No objection here to your detaining him if you wish.' The Irish reply was dispatched by Frederick Boland at External Affairs: 'No objection to Lenihan coming for a short visit. The authorities concerned will do their best to keep him under constant observation but they hesitate to guarantee a 100%, fool-proof check on his doings owing to the man's habit and character.'[149] It is not recorded in the files at either the Irish Military Archives or the National Archives whether Lenihan ever had his holiday in Ireland. Interestingly, the impression given by the documents preserved at the National Archives of Ireland is that all communication between MI5 and G2 was routed through the diplomats. This is false. More direct lines of inquiry existed previous to the Lenihan case and would continue to the end of the war.

In *Neutral Ireland and the Third Reich*, historian John Duggan (the first researcher to mention Lenihan) noted that the Lenihan family did not have regular contact with Joseph after the war. Duggan learned that he subsequently moved to Manchester and that he died in the 1970s and was buried in Esker, Lucan, Co. Dublin. Lenihan never attempted to profit from telling his story about working with the German and British Intelligence services.[150]

JAN VAN LOON: THE FLYING DUTCHMAN

Of all the persons interned for espionage-related activity during the Second World War, the case of Jan van Loon is unique. Alone among the others, there is no available evidence that he acted on behalf of the Abwehr, or that he had received any training or instructions in the matter of intelligence collection and reporting.

Born on 29 March 1917 in Rotterdam, van Loon had been a member of the Dutch version of the German National Socialist Party, the Nationaal Socialistische Beweging, organized and led by Anton Mussert.[151] He was also a member of another Dutch national socialist organization, the WA (Werafdeling – 'defence unit'), called the 'Young Lions', which was disguised as a hiking club. Van Loon had earlier been a member of the merchant marine when he was drafted into the Royal Dutch Navy in March 1938 for a period of twelve months.[152] Aged 21 at this point, he was assigned to the HMS *Van Meerlant*, a minelayer. As the Germans invaded Holland in May 1940, the *Van Meerlant* set sail and van Loon watched the destruction of his home town from aboard the fleeing warship. The surviving ships of the Royal Dutch Navy were merged with the Royal Navy and van Loon was transferred to the HMS *Jacob van Heemskerck*, an anti-aircraft ship, on 26 March 1941. At the time the ship was assigned the role of convoy escort duty. Van Loon performed with distinction, shooting down a He-111 and two German Ju-87 Stukas while aboard the *van Heemskerck* in Dutch waters. Despite his extraordinary service as a sailor, van Loon remained in a quandary about the nature of the war. He was, by political conviction, a national socialist, and his patriotic ties to Holland were strained when the Dutch royal family, including Queen Wilhelmina and the Crown Prince, along with the entire civilian cabinet, fled before the advancing Germans on 13 May and thereafter set up the Dutch Government in Exile, based in London. The implication for van Loon was that the leaders had abandoned the soldiers to fight on alone.

His conflicting emotions under the stress of military active duty helped van Loon make the decision to try to return to Holland. In a letter to his girlfriend during internment, he said that he could not accept the idea that he was to 'sacrifice my life for the English and other capitalists and all that in direct opposition to my conscience'. Additionally, the German invasion of Russia on 22 June 1941 provided evidence to van Loon that Germany was the only major power fighting the communist enemy, a cornerstone of his political beliefs. Consequently, he thought that his moral duty was with the German armed forces, not on board a ship of the Dutch Government in Exile. When the *van Heemskerck* docked at Belfast in September 1941, he saw this as his chance. The ship's company had leave from 8 to 18 September; van Loon left Belfast by train on 11 September and arrived in Dublin at 1330 on the same day. Prior to leaving Belfast, he had acquired a British national registration card (no. UAJW/947/8) which belonged to a Daniel Dunne and listed his address as 6 Galway Street, Belfast.[153] According to van Loon, the identity card and a set of civilian clothes were provided by a British Army lieutenant who was sympathetic to his aim of returning to the Netherlands.[154] It was, however, forbidden for any member of the serving forces to visit Ireland, other than those who had listed the country as a home-of-record. Van Loon did not fall into this category, and consequently, when he crossed the border, he had violated the terms of his leave.

According to a statement he later made to the Garda Special Branch, van Loon spent the first few hours in Dublin at the movies and eating, and checked into O'Neill's Hotel on Westland Row at about 2200 hours. He brought no luggage and gave his national registration card as proof of identity. However, the telephone intercept record for the German Legation in Northumberland Road adds significant detail to this itinerary and was ultimately the reason that van Loon found himself in custody.

According to the intercept transcript, an unknown caller phoned the legation at 1759 and asked to 'talk to the Ambassador tonight'. The female voice who answered the phone (presumably one of the legation secretaries) told the caller that no one was present who could help him at the moment. The caller did not want to discuss the nature of his business at the legation, preferring to do that in person. The embassy worker then suggested that he could call at the legation between 1000 and 1200 hours the following day to speak to an official.[155]

On the morning of 12 September, van Loon took a tram to the German Legation on Northumberland Road and entered the building at almost exactly 1100. He left the building at approximately 1120 and what was discussed inside is still debated. According to van Loon at his interrogation, he merely asked if the German official, Herr Müller, could help him locate a friend from Rotterdam, Hermann Krause.[156] Irish officials were fairly sure that van Loon was offering to trade or sell information about Allied convoys to the Germans. Van Loon himself states that he was asking for help in getting back to his family in Holland.[157]

Van Loon left the legation building, tailed by Detective Sergeant Michael Wymes of the Garda. The subject stopped at the Shipping Federation office on the quay, where he asked about signing on board an Irish ship, producing his seaman's book as proof of qualification. He was told to call back the next day to find out if he could ship out. Leaving the quay, van Loon was observed making a phone call in Lincoln Place and was arrested by the Garda. When initially stopped, he gave his correct name and said he was on 'holidays'. D/Sgt Wymes remarked that he seemed intelligent and that his English was good. In his possession were several items: a red address book/diary, a map of Dublin and two photographs.[158] He admitted to D/Sgt. Wymes that he was thinking about returning to Holland and had no plans to go back to Belfast. At this point, van Loon seemed to think that the Gardaí were questioning him only in relation to the charge of desertion, but that they did not know about his earlier visit to the German Legation. When examined, the address book had the notation '58 Northumberland Rd 61986' – the address and phone number of the legation. Van Loon also had £1 2s.6½d. on him, having already paid 6s.6d. for his room at O'Neill's Hotel.

Van Loon's diary was more problematic, in that it contained the dates of convoy missions while on board the *van Heemskerck*. The obvious conclusion, at least to the Garda, was that van Loon had been attempting to sell or trade information to Nazi Germany's representative in Ireland. However, information about past convoy escort missions would have had no relevance to anyone and van Loon was hardly privy to details about upcoming assignments. Van Loon admitted to writing the entry 'DL 10–12' in the diary – presumably meaning 'Deutsche Legation 1000–1200 hrs.' On being shown the map of Dublin with the position of the German Legation marked in pencil, van Loon attempted to erase the mark before handing the map back, according to the Garda interrogators.[159]

The interrogation posed a few more problems for Jan van Loon as well. When asked by detectives why he was making a phone call at Lincoln Place, he said he was not, only trying to get the address of the German Legation. This was a ridiculous statement in view of the telephone intercept and the surveillance which showed him entering and leaving the legation, and the map with the location marked on it, not to mention the address book with the address and phone number already written in. Though van Loon's exact motives in contacting the German Legation remained a mystery, it was clear that he was a foreign national who had illegally entered Ireland and that he had been in contact with a representative of one of the belligerent powers. Further, he had lied to the Garda about certain aspects of his contact, increasing the suspicion that his activities might prove to be hostile to the state and potentially upset the official position of neutrality. By the decision of Minister for Justice Gerald Boland, he was to be held under the Emergency Powers (No. 20) Order and was transferred to the former women's section of Mountjoy Prison on 20 September 1941.[160]

Van Loon attempted to resolve the situation with the Irish authorities by appealing for help from his commanding officer on the *van Heemskerck*, as well as from the Dutch Government in Exile's consul in Dublin. Perhaps wisely, neither decided to intervene.[161] Van Loon maintained this position, at least officially, until October 1943, when he sent a letter to the Dutch Consulate in Dublin which stated that 'As a National Socialist, I am obliged to inform you that the undersigned no longer recognizes the Dutch Government in London as the lawful Dutch Government. I place myself in the ranks of the fighters for the freedom of Europe, in order to protect our fatherland against the communist dánger.' In a letter written the same day, he made essentially the same statement to the German Legation, adding that 'I place myself under the protection of the German Legation in Dublin'.[162]

RYAN AND FURTHER ABWEHR OPERATIONS – SEA EAGLE

While the Abwehr's Irish plans were quickly cascading into nothingness during 1941, the German Foreign Ministry expert Dr Veesenmayer had developed a plan that involved the re-emergence of Frank Ryan and an ambitious plan concerning Ireland. Since returning from the ill-fated attempt to reach Ireland in August 1940, Ryan had little to do. He met with Francis Stuart on occasion and discussed Stuart's radio commentaries to Ireland, which began in March 1942, though Ryan never actually wrote any of the material himself.[163] Stuart's view of Ryan is interesting, and it changed in the years since the war. In a 1950 article on Frank Ryan's years in Germany, Stuart gave the impression that he and Ryan had a cordial relationship: 'It was then that I got to know him well and we became close friends.'[164] David O'Donoghue logically speculates that Stuart was trying to give a deliberately false impression. 'This could have been to ingratiate himself within the Republican circles in Ireland. More likely, it was to win favour with his brother-in-law, the then Foreign Minister Seán MacBride, who was angry with the writer for having abandoned his wife Iseult (MacBride's half-sister).'[165] Stuart's recent comments are more revealing.

> Ryan was in a very ambiguous position; starting off fighting for the International Brigade and ending up as an adviser to the SS Colonel Veesenmayer, a Jew exterminator. I never liked Ryan, we really didn't get on. ... He should have made up his mind what he was doing. Then this hobnobbing with the Germans. As long as the Germans were planning an invasion of England, Ryan was treated like a VIP. ... I remember one day we were both walking down to the university where I had a class. We disagreed over something. He said to me, 'When' – not 'if', mind you – 'Germany wins the war I will be a minister in the Irish government'. I took this as some sort of threat to me to keep in with him. I took that very much amiss. I didn't like this 'When Germany wins the war'.[166]

In a more recent interview, Stuart has commented that Ryan 'was always making these promises – "Now Frank [Francis], when we win the war, you will be this, that, and the other." ... I didn't say anything because I didn't like him anyhow.'[167]

Though Ryan might have failed to live up to Veesenmayer's hopes for the Russell operation, he was still a useful pawn in other active Foreign Ministry schemes. As early as November 1940, Veesenmayer worked out the details for *Unternehmen Wal* ('Operation Whale'), which envisioned a seaplane landing on an Irish lake.[168] Veesenmayer was working under the questionable assumption that an Allied occupation of Ireland was imminent and that it would be important to have a military-political link to the IRA and Irish government in such an eventuality.[169] This operation was rejected, only to be replaced by another variation in May 1941 involving a seaplane landing on the Irish west coast to resupply the IRA with money and a transmitter.[170] Under State Secretary Dr Ernst Woermann initially approved the enhanced project, code-named *Seeadler* ('Sea Eagle'). Helmut Clissmann and Corporal Bruno Rieger were attached to the Foreign Ministry for the planning phase.[171] At a later date, Frank Ryan was brought into the project when the mission expanded to include a direct liaison with the IRA.

Between July and August, the Abwehr's role had expanded in the Foreign Ministry scheme: 'In contrast to his earlier view, the Reich Foreign Minister now attaches importance to the participation of the Wehrmacht. It is of particular value to the Wehrmacht to have wireless contact with the IRA and thereby receive wireless reports for the Luftwaffe, as the Irish government has raised objections to the transmission of further weather reports by the embassy wireless set.'[172] This would necessarily imply that there was no existing IRA–Abwehr link through Görtz. Veesenmayer formally outlined his improved plan in a secret memorandum to the Foreign Minister on 24 August 1941.

Prior to this, the Abwehr II diary records what seems like a loss of face for the Abwehr in its continuing battle for parity with the Foreign Ministry. As of 21 June 1941 (the day before the German invasion of Russia), following the failure of almost every Abwehr and Foreign Ministry mission to Ireland, it was decided that all future operations to Ireland would be carried out only with the express approval of Dr Veesenmayer. Military missions to Ireland seem to have taken second place to political concerns, and the Abwehr was reduced to the level of a child asking permission from a moody parent, but if this state of affairs was disputed between the OKW and the Foreign Ministry, the official records do not reveal it.

Veesenmayer's written proposal for *Seeadler* was quite general but covered all the basics. He projected that the best time for the operation is between 15 and 25 September 1941. Veesenmayer reported that he had consulted Oberstleutnant von Harlinghausen (holder of the Knight's Cross with Oak Leaves) of the Luftwaffe.[173] Harlinghausen agreed that the operation was feasible and had assigned an experienced pilot for the He-59 (seaplane) that was to be used. As with covert parachute drops, the seaplane would cut its motor on descent and glide to an agreed landing point. The personnel would disembark into an inflatable rubber boat and carry folding bicycles for use on land. After careful study of alternatives, it was decided that the area of Brandon Bay in Kerry was the most suited to the operation.

Ryan was included in the plan because 'he is one of the leading Irish nationalists [and] has been for many years a member of the leader's council of the Irish Republican Army, and a participant in numerous fights against England'. This was, of course, untrue. Ryan was never a member of the Army Council, but it certainly gave more weight for the proposal to include him in the operation. As if for good measure, Veesenmayer threw in another biographical untruth: 'In 1929 the [British] Secret Service carried out an unsuccessful assassination attempt against him and he has often been in jail since.' The experienced Veesenmayer also highlighted his subject's familiarity with people in power: 'He has extensive connections with the Irish republican circles up to de Valera's closest entourage and with de Valera himself, as well as to the Irish regular army, the nationalist Irishmen in Northern Ireland and especially to leading Irishmen in America.'[174] If Ryan told the Secret Service story to Veesenmayer, he lied. In all probability, Veesenmayer was using the fictitious incident to bolster Ryan's image with the Foreign Ministry. Veesenmayer himself considered Ryan to be little better than a communist, but he was a communist who could serve the greater interests of the Third Reich.[175]

Veesenmayer then went on to recommend the talents of Sergeant Helmut Clissmann and Private Rieger. He notes Clissmann's familiarity with Ireland, marriage to an Irish national and language ability ('English with an Irish accent' – Clissmann's English was excellent, but he retained his German accent).[176] The mission specifications of Sea Eagle were as follows:

1. Establish a liaison with the IRA and activate their sabotage operations in England, and to 'bring the Irish Republican Army the sum of money it is expecting';
2. Establish radio communication by means of a transmitter that is to be taken along;
3. Transmit military information, to include weather reports – in view of de Valera's order to hold Dublin Legation traffic to a minimum;
4. Preparation of underground resistance in the event of Ireland's occupation by the English or Americans.[177]

In addition to the 'military tasks' set out above, Veesenmayer also identified several 'political tasks' that Sea Eagle was designed to address. These included 'bringing about an understanding between the IRA and de Valera'; 'influencing through Clissmann the attitude and policies of the Irish nationalist activities'; 'to furnish the Reich with a clear picture of Ireland's domestic and external situation through objective reporting'; and 'in the event of Ireland's occupation by England or America, to organize the resistance, thereby to tie down enemy forces to the greatest possible extent'.[178]

Veesenmayer's plan was shown to Hitler, with a recommendation from von Ribbentrop. Following a conference on 6 September 1941, Hitler decided to postpone the operation, with the note that the possibility of delaying it until October, November or December would be examined. German forces were already heavily committed in Russia and Sea Eagle was, at least for the moment, extraneous. It was ultimately cancelled.[179] It was, however, not yet deceased.

In 1942, after the first US troops landed in Northern Ireland, Veesenmayer, this time in co-operation with the SD chief Walter Schellenburg, planned another Irish mission along the same lines.[180] In January 1943, Helmut Clissmann was dispatched to the SS Totenkopf Kaserne at Berlin-Oranienburg to screen SS volunteers from the First SS Special Service Troop for their suitability. The mission presupposed that the Americans would attempt to occupy the whole of Ireland and that this elite SS assault team would fly to Ireland, land by parachute, and provide tactical support and training to the IRA and Irish Army so that they might better resist the invaders. Clissmann was not impressed with the level of English fluency among the volunteers, but the operation was eventually cancelled when the expected American offensive did not materialize.[181] It did, however, mark the introduction of active participation by the SS and its intelligence section, the SD, in Irish affairs.

After the failure of the revised Operation Sea Eagle, Ryan was dropped as a mission specialist in further covert Abwehr and Foreign Ministry plans and operations. He was approached in late 1943 for his view on a *Geheimsender* (secret transmitter) propaganda operation for broadcast to the United States, but the plan never reached fruition before Ryan's health declined.[182] He died in June 1944 at a hospital in Dresden-Loschwitz. Like Russell before him, Ryan's death was not immediately reported and continued to prompt speculation as to his whereabouts and fate. He was buried in Dresden, where his grave was located by Enno Stephan in 1963.[183] Stephan paid a fee to keep the grave from being destroyed and Ryan's body was eventually sent back for burial in Ireland.

VEESENMAYER AND KERNEY

In fulfilment of his mission as the Foreign Ministry's 'special adviser' on Ireland, Veesenmayer was always alert to new possibilities that offered the chance to advance German political objectives. Though the Russell/Ryan missions had failed and the revamped Sea Eagle had been ultimately disapproved, another opportunity presented itself in late 1941. The Irish contact was more influential than he could have hoped for: the Irish Minister to Spain, Leopold Kerney. Charles Bewley, the former Irish minister to Berlin and a pro-Nazi, may have been the genesis for the contact. In the period since the war, Bewley developed and maintained contact with the Germans on a regular basis, with his pro-fascist bias evidently taking precedence over his national allegiance. Bewley's actual agenda and activities are difficult to discern. William Warnock observed him in Berlin in 1940, when Bewley was said to be working with the anti-Comintern organization. The Swedish Minister in Rome noted that the 'Swedish news agency for which Bewley worked was possibly part of a German organization "directed by a gentleman with a clubbed foot"'. In Michael MacWhite's (the Irish Free State's Envoy to Rome) report back to the Irish government, Bewley's sponsor was specifically identified as Joseph Goebbels and Warnock later reported stories that Bewley was working for the Ministry of Propaganda.[184]

A British diplomat who met Bewley in 1940 reported that he was ostensibly working for 'a Swedish news agency known as the "Scandia Presse" ... he showed me a three-page typewritten letter which made it clear that the Scandia Press is virtually for promoting German interests ... He also confessed that his duties would include the placing of articles and propaganda in Italy. This does not normally come within the duties of a press correspondent but is the work of a propagandist.' The British Foreign Office considered trying to get Bewley removed from Rome, but decided that it would be difficult to get the Irish government to comply and that 'Mr Bewley's presence in Rome will have to be endured'. Irish Minister to the Vatican Thomas Kiernan was sympathetic to the British plight: he advised that 'Bewley was got rid of from Berlin, and that we should be very careful in our dealings with him'.[185]

Further reports from Michael MacWhite in Rome in 1941, suggested that Bewley was an informant for the German Minister in Rome and that 'his information about England and other countries is held to be incalculable. According to the same source, his work in Rome is to keep the Germans posted about things that might otherwise escape purely German ears.'[186] The Germans obviously thought highly of Bewley. One Foreign Ministry official stated that 'Bewley is ein uberzeugter Freund des nationalsocialistischen Deutschland und fanatischer irischer Freiheitskampfer. Er ist eine in jeder Hinsicht seriöse Personlichkeit, die Zugang zu hohen und höchstens italienschen und vatikanischen Stellen hat' (Bewley is a convinced friend of National Socialist Germany and a fanatical Irish freedom fighter. He is in every respect a trustworthy personality [and] has access to high level Italian and Vatican places).[187] Bewley's connection to the Germans was of a continuous nature and hardly passive. German documents indicate that Bewley suggested the Veesenmayer–Kerney liaison, though this does not preclude the possibility that it was already something under consideration before Bewley's gratuitous suggestion. In an SD report to the Foreign Ministry in early 1941, Bewley is quite complementary about Kerney, whom he describes as the only '"real Irish nationalist" among the Irish diplomats serving abroad'.[188]

By this point, Kerney had an existing history with German Intelligence, and it was assumed that a further connection to the Reich would not be unwelcome. Kerney had worked with the Abwehr in freeing Frank Ryan, and had made it possible for Abwehr courier Mary Mains to funnel money and materials to Hermann Görtz. He was an old associate of de Valera, and Veesenmayer apparently agreed with Bewley's suggestion that Kerney could be an information conduit to the Irish government in a way that would serve German interests. The Irish Minister to Spain could also serve as a barometer for actual – as opposed to public – Irish governmental attitudes towards the Third Reich.

The series of meetings between Kerney and representatives of the German Foreign Ministry and German Intelligence was the subject of a series of articles by the noted Irish historian Desmond Williams.[189] Williams maintained that 'these secret meetings between the Veesenmayer group and the unnamed diplomat were said to have gone on for months and had it not been for the great set-backs on the Russian front, might have encouraged Hitler to throw the advice of his ambassador in Dublin to the wind and to act on de Valera's alleged promise of help'.

In short, Kerney had five separate meetings with Helmut Clissmann from November 1941 to July 1943. On two of these occasions, Clissmann was accompanied by Veesenmayer. When the Williams articles, 'A Study in Neutrality', were published in the *Irish Press*, Kerney sued him for libel, asserting that 'an Irish diplomat in a neutral European country' could only refer to himself, though Williams never referred to Kerney by name. In preparation for the lawsuit, Clissmann, then living in Ireland, was asked to prepare a statement of what happened.

Clissmann claimed that he never told Kerney that he was on active duty with the Brandenburg Regiment, but merely that he was still representing the German Academic Exchange Service. Clissmann reported that Kerney agreed that partition was inevitable unless British power collapsed through a German victory. For one who allegedly gave the impression of working only for the German Academic Exchange Service, Clissmann's next point is curious: he mentioned to Kerney that Germany had a large supply of captured British war material and that such material could be sent to Ireland. Clissmann, again according to his post-war recollection, asked Kerney for his thoughts on Ireland's position if Germany was victorious in the East and again turned its attention to the West. Kerney was said to have responded that Ireland's position would have to be re-examined and that de Valera would then 'announce his claim to the Six Northern Counties'.[190]

If such meetings and discussions were not sufficiently incendiary, Kerney followed this up by personal meetings with Veesenmayer in August 1942 and a subsequent meeting in July 1943. Clissmann maintained that Kerney was under the impression that Veesenmayer was 'an important personality in German political life, and an official in the German Railways, who had direct access to Ribbentrop, who had a high opinion of his experience and judgement'. If Kerney actually believed this fairy tale, he did not take any steps to investigate Veesenmayer's true identity, something that could have been accomplished in a coded cable to the Irish Chargé d'Affaires in Berlin. By at least October 1942, both G2 and the Department of External Affairs were aware that Clissmann 'is an intelligence officer in the German Army'.[191] Kerney could hardly have been unaware of what was already known to his own government. Clissmann maintained that the talks were inconsequential from a German point of view and that they covered such esoteric subjects as a comparison between the personalities of Ryan and Russell. Professor Williams maintained that Kerney ('The Irish diplomat') 'hoped indeed one day to see Ryan as the liaison officer between Germany and the Irish government'. Clissmann later wrote: 'This does not reflect Kerney's views but German views at that time.'[192] The 1941 interview between G2's Joseph Healy and Kerney suggests something quite to the contrary.

What is one to make of this episode? Desmond Williams was relying on the contemporaneous written reports filed by Veesenmayer and Clissmann when they returned from the meetings. The Veesenmayer report is unambiguous and certainly makes the point that Kerney was something more than a passive Irish pawn. Veesenmayer's version was that Kerney intimated that de Valera would ask Germany for help if the US or Britain invaded Ireland and, if such a thing occurred, the government and the IRA would have common ground. Kerney said that de Valera was not fanatical about neutrality and would enter the war against the Allies as soon as any chance of liberating Northern Ireland presented itself. If Germany chose to aid this move, she would need to publicly deny any interest in Ireland and German troops would only remain to complete the war against England.[193]

It is, of course, possible that the two German officers lied in an effort to convince Berlin that something more significant had occurred, and that this was done in concert with Veesenmayer's pre-conceived plan of action in Ireland. Clissmann, however, did have a motive to play down any active role by Kerney: he had been granted a visa to live in Ireland, and his own position might have been jeopardized if he implied that an Irish diplomat was entering into treasonous talks with the representative of Nazi Germany. Veesenmayer himself said that 'the tenor of the conversations could be put this way: to such an extent as Germany's chances of winning the war improved, so would "official" and "unofficial" Ireland be prepared indirectly to give Germany useful help within the framework of her own efforts to gain independence'.[194]

Kerney himself did not report the meetings with the Germans until well after the event – certainly after British Intelligence learned of them. In the same way, he was reticent to 'come clean' in his precise dealings connected to Frank Ryan's escape, and never admitted culpability in helping Mary Mains complete her espionage mission for the Abwehr. When specifically questioned, Kerney admitted to G2 that he had known all along that Ryan was being released at the behest of German Intelligence. Complicity with the intelligence service of a belligerent power was not a minor diplomatic gaffe. The additional fact that Kerney did not willingly reveal the extent of his contacts with Ryan and Clissmann would raise the possibility that he had something to hide from his own government.[195] In any event, Kerney did not speak for de Valera, to the Germans or to anyone else. Though recalled to Dublin in 1943 after G2 became fully appraised of his contact with German Intelligence and the German Foreign Office, Kerney was returned to his post in Madrid.[196] Regardless of Kerney's intent, the effect was to give German Intelligence a green light in Irish affairs. Whereas before, the German Foreign Office was understandably cautious in potentially upsetting Irish neutrality, confirmation from the Irish minister in Spain opened new possibilities. Professor Williams's contention seems to be historically sound: only the increasingly disastrous situation in Russia forced a cancellation of any meaningful German initiative in the direction of the Ireland. Perhaps significantly, the Foreign Ministry closed its Ireland office in 1943.[197]

GÖRTZ IN CUSTODY

Görtz was initially imprisoned at Arbour Hill and Irish officers had no difficulty establishing his true identity, which they had known for some months. Hempel stayed at a distance from the new prisoner, but Görtz wrote to him in early January 1942 stating 'I am an officer of the Luftwaffe. ... I ask you urgently to get in contact with me as I feel the honour of the German Wehrmacht is involved. Heil Hitler.'[198] Görtz's situation was already causing confusion in Germany. The DNB office in Stockholm reported his arrest on 5 December 1941, and accurately summarized his pre-war spying in England and the discoveries in the wake of the Held raid. Hempel sent a telegram in December to the Foreign Ministry. The Foreign Ministry replied with a statement to aid Hempel in drafting a formal reply to the Irish government: Görtz's mission was simple – to facilitate the possibility of attacks on England with the assistance of the IRA. Görtz was specifically warned to avoid interference with the Irish government. Berlin also reported the last radio contact with Görtz in which he suggested a German proclamation for 'Irish freedom and reunification of the occupied North with the South on the principle of Irish neutrality'. The Foreign Ministry correctly concluded that 'This was a complete misunderstanding of his mission'. Görtz's irrational conduct could only be explained by the fact that he had 'lost his nerve and perspective in the previous eighteen months' and that he had been attempting all possible means of returning to Germany.[199] Accordingly, when Hempel met with Joseph Walshe of External Affairs to discuss the Görtz case, he kept to the prepared text and stated that 'if Görtz was active in a political way it could only be because he had acted on his own responsibility or through personal anxiety and a disturbed state of mind'.[200] Görtz's mental peculiarities provided Hempel with a plausible denial.

Görtz's arrest also puzzled the Luftwaffe personnel department. On reading the article about his arrest in the *Daily Express*, it wrote to the Abwehr asking whether Görtz was known there.[201] As late as 1 December 1941, Abwehr II was exploring with Dr Woermann at the Foreign Ministry the possibility of picking Görtz up by seaplane – Lahousen had not yet heard of his arrest – concluding that Görtz's hope of an Irish plane to bring him back to Germany was not feasible.[202] According to the Abwehr II war diary, the Abwehr did not learn of Görtz's arrest until 8 December, when Veesenmayer informed Hauptmann Astor. The German Intelligence service was seemingly the last to learn of its agent's fate. The Abwehr and the Foreign Ministry discussed the official version that was to be circulated by Hempel: 'Hauptmann Görtz had a mission as a German officer against

England, but was unfortunately delayed in Ireland en route to England.'[203]
Görtz is referred to here as 'Hauptmann' (captain). He had been promoted
to Oberleutnant (first lieutenant) in September 1940 and to Hauptmann in
April 1941 (because he volunteered 'for an extraordinarily dangerous
special mission overseas'). He was never promoted above that grade, at
least by the Germans.[204]

The Foreign Ministry did not seem particularly upset by Görtz's arrest,
to judge from Frank Ryan's comments: 'The Görtz affair ends happily for
all concerned. So far as I hear, they were trying to get him home, for a while
past, as he had exceeded his instructions by meddling in our internal affairs.
His encounter with the General was the last straw. They blame that for his
arrest, and say "Serve him right!" They are gratified there is no sign of a
trial; that, they wouldn't like.'[205] Ryan was still in Berlin, and through his
contact with Veesenmayer would presumably have an insight into the
Foreign Ministry position. In Dublin, Hempel certainly was relieved, now
that a danger to his own position had been removed.

Görtz was interrogated immediately by both the Garda Síochána and
G2. Most of the interrogations were conducted by Commandant Eamon de
Buitléar and Dr Richard Hayes, both German linguists available in G2. Dr
Hayes wanted to explore the topic of Görtz's coded messages, several of
which had been found during the Held raid the previous year.

German Intelligence operations, 1943

JOSEPH ANDREWS AND THE DUBLIN LINK

A disturbing event occurred in 1943, when MI5, using the 'Dublin Link' notified G2 of another potential German agent. In February 1943, Bletchley Park decrypted a message from the SD in Lisbon notifying headquarters that they had received a message from a Irish crew member named Christopher Eastwood on the SS *Edenvale*. At approximately the same moment, MI6 reported that they received a coded message from 'Tomas', a Portuguese worker who was supposed to convey the message to the Abwehr, but who had taken it to MI6 instead. Tomas was a low-level native recruit of MI6 in Lisbon and certainly could not believe his luck when he was chosen as the go-between for Eastwood. Tomas agreed to bring all messages to the SIS before delivering them to the Germans. It turned out that the messages did not originate with Eastwood, but with another Irishman, Joseph Andrews.[1]

BACKGROUND

Andrews operated a jewellery shop in Dublin's fashionable Grafton Street. He had been an Irish Hospitals Trust employee, but was fired for suspected dishonesty. His former contacts at the Hospitals Trust included Maisie O'Mahony and Helena Kelly. It was thought that by this route he wormed his way into the Görtz circle. His wife, a sometime courier for the German agent, is believed to have had a special relationship with Görtz and, by that means, acquired the code that her husband used. Andrews himself acted as a driver for Görtz and assisted him in locating safe houses. He also relayed messages from Görtz to Brenda Brugha, which were then sent to Anthony Deery for transmission to Germany. According to his later statements, Andrews was trying to set up an alternative channel between Germany and Görtz, using money transfers through a Swiss jeweller, but Andrews and Görtz were both arrested before the system could be established. He mentioned that Görtz had been in touch with a priest, the Reverend Fuller Weldon, OSF, who was attempting to mediate between the IRA and the government. Andrews was also a member of the People's National Party and Coras na Poblachta, both extreme anti-Semitic political groups.[2]

Colonel Bryan eventually concluded that 'Andrews is an astute and plausible rogue without any fixed convictions and mainly actuated by a desire to obtain money rapidly without any due regard as to the honesty of the methods used to secure his ends'.[3] This was an accurate assessment. As soon as Andrews obtained the Görtz code he took it to the American Legation and offered it in exchange for money. He was refused. Because of his proven connection to O'Mahony and others in the Görtz ring, he was arrested on 21 November 1941 and detained in the Curragh until April 1942. After his release, he approached Carlheinz Petersen at the German Legation for material on a lecture he was giving on Germany. Using Mrs Andrews as a courier, he soon began sending coded messages to Petersen; two were sent in December 1942, and two more sets of messages were routed through a Stephen Kelly to Petersen. When Andrews received no answer from the legation, he began the contact through Christopher Eastwood on the SS *Edenvale*. After the second delivery by this route, Andrews received two £50 notes from the Germans.[4]

Andrews had some difficulty with these communications, owing to the delay in the round trip. The route from Dublin to Lisbon generally took a month, and 'on one occasion the ship did not call at Lisbon for two trips, so that messages handed to the courier in April were not delivered until July'. Another aggravating factor was that the Germans had insufficient time to respond to the messages while Eastwood was in port, meaning that such replies would have to wait until the next scheduled run.[5] Eastwood himself was not the most reliable character. In one instance, he lost his job as ship's cook when he arrived on board drunk and late. Only the insistence of his fellow crew members prevented his discharge, which would have broken Andrew's only reliable communications link with German Intelligence.[6]

The Abwehr did not know what to make of the messages at first, and had difficulty deciphering them, as they were unaware of the keyword. In several parts, Andrews identified himself and added that 'I am a member of his [Görtz's] personal organization, which is independent of the IRA.' Andrews boasted that he had 'complete knowledge of plans for projected active organization under General O'Duffy. O'Duffy willing to cooperate in active work, especially in occupied Ireland.' He also added: 'Major-General McNeill sympathetic'. Andrews suggested that he be picked up and taken to Germany, or alternatively, that Germany could send another agent, a radio and especially money directly to Andrews. In the text of one message, he mentioned that O'Duffy wanted to recruit a 'green division' to fight with Germany on the Eastern Front.[7]

Back in Germany, the messages from Andrews attracted the attention of Dr Veesenmayer at the Foreign Ministry. In a letter to Ribbentrop on 5 May 1943 – well after the Irish and British closed Andrews's channel –

Veesenmayer outlined O'Duffy's background and detailed his tenuous relationship with Görtz. While the 'Special Adviser on Ireland' considered Andrews's offers and suggestions totally impractical, he thought that there might some utility in the 'green division' suggestion, not as a real fighting force but for propaganda value. Clearly, even if such a mythical force had existed, it would be impossible to transport it anywhere, but Veesenmayer advised keeping the Abwehr channel open, encouraging Andrews and allowing the situation to develop.[8] Although SIS had the messages, they could not break this particular hand-cipher code. The 'Dublin Link' *had* to provide the answer. The British had gleaned the keyword from ISOS intercepts. Dr Hayes succeeded in unscrambling Görtz's coding system in March 1943, and was thus the ideal person to decipher the text. Unfortunately, British Intelligence could not reveal the Bletchley intercepts and the source of the keyword without revealing the secret of their intercept programme. G2 invited MI5's Cecil Liddell and an officer from the GC&CS (the British Government Code and Cipher School) to Dublin, where Dr Hayes explained the workings of the German system.[9] As Liddell observed, 'His [Hayes's] gifts in this direction amounted almost to genius'. With G2's cooperation, the British were able to read the plain text of the Andrews messages without compromising the ISOS programme. Colonel Bryan's cooperation even went further.

> The real Irish co-operation in this was that they voluntarily agreed to allow the messages to run on, and enabled the British to read them without knowing what they might reveal or what Irish nationals might be compromised; in fact the messages did indicate that the GOC of the 2nd Division of the Eire Army [Hugo MacNeill], who was well known to be anti-British and pro-German, had been in touch with Goertz before his arrest.[10]

On several occasions, Colonel Bryan was presented with the opportunity of running double agents, but declined. MI5 made this offer once information established that German Intelligence agents in Portugal were trying to obtain information about Allied ships and routes from Irish sailors. The Germans were also very anxious to know about American troops stationed in Northern Ireland.

> This information was passed to Colonel Bryan with the suggestion that he might make use of a reliable man as a double-agent, but it is not thought that this was followed. ... Colonel Bryan's view was that while he would shut his eyes to anything we might do on Eire soil, of course with his knowledge, he could not in his position run a double agent outside Eire.[11]

Once the nature of Andrews's communication was determined by MI5, there was no further point in allowing him to continue. Accordingly, he was arrested in August 1943 and held until May 1945. Eastwood was also arrested and interned. When Andrews's house was searched, copies of many of his messages were found. Charred papers found in the fireplace were sent to the Garda Technical Bureau at Kilmainham, sprayed with cellulose acetate and then mounted on glass slides in acetone, revealing the original messages.[12]

O'REILLY AND KENNY

Although there had been periodic scares since the last landing on Irish soil (Lenihan), by 1943 it seemed to G2 that all German interest in Ireland had evaporated, largely because it was obvious that Germany no longer had the means or will to invade Great Britain after 1942 and was trying to cope with a steadily worsening situation in Russia. However, such an opinion was mistaken. While Abwehr influence declined following a number of glaring intelligence failures, the standing of the rival SS intelligence service – the SD – was increasing.

On the morning of 16 December 1943, the family and friends of John Francis O'Reilly were quite surprised to find that he had finally come home. To the best of their knowledge, he was still in Germany and it was strange, at the very least, to find him once again in County Clare after an absence of three years.

BACKGROUND

O'Reilly's family already had connections to German espionage – though not of the kind with which John Francis was to become familiar. His father, Bernard, was the Royal Irish Constabulary sergeant who had helped arrest Sir Roger Casement in April 1916 when Casement alighted from a German U-boat with the intent of participating in the Easter Rebellion. Thereafter nicknamed 'Casement O'Reilly,' Bernard had long since retired and moved to Kilkee, County Clare, by the time his son John Francis returned home in 1943.[13] Born in County Kerry on 7 August 1916, John Francis attended the Christian Brothers school in Kilrush and went on to join the Irish Customs Service in Rosslare in 1936. Apparently he failed the statutory Irish language examination and then decided, briefly, to join the priesthood. He entered Buckfast Abbey in England, but left after just two weeks. Moving on, he was working as a hotel receptionist in London when war was declared in September 1939. Shortly afterwards, O'Reilly decided to leave his hotel position and move to the island of Jersey, where he was employed as a seasonal worker with the potato harvest at Beaumont Farm, St Helier. Later he transferred to a tomato plantation and performed similar work. Though some workers were evacuated when Germany invaded France in June 1940, O'Reilly stayed on and was present when German forces occupied the island on 2 July. Jersey proved a fruitful breeding ground for Nazi collaborators.[14]

FROM JERSEY TO GERMANY

O'Reilly ingratiated himself with the German forces, working his way up the collaboration ladder from a menial job at the Luftwaffe airfield to eventually acting as a translator between the island commander, Major Georg Wilhelm Prinz zu Waldeck und Pyrmont, and the Irish workers who decided to remain on Jersey. He eventually approached zu Waldeck about the possibility of getting permission to travel and work in Germany; and later said that this was done with the idea of contacting the Irish Legation in Berlin to return home to Ireland.[15] Zu Waldeck agreed, provided that O'Reilly would recruit other Irish workers for employment in Germany. The Irishman diligently pursued his new task and managed, by means of a creative incentive plan (including pay, holidays and paid return to Ireland once the war was over), to induce seventy-two Irish workers to transfer to Germany with him.

For the Germans, the band of Irish workers hardly exemplified the self-discipline and conduct that they desired. The train journey from the French coast to the Hermann Göring plant at Watenstedt was later described in an Irish Intelligence report:

> [T]he party was anything but well-behaved. They had a fair amount of money saved and proceeded at once to get completely drunk and out of hand ... the train was divided into various compartments according to nationality. O'Reilly's party invaded all compartments of the train and on several occasions pulled the communication cords causing an amount of confusion. As accepted leader of the party, he had to bear the brunt of criticism.

Once at Watenstedt, O'Reilly again managed to gain access to the authorities by acting as an interpreter to the German forces.[16] However, his Irish comrades never fitted into the German scheme of things at Watenstedt; they habitually 'disregarded the rules, coming back late at night, singing and shouting, and – most dangerously from the German point of view – switching on factory lights during the blackout'.[17]

O'Reilly soon tired of this company and in September 1941 applied for a job writing articles for the Irish service of German Radio, the Irland-Redaktion.[18] As a genuine Irish national, he was a valuable find for the head of the Irland-Redaktion, Dr Hans Hartmann, and he was immediately put into broadcasting. While in the Irish section, O'Reilly came into contact with a number of Irish and pseudo-Irish nationals. Chief among these were the writer Francis Stuart and Nora O'Mara, who claimed to be Irish. O'Reilly began broadcasting to Ireland under the pseudonym of 'Pat O'Brien', but started using his real name in October 1941. Despite his lack of formal training in radio broadcasting, he started making waves almost immediately. Though generally kept on a short leash by Dr Hartmann, O'Reilly made the situation impossible when he refused to read the suggested text of Wolfe Tone's diaries, calling them 'uninteresting', but ultimately gave in and read the script as ordered. He also criticized the music selections played on the Irland-Redaktion as 'having no actual Irish basis'. Things did not improve and in 1942, O'Reilly began to seek other employment. In June 1942, he claimed to have met an American working for the SS, who told him that there could be work for him in Spain, contacting sailors who might have news of Northern Ireland.[19] MI5 later identified the American as Howard Marggraff – an individual who served in the Waffen-SS, worked with German radio and had assisted Norman Baillie-Stewart in getting work in Germany.[20] Marggraff was most likely a freelance recruiter for both the Abwehr and its competitor, the SD.

O'Reilly allegedly replied that he would prefer to be sent on a mission to Northern Ireland. When asked to report back to the SS Bureau (probably the SD), he was told that his application to work for German Intelligence had been approved. O'Reilly's narrative is confusing on a few points. He subsequently went to work for the Abwehr and only worked with the SD later. In the meantime, however, O'Reilly was to continue to work for the Irland-Redaktion until his training cycle began.[21]

When Dr Hartmann learned of O'Reilly's decision to leave the radio, he attempted to get him to stay. Though O'Reilly was undoubtedly a poor subordinate, the fact that he was actually Irish in the Irish section almost made up for the difficulty in working with him. Hartmann approached Helmut Clissmann (then assigned to the Brandenburg Regiment) to help persuade O'Reilly. O'Reilly had earlier met Clissmann at one of the St Patrick's Day functions at the Irish Legation in Berlin. Clissmann failed, but O'Reilly did agree to find a substitute announcer, nominating his friend Liam Mullally, formerly of the Berlin Berlitz School, who shared an apartment with him at Kladow.[22] O'Reilly began training with the Marineabteilung (Naval section or I-M) of Abwehr I at Bremen from September 1942 in preparation for a mission in Northern Ireland.

Code-named 'Agent Rush' and given the Abwehr numerical designation RR 2261, O'Reilly's secret mission was called 'Isolde'. At this stage, the Germans described him as 'an enthusiastic Irish patriot and has been active since his boyhood in the IRA movement. He maintains that he has close connections with the other friends in the IRA movement. He is modest in his way of life and reserved. He makes an excellent and trustworthy impression.' The mission for this 'typically Irish looking' agent was to discover naval and air intelligence information from Londonderry, Belfast, Liverpool and Lough Foyle.[23] At the initial stages, the Abwehr considered basing O'Reilly in London and having his 'IRA connections' funnel information to him from various sites of interest. They also considered a sea insertion by cutter on the Irish west coast, travel via Lisbon ('Country 18'), and a parachute drop into Ireland ('Country 32'). In the event of O'Reilly being transported through Portugal, which was neutral, the

Bremen Ast trained him to build and repair his own version of an agent's transmitter.[24] O'Reilly furnished considerable information to the Germans, both geographic and political, to assist in the mission planning.

WITH THE ABWEHR

While at the Bremen school, O'Reilly was given a thorough course designed to turn the raw recruit into a competent intelligence agent. His primary area was radio communications and he began an intensive radio course from October to December 1942. He achieved (or so he said) a Morse speed of 100 letters per minute – a rate far ahead of the other German agents inserted into Ireland. O'Reilly later reported that his radio handler in Germany knew his method and habits of transmission, as a way to detect if his station had been compromised and was being run by the enemy. He also received training in both normal photography and microphotography. In his rambling account of his secret training, O'Reilly said that the Abwehr controllers prescribed table tennis as the proper exercise for radio operators, and claimed that he sometimes played against former world heavyweight boxing champion Max Schmeling.[25] According to O'Reilly, his commander at Bremen, Kapitän Seemann, was pleased with his work and they both took part in the operational planning.[26] The plan was to return O'Reilly by U-boat to the Irish west coast, near his home in Kilkee, but when he returned from Christmas leave in January 1943, he was informed that the U-boat plan had been scrapped. The Abwehr briefly considered the feasibility of obtaining a transit visa from the Irish consulate in Berlin, but this plan was also abandoned.[27]

Ultimately the decision to return O'Reilly at that time was scuttled by Dr Edmund Veesenmayer, the Irish specialist in the Foreign Ministry. Veesenmayer, still anxious to secure Frank Ryan's return to Ireland, thought that the O'Reilly mission was a waste of precious resources and might interfere with the larger and more politically significant Ryan operation. Veesenmayer contacted the commander of I-L at the Bremen Ast, Kapitän-Leutnant Heinrich Ahlrichs, to express his view, prompting a second meeting on 8 December with Admiral Canaris and Abwehr I-M chief, Kapitän zur See Menzel in an effort to deflate the O'Reilly mission.[28] He also directed Sonderführer Kurt Haller to compile a personal assessment of O'Reilly and Liam Mullally. Haller described O'Reilly as a 'pig-headed opportunist'. Ahlrichs attempted to revise the mission and to overcome the Foreign Ministry's objections, suggesting that O'Reilly could approach William Warnock and obtain the necessary travel papers, obviating the need for a naval insertion into Ireland. Despite this, the Abwehr operation, with Canaris's approval, was effectively cancelled.[29] O'Reilly subsequently attended a refresher course in telegraphy on the outskirts of Hamburg, but was ultimately released from Abwehr service.

The SD, however, had other ideas. Though the Abwehr mission was torpedoed, they continued to press ahead with their own plan, unbeknownst to either Veesenmayer or the Abwehr. Whereas the Abwehr was primarily concerned with military intelligence objectives, the SD was almost exclusively devoted to gathering political intelligence. Bolstered by his own inflated version of his background and contacts, O'Reilly seemed an ideal candidate to fulfill the particular needs of the SS intelligence service.

Following the Abwehr mission cancellation, O'Reilly returned to Berlin with the intention to rejoin the Irland-Redaktion team. However, he seems to have decided to remain in Berlin rather than return to work – prompting a mildly threatening phone call from Sonderführer Dr Kurt Haller. In his post-war memoirs, O'Reilly described a conversation he had with Nora O'Mara (whom he refers to as 'Deirdre'), a fellow worker at the Irland-Redaktion. O'Reilly recalled that, in the course of this conversation, she claimed Sean Russell had been secretly poisoned by Kurt Haller before boarding the submarine bound for Ireland. She then offered to help O'Reilly return to his native land.[30] He subsequently received a call from SS-Obersturmführer Geisler, who made an offer of employment with the SS.

FROM ABWEHR AGENT TO SS RECRUIT

From O'Reilly's frequently incomplete narrative, it appears that he trained with the SD Leitstelle, Berlin, until he parachuted back into Ireland. He received more wireless training at the Havel Institute, Wannsee, under the command of SS-Sturmbannführer Peter Siepen. Although many of the trainers had previously worked for the Abwehr, O'Reilly learned that the SD procedure varied somewhat. His immediate supervisor was Geisler, but SS-Sturmbannführer Dr Peters shadowed his overall training.[31] His mission specification had changed, however. In consideration of the fact that the Luftwaffe was providing the transport to the SD operation, O'Reilly was trained to supply requested air intelligence data from Northern Ireland and England. To enable him to competently perform this task, he was taken to a secret Luftwaffe airfield and shown captured Allied aircraft, as well as shoulder boards and RAF unit patches that the Luftwaffe intelligence people wanted him to identify.[32]

By contrast, his SD mission was more subtle. His task was to collect political intelligence in England, with particular emphasis on inter-party political conflicts in the government.[33] Of particular interest were the reported comments of Russian delegates at the 1943 Trades Union Congress meeting in Bristol. Once in England (having crossed over from Ireland), O'Reilly was to contact the Labour Party and hopefully secure employment with them as a means of worming his way into the British political structure.[34] He was also to make contact with the Scottish and Welsh nationalist movements.[35] He was briefed for this aspect by Norman

Baillie-Stewart, a court-martialled British Army officer who had launched a
second career broadcasting for Nazi radio.[36] O'Reilly also revealed that
part of his mission specification required him to go to Northern Ireland,
where he was to note the relationship between British and American troops,
British convoys and destroyer escorts, shipping and the American Air
Force.[37] He also met Oscar Pfaus, who said to pass on his greetings to
former IRA Chief of Staff Maurice Twomey.[38] With the threat to Fortress
Europe from the impending Allied invasion, it is curious that O'Reilly was
assigned only a secondary military mission. Given O'Reilly's tendency to
tell less than the full truth, his own explanation of his mission should be
regarded with caution.

O'Reilly's activities during September were not totally taken up with
training for his mission; he also worked with the SS to provide another
candidate for an espionage mission to Ireland. The selection of John Kenny
proved to be an uninspired choice.

JOHN KENNY

Kenny was born in Dublin on 27 March 1916. His father died while he was
very young and his mother, later remarried to a man named Healy, seems to
have little to do with him. Kenny was principally raised by his uncle, John
Sullivan, in Kilcummin, Killarney, County Kerry. He claimed to be a
'nominal' member of the IRA in 1936, but left for England in 1937 to take
up a continuous series of menial jobs. He worked for Greystone's Radio in
London, but he cut his face in a bar fight, was accordingly told that he
could no longer work with customers and was laid off. The outbreak of war
meant that he would be liable for conscription into the British forces, so
Kenny emigrated to Jersey as a seasonal worker picking potatoes.
According to Kenny himself, 'I left London early in 1940 after I was called
up as cannon fodder for the Jewes [*sic*]. I certainly did not mind being a
soldier but I certainly did not feel like fighting for "John Bull" so I left.'
Another more likely scenario was that he was about to be arrested. A
Prevention of Violence Act expulsion order on Kenny had been issued, but
he left of his own accord first. The British were evidently acting on
information that Kenny had been a member of the Irish Republican
Defence Association in Ilford from 1937 to 1940 and as such was a danger
to the realm.[39] It seems likely that Kenny was sent to Jersey with the
assistance of the Peace Pledge Union, an anti-war group dedicated to
helping otherwise able-bodied men avoid conscription.

Like O'Reilly, Kenny found employment with the German occupation
forces, first as a waiter in a hotel, then checking the mileage on vehicles in
the German motor pool, and finally as a driver for a Naval engineering
officer from 1942 until he was recruited by O'Reilly in September 1943.[40]
His job as a staff car driver came about by accident; the existing driver, an

Irishman named Sargent, ran down and killed a local boy while driving drunk, receiving a two-year sentence from the Germans, and Kenny was promoted to drive in his place.[41]

In September 1943, Kenny was visited on Jersey by O'Reilly and 'a Gestapo officer', and volunteered to accompany them back for espionage training.[42] Largely, this was as a result of three promises made to Kenny: that he could go to Germany; that he would not have to do factory work (he had apparently talked to some of the other Irish sent to Watenstedt); and that he would be home in Ireland by Christmas. In retrospect, O'Reilly and the 'Gestapo officer' kept all three of their promises. Kenny was sent to Berlin, paid a salary of 450 Marks a month, and sat in the Hotel Roxy for three weeks with no assignment whatsoever.

Eventually, Kenny was summoned to a meeting with an Oberleutnant Geeser at the SD headquarters, 32–35 Berkaerstrasse, Berlin. In a later statement to G2, he noted that Geeser's office (Room 228) also contained a girl whose job seemed to be to read and mark copies of Irish daily newspapers.[43] Kenny was detailed to Lehnitz for an SD course in the repair and maintenance of various transmitter sets.[44] His classmates included a Croatian, a Frenchman, a 65- to 70-year-old Greek, a Turk, two Algerians and three Arabs. While at Lehnitz, Kenny met another Irishman, John Collins, who had served with the British Army at Dunkirk. Collins, then in training for an undisclosed SD mission of his own, had been working as a physical drill instructor for the Germans.[45]

Kenny, who was described by a G2 interrogator as having 'little education and limited intelligence', did not make rapid progress in his class at Lehnitz. He later admitted that he did not really understand the book code and that his instructors did not seem pleased with his progress. At the conclusion of his hurried course, where he also learned rudimentary RT procedure and Morse code, he was accompanied by an Oberleutnant Dr Schüttenkoff – this is probably a reference to SS-Sturmbannführer Dr Otto-Ernst Schüddenkopf, the SD chief of Group D, Desk 2, responsible for Great Britain – to occupied Brittany, in preparation for his flight.[46]

O'Reilly and Kenny reported to Rennes on 15 December 1943. Even at this late stage in the mission, O'Reilly seems to have tried to talk the Germans out of sending Kenny, deciding that his limited skills were likely to jeopardize the mission's objectives.[47] This is a striking contrast to the story O'Reilly later told G2, of how he merely used the Germans for a free ticket back to Ireland. Originally, Kenny and O'Reilly were to have been dropped on 16 December, but the pilot expressed doubts about whether he could guarantee a precise drop of two men and equipment in such a narrow drop zone. It was decided to fly Kenny the following night, 17 December, but the Luftwaffe pilot of Kenny's aircraft found the conditions too foggy over the drop zone and he was returned to France. En route, Allied fighters attacked the He-111 and the crew (including Kenny) baled out over the airfield at Rennes while the pilot attempted an emergency landing. The aircraft was repaired and Kenny successfully parachuted into Ireland on 19 December. Radio warning of Kenny's aborted attempt to reach Ireland was intercepted by the British Radio Surveillance Service (RSS), which monitored the plane's return to Morlaix.[48]

Kenny and O'Reilly were to be flown by Luftwaffe Specialist Group 3F 123, normally based at Brest.[49] The Luftwaffe had done some degree of advanced planning for the mission and had timed the landing at Kilkee to coincide with the arrival of the scheduled transatlantic flight from New York to Shannon, with the idea that the sounds of the twin-engine He-111 would be masked by the four-engine Clipper. The mission also called for O'Reilly to jump from an altitude of only 300 metres.[50] To avoid a repetition of Görtz's landing, O'Reilly and his suitcase were weighed separately so that the descent of both parachutes could be timed more precisely. He was also given a red/green signal light so that he could indicate his safe landing to the bomber crew.[51]

JOHN FRANCIS RETURNS HOME

When finally dropped approximately a mile from his family home in Kilkee at 0200 on 16 December, O'Reilly made his way almost directly to his house. Though originally dropped with £300, he only had £143 on him when he was later arrested. The O'Reilly family did not notify the Garda that John Francis had landed. Their delight at having him home again invariably spread by word of mouth, and the Garda – fully aware of the recent broadcast activities of their 'local boy' – heard the same rumours. They initially became interested when reports reached them that a strange man with a heavy case stopped at Moveen asking the way to Kilkee. Despite this information, Gardaí; did not seem to be in hurry to arrest O'Reilly. When they arrived at the O'Reilly house, John Francis was not at home – he had gone on a shopping trip to town – and the officers merely asked his mother to have him stop by the police station. He did so at 2300 hours, but was questioned and released, and was only taken into custody at 1130 the next day (17 December).[52] Investigation revealed the landing site and the presence of two parachutes, one with a harness and one without, two spades, and eight shock-absorbing pads.[53] He also carried a standard Abwehr-issue suitcase with an a.c. mains transmitter/receiver and also a battery-operated telegraph transmitter/receiver, Morse key and, unusually, a code-wheel for enciphering and deciphering messages.[54]

Kenny's arrival, as might be expected, was hardly error-free. When he descended at approximately 0235 on the morning of 19 December, he seemed to have forgotten the basic airborne rule to collapse the parachute immediately upon landing. As a result, his parachute picked up a wind gust, dragged him through several fields and over a few low walls, and stopped only when he hit a more formidable stone wall. Kenny suffered a moderately deep cut to his head, injured his back and was covered in bruises. He walked to a neighbouring house and the occupants, sensing that something was definitely out of the ordinary, called the Garda. Kenny's only possessions were £94 and a camouflage parachute. In a later statement, he said that he had been given £100 before leaving France, but could not understand what happened to the missing £6.[55] Kenny was later taken to Kilrush Hospital and eventually transferred to the county hospital at Ennis.

The aftermath of the O'Reilly and Kenny episodes meant the end of active German Intelligence initiatives in Ireland. Following a concerned telegram from Hempel in Dublin, Ribbentrop ordered meetings with both the SD and the Abwehr to warn them against future covert operations in Ireland. With the run-up to the invasion, the Foreign Ministry (and Hempel) feared that Ireland would give into British and American demands and expel the German Legation from Dublin. The Abwehr reaffirmed that it had 'no further action plans for Ireland'. The SD likewise deferred to the Foreign Ministry.[56]

There was one further and final attempt to involve the Irish in the plans of the Third Reich: a half-baked operation was organized by Heinrich Himmler in July 1944 to corral approximately 1,200 Irishmen from among British prisoners of war, based on their theoretical anti-communist and anti-English position. The SS plan was essentially to create a foreign legion based on the existing model of the British Free Corps/Legion of St George for purposes of propaganda, not as a reservoir of needed military manpower. The Irish were sent to a special camp at Buchenwald, but proved impervious 'against every influence'.[57] Germany's worsening military situation might have had something to do with the lacklustre response; Himmler abandoned the idea in early 1945. The inevitable course of the war ensured that no further action was taken in relation to Ireland.

8
Irish in Germany

Espionage activities directed against Ireland were in no way limited to actions that took place on Irish soil. The presence of a small and diverse Irish community in Nazi Germany contributed to the ability of the German Intelligence services (the Abwehr and the SD) to plan and mount covert activities in Ireland itself by providing crucial information, moral support, undoubted propaganda value and even the odd volunteer spy. The Irish community in wartime Germany was never large, but several Irish expatriates did serve Nazi Germany. Though they generally did not use these sources wisely, the various German Intelligence services had access to a ready-made pool of expertise on Ireland and Irish matters.

The question of Irish citizens aiding and assisting the German war effort is one that has legal and practical considerations. While Ireland was a 'Free State' and issued passports under its own name, it maintained a legal relationship to England. The 1937 Irish Constitution, despite its delicate wording, did not declare Ireland independent, but rather left it squarely inside the British Commonwealth as a dominion. As MI5 noted, under the 1931 Statute of Westminster, Ireland had a right to declare neutrality, but that 'as British subjects, those who give aid and assistance to the King's enemies rendered themselves liable to be charged with treason'.[1] Whether Irish citizens who sided with Hitler were or were not traitors was never established in a court of law. British renegades, on the other hand, risked receiving the death penalty.[2]

British Intelligence took collaboration seriously. They formed a special unit, SLB3, to deal with renegades, 'both British and Irish'. The British were also concerned that William Warnock issued passports

> on the flimsiest grounds and on occasion to persons having little or no claim to Eireann nationality, who wished to escape internment. The excuse given by [Warnock] was that this was done on humanitarian grounds, but there have been indications that these passports were not acquired without consideration and that the Germans were often a party to these transactions in the case of persons of whom they hoped subsequently to make use.[3]

The Germans obviously regarded Warnock as 'approachable' (as in the Schütz case) but there is no released document that proves that he acted from motives of 'consideration' of one kind or another. One of the questionable passports would have been that issued to Nora O'Mara, who apparently started using this *nom de guerre* in connection with the issuance of her Irish passport, having previously been a British citizen.

CHARLES BEWLEY

Bewley, who had last been active recommending Leopold Kerney's republican qualifications in 1941, was still promoting himself as an expert on Irish affairs later in the war. The former Irish minister to Germany arrived uninvited in Berlin in December 1942 and proceeded to give Foreign Ministry Under-Secretary of State Ernst Woermann gratuitous advice on how to destabilize the de Valera government. Bewley suggested an association with Irish clerics and 'Republican forces'.[4] Bewley's advice also extended to strategy concerning the Irish in the United States – Bewley suggested promising Irish-Americans that in the event of a German victory, Germany would oversee the creation of a united Irish republic, to include Ulster.[5] In another German Foreign Ministry report from December 1942, Bewley told the Germans that de Valera 'was in reality, a friend of England' who wants to 'maintain Ireland in the British Commonwealth'. He also offered the sage advice that an English or American occupation of Ireland was not anticipated.[6] The full extent of Bewley's activities from 1943 to 1945 are still shrouded in secrecy.

His pleas of good conduct and neutrality aside, Bewley was arrested by the United States Army on 17 June 1945. The Americans turned the erstwhile Irish patriot over to the British, who imprisoned him for six months in a cell in Terni together with the renegade John Amery. Despite Bewley's unabashed fascism, the Irish Department of External Affairs went to great lengths to assist their former minister to Germany once the Allies arrested him; Joseph Walshe addressed a plea for leniency to the British representative in Ireland, Sir John Maffey. Bewley was released without trial on 15 December 1945. Though sympathy for Bewley existed in political quarters, G2's Dan Bryan was under no illusion about his conduct. An MI5 report stated that Bewley had been a paid adviser to the Propaganda Ministry in connection with German initiatives in Ireland and the Vatican. The British also alleged that Bewley eventually worked for RSHA Amt VI – the SD. While some of the more elaborate charges against Bewley were thought to be lacking in foundation, Bryan concluded that 'there is little doubt that Bewley was working for the German Intelligence Service and Amt VI in Rome and was being regularly paid by them'.[7] German records indicate that Bewley offered his services to the SD, but was turned down – 'rejected as a staff member by Amt VI D because [he is] too lazy and very timid'.[8]

FRANCIS STUART

Following his initial encounter with German Intelligence in 1940 as an IRA courier, Stuart was soon approached by the ubiquitous Franz Fromme and asked if he would be willing to write radio scripts for broadcast to England and Ireland. These duties would also involve translating German news items into English. Stuart agreed and found himself writing scripts that were broadcast by William Joyce, though Stuart claimed that he did not initially know this.[9] This eventually led to Stuart's more notorious work with the Irish-language section of the Foreign Ministry's radio propaganda broadcast team, the Irland-Redaktion.

It was about this time that Stuart became somewhat friendly with the Irish Chargé d'Affaires in Berlin, William Warnock. Stuart said that the two of them would sometimes play golf together, joined by Eileen Walsh, the legation secretary. Warnock also invited Stuart to listen to foreign broadcasts on his short-wave radio and likewise agreed to forward Stuart's mail to Ireland in the diplomatic bag. Stuart says that this was done rather surreptitiously, and that he left his outgoing mail on the piano in the legation. He suggested that this was done with the complicity of Miss Walsh.[10]

While at this point (April 1940) Stuart was doing only light work for the Berlin Rundfunkhaus (broadcasting centre), Franz Fromme suddenly reappeared and introduced him to Dr Hermann Görtz. Görtz was temporarily assigned to the Brandenburg Regiment for training and was preparing for his scheduled espionage mission to Ireland. The evident purpose of this meeting in the fashionable Kurfürstendam was for Stuart to provide details about Ireland that might be useful to Görtz. In Stuart's version of events, he gave Görtz a £1 note and some change, and provided his Laragh Castle address to be used only in case of an emergency. Describing Görtz as a 'very honourable person', Stuart said he liked him very much.[11] Görtz apparently reciprocated the feeling. In part two of a series of articles allegedly written by Görtz that appeared posthumously in the *Irish Times*, he described his contact with Stuart:

> I got in touch with a number of Irish persons living in Germany. Among them was Mr. F. S[tuart], towards whom I felt a strong personal sympathy. Mr. S[tuart] was not connected with the German Intelligence. I made a point of meeting him when I heard that an Irishman was a lecturer at the University of Berlin. He was not politically-minded, and had no contact with, or knowledge of, the IRA, but he was an ardent Irish patriot, the prototype of these people who later became my friends in Eire. ... I was warned by the Irishmen I met in Germany not to expect too much from the IRA, either as a political body, the torch-bearer of a national movement, or as a military body. I think it was Mr. S[tuart] who described the organisation as the expression of an embittered and disappointed longing for the national unity of Ireland. [12]

There are a few problems with this account, leaving aside the obvious differences in syntax used by Görtz in these articles and in all other examples of his genuine correspondence and writing. Despite the published Görtz contention that Stuart was not connected with the IRA, this was clearly false. Fromme certainly knew that Stuart made no secret of his connection with the organization, and since Görtz's brief was to act as a liaison between the IRA and the Abwehr, it would be reasonable to assume that he too knew Stuart's background. In any event, Görtz made a beeline for Laragh Castle upon landing, which served once again to attract the attention of Irish Intelligence to Francis and Iseult Stuart.[13]

NORA O'MARA

During the transitory meeting between Stuart and Hermann Görtz, the German mentioned to Stuart that he knew another Irish person who was acting as his secretary.[14] This woman, Nora O'Mara, was introduced to Stuart a few days later and he was disturbed by her personal circumstances. Lacking a permanent place to live, she was temporarily staying in a sitting room belonging to two Russian sisters. O'Mara was also obviously pregnant, the Ukrainian father of her child having abandoned her. Stuart offered to let her stay in part of his apartment and soon offered her a job as his secretary at the Drahtlose Dienst (wireless service), where he translated news articles from German to English. Stuart and O'Mara descended into a romantic relationship after the birth of her daughter, Nadejda Agnes.

Though she presented herself to Stuart and Görtz as Irish – indeed, she continues to make this claim – the evidence for this is sparse. Like many of the details that O'Mara gives about herself, there are strong elements of fantasy and deception about her actual origins. According to a questionnaire she completed in 1942 for the German authorities, she lists her place of birth as Philadelphia.[15] However, in another questionnaire for the Reichstheaterkammer in 1944, she states that she was born in London. In a reference to her by MI5, her correct birth name is given as Rosaleen James, born in 1918.[16] By contrast, in her self-serving and highly fictive autobiography, she ignores this question entirely, stating only that her father was Irish and that she was a 'war orphan of the 1914–18 war whose father had been seduced by lies to fight on England's side'.[17] She further states, without corroboration, that she was adopted by Sir Ian Hamilton and lived the life of high English society, attending only the best finishing schools in Paris and Munich.[18]

This 'strikingly beautiful Irish colleen' (to use Uinseann MacEoin's phrase) ended up in wartime Berlin, pregnant and essentially homeless.[19] At some point during this poignant voyage of self-discovery, she decided that she was Irish and claims to have authored a work while in Germany called *Irische Freiheitskämpfer* (Irish Freedom Fighters).[20] She further claims that Hermann Görtz asked her to act as a recipient of radio messages that he would send back from Ireland.[21] In an even more puzzling leap of credibility, O'Mara also maintains that coincident with the projected Operation Sealion, Graf von Stauffenberg (presumably the one who planted the bomb at Hitler's headquarters in the 20 July 1944 plot) approached her to act as the vanguard of the German invasion of England and asked if she could assist them by being in Surrey and leading the victorious German troops to Chartwell, the home of Winston Churchill.

It is known that O'Mara eventually transferred in 1943 with Francis Stuartto the Irland-Redaktion, where she gave a few radio talks under the direction of Dr Hans Hartmann.[22] According to the dubious recollections of O'Mara herself, she had earlier broadcast for German radio during the Polish campaign of 1939 – though she seems to have neglected to provide this information to the Germans when completing her personnel documents in 1942 and 1944.

Kurt Haller remembered her as 'Kitty' O'Mara and noted that she was 'not the type of woman that one treats lightly'. He also said that she had a second illegitimate child sometime during the course of the war and became associated with members of the French resistance.[23]

O'Mara's connections to the German Intelligence missions in Ireland, whether real or imagined, are largely conjectural. Writing in his serialized memoirs published in 1952, John O'Reilly gave some attention to Nora O'Mara. He noted that she

> was slightly built, pretty but not strikingly so, with very little colour in her cheeks. Her hair was long, jet black, and parted severely in the middle. ... Although she appeared to have some Irish background I never learned what it was or whether she had Irish parentage. Despite her good looks and her enigmatic personality there was very little of the glamorous Mata Hari about 'Deidre'. What puzzled me most about her was that she appeared to maintain equally friendly contacts with the various espionage groups of the Wehrmacht, the Admiralty, and the SS. Their intelligence departments usually maintained completely separate identities. They exchanged neither agents nor information, though their activities frequently overlapped. Yet here was 'Deirdre', attached to every group, but tied to none.[24]

MI5 was also keeping track of this renegade: 'She claims that her parents were English and that she is the adopted daughter of Sir Ian Hamilton, but has no papers to establish her claim. She is supposed to be married to a Russian nobleman, present whereabouts unknown, and has a three year old child, but still uses the name Nora O'Mara in her correspondence.'[25] Another equally puzzling picture of O'Mara is drawn by the wartime Irish Chargé d'Affaires in Berlin, William Warnock. Meeting her at a theatre opening in Berlin, he was perplexed by her attitude. O'Mara, now playing the part of an actress, had volunteered to perform for the show, but had been turned away at the door. She made a rigorous complaint to Warnock:

> She did not appear to him [Warnock] to be quite sensible on the occasion. She was obviously pregnant although she was emphasising that she was 'Miss'. He had no information of her 'liaison' with a Russian count ... he could not understand the part she was playing. Mr. Warnock was of the opinion that she was responsible for a raid by the SS on [Liam] Mullally's flat, as the latter did not like her, and was rather outspoken where she was concerned.[26]

In his report back to the Department of External Affairs, Warnock 'could not throw any light on the point as to whether she was an illegitimate daughter, or a ward, or adopted daughter of Sir Ian [Hamilton]'.[27] According to her Nazi file, O'Mara drifted somewhat after leaving the Irland-Redaktion. She apparently worked for a time as an actress in Vienna and involved herself with several theatre companies. In 1992, after almost fifty years of blissful silence, she was again in the headlines on the publication of her memoir, *Cé Hí Seo Amuigh?* Using her adopted name of Róisín Ní Mheara-Vinard, Nora O'Mara/Rosaleen James managed to generate controversy when she claimed in her book, among other things, that the photographs of German extermination camp victims were false and that the dead were really German civilians killed in Allied bombing raids. Most significantly, she alleged that Jews in the camps died from typhoid, not Zyklon-B gas.[28] These outrageous opinions were made even more objectionable when it was revealed that her publisher would be eligible for an Irish government grant since the book was published in the Irish language. To their credit, most newspapers published scathing reviews of the work, in one case pointing to the distinct similarity between the writing of Miss Ní Mheara-Vinard and that of Ciaran O Coigligh.[29] In the years since, she has occasionally worked at the Cardinal Tomás O Fiach Library in Armagh, but lives in Klosterneuberg, Austria.[30]

WILLIAM JOSEPH MURPHY

Originally from Bessbrook, County Armagh, William Joseph Murphy worked for Berlitz language schools in Germany, Holland, Belgium and Yugoslavia in the years before the war began. Teaching in Essen when war was declared, Murphy was arrested and jailed by the Gestapo for two days and released when they grudgingly accepted his protestations of Irish nationality. In mid-1942, Murphy was contacted by an Irishman named John Freeman, who said he worked for the Essen publishing company Verlag Girardet. Freeman mentioned that Murphy would find easy employment at the Abwehr, where his talents could be put to better use. Somewhat bored by his work at Berlitz, and having already been arrested three times by the Gestapo, Murphy accepted Freeman's invitation to the

Abwehr Ast in Bremen. Once there, he was interviewed by a Hauptmann Steffens, who asked if he would be willing to return to Northern Ireland and report on the damage caused by German air attacks. Steffens gave Murphy 1000 Reichsmarks as an advance payment.[31]

Murphy applied to William Warnock at the Irish Legation for an Irish passport, surrendering his British passport at the same time. He was issued an Irish passport.[32] For reasons that are not entirely clear, the mission was abandoned after Allied bombing raids on Essen, and Murphy took a job with Berlitz in Berlin. Murphy was again unemployed after an air raid on 22 November 1943 destroyed the Berlitz school two days after his arrival. Remembering the promise of the Irish mission with the Abwehr, Murphy traced John Freeman to a house on Florastrasse, Berlin and he attempted to reactivate interest in the espionage mission.

At about the same time, Murphy met an American writer, Andre Gotzien, who introduced to him to William Joyce, leading to a one-month studio trial with the English service of Berlin Radio at a rate of 20 Reichsmarks a day. He briefly joined Dr Hartmann's Irland-Redaktion team in Luxembourg, but he failed the voice test and was told his language skills were not suitable for employment as a translator – which makes one wonder how he managed to work for Berlitz. One week after arriving in Luxembourg – and still on his one-month guaranteed employment period – he was introduced to a man calling himself Henry Freeman. Freeman said he was John's brother, that John was ill, and that he had taken over the assignment. Murphy again met with Hauptmann Steffens at the Bremen Ast in March 1944 and was given a list of information that the Abwehr wanted from Britain and Northern Ireland, now including details of factories supplying the Allied war effort. Murphy, agreeable to the German plan, was sent to Berlin to get a visa for Ireland from the Irish legation with the idea that he could be infiltrated to Ireland via Spain and Portugal. Before leaving, he was given an additional 50 Marks and an Abwehr cover address in Madrid. As an incentive, Steffens promised him that if he returned to Germany from the mission, the Abwehr would support his professional goal of setting up his own language school and pay him an additional £20,000.[33]

At the Irish Legation, Murphy found that Warnock had been recalled to Dublin and Con Cremin was in charge of the new legation offices.[34] Cremin was obviously suspicious and told Murphy: 'I hope you have no idea of working for the Germans over there, because you'll be put in jail'. Cremin informed him about John O'Reilly, now detained in Arbour Hill. Cremin's suspicions were such that he did not issue the visa.[35]

Murphy then went to see Francis Stuart, whom he first met in Luxembourg. Earlier, Stuart had mentioned that he could help Murphy with a job at Berlin University. According to Murphy's statement to MI5, Stuart boasted that he was part of the Ryan/Russell operation in 1940 and that he was scheduled to travel to Ireland carrying arms once the advance party landed. Stuart suggested to Murphy that they both return to the Bremen Ast and ask the Abwehr to land them both in Ireland by submarine, along with a transmitter for the IRA. When Murphy put Stuart's suggestion to an Abwehr officer named König, the German dismissed the whole idea as 'nonsense' and thereafter refused to have anything to do with Murphy or Stuart.[36]

Murphy said that Stuart introduced him to officials at the Büro Concordia, the German 'black propaganda' radio station located in the Reichssportsfeld, Berlin, where he secured another one-month trial period and was paid 600 Marks a month.[37] Realizing that the war was getting dangerous even for foreign civilians in the service of the German Reich, Murphy decided to leave Germany and returned to Luxembourg on the pretext of collecting his luggage. He stayed in a hotel until the area was liberated by the US Army on 10 September 1944; he surrendered to the Americans and asked to be put in touch with British Intelligence.

The Freeman brothers are slightly mysterious, but they did exist. Their respective Nazi files at the Bundesarchiv-Berlin reveal that they were the sons of George Freeman, an Irishman who died in 1915. Henry was born in 1902 in Emden, lived in Düsseldorf and had been a Nazi party member since 1937. He was the author of the books *Technisches Englisch* and *Das Englische Fachwort*. According to a Gestapo report of March 1941, he had no criminal record and the Gestapo was pleased to recommend his candidacy for the Reichsschrifttumskammer.[38]

Johann Freeman (a.k.a. John Freeman) was born in 1886 in Emden and was a professional writer/salesman. He was the author of the novel *Michel*, published in 1918. According to his application for membership in the Reichsverband Deutscher Schriftsteller, he had a prior relationship to the World War One German secret intelligence services.[39] It is also noteworthy that German Military Intelligence would even consider another agent insertion into Ireland or Northern Ireland well into 1944, clearly after the point when such an action would serve any legitimate military purpose. The Freeman brothers, collectively, seem to have been freelance recruitment agents for the Abwehr, clearly specializing in attracting English-speaking people for potential espionage work.

STUART DABBLES WITH ESPIONAGE, AGAIN

When Francis Stuart arrived in Berlin in January 1940, he renewed his acquaintance with Helmut Clissmann, then stationed in Berlin and detached from his military assignment with the Brandenburg Regiment to act as an adviser to the Foreign Ministry specialist on Ireland, Dr Edmund Veesenmayer. Through Clissmann, Stuart was introduced to Sonderführer Kurt Haller. Haller was an attorney who, due to a childhood illness that resulted in a club foot, was not eligible for active service with the German Army. With a rank approximating that of a US Army Warrant Officer, Haller was assigned to Abwehr II, acting as a liaison between the Abwehr and Dr Veesenmayer in the Foreign Ministry.[40] In August 1940, Haller approached Stuart and asked if he would consider sailing to Ireland in a Breton boat piloted by Christian Nissen to act as an advance detachment for Frank Ryan and Helmut Clissmann. Stuart agreed to participate, but the plan was soon dropped in favour of the mission to transport Ryan and Sean Russell to Ireland by submarine.[41]

Stuart broadcast for the Germans from March 1942 until January 1944, when he objected to the inclusion of anti-Soviet material that was then deemed essential by his supervisors at the Irland-Redaktion. He had no further known connection with German espionage, but did maintain contact with Frank Ryan until the latter's death in June 1944.

LIAM MULLALLY

Mullally (also spelled Mulally) was born in London on 10 June 1908 to an Irish father and an English mother. He had an amazing ability for languages and by the Second World War, spoke at least six. He worked on the Continent for most of the 1930s in various Berlitz language schools, from Hungary to Germany. Returning to Ireland in 1938, he joined the Irish Defence Forces in June 1939, and was attached to the anti-aircraft battalion at McKee Barracks, but applied for an exemption in November 1939 so that he could return to a more lucrative job with the Berlitz school in Berlin.[42] He was separated from his wife, who lived with their son in Mullingar. Mullally started working for the Irland-Redaktion as O'Reilly's replacement in September 1942 (he had been sharing a flat with O'Reilly in the Berlin suburb of Kladow).[43]

According to an MI5 report, Mullally 'wrote broadcast scripts, translated songs and acted as monitor for the Irish and American programmes'.[44] Francis Stuart knew Mullally from the Rundfunkhaus – and didn't think much of him:

> There was an Irishman called Liam Mullally. He used to broadcast but, now I don't want to criticize any [body] ... he seemed to me to be a bit malleable in the German hands. He would go in for a certain amount of anti-Russian [material]. I remember once in Berlin, I used to see him, very seldom, but I said, and that was towards the end of the war, 'I wouldn't like to be in your shoes if you're here when the Russians come.' If they knew, the Russians couldn't care less and didn't have any record in my opinion, but that terrified poor Mullally, between not being able to give it [his radio job] up and dreading what would happen if the Russians came. He lived life on the black market like many of these foreigners did.[45]

When the Abwehr naval section was still employing O'Reilly in 1942–3, it contemplated using Mullally as his espionage companion. When word of the plan leaked to Dr Veesenmayer at the Foreign Ministry, he was concerned that the use of O'Reilly and Mullally would compromise what were, in his view, more significant operations involving Frank Ryan. Intelligence resources were scarce and Veesenmayer had no intention of squandering them. In the same critical report written by Kurt Haller on John F. O'Reilly, Mullally was described as an 'irresponsible, albeit affable, chatterbox.' Veesenmayer's efforts had the desired effect: Mullally was dropped from the plan and the mission was cancelled shortly thereafter.[46] Mullally eventually left broadcasting and managed to find a job in Vienna working as a valet to former British officer turned Nazi broadcaster Norman Baillie-Stewart. According to Stuart, Mullally:

> went to Vienna. There was this ex-British officer Baillie-Stewart. Before the war he'd betrayed some secrets. He was living in Vienna, and Mullally went to Vienna as his valet ... he said 'I have an easy job. Baillie-Stewart gets special rations on the black market, and all I have to do is exercise his dog mornings and evenings.[47]

Mullally returned to Ireland after the war.[48] Baillie-Stewart returned to jail.

FRIESACK CAMP

Once again in Germany following the death of Seán Russell, Frank Ryan continued to play an active part in the German war effort, though whether he pursued own agenda or that of the Germans in not clear. Part of this assistance related to the recruitment of Irish personnel for active use by the German Intelligence community, particularly revolving around the prisoner-of-war camp at Friesack.

The German idea was to try and improve upon Roger Casement's abortive 1916 attempt to recruit Irish volunteers from a special POW camp at Limburg. Casement's plan was to recruit an 'Irish Brigade' from among captured British Army prisoners that would then be transported by the Germans to Ireland. At best naïve, the plan was a failure. Only some 56 ethnic Irish reported to the Limburg camp. Casement apparently had hoped to recreate the historical participation of earlier Irish contingents in foreign armies (from the *Légion Irlandaise* in Napoleon's service to John MacBride's 'Irish Brigade' in the Boer War), but his appeal was an exercise in futility.[49] Germany hoped to improve on its earlier record with the help of some expert advice.

The special Alt Damm camp was constructed near the village of Friesack. The camp was not large, originally holding some eighty prisoners and later rising to around 180.[50] While the original plan had envisioned using as many officers as possible, Jupp Hoven recalled that the number was *weniger als Finger an einer Hand* ('fewer than the fingers on one hand').[51] Clissmann, Hoven, Haller, Ryan, and even Francis Stuart were some of the visitors to Friesack.[52] The German screening process also left something to be desired. Of the original eight officers selected by Hoven, three were mistakenly picked because the Germans did not understand their responses, two were doctors who wanted better rations than they received at their Stalag, one was a (non-Irish) journalist who saw the possibility of a good story and the remaining three had War Office codes for use in letters home smuggled to them before they were transferred to Stalag III B.[53]

SERGEANT JOHN CODD

One of the soldiers concentrated here was Sergeant John Codd. Originally from Dublin, Codd emigrated to Canada in 1929, but moved to England in 1931 to enlist in the Royal Welsh Fusiliers. He served in this unit in the Far East until 1938 and was recalled on the outbreak of war in 1939. Though of limited education, Codd spoke an interesting variety of languages, including Spanish, French and Chinese. His unit was part of the British Expeditionary Force (BEF) in France, where he was wounded covering the British forces' withdrawal at Dunkirk. After a time in a German field hospital, he was transferred to Stalag III B at Lannesdorf, and was interned from December 1940 to January 1941.[54] Stalag III B was apparently a screening camp of sorts for Irish personnel who would ultimately be selected for Stalag XX A (301) at Friesack. While at Stalag III B, the Irish prisoners were contacted by a German nicknamed 'American Joe' (also known as 'Gestapo Joe'), who promised them improved conditions and the possibility of early release if they would consider working for Ireland and against the British. Codd was among those who, for reasons either practical or patriotic, agreed. He was sent to an intermediate camp at Luckenwalde and then on to Friesack in the middle of February 1941. At the time of his arrival, he reported that there were approximately 120 to 125 other Irish there, from Stalags all over Germany. At the time the senior officer was an Irishman named Lieutenant Birrell from County Clare who was trying to ingratiate himself with both the Germans and the other prisoners. A lapse in judgement involving alcohol at a prisoners' concert resulted in Lt. Birrell being removed, and a Major John McGrath was eventually brought in to act as senior officer for the prisoners. British Intelligence was aware of the existence of Friesack since the autumn of 1940.[55]

Major (later Colonel McGrath) was a genuine hero. He had been ordered to infiltrate the other prisoners at Friesack, and try to counter the German propaganda, as well as make an accurate report of what occurred. To his credit, McGrath later tried to protect the reputation of the prisoners at Friesack, though in doing so he disregarded the truth. On his return to Dublin in 1954, where he took over as manager of the Theatre Royal,

McGrath was interviewed by the major Irish newspapers. Recounting the story ('The Germans gathered 180 Irish prisoners of war together in a special camp outside Berlin...'), McGrath concluded by saying that 'the Irishmen under me were magnificent ... nobody did anything to be ashamed of'.[56] Previously he had made a similar statement: 'Not one of the 180 gave in.'[57] However, this wasn't true.

Upon arrival in Stalag XX A (301), Codd was visited by a Herr Bruckner who made the initial approach for volunteers. Spurred on by the promise of freedom, money and an eventual return to Ireland, Codd and several others volunteered for German service. His fellow volunteers were:

> **Private James Brady**: Originally from Strokestown, Roscommon, he had been stationed in Norway with the British Army, but at the time of the German occupation of the Channel Islands, was in jail on Guernsey, convicted of the attempted murder of a police officer, and was set free by the Wehrmacht. The Germans issued him a South American passport in the name of de Lacy.
>
> **Private Frank Stringer**: Gravelstown, Carlanstown, Kells, County Meath. Born in 1922, he had been arrested for stealing turf at age 15. Stringer joined the British Navy but was dismissed, later joining the Royal Irish Fusiliers of the British Army. He was charged and convicted for attempted murder while on Jersey and was released when German forces took control of the island in July 1940.
>
> **Private William Murphy**: Enniscorthy, County Wexford. According to fellow Friesack prisoner Timothy Ronan, Murphy 'went off his head and became dangerous', and was, in the post-war period, confined to Nutely, the asylum for servicemen. Murphy reportedly died there a year later.[58]
>
> **Private Patrick O'Brien**: Nenagh, County Tipperary. Like Stringer, he had a juvenile record – breaking into the Nenagh Co-Operative Creamery and stealing a fountain pen and several pencils, sentenced to two months but placed on twelve months' probation.[59] He joined the British Army and was assigned to the First Battalion, East Lancashire Regiment, and was captured at Dunkirk. He was vetted for espionage and taken to Berlin, but was arrested on a rape charge in May 1942. He was later returned to Stalag III D (961).[60]
>
> **Private Strogen**: Duleek, County Louth.
> **Private Crawley**: Bridge Street, Mountmellick.
> **Private Thomas J. Cushing**: Tipperary Town, County Tipperary.
> **Private Andrew Walsh**: Fethard, County Tipperary.[61]

Stalag XX A (301) was visited by Jupp Hoven and Helmut Clissmann, both assigned to the Abwehr, in June 1941. Hoven, who had previous experience in Ireland as an exchange student in anthropology, was the one nicknamed 'Gestapo Joe' by the Irishmen at Friesack. Hoven's visit was followed by that of Sonderführer Kurt Haller, who represented both Abwehr and the Foreign Ministry. Haller approved Codd's recruitment to Abwehr and assigned a Abwehr officer Harold Leichtweiss (described as being from 'the same bureau as Hoven') to act as Codd's chaperone during his move from Friesack to Berlin.[62] Codd was given the false name and accompanying identity card of Juan Louii along with fictitious US citizenship. In the company of Leichtweiss, Codd was taken by train to Berlin and installed in an apartment at Ludwigskirchestraße.

Despite Codd's own version of himself as a leader at Stalag XX A (301), there is a contrary viewpoint. An Irish priest, Father Thomas O'Shaughnessy, was also a witness at Friesack, though an unwilling one. According to a G2 report, based on Father O'Shaughnessy's statement, he was seconded to the Germans following a visit by Helmut Clissmann to the African Missions College in Rome, where O'Shaughnessy was working.[63] After explaining to him that Irish prisoners in Germany needed the services of an Irish priest, O'Shaughnessy's supervisors assigned him to the mission, largely in view of the fact that he spoke fluent German. Jupp Hoven (using the pseudonym Reiners) took him to Friesack where he met most of the other Irish prisoners, including Codd. On meeting this last gentleman, O'Shaughnessy 'formed the impression that his fellow prisoners would like to kill him [Codd]'.[64] He also characterized Codd as 'a tough, owing to his pro-Fenian attitude'.

Codd's exact mission was soon spelled out. The 6 October 1941 entry in the Abwehr II war diary states: 'Das Referat WN bereitet ein Unternehmen unter dem Decknamen "Gastwirt" vor. Es is beabsichtigt, zwei einsatzbereite Iren mit S[abotage]-Aufträgen nach London zu entsenden und ihnen einen Funkapparat mitzugeben. Am 5.10. hat die Funkausbildung der Iren begonnen' ('Office WN has prepared an operation under the code name "Innkeeper". It is intended to send two trained Irishmen on a sabotage mission to London and to give them a radio/transmitter. The radio training for the Irish began on 5 October'). In the projected operation, Codd and Stringer (using the pseudonym of William Martial LePage) were to be sent in together. Until that time, they were given civilian clothes and the relative freedom of wartime Berlin.

The Germans made a serious effort to wine and dine the new recruits. Codd was invited to dinners with an SS soldier named Bruggermann, along with Helmut Clissmann and Dr Schreiber of the Abwehr. On one of these occasions, he was introduced to a mysterious man who spoke passable Spanish. Codd had never encountered this gentleman before, but the man was said to have 'fought in Spain', and was introduced as Frank Richards. This was, of course, Frank Ryan, though Codd does not seem to have known this at the time. Codd subsequently visited Ryan at his bungalow in the Nicholasee (complete with a large garden). According to Codd, Ryan said that 'anything he [Codd] might do to help the Germans would be all right'. Other than expressing a fondness for the game of draughts (checkers), Ryan inexplicably mentioned that he had a Russian woman who mended his socks![65]

Codd was ordered to report to the demolition school near Potsdam for one week of intensive training under a Dr Koch. This was followed by a course under a radio instructor named Bublitz that lasted until the end of January 1942. Hoven replaced Herr Leichtweiss with another officer named Stinzing, who was now tasked with looking after Sergeant Codd. At this point, Codd was told that his projected mission was to involve a submarine landing in the US and he was to be allotted £35,000 for the two-year sabotage project in the form of US dollars, British pounds and gold bars. Codd's current salary was 400 Reichsmarks per month, meaning that he could look forward to a substantial increase in his standard of living.

However, in March 1942, the mission particulars were changed. Hoven ordered Codd to report to the *Truppenübungsplatz* (troop training area) at Roesrath, near Cologne. He was there met by a new RT (radio-telegraph) instructor, Private Kumbach, and put through another course in Morse and transmission procedures. On 1 April, Codd was taken to Dusseldorf and given an apartment in Strasse der SA, with a salary increase to 600 Reichsmarks a month. Haller later told author Enno Stephan that Codd was removed from Berlin because he was neglecting his training in pursuit of women. About the same time, his Friesack companion Frank Stringer was sent to Bonn for additional training. Hoven, now with orders to join an active-duty parachute unit at the front, turned Codd over to the control of a Herr Holborn, who supervised his training through the summer of 1942.

The news that several of their operational agents had been arrested by the Americans effectively changed the Abwehr's priorities yet again. The Friesack spies-to-be were put in cold storage. About this time, Codd lost contact with Stringer and on 25 September he was arrested by the Gestapo and thrown into prison in Dusseldorf. Again, maintained Haller, Codd had lost his mission focus, having decided that '*Mädchen vom Rhein*' were equally as enticing as the women in Berlin. His arrest was by way of a disciplinary measure and an indication that the Abwehr did not think him sufficiently serious for successful espionage work.[66] He was to remain there, uncharged, until 20 March 1943. While in jail, Codd was visited by Frank Ryan (now using the pseudonym of Mr Maloney) and Kurt Haller. Ryan again urged him to play draughts to pass the time in prison.[67] Haller and Ryan finally liberated Codd from prison and travelled with him to Berlin. Upon his release – with no explanation – Codd was sent to SS-Hauptsturmführer (Captain) Drescher at Berlin-Wilmersdorf, who informed him that he was once again scheduled for espionage work, but that he had been released from the Abwehr and was now under the authority of the SD. Unknown to Codd, two of his fellow prisoners at Friesack had been responsible for his confinement.

With the collapse of *Unternehmen Gastwirt* (Operation Innkeeper), the Abwehr turned its attention to other strategic targets. The 16 May 1942 entry for the Abwehr II war diary notes that Haller, in consultation with an expert on electricity supply from the Economic Group, formed a plan to attack the North Scottish power station at Fort William. This new operation, code-named *Möwe I* (Seagull I) planned to use a sabotage operative from Abwehr II. Andrew Walsh and Thomas Cushing were assigned a separate mission by the Abwehr.[68] The plan was further refined by the time of the next diary entry on 22 June and was subdivided into two sections, Seagull I and Seagull II. Seagull I was to use an Irish agent (*irishche V-Manner*), who would parachute in the vicinity of Glasgow. He was to form a three-man sabotage operational group from Irish friends in Scotland and then attack the electric power station at Fort William and the hydroelectric production facility at Kinlochleven. Seagull II would also be a parachute insertion. In this instance, Agent Metzger would land south-east of Ballycastle in Northern Ireland, recruit his sabotage team from any willing IRA personnel in the area, and take out important 'targets of opportunity'. Both sabotage operations were to be controlled by radio. Agent (*V-Mann*) Vickers was none other than Andrew Walsh; Metzger was actually James Brady. Following the completion of their training, which included an intensive radio course at the Abwehr school at Stettin, the pair set off with Haller for occupied Norway where they were to fly to their respective destinations in a converted Focke-Wulf 200 Condor.

Shortly before takeoff, Haller received a call from Hauptmann Astor at Office WN (Abwehr II headquarters in Berlin), who would only say that 'something happened' and that he was to return to Berlin with his would-be agents. Upon arrival in Berlin, Haller learned the nature of the problem. Prior to the departure for Norway, Walsh (a.k.a. Vickers) confided to fellow Irish POW Thomas Cushing that he was planning to turn himself into the police on landing in England, after hiding his German espionage money. Cushing, now a devoted German stooge, reported his fellow Irishman's comments and the two found themselves in the 'protective custody' of the Gestapo.[69] Their exact fate remains unknown.[70] The remainder of the group, except for Codd, were sent to a farm in Silesia for forced manual labour, better than a concentration camp, but hardly what they were led to expect.

Codd was given a new mission, this time to Northern Ireland, and was photographed for a passport issued under his new cover name, Jacob Collins, a German born in Metz, France). His prior Abwehr training was apparently deemed insufficient and he was given a two-week course in cryptology from a Frau Dr Heimpel. Ireland's wartime cryptology expert, Dr Richard Hayes, made the point that the Germans followed a pattern with the encoding methods taught to their agents; the complexity of the ciphers depended on the relative importance of the particular mission and the capability of the operator.

Using this standard, Codd was not put into the same class as Görtz or O'Reilly. Codd was taught several relatively low-grade ciphering methods. The first was a simple substitution, with a key word being written out (for example, 'Dusseldorf,' which was always the keyword chosen for Codd's training exercises). This word was followed by all the remaining letters of the alphabet, with duplicate letters removed. Below the first line, the normal alphabet was written and for encoding the letters in the top line were simply substituted. Since there was no difficulty in breaking this type of cipher, its use was restricted to ordinary letters in the post in which the first letter of every third word was the only letter intended to be read.

Codd's second cipher was based on the 25-letter square that was used in the preliminary steps of the Görtz code – see Table 8. The clear text is converted into a row of figures – two figures for each letter, e.g. 11245131214 and so on. The first figure ('1') is switched from the beginning to the end to make the series 12451312141. This set of figures is put back into letters by means of the square and this gives the enciphered text.

A third cipher variation also used the 25-letter square, but without the marginal numerals. The ciphered letter is obtained by showing the intersection point of the column and the row. For example, the letter R would be represented as OW, OU, BU, UB or BW. This system gave a substitution in the ciphered text that was double the length of the original message (presenting a complication in terms of transmission time). If desired, the first letter could be again be placed at the end of the series and the message could be substituted back by using the square to halve the number of letters to a length equal to the original text.

A further variation taught to Codd involved the SD disc cipher that was also used by O'Reilly. The series of jumbled figures needed was obtained by listing the date and then adding the numbered text, e.g. for 1 October:

Table 8

	1	2	3	4	5
1	D	U	S	E	L
2	O	R	F	A	B
3	C	G	H	I	K
4	M	N	P	Q	T
5	V	W	X	Y	Z

D is 11: U is 12: A is 24. etc.

01101133553298 etc. Codd told G2 he had never heard of the micro-photographic list of 400 five-number sets that was provided to O'Reilly and had no idea as to its use.

The only remaining enciphering system taught to Codd was another – and simpler – variation of the one used by Görtz. A keyword and phrase was used and listed as in Table 9. The cipher was extracted by numerically ordered columns using the sequence on the top of the cipher (which is based on the position of the letters in keyword/phrase) e.g. TLLUT TEFWX EYIRR XTENL and so on.[71]

Codd's training was supervised by SS-Hauptsturmführer Schultz. He was then posted to a ten-day demolition course at Hubertusallee, near Hallensee. This consisted of a series of classes and practical exercises in the use and manufacture of explosives and booby traps, followed by a heavy and light weapons course at Berlin-Zehlendorf. Rather than being sent on his mission immediately, Codd was detailed to act as an interpreter for a group of twelve Arabs (mostly from Tunisia and Algeria) who were undergoing various courses in telegraphy at the SD espionage school. The Arabs spoke only French and Arabic, so Codd was to translate the German instructions into French for the Arabs, and then translate their questions back into German for the benefit of the instructor. Codd's fiancée arrived in Berlin about this time and they married. Irmgard Kensky née Schoenhoff, from Cologne, had struck up an acquaintance with Codd in March 1942.

On 23 April 1943, SS-Hauptsturmführer Giese took over from Drescher and Codd was again ordered to report for RT training, this time at the SD school at Lehnitz. His operational task was again reworked, now assigning him as a radio operator for the Northern Ireland mission. Codd remained at Lehnitz until May 1944. During his stay there, he received instruction from a Dutch SD man named Bakker, the school specialist in coded radio transmissions and disc ciphers, and Morse classes from SS-Scharführer

Table 9

2	17	12	13	4	7	3	9	11	5	14	15	1	16	6	10	8
D	U	S	S	E	L	D	O	R	F	S	T	A	T	I	O	N
1 T	H	E	T	E	X	T	I	S	W	R	I	T				
2 T																
3 E	N	I	N	T	H	E										
4 F	O	L	L	O												
5 W	I	N	G	M	A	N	N	E	R							
6 X	Y	O	U	F	I	L	L	E	A	C	H	L	I	N		
7 E	U	N	T	I	L											
8 Y	O	U	M	E	E	T	T	H	E	C	O	L	U	M	N	W
9 I	T	H	T	H	E	C	O									
10 R	R	E	S	P	O	N	D	I	N	G	N	U	M	B	E	
11 R	A	T	T	H	E	T	O	P								
12 X	X	X														

(Sergeant) Odenthal. Codd also confirmed the independent testimony given by John Kenny during the course of occasional visits to the SD headquarters at 32–35 Berkärstrasse on the Elsterplatz. The section leader of the SD espionage section, Abteilung VI A, was SS-Hauptsturmbannführer Otto Skorzeny, followed by SS-Obersturmbannführer Schüddekopf and then SS-Hauptsturmführer Giese.[72] Codd also mentioned the presence of a Dr Todt from the Gestapo.[73]

Codd's information about the SD espionage section usually dovetails with that given independently by O'Reilly and Kenny, including the office at SD headquarters where girls marked items of Irish interest from newspapers, cut them out and pasted them on separate sheets of paper. Codd met John F. O'Reilly in September/October 1943 and, with Giese, discussed the possibility of a joint operation to Ireland.[74] Codd maintained that he did not want an Irish mission, but O'Reilly's version of this encounter is slightly different.

O'Reilly later said that SS-Sturmbannführer (Major) Dr Peters told him to visit a certain address in West Berlin where he was to meet 'the man we have tentatively selected to be your companion'. O'Reilly was initially impressed with Codd's appearance, 'powerful body, with heavy muscular shoulders and large capable hands. A good man in a rough-and-tumble, I considered.' He then went on to describe Codd as having the 'broad-cheeked features and distinctive eyes which characterize the typical Irishman'. In O'Reilly's version of events, he questioned Codd at length and the POW told him a story about being in the IRA under orders to infiltrate the British Army to get military information. O'Reilly did not believe this version of the truth and decided that 'when my feet touched Ireland, Private [*sic*] C[odd] would not be there to witness the exile's return'. O'Reilly then told Peters that Codd would be unsuitable for his mission to County Clare.[75]

At the end of May 1944, Codd was again transferred to a new SD espionage school, this time near The Hague. This particular facility, called 'A-Schule West', was located between The Hague and Scheveningen, on an estate park.[76] Once in the Netherlands, Codd was introduced to a fellow agent named Koller, also of SD VI A. Koller's real name was William Colepaugh. He was born in the United States and had worked as a sailor while engaging in minor missions for the Abwehr in the pre-war period in Latin America. He later joined the US Navy, but had been dismissed on unspecified grounds. Codd said that Skorzeny made the decision to send himself and Colepaugh on a new mission to the US, but that a last-minute change resulted in Koller and another agent named Erich Gimpel being sent on the US assignment. They were later captured and narrowly escaped execution.

Meanwhile, Codd was finding the SS Training School at The Hague to be analogous to an espionage holiday camp. Classes were held from 0800 to 1200 and from 1400 to 1700 daily, under the overall supervision of Dr Peters, chief of the school. Students were taught demolition techniques (both anti-material and anti-personnel), sports, horse riding, motorcycling, swimming and the construction of miniature models and radio sets. While at The Hague, Codd was asked whether he wanted to join John Amery's collaborator unit, the British Free Corps, also known as the Legion of St. George. He wisely refused.[77]

Codd was never used as a secret agent by either the Abwehr or the SD. With the invasion of Normandy on 6 June 1944, even the very idea of using espionage agents against Allied countries became ludicrous. Codd was again attached to the SD school at Lehnitz and along with the other personnel was principally hoping to be seen as vital to the war effort and thereby to avoid front-line service. In March 1945, he and his wife successfully infiltrated a group of French refugees and made it safely to newly liberated France. Codd and his wife returned to Dublin after the war and lived at 59 Montpelier Hill. He was arrested on entering the country – his name being on the G2 'wanted list' – but was released after interrogation with no charges preferred. The British might have had other ideas had they known of his whereabouts. Codd was not able to find a job, but with four years of extensive (and repetitive) German military training behind him, decided on another tack. In July 1948, he wrote to the secretary to the Minister of Defence in Dublin and offered to demonstrate his ability in areas such as 'small arms, grenades – all nations, patrolling'. The secretary, like the German Intelligence services before him, does not seem to have taken Codd up on his generous offer to demonstrate his ability.[78]

JAMES O'NEILL: THE SPY WHO NEVER WAS

The Abwehr also selected another Friesack prisoner for special duty: James Cromwell O'Neill of County Wexford. O'Neill was captured on a freighter and sent to Friesack (though as civilian, he would not normally have qualified for placement in a Stalag) for further screening. He accepted the Abwehr's offer of work in Ireland. Code-named 'Eisenbart', he was trained in Hamburg as a radio operator for a mission in Northern Ireland, where he was expected to report on items similar to those in the brief given to Günther Schütz.[79] He was taken to a point at the Franco-Spanish border and told to make his own way back home, preferably by contacting Minister Kerney in Madrid. O'Neill was given cover addresses in Sweden and Spain, to use if radio communication with Germany was impossible. His cipher code was perhaps the simplest given to any German agent, an indication that the Abwehr did not rate him too highly. It was operated by a sliding rule and used a poem to provide the letter positions before enciphering them.[80] O'Neill eventually reached Portugal where he surrendered to the British.[81]

O'Neill's mission to Northern Ireland had been designed to sidestep the Foreign Ministry's ban on operations in Ireland proper, but after O'Neill's departure, the Abwehr was under pressure to produce a progress report on his operation. They stalled with the story that he was under orders to wait two or three months before making contact. Actually, O'Neill had turned himself in to British intelligence as soon as possible. He was interrogated in London and then sent on his way; like Lenihan, O'Neill was considered unsuitable for a Double-Cross operation, but was inexplicably turned loose, rather than being interned. The dividing line seems to have been that they voluntarily surrendered, rather than attempting to carry out their Abwehr missions.[82]

IRISH CIVILIANS IN GERMANY

Other than the aforementioned individuals, there was additionally another class of Irish who were living and working in Germany. The reasons for their presence in the Third Reich varied; some were married to German civilians or soldiers, while others appeared to be in Germany for no particular reason. Irish Intelligence kept a continual track of the people and updated rosters as more information became available. There were at least 85 Irish women residing in Germany, some of whom were said to work for the German propaganda services.[83] G2 kept a particular watch on Maura Lydon (Gortmore, Tourmakeady, County Mayo) after she mentioned in a 1943 letter to her sister Delia that she was broadcasting 'for Germany calling Ireland' from 8:15 to 8:45 p.m., which seemed to match up with an unidentified voice on the Irland-Redaktion transmissions.[84] In another case, that of Peggy Keaney, who had previously been on Jersey, G2 noted that she 'has no respect for her Irish upbringing'.[85] Other women were also monitored, as their names became known. Ella Kavanagh and Maureen Petrie were both put on the 'suspect list' when these names were used on the German radio propaganda broadcasts to Ireland – though in retrospect it was considered that they might have been pseudonyms for other announcers.[86]

The number of Irish men resident in wartime Germany was also a statistical problem for Irish Intelligence. Some were civilian internees who had been taken off merchant ships, while others fell into a more general category.[87] One Edward Bowlby (born on 22 June 1911) was said to be working for the German Foreign Ministry and another, John McCarthy (Rose Cottage, Doneraile, County Cork) was reported to be in the German merchant marine service (the DDG Hansa), assigned to the SS *Treuenfels*.[88] Irish Intelligence got Edward Bowlby wrong: he was actually a member of the renegade unit, the British Free Corps – a group of traitors organized by John Amery and the SS to fight for Nazi Germany.[89] Also included on the list was another John McCarthy (from Bandon, County Cork), who was born in 1864. Other than the 'suspect' Irish nationals known to be at Friesack, were William Sargent (or Sergeant) from Kilmallock, County Limerick – who had been mentioned by John Kenny – Liam Mullally, from the Berlitz school, and Dan Reeves (Dublin), who was working for the German Fichte-Bund.[90]

One Irishman, Owen Corr (Rush, County Dublin), was also of interest to G2. Born on 22 January 1916, he was a sailor whose merchant ship, the MV *Silverfix*, was sunk by a German raider. He was interned in Marlag and Milag Nord (the internment camp for enemy merchant sailors) near Bremen. For reasons that are not entirely clear, he was released on 27 January 1943 for civilian work at the Bremen Labour Office. Corr's name was given by Joseph Andrews – Görtz's would-be successor – as a character reference to Irish Intelligence interrogators. Since by this time Irish Intelligence had determined that Andrews had no character to speak of, this made Corr a suspect by default. According to a file notation, he died some time during the war.[91]

British Intelligence was also interested in another Irish graduate of Marlag and Milag Nord, Patrick Joseph Dillon, who was said to be working for the SD.[92] Thomas Gunning, former secretary to Blueshirt leader Eoin O'Duffy, had accompanied the Irish volunteers for Franco, but remained in Spain when the remainder of the brigade departed under a cloud of recrimination. He worked as a newspaper correspondent for a short time before making his way to Berlin, where he worked for the Propaganda Ministry until his death from tuberculosis in 1940.[93]

9
Agents in custody

The German Intelligence internees in Ireland were held in a variety of locations at one time or another: Sligo Jail, Arbour Hill Prison, Mountjoy, Bridewell Jail and finally Custume Barracks, Athlone. Though three of them (Görtz, Tributh and Gärtner) were serving members of the German Wehrmacht, the special nature of their activities in Ireland was considered sufficient to separate them from the strictly military German internees (Navy and Luftwaffe) who were kept in the Curragh; spies needed to be kept separate. For security purposes it was decided to incarcerate them together in a secure facility, and the military detention block at Mountjoy was deemed appropriate, despite its proximity to downtown Dublin. Curiously, O'Reilly and Kenny were never mixed with the other Abwehr internees, but remained at Arbour Hill.

Soon after the initial concentration of 'special' prisoners at Mountjoy, Dutchman Jan van Loon, agreed to assist Schütz in his planned escape from the prison. The two first attempted to dig a tunnel under van Loon's bunk. They worked diligently for several weeks, only to have to abandon the project when the tunnel filled up with water.[1] Schütz organized the next attempt very thoroughly. The first part of the plan involved buying women's clothing: a hat, silk stockings, shoes, a winter coat and several yards of curtain material. The Irish authorities generously allowed him to spend the English money he brought to Ireland and he soon obtained the Mountjoy governor's approval for the purchases by explaining that he wanted to send the items to his fiancée in Germany. Governor Kavanagh was doubtful and had guards check the shoe size – too small for Schütz – before he would allow the purchase.[2]

The next part of the plan required a working knowledge of the outside. Schütz had noticed that German and IRA prisoners, normally kept strictly segregated, were allowed to mix together on sick call; Schütz made a point of reporting sick on a regular basis. In this way, he made contact with IRA internee Jim O'Hanlon. O'Hanlon obligingly provided his own address, and those of several others, to the German prisoner. Schütz obtained two miniature hacksaws from an English prisoner and set to work on the bars in the lavatory window. He and van Loon spent the next six weeks sawing the steel bar and then covering over the cut marks with shoe polish. The pair apparently had extensive freedom of movement, because in addition to working at the window, they managed to fashion a disused heating pipe into a hook, which would then be thrown over the outer wall during the escape.[3]

On 15 February 1942 at 2130 hours, the moment finally arrived.[4] Schütz made up his bed to create the impression of a sleeping prisoner and then walked out of the unlocked room to join van Loon in the latrine. Earlier he had asked Dieter Gärtner to distract the guard as long as possible and had given him the list of safe houses, in case he could follow the escape route himself. Schütz and van Loon punched out the bar, threw out the change of clothes and pushed the heating pipe before them. They followed and then placed the pipe with the attached curtain material over the final wall to freedom. Schütz successfully negotiated the wall, but van Loon fell as he attempted to climb up, breaking his rib. Schütz, already wearing his frock and scarf, dropped down on the other side – a distance of seven metres – and hurried away. Within five minutes, and with a sprained ankle, he had arrived at O'Hanlon's house in Innisfallen Parade. Back in Mountjoy, the guards had been alerted by van Loon's fall. In Schütz's cell, they discovered a list of addresses – minus O'Hanlon's house.[5]

Telling them that he brought a message from their son in Mountjoy, Schütz was admitted to Joe O'Hanlon's door. He explained that he was an escaped German, but the imminent danger from the searching police meant that there was no time for further explanations. Mr and Mrs O'Hanlon went to work perfecting Schütz's disguise with a wig, lipstick and an eyebrow pencil. Within a half-hour of his escape, the sirens from Mountjoy could be heard, and it was necessary to move Schütz to a safer location. Accompanied by the O'Hanlons, he walked across Drumcondra Bridge – and noticed that it was guarded. O'Hanlon identified his wife and his 'daughter-in-law' and was allowed to proceed. Schütz was taken to the house of Joe O'Hanlon's sister. A short while later, Garda cars pulled in across the street and searched Drumcondra Church. Schütz bolted out of the back door and into the garden of the neighbouring house. To the surprise of the two old women who lived in the house, this stranger invited himself to the use of their cellar until he was given the all-clear by Joe O'Hanlon about two hours later. In the meantime, other accommodations had been located; O'Hanlon phoned Caitlin Brugha who, as she was wont to do, took command of this particular operation.[6] Though his Abwehr superiors had strenuously warned him against it, Schütz now was deep within the inner circles of the IRA.

CAITLIN BRUGHA

A successful businesswoman (she owned Kingston Shirts), Caitlin Brugha was also a legend in the underground community. The widow of Cathal Brugha (a.k.a. Charles Burgess), she had been active for many years in the

IRA – hiding wanted fugitives and delivering arms and munitions to gunmen. She had also financially supported Hermann Görtz during his eighteen-month flight from Irish justice. Mrs Brugha arranged for Schütz to hide at the home of an elderly couple named Cowman in Blackrock. Though he had already had enough excitement for one night, Schütz had to move to his new hiding place immediately. Provided with a new wig and accompanied by Mrs Brugha's daughters, Neassa and Nóinín, Schütz took a bus to Blackrock.[7] He remained there for four days. In the meantime, the government circulated a wanted poster, advertising a £500 reward for information leading to the arrest and capture of Hans Marschner. The photograph from Schütz's fake South African passport illustrated the poster. Due to censorship issues, the poster was not distributed until four days after his escape, raising the issue of whether he might have been arrested sooner, had Irish newspapers been allowed to report the story.[8]

The Cowmans introduced Schütz as a French student trapped in Ireland by the war. However, they had another lodger and were concerned that he might inadvertently mention the strange foreigner who spoke French with a German accent. To avoid this, they decided to transfer Schütz to Mrs Brugha's house, 'Ros na Riogh', Temple Gardens, Rathmines. Her son Rory (who later became a Fianna Fáil TD) had also recently left Mountjoy on a temporary pass. Neassa and Nóinín Brugha arrived again, and for the third time in four days, Schütz assumed the guise of a woman. This time he went by bicycle and arrived at Mrs Brugha's house that evening.

Mrs Brugha had definite ideas about how Schütz should spend his time. She explained that the communication link between Germany and Ireland had been severed with Görtz's arrest, that Schütz must see about re-establishing that channel, and that he was to facilitate a resupply of arms, ammunition and equipment for the IRA. Though it is contradictory, Mrs Brugha informed him that there was a radio link operational in Northern Ireland that had the capability to transmit to Germany.[9] While he was staying in the house, Schütz was expected to hide in a prepared cellar at a moment's notice; Mrs Brugha conducted drills with a stopwatch to ensure that he knew what was expected of him. During his stay, Schütz witnessed the arrival of explosive material bound for Northern Ireland.

Mrs Brugha oversaw an amateur courier network operated by her obedient children. Using their bicycles as their primary means of transportation, the Brugha girls transmitted messages and documents to various IRA members scattered across the city. Schütz's presence in the Brugha household did not remain a secret long. Though the courier network functioned to some extent, it necessarily depended on word of mouth – with all the weaknesses that such a system invites.

Through Mrs Brugha's many illicit contacts, Schütz soon met the representatives of the 'Northern Group' – the Belfast IRA, who had practically taken over the shattered organization following the Stephen Hayes affair the previous year. The men had a plan: they wanted communications equipment, arms and ammunition and money to rebuild the IRA; in exchange, they would make arrangements for Schütz to leave Ireland and arrive in occupied France. In a subsequent meeting with Eoin McNamee (the new IRA adjutant-general), and a nameless senior IRA member (presumably Seán McCool), Schütz was told that a courier to the German Legation had received £300 for the purchase of a boat to take him to Brest. Schütz was only told that the pilot was an Irish naval officer and that three other passengers would accompany him.[10] As Schütz learned later in Arbour Hill, the intended captain of his escape vessel was Charles McGuinness of the Irish Naval Service.

CHARLES McGUINNESS

McGuinness had much in common with Görtz: a tendency to tell tall-tales and to be dogged with consistently poor luck. McGuinness had been an IRA gun-runner in the early 1920s (with future TD Robert Briscoe) and had been a sailor for most of his adult life. He published a book, *Nomad*, which purported to chronicle his adventurous life. In the book, McGuinness claimed, among other things, to have been the first harbour commander of Leningrad during the October 1917 Revolution, the president of a Central American republic, a Loyalist volunteer during the Spanish Civil War and a member of Admiral Byrd's Polar expedition. When the Irish Marine Service was formed in 1940, McGuinness saw himself as the natural leader for an important command, but he was instead made a chief petty officer and assigned to Haulbowline station.

Probably more out of a desire to do something exciting than an impetus to commit high treason, the erstwhile explorer found himself embroiled in a series of contacts with German agents. He was on Walter Simon's list of potential Irish contacts; at least Simon knew his name. He also met with Joseph Lenihan in July 1941, though that agent is not known to have made any other attempt to fulfil his espionage mission.

McGuinness also attracted attention from the Germans in September 1941 due to his connection with a German national named Wilhelm Masgeik, a steelworker at Haulbowline. According to a message from Dr Hempel to the Foreign Ministry, McGuinness was offering to pilot Masgeik in a motorboat to France. Fearing some sort of plot that might tarnish him, Hempel urged that the plan be dropped, with the additional note that Masgeik might be suspicious since he left Germany to work for a Jewish firm in London.[11] Former Free State General Richard Mulcahy (then a Fine Gael TD) had earlier noted in a letter to Frederick Boland that Masgeik was a potential Nazi sympathizer, but no proof of this was ever uncovered by G2 or the Garda.[12]

The planned rendezvous with Schütz never took place, but McGuinness was not long out of the spotlight. Lacking the good judgement to withdraw from the fluid world of intrigue, McGuinness's sense of adventure was overwhelmed by a motive of an altogether different sort. On 6 April 1942, he sent a message to Dr Carlheinz Petersen at the German Legation and informed the press attaché that he was in a position to assist Axis nationals who wanted to leave Ireland, that he had important information about Allied shipping and that he wanted to contribute to the Axis war effort. It never seems to have occurred to McGuinness that mail to the German embassy might be subject to examination. He was arrested. On 5 June 1942, McGuinness was sentenced to seven years in prison for attempting to report information to a belligerent power. While at Athlone, he met Schütz and told him that he was to have been the captain of the boat to Brest. McGuinness was released at the end of the war, before his full sentence had been served. He later applied to have his government pension restored and the authorities seem to have been sympathetic, writing that he had become involved with the Germans 'out of a sense of adventure, not the intent to seriously engage in espionage'. The issue of his government pension soon became academic, however; McGuinness drowned on 6 December 1947 off Ballymoney, County Wexford, when his Bermuda-bound yacht, the *Isallt*, capsized in rough water.[13]

McGuinness's frequent contacts with German agents make it likely that he was slightly more involved with the periphery of espionage than is generally supposed. Like many others, he was never a major player, but he could be counted on – up to a point – by any German agents who needed assistance.

SCHÜTZ'S RE-ARREST

While waiting for his planned departure on 30 April, Schütz didn't lack for things to do. While at the Brugha household, he was brought a typed copy of the Stephen Hayes confession. Mrs Brugha told him to translate sections of it into German. Under her supervision, he also prepared a situation report on the Irish political climate, to include several not-so-flattering references to de Valera's 'dictatorship'. This certainly reflected Mrs Brugha's jaundiced views; Schütz did not have enough Irish experience of his own to draw upon. He also prepared a coded signal for the German Legation to transmit to Abwehr headquarters. The message read:

> I am safe for the last four weeks with help from the IRA. Country organized. Require 10 transmitter cases to be sent. Important plan for Northern Ireland urgently waits on your help. To stay is very dangerous. Cause Embassy Dublin to deliver 1000 Pounds to me at Klingston private. Embassy behaves as if to put me off. Wait on U-boat or flying boat. Arrange with Minister. Have valuable material. Greetings to Lilo, Parents. Gunther.[14]

Schütz's theory that the embassy was trying to distance itself from him was correct. During the time that he was free and seeking to return to Germany, the German Minister provided, at best, anaemic support to him, seeking to protect his own delicate position. Hempel notified Berlin of the escape on 18 February, noting that Schütz had requested money from the legation and was planning to leave Ireland by boat. Hempel noted that he had provided £80 to the escapee and would accordingly charge this amount to the German authorities. The Abwehr – through the Foreign Ministry radio link with Dublin – asked a series of inane questions about Schütz's current situation, with the idea that he should remain in place and continue his mission. Though they certainly knew the events surrounding his arrest, his superiors asked Hempel to find out if he still had his radio transmitter! They requested that Hempel provide enough money for six months and assist him in getting new identity documents. Carolle Carter noted that the go-between the legation and Schütz was 'MB' – said to be affiliated with the Brughas – and the same person who was earlier in contact with Ernst Weber-Drohl; Seán MacBride is the obvious candidate.

According to Foreign Ministry records, Schütz was successful in getting his coded message to the legation and they transmitted it. Hempel also wired a report of his own, asking that Berlin contact some third party for further assistance and that this emissary should inform Schütz that the legation was unable to offer any further assistance. Hauptmann Eduard Schauenburg, the commander of the Hamburg Ast I-Wi section, wired back – again through the Foreign Ministry – that the agent should stay in place and send any information via a new cover address in Spain. The Abwehr also requested that the Dublin Legation pay Schütz £600 and added that it could drop him a new transmitter if necessary. There is no indication that Hempel ever communicated this information to Schütz.[15]

Schütz prepared a letter to the German Legation asking them to inform Major Dr P[raetorius] or 'Captain Ritter' of his situation. He likewise drafted a cipher to the German legation, asking them to inform his headquarters that he planned to return to Germany. But his return to Germany was going to have to wait a little longer than he planned. On 30 April, Schütz was to be collected at 1800 hours and taken to the boat at Bray, twelve miles south of Dublin. Mrs Brugha went into Dublin, leaving her daughter Delma to look after Schütz. Just after midday, there was a knock at the door and Delma inexplicably forgot first to check who was outside. When she opened the door, several detectives burst in, and a startled Schütz was found in a chair on the veranda, reading a book. When asked his name, he responded with 'Graves'. When prompted, he told the Special Branch men that he was a visitor from Sligo. Things were going well up to this point, until the detective asked him the exact address in Sligo. Schütz, who knew only the accommodations in Sligo Jail, answered 'Webster Gardens' – his pre-war address in London. The detectives clearly didn't believe him and he finally said, 'I'm the one you're looking for'. The surprised detectives responded that they weren't looking for him at all, but finally realized who they were looking at. Schütz was put under arrest.

The irony was that the detectives really weren't looking for Schütz during that raid. They were expecting to arrest Nóinín Brugha. One of her couriers had been caught earlier with documents that clearly incriminated her in IRA activity. A simultaneous raid was executed on Kingston Shirts and the Brugha home. Both Nóinín and Mrs Caitlin Brugha were later arrested and interned. Schütz was returned to the Bridewell Jail and eventually transferred to Arbour Hill Military Prison. He expected a three-month spell in 'solitary', but his room (which, his guard told him, once housed Eamon de Valera) was fitted with a carpet and a radio. He also had a boy to clean his room. Schütz later smuggled a letter to the Brughas via the cleaning boy.[16]

Though the German minister probably wouldn't have approved, the Abwehr was pleased with his escape. In recognition, Schütz was promoted to Leutnant, effective 1 February 1943.[17]

LIFE BEHIND BARS

Schütz's escape demonstrated that Mountjoy was imperfectly secure. With the later exceptions of O'Reilly and Kenny, all the German agents active in Ireland were eventually at No. 3 Internment Camp, Custume Barracks, Athlone, starting in early June 1942. The prisoners brought all their personal belongings with them, including pets. Van Loon, who was still recovering from broken ribs received in his attempted escape, joined the others on 9 June.

Though provided with a radio, library materials, a garden and an exercise area, several of the inmates still found planning escapes to be a more rewarding pastime. Schütz's brief experience with the outside world inspired him to attempt a number of escape schemes, though none as successful as his first. Internal security remained a consideration, and Schütz was as worried about his fellow Germans foiling his plans as he was about the Irish guards. Once ensconced at Custume Barracks, the prisoners took over a military detention section that had been modified for their confinement. Van Loon and the other inmates gradually became accustomed to the new routine. Relationships between the prisoners varied as time went on. 'Cabin fever' certainly contributed to a number of incidents that drove a wedge in the group. For example, there was only the one radio in the common room at Athlone and there were frequent disagreements over the choice of stations. Music programmes provoked the least dissension – classical was preferred – and the internees were able to tune into German stations. Van Loon copied out the military situation reports announced in the *Wehrmacht Bericht* and posted them in the common room.[18]

Van Loon became increasingly attached to Hermann Görtz and in the next several years of confinement became his closest friend among the internees. During the extended period when Görtz was sending messages to the outside – the ones he mistakenly thought were bound for Germany, but were really intercepted and answered by G2 – van Loon encrypted and deciphered the complicated messages, usually working under a table a night with a candle, shielded from the guards only by the tablecloth.[19] The messages were taken out to Irish collaborators (the O'Farrell sisters, Mrs Austin Stack, Mrs Cantwell) by either Sergeant John Power or Corporal Joseph Lynch. Van Loon remembers that Görtz always gave the soldiers messages in open envelopes, perhaps to show a measure of trust for them.

Van Loon was also Görtz's companion on several of the planned escape attempts from Athlone. Though he never realized that his code was compromised, and certainly never had any idea that he was playing a *Funkspiel* with G2, Görtz made requests to Berlin to provide the would-be escapees with supplies – including 'cholera belts' for the period that they would be forced to sleep in the outdoors.[20] Görtz reciprocated van Loon's loyalty and – citing his authority as a German officer – 'enrolled' van Loon into the Waffen-SS and even produced a certificate to that effect. Though as a Reserve Luftwaffe Hauptmann this would be slightly beyond his authority, Görtz seemed to genuinely believe that such an act was within his purview as senior officer at Athlone. G2, somewhat amused by this turn of events, sent a confirming message into Athlone that van Loon had been duly enrolled.[21]

Another diversion was the availability of medical care. Though not the equivalent of a successful jailbreak, it did provide for a break in the camp routine and a chance to visit the medical barracks. Weber-Drohl, in particular, used this dodge at every opportunity. In an example of the somewhat heavy bureaucracy that permeated the system at No. 3 Internment Camp, there was a volume of official correspondence before the Irish government would agree to provide van Loon with required dental care: 'Regarding the supplying of dentures at Public Expense to the abovenamed, it will be necessary to obtain a certificate from the Medical Officer to the effect that the Internee's health is deteriorating because of lack of teeth.' Eventually the request for dentures was approved, with the stipulation 'cost not to exceed £2 16s. 0d.'[22]

Much of the time in Athlone was spent writing letters and van Loon kept up a regular correspondence to his family and a girlfriend in Rotterdam. Mail sent from occupied Holland to prisoners in Ireland, labelled *Internierten Sendung* did not require stamps but was passed through the German postal censors. Mail generally took about five weeks to receive. All mail to and from internees was examined and copied by Irish military censors, and in the case of van Loon, translated from Dutch into English, with a summary being placed in his active file. Letters sent to

Rotterdam were routed through Lisbon and also took many weeks to receive. Mail occasionally came to the prisoners from inside the country. On one occasion, both van Loon and Görtz received parcels from Neassa Brugha, who had earlier aided Schütz's escape.[23]

Though he continued to plan escapes with Görtz, van Loon spent the rest of his time in internment without making trouble for the military authorities. After the war ended, and the internees were still being held pending a decision on their status under international law, several changes took place that affected van Loon. Following a letter from his father in Rotterdam that said the Dutch authorities considered him a deserter, van Loon wrote a letter on 25 November 1945 to the Consul-General of the Netherlands stating that he was not a deserter, 'only a person from a belligerent state in a neutral country without permission'.[24] This letter apparently did not have the desired effect; Van Loon was officially exiled from the Netherlands for a period of twenty-five years, though he kept his Dutch citizenship.[25]

The prisoners were informally members of rival cliques that essentially divided into the pro- and anti-Görtz factions. Schütz, along with Tributh and Gärtner, were not remarkably cooperative with the other group, consisting of Görtz, Preetz and van Loon. Obéd was excluded from mainstream membership of either group for ethnic reasons, but found more sympathy from Schütz and his friends. Weber-Drohl and Simon were older than the rest and had no distinct loyalty to either side. Unland was officially the prisoners' spokesman and was more neutral. Part of the difficulty lay in the fact that only Görtz, Schütz, Tributh and Gärtner were German soldiers; the rest were civilian agents (or, in van Loon's case, a non-German sailor), so the normal command hierarchy of a prisoner-of-war camp did not exist. An additional complicating factor was that Görtz, Preetz and van Loon were doctrinaire National Socialists, these three having been the only ones with pre-war party membership.[26]

Schütz, whether because of his personality or because he had made a semi-successful escape, did not mix well with Görtz. Schütz made a point of listening to English broadcasts on the common radio, something that Görtz considered treasonous. At one of Görtz's impromptu meetings, he announced that he would have Schütz executed when they reached Germany. In another instance, Schütz asked a military doctor to send some silk stockings and candy to Lilo in Hamburg. Görtz and Preetz apparently eavesdropped on the conversation, because at another of Görtz's periodic gatherings, he said 'I think there must be a traitor among us and I think the traitor is Marschner'. Görtz's allegation was that Schütz was passing along secret information to Irish Intelligence in the guise of silk stockings and chocolate. A fight developed and Tributh even attacked the paranoid Dr Görtz.[27] Schütz also had difficulty with Simon, who repeatedly called him a 'dirty Jew boy' and threatened to beat him up.[28]

Weber-Drohl had been finally arrested for good on 13 August 1942, but even then, his confinement was not without periodic interference from the Department of Justice.[29] The reason for Weber-Drohl's sudden arrest is unclear; he had been free for a year and a half when taken into custody. The only likely source of information would have been Hermann Görtz, who by that point, had been under semi-regular interrogation for ten months, having been arrested in November 1941. Government documents mention only that 'evidence became available that he had arrived in February 1940 by submarine', but there is no source given for the information.[30]

When pressed by the Department of Justice on the issue of Weber-Drohl's release, shortly after the last arrest, G2's Colonel Bryan remarked that 'consideration of Drohl's moral character does not incline me to the view that he would be an asset socially to any urban or local community'.[31] In an even more witty commentary, Bryan added: 'As you sow, so shall ye reap. And if what we know regarding Weber-Drohl's amorous activities is but partially correct, he is due a harvest which will not be evaded by such ordinary means as changing his earthly location.'[32]

Weber-Drohl was kept in custody and soon began his campaign to force the Irish government to stand up and take notice. For the next several years, his various stratagems served only to cause G2 and the prison authorities to regard anything he said with suspicion. He wrote constantly. Depending on his momentary attitude, the letters were praising, complaining, whining about his physical condition or threatening some sort of self-destructive action.

Weber-Drohl did not fit in with the other internees at Mountjoy Prison and the Athlone internment camp for several reasons. He was the oldest among them, an Austrian, and he correctly believed that close ties with known German agents would prejudice any chances he might have of early release. He also had moderately severe medical problems and was constantly in and out of the Curragh Military Hospital. He was admitted there on 9 March 1943 (listing his civilian address as 10 Howard Terrace, Ringsend St., Dublin) and was finally diagnosed as having 'degeneration of the anterior horn cells of his spinal cord'. The prognosis was 'a steady progress to a fatal termination'. Presumably in response to this information, the Department of Justice again suggested Weber-Drohl's release on a six-month parole. This time, however, military considerations prevailed and he remained in Athlone. His periodic visits to the Curragh Hospital were not without incident: 'He has been discharged from the Internee Hospital because he insulted an Irish nurse in such a sexually filthy way that the doctor refused to keep him in any longer.'[33]

In many instances, he was unable to walk up and down stairs unassisted. Nevertheless, experience in the internment camp demonstrated to the authorities that Weber-Drohl was not above pretending to be more disabled than he was in actuality. His failure to be released on medical grounds prompted a change of strategy. Beginning in September 1943, he continually suggested that it was merely a matter of time before the combination of his incarceration and medical condition would kill him. In a letter, he predicted that 'it will not be long until a stroke will reliefe [*sic*] me of all my suffering of which I have had enough in my 65 years of life, especially lately'. He thereafter started using the one course of action that had secured his release in the past – the hunger strike. After three weeks, he sent a telegram – returned by the military authorities – to his son Emil. Weber-Drohl succinctly said: 'Expecting to die in very few days and wish to see you. Father.' The hunger strike officially lasted from September to December 1943. A medical check-up following the event diagnosed him as suffering from a wasting of muscle tissue in his hand and scabies.[34]

He frequently wrote letters to people on the outside that he knew would be refused by the military censors. These included messages to the German Legation and others outside the permitted list. Another tack was to try and get transferred out of Athlone and to a camp away from the other inmates. He seemed to get on fairly well with Henry Obéd, the Indian, but did not have much contact with the other Germans or Jan van Loon. In a letter on 26 June 1944, also stopped by the military censors, he asked the German Legation to encourage the Irish authorities to 'grant my transfer as soon as possible, but before I will become a lost victim, and before my lips will close forever'. He then went on in the letter to describe his stamp-collecting hobby and then, in a logical anomaly, mentioned that a piece of paper with a skull and crossbones had been placed on Obéd's door.[35] During this period, Weber-Drohl was on another hunger strike that lasted from May to July 1944. Another hunger strike followed in November, lasting until the Christmas season.

A report from Corporal Thomas Malloy suggests that the hunger strikes were not all they were made out to be. He escorted Weber-Drohl to lunch on 5 December, but the prisoner refused to eat (he was on a hunger strike) and Malloy accompanied him back to his room. The Corporal returned about fifteen minutes later and noticed that Weber-Drohl seemed nervous and expectant. Suddenly, Henry Obéd entered the room bearing a plate of food. Both Obéd and Weber-Drohl clearly looked embarrassed and finally after several seconds of silence, the German asked Obéd if he wanted some pepper, reached over to the table and pretended to sprinkle pepper on the meal. Obéd thanked him and left.[36]

In a letter to the Irish Department of Defence on 22 November, Weber-Drohl again asked for a transfer to another prison. Explaining that he was a refugee, not a war criminal, he stated that he was on a hunger strike until someone listened to him:

> I have become the target of mean and filthy lies and conspiracy of the Germans in the camp ... because I am an 'Austrian' and because I refuse to

put myself under their command and jurisdiction in the camp, where Internee Unland reigns as 'Overlord' over the others. ... Internee Marchinger [*sic*] told me when I came back from the Hospital that Preetz told everyone in the camp that I was a Traitor to my Fatherland, and he also told other lies about me. ... I surely did not come to Eire to fight with big-mouthed 'German Internees' who have proven themselves already here at times they had scraps to be 'tea-pot throwers', such as internee Preetz when he had several fights with Internee Marchinger [*sic*], and smashed the pot on his head. I will never consume food as long as I have to remain here with those fellows.[37]

Not one to rest on his literary laurels, Weber-Drohl then took his appeal to the United States' Minister, David Gray. Weber-Drohl wrote several letters to the American diplomat – all stopped at the censor – in which he gave a wordy version of his career (including a stint 'in the Regiment Estranger [*sic*] in the French Foreign Legion in Sidi Bel Abes in Africa') and asked Gray to help get him transferred, released and finally sent to America.[38] He closes one letter with 'I ask and adore [*sic* – probably he meant 'implore'] you Sir Gray from the bottom of my heart'. In a follow-up letter, Weber-Drohl asked Minister Gray for an application for US citizenship, explaining that he had filled out the paperwork in the US in the 1920s but had to return to Germany to handle a will and could not return.[39]

The mail from Weber-Drohl did not become any more uplifting in 1945. In June of that year, he wrote what was essentially a seventeen-page suicide note to his son Emil, describing himself in the most pathetic manner imaginable, 'internee in sorrow and agony' being among the most positive references. The letter was appropriately signed 'your suffering dad'. In October, he returned to the theme of the German conspiracy, writing that 'I fear I will become a victim of foul-play, arranged by the Hitler-worshippers in Internment Camp No. 3'. This from a man who had an iron cross tattooed on his chest. Weber-Drohl's attitude varied, depending on the recipient of his correspondence. In a remarkable about-face, he wrote to Görtz that 'above all I would not wish you to doubt my "German Fidelity", uprightness and honour as regards yourself and as regards my Fatherland. ... I am a grown man with a German mind and character ... and therefore you should respect me.'[40]

In January 1941, Simon had been transferred from the Bridewell to Mountjoy, where Henry Obéd, Herbert Tributh, Dieter Gärtner and Wilhelm Preetz soon joined him. Preetz's arrival caused some initial hostility. They had trained together in Hamburg-Wohldorf. Simon was still insisting that his name was Karl Anderson; when Preetz shouted 'Walter, are you here, too?', Simon's response was 'You idiot!'[41] Housed in the disused women's wing of the prison, their cells were open all day and not locked until 2100. They listened to music from home, broadcasts of Hitler's speeches, and those of 'Lord Haw-Haw'. Prison officers asked the German prisoners to saw logs, but they refused as part of the general IRA (also interned in Mountjoy) refusal to do work. They finally relented, preferring exercise to inactivity. To Simon, 'all the IRA men appear as fools and rogues; in what they propose to do they are only tearing their own land to destruction and through their folly playing into the hands of the English whom they hate'.[42] On 3 October 1942, Minister for Justice Gerald Boland ordered Simon released from penal servitude (following ordinary remission of a quarter of his sentence) and had him re-arrested under the Emergency Powers (No. 20) order.[43]

Simon, who was eventually transferred to Athlone with Weber-Drohl and the others, had very definite opinions about his fellow prisoners, most not very complimentary. Speaking of Tributh, Simon said: 'I can't bear him, have the greatest antipathy for him and always have from the first moment ... he walks and talks like an old pedantic schoolmaster.' Obéd (whom Simon consistently referred to as 'prisoner no. 4') did not fare much better: 'How no. 4 came to be sent on such a delicate mission apparently, God only knows ... a really volatile chap, a proper Asiatic ... suffers from an inferiority complex, and thinks that others are up against him. Such people are unpleasant.' Regarding Unland, Simon said that he asked after 'friends in Langenreihe' and that 'he made it his business inside the first half-hour to make us aware that he was an officer'.[44] Simon also told of Marschner (Schütz) and Tributh almost fighting over cleanliness in the food preparation area – Obéd and Tributh had been made permanent orderlies by the others – and how Marschner and Preetz fought over precedence for a hot bath.

Simon seems to have left a few problems back in Germany. His former superior at Hamburg reported that Simon 'had a girlfriend in Hamburg who constantly made claims against him. These cases were settled in his absence by Dr Schütze out of Ast funds.'[45] Simon had some suspicious contacts with the outside while in prison. While interned in 1943, Simon asked for a consultation with 'barrister MacBride, who had been recommended to me'. This request was refused.

Though he initially liked Schütz ('a very alert minded fellow, witty, merry and always ready with a joke') this opinion changed within five months. By October 1941, Simon was speaking of him in less friendly terms: 'He appears to me, in his outward appearance and mental and moral constitution to be nothing but a despicable Jewish clod.' Simon wrote that he told Schütz 'Put that radio loud again and I will give you a punch in the nose, you impudent Jewish clown.' According to a report by Dr Richard Hayes after visiting the internees, Simon had called Schütz '"a dirty Jew boy", which is one of the most serious forms of actionable abuse in Germany'.[46]

Simon evidently had difficulties mixing well with the other internees, and he busied himself with reading and writing. On 3 February 1943, he ordered two copies of *The Social Policy of Nazi Germany* from publishers Browne and Noland Ltd. G2's Joseph Healy observed that 'Anderson/Simon ... is anything but the common sailor he gave himself out to be – he is, on the contrary, well-educated'.[47] Simon's attempts at writing were mainly concerned with political issues, and he was a committed National Socialist in beliefs, but not actually a party member. By 1945 he had completed several chapters in a book on National Socialism that he wanted sent to Brian Higgins, Upper O'Connell Street, Dublin. Chapter 10 of his magnum opus, 'On Jews', went on at some length about the 'true nature' of Jews versus the superior Aryans. He further attacked the 'power of Jewry and International Big Capital'. G2 decided that the manuscript outline did not fit within the postal censorship guidelines and returned the work to Simon.[48]

Wilhelm Preetz was held under the Emergency Powers (No. 20) Order and confined to Mountjoy, later moved to Athlone. He was not much appreciated by the prison officials or G2, who described him as 'a proper thug'. He had several fights with Obéd and Schütz, and generally did not mix well with the others.[49] On occasion, he was involved in Görtz's plans for escape, once offering Sergeant Power $2,000 if he would assist the escape plan; G2 told Power to refuse, but to stay on friendly terms with the inmates.[50] Preetz received fairly regular visits from his mother-in-law, Margaret Reynolds, and from his brother-in-law, T.J. Reynolds. These visits ceased in 1944–5, presumably after the family received word of some of his more unsavoury familial activities.[51] While they were still in contact, it is likely that Preetz's extended family continued to assist the Germans.[52] Preetz suffered from a moderately severe case of rheumatoid arthritis and joined Weber-Drohl in the Curragh Military Hospital on a semi-regular basis.

Henry Obéd spent much of his time in Athlone writing to his wife in Antwerp. To ease the delay in receiving mail due to translation problems, he encouraged her to write in English and asked a friend to assist her. Obéd's English was distinctly better than that of the other prisoners, with Görtz following close behind. Obéd asked his wife not to write anything controversial and noted that the censors were still holding some of her mail. In one letter, his wife remarked: 'You should not have been so frightened and stay home, nobody would have trouble you, here are still a lot of foreigner free'. By and large, the Obéds' correspondence was kind and affectionate, in marked contrast to that of the other prisoners and their wives.

All incoming and outgoing mail was carefully monitored by the military authorities, and there was seldom anything suspicious to record. In one puzzling coincidence, G2 discovered that both Tributh and Gärtner were writing to the same woman, a Fraulein Erika Kuhlmann. Their correspondence indicates that this woman knew each man from Brandenburg – an interesting event since, at that time, both were assigned to the Brandenburg Regiment and in training for their sabotage mission. It is possible that this was an Abwehr cover address and that the mysterious Fraulein did not exist. However, G2's knowledge of Germany was insufficient to determine if this was the case.[53]

Obéd frequently suffered at the hands of the other internees. In a 1943 letter to Irish Justice Minister Gerald Boland, he stated that 'I am kept in company with a number of Germans who are differently disposed than I am politically, and this makes things much harder for me. I am more or less ostracized by them, they seldom or ever speak to me or I to them. We have nothing in common. I am by no means a sympathizer of Hitler and they know this.'[54] By force of numbers, Obéd was the permanent orderly for the rest of the prisoners and did whatever tasks he was assigned. He was diagnosed with chronic bronchitis and, according to the medical officer, 'the climate in Ireland has an adverse effect on his health'. During his entire time in Athlone, he was essentially an outcast.[55] Walter Simon noted that Obéd 'insisted on playing nigger music', but that he was persuaded by the others not to do so.[56] After an inspection tour of the prisoners' quarters in 1942, Captain Joseph Healy observed that 'Obéd is not popular with the others, and is eager to get away from them. An attempt was made by Preetz to "beat him up".'[57] Although Görtz made a show of being the senior military prisoner and having a code of honour that went with that responsibility, he openly accused Obéd of being an informer and of betraying numerous escape attempts.[58] Ironically, it was Görtz himself who gave away the escapes in his coded messages which he believed were received by his loyal supporters on the outside.

Gärtner and Tributh were relatively close to Görtz during captivity. While Tributh's time at Athlone was far more pleasant than Obéd's, he managed to go almost completely bald during his six years in custody. At one point, in March 1946, Görtz was on another of his pseudo-hunger strikes and refusing (again) to write to his family in Germany. In a thinly disguised end-run around his public refusal to write, Görtz apparently had Gärtner make contact instead. In the letter, addressed to 'Aunt Fanny' Aschenborn (actually Ellen Görtz née Aschenborn), Gärtner enquired whether Mrs Görtz had word from his 'lady friend at the World Economic Institute' and that he had 'heard nothing of the Aschenborns either. They must be living somewhere in the Union if they have not been expelled by now.' The letter was signed 'your nephew, Dieter'.[59] Clearly the possibility of coded jargon phrases in such a letter is high. Covert messages to and from the prison were a constant problem for the authorities. According to a secret memorandum from a source identified only as 'D', an Englishman named Rosbane (who had been sentenced for fraud) was the contact between the prisoners and the outside IRA. Rosbane asked a visiting journalist to bring in copies of the *Evening Mail* or the *Kerryman*, specifically the part of the paper devoted to advertisements from dance bands, which was apparently the means by which the outside contacts communicated with the interned Germans. The same source also noted that messages were being smuggled in rolled cigarettes and then being passed on to the Germans.[60]

Once at Athlone, Hermann Görtz set to work getting messages to his supporters on the outside. These assistants consisted of the same small group that sheltered him while on the run; the Farrell sisters, Mrs Cantwell and Mrs Austin Stack.[61] Görtz approached two military guards at Athlone to carry his messages, Sergeant Power and Corporal Lynch. The German offered to pay Power, but the sergeant refused. Powers then took the messages to G2 where they were copied and eventually deciphered by G2's secret weapon: Dr Richard Hayes. As the pre-war director of the National Library, Dr Hayes had been approached by the Army to try his hand at decoding the messages recovered from German agents. The Irish military had no cryptology section, forcing Hayes to work without support and almost exclusively on his own.[62] Hayes's method was to work out a mathematical solution to the ciphers based on letter frequency and his estimation of the weaknesses of the given cipher. An explanation of the older coding systems had been published in the pre-war treatise *The American Black Chamber* by Herbert Yardly, but the mental work involved was considerable. Though shown the Görtz messages captured after the Held raid in May 1940, Dr Hayes was unable to break the cipher without knowledge of the keyword or a better understanding of the intricacies involved in the particular system. He had better luck with the relatively simpler system used by Wilhelm Preetz and was able mathematically to extrapolate one of his stranger keywords: *Analecta Hibernicamar*.[63] Interrogated by both Hayes and Commandant Eamon de Buitléar, Görtz was asked to explain his coding system. Görtz complied – to a point. He agreed to demonstrate the procedure for enciphering and deciphering messages, but refused to provide the necessary keyword. Görtz obligingly translated a few of the Held messages in an attempt to show that his mission was benign, but his efforts did not convince Dr Hayes, who eventually reconstructed the keywords on his own.[64] Görtz's own half-truths to G2 interrogators, combined with his messages to supporters on the outside, allowed Hayes to make a breakthrough in 1943 that led to the complete decipherment of Görtz's system.

This was the genesis of the ultimate *Funkspiel* – G2 kept Görtz believing that his messages were faithfully transmitted to his supporters on the outside, and then on to Germany. Görtz did not know the truth until his release. The ultimate test of this game was when G2 – through the intermediaries – persuaded Görtz to make a report of his activities since arriving in Ireland, with the impression that this information was wanted by the OKW. Görtz complied with an 80-page coded report listing his activities and contacts since his arrival in Ireland. G2 was also confident enough to promote Görtz to Major, though the German military knew nothing about it. Working this double-game was not always easy for Sergeant Power. In late 1944, his wife received a message from Mrs Cantwell, who asked that Sergeant Power visit her. Mrs Power jealously assumed that Mrs Cantwell was 'the other woman' and went to see her. The perplexed Mrs Power left the Cantwell house with a coded message to give to her husband.[65]

Sometimes, the interception system was not foolproof. At Christmas 1941, Görtz persuaded Corporal Joseph Lynch to smuggle letters out from Arbour Hill Detention Barracks. Lynch, who was being paid small amounts by Görtz, did not alert Irish Intelligence to this and continued to take occasional letters until 1944. Lynch first took a sealed envelope to Mrs Austin Stack – Görtz had told Lynch that it concerned his family and an attempt to arrange an escape. Stack took the letter and gave the corporal a compass and a Dublin map to take back to Görtz. Future letters were taken to Mrs Maeve McDowell (who worked at Lee's in Rathmines). He took several more letters, meeting McDowell at Mount Argus Church for her written replies. G2 eventually noticed Lynch's activities and used him to send several bogus letters purportedly from Görtz. However, Lynch continued to act as postman for letters unknown to G2, and smuggled at least three between February and July 1943. This deception was discovered in 1944 and Lynch was interrogated. According to LTC Joseph Guilfoyle, because of 'grave domestic difficulties and the position in which he finds himself, he appears to be on the verge of a nervous breakdown'.[66] During this examination, Lynch admitted to accepting money from Görtz and remembered that the German 'talked of his work for the German Secret Service during the last war'.[67]

Keeping track of Görtz's messages became a full-time job for G2. As Dr Hayes pointed out, 'obviously we had to intercept all [the messages] or none'. With the exception of the few letters Lynch delivered, Irish Intelligence appears to have been able to maintain the charade. Many of Görtz's attempts to communicate with his supporters were patently amateurish: in once instance he threw a matchbox from his cell window to a passing girl. The enclosed message read: 'Please meet Bridie Farrell of 7 Spencer Villas, Glenageary, who will tell you what a good friend of Ireland I am.'[68] In a repetition of this tactic, he managed to get a girl named Ethel Phillips, who lived at Arbour Hill Terrace, to pass along a message to the Farrell sisters. Görtz asked for a hacksaw blade, a glass cutter, a wire cutter and £3 to be left at Del Rio's café, where they would be picked up 'by a messenger from Preetz'. The Farrells were to indicate receipt and compliance by posting an ad in the 'In Memoriam' section of the *Irish Independent*, mentioning the name 'Sean Hogan'. Sergeant Power dutifully collected the material from the Farrell sisters and delivered it to Görtz, minus the hacksaw blade. SD agent John O'Reilly's landing immediately thereafter gave G2 the excuse to conduct a thorough search of the cells and the contraband material was recovered by the Athlone authorities.[69]

Several messages could have posed a genuine threat had Görtz been able to establish legitimate and uncensored contact with the outside. In a message from June 1943, Görtz wrote: 'Ask Hempel whether prepared to put money at disposal immediatly [sic] after success. The more the more chances. IRA must not know of it. Discret [sic]. Way is up to you.'[70] Görtz typically requested replies to appear as advertisements in Irish newspapers, often in the section for dance bands; this confirmed the information passed by G2 source 'D'. Görtz planned innumerable escapes, some more clever than others. During his incarceration, Görtz and his followers expanded their network. They used legitimate businesses as drops: the Café del Rio (run by Italian sympathizer Amadeo del Rio) and the shop owned by the butcher George Hick. Hick was a second-generation German with an Italian wife; they were approached by Bernard O'Donnell and Nicholas Stack to act as a letter-drop as a way of doing 'something for Germany'. O'Donnell and his wife collected the messages.

Another member of the chain was William Carter, the leader of the Selma Follies Dance Band. Carter had been active for some time, having passed messages from Görtz to the *Fushimi Maru* when it docked in November 1940. He also helped to transport and shelter Anthony Deery, Görtz's radio operator. Dr P.J. Brennan, a former TD and Dublin City Coroner, was also part of the network. Brennan had attended Görtz while he was at large, and continued to be of assistance when he was incarcerated.

In August 1943, Görtz was transferred from Arbour Hill to Athlone. He protested against the move and demanded to see a lawyer. Specifically, he wanted to contact the German Legation, wanted to be treated 'as an officer' and objected to the seizure of his property (books and clothes), noting that his request was 'based on domestic Irish law'. [71] Prior to this latest quasi-legal objection, Görtz had been refusing to write to his family in Germany, though the Irish authorities assured him that they would forward all prisoner mail. He would not write, he said, 'for fear of incriminating other persons to whom he has written'.[72] This is another example of the disintegration of Görtz's mental health: there was already ample evidence in his previous letters to incriminate those with whom he corresponded, both in Ireland and England. The German Minister also tried, without success, to get him to write to his family.

Though most of Görtz's messages to and from the outside were well under control, Irish authorities realized in 1942 that they had a new problem: someone else was using Görtz's code. In September 1942, an Irish customs officer at Swanlinbar stopped a man crossing from Éire to Northern Ireland. A search of his pockets revealed a piece of paper with what looked like code groups. However, as he had no official contraband, the stranger was allowed to proceed – without the customs official notifying any security authorities – and without even making a note of the man's name and address. When G2 eventually received the coded message, they saw that it read:

BNIM	BIYU	UKZT	EOUP	BUTB
TBCK	GXUN	RHCC	WNPG	KNUR
TNLM	IMLA	QNNN	VEML	EBXQ
QLTR	NAZR	VPDX		

Dr Hayes quickly discovered that this message was sent using Görtz's code, though the format was in four-letter groups, instead of the five-letter style favoured by German intelligence. The message, once deciphered, indicated that someone in Ireland was still active in passing messages to the Germans: 'WOB (or BOW) confirms Dev partition pact England/USA support help call Germany. Confident RKY (or RYK) arrived. GR.' Unfortunately, as a result of the incompetence at the customs post, it was impossible to identify either the sender or the intended recipient. This mystery was never solved.

This was not the only example of continuing interest in Northern Ireland. On 9 February 1942, a man named Henry Lundborg was arrested in Belfast. Lundborg was a restaurant car attendant on the Great Northern Railway between Dublin and Belfast, and was found in possession of three letters intended for the IRA Northern Command. The letters requested a meeting in Dublin between the Northern and the Southern IRA groups, and asked for a comprehensive report on US, British and colonial forces stationed in Northern Ireland. Under questioning, Lundborg claimed ignorance, stating that he had been asked to carry the letters by his predecessor, a man named Lawlor, that the material originated at Kingston Shirts (the company owned by Caitlín Brugha) and that his contact was a nameless woman in a black raincoat. For his trouble, Lundborg was sentenced to two years' imprisonment.[73] Though Görtz was behind bars, the IRA was clearly still interested in the status of Allied forces in Northern Ireland, but whether it wanted this information to give to the Germans or for its own nefarious purposes is unclear.

Meanwhile, Görtz continued to labour under the impression that his messages, in their original forms, were being received by the intended recipient. His faith in his success allowed G2 and the Garda to gather evidence on his accomplices and to reconstruct his activities prior to arrest. In a series of messages and answers from January 1944, G2 learned the name of another supporter – Dr Kathleen Lynn ('KL').

> **Görtz**: Is Miss KL from Gold Queen [Maisie O'Mahony] safe receive verbal message after escape? Do you know whereabouts of Kielty IRA friend of Preetz here and O'Duffy? Valuable afterwards.

O'Mahony: Do not write to Ethel again. Father dangerous. Write to Miss Cantwell, 37 Pembrook Road, Dublin. Love.

Dr Lynn was an old Republican supporter and a long-time friend of Helena Moloney, whom she was treating for alcoholism. Lynn and Moloney again came to the attention of G2 in September 1944, when in a meeting at the All-Ireland Hurling Final – also attended by Maurice Twomey, Mrs Austin Stack, Helena Moloney and Kathleen Lynn – they allegedly discussed a strategy of bank robberies to provide funds for the fiscally-strapped IRA.[74]

Undaunted by his previous failures, Görtz continued to dream of escaping. In 1944, in yet another escape plan that he attempted to smuggle to the outside, he appealed to his friends the O'Farrell sisters for help:

> I ask you to help me get out of this prison. After a failure due to the elements it has become impossible for me to get out without your help from outside. I lost my freedom during your internal crisis, mainly by this crisis. I have the feeling that you have overcome this crisis by the national feeling of your men. At the first opportunity I had sent from here an urgent message to Germany to support you with all means in your fight against our common enemy England. I have reason to believe that this message has reached my country, but I also have reason to believe that in order to make this help real it needs personal contact and explanation. There has been much misunderstanding, and the fault was not on Germany's side. I still think that I am the best man to re-establish this contact, perhaps the only one.

Görtz intended to go through the ceiling in the common room at Athlone and then make his way down the walls. He asked for a bicycle and a few trusted men, with the stipulation 'let the men darken their faces and have gloves on'. Needless to say, this message was stopped by the censors. In a subsequent escape plan, Görtz muses that it would be 'easy for me to use physical force' to effect his escape, but that he does not want to resort to that extreme. Subsequent letters also make increasingly maudlin appeals to the Irish character: 'I would not dare ask you if it were only for me. I am convinced it is for Ireland, and for the friendship and the unbelievable kindness of hearts I have found here. It has become to me a kind of second home ... nobody expects that you slip out of neutrality, but you must show that there is an Irish spirit, not only by Irish dancing. I know it is there.'[75]

Failure to organize a successful escape led Görtz to resort to a hunger strike, the first lasting twenty-one days. He was eventually fed through an intravenous tube and opted to quit the hunger strike soon thereafter. Görtz became increasingly depressed in Athlone, though he continued to write short stories, a play based on Stephen Hayes (*The Mirror*) and a novel detailing his unsuccessful pre-war spying adventure in England. Increasingly, he became more despondent, as his writing reflected: 'Death.

I fear him and I love him. His eyes are hard and merciless. Duty. I try to ask him – but my voice fails. He only looks at me – and I know. He comes when I try to think, he comes when I try to dream. He never says a word. My life is unreal.'[76]

The knowledge that he had ultimately failed in his mission may have begun to weigh on Görtz's mind. He certainly began to make increasingly irrational statements as the war turned inexorably against Germany. In 1944, at about the time he convinced his fellow internee Jan van Loon that he was empowered to enrol him into the Waffen-SS, Görtz began to manufacture a past for himself. He spoke of the SS and the OKW, commenting that 'it is known that I belonged to both organizations as a senior officer'. He seems to have been fixated on the SS in particular, as the perfect embodiment of his hopes. In a later letter, he stated that he was in the 'SD of the Supreme Command' as well as a 'Squadron Leader and Wing Commander in the Air SS'. Still later, he told Minister Hempel that he had 'belonged only to the Waffen SS, as a former member of the so-called Black Reichswehr, which had been legalized after Hitler came to power, he felt very serious apprehensions that he would be in some or other way persecuted by enemies, particularly Communists'.[77] Görtz's service record is unambiguous on this point: at no time did he belong to the SS and he had resigned his Nazi Party membership in 1935.

He also made repeated – and legally and logically questionable – appeals to Irish justice: 'As I have landed in full German uniform against my will in this country, I have the right to be treated according to International Law.'[78] His attempts to gain access to the legal process, many of them patently unworthy of a man who had styled himself as an 'expert in international law', seldom made it beyond the prison censor and those that did were not approved.

POST-WAR STATUS

The end of the war in Europe in May 1945 finally brought peace to the continent, but no appreciable change in circumstances for the German internees in Athlone. The British Representative provided a list to the Irish government of German agents, to include Görtz, with the view that 'it would be most undesirable that these agents should be released and allowed to be at large in Eire after the war'. The initial position of the Irish government was to refuse any suggestion that the agents should be deported back to the Allied-controlled sectors, but it agreed that they would remain interned until such time as an arrangement could be worked out: 'The British government made it clear that they would only agree to their release subject to an effective Deportation Order [to Germany].'[79] Görtz wrote to Minister for Justice Gerald Boland in June 1945, asking for political asylum in Ireland, but this request was stopped by G2.

Irish Intelligence also wanted to be rid of the German problem. Writing to Frederick Boland of External Affairs, Colonel Bryan stated: 'I need hardly say that I am anxious to have the disposal of the internees solved as early as possible and for that reason I think that the prospects of the treatment of any one of them after leaving our hands should be sufficiently attractive to encourage the others to follow suit.'[80]

The problem of repatriation also included the German diplomats. In June 1945, American Minister David Gray submitted a list of German diplomats, agents and 'other German nationals deemed to be inimical to the United Nations'. The Irish government's response was a blanket refusal to deport any of those listed unless the deportation was voluntary. The Allied Control Commission, which had legal jurisdiction over all former German personnel, including diplomats and spies, issued an order that such persons would be returned to Germany. Both the Irish government and the Germans concerned apparently ignored this order. Behind the scenes, however, a different dialogue was occurring. After a meeting with Joseph Walshe, Sir John Maffey, British Representative in Éire, wrote back to his own government about the actual Irish position, at least as it related to agents, not diplomats:

> I got the impression that these men could be handed over to us if we sent the Germans to Germany and the rest to their own country as soon as convenient, all of them to be dealt with in such a manner as we saw fit on arrival, but on the understanding that their position would not be worse than it is here. That's to say ... that we could imprison them but not execute them.[81]

For his part, de Valera clung to his cherished myth about the German Minister's wartime conduct:

> The Irish people set great store by the right of asylum and would be unable to understand his [de Valera's] actions in the case that he gave up German officials and agents. ... The German Minister, to the best of his [de Valera's] knowledge and belief, had behaved with correctness during the period of the war ... the Minister was a very decent man and he [de Valera] could not bring himself to return him [Hempel] to a Germany without a government of its own and in extreme economic disorder.[82]

Whatever de Valera's personal feelings for Hempel, the Irish leader was forced to order the surrender of the German Legation's transmitter in 1943, and his intelligence service was well aware of Hempel's wartime role. Hempel's conduct, far from spotless, was merely better disguised; he was as deeply involved in the cases of espionage as far as his keen sense of propriety and self-preservation would allow.

De Valera's loyalty to Hempel was more poignantly expressed when, on 2 May 1945, he visited the German Minister to offer his sympathy following Hitler's death. Interestingly, de Valera had not followed this protocol when

Franklin D. Roosevelt died eighteen days earlier, probably because of his animosity toward the American Minister in Dublin. In a feeble attempt to justify his conduct on that occasion, de Valera said that 'to have failed to call upon the German representative would have been an act of unpardonable discourtesy to the German nation and Dr Hempel himself. During the whole of the war, Dr Hempel's conduct was irreproachable. ... I certainly was not going to add to his humiliation in the hour of defeat.'[83] Coming from a man who was aware of the Holocaust before it became general knowledge in Ireland – and well after the lifting of wartime censorship had finally allowed Irish audiences to see newsreels of unburied corpses at Buchenwald – it remains an unnerving sentiment.[84] If avoiding an 'unpardonable discourtesy to the German nation' was the motive for his conduct, he would appear to have missed the overriding moral lesson to emerge from what Ireland euphemistically called 'The Emergency'. In all likelihood, de Valera was making a public point about his neutrality doctrine, albeit in a manner that would certainly give offence to the Allies and the death camp survivors.

In considering the ultimate fate of the internees, Schütz was seen as a particular problem for both Dr Hempel and the Irish government. Standing by the false statement that Hempel 'behaved correctly' during the war and was not involved in espionage activities, the Irish government found Schütz to be something of an embarrassment; he could tell stories about Hempel and the legation that many people did not want told. Frederick Boland was clearly aware of this danger: 'Marschner is clearly a man of little character, and he is just the sort of person who might try and ingratiate himself with the Allied authorities by making false statements about German activities here during the war' – for example, 'in his statement that the German Legation were informed beforehand of his arrival here. We are satisfied from inquiries we have made that that statement is false.'[85] Historically, it is difficult to determine the exact relationship between the Irish government and the German Legation, in that de Valera ordered destroyed all records of discussions with foreign diplomats.[86]

G2 had already deciphered Schütz's microdot instructions that clearly state the Legation *did* know about his arrival beforehand and agreed to use Carlheinz Petersen as a contact man. The legation also provided funds to Schütz during his 1942 escape and, grudgingly, facilitated his coded messages to Germany. Hempel, by deliberately avoiding Schütz from the moment of his capture, seems to have been aware of the danger that Schütz represented to his image of impeccably correct diplomatic behaviour in a neutral country. Hempel was an unimaginative and cautious intelligence-gatherer, but was still involved. He had undeniable contact with several other agents (Unland, Weber-Drohl and Görtz), as well as incidental association with a host of would-be Irish collaborators. The fact that he handled these contacts in a maladroit manner does not mean that they did not occur. For his part, Schütz was not exactly pleased with the conduct of the legation. Upon his recapture in 1942, he said that he 'resented the attitude of the German Legation and intended to complain to his chief in Hamburg'.[87] He did not, however, attempt to blackmail Dr Hempel or reveal any information which might prove embarrassing to the diplomat, much to Hempel's relief.

By contrast, Tributh and Gärtner did not present a serious problem, at least in G2's opinion. Considering the idea of allowing the prisoners a parole from Athlone in 1946, Colonel Bryan of G2 reviewed the files on both Tributh and Gärtner, and remarked: 'I regard them as more soldiers than spies. They are the only people whose word of parole might seriously be entertained.'[88]

While the diplomatic debate ebbed and flowed between de Valera and the Allies, Dan Bryan again considered the spies under his control and what was to be done with them. Clearly a major concern was Hauptmann Dr Hermann Görtz:

> Goertz, who is a dangerous person (notwithstanding the ill-informed views to the contrary expressed by some people) will certainly, if given any kind of facilities, resume some of his former contacts. These contacts lead straight to certain groups in this country who were pro-German in the war years and are now interested in the project to bring German children here ... a certain clique in the group seeks to give it an anti-British and almost pro-Nazi bias.[89]

The organization Bryan referred to, the Save the German Children Fund, eventually brought forward a plan in 1945 called Operation Shamrock. The aim was to bring over 400 Catholic German children, mostly from the Rhineland, for foster placement in Ireland. Görtz was eventually employed as secretary of this organization, at a wage of £2 per month. Ironically, Jewish groups had difficulty getting official permission for refugee children to come to Ireland under a similar scheme, but the post-war Irish public embraced the idea of fostering German children.[90] At the same time as de Valera was trying to find a plausible reason to grant Hempel asylum, the Department of Justice was writing that 'It has always been the policy of the Minister for Justice to restrict the admission of Jewish aliens, for the reason that any substantial increase in our Jewish population might give rise to an anti-Semitic problem.'[91]

However, bowing to political realities, including the undeniable fact that the Allies were clearly the post-war leaders, de Valera decided to reverse his broad policy of political sanctuary, at least as it pertained to spies. On 26 August 1946, with the larger issue still unresolved with the Allies, Gerald Boland ordered Görtz and the others to be released from custody under the Emergency Powers Act – and simultaneously ordered that they be deported and detained until this departure could be arranged.[92] Weber-Drohl was finally transferred from Athlone to Mountjoy in September 1946 and was ordered released from custody on 24 October. His plans for asylum in a private residence seem to have fallen through and he continued to reside at Mountjoy, making daily excursions into the city. The government gave him an allowance of £2 per month.[93]

Görtz continued to be a problem. Further attempts to clarify his status – and to avoid forced deportation to Allied-controlled Germany – inspired another hunger strike in September 1946. Görtz commented: 'I am treated as an outlaw. There are no other means left to fight for my right but to take refuge to passive resistance.'[94] This hunger strike was shorter than the previous attempt and Görtz decided to desist when he read a newspaper ad that mentioned an Estonian ship bound for Spain, which was looking for an 'experienced helmsman'. Despite his rather lacklustre performance as a sailor during his escape attempts in 1941, Görtz wrote to the Irish government asking permission to join the crew, noting 'it is a question of death and life for me'. Predictably, permission was refused.[95]

Görtz was clearly getting more and more paranoid. He still would not to write to his family, even after the war. Instead, he tried to contact Maeve McDowell, asking her to contact his daughter Wiebke, who was then living in Madrid. Wiebke was to be told only that 'Chatterbox' was asking after her and for her not to use his proper name or 'father'. The Irish authorities freely passed Red Cross messages from Görtz's family to Athlone, but he would not reciprocate.[96] G2 initially tried to assure Görtz that his family was safe, but they were still puzzled by his failure to communicate with them. In one report, Irish Intelligence observed that 'Görtz has a rather strange personality' but that 'he has always acted more favourably, from the point of view of our interests, by indulging within limits various of his little humours'.[97]

Görtz repeated his request for permission to travel to Valencia Harbour to make contact with Spanish ships and secure passage to Spain. He erroneously cited the precedent of Leon Degrelle to induce the Irish authorities to permit his exit. They refused.[98] Görtz and the other inmates had been allowed out of Athlone on day-passes from the end of the war, and in September 1946 they were given parole to stay in the Dublin area, provided they reported at specified intervals. Van Loon was permitted to reside at 7 Spencer Villas, Dublin, in the home of Mary and Bridie O'Farrell. This temporary parole was conditional on van Loon not discussing his 'past activities, those of other aliens, or the conditions of detention'.[99] Given that the Farrell sisters had been deeply involved in aiding and abetting the German espionage effort in Ireland, particularly Hermann Görtz – who also lived there on parole – there would be little that they would not already know, other than that their supposedly secure message system had been compromised. At a party in the garden of Bridie and Mary Farrell's house in Dún Laoghaire, van Loon and Görtz were joined by Tributh and Gärtner to celebrate the end of their captivity.[100] Also present were Tributh's fiancée

Paula and Captain J. Kirby, a former Irish Army officer from No. 3 Camp, Athlone, who had since gone into business with ex-Nazi spy Werner Unland.

Unland had earlier requested an unsupervised visit with his wife, which was granted by the military authorities. Colonel Bryan's only stipulation was that Mrs Unland should be made aware of the rules regarding contraband. His comment on Unland was more colourful: 'As Unland is a person of no status and something of a crook, I am not suggesting that any guarantee should be asked of him.'

Walter Simon was paroled along with the other internees on 9 September 1946 and finally released on 26 October 1946. He was unable to find suitable employment in Ireland and in December 1946 he asked to be repatriated to Germany. He left on the SS *Travemunde* on 9 January 1947, bound for Bremen, the first of the internees to depart. He asked that his books and personal papers be forwarded to Dr Prionnsias O'Suilleabhain.[101] Simon's return to Germany did nothing to improve his circumstances. By 1959, he was living in a nursing home in Hamburg-Bahrenfeld and was so destitute that he could not even afford the price of a cigarette. Author Enno Stephan, who discovered Simon while researching his book *Geheimauftrag Irland*, organized an unofficial monthly allocation of 100 Marks, subscribed to by himself and former Abwehr officers Herbert Wichmann and Nikolaus Ritter.[102] By the autumn of 1961, Simon's health had deteriorated even further – he was 79 years old – and he died on 27 October of that year. He was buried in a mass grave in the cemetery at Hamburg-Altona. The brief ceremony was attended by Stephan, Wichmann, Ritter and one of Simon's former neighbours.

SUICIDE

The idyll for the remaining prisoners ended on 12 April 1947 when Görtz and the others were re-arrested and taken to Mountjoy Prison pending deportation. The Irish government had made its decision: the diplomats would stay, but the agents were to be returned. To the great relief of his captors, Weber-Drohl was placed on an American aircraft at Baldonnell Aerodrome and flown to Germany on 15 April, along with Wilhelm Preetz, Dieter Gärtner and Herbert Tributh.[103] He was presumably interrogated for a brief period by the Allies at either Bad Nenndorf or Oberursel and then released to his family. Nothing further was heard of him and his exact fate remains unknown.

Preetz was part of the general internee release in September 1946, but he could not seem to stay out of trouble. He was arrested by the Garda in December 1946 and charged with dangerous driving and not being insured. The car belonged to Dr Philomena Turbridy Evers, one of his new acquaintances, but Preetz's case never came to trial.[104] He listed his next of kin as Mrs Margaret Reynolds, Bishop Street, Tuam, rather than his wife.[105] Sally Josephine Preetz, who spent the entire war with Preetz's in-laws in Bremen, returned to Ireland after VE Day in May 1945, but did not return to live with Preetz. In 1949, G2 reported that Sarah Josephine Reynolds, *former* wife of Wilhelm Preetz, made a successful application to go to the United States.[106] Preetz was contacted by Enno Stephan during the research for *Geheimauftrag Irland*, but declined to participate or be interviewed. Nothing further is known of him.

Gärtner returned to Swakopmund, South West Africa (now Namibia), where he still lives. Tributh settled in Markheidenfeld, Germany. He died in 1996.[107] Obéd was flown from Ireland to London and then deported back to India, rather than to his wife in Antwerp. Before his deportation order was issued, and while he was still in Athlone, Obéd had successfully obtained (via his wife) a certificate of good conduct from the Antwerp police in the hope that he would be returned there. According to a statement made in 1948, he had approached the India League in Dublin after release and this group had arranged his return to India (return to Belgium being disallowed) after consulting the High Commissioner for India in London. Once in India, he applied for a passport in order to return to Antwerp. Based on his earlier history with illegal weapons, his application was rejected and he accordingly made an application directly to Nehru once India became independent from Great Britain (1947). In the end, both he and his German-born wife were granted Indian passports and Obéd was finally free to return to Antwerp.[108] His story, like that of Hermann Görtz, ended tragically. In 1952, Henry Obéd was murdered by his wife – allegedly after she discovered an affair between her husband and the daughter of a local police official.[109]

The only exceptions to the Irish policy were Unland (who had been an Irish resident before the war) and van Loon (who risked execution if he was returned to the Netherlands). Goertz legally challenged the deportation order through a *habeas corpus* motion, and Mr Justice Maguire heard his case from 21 to 23 April 1947. The court ruled against him and an appeal to the Supreme Court on 5 May was likewise refused.[110] With this decision, Görtz slipped into the final grips of paranoia. Despite assurances from the Allies, the Irish government and even from Dr Hempel, Görtz believed that he would be killed if he returned to Germany and said that he would never go back. According to Günther Schütz, the elderly spy said: 'Whatever happens they will never get me. My phial of cyanide will be my last resort.'[111] Even the Americans were concerned about Görtz. Minister David Gray, writing to US General Lucius Clay reported 'the Minister of Justice further told us (on May 10) that his police officers in charge of Görtz reported that in their opinion Görtz would kill himself rather than return to Germany'.[112] Görtz, always quick to defend his bruised honour, brought a libel suit against the *Daily Mail* and John Murdoch for referring to him and his fellow agent Werner Unland as 'spies'.[113]

Görtz made a point of telling several people that he was planning suicide. In addition to Schütz, he also dropped hints to former internee Jan van Loon. With this danger in mind, Frederick Boland asked Dr Hempel to intervene and try to talk to Görtz. Boland stressed, in a convoluted statement quoted by Hempel, that it was always the intention of the Irish government 'not to give the right of permanent residence in Ireland to German agents who had come to Ireland illegally during the war, and only to let them stay here so long as the government could not be satisfied that they would not be exposed to any danger of persecution and punishment when they would be sent back to Germany. The moment had come now.'[114]

Hempel met with Görtz on the evening of 14 May. In his statement to the Irish government, Hempel conveniently forgot that he had met and assisted Görtz during his wartime liberty: 'I had met Dr Görtz before. He had called on me shortly after his release from Athlone in September or October 1946, and I had seen him since a few times in my house.' Görtz told Hempel that he was afraid for several reasons: first 'that all countries which hold now [sic] Germany occupied, were out for the extermination of the classes of Germans to whom he belonged'; second, 'he felt very serious apprehensions that he would be in some or other way persecuted by enemies, particularly Communists, against whom he had been fighting after the last war'; third, 'he could not expect to get any chance to earn his livelihood and would therefore only be a burden to his family, who was already living in distress.' Görtz also complained about his re-arrest in April, noting that 'he had been confined in the cell for people condemned to death because he was told it had the advantage of having an open fireplace. The fact that the electric light was not switched off during the whole night and that in short intervals a guard looked into his cell, had been a great strain on him.'[115] This has all the outward appearances of a suicide watch.

Hempel thought that Görtz would benefit from meeting with Frederick Boland in person and a second rendezvous at Hempel's house was organized for 15 May. Boland assured Görtz that he would, at maximum, be held for a few weeks in Germany and that after that, he could go where he pleased. Görtz replied that 'he could not face a possible new period of internment or imprisonment for years and was absolutely not convinced that this could not happen'. In concern for Görtz, Boland arranged an immediate parole for the German, and Görtz and Hempel met again on 18 May. Görtz told Hempel that if he had had to return to Mountjoy on 15 May, 'he would have taken his life'. At their parting, the former minister and the former spy agreed to meet again on the evening of 23 May for dinner.[116]

When he appeared at the Aliens Office in Palace Street (just outside Dublin Castle) to renew his parole on the morning of 23 May 1947, Detective Sergeant Patrick O'Connor informed Görtz that a plane was waiting to fly him back to Germany and that he would be detained until the time of departure. Görtz did not ask to telephone either Hempel or Boland, but sat in the waiting room, smoking his pipe. In an adjoining room Günther Schütz and his new bride, an Irish nurse, also waited. In a casual manner, Görtz calmly removed his pipe, took his hand from his trouser pocket, and bit down on the glass capsule. Detective Gordon said 'That man is taking something,' and tried to get the ampoule out of Görtz's mouth. Görtz responded with 'That is none of your business' and collapsed. He was immediately rushed downstairs through the Passport Office and into an ambulance and taken to Mercer's Hospital, where he died at 11:15.[117]

The inquest into Görtz's death was a relatively short affair. The Dublin City Coroner, Dr D.A. MacErlean held hearings but was met with a noticeable lack of cooperation from the Fianna Fáil government. Eamon de Valera issued the following memorandum:

> I have considered the communications relating directly or indirectly to the late Dr Herman [*sic*] Goertz which have passed between myself, the officers of my department, and other Ministers and between myself or my officials and representatives of other Governments. I am satisfied that it would be injurious to the public interest that any of the said communications should be disclosed to any person. I am also aware of communications which have passed between departmental officials relating directly or indirectly to the late Dr Herman Goertz. I consider it would be injurious to the public interest that any communication passing between such officials should be disclosed to any person. I accordingly direct Mr Boland not to disclose any of the said communications and to claim privilege in respect thereof on the aforesaid ground.[118]

It was clearly not in the government's interest to have the disparate treatment of spies and diplomats scrutinized too closely, though, to be fair, diplomats might be hypothetically covered by diplomatic immunity, while agents had no such protection. De Valera's dictum was apparently carried out – no official correspondence regarding this matter is preserved in the Irish governmental files, even more than fifty years after the events. John Costello, representing Görtz's estate at the inquest, sought to delay the deportation of Günther Schütz, but was unsuccessful. Costello also intended to widen the net of responsibility, formally asking that Frederick Boland in the Department of External Affairs and J.P. Berry of the Department of Justice be summoned to give evidence.[119] Following de Valera's decision, that potential line of inquiry collapsed of its own weight. Eventually, the coroner returned a verdict of suicide – which it obviously was – and listed the cause of death as heart failure brought on by lethal ingestion of potassium cyanide.[120]

The reasons for Görtz's suicide remain conjectural. He was obviously possessed of an irrational fear of being deported, a fear so strong that no assurance was ultimately sufficient to convince him of his safety. Another contributing factor was that during the last few months he finally became aware that his carefully crafted image of 'master spy' was becoming unravelled. Görtz learned that his prison messages were intercepted, that G2 had broken his code and that his comprehensive report to the OKW was nothing more than a clever charade by Irish Intelligence.[121] Speaking many years later, Günther Schütz adequately summed up Görtz, saying: 'He was a tragic figure because he always failed. He failed as a lawyer; he failed as an agent in England; he failed as an agent in Ireland. He even failed to escape. Between fifty and a hundred people were arrested in Ireland because of his activities.'[122] Prior to his discovery about the intercepted prison messages, Görtz had always clung to the illusion that he was the lone island of competence in a raging sea of betrayal. Writing about his mission from his cell in Athlone, he said that 'I don't believe in a blunder. I am convinced of an intrigue.'[123] The facts, as he finally came to understand, were quite different. For the second time in his life, he had been given an important espionage mission and had bungled it. By the time of his imminent deportation, there was no illusion left, and, consequently, nothing left for Hermann Görtz to live for. His distorted concept of honour demanded no less.

Görtz's funeral on 26 May 1947 was a public event. A military ceremony was refused and crowds thronged the route to Dean's Grange cemetery. Görtz was clad in a Luftwaffe greatcoat, borrowed from former internee Georg Fleishmann, and his coffin was decorated with a swastika flag. In attendance among the estimated 600–800 people were Werner Unland, Jan van Loon, Charles McGuinness, Dan Breen, TD and Jim O'Donovan. Hempel had enquired if he might go, but Frederick Boland advised against it, so he stayed at home. In tribute to Görtz, the Farrell sisters wore his military decorations, though this would have been gross violation of protocol at a military service. As the coffin was carried out, unnamed Irish citizens raised their hands in the Nazi salute. The service was directed by the Revd. K.D.B. Dobbs of the Church of Ireland – Görtz was officially listed as 'Protestant' – and he was finally interred at 1100 hours. He was originally given a simple marker, but Frau Görtz later successfully petitioned the Irish government for a stone that Görtz had carved while at Athlone. It was not originally – as has been reported by others – meant to be Görtz's tombstone, merely another artistic project that he began in internment. The Farrell sisters added a plaque naming the deceased as 'Lt. Colonel Hermann Görtz', seemingly unaware that his actual rank when the war ended had never risen above captain.[124] In 1974, Görtz's body was exhumed and transferred to the picturesque and dignified German Military Cemetery at Glencree, County Wicklow. Today he lies under a common marker, identical in every way to the other German soldiers and sailors who are buried there. In a final but unconscious tribute to the ingenuity and finesse of Irish Army Intelligence, his rank is listed as 'Major'.

While the former internees waited to hear the decision of the Irish government on their post-war status, van Loon stayed in contact with Görtz, who had been returned to Mountjoy Prison on 12 April. On the day before Görtz's appointment at the Aliens Office at Dublin Castle, van Loon had a meal with him. He said that he knew Görtz was planning to take some action, but he was not sure what it was. Görtz's suicide still came as a shock and van Loon believes that Görtz kept the cyanide capsule with him throughout his internment. Görtz made a powerful impression on Jan van Loon and even almost sixty years after the events, he describes him as 'very human' and 'gifted' with a wide range of intellectual and artistic interests.[125]

Schütz himself began asking permission to return to occupied Germany in February 1946. Lilo was seriously ill in a hospital in Bremen, and life in Ireland in the post-war period did not hold any obvious attraction for him. At some point, his plans changed. With the German surrender in May 1945, the German internees were allowed out on day passes from Athlone. At a dance in Athlone, he met 25-year-old Una Mackey. Miss Mackey was employed as a ward sister at Paddington Hospital in London and had been visiting friends in Athlone. Sometime after April 1946, there is no further mention of Lilo, and Schütz and Una Mackey decided to get married.

Nevertheless, the Allied authorities insisted that Schütz and the other internees be transferred to Germany for interrogation. Neither de Valera nor any other member of the government attempted to protect the agents as they so strenuously – and successfully – protected Dr Hempel. Elizabeth Clissmann suggests that de Valera engaged in what she called a *Kuhhändel* (cow trade): the Allies could have the agents in exchange for Dr Hempel being allowed to claim sanctuary.[126] Such an allegation is unprovable, but it does fit in with events: the agents were deported and interrogated in Germany, Hempel safely stayed in Ireland.

Though on the list for deportation, Schütz married Una Mackey on 1 May 1947. By this time, Schütz was on permanent parole, and had a flat at Haddington Road, Dublin. He was briefly re-arrested in anticipation of being sent back, but through the intercession of Archbishop John Charles McQuaid he was again released on parole. Schütz received orders to report to the Aliens Registration Office, Palace Street, Dublin on 24 May. While waiting there with his wife, Schütz heard a commotion from the next room and several officers hurriedly entered the room and searched him. The commotion had been the sound of Dr Görtz taking cyanide in the next room and the authorities thought that Schutz might have similar ideas; he did not.[127] Schütz was taken back into custody the next day and flown from Baldonnell to Frankfurt. He was taken to a US Army interrogation camp near Oberursel and was released soon thereafter.

While on his initial parole from Athlone, Schütz began a small business making desk lamps, but on his return from Germany, he expanded his concept. After his release from interrogation, he and his wife had to start all over again, this time in Hamburg. He successfully established his own import/export company and eventually moved back to Ireland in the 1960s.[128] With financial help from Irish friends in the ESB, he began buying surplus military materials and converting them to civilian use. Pontoon tanks from the Normandy invasion became oil storage units; 200,000 yards of British field cable were purchased by the ESB.[129] Schütz was fortunate in that he did not have to front the money himself, but received a commission for finding the items and eventually saved enough to buy his own Riley convertible, a rare event in a time when most people did not own automobiles. For some years he ran a hotel in County Wicklow and eventually retired to his home in Avoca.[130] Günther Schütz died in Shankill, County Dublin in 1991.

While he was still on parole, the 15 April 1947 publication of an article in the *Daily Mail* caused Unland to emerge from his cocoon. Under the headline 'Deportation by Air Order – De Valera Rounds Up German Spies – Court Writs due Today' the paper told the story about the remaining German agents being prepared for transfer back to Germany. Both Görtz and Unland, jointly represented by Counsel John A. Costello, filed suit against the *Daily Mail* and their correspondent John Murdoch, claiming libel.[131] Their objection was to the word 'spy' in the headline and the suggestion in the story that they were Nazis. In his complaint, which was immediately reported by the press, Unland lied: 'I have never at any time directly or indirectly associated with espionage. I have never been associated with any Nazi organization either in this country or elsewhere.'[132]

Though the Irish Intelligence branch could certainly prove otherwise, it would be difficult for the *Daily Mail* to obtain the hard evidence to show with a preponderance of evidence that Unland was an espionage agent. Görtz went back to his usual refrain that he was not a spy but a military officer on a legitimate mission – despite the fact that he had operated in a neutral country without the benefit of his uniform. Görtz's premature death had the effect of dropping him as a plaintiff, but Unland's claim was eventually settled out of court in November 1947 for an unspecified amount of damages. In its story covering the settlement, the *Evening Herald* mentioned that Unland was in partnership with a former Irish Army officer from Internment Camp No. 3, Captain J. Kirby.[133] This was said to be an import/export business based in Dublin and one story had them selling women's scarves, among other things.[134] Werner Unland died in Dublin on 20 August 1962 from a heart attack at the age of 70.[135]

While most of the other internees were flown back to Germany, van Loon was not deported back to the Netherlands. He was allowed, with Unland, to remain in Ireland.[136] After a successful business career in manufacturing and retail sales, he is retired and still lives in Howth, a Dublin suburb.

O'REILLY AND KENNY AT ARBOUR HILL

John O'Reilly and John Kenny were treated quite differently from the other foreign nationals – and, indeed, from Joseph Lenihan. While the other internees were subject to rather Spartan surroundings at Mountjoy and Athlone, O'Reilly and Kenny were housed in relative comfort (as the surviving photographs demonstrate) at Arbour Hill Prison.

Once in G2 custody and interned at Arbour Hill Prison, Kenny was interrogated, but nothing useful came out of the sessions. The official conclusion was that Kenny simply did not have the information to begin with. He stated his mission was something to do with 'collecting information on ships', but did not seem to know any of the details.[137] His actual function seems to have been to act as O'Reilly's RTO (radio-telegraph operator), but his training was obviously insufficient to perform this task reliably. Fearing the worst, O'Reilly had instructed him to go home and wait until he was called. The only statement that Kenny made on this subject was to say that he 'came to Ireland, not with the intention of doing Ireland any harm, but for the purpose of getting to England to work there against a country he did not like for another country who [*sic*] was at war with England'. Kenny also added that he would not 'squeal on his friends'.[138]

Kenny's time in Arbour Hill seems to have passed rather peacefully, but he was diagnosed with 'traumatic neurasthenia' due to his back injury and being kept in an unheated cell. He was released from internment on 11 May 1945. The only further mention of him is a newspaper report from May 1949, which states that John Kenny of Jones Road, Dublin, 'former parachutist', had been charged with arson. His age was given as 32 and his occupation was listed as mechanic. There is no disposition given for the arson charge and Kenny seems to have subsequently disappeared from the headlines.[139]

In a curious, and possibly important development, there was some doubt about whether O'Reilly and Kenny were the only two German parachutists dropped over Ireland during December 1943. The mystery was initiated by a report filed by Captain Wellwood, a member of the Irish Army's First Division legal staff. While on leave in December 1943 – and before the arrival of O'Reilly had been announced or was even known beyond a relatively small group – he happened to visit a pub at Brendan's Corner, Galway. While there, he met a former University College, Galway, student named Tim Kelly. Mr Kelly appeared to be under the influence of alcohol, but mentioned that he had been an exchange student at Toulouse University at the time of the German occupation of France. Mr Kelly continued this narrative by saying that he had been parachuted back into Ireland along with two other Irishmen, one Englishman and three Germans. He specifically mentioned O'Reilly of Kilkee, and that O'Reilly's 'relation had been with Casement'. The Irish Intelligence officer of the Southern Command, Florence O'Donoghue, thought this report was serious enough to warrant further investigation. In a witness statement taken during the G2 inquiry, a man named Roddy Heron said he recalled the conversation between Wellwood and Kelly at Brendan's Tavern and that Kelly even gave William Joyce's Irish address – though Heron could not say whether or not it was correct. No further reference to this case appears in the G2 files.[140]

O'Reilly's arrival did attract the attention of the Americans at the US Legation in Dublin. Writing home on 30 December 1943, Daniel Terrell of the Office of War Information (OWI) notes that 'for the Christmas holidays, the Germans dropped a few presents on Eire. Further details cannot be disclosed a this time, but life here does have an interesting item now and again.'[141] Terrell followed this up on 20 January 1944 when he added

> One month after it happened, the Irish public was informed this week about the two parachutists who were dropped from German planes. Both Irish, of course. Our favourite angle: John P. O'Reilly, 28-year-old Irish 'Haw-Haw,' left Berlin with paper permitting him both to leave Germany and land in Eire – even down to an exit permit visaed by the Irish Charge d'Affaires in Berlin! (Such detail, of course, was censored by our old friend, censor Thomas Coyne).[142]

In addition to the code-wheel cipher device that O'Reilly brought with him, the Irish Intelligence authorities were also anxious to learn the circumstances surrounding his possession of what seemed a genuine Irish passport, complete with an exit permit signed by the Irish Chargé d'Affaires, William Warnock. O'Reilly undoubtedly had contact with Warnock during his time in Berlin while attached to the Irland-Redaktion, but the Irish visa was a problem for the Irish authorities, who were astute enough to anticipate the potential political fallout. O'Reilly admitted that his passport visas for Spain and Portugal were forged, but continued to maintain that the Irish stamps were genuine. Irish Intelligence had an initial difficulty proving otherwise. Dr Richard Hayes, while working with the Garda forensic laboratory at Kilmainham, successfully examined the passport under ultraviolet light and made further examinations by using infra-red photographs. He determined that the passport was genuine other than the suspect page 12, which had been cleverly substituted. The visa stamp was originally from one issued on 15 May 1939 (No. 213/39) which had been altered to read No. 213/43. Despite the clever manipulation, the German experts had missed a few points: Warnock's title was given as 'Secretary of the Legation', the job he held in 1939, but by 1943 he had been promoted to Chargé d'Affaires. Further, the passport bore a code-number

(H/RHT/662). Code numbers had been discontinued since the outbreak of the war.[143]

It would have been too much to expect that O'Reilly would become just another prisoner who served his time in relative quiet. On 6 July 1944, O'Reilly successfully escaped from Arbour Hill Prison by squeezing between the bars of his cell window.[144] Having obviously reconnoitred the area before, he climbed on top of an unused sentry tower, loosened the barbed wire, made it over the wall and managed to board the next train home to County Clare.[145] A subsequent investigation of the escape by the Irish military revealed some major lapses in security. First, O'Reilly had presumably escaped at approximately 01:00, but the next check of his cell was not until 0830.[146] During the course of the investigation, an anonymous letter was received that suggested the duty officer had left the key to O'Reilly's cell in the lock, and testimony from the investigation seemed to suggest that this had happened on other occasions. Key security did not seem to have been a priority. However, before any of the responsible personnel could be seriously embarrassed by their failings, O'Reilly was recaptured and the investigation was quickly terminated without any finding of misconduct. The *Daily Press* (an English paper) reported that he 'opened the cell door with a key that had been smuggled to him'.[147] In his post-war memoirs, O'Reilly also added that the duty officer had thoughtfully acceded to his request for a Dublin map, without bothering to question O'Reilly's intended purpose.[148]

A £500 reward was offered by the Irish government for information leading to the capture of John Francis O'Reilly. Wanted posters were quickly circulated across the country. Unexpectedly, the claimant was John O'Reilly's father, Bernard. According to his statement to the investigating Gardaí, John had arrived home at 19:00 on 9 May and was re-arrested at 21:00 the same evening. Bernard dutifully applied for and collected the reward money for his son, though there was discussion between Justice Minister Gerald Boland and G2's Dan Bryan about the legitimacy of paying in this instance. It was finally agreed that the government should pay so as not to damage the public response to any future reward offers.

Following his recapture, O'Reilly amused himself by periodically speaking to interrogators from Irish Intelligence. British Intelligence, making full use of the 'Dublin Link' passed along questions and material for G2 to assist in the interrogation of O'Reilly. In a reciprocal gesture, G2 gave MI5 (specifically Cecil Liddell's B.1.H Ireland section) copies of the Irish Intelligence reports from the interrogations.[149] In 1944 O'Reilly applied to have his £143 in German espionage funds applied to his account at Arbour Hill. In what has to be one of the wittiest items to come out of the Military Archives files, O'Reilly penned this poem to Major Guilfoyle of G2:

I'm quite 'on the rocks' – eight-and-thrupence, approx.
(though my spiritual wealth is unbounded)
Admitting you dread it – please place to my credit,
The cash you've so kindly impounded.

And now, to my grief, the State, like a thief,
Camouflaged by Emergency Orders,
Just pockets the coin, with most knavish design,
To bolster its Budget disorders.

Without hesitation, you'll counter – "Inflation
Is causing us fits of the jitters!"
But no one disputes, you've gained three parachutes,
Not to mention two handsome transmitters![150]

O'Reilly's money was returned to him upon release from Arbour Hill after the war. One important issue that confounded G2 was the nature of O'Reilly's ciphers. They quickly determined that O'Reilly had the capability to use three different encoding systems: the book cipher, the revolving disc, and an alpha-numeric code based on a microphotographic list of 400 five-figure groups, which had been intercepted when O'Reilly was arrested.

Dr Hayes, in the course of several interviews with O'Reilly managed to develop a theory about the code-wheel (which he called an 'autoclave') and speculated that it could be used as a separate coding device or in conjunction with the microphotographic list. By this time, the autoclave was seemingly an exclusive toy of the SD and there were no reported instances of the Abwehr using this device in Ireland, though the Abwehr did issue the disc cipher to an agent sent to England in September 1940. Dr Hayes would have been interested to learn that O'Reilly's code and cipher keys (which explained the use and relationship between the microphotographic list) had been overlooked by Gardaí in their search of the O'Reilly house at Kilkee. They were in a cardboard folder hidden beneath the front door mat. His father later burned them.

O'Reilly looked on the Irish decoding attempts on the autoclave or the list as a source of entertainment. Again, though O'Reilly maintained, after the fact, that he was merely using the Germans as a means of returning home, he steadfastly refused to provide Irish Intelligence with any useful information on his coding system, and was considered less-than-candid in other aspects of his testimony. O'Reilly's main code was nevertheless broken. According to Dr Hayes, O'Reilly 'was a cocky young man who believed that the cipher methods he had been taught in Germany were impenetrable and he fell for a challenge'.[151] O'Reilly accepted the task of enciphering an 'unbreakable message' but Dr Hayes recovered the burned notes O'Reilly used while the spy was out of his cell on an exercise period.[152] Hayes had the burned pages treated at the Garda Forensic Laboratory at Kilmainham using the same process that had been successfully applied to Joseph Andrews's notes from the previous year. The paper fragments were sprayed with a cellulose acetate and then mounted on glass slides that were exposed to acetone.[153] On 21 January 1944, barely four weeks after O'Reilly's arrival, Dan Bryan telegraphed Cecil Liddell in London: 'Messages just read, Doctor's notes provided solution.'

O'Reilly apparently sent a message to a prominent Irish political figure, because Colonel Bryan noted that 'O'Reilly was in touch with Seán McBride and has given McBride information concerning Francis Stuart which was not given us by O'Reilly'.[154] Though Dr Hayes had defeated O'Reilly's attempts to block a solution to his coding systems, O'Reilly continued to want to play the game. 'I am no longer surprised at the ingenuity of some of his red herrings,' remarked Dr Hayes.[155] Working in concert, G2 and MI5 were able to identify most of the code secrets.

In one interesting discovery, the intelligence agencies learned that the SD, to maximize security, even had the numerals transmitted in a way to foil would-be decipherers. Rather than transmit the numbers as normal (e.g. *eins, zwei, drei, vier, fünf, sechs,* etc.) the SD introduced alternative spellings: ein, zwo, dri, vir ... seqs and so on. As with various peculiarities in the main message, these features would, in theory, ensure that an incoming message was actually from the agent and not from a captured transmitter. O'Reilly was also trained to mathematically arrive at a new call-sign for each day's transmissions, avoiding the type of problems that had plagued Preetz. An alternative method for generating call-signs was from the book *Îles de Lumière* by Henriette Celarie, using different pages for even and odd months.[156]

Typically, O'Reilly did not vanish gracefully into obscurity upon his release from Arbour Hill. Unlike the German agents kept at Athlone, who were incarcerated for almost two years after the war's end, O'Reilly and Kenny were released soon after VE Day, Kenny on 11 May and O'Reilly on 24 May. Returning home to Kilkee and his family, O'Reilly found a warm welcome. Apparently as part of a pre-arranged plan, his father had combined the reward money for his son with the remainder of his espionage funds (only part of which had been found by the Garda) meaning that O'Reilly ended the war on a profitable note.[157]

In October 1945, O'Reilly purchased the Esplanade Hotel in Dublin for £7,100 and somewhat later opened a pub in Parkgate Street, just down from the former headquarters of Irish Intelligence. Though actually called 'O'Reilly's', the pub was commonly known as the Parachute Bar and O'Reilly as 'the Parachutist'.[158] O'Reilly's first wife, Helen, was the celebrated fatal victim of Dublin's infamous American abortionist, nurse Maimie Cadden.[159] He soon tired of the monotony of being a hotel and pub owner.[160] In 1952 he serialized his memoirs of the war years in the *Sunday Dispatch* (London), which ran them for six weeks. Leaving Ireland yet again for the lure of adventure overseas, he lived for a time in both Nigeria and Lima, Peru, working as an electrician and, allegedly, as a radio operator for the British in Cairo during the 1967 Six Day War between Israel and the Arab states.[161] He had moved to Westminster, London, in 1957. Fourteen years later, O'Reilly was critically injured in a car accident and spent his final months in a hospital in Middlesex, England. He died there on 4 May 1971 and was subsequently buried on 13 May in Glasnevin Cemetery, Dublin.[162]

(25) Dutch naval photograph of a young Jan van Loon (IMA).

(26) John Francis O'Reilly (PRO).

(27) John Kenny, potato picker and SD agent (PRO).

(28) Colonel Dan Bryan, head of Irish G-2 (IMA).

(29) John O'Reilly's Abwehr 'Afu' transmitter (IMA).

61	1	2	3	4
25	28798	27564	46355	32124
70	18675	15243	37563	15211
09	28672	17564	18876	29972
53	18675	18867	15243	36541
42	17765	14325	96785	75643
74	85346	16243	36544	48675

(30) O'Reilly's microphotographic code list (NLI).

(31) Tributh, Görtz and Gärtner at a post-war party of former spies at the O'Farrell House (van Loon).

(32) Görtz and the O'Farrell sisters (van Loon).

(33) Dr Richard Hayes, code breaker, library director (NLI).

(34) Joseph Andrews, Görtz's assistant and would-be spy (IMA).

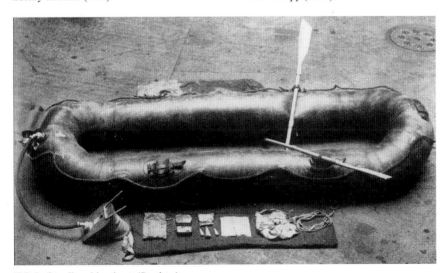

(35) Luftwaffe rubber boat (Stephan).

(36) Dr Edmund Veesenmayer, Foreign Office specialist on Ireland and SS general (BA).

(37) A worried-looking Oscar Pfaus in 1944/5 (Stephan).

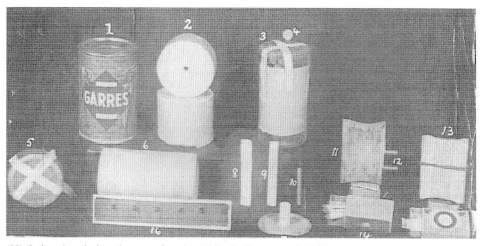

(38) 'Lobster' explosives that were found on Tributh, Gärtner and Obéd (IMA).

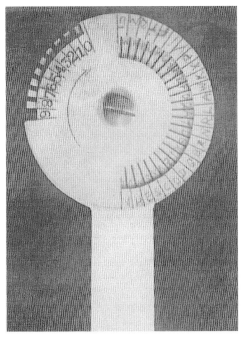

(39) O'Reilly's encoding device (IMA).

(40) Oberst Nikolaus Ritter, chief of Abwehr I-L (air intelligence section) (PRO).

(41) Walter Schellenberg (PRO).

(42) Charles McGuinness, adventurer, sailor, and would-be German spy.

No. 0094 A/N

IRISH REPUBLICAN 3½% WAR LOAN GOVERNMENT BOND.

(ISSUE OF MAY, 1941).

This script represents £............ (............... Pounds) stock, and is repayable at its face value plus three and one half per cent interest per annum from date of issue to holder. Date of payment shall be any day six months after the Government of the Irish Republic has begun to function in the exercise of sovereign control over the territory of all Ireland.

Date .... 1941.

Signed : ....

For the Army of the Irish Republic.

No. 0094 A/N

IRISH REPUBLICAN 3½% WAR LOAN GOVERNMENT BOND.

(ISSUE OF MAY, 1941).

£...

(...Pounds

....

....

Date ...., 1941.

Signed : ....

For the Army of the Irish Republic.

(43) IRA bond (Stephan).

WHO IS YOUR ENEMY ?

WHO has for centuries trampled you in the dust?

WHO engineered the artificial famine of 1846-48 when two million of our people perished amidst plenty and which forced millions of our people into exile?

WHO let loose the scum of England — the Jew Greenwood's Black and Tans — to murder, burn and loot in our country?

WHO is maintaining the inhuman partition of our country?

WHO is persecuting and victimising our fellow-countrymen in the enemy occupied area of our country?.

WHO has unceasingly endeavoured to represent us to all nations as a race of clowns and half wits?

WHO are the self-chosen "protectors and patrons of Christianity" who organised the Priest hunts, despoiled our Churches, and even excluded His Holiness the Pope from the Peace Conference of Versailles?

WHO is flooding Ireland with Jewish-Masonic drivel and filth insulting to our national aspirations and the Christian religion, paralysing your mind and warping your judgement?

THE ANSWER IS ENLAND — IRELAND'S ONLY ENEMY.

England's foes are Ireland's friends — May they increase and multiply ! Moladh go deo leo !

WHO HAS NEVER CONCEALED ITS SYMPATHY WITH THE IRISH PEOPLE AND THEIR CAUSE THE GERMAN NATION.

Success to Ireland's friends.

WHERE DO YOU STAND IN THIS WAR?

(44) Irish Friends of Germany leaflet; spelling seems to have been a problem (IMA).

'ASP

SERVES THE
BY SERVING

NEVER FAILS TO STOP
COLD

45 Barrington Road,
Brixton, S.W.9,

Gentlemen,

About 3 years ago I wrote to inform you of the great benefit my wife and myself had received from 'ASPRO'. I thought it might interest you to know that I recently recommended 'ASPRO' to a friend who has been troubled with rheumatism. He tells me that not only did he secure immediate relief, but the improvement appears to have been permanent. My step-son has also found 'ASPRO' wonderfully efficacious in an attack of violent toothache. May I add that I have never known 'ASPRO' fail to stop a cold if taken at bedtime with hot milk. I may say that I should not care to be without some in the house.—Yours faithfully.

W. T. WILKINSON.

RHEUMATIC PAINS GO
—NURSE WRITES

Brighton.

Dear Sirs,

Finding 'ASPRO' all that it states, I feel I must write you as I shall be eternally grateful to you after my past experience. I am a trained nurse and I developed a nasty pain in my right side. It seemed to envelop the whole of my hip, so much so that it must be rheumatism, developed from a severe chill from swimming in very cold water. Well, yesterday, I took 2 'ASPRO' tablets after every meal. I slept throughout the whole of last night and awoke a changed being. You can imagine my joy throughout to-day when I found no pain returning. It has done the trick and I can shout from the house tops, "ASPRO for ever."

Thank you again and again. I shall always recommend it now in the most stubborn cases. Excuse my hilarity but I am so very happy at bei

(45) The fake 'Aspro' advertisement with microdots which encoded Schütz's mission information (IMA).

(47) Page two of Görtz's paybook with his signature of 'Dr. Hermann Kruse', p. 2 (IMA).

(46) The first page of Görtz's Luftwaffe paybook, giving his pseudonym of 'Leutnant Kruse' (IMA).

10
The end of the Abwehr

German Military Intelligence last considered the Irish question in early 1944, with the tepid offer to William Murphy. It was truly the last gasp. On 12 February 1944, after a string of glaring Abwehr failures and defections, Hitler formerly transferred the responsibility for German Intelligence gathering to the SD. Canaris was removed as head of the Abwehr and transferred to an insignificant post at the Reich Economic Warfare Office. The functional hand-over was delayed until May, when the remaining Abwehr leadership was summoned to a meeting in Salzburg to learn the specifics: Abwehr I and II were re-named 'Militärisches Amt' (Mil Amt or Military Department) and would be absorbed by RSHA Amt VI (the SD). Abwehr III (counter-intelligence) was placed under Gestapo control. The Asts were renamed 'command report areas' (Kommando Meldgebiete) and were likewise subject to the SD. The OKW successfully argued that it should retain some of the Abwehr responsibilities and personnel under the OKW operations staff (Generaloberst Alfred Jodl), keeping the Foreign Intelligence Group, the combat intelligence sections of Abwehr I and the troop security and military counter-espionage missions of Abwehr III. Oberst Georg Hansen (of old Abwehr I) was initially given command of Mil Amt, but was arrested and executed following the July 1944 attempt to assassinate Hitler. From that point forward, SS-Brigadeführer Walter Schellenberg personally directed the organization.[1]

Like its Abwehr predecessor, the Mil Amt had a section devoted to intelligence collection in the West, Abteilung B, and a sub-section (B/I – Nord) responsible for Great Britain and Ireland.[2] This command operated no agents, but was reduced to collating wireless information and whatever else could be gleaned from neutral sources and the world press.[3] Most Abwehr officers found positions in the new RSHA organization, and military personnel continued to belong to their original services for purposes of rank and pay.

With the Allied invasion of France in June 1944, even the radical reorganization of German Military Intelligence failed to produce any positive results. Events had moved from the point where foreign intelligence operations had any meaning to the Third Reich. The planned invasion of Britain and the implied importance of Ireland were an anachronism. Nazi

Germany was engaged in a fight for survival and Ireland was relegated to the distant sidelines.

Canaris, who bore the responsibility for many of Germany's Intelligence difficulties, died before the Allied victory. He was arrested on 23 July 1944 and remained in confinement until 8 April 1945 when he was strangled, suspended from an iron collar, at Flössenburg concentration camp. His ten-year tenure as chief of German Military Intelligence had been a failure, at least in so far as it served military interests of Nazi Germany. His real motives and actions remain a mystery.

Conclusion

Only now has it become possible to examine the scope of Germany's espionage activities in Ireland during the Second World War. For obvious reasons, the German authorities never wrote an after-action report on their espionage activities; for less obvious reasons, the Irish counter-intelligence personnel did not report on their wartime achievements in foiling the German Intelligence initiatives. MI5, however, gave this matter careful attention. During the war, they had access to the largest collection of captive German agents at Camp 020 near Ham Common in Richmond upon Thames, and successfully ran a host of double-agent networks. More than anyone else – perhaps more than the Germans themselves – MI5 was in an ideal position to evaluate the efficiency of German Intelligence.

In the 1945 'Baird Report', MI5 examined the first of the failings of German Intelligence: personnel acquisition.

> In view of the manner in which the spies were recruited it is hardly surprising that almost without exception, they proved to be extremely poor material. In most cases they were men devoid of moral principles, who would have worked for any side that paid them. Many had drifted from one job to another without making good; many had been sentenced for various offences; a high proportion suffered from venereal disease. It was reported by a number of agents that the recruiters of the Abwehr were keen on showing results to their superiors by dispatching as many agents as possible, and that in many cases they did not expect results. Their aim was quantity rather than quality.[1]

The German civilian personnel selected for Irish missions fell squarely in the middle of this category and, by their very selection, gave evidence that the Abwehr was an organization in trouble. The ideal (and usually hypothetical) recruit for espionage work combines initiative, intelligence, loyalty and a sense of mission priorities. While German forces, particularly the Lehr Regiment Brandenburg, possessed such men, they were inexplicably not chosen for missions to Ireland or anywhere else.[2] The selected few were the exact antithesis – lacking in judgement, wasteful and focused on anything but the task at hand. Selection was based on any number of inane factors: Preetz was in possession of an Irish passport; Weber-Drohl had a false alibi that could, in a ridiculous sense, explain his interest and presence in Ireland; Hermann Görtz, popularly considered the best agent dispatched to Ireland, had nothing but a history of failure as a spy.

As MI5 noted, another trait characteristic of Abwehr recruits was their inability to speak English fluently, making it impossible for them to pass as natives.[3] Of the agents dispatched to Ireland, several had only a rudimentary grasp of the language; and even though Obéd, Görtz, Schütz and Preetz spoke English well, it was accented – in the relatively homogeneous Irish population, each would stand out as a foreigner in even the most casual conversation. Aside from the shocking lack of selection standards, the problem was further complicated by the failure of Abwehr controllers properly to brief their chosen agents. Elementary mistakes – such as not knowing the accepted currency (Görtz), a fundamental misunderstanding of the relationship of the IRA to the Irish Army (Schütz) or not being able to distinguish between an active and a long inactive rail line (Simon) – were all easily avoidable. With so little pre-war planning, and minimal cooperation from the German Legation, the Abwehr essentially had the agents figure out the situation on their own and provided only a bare minimum of information regarding local contacts and safe houses. The fact that Preetz was able to operate for almost three months is a testament to his luck, not to the quality of his instruction.

Another disabling factor for German Intelligence was a lack of proper command and control. With the IRA's only transmitter seized shortly after the outbreak of the war, Germany had no reliable means of knowing the status of the agents or their missions. Replacement sets were lost through carelessness, and the legation was unable to risk its own position to maintain a constant watch over espionage operations. Moreover, it would probably have been foolish to do so. This interruption in the flow of situational, tactical and strategic intelligence seemingly did not deter the Hamburg and Bremen Asts, among others, from sending in a steady stream of agents without first establishing the status of the previous missions. Allied interrogation reports of senior Abwehr officers had a common denominator: the commanders ultimately responsible for the missions had almost no idea of what was going on in their own commands. Part of this intelligence gap is attributable to a lack of information from the field, but some of it is simply due to profound professional incompetence.

Likewise, attempts by headquarters to monitor the progress of agents in the field were similarly inept. Agent codes, with the exception of that used by Görtz, were of a type known to be vulnerable to enemy decoding. Rather than provide the agents with more advanced and secure means of communications, the negligence of the OKW cipher branch and the Abwehr made it likely that the enemy would ultimately discover the agents and intercept and read what was supposed to be secret traffic. Dr Richard Hayes observed that 'the educational standard of the agent as well as the importance of his mission has to be taken into account by an intelligence service when selecting a cipher for him. It might be laid down as a general principle that the relative complexity of an agent's cipher gives a fair measure of the relative importance of his mission and of his rank in the intelligence service which employs him.'[4] However, this begs the question of why Germany would send agents into the field that were not capable – practically or intellectually – of working with more complex ciphers. The majority of the spies in Ireland were sent in 1940, well before a severe manpower shortage would explain the degradation in the quality of available agents. The answer might be, as suggested by MI5, that the Abwehr was going for quantity, rather than quality, and that 'they did not expect results'. The lack of intelligible reports from Abwehr agents had caused the OKW and lower echelon commanders to regard agent reports as practically worthless. In addition, Foreign Armies West (the OKH intelligence evaluation branch for Western Europe) usually exaggerated enemy strength reports – because, they felt, the OKW operations staff halved their estimates before reporting them to Hitler. Thus was created a farcical situation where no intelligence of any accuracy found its way to the German High Command.

One factor common to all German agents sent to Ireland was a profound absence of good judgement, which goes back to the selection of personnel. This could be illustrated by Simon asking an undercover policeman if he knew anyone in the IRA; Preetz using his espionage money to buy a new Chrysler; or even Görtz, in partial Luftwaffe uniform, asking the way to Laragh at a local police station. Indeed, all the German spies seemed abundantly blessed by a lack of common sense. Their Abwehr controllers were no better: Sending Henry Obéd to Ireland – even as a guide for a mission to England – was the epitome of carelessness. Likewise, even a quick review of Görtz's personnel dossier should have convinced even the dimmest officer that he was not a viable candidate for an extended foreign mission. The Abwehr was similarly careless in the smaller details, such as providing the agents with their identity papers. For example, Görtz's pay book in a false name was not filled out completely or correctly. Schëtz, for his part, had a competently forged passport but no visa stamp; Joseph Lenihan carried his radio instructions on a typed piece of paper, without even a half-hearted attempt to conceal them.

The pertinent question is: was the failure of German espionage occasioned by negligence or design? It stretches the bounds of probability that every responsible officer in the Abwehr was an opponent of the Nazi regime and therefore committed to its downfall by deliberately sabotaging its own espionage effort. Certainly Admiral Canaris was opposed, or became opposed, to Hitler, but did his personal disloyalty sabotage the goals of the entire German intelligence service? Canaris seems to have picked as his key subordinates those who were of like mind (e.g. Lahousen and Oster). Conversely, there seems to have been an effort to actually do the job he was paid to do, at least on occasion, although in an inept manner. The probable answer is that Canaris was both an opponent of the regime and a poor supervisor of intelligence activities, hardly the qualities suited to the successful management of a global spy empire.

Both time and increasing numbers worked against the German intelligence community. Prior to Hitler's ascent to power, Germany was limited by the Versailles Treaty to an army of 100,000 men, including some 4,000 officers. General military rearmament began in 1935 and the Second World War started a mere four years later. By 1944, at the high point of recruitment, some twelve million soldiers and 250,000 officers were under arms. It was a logistical impossibility to expect such a rapid numerical expansion to be accompanied by a matching rise in experience and quality. The Abwehr did not – and probably could not – effectively correlate the increase in personnel with the intelligence-gathering tasks expected of it. Too many officers with too little experience were necessarily forced into situations where their presence had the effect of compromising the results. Decisions were made on a local level by unqualified personnel, which had a devastating impact on the organization as a whole. Combined with equally nebulous direction from headquarters, it was a certain recipe for disaster.

The Abwehr's decision to ally itself with the IRA was misplaced, but based on previous experience with other discontented racial/ethnic minorities. In earlier campaigns, German Intelligence had successfully manipulated such diverse groups as the Breton nationalists, Indians and Croats, not to mention acting as an ideological and financial sponsor to burgeoning fascist groups across Europe. While Ireland did not have a promising fascist movement in the late 1930s – the Blueshirts having long since self-destructed – German planners reasonably believed that the IRA was sufficiently organized, popularly supported and ideologically committed to the destruction of Britain, both at home and abroad. German Intelligence was initially impressed – and confused – by the S-Plan bombing campaign in England and the Magazine Fort raid. These actions gave the mistaken impression that the IRA was a paramilitary force to be reckoned with, and it seemed a natural counterpart to general German intentions against England. Though there were hints that the IRA was, in reality, hopelessly amateurish and readily contained by the Irish government, these indications came too little and much too late, Minister Hempel's doubts notwithstanding. Liaison with the IRA formed the core of both the Weber-Drohl and Görtz missions, but as Görtz discovered to his detriment, German inducements were insufficient to redirect the IRA from its campaign of sporadic mayhem in Ireland to more suitable and more strategically important targets elsewhere. Germany should have realized this in 1940, but still had not learned this lesson by 1944. Ironically, the German Minister, Dr Hempel, who consistently refused to support ongoing Abwehr operations in a meaningful way, was exactly right in his 1939 opinion that the IRA was not a suitable vehicle to further German strategic interests. Situational analysis, never a strong point with Canaris's

Abwehr, should have demonstrated the folly of a German–IRA link before it ever got off the ground.

Part of the blame for this overall intelligence failure must be laid at the feet of both Hitler and the OKW. Historically, intelligence was a non-existent component of the great general staff, and relegated to a sub-level of the operations staff. The OKW continued this tradition. Though larger battlefield commands had an organic intelligence officer (Ic), it was considered heretical that the military intelligence service was an integral part of the decision-making process on a par with the operations staff (Ia). Thus, ambitious and intelligent young officers sensed that operations was a path to promotion, whereas intelligence was a career quagmire. When the OKW finally relented in 1943 and gave intelligence its own billet on the staff (Ic to the OKW) – and a grand total of three officers – it was far too little, and much too late to affect the outcome of the war.

The Germans in Ireland typically suffered from a lack of clear mission objectives and were frequently given tasks that could be better accomplished by other means. Schütz and Lenihan were parachuted into Ireland for the primary purpose of acting as human weather stations. In addition to being politically dangerous (as the Foreign Ministry was quick to point out) the missions offered almost no significant intelligence advantage. The same task could be accomplished by air, using the FW 200 Condor, by automated weather collection devices (such as those discovered off the Galway coast) or, in important cases, by having the on-site legation personnel collect the necessary data and radio it to Germany.[5] There was no need to risk an agent to accomplish something that could be more efficiently and more accurately acquired elsewhere. Preetz and Simon also had a weather component in their missions, in addition to reporting on shipping and convoys. Gärtner, Tributh and Obéd seemed to have had no Irish mission at all. Rather, they were rather to make their way across the country using Obéd's dormant Irish contacts and his non-existent local know-how. Such a mission as they did have in England was equally ill-defined. Being caught in Ireland was probably the best thing that could have happened to them; a more unpleasant fate awaited them at their intended destination.

The Ryan and Russell mission in 1940 is a case in point. Though the mission was organized and executed at considerable expense, Russell's individual objective – if we can accept Dr Veesenmayer's version of it – was vague, at best. The premature death of Seán Russell en route to Ireland almost certainly saved the Abwehr and the Foreign Ministry from an even bigger and more public failure. Görtz's mission seemed the clearest of the lot: liaise with the IRA and direct their attacks against English military targets in Northern Ireland. In his case, the mission was both important and clear, but they sent someone who was mentally and temperamentally incapable of executing it. But who is correctly answerable for this failure, the defective messenger or the organization that sends him? A universal principle of war is that the commander is responsible for everything his people do or fail to do. Individual failure, therefore, comes back to the Abwehr headquarters. MI5's conclusion was that 'There were few signs of a well coordinated plan of German espionage, and the various offices of the Abwehr seemed to be working without reference to each other. In short, the German espionage effort made the impression of being patchy, disjointed and ineffective.'[6] This is abundantly clear in the Abwehr and SD missions to Ireland.

Of course, the initial failure to outline mission objectives was beyond the control of even the Abwehr, and rested with Adolf Hitler. During the difficult early years of Canaris's stewardship, from 1935 to 1937, Hitler officially excluded Britain from the list of target countries and neglected the period when more agents could have been inserted or cultivated in what was logically the most immediate military threat. His misreading of the British character was duplicated down the command line, lulling the OKW and the Abwehr into a false sense of security and preventing Germany from capitalizing on the rare tactical and intelligence windows of opportunity. Both Hitler and his military intelligence service committed the most single catastrophic error in warfare: underestimating the enemy based on insufficient data while simultaneously overestimating their own capabilities.

To add to a host of other grievous command and control problems, duplication and competition from inside Nazi Germany doubly plagued the situation. Foreign Ministry objectives regularly clashed with Abwehr priorities, wasting resources and even actively working against one another. Even assuming that the Abwehr had only minor efficiency difficulties – which was clearly not the case – the fact that intelligence collection was decentralized made the effective gathering and processing of intelligence impossible. The ravenous SD expansion in the area of foreign intelligence collection simply reduced effective acquisition and processing of information. When, in 1944, the SD finally emerged as the victor in the struggle and established a single intelligence-collection agency, it no longer made any qualitative or quantitative difference. The war was already lost.

With a minimum of ten separate intelligence collection agencies, there was no level of command where synthesis could take place. Information critical to the outcome of the war was fragmented into isolated cells and never pieced together with other related data to form a coherent picture. Intelligence is supposed to assist a commander's decision-making process, but the German system did exactly the opposite. Information of questionable veracity was accepted, because the people responsible for intelligence collation and analysis worked in different departments in ideologically different agencies. Rather than providing soldiers in the field with accurate and balanced estimates of enemy intentions – the goal of military intelligence work – the various appendages of the Nazi state, in the best cases, issued estimates of the 'could be' or 'might be' variety. They lacked the hard data to do otherwise.

Ultimately, the fundamental reason for German Intelligence failures in Ireland went beyond the negligence and inattention of the OKW and the Abwehr. Perhaps the central reason for these failures was the system of brilliantly effective counter-intelligence operations run by both Ireland and Britain. To Ireland, counter-intelligence was more than a mere luxury; it was a fundamental line of defence. The strength of the regular Irish Army at the start of the 'Emergency' consisted of 7,494 men – about the size of a single US-reinforced infantry brigade. Any comparison between US and Irish forces ends there; Ireland had almost no air or naval defence to speak of, no armoured force at all, outdated basic weapons and no one with any experience of facing a professional army in a conventional scenario.[7] A determined attack by even a token German force of a few divisions, with modern tactics and equipment, would almost certainly have resulted in total defeat for the Irish troops, barring the intervention of a third party. Defensive use of intelligence – counter-intelligence – was therefore the only viable strategy in an effort to blunt any belligerent power's efforts to gather information or prepare for a landing of military personnel.

Though G2's financial resources were insignificant compared to those of the major belligerent powers, they more than made up for their lack of funding with first-class personnel. The men who headed wartime Irish Intelligence, Colonels Liam Archer and Dan Bryan, were dynamic and intelligent officers who understood both the nature of the threat and the mechanics of counter-intelligence operations in Ireland. Their training and experience, as contrasted with that of the Germans, was forged in the War of Independence (1919–21) and the Civil War (1922–3), when intelligence and counter-intelligence literally meant the difference between victory and defeat. The subtlety of Archer and Bryan was reflected in their inspired choice of subordinates and in generally positive relations with the Garda, the Irish government and the Allies. In short, they knew what was happening in their own backyard and were in a position to make proactive choices rather than letting events spin out of control. Bryan had been giving practical thought to security issues since the mid-1930s (his *Fundamental Factors* paper) and by 1939, G2 had the tools necessary to contain any major or minor incident that threatened state security. Both Archer and Bryan established a working link with Superintendent Carroll in C3, the Garda special branch. This formidable counter-intelligence alliance was aided by the powers of physical, telephone and postal surveillance on a massive scale, so that there was little mathematical chance that any potential threat (Allied, Axis or IRA) would go undetected.

Another key to winning the counter-intelligence war was the Dublin Link with Britain. While no power could replace the local and psychological advantage enjoyed by G2 in Ireland, no other European power could match the domestic intelligence service (MI5) fielded by Great Britain. Their expertise had been sharpened in the pre-war period and, perhaps unlike de Valera at times, they clearly understood the global threat from Nazi Germany and its intelligence services.[8] The British were aware that an intelligence failure against Hitler would mean annihilation. Experience and innovation allowed them to get inside the German military intelligence system and elevate strategic deception to a new level. The pre-war establishment of the Dublin Link allowed Irish Intelligence to call upon MI5's expertise in handling and evaluating German spies and information. In turn, G2's adept handling and debriefing of captured German agents helped to complete the British counter-intelligence picture, and allowed even more insight into the enemy's mind and methods.

Part of this success is due to official cooperation between the two governments dating back to 1938. On a more important level, however, the day-to-day decisions, particularly those made by Dan Bryan, helped this system function in a manner that circumvented the periodic wartime upheavals in British–Irish political relations. De Valera and his ministers occasionally wavered in their belief in an Allied victory, particularly when Germany was ascendant, but Bryan had no difficulty seeing both the advantages of intelligence cooperation with England and the inherent danger in a German victory. With an exception in the case of Hermann Görtz, where the Irish did not volunteer information about a captured agent, the degree of intelligence exchange between the two nominal Commonwealth partners was exceptional.

This was not accomplished without friction, even from inside Irish Intelligence. Major (later Colonel) Éamon de Buitléar, for example, did not approve of the intelligence exchange – or even admit Bryan's competency to run G2 – and took the extraordinary step of not informing Bryan that Dr Hayes had broken Görtz's code for fear that his chief would share the information with MI5.[9] Bryan, for his part, respected de Buitléar's ability, despite this lapse in his judgement, and took no action in such a case of open insubordination. Even with this minor bump in the road, Bryan was also fortunate in having a competent staff, something that the larger Abwehr lacked. In addition to the code-breaking brilliance of Dr Richard Hayes, G2 could rely on the linguistic talents of another young officer, Captain Joseph Healy.[10] Working with both Dr Hayes, de Buitléar and a young German linguist named Douglas Gageby (later managing director of the *Irish Times*), Healy was an integral part of the team that effectively neutralized German espionage in Ireland before it became a serious threat. Their actions – making the right decisions at the appropriate time – secured the survival of neutral Ireland and made a critical contribution to the defence of the British realm.

Ireland was never a military target of German Intelligence, though that hardly made a difference to the effectiveness of its operations. Britain, arguably the main European threat to Nazi Germany, was repeatedly subjected to agent incursions that were on an equally low par with those mounted in Ireland. Ireland was, however, a potential political asset and its neutrality policy served the short-term interests of the Reich. Ireland's role in Germany's planned choreography for Europe was to act as a foil for British interests and as a diversion for their military and political resources. Allied concern focused on Ireland was concern that could not be more profitably directed elsewhere. In terms of military intelligence, Ireland was, at best, one of its capabilities, a reserve plan, but never one that was vigorously or convincingly pursued. Ireland's utility to Germany necessarily depended on a pivotal event: the invasion of England. As the feasibility of Operation Sealion receded in the autumn of 1940, so too did German interest in Ireland. After that point, Ireland held a distant place of secondary importance as a weather observation platform, but had little continuing tactical viability. Incompetence and poor preparation at all levels of the German Intelligence hierarchy prevented even the secondary missions in Ireland from being conducted with efficiency.

Ironically, it was the Görtz mission that caused the greatest danger to Ireland, not because he was following his instructions, but precisely the opposite. His mercurial and irresponsible actions almost succeeded in driving a rift in the Irish Army and temporarily gave rise to English fears that Irish security forces were unable to contain the threat. On the other hand, Görtz was about the best agent that Ireland could hope for; a more balanced individual might have succeeded in actually fulfilling the terms of his mission and possibly dragging neutral Ireland into the war.

Irish sovereignty was also threatened at times from within its own ranks. Diplomats such as Leopold Kerney in Madrid, Charles Bewley, formerly Irish Minister to Germany, and, on one occasion, Secretary to the Department of External Affairs Joseph Walshe, kept alive the faint German hope that Ireland could have a part to play against England. Bewley, as unofficial Irish advisor to Nazi Germany, was easily the most sinister, and the scope of his activities, as nefarious as they were, is only partially reflected in the documents that have been declassified thus far. Kerney, by contrast, also played his part in furthering German plans for Ireland, but seemingly through bad judgement and ignorance, rather than a desire to commit treason. Joseph Walshe's contribution to the German misperception about Irish attitudes – his expressed hope to Minister Hempel that Germany would not forget Ireland at the peace conference after the war – was made during the period when the Swastika was ascendant and expectations were, in some quarters, that German victory was inevitable. Only the course of the war against Hitler kept these actions by Irish diplomats and officials from having more dire consequences. Irish citizens in Germany, too, did varying degrees of work for the Nazi regime, but other than creating a dubious resource for equally dubious intelligence missions, the amount of harm they did was limited by their own insignificance. Francis Stuart was the most visible and vocal, but his service to Germany – regardless of his real motive – was ultimately unimportant. The same is true of the Irish volunteers to German Intelligence, Joseph Lenihan, John O'Reilly and John Kenny, whose collective missions accomplished nothing of substance. In any event, the thousands of Irish volunteers within the British forces more than made up in post-war goodwill for the negligible wartime damage caused by such a tiny handful of miscreants.[11]

The absolute failure of the various German Intelligence services had a predictable result. Deprived of any semblance of an accurate estimate of enemy plans and intentions, Germany was forced, for the second time in the twentieth century, into a losing war of attrition. An army deprived of its eyes and ears simply does not win battles. Despite having sent ten agents (excepting Unland and van Loon) to Ireland, neither the Abwehr nor the SD received so much as a single report of any military significance. Unlike the German military reverses resulting from the Enigma interceptions or the wrong-headed strategic complacency developed through reliance on the Double-Cross agents, German failure in Ireland was caused by systemic, organizational failure – a debilitating and ultimately fatal disease that destroyed the heart of its intelligence system. Hazy objectives, inter-agency rivalry, poor personnel screening, and dubious leadership, combined with an efficient Irish and British counter-intelligence system, proved to be hurdles that were simply too high to be overcome by German Intelligence.

Appendices

Table of equivalent ranks in the Second World War – German and US

Waffen SS	German Army	US Army
Oberstgruppenführer u. Generaloberst der Waffen SS	Generaloberst	General of the Army
Obergruppenführer u. General der Waffen SS		General
SS-Gruppenführer u. Generalleutnant der Waffen SS	Generalleutnant	Lieutenant General
SS-Brigadeführer u. Generalmajor der Waffen SS	Generalmajor	Major General
SS-Oberführer	N/A	Brigadier General
SS-Standartenführer	Oberst	Colonel
SS-Obersturmbannführer	Oberstleutnant	Lieutenant Colonel
SS-Sturmbannführer	Major	Major
SS-Hauptsturmführer	Hauptmann	Captain
SS-Obersturmführer	Oberleutnant	1st Lieutenant
SS-Untersturmführer	Leutnant	2nd Lieutenant
SS-Sturmscharführer	Stabsfeldwebel	Command SGM
SS-Hauptscharführer	Oberfeldwebel	Sergeant Major
SS-Oberscharführer	Feldwebel	Platoon Sergeant
SS-Scharführer	Unterfeldwebel	Sergeant
SS-Unterscharführer	Unteroffizier	Corporal
SS-Rottenführer	Obergefreiter	N/A
SS-Sturmmann	Gefreiter	N/A
SS-Oberschutze	Oberschutze	Senior Private (E-3)
SS-Schutze (Kanonier, Pioneer, etc.)	Schutze	Private

Abwehr organization

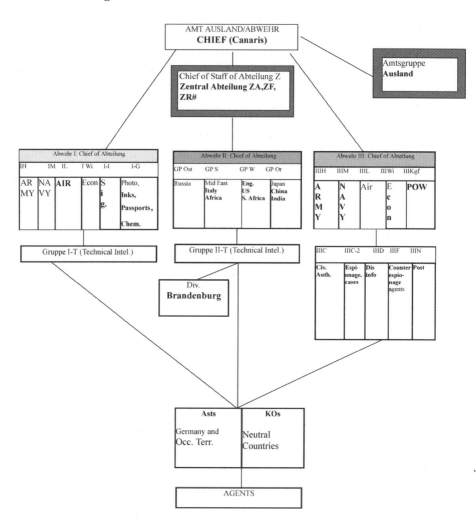

APPENDIX III

Wartime organization of MI5

Wartime organization of MI5

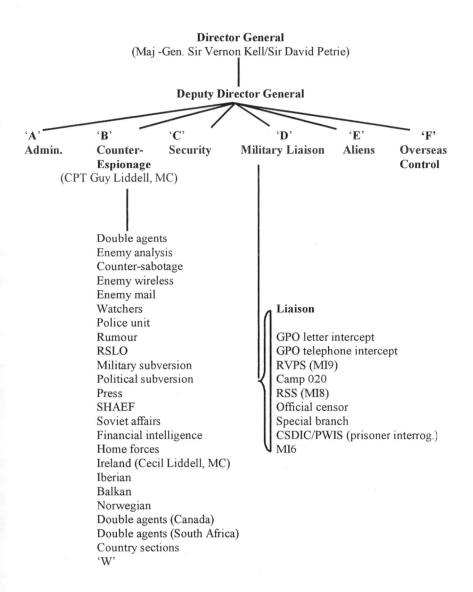

Director General
(Maj -Gen. Sir Vernon Kell/Sir David Petrie)

Deputy Director General

'**A**'	'**B**'	'**C**'	'**D**'	'**E**'	'**F**'
Admin.	**Counter-Espionage**	**Security**	**Military Liaison**	**Aliens**	**Overseas Control**

(CPT Guy Liddell, MC)

Double agents
Enemy analysis
Counter-sabotage
Enemy wireless
Enemy mail
Watchers
Police unit
Rumour
RSLO
Military subversion
Political subversion
Press
SHAEF
Soviet affairs
Financial intelligence
Home forces
Ireland (Cecil Liddell, MC)
Iberian
Balkan
Norwegian
Double agents (Canada)
Double agents (South Africa)
Country sections
'W'

Liaison

GPO letter intercept
GPO telephone intercept
RVPS (MI9)
Camp 020
RSS (MI8)
Official censor
Special branch
CSDIC/PWIS (prisoner interrog.)
MI6

Organization of Militärisches Amt (1944/45)

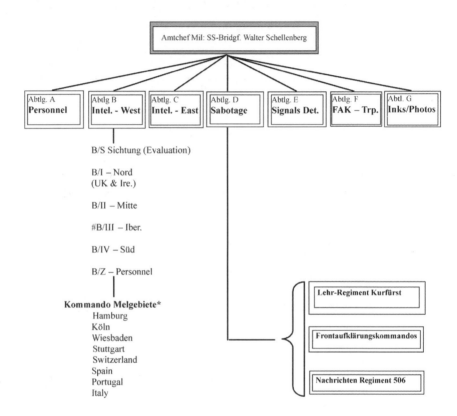

Amtchef Mil: SS-Bridgf. Walter Schellenberg

| Abtlg. A Personnel | Abtlg B Intel. - West | Abtlg. C Intel. - East | Abtlg. D Sabotage | Abtlg. E Signals Det. | Abtlg. F FAK – Trp. | Abtl. G Inks/Photos |

B/S Sichtung (Evaluation)

B/I – Nord
(UK & Ire.)

B/II – Mitte

#B/III – Iber.

B/IV – Süd

B/Z – Personnel

Kommando Melgebiete*
Hamburg
Köln
Wiesbaden
Stuttgart
Switzerland
Spain
Portugal
Italy

Lehr-Regiment Kurfürst

Frontaufklärungskommandos

Nachrichten Regiment 506

*Formerly Abwehrstellen (Asts) and Kriegsorganisationen (KOs)

Organization of Irish Military Intelligence (G2)

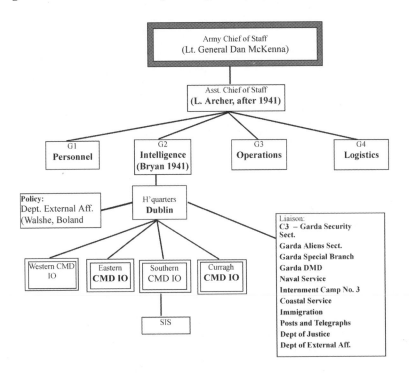

APPENDIX VI

Abwehr order concerning John O'Reilly (with translation)

Abwehrnebenstelle Bremen
Dizns des Reichs, Postnummer 25
Ruf: 28252, 28354, 28057
Nachr. ....

Bremen, den 9. Dezember 1942.

221

Geheime Kommandosache!

An

Abwehrabteilung I M
am 12. DEZ 1942
B. Nr. ....

das O.K.W., A Ausl/Abw.Abt. IM,
z.Hd. Herrn Kapt.z.See Menzel o.V.i.A.,

B e r l i n .

Betrifft: Unternehmen "ISOLDE" – Einsatz des V-Mannes Nest
Bremen RR 2621 "Rush". ....

Vorgang : Nest Bremen gKdos 247/42LI v. 21.11.42,
gestr. Besprechung Kaptltn.(S) Ahlrichs mit Sdfr.
Dr. Bensmann, Nest Bremen, in Berlin.

 Die aufgrund o.a. Vorgangs Nest Bremen am 8.12.42
geführte Besprechung ergab, dass die mit o.a. Vorgang unter
Ziffer 2.) gemachten Vorschläge wegen des entgegenstehenden
Verbotes des Auswärtigen Amtes, V-Leute in Land 32 abzusetzen,
nicht in der vorgeschlagenen Form durchführbar ist. Nest Bremen
ändert daher den gemachten Vorschlag wie folgt :

1.) Die Verbringung mittels Kutter bleibt nur als sekundäre
Verbringungsart bestehen. Der Absatzort wird gegebenenfalls
zu gegebener Zeit von Abw. IM, Berlin, mitgeteilt.

2.) RR 2621 soll nunmehr legal nach Land 32 via Land 18 aus-
reisen. Er soll sich zu diesem Zweck mit der Botschaft
des Landes 32 in Berlin in Verbindung setzen. Verweigert
diese die Erteilung eines Visums oder entstehen andere,
unüberwindliche Schwierigkeiten, so wird RR 2621 von
Bremen nach Land 18 verbracht, um von dort aus alsdann
Ausreise vorzunehmen.

Mitnahme eines Afu-Gerätes kommt nicht in Frage; vielmehr
soll die Afu-Ausbildung so weit ausgedehnt werden, dass
RR 2621 im Bau von Geräten genügend Erfahrung besitzt, um
mit einem selbst erbauten Gerät Verbindung mit Meldekopf
Le Havre aufnehmen zu können. Er soll ferner versuchen,

b.w.

durch seine IRA-Freunde ein Gerät an Ort und Stelle zu erhalten.

Da von Abw. IM ein weiteres Kutter-Unternehmen geplant ist, besteht die Möglichkeit, ein Afu-Gerät für RR 2621 nach Land 32 zu verbringen und ihm dort auszuhändigen. Aufgrund dieser Möglichkeit soll RR 2621 befragt werden, wo er ein Afu-Gerät in Land 32 in Empfang zu nehmen in der Lage ist. Die von ihm gemachten Angaben sind Abw. IM vorzulegen.

Unter Berücksichtigung der obigen Änderungen wird nunmehr um Genehmigung des Einsatzes gebeten.

Translation

Bremen
9 December 1942

To: OKW, Amt Ausland/Abw.Abt IM,
For the attention of Naval Captain Menzel, o.V.i.A., Berlin

Concerning: Enterprise 'ISOLDE' – Placing of the V-Man of Nest Bremen RR. 2621 'Rush'

Reference: Nest Bremen gKdos 247/42/LI of 21.11.42 – yesterday's conversation between Naval KL (S) Ahlrichs with Sdfr. Dr Bensmann, Nest Bremen, in Berlin.

The conversation which took place at Bremen on 8.12.42 in accordance with the above mentioned plan settled that owing to the ban of the Foreign Office, V-people are not to be landed in Country 32, and the plan therefore cannot be undertaken in the proposed form. Nest Bremen therefore alters it and make the following proposal.

1. The transport by cutter is only to be considered as a secondary possibility. The place of landing will be given at the appropriate time by Abw. I-M, Berlin.
2. RR 2621 is to travel legally to Country 32 via Country 18. For this purpose he is to get in communication with the Embassy of Country 32 in Berlin. If they refuse a visa or if other insurmountable difficulties arise, RR 2621 will be taken from Bremen to Country 18 so as to start his journey from there.

Taking with him an Afu apparatus does not come into consideration, but the Afu. training is to be so detailed that RR 2621 has enough experience to build such an apparatus so that he can get into communication with station Le Havre with his self-built instrument. Further, he is to make efforts to obtain an apparatus through his IRA friends.

As Abw. I-M are planning a further cutter undertaking, there is the possibility of taking an Afu. apparatus for RR 2621 to Country 32 and to hand it over to him there. On account of this possibility, RR 2621 is to be asked where it will be possible for him to receive this Afu apparatus in Country 32. The place mentioned by him to be submitted to Abw. I-M.

In consideration of the above alterations it is now requested that concurrence may be given for the placing of the V-man.

Notes

INTRODUCTION

1. Robert Fisk, *In Time of War: Ireland, Ulster and the Price of Neutrality 1939–1945* (London: Paladin Grafton, 1983), p. 129 and Reinhard R. Doerries, *Prelude to the Easter Rising: Sir Roger Casement in Imperial Germany* (London: Frank Cass, 2000), pp. 9–18.
2. Lauran Paine, *The Story of German Military Intelligence in World War II: The Abwehr* (New York, Stein and Day, 1984), pp. 81–4; David Johnson, *Germany's Spies and Saboteurs* (Osceola, WI: MBI Publishing Co., 1998, pp. 9–19, 145–9.
3. Seán O'Callaghan, *The Jackboot in Ireland* (London: Allan Wingate Ltd., 1958)
4. These areas are covered in considerable depth by Robert Fisk (*In Time of War: Ireland, Ulster and the Price of Neutrality 1939–1945*), Dermot Keogh (*Jews in Twentieth Century Ireland: Refugees, Anti-Semitism and the Holocaust* and *Twentieth Century Ireland: Nation and State*), Eunan O'Halpin (*Defending Ireland*), Professor J. J. Lee (*Ireland 1912–1985: Politics and Society*) and John Duggan (*A History of the Irish Army*).
5. These files, broadly classified as IMA G2/0002, are retained in the Irish Military Archives, but not scheduled for release. Part of this is due to the fact that the much of the G2 surveillance on the Axis (and Allied) legations might well have been considered a violation of diplomatic and international law.

CHAPTER 1

1. Sun Tzu, *The Art of War* (London: Hodder & Stoughton, 1981), p. 7. Sun Tzu devoted an entire chapter to the use of spies in war and his subtle understanding of this art is one of the reasons that his work is standard reading at the US Army Command and General Staff College, Ft. Leavenworth, Kansas, and other comparable higher-echelon professional military staff colleges all over the world.
2. Clausewitz made some prescient observations on the role of intelligence in war: 'Many intelligence reports in war are contradictory; even more are false, and most are uncertain. What one can reasonably ask of an officer is that he should possess a standard of judgment, which he can gain only from

knowledge of men and affairs and from common sense ... in short, most intelligence is false, and the effect of fear is to multiply lies and inaccuracies.' (Carl von Clausewitz, *On War* [London: Everyman's Library, 1993], p. 136.)

3. Oberst Nicolai, whose espionage career ended in 1918, was captured by the Russians in 1945 and never heard from again (Anthony Powell, 'Our Gallant Allies: A Tale of Germany and Ireland', unpublished manuscript, p. 301). Patzig's career did not suffer following his stint at Abwehr. He was subsequently ordered to command the pocket-battleship *Admiral Scheer* (Alan Wykes, *Heydrich* [New York: Ballantine Books, 1973], p. 107). The more detailed list of Abwehr command succession: Oberst Gempp (1919–27), Major i.G Günther Schwantes 1927–9), Oberst i.G Ferdinand v. Bredow (1929–32), and Kapitän z.S. Patzig (1932–4). (Uwe Brammer, *Spionage und Geheimer Meldedienst: Die Abwehrstelle X im Wehrkreis Hamburg 1935–1945* [Freiburg: Rombach Verlag, 1989], p. 149.)

4. Christian Zeutner and Friedemann Bedürftig (eds), *Encyclopedia of the Third Reich* (New York: Da Capo, 1997), p. 2.

5. The actual name of the German Intelligence Service was *Amt Ausland/Abwehr* – usually shortened to *Abwehr*. *Abwehr* actually means to 'fend off' or to 'repulse' in the sense of defending oneself. The word *Abwehr* itself entered the German military lexicon as 'counter-intelligence'. *Amt Ausland* means 'overseas department/office'.

6. The OKW did not establish an Intelligence Branch in the Operations Staff until 1943, and even then it consisted of only three officers. The chief of FAO – *Fremde Heere Ost* – Foreign Armies East, General Reinhard Gehlen, had an interesting post-war career that included providing cold war intelligence information concerning the numbers and strength of Soviet Bloc forces through agents employed by his Gehlen Organization ('the Org'). Gehlen became the first chief of the German Federal Intelligence Service, the BND (*Bundesnachrichtendienst*) on the basis of this work (*World War II German Military Studies*, Vol. 4, Part III: Command Structure, Ms T-101, Chap. B1 f – Intelligence, pp. 2–3).

7. Basically, all intelligence gathering can be classed as either HUMINT (human intelligence – reports from agents or other live sources) or SIGINT (signals intelligence – interception of radio/telephone traffic). Interception of computer-generated messages such as email and other communications transferred via the Internet would fall under the heading of SIGINT, as would the Ultra intercepts from the German Enigma machine. In modern times, this traditional duo of intelligence gathering would be augmented by a third medium, aerial or satellite photo reconnaissance.

8. See Appendix II – Abwehr organization.

9. *World War II German Military Studies*, Vol. 5, Part III (Command Structure), Ms T-101, Annex 3, p. 3.

10. *World War II German Military Studies*, Vol. 4, p. 103.

11. TO&E – Table of Organization and Equipment, the exact listing of what is deemed necessary for any military unit to be at full operational strength. The exception to this rule of Ast organization was Hamburg, which alone had no permanent Abwehr II presence (Public Record Office [PRO] KV 2/170, Memorandum, 11 Oct. 1945).

12. David Kahn astutely pointed out that 'No spies ... meant no Abwehr and that could mean, for its members, winding up on the Russian front.' (David Kahn, *Hitler's Spies* [New York: Macmillan], p. 363.) In practical terms it meant that numbers of agents, and not the efficiency of the service, had an attraction all of its own.

13. By 1942, the Abwehr had ten KO stations: Portugal, Spain, Switzerland, Sweden, Finland, Bulgaria, Croatia, Morocco, Turkey and Shanghai (Kahn, *Hitler's Spies*, p. 243.).

14. The standard acronym for this is MICE. The theory is that many otherwise loyal people can be converted to intelligence work for a hostile power based on the factor(s) of Money, Ideology, Compromise or Ego. This works more times than not.

15. Other Schwarze Kapelle members in the Abwehr included General Hans Pieckenbrock and Oberst Georg Hanson (Abwehr I), Generalmajor v. Lahousen and Oberst v. Freytag-Loringhoven (Abwehr II), Generalleutnant Franz Eccard v. Bentivegni (Abwehr III). Oberst Hansen, Oberst Freytag-Loringhoven, Generalmajor Oster, and Hans von Dohnanyi (Oster's deputy) all died following the 20 July 1944 attempt to kill Hitler at Rastenburg, East Prussia. Cf. James Taylor and Warren Shaw, *Penguin Dictionary of the Third Reich* (London: Penguin, 1997), p. 54. The name Schwarze Kappelle was given to the group by the SD when they later became aware of its activities.

16. Ian Colvin, *Master Spy* (New York: McGraw-Hill, 1951), p. 55.

17. *Trial of German Major War Criminals* Part I, 20 Nov. 1945 to 1 Dec. 1945. Lahousen testified over a two-day period, from 30 November to 1 December. He specifically stated that Canaris was gathering evidence of Nazi atrocities and had attempted to block many such orders that came to his attention. Previously the head of the Middle Europe Department for Austrian Intelligence, Lahousen had been selected by Canaris to join the Abwehr in early 1939, where he was the expert on Czech and Polish affairs. Early in 1939, Lahousen was named to succeed Major Helmuth Grosscurth as head of Abwehr II and left the Abwehr in 1943 for a combat command in Russia.

18. PRO KV 2/173, Lahousen statement, 17 Dec. 1945.

19. In what was called the Oslo Report, the British Embassy in Oslo received a package containing technical diagrams of a new acoustic torpedo, the Würzburg and Freya radar systems, a new Luftwaffe bombing system (*X-Gerät*) and information about the *Aggregatprogramm* (rocket program) at Peenemünde. According to the head of Britain's Telecommunications Research Establishment, Dr Robert Cockburn, 'It seemed quite possible that the report was Canaris's doing. But we never found out. And we never discovered who else but Canaris or his agents could have done it.' (Cockburn interview in Anthony Cave Brown, *Bodyguard of Lies* [London: W.H. Allen, 1976], p. 199 and R.V. Jones, *Most Secret War* [London: Hamish Hamilton, 1978], p. 67).

20. Brown, *Bodyguard of Lies,* p. 207, interview with General v. Liss. Liss's successor at FHW, Oberst Freiherr Axel v. Rönne, was also a member of the anti-Hitler conspiracy. A large measure of the Abwehr's pre-invasion intelligence failure had to do with the fact that all the German agents sent to Britain were arrested and either executed or 'turned'.

21. Brown, *Bodyguard of Lies*, p. 816, interview with Sir Steward Menzies.
22. PRO WO 204/1206, interrogation file on Colonel Constantin Canaris. Oberst Canaris was principally Himmler's liaison between the Commander South-East for the Ordnungspolizei and Waffen-SS. Another nephew, Joachim Wilhelm Canaris, served as an Abwehr desk officer in Madrid (PRO KV 2/167).
23. Kahn, *Hitler's Spies*, pp. 44–5.
24. Ibid., p. 176. In the Army, signal intercepts were passed from the listening post thorough several stages before being fully analysed at Corps and Army level, a time-consuming process (*German Operational Intelligence*, Military Intelligence Division, War Department, Washington, 1947, pp. 11–14).
25. The SD was section VI of the RSHA, Kripo was section V, and the Gestapo was section IV.
26. Until his death at the hands of British-trained Czech commandos in 1942, Heydrich was arguably the most feared man in Germany. His responsibilities included the concentration camp system and it was he who organized and chaired the infamous Wannsee Conference that approved the 'Final Solution of the Jewish Problem' in January 1942. Heydrich had previously served under Canaris on board the *Schleisen* and it was widely assumed that Canaris had derogatory information on Heydrich to ensure his own survival. At any rate, Canaris's insurance policy died with Heydrich. Himmler briefly ran the RSHA directly from Heydrich's death until January 1943, when he appointed Ernst Kaltenbrunner to manage the office. Kaltenbrunner was responsible for investigating Canaris in 1944. Himmler committed suicide in 1945 and Kaltenbrunner was hanged at Nürnberg.
27. Robert Gellately, *The Gestapo and German Security* (Oxford: Clarendon Press, 1990), pp. 66–7. Schellenberg (1910–52) had previously been in charge of Amtsgruppe IV E – Domestic Counter-Espionage.
28. Canaris and Heydrich agreed to a division of responsibility in December 1936 called the 'Ten Commandments'. The splintering of Abwehr functions effectively dates from this point. (Kahn, *Hitler's Spies*, p. 60 and Reinhard Gehlen, *Der Dienst* [Mainz: Hase u. Kohler Verlag, 1971], p. 42).
29. Hitler practised this philosophy of 'divide and rule' at all levels of organization and command as a means to ensure that no one group became a political or military threat (*World War II German Military Studies*, Vol. 4, Part III (Command): Ms T-101, p. xii.).
30. This was done because of what Hitler correctly perceived as the Abwehr's inability to acquire this information.
31. The gradual absorption of Abwehr functions by the SD was slow, but deliberate – and not exclusively limited to the Abwehr. The same practice was followed with the Forschungsamt, originally Göring's private signals intelligence service. It eventually became charged with tapping phones and working on intercepted ciphers, and naturally formed a close relationship with the SD.
32. James Lucas, *Kommando* (London: Arms and Armour Press, 1985), p. 4.
33. Helmut Clissmann and Jupp Hoven were permanent-party members of the Brandenburg Regiment. Hermann Görtz was assigned to the unit for a brief period in 1940 while undergoing training for his Irish mission. Ironically,

Clissmann would have probably been an ideal choice for tactical insertion in Ireland, but despite the attempt in Operation Lobster II and the proposed Operation Sea Eagle, he was not successful in reaching the country. In full uniform, an embroidered cuff band, an indication of their elite status, distinguished the members of the Brandenburg from other units.

34. Lucas, *Kommando*, p. 17.
35. This had serious consequences for the *Fallschirmjäger* (parachute troops) and the Panzer-Lehrdivision, among others. In the case of Panzer Lehr, the cream of the armoured instructors were placed in a consolidated unit. They performed brilliantly, but high attrition rates eliminated a pool of expertise that could not be replaced so late in the war.
36. IMA G2/X/0203, interview with Günther Schütz, 11 April 1946.
37. Stanley Hilton, *Hitler's Secret War in South America, 1939–1945* (Baton Rouge, LA: Louisiana State University Press, 1981), p. 17. Ritter had been successfully sent to the United States in 1937 to receive information connected to the development of the top secret Norden bombsight. Ritter had extensive experience in the US and married a woman from Alabama (PRO KV 2/87, Ritter interview, 20 July 1945). He joined the Afrika Korps in 1941 and specialized in placing agents behind British lines in Egypt.
38. IMA G2/X/1263 (John Kenny).
39. Ibid. Students were also able to practise sending and receiving messages to and from overseas posts.
40. PRO KV 2/103, interrogation file of Kapitän zur See Herbert Wichmann.
41. IMA G2/3824, G2 Interview with John O'Reilly on 26 Jan. 1944. O'Reilly also said he was instructed to change his call sign daily.
42. IMA G2/X/0805. For some reason, despite the previous (and subsequent) use of the microdot technique, his German controllers wrote Joseph Lenihan's R/T (radio/telegraph) procedures for him on typed pages, which he obligingly carried with him. Whether this is a poor reflection on Lenihan or the German Intelligence service is difficult to say.
43. IMA G2/0265, Dr Hayes's report, 14 Oct. 1940. This also presented Dr Hayes and G2 with another problem: The German controllers also sent messages to a station DES – which did not match any of the known German agents sent to Ireland. This station – and agent – was never positively identified.
44. IMA G2/X/0203. These were included in the microdot R/T (radio/telegraph) instructions found on Günther Schütz when he was apprehended in 1941.
45. Named after the training section devoted to secret inks and codes, this invisible ink was designated 'G-Tinte' in Abwehr language. 'G' – for *geheim* (secret) – was the Abwehr I subsection devoted to clandestine communications.
46. As Hermann Görtz discovered the hard way, the Pyramidon-impregnated pads were not designed to be immersed in water. While swimming across the Boyne River, Görtz forgot about the pads and his invisible ink was ruined as a result (IMA G2/1722, Görtz report to G2, Oct. 1944, and NLI MS 21,155, Jim O'Donovan papers).
47. IMA G2/X/0805. Reagent and invisible ink were found along with Lenihan's luggage in the Lerne Hotel, Dundalk in July 1941.
48. Kahn, *Hitler's Spies*, p. 279.

49. Werner Unland spent much of his time in Dublin sending fictional reports to his case officer, Günther Schütz, via the Abwehr mail drop in Barcelona (IMA G2/026).

50. IMA G2/X/0805. These messages were given to Joseph Lenihan. His mail-drop address was Luis Fernandez de Herdia, Plaza de Jesus 3, Madrid.

51. The German Cryptographic Branch was not directed by the Abwehr, but was placed under the Signals Branch of the OKW, causing a distinct gap between HUMINT and SIGINT in any effort to determine enemy intentions. Radio intercepts from the various branches of the armed services were directed to the Signals Branch and reached the Abwehr, if at all, by a circuitous route (*World War II German Military Studies*, Vol. 4, Part III: Command Structure, Ms T-101 (Signal Communications), pp. 5–6).

52. Simon Singh, *The Code Book: The Science of Secrecy from Ancient Egypt to Quantum Cryptography* (London: Fourth Estate, 1999), p. 243.

53. Ibid., pp. 143–89. The British had specialized teams that worked on the different types of signals. The Radio Surveillance Service (RSS or MI9) was responsible for the initial signal interception, which was then passed on to the GC&CS. The RSS shared information with the Irish Army Signal Corps beginning in 1941 (PRO KV 4/9, Appendix I, p. 4). Intercepted hand-signals were designated ISOS (Intelligence Services Oliver Strachey) and Enigma ciphers were ISK (Intelligence Services Knox).

54. Richard Breitman, *Official Secrets* (London: Penguin, 1999), p. 58.

55. Görtz flagrantly violated this procedure in some of his messages from Athlone by using 'ELLEN WIEBKE ROLF UTE' as his keyword – the names of his wife and children (IMA G2/1722, Hayes report in Part XII).

56. Napoleon's system employed all the essentials later used in the Abwehr method. The first number group would indicate the page number, the second identified the line which was to be used, and the remaining numbers would be the enciphered message. The complete text was sent as a continuous line with no breaks between words (John Elting, *Swords Around A Throne* [London: Phoenix, 1997], p. 112–13).

57. In some cases, the messages followed the sequence of the page numbers. For example, on Tuesday, the correct page was 128; messages sent on the next day would use page 129. In the preferred system, the agents would be given a base number, and the day and month would be added to produce the correct page for that day's transmissions.

58. Hilton, *Hitler's Secret War in South America*, p. 43.

59. Ibid., p. 58.

60. Singh, *The Code Book*, p. 374.

61. As a safety check, it was standard practice to introduce a grammatical error into the keyword. The first keyword sent by the Abwehr to the IRA, "House of Parliaments" was an example of this. In *The Shamrock and the Swastika* (Palo Alto, CA: Pacific Book Publishers, 1977), Carolle Carter (p. 103) somewhat mistakenly calls this a 'key code word' and does not explain its use. Görtz used 'UNITED STATES NAVIES' in some of his messages found at Stephen Held's house in 1940 (IMA G2/1722, Part 2).

62. IMA G2/1722, undated Görtz to Farrell sisters, explaining his coding system.

63. IMA G2/0203. Schütz's file at the Irish Military Archives includes the original newspaper clippings, which were ostensibly ads for Aspro medicated tablets and a review of 'Oxford Pamphlets'. More than anything else, these were suspicious items for Schütz to be carrying on what was obviously an espionage mission, prompting Irish Intelligence officers to take a closer look at them. As if the possession of the clippings wasn't strange enough, Schütz was thoughtfully carrying a high-power microscope along with his Abwehr 'Afu' transmitter/receiver. Irish Intelligence was certainly capable of adding two and two.

64. IMA G2/X/0203, Schütz's microdot instructions.

65. PRO KV 2/87, Interview with Alfons Kurt Wolf, I-G, Hamburg Ast.

66. Nigel West, *MI5* (London: Triad Grafton, 1983), p. 256.

67. Singh, *The Code Book*, pp. 126–7. O'Reilly refused to tell G2 his agreed code word for communicating with SD headquarters with the disc cipher (NLI, Richard Hayes Papers, Ms 22,984).

CHAPTER 2

1. The introduction of the long-range Focke-Wülf 200 'Condor' bomber as an anti-ship weapon greatly increased German reach, but even then, operational range was limited to within 300 miles of Ireland's west coast (Alfred Price, *Luftwaffe Handbook 1939–1945* [New York: Scribner's, 1977], p. 47). Like the Abwehr, the Kriegsmarine (Navy) was unprepared for war in 1939 and possessed an insufficient number of U-boats to turn the Battle of the Atlantic conclusively in Germany's favour.

2. Though it appears contradictory, Germany also prepared an extensive and detailed assessment of Ireland, largely derived from pre-war information. Called Fall Grün (Plan Green), it will be discussed in detail later in this work. Despite having this existing body of knowledge, more current information was needed.

3. John Duggan, 'Germany and Ireland in World War II', *The Irish Sword*, 19 (1993), p. 97. Duggan gives no citation for his quote 'that possession of Ireland would mean the end of England'. Fisk (*In Time of War*, p. 225, citing A. Martienssen, *Hitler and His Admirals* [London: Secker and Warburg, 1948], Appendix II) gives the quote as 'occupation of Ireland might lead to the end of the war'. The actual quote, as reflected in the *Kriegstagebuch des Wehrmachtführungsstabes* (1 Dec. 1940–24 March 1941) from the Wehrmacht situation conference of 3 Dec. 1940, is not specifically ascribed to Hitler: 'Als Basis für Angriffe auf die nordwestlichen Häfen Englands sei Irland wichtig für die Luftwaffe. Der Besitz Irlands könne das Ende des Krieges herbeiführen' (Ireland is important to the Luftwaffe as a base for attacks on England's north-western harbours. The possession of Ireland could hasten the end of the war).

4. Estimates of German nationals in Ireland vary. John Duggan (*Neutral Ireland and the Third Reich* [Dublin: Lilliput Press, 1989], p. 58) gives the number as 529 in 1936 and 460 in 1946. Carrolle Carter (*The Shamrock and the Swastika*, p. 36) cites a number of 400 in 1939, but neither of these numbers is

authoritative. Dermot Keogh (*Jews in Twentieth Century Ireland* [Dublin: Gill and Macmillan, 1994], p. 121), using a better basis – Irish Department of Justice records and G2 files – puts the total of German aliens at 194 in 1939, plus 52 Austrians and 188 Italians. The overwhelming number of Germans lived within the Dublin metropolitan area (123 out of 194). At least thirty German aliens were members of the Nazi Party: David O'Donoghue, *Hitler's Irish Voices* (Belfast: Beyond the Pale, 1998), p. 7.

5. Zeutner and Bedürftig, *Encyclopedia of the Third Reich*, p. 178.
6. David O'Donoghue, 'Hitler's Irish Voices: The Story of German Radio's Irish Service, 1939–1945' (Ph.D. thesis, Dublin City University, 1995), p. 45. Membership in the AO was confined to persons holding German citizenship. Even more strict racial and ancestry requirements were mandated for candidates in the SS officer corps. Curiously, Nazi Party membership was not required for membership in the SS.
7. Zeutner and Bedürftig, *Encyclopedia of the Third Reich*, p. 178.
8. The *Wilhelm Gustloff* was converted to a Lazerettschiffe (hospital ship) and was carrying refugees in January 1945 when it was torpedoed in the Baltic. An estimated 9,343 people, mostly women and children, drowned, making it the most costly maritime disaster in history.
9. Other prominent Nazis in Ireland were Heinz Mecking, the chief adviser to the Turf Development Board, Friedrich Weckler, an employee of Siemens and later chief accountant with the ESB, and Oswald Müller-Dubrow, a Siemens director and deputy head of the AO in Ireland. Mecking, who took over the leadership of the AO in 1939, seems to have later entered the German Army in a quasi-officer status, and was captured in Russia, later dying in captivity. Weckler, though a Nazi party member, worked for the ESB until his death in 1943 (O'Donoghue, *Hitler's Irish Voices*, p. 220). For some reason, Fritz Brase, who had earlier asked permission from his Irish Army superiors to set up a branch of the Nazi Party, is reported by Carter (p. 96) to be 'the head of the Irish Nazis' – which is not accurate. Brase remained in Ireland and died of illness in 1940 while still serving as an officer in the Irish Army.
10. Irish Army Intelligence noted in a 1945 report that Mahr was 'an open and blatant Nazi and made many efforts to convert Irish graduates and other persons with whom he had associations to Nazi doctrines and beliefs' (IIMA G2/0130). Mahr joined the Nazi Party on 1 April 1933, just after Hitler came to power. Germans referred to these sorts of people as 'schön Wetter Nazis' (fair-weather Nazis).
11. Mervyn O'Driscoll, 'Irish-German Diplomatic Relations, 1922–1939' (MA thesis, University College, Cork, 1992), p. 310 and Duggan, *Neutral Ireland and the Third Reich*, pp. 23–4. Mahr publicized a photograph taken of von Dehn kissing the Papal Nuncio's ring, something seen as demeaning for a minister representing the Third Reich. Von Dehn was recalled from a subsequent diplomatic post and dismissed from the consular service.
12. This was probably at the behest of the German Ambassador to England, Joachim von Ribbentrop, himself a leading National Socialist, and later German Foreign Minister (1938–45), who was later hanged at Nürnberg.
13. Kahn, *Hitler's Spies*, p. 99.
14. O'Donoghue, *Hitler's Irish Voices*, p. 21.

15. PRO KV 2/170, Praetorius interview, 11 Oct. 1945. Praetorius was head of I/Wi at Hamburg.

16. O'Donoghue, *Hitler's Irish Voices*, pp. 19–20 and *Irish Times*, 20 Dec. 1937.

17. Keogh, *Jews in Twentieth Century Ireland*, p. 107, citing IMA G2/0222.

18. Ibid., p. 183.

19. Ibid., p. 63.

20. Raul Hilberg, *Die Vernichtung des europaischen Juden* (Frankfurt: Fischer-TB Verlag, 1999), pp. 160–7. 'Arbeitstagung der Judenreferenten der Deutschen Missionen in Europa' held at Krummhübel on 3 and 4 April 1944. The minutes of this meeting clearly state the overriding purpose. In his introduction to the conference, Dr Alfred Franz Six commented that 'the physical elimination of Eastern Jewry would deprive Jewry of its biological reserves'. Dr Kutscher of the Propaganda Ministry noted that 'A Jewish victory would be the end of every culture (for example, the Soviet Union). ... Germany's war against the Jews was not done for itself, but for the entire European culture. ... The Jew has, with this war, dug his own grave.' Ironically, Mahr's family later complained that he was 'badly treated' in a British internment camp (O'Donoghue, *Hitler's Irish Voices*, pp. 167–8). Despite a post-war conviction for crimes against humanity for his other activities, Dr. Six (who was the prewar chief of the SD 'Deviant Ideologies' department, and was wartime head of RSHA Amt VII, Research and Evaluation of World Affairs) was released early from prison and joined Reinhard Gehlen's intelligence group. Cf. Christopher Simpson, *Blowback: America's Recruitment of Nazis and Its Effects on the Cold War* (London: Weidenfeld & Nicolson, 1988), pp. 47–9. Adolf Mahr died in 1951.

21. Clissmann went on to join Abwehr II and was posted to the Brandenburg unit. He was later commissioned in the German Army after active military service with the Panzerarmee Afrika and graduation from officer candidate school (Elizabeth Clissmann telephone interview, 15 Feb. 1999).

22. Clissmann also worked for the Deutsche Akademie and the Goethe Institute, which had many of the same objectives for German cultural and academic exchanges (Ibid). It would be wrong to characterize Clissmann as exclusively performing intelligence-related work during his time in Ireland, since he obviously did fulfil other duties as well. The evidence of any intelligence connection before 1937–8 is lacking. Mrs Clissmann is adamant that he was not a spy in pre-war Ireland. Among other events, Clissmann arranged for the choir from his native Aachen to perform in Dublin (Ibid). After the war he worked as a businessman in Dublin and was a founding member of the Irish branch of Amnesty International. He died in 1997.

23. The only two minor successes in this area were Trinity students Sidney Ievers and another named McCutcheon, who participated in academic exchange programmes to Germany. Ievers was a sometime neighbour of Francis and Iseult Stuart at Laragh, who studied at the University of Bonn, and later went to America. His presence in Germany was of concern to the Irish Department of External Affairs. Ievers apparently had connections with the Breton autonomist movement from his time in Paris in 1938 and with Leon Mill-Arden, who worked for German Intelligence. In *The Shamrock and the Swastika* (p. 95), Carter mistakenly spells his surname as Eivars, and gives no

first name. Cf. IMA G2/0214 and NAI A66 (restricted). Contrasted with KGB penetration of leftist students at Cambridge, the Abwehr had neither the time necessary nor the organization to make this system work more effectively. One of the primary jobs of agents operating under cover of academic exchange organizations is to vet candidates for potential recruitment by the host country intelligence services. Francis Stuart would be a case in point.

24. NAI, DFA 238/59, Clissmann to Secretary of the Department of Education, 10 March 1939, quoted in O'Driscoll, MA thesis, p. 317. To emphasize the folksy nature of the organization, the party youth authorities in München used the word *Mädel*, a somewhat archaic regional variation of the word for girl (*Mädchen*).

25. Ibid., Walshe to Secretary of the Department of Education, 2 May 1939.

26. John Duggan, 'Herr Hempel at the German Legation in Dublin, 1937–1945' (D.Litt. thesis, Trinity College, Dublin), p. 97.

27. Enno Stephan, *Spies in Ireland* (London: Four Square, 1965), p. 29. Clissmann was told this by Hauptmann Marwede, who was later involved with Oscar Pfaus, Ernst Weber-Drohl and Hermann Görtz. However, in an interview with author Horst Dickel, Clissmann said that his Abwehr contact was Kurt Jahnke, who had been involved with Irish affairs since World War One (Dickel, *Die deutsche Außenpolitik und die irische Frage von 1932 bis 1944* (Wiesbaden: Franz Steiner Verlag, 1983), p. 78, fn. 196). Jahnke was a shadowy figure who worked as a German Intelligence agent in the US from 1914 to 1917 and was then an intelligence adviser to both Rudolf Hess and Reinhard Heydrich (Reinhard Doerries, 'Tracing Kurt Jahnke: Aspects of the Study of German Intelligence', in George O. Kent [ed.], *Historians and Archivists* [Fairfax, VA: George Mason University, 1991], pp. 27–44, and Richard Spence, 'K.A. Jahnke and the German Sabotage Campaign in the United States and Mexico, 1914–1918', *The Historian*, 1998, pp. 89–112.).

28. PRO FO 940/49. According to MI5, Clissmann had been in Ireland during the summers of 1930–2, 1934, and full-time from 1938–9. Clissmann performed his front line service (*Wehrdienst*) in North Africa and returned to the officer candidate school in Hanover. He finished the war as a lieutenant in a British POW camp/interrogation centre at Bad Nenndorf (Elizabeth Clissmann, telephone interview, 15 Feb. 1999). His MI5 interrogation file has not been released to the Public Records Office.

29. Carter, *The Shamrock and the Swastika*, p. 28.

30. Ibid.

31. These included such minor matters as what to say in a courtesy call to Irish President Dr Douglas Hyde (whether congratulations should come from Hitler or the German government); whether Hempel should pay a monthly allowance to the family of a German internee; and if he should provide money to assist Hermann Görtz's escape back to Germany. According to the replies from the Foreign Ministry, the correct answers to Hempel's questions were: Hitler *and* the German Government; yes; and it was up to Hempel to make up his own mind.

32. According to the data provided in the Foreign Ministry publication *Jahrbuch für Austwärtiges Politik 1940*, the Germans also had a consulate in Limerick. This office was supervised by one James O'Keeffe and was responsible for the

counties of Galway, Clare, Limerick, Kerry and Cork. No mention is made of this consulate in any available Irish documents. The current policy calls for an Irish national to act as the German consul in satellite offices (Interview with German Cultural Attaché, Dublin, 31 Trimleston Avenue, Booterstown, Co. Dublin, 25 Oct. 1999).

33. Though Carter (*The Shamrock and the Swastika*, p. 28) said that Hempel was 'not a Nazi himself', he was; he joined the NSDAP on 1 July 1938. Thomsen had joined a year earlier, on 1 Aug. 1937 (O'Donoghue, *Hitler's Irish Voices*, p. 219). Thomsen was also a member of the 'Reiter-SS' – an SS affiliate organization (Duggan, D.Litt. thesis, p. 326). Carter is not alone in this error; several other historians make the same mistake. Those that do get the information correct usually do so in an apologetic manner, and maintain that Hempel was not a 'hardcore' Nazi (Duggan, *Neutral Ireland and the Third Reich*, p. 25). Judging from Hempel's periodic anti-Semitic references, this conclusion is debatable.

34. PRO KV 2/173, Lahousen statement, 17 Dec. 1945, p. 2.

35. There were four women who had this job at various times during the war, Ina Foley, Helene Neugebauer, Edeltrude Freidinger and Hilda Mallie née Six. Neugebauer left Ireland on 11 Sept. 1939 and later married Celtic scholar turned radio propagandist Dr Hans Hartmann. Mrs Mallie worked for the German Legation from 1937 to 1940 and left when she married Dr Mallie in Dublin (Mallie telephone interview, 4 Feb. 2000). Cathy Molohan, citing PRO FO 371/55358, also includes a Frl. Lackkamp (Cathy Molohan, *Germany and Ireland 1945–1955: Two Nations' Friendship* [Dublin: Irish Academic Press, 1999], p. 25). A Dr Heinrich Becker, a German teacher and cultural affairs expert, was sometimes employed on an unofficial basis.

36. Carter, *The Shamrock and the Swastika*, p. 29.

37. IMA G2/2457. Günther seemed to be preoccupied by other prurient interests. He maintained an aggressive correspondence schedule with the female students of his private German classes. G2's Colonel Bryan wrote 'he is, in fact, an expert in sexual psychology'. (Bryan to F. Boland, 2 Jan. 1944.)

38. NLI Ms 22,982 and 22,983, Richard Hayes Papers. The Irish attempted to break the cipher transmissions of most foreign diplomatic missions. G2 apparently had someone on the inside of the US Legation, because copies of internal documents found their way to G2. The US personnel had a thing or two to learn about communications security. In one instance, G2 tapped a telephone conversation between the US station at Foynes and the legation in Dublin. The Foynes station was having difficulty decoding a particular message. The Americans in Dublin helpfully supplied the clear text translation, reminding the Foynes caller that it was in the 'Orange Code'. The Italian Legation was directly opposite the German one in Northumberland Road, providing a 'two for one' situation when placing a hard-line phone tap.

39. The Irish papers were singularly uninformative; censorship ensured that everything but the drollest items were reported in a redacted format (Donal Ó Drisceoil, *Censorship in Ireland, 1939–1945* [Cork: Cork University Press, 1996], pp. 95–148).

40. In one telegram, Hempel asks the Foreign Ministry whether he should destroy all his secret materials before letting the British take him or run the risk of trying to hide his transmitter and codes. He apparently did destroy some of his secret papers before the scare ran its course (Carter, *The Shamrock and the Swastika*, p. 55 and USNA II, A.A., Hempel to Woermann, reel 89, frames 100406 and 1004455, documents of 3 Oct. 1940 and 27 Nov. 1940).

41. John Cornwell, *Hitler's Pope: The Secret History of Pius XII* (London: Viking, 1999), p. 228.

42. The Japanese also maintained a tiny diplomatic presence in Ireland. There has been some suggestion of incidental contact between the IRA and the Japanese Vice-Consul Kazuo Ichihashi in 1942 and 1943 (J. Bowyer Bell, *The Secret Army: The IRA 1916–1979* [Dublin Poolbeg Press, 1989], p. 236, citing Michael McInerney, 'Gerald Boland's Story', *Irish Times*, 18 Oct. 1968). This is borne out by G2 reports, which suggest that the vice-consul was active in a number of spheres. The Japanese Minister, Setsuya Beppu, maintained an extremely low profile during the war and stayed in Ireland for three years after the end of the war despite orders by the Japanese Foreign Ministry to return home. He was arrested upon arrival in Yokohama in 1948 (*Evening Herald*, 14 Aug. 1948).

43. PRO KV 4/9, Liddell report, pp. 28–9.

44. The DNB, the German Press Agency, had reporters and contributors in most capitals, who had the dual function of acting as press spokesmen and propaganda distributors for the various German legations. The Graf Reischach-Pressedienstes had been earlier founded by Hans Graf Reischach. Petersen's name is spelled as it appears on official German documents. Historians in this field often succumb to the temptation to rename him 'Carl Heinz', 'Karl Heinz', 'Karl' or 'Karlheinz'.

45. Ó Drisceoil, *Censorship in Ireland 1939–1945*, pp. 141–3

46. Petersen later married Mary Kay Lynch of Sligo – a friend of Elizabeth Clissmann. During the war, Petersen had been denied official permission to marry her, but they lived together. The marriage broke up after the war and Ms Lynch opened a highly successful retail women's clothing business at her Dublin store, Anna Livia's. Petersen and his girlfriend, referred to as his 'cousin', committed suicide in 1970 in the kitchen of his Hamburg flat, after inhaling gas from the stove (Elizabeth Clissmann interview; Letter of Enno Stephan; Carter, *The Shamrock and the Swastika*, p. 32).

47. Carter, p. 34, cites USNA II, A.A. Reel 89, Frame 100102, document of 11 Nov. 1939.

48. IMA G2/1722, Garda report, 26 Sept. 26, 1941 (clandestine meeting between Petersen and Tom Mullins of the *Irish Press*); IMA G2/0261, surveillance reports of 27 May and 3 June 1940, et al.

49. IMA G2/3261, summary, September 1945 and NAI S/12860, Charles McGuinness file.

50. Duggan interview with Dr Edmund Veesenmayer, 1977. According to Veesenmayer, Hempel 'hatte keine Meinung, keine Empfehlung' (had no opinion, no recommendation). (Duggan, D.Litt. thesis, p. 425.)

51. Keogh, *Jews in Twentieth Century Ireland*, pp. 74–5.

52. Ibid., pp. 99–103. There is no evidence that Bewley's reports directly influenced Irish policy, which in any event did not respond either favourably or charitably during the time that some Jews could leave Hitler's Germany in the 1930s. However, Bewley's attitude was shared by at least one official in the Department of Justice, as noted later in this work.
53. O'Driscoll, MA thesis, pp. 294–305.
54. Keogh, *Jews in Twentieth Century Ireland*, p. 135–6.
55. Charles Bewley, *Memoirs of a Wild Goose* (Dublin: Lilliput Press, 1990), pp. 197–8. This was in fact his analysis of the key people in Irish diplomatic circles. It was characteristically condescending, (PAAA, Dienstelle Ribbentrop, Ribbentrop persönlich, microfiche No. 2793, document of 12 Oct. 1940). A second missive indirectly sent to Minister Hempel in Dublin proposed sending a 'Republican' representative to Bewley in Rome. The two would then venture to Berlin in an effort to convince the Germans that a Republican government in Ireland would benefit Germany. In essence, it called for de Valera's overthrow (PAAA, microfiche No. 473 and Botschaft Rom (Quirinal) geheim, vol. 7; Andreas Roth, *Mr Bewley in Berlin* [Dublin: Four Courts Press, 2000], pp. 100–1).
56. Bewley, *Memoirs of a Wild Goose*, p. 189.
57. Eunan O'Halpin, 'Aspects of intelligence', *The Irish Sword*, 19 (1993), p. 59.
58. Ibid., p. 62 and IMA G2/0363.
59. Douglas Gageby telephone interview, 29 April 1999.
60. The 'official' wartime history of MI5 (F.H. Hinsley and C.A.G. Simkins, *British Intelligence in the Second World War*, Vol. 4: Security and Counter-Intelligence [London: H.M.S.O., 1990], p. 17) gives the date of the Walshe–MI5 correspondence as 31 Aug. 1939, rather than 1938. However, the reliable Liddell history in PRO KV 4/8 and other documents point to 1938 as the correct year.
61. Eunan O'Halpin, 'MI5's Irish Memories: Fresh Light on the Origins and Rationale of Anglo-Irish Security Liaison in the Second World War', in Brian Girvin and Geoff Roberts (eds), *Ireland in the Second World War* (London and Portland, OR: Frank Cass, 2000).p. 8.
62. PRO KV 4/9, Liddell report, p. 6.
63. As editor of *An Phoblacht*, the IRA newspaper, Ryan was not above inciting people to violence: 'No matter what anyone says to the contrary, while we have fists, hands and boots to use, and guns if necessary, we will not allow free speech to traitors.' (Bell, *The Secret Army*, p. 103.)
64. Murders, robberies and beatings continued to be the main cards played during this period, though the IRA was not the exclusive purveyor of these methods. Blueshirts (in the South) and Loyalists (in the North) alike seemingly relied on violence as an old and trusted friend. Uinseann MacEoin paints a year-by-year picture of the movements in *The IRA in the Twilight Years, 1923–1948* (Dublin: Argenta Publications, 1997).
65. Mary McSwiney was the widow of Terrence McSwiney, the Lord Mayor of Cork executed by the British in 1920. She was a strident supporter of a number of Republican issues. Moloney was active since before the 1916 Rebellion as a member of James Connolly's Citizen Army and later as a socialist labour organizer.

66. O'Duffy has recently come to public attention again with the allegation that he carried on a homosexual affair with noted Irish actor Micheal MacLiammoir ('The Odd Couple: MacLiammoir's "affair" with Blueshirt General', *Irish Independent*, 21 Oct. 1999, p. 12).

67. The name National Guard was also short-lived. It was banned under that name in August 1933 and metamorphosed into the Young Ireland Association. The organization under this title was banned in December 1933 (MacEoin, *The IRA in the Twilight Years*, p. 263). The name was later changed to the League of Youth (1934) and O'Duffy also founded the equally temporary National Corporate Party in 1935 (Maurice Manning, *The Blueshirts* [London: Gill and Macmillan, 1970], p. 199 and Fearghal McGarry, *Irish Politics and the Spanish Civil War* [Cork: Cork University Press, 1999], pp. 22–3). The brown shirt was also worn by other organizations in the NSDAP fold, to include the *Hitler Jugend*.

68. 'Blueshirt' was actually the name of the party newspaper, but never the official name of the organization. The uniform made its first public appearance in Kilkenny in April 1933, being worn by all the leadership except W.T. Cosgrave. The terms of membership did not specifically exclude Jews, but the wording left little doubt of the intent; members had to be Irish or have had parents who 'profess the Christian faith'. Members of secret organizations (e.g. Freemasons) were likewise excluded (Dermot Keogh, *Ireland and Europe, 1919–1948* [Dublin: Gill and Macmillan, 1994], p. 43).

69. MacEoin, *The IRA in the Twilight Years*, p. 251.

70. Manning, *The Blueshirts*, p. 172.

71. MacEoin, *The IRA in the Twilight Years*, p. 383.

72. Bell, *The Secret Army*, p. 131.

73. The significance of the various international contingents soon outweighed that of the native Spanish soldiers. Germany sent a sizeable force, the Condor Legion, which used the Spanish Civil War as a testing laboratory for close-air support tactics and a working trial for the new Me-109 B fighter aircraft. German Ju-86 planes from the Condor Legion bombed the town of Guernica in 1937 in what became one of the most publicized tragedies of the war. A total of 16,000 German troops saw action in Spain, including future Luftwaffe fighter aces Adolf Galland and Werner Mölders (Taylor and Shaw, *Penguin Dictionary of the Third Reich*, p. 203). Soviet Russia sent millions of dollars' worth in equipment and personnel, including NKVD troops (Christopher Andrew, The *Sword and the Shield: The Mitrohkin Archive and the Secret History of the KGB* (New York: Basic Books, 1999), pp. 72–4).

74. MacEoin, *The IRA in the Twilight Years*, p. 386. The bulk of the troops left in December aboard the German vessel *Urundi*. Some fifty changed their minds at the last minute because 'their officers were referring to them in demeaning terms'.

75. Keogh, *Ireland and Europe*, pp. 83–4.

76. Ibid., p. 393. The Spanish Nationalist leaders apparently requested that O'Duffy and his unit vacate Spain due to their unsuitability for combat operations. Manning (*The Blueshirts*, p. 206) reports that there were seven deaths from the group, including two due to 'friendly fire' and four during an all too brief advance.

77. They were initially formed into the 'James Connolly section' of the Abraham Lincoln Battalion, International Brigade. The total number of Irish volunteers to the Republican side was approximately 400, of whom there were forty-two killed, 114 wounded and twelve captured (Bell, *The Secret Army*, p. 134). Despite specious statements to the contrary, there was never a 'Connolly Column' and even the name 'James Connolly section' was unofficial. Irish volunteers were attached to either the American or British battalions (McGarry, *Irish Politics and the Spanish Civil War*, pp. 66–7.)

78. Other than to send Enquiries about the ages of some of the volunteers, the Irish government made no effort to stop either Ryan's or O'Duffy's volunteers from going to Spain (NAI S/5631). Though the Foreign Enlistment Act and a Non-Intervention Pact were passed by the Dáil, the latter making participation in the Spanish Civil War punishable by two-year imprisonment, popular support for the Nationalists made enforcement of the law politically indiscreet (Manning, *The Blueshirts*, pp. 200–2).

79. De Valera jailed Blueshirts and IRA men in exactly equal numbers in the period from 1934 to 1937, the annual differences between the arrest totals accurately reflecting which group was perceived to be the greater social threat: Tim Pat Coogan, *Eamon De Valera, The Man Who Was Ireland* (New York: Harper Perennial, 1995), p. 479.

80. Ibid. The Republican Congress split at its convention in September, when Michael Price left the group.

81. Ibid., p. 480. This situation was probably not helped by an incident during de Valera's 1936 St Patrick's Day radio address. An illegal IRA transmitter jammed much of the broadcast and even interjected 'Hello comrades! For the last half-hour we have just witnessed a very fine display of English militarism.' The IRA was later re-banned in 1939, after a brief period of legality.

82. Barry, possibly with connivance from the Germans, promoted the idea of an attack on British installations in Northern Ireland, beginning with Gough Barracks, Armagh. The 1938 convention also marked Sean MacBride's gradual withdrawal from overt IRA activity (MacEoin, *The IRA in the Twilight Years*, pp. 845–6).

83. Carter, *The Shamrock and the Swastika*, p. 24. The British press interpreted the S-Plan to be the work of the German General Staff – something that the OKW would probably not have viewed as a compliment ('How Hitler Got a Foothold in Ireland', *P.M.*, 17 March 1944).

84. Enno Stephan, 'Studie B, Die IRA im Spiegel der Weltpresse, 1936–1944', unpublished ms, p. 17.

85. Coogan, *The IRA: A History* (New York: Roberts Rinehart, 1994), p. 172.

86. Letter of Stephan Hayes to Jim O'Donovan, 2 May 1941, in the possession of Enno Stephan. De Valera and Joseph McGarrity, the leader of the Clann na Gael, split in 1936 when de Valera refused to declare Ireland a Republic. McGarrity then threw his weight behind the IRA and, specifically, Seán Russell (Coogan, *De Valera*, p. 484).

87. Stephan, 'Die IRA im Spiegel der Weltpresse', p. 14, interviews with Jim O'Donovan and Moss Twomey.

88. In addition to performing a number of other functions, Abwehr II was responsible for contacting and coordinating intelligence operations with

disaffected nationalist groups in foreign countries. These contacts ranged from the Welsh and Scottish independence groups, the Breton separatists in France, a Flemish movement in Belgium and the Indian nationalists (Azad Hind) under the uneven leadership of Subhas Chandra Bose. For purposes of propaganda, the German postal system optimistically issued commemorative stamps for use by Bose's government once in power. The IRA never rose to the level necessary to merit this type of attention.

89. *Documents on German Foreign Policy, 1918–1945*, Series D, Vol. VIII, pp. 405–6, Hempel to Woermann, 14 Nov. 1939.
90. West, *MI5*, p. 114.

CHAPTER 3

1. IMA G2/0238, 3 Oct. 1938 summary.
2. PRO KV 4/9, Liddell report, pp. 34–7 and IMA G2/0238, summary.
3. IMA G2/X/1091, note of 2 Jan. 1943. There was some evidence, however, that he next went to the United States on behalf of the Abwehr (PRO KV 2/87, Ritter interview, responding to a query from the FBI).
4. IMA G2/1722, report entitled 'Summary of German Activities'.
5. IMA G2/2146, undated summary.
6. IMA G2/0257, memorandum on Frank Ryan, 20 Oct. 1941.
7. Maud Gonne had divorced 'Major' John MacBride. She had a daughter, Iseult, from an earlier liaison with French extremist politician Lucien Millevoye. Iseult married Francis Stuart in 1920 (O'Donoghue, Ph.D. thesis, p. 76; Ion Stuart interview, June 1999). MacBride's contacts with Hempel were regular throughout the war, and some were held under circumstances that suggested covert activity (IMA G2/0214).
8. Elizabeth Clissmann telephone interview, 15 Feb. 1999 and IMA G2/0089, summary.
9. In a 1943 FBI report it was noted that 'Tom Barry of Cork, the then Chief of Staff of the IRA, visited Germany in 1937 where he was known to have been treated as a distinguished visitor' (Hoover to Adolf Berle, Jr., 30 Sept. 1943, No. 841D.00/1421, courtesy of Professor Eunan O'Halpin.) Though the date of 1938 is given for the visit in G2 records, January 1937 is more probable (Dickel, *Die deutsche Außenpolitik und die irische Frage*, p. 78). Dickel refers to a trip note in the possession of Frau Hoven and an interview with Helmut Clissmann in 1976.
10. According to Carter (*The Shamrock and the Swastika*, p. 94), citing her 'Confidential Government Source' (Col. Bryan): 'Hoven became acquainted with ... a former IRA man for whom he arranged a trip to Germany. This man had been one of the principal guerrilla chiefs during the Black and Tan War but had done little but write his memoirs [*Guerrilla Days in Ireland*] since that time. The trip was probably arranged so the IRA man could discuss the bomb campaign that had started in England around that time, and IRA-German cooperation.'
11. IMA G2/0089, DMD reports, 23 Feb. and 18 July 1939.
12. IMA G2/0093, Foley report, June 1940.

13. IMA G2/X/0093, Captain Butler report, 23 Nov. 1943.
14. IMA G2/1722, summary of German activities.
15. IMA G2/0265, German–IRA contacts.
16. Carter, *The Shamrock and the Swastika*, p. 144, fn. 24, cites A.A. Reel 89, Frames 100166, 100168 and 100173, 5 March, 6 March and 21 March 1940. MacBride spent part of his youth in Switzerland and spoke French.
17. Carter, *The Shamrock and the Swastika*, p. 209, Günther Schütz interview.
18. The records of MacBride's telephone and mail surveillance exist, but are not open to the public at the present time. The Irish government's wartime policy was curiously uneven. Many lesser IRA figures were interned, but many of the leaders escaped long-term confinement, particularly the pre-war leaders.
19. PRO KV 4/8, Liddell report, p. 38.
20. IMA G2/0184, Phillips's statement, 9 April 1943.
21. Frigattenkapitän Dr Erich Pheiffer was commander of the Bremen Nest, a subordinate post of the Hamburg Ast (KV 2/170, Praetorius interview, 11 Oct. 1945). Brammer (pp. 10, 36) gives the name as 'Pfeiffer' – a more likely spelling.
22. IMA G2/0184.
23. Fisk, *In Time of War*, pp. 1–2.
24. IMA G2/0184, Sept. 1945 summary.
25. Ibid.
26. Ibid., Commandant Harrington to Bryan, 5 Dec. 1942.
27. Ibid., pp. 38–9. The Gardaí also reported that a 'Phillip Bernard Richards' was in contact with Werner Unland in February 1940. Though the names are similar, there is no mention of a clear connection or further investigation in the G2 file (IMA G2/0261, Garda report, March 1940).
28. The Czech information was relayed by a cut-out named Lisicky (FO 371/24962). The reasons for a Czech consul in Ireland are ambiguous. Czechoslovakia was completely occupied by German troops in March 1939 and administratively renamed as the 'Reichsprotektorat Böhmen und Mähren' (Reich Protectorate of Bohemia and Moravia).
29. Fisk, *In Time of War*, pp. 144–7. Hemersbach's daughters confirmed that legation personnel stayed there but denied that there was anything sinister. Stumpf was a radiologist at Baggot Street Hospital and a Nazi Party member, but did not work at the German Legation.
30. PRO KV 4/9, Liddell report, p. 31.
31. IMA G2/X/0581, DMD report, 25 Sept. 1939.
32. *Birmingham Post*, 7 Aug. 1939, copy in IMA G2/X/0581.
33. PRO KV 4/9, Liddell report, p. 32.
34. Pfaus had an affinity for being photographed in various uniforms. Posed photographs exist of him wearing the uniform of the US Army, the Chicago police, the German Army (enlisted) of the First World War and the German Army (enlisted) in the Second World War, and there are numerous shots of him in civilian clothes. The National Personnel Records Center in St Louis, Missouri, has no record of Pfaus serving in the US Army, at least under that name.
35. Pfaus believed that General Mosely was sympathetic to his fascist propaganda activities. He asked an American sympathizer, Dr Anna Sloane to contact the

General concerning the Fichte-Bund (Pfaus to Sloane, 3 June 1939, courtesy of Enno Stephan).

36. *California Journal*, 26 Feb. 1932. The article appears under the banner headline 'Antrag auf Nobelpreis-Verliehung an Oscar Pfaus' (Nomination of Oscar Pfaus for the Nobel Prize Award).

37. In fact, there was no Peace Prize awarded in 1932, the money going the Special Fund.

38. Pfaus to Dr Anna Sloane, 3 June 1939. Pfaus also gave Dr. Sloane his private address, Steindamm 22, III, Hamburg.

39. Pfaus joined the Nazi party on 1 Dec. 1937 (USNA, RG Zentralkartei, roll L-0126).

40. According to the Fichte-Bund letterhead, the organization was founded 'in memory of the great German philosopher Fichte'. The word 'great' in connection with Johann Gottlieb Fichte (1762–1814), a nationalist and philosopher during the time Napoleon was humiliating Prussia, might be something of an overstatement. He was, however, important in the development of German Romanticism, continuing the philosophical tradition of Immanuel Kant. His chief political treatise was *Reden an die deutsche Nation* (Addresses to the German Nation), in which he corrected his earlier endorsement of the French Revolution, substituting the hope that Germany would unite Europe against French rule. Part of this proposed unity was based on the racial strength of the German people, but Fichte was not specifically anti-Semitic, as was the organization bearing his name.

41. Coincidentally or not, an adjacent address, Jungfernstieg 2 was an Abwehr live letter drop at the non-existent firm of Patterson and Morton (PRO KV 2/103) and Jungfernstieg 7/8 was a cover address for Abwehr I/Wi (PRO KV 1/170, Praetorius interview, 11 Oct. 1945).

42. Shortly after the Pfaus mission, Schneidewind was transferred to another post and the Hamburg Ast never filled the vacancy for an Abwehr II officer (PRO KV 2/170, memorandum of 11 Oct. 1945 and KV 2/103, summary of Wichmann interrogations).

43. Tom Clarke was among the executed leaders of the 1916 Rebellion, and Cathal Brugha, a member of the anti-Treaty IRA, was killed by Free State soldiers at the Four Courts siege in Dublin (1922).

44. Róisín Ní Mheara-Vinard [Nora O'Mara], *Cé Hí Seo Amuigh?* (Dublin: Coiscéim, 1992), p. 138.

45. This information seems to agree with the information contained in the Abwehr II Kriegstagebuch and with Kurt Haller's statement to Enno Stephan. O'Mara, however, makes a number of factual errors in her account, and refers to Abwehr II as the 'the counter-intelligence department' – which it certainly was not. Abwehr III was the counter-intelligence section of German military intelligence. Abwehr II dealt with sabotage and discontented minorities.

46. Ní Mheara-Vinard, *Cé Hí Seo Amuigh?*, p. 138.

47. Enno Stephan, 'Die Vergessene Episode: Deutsche Agenten im irischen Untergrundkampf', unpublished MS, p. 14.

48. This is probably the same tour mentioned in IMA G2/X/0703. A group of Irish singers visited Hamburg in 1937 as part of a Nazi 'Kraft durch Freude'

(Strength Through Joy) outing, complete with Abwehr Sonderführer Hans Blau as tour guide.

49. IMA G2/0054. Friedrich Herkner was a Nazi Party member in Ireland. He left the country with the other German nationals in September 1939. However, in a magnanimous spirit of forgiveness after the war – and after the photos of Buchenwald were shown around the world – Herkner was invited back to Ireland by the Department of Education and returned to his art teaching job in 1947 (O'Donoghue, *Hitler's Irish Voices*, p. 178). Dr Adolf Mahr, the head of the AO in Ireland, who held a civil service position as Director of the National Museum, was frustrated in his efforts to return to his job when his wartime role became public. He was pensioned off by the Irish government with 12 years of active service (1927–39) (Ibid., pp. 167–72).

50. Pfaus letter to Enno Stephan, 5 May 1959.

51. IMA G2/0246, summary of 3 May 1944. Walsh later penned a sympathetic but unpublished biography of Eoin O'Duffy, *General Eoin O'Duffy – His Life and Battle*, now in the NAI.

52. Pfaus to Stephan, 5 May 1959.

53. IMA G2/0246. Mrs Martin was one of several Hospitals Trust employees that had direct contact with the Germans or their sympathizers.

54. Pfaus later listed Diarmuid E.O. Dubhghaill, Criostoir Mac Aonghusa (Galway), Peadar O'Mongaigh (Roscommon), Brendan Mooney (Wicklow), Peter F. Loftus (Sligo), Edward Russell (Cork), T. Kenny (Carlow) and Commandant Brendan-Whitmore (Wexford). (Pfaus to Stephan, 10 May 1959.)

55. Stephan, 'Die Vergessene Episode', pp. 9–10; Pfaus to Stephan, 5 May 1959.

56. Twomey was IRA Chief of Staff from 1926–1936 and was followed in that office by Seán MacBride, Tom Barry, Michael Fitzpatrick, and Seán Russell. Pfaus's contention that he was carrying a .45 automatic is probably apocryphal, like several of his other details. He cultivated the James Bond image years before Ian Fleming wrote his first novel.

57. IMA G2/0246. This was probably misinterpreted. It fits in with Pfaus's own description of what happened before Twomey picked him up. It seems strange that the surveillance team would see this incident yet completely miss the fact of the meeting with the IRA leadership.

58. IMA G2/1722 and G2/0261.

59. In his telegram of 16 Dec. 1939 to the Foreign Ministry, Dr Hempel complained that Pfaus 'has lately again been sending propaganda material, some of which is allegedly very strong, to radical Irish-nationalist personalities'. Hempel theorized, correctly, that the authorities were permitting the material to pass in to the country as a means of noting the addresses of security threats. Asking that the material be stopped, Hempel continued that he wanted the issue handled 'with the greatest caution and without any mention of my part, since I must in no case be compromised in connection with the Irish nationalist movement' (*Documents on German Foreign Policy*, Series D, Vol. VIII, p. 545, No. 465, 91/100122–23, Telegram No. 182 of 16 Dec. 1939).

60. Stephan, 'Die Vergessene Episode', p. 13.

61. Ibid., interview with Oscar Pfaus.

62. IMA G2/2244, Pfaus to T. Kelly, 31 March 1939.

63. IMA G2/2278, Pfaus to Maud Gonne MacBride, 31 July 1939. Mrs MacBride was also a supporter of the Save the German Children organization and wrote the occasional editorial letter on its behalf.

64. According to Pfaus (letter of 5 May 1959), Walsh visited him twice in Germany, but the Irish records mention only the one visit. G2 thought that Kessenmeier and Leiter were two separate individuals, but Leiter was actually Kessenmeier's cover-name (Pfaus to Stephan, 9 Nov. 1959).

65. Pfaus to Stephan, 5 May 1959.

66. Walsh to Gaffney, 22 June 1939, courtesy of Enno Stephan.

67. PRO KV 4/9, Liddell report, p. 31 and FO 371/24962.

68. Walsh was also in contact with Sir Oswald Mosley of the British Union of Fascists (IMA G2/0246, summary).

69. IMA G2/0289, letter of 15 Feb. 1940.

70. Ibid., memorandum of 1 July 1943.

71. Pfaus to Stephan, 29 July 1959; Stephan to author, 17 Oct. 1999. Pfaus theorized that meeting with her in his hotel room was sufficient to attract the attention of the resistance.

72. Apparently unknown to Pfaus, Father Monaghan was a British Army chaplain who had been ordered back to Paris to establish links between MI6 and the resistance. Arrested and interrogated by the Gestapo in 1940, he was later released. This would obviously explain the failure of Pfaus's mission (O'Donoghue, *Hitler's Irish Voices*, p. 196).

73. IMA G2/3783, summary, September 1945.

74. Ibid.

75. O'Donovan was credited with creating new types of explosives and with importing the necessary ingredients in the guise of salt, Paxo stuffing, and baking powder (Stephan, 'Die Vergessene Episode', p. 38).

76. Despite his later activity, which included three years behind bars, O'Donovan remained with the ESB until his retirement in 1961.

77. O'Donovan himself described the bombing campaign as 'hastily conceived, scheduled to a premature start, with ill-equipped and inadequately-trained personnel, too few men and too little money ... unable to sustain the vital spark of what must be confessed to have fizzled out like a damp and inglorious squib' (O'Donovan diary, 23 Aug. 1939, courtesy of Donal O'Donovan.).

78. Stephan, 'Die Vergessene Episode', p. 40. This introductory meeting should have told the IRA what they needed to know about German military priorities. The German position remained remarkably consistent even through the Görtz mission.

79. Ibid., p. 44. The Abwehr had designated a Breton nationalist named Paul Moyse as their operational courier. The Bretons were widely recruited to Abwehr, mostly by their Breton specialists, Hans Otto Wagner and Hans Scharf (PRO KV 2/207–209). The Waffen-SS also recruited approximately 200 Bretons for a small but special national fighting unit. In 1945 it took part in the fighting around Hanover (Saint Loup, *Les Hérétiques* [Paris: Presse de la Cité, 1965], p. 517).

80. Hayes was already the Adjutant-General of the IRA. Russell had been the chief of staff since the 1938 IRA split over the bombing campaign (Carter, *The Shamrock and the Swastika*, p. 112).

81. Stephan, 'Die Vergessene Episode', pp. 147–8, interview with Jim O'Donovan. As is noted in other sections of this thesis, several members of the Hospital Sweepstakes organization were more than willing to help German agents as the need arose. Even under wartime censorship, the Irish government assisted the sweepstakes in violating internal postal laws. Sweepstakes material was sent to the censor complete with unmarked envelopes that were then forwarded by the Irish postal system to countries where the lottery was illegal (O'Drisceoil, *Censorship in Ireland*, p. 73).

82. IMA G2/3010, Bryan memorandum on Bridie Clyne, 21 March 1939.

83. IMA G2/X/0093, file memorandum, 'Germans and the IRA', 20 March 1946.

84. PRO KV 4/9, Liddell report, pp. 31–2.

85. Carter, *The Shamrock and the Swastika*, p. 103. Duggan, (*Neutral Ireland and the Third Reich*, p. 61) refers to Mrs O'Donovan having 'an undeclared packet of cigarettes'. Stephan reports that Monty was a chain-smoker and that she would smoke from several packs simultaneously and discard the half-used packs in her handbag or case. The customs official was seemingly not impressed with this explanation.

86. Stephan, 'Die Vergessene Episode', p. 57, quoting from an interview with Oscar Pfaus.

87. According to Pfaus, Mrs O'Donovan went on something of a spending spree: 'It didn't please me, but it was not my business to be critical about it.' At his request, Pfaus also took Jim to see the 'Blessings of the Sea' plant and flower exhibition in Hamburg (Pfaus to Stephan, 10 May 1959).

88. Neumeister later took the 'House of Parliaments' code from Berlin to Paul Moyse in Brussels (Stephan to author, 12 Sept. 1999).

89. O'Donovan diary, 23 Aug. 1939.

90. Ibid. On his return, McGarrity wrote a letter to one of the German hosts: 'A great country and a fine people, hope all are tending to their task. Now is the day and now is the hour.' (NLI, McGarrity papers, 17/645/1, McGarrity to 'General', 4 September 1939.

91. Though it is not stated in any source, the Abwehr must have spent time during either the May or August visit teaching O'Donovan the basic enciphering system. Messages encoded by him appear in his papers at the National Library of Ireland (MS 21,155) using the agreed keyword.

92. Carter (*The Shamrock and the Swastika*, p. 103) states that 'Kurt Haller, a club-footed civilian attached to the Abwehr, thereupon selected 'House of Parliaments'. Other than Carter's questionable choice of adjectives, it should be noted that Haller's disability was the result of childhood poliomyelitis. His rank, Sonderführer ('Special Leader') was a quasi-officer's rank reflecting that he had specialist military responsibilities, but was not a regular soldier or officer (Stephan to author, 25 June 1999).

93. Stephan, 'Die Vergessene Episode', p. 58. This was Moyse's last mission for Abwehr II. After returning, he decided that he was no longer safe in Brussels (his home) and moved with his Flemish bride to Berlin, where he began work with the Breton nationalist group Breiz Atao, which was covertly funded and organized by Abwehr II.

94. Bundesarchiv-Militärarchiv (BMA), RW5/ v. 497, Abwehr II Kriegstagebuch, 29 Oct. 1939.

95. Carter, *The Shamrock and the Swastika*, p. 104. She also incorrectly identifies it as a 'Scott radio', apparently based on an interview with Jim O'Donovan in 1969. This does raise the question of whether there were two different transmitters. Carter (and O'Donovan) probably confused the Ashgrove House transmitter with the one that was later seized in the raid on Stephen Held's house in May 1940. That particular set was acceptable for localized internal transmissions, but unsuitable for international contact (IMA G2/X/0114). To make matters even more confusing, a Mattie O'Neill remembers going to O'Donovan's house in 1940 to diagnose a problem with his transmitter 'for keeping in contact with Germany'. This would presumably be a third set, or the same set that was delivered to Held's house (most probable) – in which case O'Neill was wrong about its use (MacEoin, *The IRA in the Twilight Years*, p. 722).
96. IMA G2/X/1164, memorandum from 2LT Greene to G2, 30 Jan. 1940.
97. The four were Jack McNeela, Jack Plunkett, James Byrne and Seamus Mongen. Plunkett was also an ESB employee. (Stephan, 'Die Vergessene Episode', p. 336; Maurice Cogan interview, 6 Jan. 2000.)
98. IRA Transmission Log, courtesy of Mr Michael Hill. The log was found when a subsequent owner of Jim O'Donovan's house, 'Florenceville', discovered the papers stashed in a recess of the garage.

CHAPTER 4

1. The primary goal of the raid might have been to secure a supply of .45 ammunition for the IRA's Thompson machine guns. The only large supply of this ammunition outside of the United States was the Irish Army (Bell, *The Secret Army*, p. 172).
2. According to Stephan (*Spies in Ireland*, p. 59) the IRA message about the Magazine Fort raid was among the last to be sent via the IRA transmitter before its capture. The transmitter seizure was accurately reported in the 1 January edition of the *Kölnische Zeitung*: 'Gestern Abend ist in der Nähe von Dublin ein Geheimsender der IRA beschlagnahmt wordern. Vier Personen wurden verhaftet.'
3. This view was evidently shared by the German press. Following a description of the Magazine Fort raid, the 30 December 1939 edition of the *Kölnische Zeitung* gave the view that 'They [the IRA] possess in Seán Russell a talented leader, who many people see as the successor to the current Minister-President de Valera.'
4. Representing the prisoners, Seán MacBride successfully argued for their release on a habeas corpus motion. This was based on the fact that none of the sections in the new or existing legislation provided for preventive detention. The prisoners were released in December 1939, only to end up back in jail when the situation had worsened and the legal loopholes had been plugged. This was also reported in the *Deutsche Allgemeine Zeitung* on 21 January 1940 in a story filed by Carlheinz Petersen.
5. Carter, *The Shamrock and the Swastika*, pp. 26–7.

6. Maud Gonne and MacBride married in 1903, had their son in 1904 and separated in 1905. MacBride was executed in 1916 for his part in the Easter Rising. Stuart could not understand why Maud Gonne thereafter wore her trademark 'widow's black' in view of her venomous hatred for her departed husband (Stuart interview, 15 July 1999). Though she jettisoned the husband, her preferred form of address was 'Madame MacBride'.

7. Geoffrey Elborn, *Francis Stuart: A Life* (Dublin: Raven Arts Press, 1990), p. 23.

8. Ibid. p. 57.

9. O'Donoghue, Ph.D. thesis, p. 78.

10. Stuart was intelligent enough to recognize anti-Semitism. In speaking of framed articles and pictures he saw in Berlin, he wrote that 'These are mostly pages from newspapers – especially *The Sturmer* [sic], the special anti-semitic one'. In the same letter he remarked: 'I have heard something of the Jewish activities prior to 1933 here and in cooperation with the communists – they were in many instances appalling.' There is no evidence that Stuart had actual information about the extermination camps, which, in any case, was not publicly advertised (Elborn, *Francis Stuart*, p. 113). There is likewise little evidence that Stuart was anti-Semitic, other than one mention in his first broadcast on behalf of the Irland-Redaktion.

11. Ibid., p. 116. Stuart described one such event at the Berlin Olympic stadium in June 1939: 'A most amazing thing. Such a spectacle and organization.'

12. Under Article 17 of the British Defence Regulations, 'any British subject who visits Germany during the war can expect 5 years and a £500 fine'. The Irish Department of External Affairs position was that 'while we do not admit for a moment that Irish citizens are British subjects, we have no effective means of protecting them from being penalized under British law. No passport will be issued for travel to Germany without special reference to this department.' (NA DFA 202/664, Dept. External Affairs circular of 6 Feb. 1940 and letter of F.H. Boland to Liam Bergin, 26 Jan. 1940.) Mr Bergin, a newspaper editor, wanted permission to travel to Germany, get married and then bring his new wife back to Ireland as an Irish citizen.

13. IMA G2/0214, mail surveillance report, 15 June 1939, et al.

14. Ibid., DMD report, 27 April 1939.

15. Ibid., report of 7 July 1939.

16. IMA G2/1722, report of 26 July 1941.

17. 'Either they believed me when I got to Germany or they didn't. I couldn't care less really.' (Stuart interview, 17 Nov. 1989, O'Donoghue, Ph.D. thesis, p. 79). Elborn (*Francis Stuart*, p. 121) gives the above version of Stuart disposing of the Abwehr paper. When interviewed by David O'Donoghue, Stuart changed his story, stating that he got rid of the paper because it was 'playacting like you read about in old spy books' (O'Donoghue, *Hitler's Irish Voices*, p. 41).

18. Stuart said that Joyce was 'winning the war single-handed for Germany' (Stuart interview, 15 July 1999). Cf. O'Donoghue, *Hitler's Irish Voices*, pp. 43 and 45.

19. In the July 1999 interview with this author, Stuart said that O'Donovan told him that 'there was a Dr Fromme who would vouch for me being Francis Stuart ... when I got there'. There is probably something missing in the details

of Stuart's mission. The message he said he delivered could more easily – and more reliably – have been transmitted in code by the German Legation. There was likely some other purpose involved, but with Stuart and the others now deceased, little additional information is likely to surface.

20. Ibid.

21. 'Der seinerzeit von USA gelieferte Sender ist, entgegen den seinerzeit gegebenen Anweisungen, nach jeweils kurze Zeit für den Verkehr mit Deutschland, sondern ausserdem auch häufig für die Propaganda im Innern des Landes verwendet worden.' (BMA, RW5/v. 497, Abwehr II Kriegstagebuch, 4 Feb. 1940.) The Abwehr was also aware that the code between the IRA and the Abwehr might be compromised. In response to O'Donovan's request through Stuart for a replacement transmitter, the Abwehr agreed to investigate the possibility.

22. Hempel had previously urged that Stuart be given assistance to travel to Germany. 'On January 26, 1940, Under Secretary of State Ernst Woermann recorded a memorandum (91/100147) that Stuart had reached Berlin and visited him. Hempel transmitted through Stuart a repetition of his request that the propaganda efforts of the Fichte-Bund be stopped. Woermann assigned further liaison with Stuart to Stolzmann of the Cultural Policy Department.' (*Documents on German Foreign Policy*, p. 546, Telegram 91/ 100122-23, 16 Dec. 1939.)

23. Letter, Hilde Spickernagel to David O'Donoghue, 9 Feb. 1992.

24. Letter of 2 Oct. 1939, BdU (Dönitz) to Abwehrabteilung. According to the document heading, the Navy was responding to an Abwehr request from 27 Sept. 1939. Cf. BMA, Rw5/v. 497, Abwehr II Kriegstagebuch, 28 Nov. 1939 – which specifically refers to the question of a landing an agent in Ireland. Dönitz later became Commander-in-Chief of the Navy and, briefly, Hitler's chosen successor.

25. Abwehr II Kriegstagebuch, 11 Dec. and 29 Dec. 1939. Despite the Navy's misgivings, three agents were landed in Ireland by submarine in 1940.

26. Ibid., 23 January and 26 January 1940.

27. Ibid., 28 January 1940. The Navy was slightly less hurried about reporting that the mission had been accomplished. Korvettenkapitän Hartmann was ordered to report completion of the mission orally, not by radio. Accordingly, the first report to the Abwehr was not until 15 February.

28. He was described as 'being as wide as he was tall, but terribly strong'. (Stephan, 'Die Vergessene Episode', p. 103.) According to his vital statistics form on entering Athlone, he was 5ft 5in. and weighed 196 pounds (14 stone) and also had an iron cross tattooed on his chest (IMA G2/1928).

29. According to Weber-Drohl, 'I am a Chiropractor and Homeopathy [sic] and a full graduate of the Manhattan College of Chiropractic ... [and] the American Chiropractic College in Chicago, Illinois'. He also claimed to have lived in the US for 23 years (IMA G2/1928, Weber-Drohl to Minister David Gray, 8 Nov. 1944). Kurt Haller stated that the doctorate was purchased (Stephan, 'Die Vergessene Episode', p. 103).

30. IMA G2/1928 Part II, Weber-Drohl summary.

31. USNA T-1022, pg. 32419, BdU operations order, Dönitz to Cdr. U-37, 22 Jan. 1940. The order was marked 'Geheime Kommandosache' (Secret

Command Matter) and 'Chefsache Nur durch Offizier' (Top Secret – transmission by officer only). There were only three copies of this order, one to Dönitz (BdU operations), and one each to the 1/Skl and the commander of U-37.

32. Stephan, 'Die Vergessene Episode', p. 104.

33. This landing site is reflected in the U-37 log. O'Halpin (*Defending Ireland*, p. 241) reports Sligo and Robert Fisk (*In Time of War*, p. 138) identifies the site as being in Sligo Bay. Stephan (*Spies in Ireland*, p. 66) is unclear.

34. Ibid. and Hartmann's log, entries for 8 and 9 Feb. 1940, courtesy of Enno Stephan.

35. IMA G2/1928, Healy to Bryan, 10 Feb. 1942.

36. IMA G2/1928, DMD Summary, 29 April 1940. Weber-Drohl didn't let this newly found wealth burn a hole in his pocket. He purchased a diamond ring for £150 at Barton's Jewellers and a further £45 in jewellery from the Dublin Smelting Company.

37. Ibid.

38. Ibid. The G2 report on the trial noted that Weber-Drohl told the arresting Gardaí that he lost his passport in Antwerp, but that he told the court he lost it when the boat capsized. He later confided to G2 that he and Görtz had developed this elaborate cover story before he left for Ireland on U-37. The G2 report went on to doubt that any wife would give her life savings to her husband so that he could go in search for his illegitimate children.

39. Ibid., statement of Anne Brady, 27 April 1940.

40. BIMA, Rw5/v. 497, Abwehr II Kriegstagebuch, 27 March 1940.

41. NA DFA A34, Summary of Persons detained under the Emergency Powers (No. 20) Order.

42. Görtz consistently had trouble with uncountable nouns, and would frequently use 'informations' – a perfectly valid construction in German – when writing in English. He also had periodic difficulty with subject-verb agreement. His posthumous articles in the *Irish Times* (Aug.–Sept. 1947) use a style and syntax quite distinct from the original Görtz material and were, in fact, written by a Dublin tax accountant named Joe Charleton (Information supplied to author from Tim Pat Coogan).

43. Bundesarchiv-Aachen Zentralnachweissstelle, Görtz personnel file. The routes to a direct commission were either entry into a university cadet corps and attendance at the training school of Gross Lichterfelde or application based on educational qualifications. In the later case, the other officers could blackball a prospective regimental candidate.

44. Stephan, 'Die Vergessene Episode', p. 123, based on interview with Ellen Görtz.

45. Bundesarchiv-Aachen, Görtz file.

46. Görtz carried an Imperial German pilot's badge to Ireland, and his promotion recommendation completed by Abwehr II suggests that he was also pilot, but his own statement to the Luftwaffe stops short. 'During my stay in Schwerin I went to school. In the field, I occasionally flew as a pilot.' Typically, the flight qualification course at Schwerin took at least seven months and his service record precludes a posting of this length. It is possible that Görtz was wearing a decoration to which he was not entitled.

47. Görtz to Air Ministry, 20 Aug. 1934. The details in Görtz's statements, personnel file and his promotion request from the Abwehr contain contradictory details and dates.
48. Stephan, 'Die Vergessene Episode', p. 124, based on interview with Ellen Görtz.
49. In another statement to the Luftwaffe, Görtz stated that at the time of the armistice, he was with a Gotha (bomber) detachment at Habay la Neuve, France, under the Fifth German Army (AOK 5): PRO, CRIM 1/813, Görtz to Reichministerium der Luftfahrt, 15 Sept. 1934.
50. Ibid., p. 5. In his statement, he quickly mentions another incident: 'After the end of the war, I next led a machinegun detachment under General v. Morgen in the Lübeck civil war.' This brief reference to Freikorps service, if it actually happened, is not repeated in earlier or subsequent statements to the Luftwaffe.
51. 'Mission to Ireland', *Irish Times*, 27 Aug. 1947.
52. PRO, CRIM 1/813, Görtz's *Lebenslauf*, 15 Sept. 1934.
53. Ibid.
54. IMA G2/1722, G2 report of July 1942. Dr Heinz Ehlers sent an angry letter to Enno Stephan, objecting to his being mentioned in the German version of *Spies in Ireland*, though he was identified only as 'a friend' of Görtz (Stephan to author, 26 July 1999).
55. PRO CRIM 1/813, Görtz to Commodore Hermann, 4 March 1935.
56. Bundesarchiv, Berlin, *Fragebogen zur Bearbeitung des Aufnahmeantrages für die Reichsschrifttumskammer*, 13 Nov. 1939. This was a personal history questionnaire completed by Görtz when he applied for membership in the Reich Literary Chamber.
57. Bundesarchiv, Aachen Zentralnachweissstelle, Görtz file.
58. *Irish Times*, 27 Aug. 1947. In the same article, Görtz refers to 'my activity in England as an Intelligence Officer'. Though he certainly understood the distinction between 'intelligence officer' and 'spy', he chose to blur the truth. In a military context, intelligence officers wear uniforms; spies don't.
59. According to Felstead, Görtz received 2000 RM as expenses and the promise of 20,000 RM upon successful completion of the mission. Görtz certainly needed an escape from his desperate financial position, but Felstead does not list his sources of information (S. Theodore Felstead, *Germany and Her Spies* [London: Hutchinson, 1940], p. 93). Görtz, however, inadvertently gave evidence against himself. In a letter to a Hamburg solicitor, he stated that he decided to 'accept an offer in England which gives me the prospect to make earnings enabling me to pay my debts. ... I had to accept the offer, that up to the end of the year only my bare expenses would be guaranteed.' (PRO CRIM 1/813, Görtz to Koob, 15 Sept. 1935.)
60. West, *MI5*, p. 114.
61. Bundesarchiv, Berlin, *Fragebogen*. Görtz later had difficulty explaining why he resigned from the party. In his application to the Reich Literary Chamber, he explained that he 'resigned due to a special mission of the Oberkommando der Wehrmacht (OKW)'. In the same application, he had to admit his prison sentence in England, but described it as a 'political' crime and that the 'OKW, Abteilung Abwehr, Luft I, will be able to explain'. So much for operational security.

62. PRO, CRIM 1/813, Görtz to Air Ministry, 15 Sept. 1934. Görtz also mentioned that he had passed his French and English interpreter tests and that 'until recently I was official interpreter to the Lübeck Provincial Court' – the first time he mentions this position in the several biographical letters to various German agencies.

63. PRO CRIM 1/813, statement of Kenneth Lewis, 13 Oct. 1935. Lewis was a glider pilot stationed at Lee-on-Solvent. He was not prosecuted, as his interest in Emig was more likely predicated on hormones than a desire to commit high treason. The same technique – using sex as a lure to commit espionage – was used by the KGB (and others) with predictable success.

64. In a contradictory statement in the Richard Hayes Papers (NLI, MS 22, 981), there is a note that Görtz had asked Mrs Johnson to send his luggage to Hospiz am Gendarmenmarkt, Mohren Str. 27–28, Berlin, and that Emig had earlier used this address. Görtz had an office at Rathausstr. 29–31, Hamburg.

65. In this application, written by Görtz himself, he states that the Allies branded him as a 'particularly dangerous' interrogator.

66. The immigration alert message described Marianne Emig as 'born in 1916, 5′ 7″, well-built, dark brown hair, fresh complexion, walks erect'. (IMA G2/ 1722.) It also noted that she developed 'personal relationships' with 'young aircraftmen from whom she obtained photos of aircraft'. Emig's physical charms seem to have worked wonders on Görtz, too. In later captivity, he half-finished a novel on his English spying episode and devoted an entire chapter, 'The Rose', to Emig. 'She is tall, slim and supple, but not meagre [sic] ... her boyish shoulders are straight and somewhat broader than her hips. Her hands are firm and hard, her thighs long and slim.'

67. Görtz made a rambling written statement to British police when arrested, including an unconvincing defence: 'I don't think that I hurt in any way the law. In any case I did not intend to offend the hospitality I enjoy in England. These are the facts.' (PRO, CRIM 1/813, Görtz statement, 9 Nov. 1935.)

68. West, *MI5*, pp. 116–22; Stephan, 'Die Vergessene Episode', pp. 126–7; Felstead, *Germany and her Spies*, pp. 95–7. Felstead claimed that Görtz, out of money, begged £10 from the 'Brown House', Cleveland Terrace, Paddington – the Nazi AO headquarters for England. Police found this address in Görtz's notebook.

69. PRO CRIM 1/813 (Rex v. Goertz), RLFM to Görtz, 29 Jan. 1935.

70. Ibid., Anwaltskammer to Görtz, 12 Jan. 1935.

71. Ibid., Görtz to Doerderlein, 2 Nov. 1935.

72. *Irish Times*, 27 Aug. 1947.

73. West, *MI5*, p. 122.

74. IMA G2/1722, Görtz to Iseult Stuart, 6 Jan. 1945.

75. Ibid. G2 interview with Görtz, 27 Jan. 1942.

76. Bundesarchiv, Berlin, Görtz file, document of 16 May 1939.

77. Bundesarchiv, Aachen, Görtz Personnel File, document of 19 Feb. 1941.

78. *Irish Times*, 27 Aug. 1947.

79. The *Zehn Gebote* also prescribed the proper conduct pertaining to taking prisoners (not to be killed, including partisans and spies), the ban on dum-dum bullets, respect for the Red Cross sign, treatment of civilian population, and the duties of German soldiers taken prisoner (had to give name and rank,

but 'under no circumstances' was he to reveal his unit, or make statements concerning German military, political or economic matters. Görtz seems not to have read this part, either.

80. IMA G2/1722, paybook in the Görtz file.
81. *Irish Times*, 29 Aug. 1947.
82. *Oberkommando*, in its most accurate translation, means 'High Command'. The German word for 'supreme' is *höchst*.
83. *Irish Times*, 27 Aug. 1947. This group could have included the former Irish Minister to Berlin, Charles Bewley, who was living in Italy at the time and was avowedly pro-German.
84. Ibid.
85. Francis Stuart interview, 7 July 1999.
86. *Irish Times*, 27 Aug. 1947. The Abwehr was known to have used live letter drops (LLDs) in both places, but there is no other documentation indicating that they were used in this operation.
87. *Documents on German Foreign Policy*, 1918–1945, Series D, Vol. VIII, document of 1 June 1940, Dr Ernst Woermann to Dr Eduard Hempel. Cf. O'Halpin, *Defending Ireland*, p. 244 and Görtz's statement in the *Irish Times*, 25 Aug. 1947, p. 4. Generalmajor von Lahousen stated that Görtz also had a weather-reporting component to his mission, in large part as a concession to the Luftwaffe to secure his transport (PRO KV 2/173, Special Interrogation Report on General-Major Lahousen and Sdf. (2) Kurt Haller, 15 July 1946, p. 3).
88. Enno Stephan to author, 18 May 1999. Out of respect for Frau Görtz – now deceased – Stephan obliged and though he mentioned Hauptmann Kaupert's report (*Spies in Ireland*, p. 113) he omitted the part about the mystery woman. Görtz also requested that this woman be informed of his landing in Ireland (Stephan, 'Die Vergessene Episode', based on Kaupert interview, p. 161).
89. Stephan, 'Die Vergessene Episode', p. 140. Canaris also had a marked distrust for Nazi Party members, which probably didn't improve his relations with Görtz. There are no other instances of German agents being equipped with cyanide.
90. Mainau is the name of a small island on the Bodensee. It was presumably chosen because of its analogous relationship to the island of Ireland. Mainau was also the site of an SD agent training centre (Kahn, *Hitler's Spies*, p. 276). The author of the 'Gilka' code-name is anyone's guess.
91. Oberleutnant (later Hauptmann) Gartenfeld eventually become proficient enough at this work to command his own squadron, the Second Test Formation. This unit was eventually merged into Kampfgruppe 200, under the command of Oberstleutnant Werner Baumbach (Kahn, *Hitler's Spies*, p. 285).
92. Stephan, 'Die Vergessene Episode', p. 162.
93. Abwehr II Kriegstagebuch, 6 May 1940. The war diary records that Haller was present at Kassel with Görtz.
94. The Germans would later refine the technique to allow for the radio to be dropped inside a florescent bag, so that it could be quickly located in darkness. Standard Allied practice would have been to suspend a line from the main parachute harness so that man and equipment would land together.

Subsequent to this mission, the Abwehr began issuing a smaller transmitter to agents, reducing the problem considerably (Stephan, 'Die Vergessene Episode', p. 163). Görtz was equipped with a white parachute. Camouflaged parachutes were introduced into the inventory following the invasion of Holland in May 1940, after Görtz's departure.

95. IMA G2/1722, Görtz report of December 1944.
96. IMA G2/1722, Report of Commandant Harrington, G2 to CSO, G2, 14 July 1941 and Garda Report of 27 May 1940. According to Gooney, 'the presence of [Reilly] who was carrying a fork gave him much more concern than did the stranger'. According to Görtz's later report, Gooney was somewhat less than truthful. He reported that Gooney took the $100 – something the Garda officer also suspected. Gardaí later re-interviewed Gooney in an effort to locate the missing transmitter. The officer believed that Gooney had it, but would only say that 'someone probably buried it and just doesn't want to get involved any more'. The police report concluded: 'Gooney is an old country man, ignorant and obstinate'. (Garda report of 7 May 1945.)
97. Ibid., Görtz report with annotations, Dec. 1944, p. 2.
98. *Irish Times*, 29 Aug. 1947. Subsequent investigation by G2 confirmed that Görtz had indeed stopped at the Garda barracks, where no one apparently noticed anything untoward (NLI MS 22, 981, Görtz chronology in the Richard Hayes Papers).
99. According to a more detailed version, Iseult had tea with her mother at Roebuck House, Clonskeagh, from where they phoned O'Donovan and the three of them returned to Laragh together (Elborn, *Francis Stuart*, p. 127).
100. Ibid., pp. 130–1.
101. In an undated letter to her, Görtz wrote, 'I would not have risked to touch you if he (A) had known anything. I have touched Cello, G.Q. [Maisie O'Mahony], and B (a year ago).' Görtz also wrote to Mrs Stuart from Athlone. Her son, Ion Stuart, told me that his mother never got over the shock of Görtz's death (author's interview with Ion Stuart, 15 June 1999). Carter incorrectly identified Cello as bandleader William Carter and incorrectly quoted Görtz's 'Cello' message (Carter, *The Shamrock and the Swastika*, p. 220). William Carter was, however, one of Görtz's supporters.
102. Görtz later claimed that O'Donovan knew of his arrival from a radio signal and that he had already searched the other drop zones in Northern Ireland and in the south (*Irish Times*, 29 Aug. 1947), but this would not seem to be the case. The radio logs kept by O'Donovan during the relevant time period show no such message from Germany (O'Donovan radio logs, courtesy of Michael Hill).
103. *Irish Times*, 29 Aug. 1947.
104. NLI, MS 22, 981, Richard Hayes papers, Held chronology and Stephan, *Spies in Ireland*, p. 106.
105. This was apparently done in direct response to Weber-Drohl's missive to O'Donovan (PRO KV 2/173, Lahousen Special Interrogation, p. 4).
106. IMA G2/3048, Hayes confession. The veracity of this is open to doubt.
107. Stephan, 'Die Vergessene Episode', p. 154, based on interview with Kurt Haller. Francis Stuart was given a torn note when he carried messages from Hayes to the Abwehr headquarters in January 1940. It is assumed that several notes were torn as recognition signals during O'Donovan's first visit to Germany. Held

maintained that the proof was a torn piece of foolscap paper and that he showed it to the Germans (IMA G2/0077, statement of 13 Oct. 1941).

108. Görtz referred to it as Plan Kathleen, but all other German documentation mentions only 'Artus Plan'.

109. IMA G2/1722, statement of Liam Gaynor, 3 Oct. 1941 and Stephan, 'Die Vergessene Episode', p. 155. The plan itself was seized by Garda in the raid on Held's home in May 1940.

110. Ibid., statement of Stephen Held at Mountjoy Prison, 13 Oct. 1941. Held also said that he met with a Dr Kessenmeir [Kessenmeier – Fichte-Bund leader].

111. BIMA, Rw5/v. 497, Abwehr II Kriegstagebuch, 24 April 1940.

112. Stephan, 'Die Vergessene Episode', p. 156.

113. IMA G2/1722, Bryan to Carroll, 21 Jan. 1939.

114. Ibid., notes on Held statement, Oct. 1941.

115. IMA G2/1722, statement of Liam Gaynor, 3 Oct. 1941. Gaynor added that Plan Kathleen was created by himself, Stephen Hayes and Stephen Held, which may explain the amateurish nature of the proposal.

116. Dan Bryan, unpublished memoirs, p. 30, courtesy of Professor Eunan O'Halpin. A note in IMA G2/0077 speaks of 'two very suspicious postcards' that were observed by postal censors.

117. IMA G2/1722, Görtz report, p. 3.

118. Görtz referred to Hayes's 'Waterford accent'. Hayes was actually born in Enniscorthy, County Wexford (MacEoin, *The IRA in the Twilight Years*, p. 382).

119. IMA G2/1722, Garda report, 19 June 1940, Ballivor, County Meath.

120. The distressed Luftwaffe tunic was found by a farmer named Hemingway in March 1941. G2 was able to identify it as a parade dress uniform of a reserve second lieutenant. Also recovered was a calfskin flight suit and quarter-inch maps of the Athlone and Dublin areas. Holes in the tunic matched to the ribbon bar recovered from Held's house in May 1940 (ibid., Garda report, 1 March 1941, Ballinkill Bog, Carbery, County Kildare).

121. IMA G2/0077, notes on Held document, 13 Oct. 1941.

122. IMA G2/1722, Görtz report, p. 4.

123. Ibid., p. 5 and *Irish Times*, 1 Sept. 1947. In his posthumous series in the *Irish Times*, Görtz changed the SA to the SS. He was mistaken on both counts. Neither organization was integrated into the German Army, as any Army veteran will be only too happy to point out.

124. In Dublin folklore, 'Konstanz' was known as the 'Swastika House' from the popular belief that it appeared to be a swastika when viewed from the air. This is a fantasy; the house is an ordinary 1930s dwelling in the shape of a quarter-circle (Letter from Dr Alf MacLochlainn, 10 May 1999).

125. The exact amount of money is disputed. Görtz himself suggests that he landed with $26,500 and that he gave $16,500 to Held and retained $10,000 for his own expenses. Brian Kennedy (*Dr Hermann Goertz – A Spy in South County Dublin* [Pub. no. 27, Foxrock Local History Club, 1989], p. 9) and Bell (*The Secret Army*, p. 185) reported that $18,500 was recovered from Held's house. G2, Garda, and Irish government reports are consistent in the amount of $20,000. *The Irish Press* (8 June 1940) reported that $18,500 was found in the safe and that a further $1,500 was discovered in two boxes in the study. Ironically, the radio in Held's house was too weak to transmit to Germany,

the three other suitable transmitters having been lost in the Ashgrove House raid in December 1939, Weber-Drohl's fiasco in February 1940 and during Görtz's landing in May 1940.

126. IMA G2/1722, G2 report of 5 Feb. 1945, summary of Görtz's report to 'Supreme Command.'
127. NAI DFA A34, G2 report, 21 April 1944.
128. IMA G2/1722, Dr Hayes decodes of Görtz material seized in Held raid.
129. *Documents on German Foreign Policy*, Vol. VIII, Series D, pp. 431–2, Document No. 314 of 24 May 1940. Hempel followed this up with a telegram the next day, informing Berlin about Mrs Stuart's arrest, noting that 'the affair has thereby turned unmistakably against us and this upsets all pretexts of English intrigues'. He also added, predictably, 'my personal position is also seriously involved. I fear indiscreet statements in Stuart's letters. ... Brandy has apparently not been apprehended yet.'
130. Ibid. Document No. 361 of 1 June 1940, Woermann to Hempel. The reference to 'Irish personalities' again brings a number of people under the spotlight, including former Irish Minister to Berlin Charles Bewley. Bewley's sympathetic interaction with the Germans is discussed later in this work.
131. Ibid. Document No. 100 of 3 July 1940, Woermann to Ribbentrop. Hempel had earlier (27 June 1941) reported on Held's trial and his sentence of five years' imprisonment.
132. She was traced through the Switzer's labels on Görtz's clothing. The actual charge against her was that she 'assisted to interfere with the apprehension of a person who had committed an offence under Section 5 of the Emergency Powers Act of 1939', and that she 'failed and refused to give all information in your possession in relation to the commission by another person of a scheduled offence'. (Elborn, *Francis Stuart*, p. 130.)
133. Interview with Ion Stuart, April 1999.
134. IMA G2/1722, summary of Görtz's report, December 1944. McDowell was the aunt of Francis Leo Redmond, who later purchased two transmitters for Görtz.
135. Interview with Francis Stuart, 15 July 1999. Helena Moloney joined Inghinidhe na Héireann (Daughters of Ireland) in 1903 and helped to found Na Fianna (forerunner of the IRA youth wing) in 1909. She served in James Connolly's Citizen Army in 1916 and supported the anti-Treaty position in the Civil War. She was formerly the President of the Irish Congress of Trades Unions.
136. IMA G2/2147. The Budinas left with most of the other German nationals in the mailboat *Cambria* on 11 Sept. 1939. John O'Reilly later encountered Karl Budina in Berlin, where he served in one of the PK (*Propaganda Kompanie*) units attached to the Wehrmacht (*Sunday Dispatch*, 27 July 1952).
137. ???, DMD report, 24 May 1940. Stuart was not in the country, having been in Germany since January 1940.
138. IMA G2/0261. M.J. Lyons, Patrick O'Connor, John Holden, Maurice O'Connor, John McGee, Thomas A. O'Gorman, Con Coughlan, Terry Trench and Dr McNally.
139. Keogh, *Jews in Twentieth Century Ireland*, p. 167.
140. IMA G2/0246, DMD report, 24 July 1940.
141. IMA G2/2468, DMD report, 8 July 1940. In addition to the above listed participants, the Garda noted the presence of Jerome Hurley, Maurice

O'Connor, Griffin's wife and sister-in-law, and a Miss K.M. O'Connor ('Glenview', St. Agnes Road, Dublin).

142. Keogh, *Jews in Twentieth Century Ireland*, p. 168.

143. IMA G2/0289. Under the banner headline 'Who is your enemy?' the leaflet asked the reader such dynamic questions as 'Who is flooding Ireland with Jewish-Masonic drivel and filth insulting to our national aspirations and the Christian religion, paralyzing [sic] you mind and warping your judgement? The answer is Enland [sic] – Ireland's only enemy. England's foes are Ireland's friends – may they increase and multiply! Moladh go deo [sic] leo!'

144. IMA G2/0246, letter of 20 June 1940; Garda report, 18 Sept. 1940. Pfaus did eventually respond, having posted his letter to a supporter in the US (E.D. Collins, 911 West Blvd., Hartford, Conn.) who then mailed it to Walsh. Mrs Walsh was assertive enough to attend the first meeting of the embryonic 'Anti-British Propaganda Committee' in December 1941. Inertia seems to have got the better of this group and nothing further was heard from them.

145. IMA G2/0267, Colonel Archer to Department of External Affairs, 29 Aug. 1940.

146. Ibid., file note.

147. Keogh, *Jews in Twentieth Century Ireland*, p. 169.

148. IMA G2/0261, DMD Report, 3 June 1940.

149. G2/0016, Brendan-Whitmore, 2 Dec. 1943, Summary.

150. Ibid., Brendan-Whitmore's manifesto, called 'A New Political and Social Philosophy for Ireland: The All-Purposes Guilds, incubator for the Celtic Confederation of Occupational Guilds', January 1939. Ms Lia Clark, formerly the DNB correspondent in Ireland (she subsequently moved to the Graf Reisach Dienst) reported on the inaugural meeting of the Celtic Confederation of Occupational Guilds. She added a pro-Nazi commentary, noting that 'Germany requires, urgently, more room for her ever-growing population. In spite of all her sufferings, she is the best organised, disciplined, and armed nation in Europe and to put it bluntly, must either expand or bust.' (Ibid., dispatch of 7 August 1939). The practical application of German expansion started three weeks later with the invasion of Poland.

151. Keogh, *Jews in Twentieth Century Ireland*, p. 149.

152. Griffin's associate founder was Patrick Moylett; George Sinclair was vice-president; Brendan Kennedy was listed as treasurer.

153. O'Drisceoil, *Censorship in Ireland*, p. 187, cites IMA OCC 2/47, Coyne to Inspector Reynolds, 16 Jan. 1941 and other correspondence, memos and reports, Dec. 1940 to June 1941, copy of *Penapa*, January 1941.

154. Ibid. cites IMA, OCC 5/32, 'Seizure of leaflet issued by the Irish Christian Rights Protection Association', June 1942.

CHAPTER 5

1. BIMA, RW5/v. 497, Abwehr II Kriegstagebuch, entry of 22 June 1940.

2. By 2 September 1940, 1000 barges had been withdrawn from the inland waterway system (*World War II German Military Studies*, Vol. 8, Part IV, MS #C-0651, OKW Conference of 2 Sept. 1940).

3. There was a German amphibious component to *Weserübung* (the invasion of Norway), but it was of reduced scale and met with no appreciable opposition. Most of the assault force was ferried by JU-52 troop transport aircraft. The concept of 'air mobile' infantry was still in its infancy.

4. *Documents on German Foreign Policy, 1918–1945*, Series D, Vol. X, Document No. 177, p. 226, Führer Directive on the Preparation of a Landing Operation Against England.

5. Göring started as a military pilot with the legendary Rittmeister Manfred Frhr. von Richthofen in the First World War, eventually becoming the commander of JG1 after von Richthofen's death, and winning the coveted *Pour le Merite* for bravery in aerial combat. Despite this, he quickly lost the confidence of the Luftwaffe leadership, and continued to make a series of disastrous operational and technical decisions. The OKW staff conference note from 5 Sept. 1940 observes that 'The Reichsmarshall is not interested in the preparations for Operation Seelöwe as he does not believe the operation will ever take place.' For once, Göring happened to be right.

6. West, *MI5*, p. 130. Those targeted for arrest included 'No. 49 Churchill Winston Spencer, Minister Präsident, Westerham/Kent, Chartwell Manor.' A copy of this manual is on permanent display at the Imperial War Museum, London. The planned Luftwaffe air offensive was slightly delayed. Though scheduled to start on 8 August, it did not actually get airborne until 14 August. Even the name *Adlertag* proved to be malleable, it was successively used on several occasions during the Battle of Britain, each time intending to be the day on which the Luftwaffe blasted the Royal Air Force out of the skies.

7. *Documents on German Foreign Policy, 1918–1945*, Series D, Vol. X, pp. 390–1 – Führer Directive of 1 Aug. 1940.

8. Hitler's meetings with Sir Oswald Mosley and the Duke of Windsor probably contributed to his mis-assessment of the English character.

9. Ibid., p. 68, memorandum by State Secretary Ernst Frhr. von Weizsäcker, 30 June 1940.

10. Ibid., Document No. 73, 1 July 1940, report of the Führer Conference.

11. David Irving, *Hitler's War* (London: Hodder & Stoughton), p. 138. Though a creditable historian in most other respects, Irving has recently brought himself into professional, popular and legal disrepute for his revisionist views on the Holocaust and Hitler's role in it.

12. *Documents on German Foreign Policy*, Document No. 166, 13 July 1940. Hitler politely rejected Il Duce's offer of Italian troops for the English operation.

13. Ibid., note to Document No. 177, Führer Directive No. 16, 16 July 1940, p. 226. This quote is from the diary of the Chief of the Army General Staff, Generaloberst Franz Halder.

14. Ibid., p. 370. The memorandum of the conference is taken from General Halder's diary and includes the following note: 'Decision: In the course of this contest Russia must be disposed of. Spring '41. The quicker we smash Russia the better.' The order to increase the size of the German army to 180 divisions was issued by the OKW on 10 September 1941, after the course of action in Russia became the new priority.

15. Irving, *Hitler's War*, p. 158.

16. Jay Baird, *The Mythical World of Nazi War Propaganda, 1939–1945* (Minneapolis, MN: University of Minnesota Press), p. 133. Lale Andersen's version of 'Lili Marlene' would soon eclipse all of them and become perhaps the most famous song of any modern war, played in equal measure by Axis and Allied soldiers alike.

17. In a meeting at Kiel during the first week of July 1940, Canaris told the assembled officers that agents sent to England/Ireland were to be given only enough money to last for six to eight weeks. By that time the invasion would have occurred or not (PRO KV 2/170, Praetorius interview, 11 Oct. 1945).

18. There were a number of pre-war German publications on Ireland on political, cultural, and geographic subjects: *Irland im Schatten Englands: Ein Kapitel britischer Ausrottungspolitik* (Robert Bauer, Berlin 1940); *Irland und das Empire* (ZfGeopolitik, 14 Jg. 1937); *Die Insel der Heiligen: Eindrücke aus Irland* (v. Dewall, Frankfurt, 1934); *Irland – Die andere Insel* (Müller-Roß, Leipzig, 1939) and so on.

19. The plan itself seems to have been widely available. Details came to the attention of Irish officials as early as 1942. A more complete version was discovered by Allied troops in 1944, at the Institut Cartographique Militaire in Brussels, where the plan was printed. An additional set was discovered by a US soldier at Luftwaffe headquarters in Bavaria. Captain Joseph Healy of G2 translated the text (Colm Cox, 'Militär Geographische Angaben über Irland', *An Cosantoir*, March 1975, p. 83).

20. Ibid., p. 92.

21. Fisk, *In Time of War*, pp. 220–33. A copy of the plan is located at the Military Archives, Cathal Brugha Barracks, Dublin.

22. Dr Ludwig Mühlhausen was among the contributors. A pre-war scholar in the Gaeltacht, his photographs of Donegal (including some taken in Teelin where he stayed) were included. Dr Mahr, as an archaeologist, had easy access to detailed topographical maps of strategically important areas in Ireland. Dr Hans Hartmann thoughtfully contributed a photo of Bunbeg, a Donegal fishing village where he stayed in 1939. Pre-war photographer Joachim Gerstenberg is thought to have taken many of the photos. He spent the summer of 1939 in Ireland taking pictures, some of which were eventually published in *Eire, ein Irlandbuch* (Hamburg, 1940). It included photos of Lough Swilly, Cobh Harbour, Killary Harbour and Bantry Bay (O'Donoghue, *Hitler's Irish Voices*, p. 16).

23. Cox, 'Militär Geographische Angaben über Irland', p. 90. Oswald Müller-Dubrow, deputy head of the AO in Ireland, was a director of Siemens.

24. Ibid., p. 94.

25. *World War II German Military Studies*, Vol. 8, Part IV, MS#C-0651, p. 27, minutes of the OKW staff conference, 3 Sept. 1940.

26. PRO KV3/4, *History of the German Secret Service* (Curry), p. 116.

27. West, *MI5*, p. 129 and Stephan, 'Die Vergessene Episode', p. 194.

28. It might have operated under Abwehr orders, but was under the control of MI5, which had penetrated the organization before it could do any actual damage. It did carry out some notional attacks during the war to increase the Abwehr's perception that it was an active unit (West, *MI5*, pp. 214–225).

Lahousen, the Abwehr II chief, discounted the reports of success, but passed them on to the OKW (PRO KV 2/173, Special Interrogation Report, 15 July 1946, p. 3).

29. PRO KV3/4, p. 116.

30. LTC Hinchley-Cooke had been the star witness for the Crown at Görtz's trial for espionage in 1936.

31. PRO KV 3/4, p. 116.

32. West, *MI5*, p. 182.

33. Stephan, 'Die Vergessene Episode', p. 196. Neither Simon nor Ritter realized that the coded diary had been successfully broken and the names of contacts noted by MI5. One of these, a Mr Durrant of Westcliff, later turned himself in to British Intelligence (PRO KV 3/4, p. 116).

34. West, *MI5*, pp. 129–30.

35. Ibid., p. 131. Though they were specifically cited in the document as being the sources of information about MI5 and other top secret British organizations and personnel, after the war both men were allowed to retire with no formal charges being brought against them.

36. Many years earlier, Simon had an operation on his larynx which left him with a very distinctive, raspy voice.

37. In yet another of his alarmist and inaccurate reports from Dublin, German Minister Dr Hempel reported that Simon had arrived with a list of 2,400 contacts (USNA, A.A. Reel 89, Frame 100388, Document of 23 Sept. 1940).

38. PRO KV 2/170, undated MI5 memorandum to Irish G2.

39. Operations order of U-38, 5 June 1940, courtesy of Enno Stephan.

40. Stephan, 'Die Vergessene Episode', pp. 197–8, interviews with Walter Simon. As was the case with Görtz before him, the sight of a stranger asking such an inane question was not reported to the local Gardaí.

41. IMA G2/2468, summary.

42. Ibid., DMD report, 20 June 1940.

43. Ibid., DMD report, 27 June 1940.

44. Stephan, 'Die Vergessene Episode', p. 201.

45. IMA G2/2468, DMD summary, 8 July 1940. Carter (pp. 191–4) reported that Simon's radio had been located by the time of his trial. No mention of this appears in his file at the Military Archives and a DEA memorandum on Simon prepared in 1946 specifically states that 'he had no technical equipment or special papers in his possession: it is thought that he may have had some and have disposed of them after landing.' (NAI DFA A34 – memorandum of 26 Nov. 1946) However, his Abwehr controller was adamant that Simon had a radio/transmitter with him (PRO KV 2/170, Liddell to Moore, 21 Oct. 1945). It may yet await discovery under a Kerry beach, somewhere on the Dingle peninsula.

46. *Dublin Evening Mail*, 22 June 1940, p. 1.

47. Ibid., 8 July 1940, p. 2.

48. IMA G2/2468, 15 June 1940, Commandant Mackey, G2 Curragh, to Archer.

49. Ibid., Walter Simon to Elizabeth Simon, March 1941. His sister Elizabeth was his most faithful correspondent. She was a student counsellor and lived at Hohenstaufenring 157, Köln. In the Seán MacEntee papers, the amount of dollars is given as $1900.

50. Ibid., Immigration Branch to Home Office, 9 March 1940.
51. IMA G2/0207. The G2 file on Walter Simon is still listed under his alias of Karl Anderson.
52. Bundesarchiv-Berlin, Abteilung R, Preetz Nazi Party file.
53. Stephan, 'Die Vergessene Episode', p. 202.
54. Of the agents sent to Ireland, only Preetz was a member of the Nazi Party. Hermann Görtz was a former member, but had resigned in the 1930s. The general policy of not employing Nazis is illustrative of Canaris's attitude towards both the political movement and its leader.
55. This was because the Royal Navy blockaded the German ports, but the mail boat continued to operate between Dún Laoghaire and Holyhead.
56. IMA G2/0265, immigration form, 5 March 1939. Other sources reported that he left in April and that he returned in September by means unknown.
57. Ibid., statement of T.J. Reynolds, 15/16 March 1943; G2 passport report; G2 report of 11 Nov. 1940.
58. Ibid. Preetz's passport is kept at the Military Archives, Dublin.
59. Ibid., Preetz chronology; G2 Report of October 1939, which speculated that the reason for the 1939 visit was to see Annie Reynolds; NLI MS 22,984, Richard Hayes Papers, letter of 13 Nov. 1973; Carter, *The Shamrock and the Swastika*, p. 216. On Hayes's advice, Carter refrained from publishing this item in her book due to Irish libel law, which, unlike its American counterpart, did not hold the truth to be an absolute legal defence.
60. Ibid., NLI MS 22,984, Richard Hayes Papers, Hayes to Carter, 13 Nov. 1973.
61. IMA G2/0265, statement of Sante Staffieri, 28 Aug. 1940.
62. Ibid., Preetz to Donohue, 13 Dec. 1939.
63. Ibid., Preetz chronology.
64. Trevor Allen, *The Storm Passed By: Ireland and the Battle of the Atlantic, 1940–41* (Dublin: Irish Academic Press, 1996), p. 72.
65. It is possible that Preetz was transported in tandem with Simon and landed closer to 12/13 June and then spent the initial period hiding with his supportive and affectionate relatives in Tuam. This theory is indirectly confirmed by Dr Günther Gellermann following interviews with crewmembers of U-38 (Stephan to author, 19 May 2000).
66. G2 IMA/0265, CPT Togher to Archer, 7 Aug. 1940. Cf. Preetz chronology in the same file.
67. Antonio Forte owned Parnell's Café. He and his brother Orazio were pro-Fascist Italians. Orazio paid the bill for Preetz's stay at O'Brien's hotel in November 1939 (IMA G2/0265, Forte statement, Aug. 1940).
68. Ibid., G2 report, 13 Sept. 1940.
69. Ibid., statement of Bernard O'Shaughnessy, 7 July 1943.
70. Ibid., Preetz chronology.
71. Ibid., report of 3 Sept. 1940, Curragh medical file.
72. Ibid., statement of Sante Staffieri, 28 Aug. 1940.
73. Ibid., Kevin Gogan statement, 28 Aug. 1940.
74. Ibid., statement of Maureen O'Hanlon, 30 Aug. 1940.
75. Preetz operated on a frequency of 7.850 Megacycles during the day and 6.222 for night-time transmissions (Hayes to Archer, 4 Oct. 1940).
76. NLI MS 22, 983, Richard Hayes papers.

77. Ibid., Dr Hayes report of 14 Oct. 1940. 'This kind of cipher is not difficult to break ... because a few of the messages contained the letter 'q' in the word 'frequenz'. The fact that 'q' was present made it clear that unless it was a null it must form part of the sequence 'equen', as was in fact the case. Preetz made the foolish mistake of ending all his messages with the same word 'grüsse.'

78. PRO KV 3/4, p. 119.

79. IMA G2/0265, Hayes to Archer, 6 Sept. 1940.

80. Ibid., Hayes to Archer, 14 October 1940.

81. In a rather puzzling statement, Carolle Carter (*The Shamrock and the Swastika*, p. 190) wrote 'Preetz, still insisting he was an Irishman named Paddy Mitchell, admitted to sending messages to Germany but denied being a German agent. One day while questioned, he made the mistake of literally translating the German idiom *"mit zusammen"* as "with together".' This makes no sense linguistically or factually. *mit zusammen* is *not* an idiom (more like an ungrammatical sentence fragment). Secondly, according to the contemporary arrest reports, Preetz admitted his true name to the arresting officers in front of Westland Row, and did not even wait for a proper interrogation.

82. IMA G2/0265, report of 14 Oct. 1940, Hayes to Archer.

83. Ibid., report of 11 Nov. 1940.

84. Ibid., G2 summary, 23 March 1944. Donohue's sister lived at Knocknacarra, Salthill, Co. Galway and he had a girlfriend, Rita McDowell, who lived at 26 Adelaide Road. Both remained under postal surveillance orders for some time due to the connection with Donohue.

85. Ibid, Boland to Archer, 6 Sept. 1940. Though Italian nationals were involved on a local level, there is no evidence of overt espionage activity.

86. IMA G2/4330, According to the file description, Arcari was '45 years of age, 5′ 5″ and Jewish looking'.

87. NAI DFA A60, Bryan to Cecil Liddell, 23 Sept. 1943. 'Arcari, Staiano, Jaconelli travelling Belfast 9 a.m. train tomorrow. Being escorted to Goraghwood for handing over.'

88. IMA G2/X/1091, memorandum, 27 April 1943.

89. O'Halpin, *Defending Ireland*, p. 240.

90. Brown, *Bodyguard of Lies*, p. 209 and Ladislas Farago, *Game of the Foxes* (New York: David McKay, 1971), pp. 223–4. A high proportion of the agents were non-German nationals, the majority being Dutch who had pre-war Nazi ties.

91. PRO KV 2/173, Lahousen Special Interrogation Report.

92. IMA G2/X/0345, report of Maj. J.P. O'Connell, Southern Command G2, to Archer, 17 July 1940.

93. Stephan, 'Die Vergessene Episode', p. 215.

94. IMA G2/X/0345, G2 memorandum of Sept. 1945

95. Gärtner telephone interview, 15 Jan. 2000.

96. IMA G2/X/0203, Bryan to Frederick Boland, June 1946.

97. IMA G2/0345, Obéd statement.

98. G2/X/0345, Obéd interrogation of 20/21 May 1943 and letter of February 1948 from Obéd to Pandit Nehru. In the letter to Nehru, Obéd understandably puts a different spin on his difficulties with the British,

claiming that the root of the problem was not gun-running, but that a certain Englishman had 'used language highly derogatory to the sanctity and greatness of Mahatama Ji [Gandhi]. I strongly resented these remarks and we came to blows. Anderson [the Englishman] was highly connected and a Freemason. He was responsible for my reputation as anti-British among British officials.'

99. Enno Stephan, *Geheimauftrag Irland* (Hamburg: Gerhard Stalling Verlag, 1961), p. 154. Obéd was supposed to smuggle the grenades onto a British ship. Obéd is alleged to have used the aliases Ahid and Muhammed Hussain (PRO KV 2/173, Lahousen Special Interrogation Report, p. 10).

100. Abwehr II Kriegstagebuch, 22 June 1940.

101. IMA G2/X/0345, Obéd statement, 9 July 1940.

102. Sardar Bahadar Khan lived in Dublin in 1936–7. While in Dublin, he dated the daughter of his landlady at 3 Mountjoy Place, but left for England in early 1939. Khan returned briefly to Ireland in 1940 to see Miss Meany. He held an Irish pedlar's certificate from August 1937 and sold drapery goods on a circuit through Ireland. His connection with Obéd, and possibly with espionage, is unknown (IMA G2/X/0345, Detective Branch report of 8 July 1940).

103. Inexplicably, Nissen later told Enno Stephan that he rowed the men ashore and returned with the launch. This is puzzling, since the *Soizic*'s boat was found at the scene (Stephan, 'Die Vergessene Episode', p. 217). In a postwar letter from the Irish consulate in Hamburg, Nissen is said to have joined the American consular service after the war and stated that he wanted to live in Ireland. In the same conversation, Nissen mentioned that he 'had occasion to ferry over to Ireland from a French port some members of the IRA. The ferrying was done in a motor-sailboat and Herr Nissen accompanied the group.' Nissen is presumably talking about Tributh, Gärtner and Obéd. (IMA G2/X/0093, Consul General to Secretary, External Affairs, 26 March 1963).

104. Gärtner says that they were not equipped with a transmitter (Gärtner interview, 15 Jan. 2000). He also makes the point that the Abwehr did not properly prepare them for the mission or tell them what to expect.

105. IMA G2/X/0345, report of Garda Superintendent James O'Gara, Skibbereen, 9 July 1940. The young Irishman first contacted by the spies has his name alternatively spelled as 'Geany' and 'Greany'. In his otherwise excellent book *In Time of War*, Robert Fisk, erroneously notes (p. 374–5) that 'Obéd had blessed his mission by setting off along the coast road in County Cork dressed in a bright silk Indian suit and a straw hat'. Photographs taken immediately upon capture and witness statements show that Obéd was wearing a conventional double-breasted suit and had earlier been wearing a 'white hat'. Fisk, citing Carter, goes on to say that the Gardaí advised G2 that 'two whites and a nigger have appeared from nowhere'. This too, is questionable. Since Carter was again quoting her ubiquitous 'Confidential Government Source' – Colonel Bryan – who has since died, there is no way of confirming what Col. Bryan did or did not say. The G2 files, which preserve every report filed on the case, have nothing like this.

106. IMA G2/X/0345.

107. IMA G2/X/0345, G2 memorandum, Sept. 1945. The addition is a little suspect – the individual totals add up to £820, not the stated figure of £829.

108. Irish Intelligence thought this might refer to a Frederick Kern, aged 37, a commercial traveller for a Viennese firm. Kern had stayed at the Victoria Hotel, Patrick Street, Cork. This apparently proved to be a wild-goose chase and there are no further notes concerning Frederick Kern (IMA G2/X/006).

109. It was (and is) standard practice for all identifying material to be removed before the start of the mission. The Abwehr supervisors seem to have dropped the ball in this instance.

110. IMA G2/0345, G2 report of 12 July 1940.

111. Ibid., unsigned memorandum of 9 July 1940.

112. Abwehr II Kriegstagebuch, 18 July 1940.

113. IMA G2/X/0345, Tributh interview, 11 July 1940.

114. West, *MI5*, p. 232. Unknown to the Abwehr, Owens was a double-cross agent.

115. NAI, S/12013 and Carter, *The Shamrock and the Swastika*, p. 197.

116. A contemporary Cork diarist, Liam de Roíste, mentioned the popular gossip that five men had landed by submarine. He also accurately summed up the Lobster I mission to Ireland: 'Unless the Germans are entirely misinformed as to the position in Éire and expect that everyone in Éire is a friend, this haphazard landing of small groups of men appears silly and not in line with German efficiency and clever planning.' (Cork Archives Institute, Liam de Roiste Papers, U 271, p. 38, entry of 10 July 1940)

117. Ryan was the subject of a sentimental television documentary by Joe Mulholland on RTE in 1979, 'Let My Tombstone be of Granite', and only one author (Sean Cronin) has so far attempted to put Ryan into a realistic, historical perspective. Bell (*The Secret Army*, p. 197) speaks of 'Ryan's continuing anti-Nazi stand during his German exile' – a misleading statement that is explored later in this thesis.

118. According to Tim Pat Coogan (*Eamon De Valera*, p. 617), the legal defence fund was authorized by de Valera. Coogan goes on to say that de Valera also cooperated in Kerney's contacts with the Red Cross and 'other bodies' in securing Ryan's 'escape' from prison and subsequent release to Germany. There is no indication that de Valera knew anything about Kerney's German connections until at least 1941.

119. Sean Cronin, *Frank Ryan: The Search for the Republic* (Dublin: Respol, 1980), p. 161. As mentioned earlier, there was a connection between Champourcin and James O'Donovan via a Breton national named Leon Mill-Arden.

120. There was no shortage of people taking credit for the idea to free Ryan. Other than Kerney and Clissmann, the honour was claimed by Seán Russell, Stephen Held, Jupp Hoven, and Hermann Görtz. Carter stated that 'The Abwehr decided to aid in Ryan's release when Jupp Hoven, its former agent/anthropologist in Ireland, and Russell requested it.' (Carter, *The Shamrock and the Swastika*, p. 114, fn. 12) The 'Frank Ryan Release Committee' in Ireland, operated out of the suspect address of 29 Gardner Place, included such luminaries as Maud Gonne McBride, Mrs Austin Stack and Mrs Aileen Walsh, all connected to various German initiatives.

121. Both Clissmann and his wife knew Ryan before the war, though they might have had quite different political agendas. Mrs Elizabeth Clissmann (née

Mulcahy) was from an old Sligo Republican family and knew Ryan from their common connection to the old IRA.

122. Blaum had a colourful career as far as Irish matters were concerned; he selected Irishwoman Mary Mains to act as a courier to Hermann Görtz in Ireland.

123. Abwehr II Kriegstagebuch, 12 July 1940.

124. Stephan, 'Die Vergessene Episode', pp. 230–1. This was not the last time that Toepfer and Haller worked together. In post-war Germany, Toepfer established a multi-million dollar import/export business and was a recognized philanthropist. Haller became the in-house counsel for the Toepfer organization (Interview with Elizabeth Clissmann, 15 Feb. 1999 and Stephan to author, 25 June 1999).

125. IMA G2/0257, 'Memorandum on Frank Ryan,' 20 Oct. 1941. This memorandum was passed along to Secretary of the Department of External Affairs, Joseph Walshe. While in Madrid, Healy had an interview with Sir Samuel Hoare, the British Minister to Spain (Mrs Jean Healy to author, 27 Jan. 2000).

126. IMA G2/0257, Ibid.

127. Seán Cronin, *The McGarrity Papers* (Dublin: Anvil, 1972), p. 171.

128. PRO DO 35/894, XII/342, Palmer to Leach, 27 July 1939.

129. According to Bell (*The Secret Army*, p. 159), Russell was detained 'for making false statements on entering the country'. Bell also states that 'the Army Council agreed that Russell, exhausted by the intensive activities of the past year, could best serve the IRA in America for the next several months. There was little dissent – the IRA needed the American money too badly.'

130. Carter, *The Shamrock and the Swastika*, p. 112. McGarrity died in August 1940.

131. Rekowski was based in Mexico City and was responsible for contacts between the IRA support groups in the United States and German Intelligence. He also had contact with 'irischen Saboteuren in Kanada' (Irish saboteurs in Canada) – actually IRA personnel in the US who might be used for such tasks. He was originally a businessman who was trapped in Germany on the outbreak of war; Abwehr II generously volunteered to finance his return in exchange for certain assistance (Stephan, 'Die Vergessene Episode', pp. 188–90). According to Haller, Rekowski's reports from the US and Mexico were 'almost too good'. The Abwehr had good reason to suspect that the successful operations he claimed against British ships were imaginary and that he had misappropriated money intended for the IRA in America. Despite this, he returned to Germany in 1941 and was made the Foreign Ministry liaison officer to the 'Arabian Bureau'. In 1944, Dr Veesenmayer took him as consul and personnel officer to the German Embassy in Hungary. Rekowski spent almost no time in post-war US captivity and moved up as an economic official to the US occupation forces. He later moved to Venezuela as a machine importer (Stephan, 'Die Vergessene Episode', p. 291).

132. Stephan, 'Die Vergessene Episode', pp. 289–92. Duggan was seemingly fixated on the idea that McCarthy and Russell were the same person, stemming from

an offhand suggestion by Dr Hempel. (Duggan, D.Litt. thesis, p. 422 and *Neutral Ireland and the Third Reich*, p. 152).

133. Stephan, 'Die Vergessene Episode' p. 291.
134. *Documents on German Foreign Policy*, Series D, Vol. XXI, No. 562, Telegram of 24 Jan. 24, 1940, 91/100144.
135. Ibid., p. 761, Document No. 605, Woermann Memorandum, 10 Feb. 1940, 91/100155-56.
136. *Dolmetscher* means 'interpreter' (Abwehr II Kriegstagebuch, 19 May 1940).
137. Lahousen reported 'the latter was a failure. There were no IRA sympathizers among the visiting Irish priests' (PRO KV 2/173, Lahousen Special Interrogation Report).
138. Colman O'Donovan, despite his familial connection to the IRA, was a member of the Irish diplomatic service assigned to the Vatican and was later appointed as wartime Minister to Portugal. Lahousen later stated that 'the brother of Jim O'Donovan had formerly been attached to the Irish Embassy in Berlin and Fromme knew him socially (PRO KV 2/173, Lahousen Special Interrogation Report).
139. Abwehr Kriegstagebuch, 21 March 1940.
140. Bundesarchiv – Berlin, Abteilung R, Veesenmayer Nazi Party file. The Allgemeine-SS, as distinct from the Waffen-SS, was the branch of the Nazi party originally recruited for Hitler's personal security detail. The SS expanded in March 1939, when the SS-VT Verfügungstruppe – active duty units – together with the SS Totenkopfverbände (death's head units) – concentration camp guards – merged together to form the Waffen SS. The Waffen-SS ('Armed SS') were more or less recruited for military service and by war's end had over thirty divisions under arms, including many composed almost exclusively of ethnic nationalities friendly to the German cause. The Waffen-SS units generally fought well, with a well-deserved reputation for fanatical resistance and high morale. However, their military reputation was compromised by involvement in a multitude of war crimes, leading the Nürnberg Trial judges to declare it a 'criminal organization'.
141. Veesenmayer file, USNA A3343-SSO-203-B and Bundesarchiv, Abteilung R, Berlin (Nazi Party File No. 873,780). Cf. Letter from Mr Aaron Kornblum, US National Holocaust Memorial Museum, 6 May 1999. Dr Wilhelm Keppler was officially listed as the 'State Secretary for Special Duties.' (*Documents on German Foreign Policy*, Series D, Vol. X, p. 68).
142. Stephan, 'Die Vergessene Episode', p. 146.
143. USNA, A3343-SSO-203 B.
144. O'Donoghue, *Hitler's Irish Voices*, p. 56. Veesenmayer testified for the defence at the 1961 trial of Adolf Eichmann, concerning Eichmann's activities in Hungary in 1944. Veesenmayer was then the German Minister to Hungary.
145. Stephan, 'Die Vergessene Episode', p. 146, interview with Kurt Haller.
146. *Documents on German Foreign Policy*, p. 37, No. 18, Woermann Memorandum of 28 March 1940, 91/1001-77/1.
147. Abwehr II Kriegstagebuch, 30 March 1940.

148. Abwehr II Kriegstagebuch, March 1940. In this entry, Fromme is described as a *Mitarbeiter* – an associate of the Abwehr.

149. Stephan, 'Die Vergessene Episode' (p. 222) refers to Fromme as 'der kauzige Professor'. A good description; *Kauz* means both 'oddball' and 'a small owl'.

150. Abwehr II Kriegstagebuch, 3 May 1940. Russell was assigned an Austrian NCO named Planer, who acted as his chaperone, bodyguard and adjutant (Stephan, 'Die Vergessene Episode', p. 158). Helmut Clissmann recalled that Russell's house was formerly the home of a bank director in the suburb of Grunewald.

151. Duggan, D.Litt. thesis, Appendix XXIV, p. 422. In fact, though he held himself out to be both 'professor' and 'doctor', Fromme was neither (Stephan, 'Die Vergessene Episode', p. 5).

152. PRO KV 2/173, Lahousen Special Interrogation Report.

153. Ibid., pp. 2–3.

154. Stephan, 'Die Vergessene Episode', p. 159, interview with Kurt Haller. It is interesting to speculate that many of Görtz's errors might have been avoided had he met with Russell. Though he spent some three months prior to departure preparing for his mission, Görtz was singularly ignorant about many aspects of the political and military situation in Ireland.

155. Abwehr Kriegstagebuch, entry of 20 May 1940.

156. Duggan, D.Litt. thesis, Appendix XXIV, p. 422, 1977 interview with Dr Veesenmayer.

157. Stephan, 'Die Vergessene Episode', p. 223, cites Dr Paul Leverkuehn, *Der geheime Nachrichtendienst der deutschen Wehrmacht im Kriege*. Leverkuehn was formerly the Abwehr KO chief in Turkey.

158. Ibid., pp. 223–4, interviews with Haller, Clissmann and Hoven and IMA G2/ 0089, report of 15 Aug. 1939.

159. Carter, *The Shamrock and the Swastika*, p. 124. The original idea was to find 200 Irish nationals to make up an 'Irish Guard'.

160. 'German Spies in Ireland', *Irish Times*, 7 June 1958. This was a serialized version of the book *They Spied on England* by Charles Wighton and Günther Peis (Odhams, 1958). It was promoted as being based on the recollections of Generalmajor von Lahousen, who died in 1955. Both the serialized version and the book include material that at times is grossly inaccurate, as well as things which are verifiable by other sources. At one point, it is stated that Russell was 'buried at sea with full military honours, his body being wrapped in the flag of the Irish Free State.' Nicely melodramatic, but it stretches credibility to imagine a covert, operational mission to Ireland coincidentally being equipped with an Irish flag. Dr Richard Hayes wrote an anonymous review of the book in the *Evening Press* (11 July 1958) which lists his doubts about several points. Cf. NLI MS 22,984, Richard Hayes papers, Letter to the Bibliothek für Zeitgeschichte, Stuttgart.

161. PRO KV 2/173, Lahousen Special Interrogation Report. According to Helmut Clissmann, one of the radio operators was to be a corporal named Bruno Rieger (Stephan, 'Die Vergessene Episode', p. 225). Rieger later accompanied Clissmann on another mission intended for Ireland.

162. Abwehr II Kriegstagebuch, 25 May 1940.

163. Ibid., 25 May 1940. It should be noted that between the entries of 23 and 25 May, the plan had changed. In the later entry, there was no mention of sending a radio operator, only a transmitter.
164. Stephan, 'Die Vergessene Episode', p. 226.
165. According to Carter (*The Shamrock and the Swastika*, p. 114), 'Soon after he arrived in Germany, Russell asked the Germans if they could arrange the release of Frank Ryan, an IRA associate, from a Spanish prison.' German involvement direct and indirect, in the Ryan affair probably predates Russell's arrival in Germany, but it was intensified at Veesenmayer's suggestion that Ryan and Russell could be used in a single operation. Cf. Keogh, *Ireland and Europe*, pp. 149–55.
166. Abwehr II Kriegstagebuch, 13 and 18 July 1940.
167. This entry followed a meeting on 4 August between Foreign Minister von Ribbentrop, Admiral Canaris, Oberst von Lahousen, Dr Veesenmayer and Russell. Haller later said that following the meeting, Ribbentrop (who had no regard for the Irish) expressed doubt as to whether Russell was *echt* (genuine). (Stephan, 'Die Vergessene Episode', p. 233). Canaris was said to have contemptuously referred to Russell as the 'music professor' (PRO KV 2/173, Lahousen Special Interrogation Report, p. 9).
168. Abwehr Kriegstagebuch, 3 August 1940. It is not beyond the bounds of possibility that the Abwehr diary entries might not tell the whole truth, as Lahousen indicated to Allied interrogators, or at least might represent a garbled version of it as regards to Russell's actual function. In any event, Hempel promptly decided to distance himself from any attendant danger; he planned to place the plant box in the embassy window permanently, so as to avoid any suggestion that he had actually signalled to Russell to do anything which might prove embarrassing (USNA, A.A. Reel 89, frame 100334, Document of 15 Aug. 1940). As Duggan observed, 'whether these putative schemes embraced a link up with the *Operation Grün* bridgehead landing in the Wexford area or not can only – as far as present documentation goes – be a matter for speculation' (Duggan, *Neutral Ireland and the Third Reich*, pp. 153–4).
169. Duggan, D.Litt. thesis, Appendix XXIV, p. 422.
170. Haller said later that one earlier idea was that Ryan be sent to the United States where he could spread anti-British propaganda with the help of American 'Reds.' (Stephan, 'Die Vergessene Episode', p. 229). Though both Ryan and Russell were IRA veterans, Ryan's leftist philosophy was anathema to Russell and most of the mainstream IRA movement.
171. Abwehr II Kriegstagebuch, 4 August, 6 August and 8 August 1941. By a linguistic irony, the mission designation (*Taube* – dove or pigeon) has a secondary meaning in German. *Der Taube* means deaf person. By the time he set out on this mission, Frank Ryan was significantly deaf. His deafness was noticeable in Ireland and worsened in Burgos prison.
172. Trevor Allen, *The Storm Passed By*, p. 73, cites 1/Skl diary entry of 14 August 1940, USNA, T1022, PG 32032.
173. Abwehr II Kriegstagebuch, 15 Aug. 1940.
174. Stephan, 'Die Vergessene Episode', p. 235 and Carter, *The Shamrock and the Swastika*, p. 115.
175. Ibid.

176. This determination was reached after consulting with the medic on U-65, Ryan, and two experts from the Berlin Charité hospital. Russell's brother Patrick confirmed after the war that he suffered from pre-existing stomach problems and, as a consequence, did not drink alcohol (Stephan, 'Die Vergessene Episode', p. 236).

177. Carter, *The Shamrock and the Swastika*, p. 118.

178. Allen, p. 73 and Jak P. Mallmann Showell, *U-Boat Commanders and Crews, 1935–1945* (Wiltshire: Crowood Press, 1998), p. 92.

179. *Irish Times*, 7 Sept. 1947. In his celebrated 'confession,' Stephen Hayes also circulated this similar version of Russell's demise: 'About July when I met Dr Ryan again he informed me that Russell had been taken off an Italian cargo boat about April and was being detained at Gibraltar. No one knew him there except the British Secret Service who had detained him at the request of the Free State Government. ... In September Dr Ryan informed me that Russell was dead as a result of an 'accident' at Gibraltar and that he was buried at sea.' (IMA G2/1722, Hayes statement of 10 Sept. 1941).

180. PRO KV 2/173, Lahousen Statement, 17 Dec. 1945, p. 13.

181. *Sunday Dispatch*, 31 Aug. 1952, p. 9 and MacEoin, *The IRA in the Twilight Years*, p. 930.

182. IMA G2/3010. Most of the erroneous information was relayed by the Eastern Command G2, Commandant Daly. Irish Friends of Germany leader Maurice O'Connor provided the information about Russell being parachuted into County Kildare.

183. Carter, *The Shamrock and the Swastika*, pp. 118–19.

184. IMA G2/0257, Ryan to Kerney, 6 Dec. 1941. Ryan's letters to the Irish Minister were only turned over to the Department of External Affairs in February 1945.

185. IMA G2/X/0093, Walsh to Bryan, 16 Jan. 1946. This was first disclosed by Stephen Hayes in a statement following his 1941 sentencing by an Irish court. Bryan noted that 'MacBride, who up to a certain date was closely involved in German activities, has never been questioned about this matter'.

186. West, *MI5*, pp. 309–16 and Brown, *???*, p. 209.

187. Stephan, *Spies in Ireland*, p. 143–59.

188. PRO KV 2/173, Lahousen Special Interrogation, p. 10; Militärarchiv, Abwehr Kriegstagebuch, entry for 11 Nov. 1940; Stephan, *Spies in Ireland*, p. 159.

189. *WWII German Military Studies*, Vol. 8, Part IV, minutes of OKW daily conference of 2 Sept. 1940.

190. Irving, *Hitler's War*, p. 158. This was almost certainly what Hitler had in mind all along, but after the Abwehr report and the Luftwaffe failure, there was no further sense in wasting valuable OKW manpower working on Sealion, when it could be more gainfully employed planning Barbarossa. The warning order for the Russian operation was issued on 18 December 1940 (Baird, *The Mythical World of Nazi War Propaganda*, p. 136, fn. 61).

191. In an ambiguous reference, Lahousen mentioned that an officer named Hollmann, apparently connected to the Brandenburg, had planned 'daredevil stunts in connection with the invasion of England'. This officer was described as a 'fanatical Nazi' and was disciplined accordingly (PRO KV 2/173, Special Interrogation Report, p. 3).

192. Duggan, D.Litt. thesis, Appendix XXIV, p. 423. Veesenmayer promised to show some derogatory material on Canaris to Duggan at a later date, but died before this could be accomplished.
193. OKW I Kriegstagebuch, entry of 27 Nov. 1940.
194. Dickel, *Die deutsche Außenpolitik und die irische Frage* p. 144, citing 1/Skl Kr. Tb., Part A, entry of 27 Nov. 1940.
195. *Documents on German Foreign Policy, 1918–1945*, Series D, Vol. XI, p. 727. Document of 3 Dec. 1940. Luftwaffe General Kurt Student, the commander of the Luftwaffe's XI Airborne Corps, proposed a diversionary landing in Northern Ireland in conjunction with a landing on the southern coast of England. Student, who planned the great German airborne actions in Holland and Crete, also envisioned dropping hundreds of *Gummipuppen* – rubber dolls – as a decoy away from the actual landing sites. Allied leaders would later use this tactic themselves in the Normandy drops. According to Student, Hitler stated: 'Eire's neutrality must be respected. A neutral Irish Free State is of greater value to us than a hostile Ireland. We must be glad that Ireland has remained neutral up to the present. But we could not avoid trespassing on a small scale, through units losing their way by emergency landings at night, by dropping in the wrong areas.' (*Irish Independent*, 25 and 26 April 1949 and B. Liddell Hart (ed.), *The Other Side of the Hill: Germany's Generals, Their Rise and Fall, With their own Account of Military Events, 1939–1945* (London: Cassel, 1948), pp. 229–30).
196. USNA, OKW/WPr., T-77, Roll 972, Frame 4458932.
197. Görtz report to G2, p. 15.
198. IMA G2/1722, statement of Leon Redmond, 6 Oct. 1941.
199. IMA G2/3261. Cahill was one of Oscar Pfaus's contacts in 1939.
200. IMA G2/3261, Michael Kinsella statement, 2 Dec. 1943. Liam Redmond, the actor, and his wife Barbara later occupied the house on Shanid Road where another Görtz transmitter was located in late 1941/early 1942 (G2 report, 11 Dec. 1943).
201. IMA G2/1722, summary of Görtz's report – with annotations – and MacEoin, *The IRA in the Twilight Years*, pp. 544, 927. Görtz apparently envisioned setting up two separate wireless stations, one as a transmitter and receiver, and the other as a pure receiver.
202. G2/1722, 'Illicit contacts and communication between Spain and Ireland, 1946'.
203. Lahousen (PRO 2/173, Special Interrogation Report, 15 July 1946, p. 10) noted that Mains met with O'Donovan and that she 'must have notified Blum in Spain of her arrival by a pre-arranged code'.
204. NA DFA A51, M.P. Mains file.
205. Stephan, 'Die Vergessene Episode', p. 265, interviews with Elizabeth and Helmut Clissmann. This scenario is unlikely. Kerney could cable messages to Ireland and could also send the diplomatic bag aboard the flying boats from Lisbon to Foynes, County Limerick. A contemporary G2 report stated that she was indeed carrying a letter for the Department of External Affairs from Kerney: a request that the DEA expedite her return to Spain (IMA G2/1722, 'Illicit contacts and communication between Spain and Ireland').
206. Abwehr II Kriegstagebuch, 14 Jan. 1941.

207. IMA G2/0093, Boland to Bryan, 29 March 1946. Also against Bryan's wishes, Francis Stuart and Stephen Held were granted passports in 1946 (IMA G2/0077, External Affairs to Bryan, 10 Oct. 1946).
208. Görtz report, p. 22.
209. *Documents on German Foreign Policy*, Vol. VIII, p. 602, document No. 473, Hempel to Foreign Ministry, 17 June 1940. 'I carried out the instructions with Walshe today. The conversation, in which Walshe expressed great admiration for the German achievements, went off in a friendly way. ... [Walshe] remarked that he hoped that the statement of the Führer in his interview with Wiegand respecting the absence of intention to destroy the British Empire, did not mean the abandonment of Ireland.' Curiously, at the same time, de Valera was giving the English mixed signals over the partition issue. According to a memorandum about a meeting between the British Minister for Health, Mr McDonald, and de Valera, the Taoiseach said that if Ireland received an English 'declaration of a united Ireland in principle' and also an agreement on its constitution, 'then the Government of Eire *might* agree to enter the war at once'. McDonald stressed that de Valera conditioned the 'might' in such a way as to guarantee nothing (PRO CAB 104/184, McDonald Memo).
210. Byrne was a Fianna Fáil TD from Wicklow, elected to the Dáil four times, lastly in 1943 (Seán Donnelly, *Elections '97* [Dublin: Brunswick Press, 1998], p. 466). Colonel Bryan later stated the correct identification was Christy Burr, Fianna Fáil TD from Wicklow ('Dan Bryan Memoirs', p. 35, courtesy of Professor Eunan O'Halpin). However, there was never a TD by the name of Burr (Donnelly, *Elections '97*, p. 466).
211. Duggan, *Neutral Ireland and the Third Reich*, p. 218.
212. As early as November 1940, the OKW had requested that 'an official or officer experienced in military reconnaissance' be sent to Dublin. The Irish government refused Hempel's request to augment his staff with such personnel. (*Documents on German Foreign Policy*, Series D, Vol. XI, pp. 572–3, Ritter Memorandum of 14 Nov. 1940).
213. Duggan, *Neutral Ireland and the Third Reich*, pp. 213–15.
214. Stephan, 'Die Vergessene Episode', p. 261. The Gardaí were slightly less complimentary. They referred to O'Mahony as 'the tall girl with the prominent teeth' (IMA G2/1722 – Detective Branch, Special Section report, 23 Oct. 1941). Görtz's romance with O'Mahony is documented by Hayes (*The People*, 18 Nov. 1967), and in several letters in Görtz's own hand in the Richard Hayes papers.
215. Michael Mac Evilly, unpublished manuscript on Dr Andrew Cooney, p. 252. Maisie O'Mahony's mother also had an interesting encounter with the law. She sued the Irish and German governments for bomb damage to her guest house, only to have the suit dismissed when it was discovered that the damage was pre-existing (IMA G2/3997).
216. IMA G2/2016, Dr A. Cooney file.
217. IMA G2/X/0058, IRA General file, 1939–1943.
218. In a separate list, G2 identified four 'possible Quislings': Eoin O'Duffy, Liam Walsh, Cecil Lavery, and Ernest Blythe (a former Minister for Trade and

Commerce, and later Minister for Finance) – all persons related to the Blueshirt movement (IMA G2/X/1091, PM1, 1941).
219. IMA G2/3997, O'Mahony file. In December 1945, she brought a suit against the Hospitals Commission for wrongful termination and asked for payment of her salary from the time of her arrest until 28 Oct. 1942. The case was dismissed with costs.

CHAPTER 6

1. NLI, James O'Donovan papers, letter of 29 Aug. 1940. 'Mr T' could refer to the Taoiseach (de Valera), or more likely German Legation Counsellor Henning Thomsen.
2. Duggan, D.Litt. thesis, p. 376, Telegram No. 502, 23 Aug. 1940.
3. IMA G2/1722, Görtz report, p. 23.
4. Abwehr II Kriegstagebuch, 29 and 30 Sept. 1940.
5. IMA G2/1722, Görtz report, p. 24.
6. *Irish Times*, 5 Sept. 1947. Görtz also wrote: 'I know that thousands are willing to die for Ireland, but very few dare to think bold.' (IMA G2/1722, Görtz to Mrs Stuart, undated.)
7. NLI, O'Donovan papers, two letters of February 1941, addressed to 'Dear Friends'.
8. IMA G2/3364, Helena Moloney file.
9. IMA G2/1722, Görtz report, p. 25.
10. Ibid.
11. IRA man John 'Machine Gun' Connor was arrested with Crofton. Crofton received a five-year sentence for his participation (MacEoin, *The IRA in the Twilight Years*, p. 685). The tip-off on Crofton apparently came from a SIS (Supplemental Intelligence Service) source in the Army's Southern Command (IMA G2/X/0363). Crofton was reportedly carrying the final £50 instalment for the boat purchase when he was arrested. According to the same source, the plan was to pick up Görtz from a smaller boat along the Kerry coast, so as not to draw attention to his presence in Fenit (Oliver Murphy, unpublished MS on Stephen Hayes, p. 23).
12. *Irish Times*, 8 Sept. 1947.
13. Abwehr II Kriegstagebuch., 4 and 6 March 1941. Hempel did continue to send messages, but they typically concerned with Görtz's various escape plans, not situational reports.
14. PRO KV 2/170–171.
15. Stephan, 'Die Vergessene Episode', pp. 299–300 and PRO 2/170, Schütz memorandum, 19 Oct. 1945. Remy & Co. was later to have another Abwehr connection. The managing partner's nephew, Rudolf Muntz, was a volunteer spy for the Hamburg Ast (PRO KV 2/103).
16. IMA G2/X/020, Schütz interview, 11 April 1946 and PRO KV 2/170. Habericter (a.k.a. Richter) was a civilian attached to I/Wi and described as 'looks a little filmstarish of Adolphe Menjou style' (PRO KV 2/170, Schütz memo, 19 Oct. 1945).

17. The name of Schütz's contact is given as 'Eibner' by Dr Praetorius (PRO KV 2/170, memorandum of 11 Oct. 1945), but is deliberately excised in the contemporary documents connected to MI5's Double Cross programme (PRO KV 4/5). The 'Pierce' identification is in West, *MI5*, pp. 220–1.
18. West, *MI5*, pp. 221–4.
19. Despite his work for Abwehr, for official (and pay) purposes, he remained attached to the 22nd Artillery Regiment – Hamburg (Bundesarchiv-Aachen, Zentralnachweissstelle, Schütz file).
20. PRO KV 2/170, undated memo to Irish G2.
21. PRO KV 2/87, Ritter interview, 20 July 1945.
22. IMA G2/X/0203, Schütz's microdot instructions as contained in the 'Aspro' newspaper cuttings.
23. PRO KV 2/170, undated MI5 memo to Irish G2.
24. Ibid., Schütz to Department of External Affairs, 8 April 1946.
25. Stephan, 'Die Vergessene Episode', pp. 301–2.
26. The original passport is in the Schütz file, IMA G2/X/0203. It reflects that Marschner was a 'pharmaceutical chemist student' (the word 'chemist' is lined through), born at Schweidnitz (Germany) on 16 June 1912, domiciled at Ludevitz, Union of South Africa. Schütz's photograph has what appear to be two genuine raised cancellation stamps.
27. IMA G2/X/0203, Schütz's microdot instructions.
28. Ibid., Schütz interrogation report, 1 and 2 April 1941.
29. Ibid., Schütz inventory.
30. Günther Schütz 'My Secret Mission to Ireland', *Sunday Press*, 31 May 1970, p. 18.
31. IMA G2/X/0203, Schütz's microdot instructions.
32. IMA G2/0402, Ernstberger file.
33. IMA G2/X/0203, Bryan to Gerald Boland, 28 May 1946.
34. Ibid., Schütz's microdot instructions.
35. PRO KV 2/170, undated memo to Irish G2.
36. Ibid., letter of 8 April 1946.
37. In 1937 Ludwig Mülhausen roomed with León Ó Broin (later the Secretary of the Department of Posts and Telegraphs, as well as a historian) in Teelin, County Galway, though the similarity in names could be merely coincidental (Ó Broin, *Just Like Yesterday, An Autobiography*, p. 132). As noted, Mülhausen was previously charged with helping Schütz obtain his visa for Ireland.
38. Ibid. Report of 1–2 April 1941 to CSO, G2 on Schütz interrogation. Cf. IMA G2/0289.
39. Ibid.
40. Ibid. Schütz interview, 11 April 1946. According to Carter (*The Shamrock and the Swastika*, p. 204) Schütz was also given the names of O'Duffy, Liam Walsh and Walter Simon. This is difficult to credit. Simon had been in jail for over a year, a fact well known to the Abwehr. Carter did, however, interview Schütz, and it is possible that his story improved with age. It certainly did as to other aspects of his testimony (unpublished interview with Schütz, 6 Sept. 1990, courtesy of David O'Donoghue). In this interview, Schütz maintained that the Abwehr should have told him that Görtz had already been arrested and that he (Schütz) did not land with a radio receiver. Neither statement is correct, but

more probably due to failing memory about events fifty years before than from any attempt to deceive.

41. Stephan, *Die Deutsche Keltologie und ihre Berliner Gelehrten bis 1945* (Berlin: Peter Lang, pp. 179–84. This is the transcript of a taped interview conducted with Schütz in September 1958.
42. The unidentified farmer never made a report to the Garda or G2.
43. Schütz, 'My Secret Mission to Ireland', p. 18.
44. According to the New Ross Garda report, she was a 'female Barrack Servant', but in the version of his story that appeared in the *Sunday Press*, the woman was identified as 'the wife of a local Garda'.
45. Ibid. and IMA G2/X/0203, M. Feeny, New Ross to O'Carroll, 4 April 1941.
46. Stephan, 'Die Vergessene Episode', p. 302.
47. IMA G2/X/0203, M. Feeny, New Ross to Garda Commissioner, 20 March 1941.
48. Ibid. Both incidents angered Irish Intelligence officers. First, that they were not notified that Schütz had even landed ('The expected co-operation from the Garda was not forthcoming,' to use Commandant Mackey's words), and second, that they allowed Schütz to spend money that was clearly intended for espionage purposes. In his report to Colonel Bryan, Mackey also thought it was strange that Schütz knew about 'following the telephone poles and knew the crossbars which carry the insulators were all fitted to the Dublin side of the poles so that by following them he could not fail to reach the city' (Ibid., Mackey report of 22 March 1941). This is a curious statement, since Schütz seemed quite puzzled about his location and once he finally learned it, was headed for Wexford, *away* from Dublin.
49. Ibid. Report of Anonymous Lieutenant, 13th Connaught Infantry to Adjutant, Curragh Command, 14 March 1941. The lieutenant probably got it wrong. Schütz's passport states that he was from Ludevitz (not Ludovig), Union of South Africa. He would have hardly called it German South West Africa, an invalid name since 1918. Schütz was unlucky, not habitually stupid.
50. The German version of 'dog-tags' (*Erkennungsmarke*) consisted of a single oval piece of tin with the wearer's unit of initial assignment and number, not the name or even the current unit. In the event of death in combat, half of the perforated disc would be retained for identification. For normal identification purposes, the soldier in the field was expected to carry his *Soldbuch* (pay book), which had a picture ID, relevant personal and service details. Schütz apparently did not have this book on his possession. Görtz retained a *Soldbuch* under an assumed name.
51. IMA G2/X/0203. The original newspaper cuttings, protected by glass slides, are in the Schütz file.
52. Stephan, 'Die Vergessene Episode', pp. 312–13. Captain Joseph Healy also interviewed Schütz on 18 March 1941. A linguist of note before and after the war, Healy noted that Schütz was intelligent and that confinement would be difficult on him for that reason. According to Schütz, he had withdrawn £600 of his own money from the Deutsche Bank, Berlin, to make purchases in Ireland of a private nature as 'there are not many things in German [*sic*]' (IMA G2/X/0203, Healy to Bryan, 18 March 1941).
53. IMA G2/X/0203, undated report, Healy to Archer.

54. Ibid., Healy report, 18 March 1941.
55. Ibid., series of letters between Col. Archer and Boland, June–July 1941. The letters between Schütz and Lilo are mostly romantic. He playfully addressed her as *Meiner Liebe Weibschen* ('My beloved little female').
56. Ibid. Walsh to Bryan, 11 Aug. 1941.
57. Ibid. undated report from 1941.
58. Schütz, 'My Secret Mission to Ireland', *Sunday Press*, 21 June 1970. Very possibly, Schütz just made a mistake, and the event happened upon his recapture in 1942. His memory became occasionally elastic in the post-war period and he often recalled events out of sequence. In his 1990 interview with David O'Donoghue, Schütz blamed the Abwehr for not telling him that Görtz had been arrested before his arrival. In fact, Görtz was still on the loose for seven months after Schütz landed in County Wexford.
59. IMA G2/0261, DMD Weekly Summary, 4 Dec. 1939; van Loon interview, May 1999. There were 28 Uhlan regiments in Imperial German service during the First World War, but none of them were based in Hamburg.
60. Ibid., statement of Muriel Unland, 21 April 1941. When initially questioned by D/Sgt. Wymes, Mrs Unland responded: 'I refuse to answer whether I ever entered any profession or took up any business.' For some reason, she changed her mind, adding to the end of her written statement, 'I now wish to say that on leaving Liverpool with my mother when I was ten years of age I was engaged as a child actress'. There is no indication as to why this confession was particularly sensitive to Mrs Unland.
61. PRO KV 2/170, undated MI5 memo to Irish G2. Dierks was the I-M chief at Hamburg. His aliases included 'Herr Müller' and he was the notional head of Hillermann AG. An effective recruiter and a womanizer of some distinction, he was killed in an automobile crash while taking three England-bound agents to their plane in 1940 (West, *MI5*, p. 215).
62. Ibid. The stationery letterhead from Ferrum reads: 'Ferrum (S.S.) LTD, 2 & 3 Philpot Lane, London, E.C.3. Director: M.W.J. Dobeyn.'
63. According to Günther Schütz, Unland was not supposed to go to Ireland, but to stay in England. Schütz also volunteered that the Hamburg Ast controlled Unland (IMA G2/X/0203, Schütz interview of 10 April 1941).
64. The Gresham was a favourite site for the Nazi Party Christmas celebrations held in Dublin, but Unland arrived about a year too late to participate in the last one held before the war (O'Donoghue, *Hitler's Irish Voices*, pp. 19–20).
65. IMA G2/0261, report on Phillip Bernard Richards, March 1940.
66. Ibid., report of 18 Oct. 1939, DC Walton, Metropolitan Police, Hendon Station, S Division. Mrs Dugarde was not charged with obstructing justice.
67. Ibid., Mrs Anna Hart, Roodborstlaan 9, The Hague to Unland.
68. Ibid., Letter of 26 Jan. 1940.
69. Apparently unaware of his reduced circumstances, Fraulein Schlattau continued to write to Unland c/o his Northern Bank address as late as 1945. When asked about these letters, Unland said he was glad the Garda had intercepted them, rather than Mrs Unland, and 'was anxious that the present letter should not go on to Merrion Square'. Report of Superintendent Carroll to G2, 5 June 1941.

70. The office of the British Representative in Éire, Sir John Maffey, was also situated in Merrion Square.
71. In a post-war interrogation, Dr Praetorius of I/Wi was asked about the esoteric references in Unland's letters. He replied that they were meaningless to the Abwehr and thought that Unland included them to give his reports an air of importance (PRO KV 2/170, MI5 memo to Irish G2).
72. IMA G2/0261, undated DMD summary.
73. The Abwehr II Kriegstagebuch first mentioned the possibility of a submarine insertion on 29 Nov. 1939, some two months before Weber-Drohl was dispatched.
74. Ibid., letter of 7 Feb. 1940.
75. PRO KV 1/173, Praetorius interview, 11 Oct. 1946.
76. IMA G2/0261, undated Garda report.
77. Ibid., DMD weekly summary, 5 Feb. 1940,
78. At one point, Unland used a mail address at the National Tourist Bureau, 14 Upper O'Connell Street. When informed of this in a report, Dan Bryan scribbled 'Black list at once!' on the cover (Ibid.).
79. IMA G2/0265 and G2/0261, inventory of Mrs Unland's bag.
80. Ibid., Unland statement, 23 April 1941, Arbour Hill Prison. Unland was also unable to explain why he had signed his letters with the names Walsh, Peters and Green, though he admitted to doing so.
81. Ibid., report of Captain J. Foley to Governor, Arbour Hill. Though this report was not dated, the subject of it would have occurred shortly after Unland was transferred to Arbour Hill on 30 April 1941. Since Unland and Schütz were detained under the Emergency Powers No. 20 Order and not on a criminal charge, it was not necessary for the government to reveal the evidence against them. Neither was aware that the microdot information had been compromised.
82. She kept the apartment on Merrion Square at the £10 per month rental. Unland was having money difficulties of his own since he no longer received monthly remittances from the Abwehr. His fellow internee Günther Schütz had to loan him £300 at one point (NAI DFA A34).
83. Ibid., p. 26.
84. *Irish Times*, 5 Sept. 1947.
85. Dan Bryan interview, p. 40, courtesy of Eunan O'Halpin.
86. Michael Mac Evilly, unpublished manuscript on Dr Andrew Cooney, p. 252, citing Liam Rice interview.
87. Fisk, *In Time of War*, p. 377.
88. IMA G2/1722, Detective Branch, Special Section report, 23 Oct. 1941. Kelly was apparently en route to a meeting with Maisie O'Mahony at University Church when arrested. The report itself is in the Görtz file.
89. Ibid., Görtz report with annotations. Deery joined Görtz in April 1941. Prior to that he was a telegraph operator at the Dundalk Post Office and was the inside man there when his IRA comrades robbed it. When interviewed by Enno Stephan, Deery told the author that he met Görtz only once, at the Coffey house, and that all messages to him were enciphered by Görtz in advance and sent through couriers.
90. *Irish Times*, 5 Sept. 1947.

91. IMA G2/1722, statement of Howard Hammond, 1 Oct. 1941. The O'Farrell sisters are alternatively referred to as the 'Farrell sisters'.
92. Hayes to O'Donovan, 2 May 1941 (courtesy of Enno Stephan).
93. IMA G2/3261, statement of James J. Murtaugh, 26 Nov. 1943. Murtaugh also said that Andrews showed him a letter to Görtz from Senator Byrne.
94. Ibid., statement of Joseph Andrews, 19 Sept. 1943.
95. IMA G2/3048, Garda report, 9 Sept. 1941.
96. The house belonged to author Uinseann MacEoin's mother (information from Michael Mac Evilly).
97. Bell, *The Secret Army*, pp. 202–3.
98. Görtz report, pp. 29–30. McCaughey took over as Chief of Staff, but was subsequently arrested and sentenced to death (sentence later commuted to life imprisonment). Joseph Atkinson, Charles McClade, Liam Rice, Andrew Skelton and Liam Burke, all prominent IRA personnel in the Hayes affair, were ultimately arrested and imprisoned. McCaughey was succeeded by Seán Harrington (arrested) and then Seán McCool (arrested in May 1942).
99. IMA G2/1722, Görtz report with annotations, Dec. 1944.
100. Abwehr Kriegstagebuch., 13 Aug. 1941.
101. Carter, *The Shamrock and the Swastika*, p. 169 and Lahousen to Foreign Ministry, 28 Aug. 1941, courtesy of Enno Stephan.
102. Hempel reported on 25 August to the Foreign Ministry that Görtz had departed Ireland. On receipt of the message, the Abwehr cancelled the plan to send the £500. The Abwehr wanted to know whether Hempel had any contact with Görtz's 'organization' or whether the departure of Görtz made that point moot (Lahousen to Foreign Ministry, 28 Aug. 1941, courtesy of Enno Stephan). In a coded telegram deciphered by the British, Hempel complains that Görtz told people that he 'has a high position of trust with the Reichsmarschall [Göring] and that he had to report to the Reich Foreign Minister'. (DO 121/86, Telegram no. 420, Hempel to Foreign Ministry, 21 Nov. 1941).
103. Abwehr II Kriegstagebuch, entry of 7 Sept. 1941.
104. Stephan, *Spies in Ireland*, pp. 226–7.
105. *Irish Times*, 1 Sept. 1947. Other than Görtz's reference to these events, there is no other mention of them from existing sources.
106. The offer was made with Jim O'Donovan acting as a go-between (IMA G2/ 1722, Görtz report with annotations, p. 34).
107. *Irish Times*, 8 Sept. 1947.
108. Interview with Commandant Peter Young. Files at the Irish Military Archives may clarify this point if and when they are identified and made available.
109. IMA G2/1722, Görtz report, pp. 35–7. O'Duffy died on 30 Nov. 1944 (Manning, *The Blueshirts*, p. 208).
110. Stephan, *Spies in Ireland*, p. 229.
111. IMA G2/3261, Andrews statement, 19 Sept. 1943. Andrews also said that Görtz was scheduled to meet with McNeill, Frank Aiken and William Norton (Labour Party), but that his arrest upset the plan. A separate G2 report from a source identified as 'Curragh' said that Görtz met with Dan Breen, McNeill, Eoin O'Duffy, Pearse Paul Kelly and Dail Secretary O'Grady in November 1941. In a note by Colonel Bryan to this report, he says that he doubts the meeting

actually took place, that it was scheduled but cancelled due to Görtz's arrest (IMA G2/1722, report of 12 May 1942).

112. IMA G2/X/1091, Garda report, 8 Dec. 1941.

113. IMA G2/1722, Görtz report with annotations, Dec. 1944. Görtz later received copies of the Hayes confession from Maura O'Brien. Walter Foley, the manager of Lee's in Rathmines, allegedly arranged for Görtz to stay at the O'Neill's.

114. Stephan, 'Die Vergessene Episode', p. 229.

115. IMA G2/X/0093, DMD report, 1 Dec. 1941. A recently released MI5 file solves the mystery: Joseph Andrews informed the police that Görtz was staying at 1 Blackheath Park, Clontarf (DO 121/86, Cecil Liddell to Sir John Stephenson, 24 Aug. 1943, p. 4).

116. Pearse Paul Kelly, 'Doing My Time' *Irish Independent*, Jan. 1969, p. 1.

117. Stephan, 'Die Vergessene Episode', p. 230.

118. Görtz's identity disc, standard issue for every German soldier, carried the name of his initial training unit from 1939, 'No. 92 1/A/Ausb. Regt. 21'.

119. IMA G2/1722, M. Lennon to Provost Martial, Department of Defence, 28 Nov. 1941.

120. IMA G2/1928.

121. IMA G2/0261, DMD Misc. Report, 27 May 1940.

122. IMA G2/1928, DMD reports of 28 Aug. and 16 Nov. 1940. These associates were Guiseppi Morrelli, Virgilio and Rudolfo Collini and Sante Staffieri. Staffieri was an associate of Preetz in 1940 (IMA G2/4330).

123. NLI, MS 21,155, O'Donovan papers, undated letter from Ernst Weber-Drohl.

124. Stephan, 'Die Vergessene Episode', pp. 120–1.

125. IMA G2/1928, DMD report, 18 July 1941.

126. Ibid., DMD report, 11 Aug. 1941.

127. Weber-Drohl did go ahead with his strongman act. The promotional photographs made the Dublin newspapers (*Evening Mail*, 25 Sept. 1941, p. 3). In the 20 Oct. 1941 edition of the same paper, he took out an ad reading 'Many thanks to Mrs Rosaline Parker and her father Mr Bracken, for assisting me in my athletic act at the Olympia last week so well – E.W. Drohl'.

128. Ibid., Statement of Mrs Rosaline Parker, 79 Glentow Row, Whitehall, Dublin, 8 Jan. 1943. In another report (29 April 1942), the postal intercept revealed that a 'person having an address as c/o Wilson, 79 Glenton [*sic*] Road [*sic*], Whitehall, whose initials are R.S. or R.D. is attempting to get money from WD.' Weber-Drohl's conduct was interesting since he also visited Mrs Parker at her father's home. A Garda surveillance noted that on 17 Jan. 1942, Weber-Drohl was at the home of Corporal Bracken, 79 Glentow Road, Larkhill and that WD is 'believed to sleep at the address mentioned on occasion'.

129. Ibid., DMD weekly report, 2 Feb. 1942. S.A. Roche, Secretary to the Department of Justice, was also the proponent of several anti-Semitic policy statements in connection with Jewish refugees (Keogh, *Jews in Twentieth Century Ireland*, p. 161).

130. G2/X/0805, undated summary, 1941.

131. According to MI5, Lenihan was said to have been 'involved in an IRA gun-running enterprise as the producer of forged frontier passes and had served a nine-month sentence on discovery of his enterprise' (PRO KV 4/14, summary, p. 177).

132. Ibid.

133. PRO KV 4/8, report on the work of Camp O20, p. 11. The preponderance of the evidence currently available suggests that Lenihan was initially supposed to be parachuted in tandem with a German agent called Josef Jacobs. Jacobs landed in England on 31 Jan. 1941. He, too, had been in The Hague for weather training, but was equipped with a disc cipher wheel for encoding messages. Lenihan's mishap with the frostbite injury delayed his own landing and possibly the destination. Jacobs was executed by firing squad in August 1941 (West, *MI5*, p. 372).

134. The twin-engine bomber/special duty aircraft He-111 should not be confused (as many historians have done) with the He-III (a biplane prototype in the early 1920s). Lenihan's story is strange; none of the German aircraft (including those of KG 200) were normally equipped with a crew-compartment heater.

135. Lenihan's secret ink was revealed with a red powder containing naphthalene, which revealed the message when heated to 60 degrees centigrade and viewed under UV light. Another Abwehr ink used a laxative tablet containing phenolphthalene, which the agent dissolved in 50 per cent alcohol solution. It was revealed with a mixture of water and cigarette ash (Kahn, *Hitler's Spies*, pp. 290–1).

136. IMAG2/X/0805, G2 report, 29 July 1941.

137. Though G2 and the Garda were satisfied that the Lenihan family was telling the complete truth about their brother, a mail intercept order was maintained for some time on Patrick and Gerald Lenihan, and on Maura Blake.

138. G2/X/0805, G2 report, 24 July 1941; NAI DFA/A27.

139. Andrew, *The Sword and the Shield*, p. 103. This was a system using the Lorenz coding machine and is explained in the section of Chapter 1 on codes and ciphers.

140. Nigel West, *MI5*, p. 212. Lenihan's MI5 file was not among those released to the Public Record Office as part of the KV series.

141. Ibid., p. 413 and IMA G2/X/0805, undated summary, 1941.

142. IMA G2/X/0805, undated summary, 1941.

143. O'Halpin, *Defending Ireland*, p. 243. Cf. John Masterman, *The Double-Cross System in the War of 1939 to 1945* (New Haven: Yale University Press, 1972), pp. 49, 99–100.

144. PRO KV 4/5, Masterman report, 22 Aug. 1945, pp. 27–8.

145. O'Halpin, 'MI5's Irish Memories', p. 6.

146. PRO KV 4/14, 'A Digest of Ham', summary, p. 177. In all British documents released by MI5, Lenihan's name has been redacted and his actual interrogation reports are still held by the Security Services.

147. This is a notable exception to the fate of most other German agents who were not used for the Double-Cross or similar double-agent operations. As cataloged by Nigel West in *MI5*, their careers usually terminated at the end of a rope at either Pentonville or Wandsworth Prison (one was executed at the Tower and two in Gibraltar) – a total of 16 Abwehr spies. By contrast, 47 participated as double agents, including those used in Double-Cross (West, *MI5*, pp. 342–3 and 307–8).

148. Cecil Liddell, MC, was the younger brother of Guy Liddell, MC, who headed MI5's 'B' Division.

149. NAI DFA A60 (30 Jan. 1943 and 4 Feb. 1943) and IMA G2/X/0805. Curiously, MI5 and G2 seem to have had a more direct line of

communication, which does not appear from the few documents on this subject in the Irish National Archive. The MI5 files, by comparison, are replete with original G2 reports that most probably did not come via the Irish Department of External Affairs channel.

150. Mrs Ann Lenihan to author, 1 Feb. 2000 and Mary O'Rourke, TD, to author, 18 Nov. 1999.

151. In the immediate post-war period, the Dutch government reintroduced the death penalty, specifically to deal with senior Nazi collaborators. Mussert was among a select few to receive personal attention.

152. Van Loon interview, 20 May 1999. This period was involuntarily extended to three years.

153. The Irish officials seemed to doubt this story but there is no record in the official file (IMA G2/3748) that this aspect of the case was investigated by either the RUC or MI5.

154. Van Loon interview, 3 Oct. 1999. He said he met the mysterious British officer in a Belfast bar.

155. MA G2/3748

156. Ibid., statement of 13 Sept. 1941. The mention of 'Hermann Krause' was unfortunate, since one of the aliases adopted by Hermann Görtz was that of 'Hermann Kruse'. The existence of a prior connection between Van Loon and Görtz, something that would certainly change the conventional picture of this episode, is still a valid question, but only one possibility. Mr van Loon does not wish to discuss this point, saying only that Hermann Krause was a friend from Holland who was thought to be in the Dublin area.

157. Van Loon interview, 20 May 1999.

158. The photographs were those of Lucie Scheurmann, his girlfriend in Holland, and of a girl he met while in Belfast.

159. IMA G2/3748, van Loon statement, 13 Sept. 1941. Van Loon admits that he did this (interview of 3 Oct. 1999).

160. Ibid., Boland order.

161. Van Loon's file does not contain any mention of an official response and the Irish files at the Irish National Archives are silent on the issue.

162. Ibid., Van Loon letters of 28 Oct. 1943.

163. Stuart to David O'Donoghue, 17 Nov. 1989.

164. Francis Stuart 'Frank Ryan in Germany', *The Bell*, Nov. 1950, p. 38.

165. O'Donoghue, *Hitler's Irish Voices*, p. 56.

166. Stuart to David O'Donoghue, 17 Nov. 1989.

167. Stuart interview, 7 July 1999, Fanore, County Clare.

168. The operation name was similar to *Unternehmen Walfisch*, the November plan to take Clissmann and Rieger to Wales by boat. *Wal* and *Walfisch* both mean 'whale'.

169. Stephan, *Spies in Ireland*, p. 203. According to Haller, the 'idea was ... for establishing a sort of listening post or telephone exchange in Southern Ireland. This listening post should be brought into use in the Irish people's struggle against the intruders in the event of an English attack against the Irish harbours.'

170. PRO KV 2/173, special interrogation report (Haller), p. 10.

171. Carter, *The Shamrock and the Swastika*, p. 120 and Abwehr II Kriegstagebuch, 7 July 1941. Haller travelled to Paris in preparation for Operation Sea Eagle. Abwehr II was 'merely' to provide assistance and

technical support to the Foreign Ministry for the operation. *Seeadler* was the Abwehr designation; the plan was called Taube II by the Foreign Ministry (PRO KV 2/173, special interrogation report, p. 10).

172. Abwehr II Kriegstagebuch, entry of 21 Aug. 1941.
173. *Documents on German Foreign Policy*, Series D, Vol. XIII, pp. 364–6, 24 Aug. 1941. Generaloberst Milch recommended Harlinghausen for this assignment.
174. Ibid.
175. Duggan, D.Litt. thesis, Appendix XXIV, p. 422, 1977 interview with Dr Veesenmayer.
176. Clissmann was extensively interviewed by Joe Mulholland for the 1979 RTE television documentary 'Let my Tombstone be of Granite', which chronicled the life of Frank Ryan.
177. *Documents on German Foreign Policy*, Series D, Vol. XIII, pp. 364-6. The reference in the first specification would seem to indicate that recent coordination with the IRA had been established at some point. Veesenmayer intended giving the IRA the sum of £40,000 that had been allocated by von Ribbentrop. By the time of this operational proposal, Ms Mary Mains had already brought $10,000 to the IRA in November 1940 and Görtz surrendered more money before that. Weber-Drohl's mission in January–February 1940 also provided operating funds for the Republicans.
178. Ibid. The reference to 'objective reporting' is an obvious slap at Dr Hempel. Veesenmayer later referred to the German Minister as someone with *keine Meinung, keine Empfehlung* ('no opinion, no recommendation') and complained that he was *immer weich* ('always soft').
179. Ibid.
180. America entered the war in December 1941, after the bombing of Pearl Harbor. US forces arrived in Northern Ireland in January 1942, provoking a statement by de Valera, who protested about the 'occupation'.
181. Stephan, *Spies in Ireland*, pp. 234–5. The SS unit did not go to waste. Renamed the SS Parachute Battalion 500, it was amalgamated with volunteers from penal battalions and participated in the assault on Tito's headquarters in 1944 (Roger Edward, *German Airborne Troops* [New York: Doubleday & Co, 1974], p. 143).
182. O'Donoghue, *Hitler's Irish Voices*, pp. 153–4.
183. Elizabeth Clissmann and Francis Stuart attended the funeral. Mrs Clissmann eventually passed word of Ryan's fate to Minister Leopold Kerney in Madrid (Stephan, *Spies in Ireland*, p. 263). According to Stuart and Clissmann, the cause of death was pleurisy and pneumonia, though Veesenmayer told author John Duggan that it was actually a venereal disease, a view discounted by everyone else, including Duggan (Duggan, D.Litt. thesis, Appendix XXIV, p. 423). Having spent almost four years in the Third Reich, there is no indication that Ryan ever approached the embassy or the Germans about returning to Ireland, other than the covert attempt in August 1940.
184. NAI, DFA SOF P. 14, MacWhite to External Affairs, 25 Aug. 1941.
185. PRO HO 371/24962, Sir Percy Loraine to P.B. Nichols, Foreign Office, 10 Feb. 1940, p. 184. A notation in the Foreign Office file laconically concluded 'Mr Bewley sounds unpleasant'.

186. NAI, DFA SOF P. 17, MacWhite to Walshe, 25 August 1941.

187. Dickel, *Die Deutsche Aussenpolitik und die Irische Frage*, cited in O'Driscoll, Ph.D. thesis, p. 377.

188. USNA, A.A., SD Hauptamt to Ausw. Amt, 5 Feb. 1941, Inland IIg, Berichte und Meldungen zur Lage in und über Irland (SD) and Dickel, *Die Deutsche Aussenpolitik und die Irische Frage*, pp. 186–7, fn. 580.

189. The Williams article ran in the *Leader* on 31 Jan. 1953 and an enhanced version appeared in the *Irish Press* on 10, 11 and 17 July 1953. Kerney knew both Clissmann and his wife, Elizabeth, from pre-war Ireland.

190. Stephan, 'Die Vergessene Episode', p. 244. The Irish claim to the Six Counties, enshrined in articles 2 and 3 of the 1937 Constitution, legally remained in place until 1999 when they were repealed as part of the Good Friday Agreement.

191. IMA G2/3010, Bryan to Walsh, 29 Oct. 1942. This letter also detailed Kerney's evasion of postal censorship by using the diplomatic bag to shuttle letters for Ryan and Elizabeth Clissmann. An additional letter raises the possibility that Kerney's complicity went even further: 'Certain remarks Mr Kerney had made indicated that he knew much more about German activities *in Ireland* [italics added] than you or I had previously been aware of.' (Bryan to Walsh, 16 Jan. 1946). The Healy interview with Kerney and the correspondence between Bryan and Walsh were not made available to Professor Williams.

192. Ibid.

193. USNA, T-120, A.A. Reel 89, Frame 101041, document of 5 Oct. 1942, and Carter, *The Shamrock and the Swastika*, p. 119. The captured German documents were not freely available to Professor Williams – though his information about them was accurate. He settled the case out of court for £500, an apology, and costs.

194. Stephan, *Spies in Ireland*, p. 227.

195. In 1945 Kerney finally gave the Department of External Affairs the letters he had received from Frank Ryan in 1940 and 1941, noting that 'hitherto I have treated them as private communications having no particular importance and to which it might not have been prudent to refer in official dispatches' (NAI DFA A52/1, Kerney to Boland, 22 Jan. 1945).

196. Ó Drisceoil, *Censorship in Ireland*, p. 73. Kerney also used the diplomatic bag to shuttle letters to and from Elizabeth Clissmann and also handled letters to and from Frank Ryan, who was then being hosted by Nazi Germany. G2's Dan Bryan, who regarded Kerney with suspicion, kept a close watch on his correspondence, official and otherwise. Kerney extended this same helping hand to former Irish Minister to Berlin, turned supporter of Hitler, Charles Bewley (Ibid.).

197. PRO FO 940/49, Clissmann file, summary.

198. Ibid., Görtz to Hempel, 5 Jan. 1942.

199. *Aufzeichnung über den in den Telegrammen aus Dublin mit K bezeichneten V-Mann*, 27 Dec. 1941, courtesy of Enno Stephan and USNA A.A. Reel 89, Frame 101360-3.

200. NAI DFA A34, Walshe to de Valera, 5 Jan. 1942.

201. Amt Ausland/Abwehr report, Kramarz to Abwehr II, 3 Jan. 1942, courtesy of Enno Stephan.
202. Lahousen to Woermann, 1 Dec. 1941, courtesy of Enno Stephan.
203. Abwehr II Kriegstagebuch, entry of 8 Dec. 1941.
204. Görtz file, Bundesarchiv Abteilung R, Berlin, Lahousen's recommendation, 19 Feb. 1941. Irish G2 later promoted Görtz to the rank of Major as part of a ruse.
205. Cronin, *Frank Ryan*, p. 212. Ryan to Kerney. One can only speculate whether the General referred to by Ryan was O'Duffy or Hugo McNeill.

CHAPTER 7

1. PRO KV 4/9, Liddell report, p. 70.
2. IMA G2/1744. In an undated speech given at a Coras na Poblachta meeting, the philosophical direction of the group is apparent: 'Engulfed in a Pagan Empire, we a Catholic people allow ourselves to be ruled and exploited by Masonry and Jewry.'
3. IMA G2/3261, summary, Sept. 1945.
4. Ibid. Andrews kept everyone in the loop. In 1941 he offered to sell the names and addresses of 1300 Hospital Trust employees in the US, stating that they were providing money to the IRA – an offer that was apparently accepted. He additionally reported on the presence of Görtz's radio at George Hick's house, and at his own home in September 1941. Though they knew of this, the Irish Government curiously took no action (DO 121/86, Cecil Liddell to Sir John Stephenson, 24 Aug. 1943, pp. 2–3).
5. PRO KV 4/9, Liddell report, pp. 70–1.
6. IMA G2/3261, summary, Sept. 1945.
7. Ibid. Andrews later said that the idea of the 'green division' originated with Görtz and that as far as Andrews was concerned, 'if the Germans got any kick out of toying with the idea, they were welcome to it'.
8. USNA, A.A.Büro Unterstaatssekretär, Reel 89, Frames 101327–9, Veesenmayer to Ribbentrop.
9. NA DFA A60, Bryan to Liddell, 24 March 1943: 'Eastwood met Andrews Saturday afternoon. Messages believed exchanged. Writing in "A" has characteristics common to Andrews. Held cipher broken. Cipher in "A" same type. Difficult explain cipher in writing but information should aid solution if you care bring expert for discussion. Groups similar cipher in Goertz all.'
10. PRO KV 4/9, Liddell report, p. 71.
11. Ibid., p. 61.
12. IMA G2/3261, search report from Andrews home, 19 and 27 Aug. 1943. This provided G2 with a complete text of the messages.
13. Bernard O'Reilly retired from the RIC in 1920 (PRO KV 2/119, file on O'Reilly and John Kenny Appendix II).
14. In addition to Lenihan, O'Reilly and Kenny, Jersey also provided two recruits (Dennis Leister and Eric Pleasants) to the SS-organized renegade unit, the British Free Corps, and at least one volunteer (Charles Patrick Gilbert) to the Nazi radio propaganda service, Büro Concordia. Several Jersey transients (Kenny, Leister and Pleasants) were sent there courtesy of

the Peace Pledge Union, an organization that actively assisted British subjects avoid military conscription by sending them to the Channel Islands (PRO HO 45/25819, Summary 26 Nov. 1945 and Eric Pleasants statement, 21 June 1945).

15. Major Prinz zu Waldeck und Pyrmont was the military commandant for only a brief period of time, from 9 Aug. to 27 Sept. 1940 (Ralph Mollet, *The German Occupation of Jersey, 1940–1945: Notes on the General Conditions, How the Population Fared* (St Helier: Société Jersiaise, 1954), p. 31). Following the death of Prinz Wilhelm von Preussen of his wounds on 26 May 1940, and the unexpected popular expression of sympathy at his funeral, Hitler ordered the removal of all princes from front-line service, the so-called *Prinzenerlass*. Zu Waldeck commanded a Panzer regiment on the Eastern Front, being promoted to Oberst by war's end. He died in 1971 (Josias Prinz zu Waldeck to author, 20 Nov. 2000).

16. The actual name for the plant was the Reichswerke Aktiengesellschaft für Erzbergbau und Eisenhütten, 'Hermann Göring' – Watenstedt. Future references will be mercifully shortened to "Watenstedt". Göring was the director of the Reich Four-Year Plan – the unrealized module for German wartime industrial development.

17. O'Donoghue, *Hitler's Irish Voices*, p. 208. O'Donoghue refers to the German commandant as "von Baldeck", a title that did not (and does not) exist in Germany.

18. O'Reilly was not alone in his dislike of things at the Watenstedt plant. When the Irish workers were granted a four-week leave back to Jersey, many of them declined to return to Germany. Jersey Commandant Major Prinz zu Waldeck und Pyrmont refused to assist the Watenstedt managers or labour authorities in Braunschweig to force their return. In the long run, both groups were probably better off (Carter, *The Shamrock and the Swastika*, p. 137). According to a contemporary G2 summary, 'They will no doubt feel much happier in the agricultural English-speaking surroundings of the Channel Islands than in the blast furnaces of the Herman Goering Works and probably the food will be better also' (IMA G2/X/0154, Department of External Affairs to Major Guilfoyle, 25 March 1943).

19. This is contradicted in O'Reilly's version in the *Sunday Dispatch*, where he alleges that Nora O'Mara was his contact to the SS (*Sunday Dispatch*, 31 Aug. 1952, p. 9).

20. PRO KV 2/119, Liddell report of 24 Feb. 1944 and FBI report of 11 Nov. 1943. The name 'Margraff' also turned up in an intercepted Abwehr message from March 1941; he was trying to infiltrate into Vichy France (PRO HW 19/5, No. 3035 of 3 March 1941).

21. O'Reilly's recollections differed substantially between his interrogation sessions with G2 and the later publication of his serialized memoirs. The version in the memoirs is that he had no contact with the SS until after his Abwehr mission was cancelled, a more logical chain of events.

22. IMA G2/3824, O'Reilly interview, 26 Jan. 1944.

23. PRO KV 2/119, O'Reilly file, Ahlrichs to Menzel, 21 Nov. 1942.

24. Ibid.

25. *Sunday Dispatch*, 17 Aug. 1952, p. 9. Schmeling did some work for the Luftwaffe prior to the 1941 invasion of Crete, but his function consisted of posing for photographs with his smaller comrades. He was shown posed in

the photographs for *Signal* and *Der Adler*, the illustrated magazines of the Wehrmacht and the Luftwaffe. He is not known to have had any ties to actual military or espionage activity. Cf. Zeutner and Bedürftig, *Encyclopedia of the Third Reich*, p. 837.

26. 'Seemann' (sailor) was most probably a cover name. According to German records, his controller was Kapitän-Leutnant Heinrich Ahlrichs. The name Seemann does not otherwise occur in either German Abwehr or British MI5 records.

27. PRO, KV, 1/119, Ahlrichs to Menzel, 9 Dec. 1942.

28. Carter, *The Shamrock and the Swastika*, p. 138. She mistakenly gives the Abwehr officer's name as 'Aldrichs'.

29. PRO KV 2/119, Ahlrichs to Menzel, 9 Dec. 1942. Ahlrichs suggested that since O'Reilly was to travel legitimately, sending a radio was impractical, but that the agent had been taught radio construction and that he should select a site with the help of 'his IRA friends'. Ahlrichs also noted that 'a further cutter-operation is planned and there exists the possibility of bringing an "Afu-apparatus" for RR 2621 to Country 32 (Ireland) and handing it over to him'.

30. As late as 1992, when she published her memoir *Cé Hí Seo Amuigh?*, O'Mara was still maintaining that Russell had been poisoned – this time on the orders of Admiral Canaris.

31. The name 'Dr Peters' does not occur in any of the SD material at the PRO London, the Militärarchiv in Freiburg, or any existing publication this author has seen. O'Reilly was probably disguising the name of his actual controller, Peter Siepen, though as head of the SD Group F-H, Siepen would not have supervised operational missions, but only radio training. SS-Sturmbannführer Schüddekopf, who should have been O'Reilly's superior, is not mentioned by him, but he is referred to by John Kenny.

32. The SD did not take this part of the mission to heart. On the way back from the airfield, Dr Peters told O'Reilly to 'forget that I had ever been to the Luftwaffe headquarters.'

33. In preparation for his mission, the SD gave him access to 'all important English newspapers, to broadcast speeches of leading British politicians and statesmen, to a comprehensive collection of political literature by prominent English authors, and to all files of information already supplied by German agents in England' (*Sunday Dispatch*, 7 Sept. 1952, p. 5).

34. IMA G2/3824, O'Reilly report, 14 Jan. 1944.

35. Ibid., O'Reilly interview, 26 Jan. 1944.

36. Originally an officer of the Seaforth Highlanders, Baillie-Stewart made a trip to Berlin in 1932. On his return he began regularly corresponding with a 'Herr Obst' and a 'Marie-Louise', signing his letters as 'Alphonse Poiret'. Investigation revealed that Baillie-Stewart had passed on classified documents from the Mechanical Warfare Experimental Establishment at Farnborough. He was convicted and sentenced to five years' imprisonment at Wormwood Scrubs and Maidstone Prison – where he met Hermann Görtz. Though Baillie-Stewart denied that there were any coded messages in the letters he sent to Germany, 'Obst' is the German word for fruit; 'Marie-Louise' is a type of French pear and 'Poiret' is a small pear. For his nefarious broadcasting activities on behalf of the Nazis, Baillie-Stewart was

lucky not to have been hanged along with William Joyce and John Amery. Again sentenced to five years, he moved to Ireland in 1949 and died under the alias 'Patrick Stewart' in Dublin in 1966 (West, *MI5*, pp. 100–10). The lure in Baillie-Stewart's case was the opportunity for sexual liaisons with German women ('Officer in the Tower was lured into spying for sex', *Daily Telegraph*, 20 April 2000, p. 15).

37. PRO KV 2/119, report of 15 Jan. 1944. This information was necessarily relayed by G2 interrogators in Dublin to MI5.
38. IMA G2/3824, O'Reilly interview, 26 Jan. 1944.
39. PRO KV 2/119, Liddell to Moore (RUC Belfast), undated Kenny memorandum.
40. O'Reilly gives the name of this officer as Naval Lieutenant Klinoke, said to be in charge of the harbour installations ('I Visit Jersey to Recruit Another Spy', *Sunday Dispatch*, 21 Sept. 1952).
41. While under interrogation, O'Reilly mentioned the name of another Irish national who was driving for the German occupation forces on Jersey, a Terrence Mooney (IMA G2/3824, O'Reilly interview of 24 April 1944). William Sargent listed his home-of-record as Kilmallock, Co. Limerick, though he was originally from Ballyhea, Charleville, Co. Cork. There is no record in the official files concerning his further activities (IMA G2/0154).
42. According to O'Reilly, the Kripo (*Kriminalpolizei* – criminal police) chief on Jersey, Herr Wolff, divided the possible candidates into two sections: the wheat and the chaff (*Sunday Dispatch*, 21 Sept. 1952, p. 9). 'SS-Sturmbahnführer' Dr Peters was presumably the 'Gestapo' man referred to by Kenny. O'Reilly consistently misspelled the SS rank; it should read 'SS-Sturmbannführer'.
43. Kenny seems to have been unaware that SD and SS officers used a different nomenclature for military ranks than that of the German army. The equivalent to Oberleutnant (Army) is SS-Obersturmführer.
44. Lehnitz was a large SS training area just outside Berlin, centred around the Totenkopf-Kaserne. It was also adjacent to the notorious Sachsenhausen concentration camp. Helmut Clissmann was sent to Lehnitz to investigate the possibility of training SS personnel in a modification of Operation Sea Eagle (Stephan, '*Die Vergessene Episode*', pp. 234–5).
45. This is almost certainly a reference to Sergeant John Codd, who was training at the centre during the same period, and who mentioned meeting Kenny.
46. IMA G2/X/1263, Kenny interview, 11 April 1944. By contrast, O'Reilly reports that the names of the accompanying SS officers were Geisler and Schaumer (*Sunday Dispatch*, 5 Oct. 1952). Kenny, who did not speak German, also referred to 'SS-Sturmführer' – not a rank in the Waffen-SS – Geisler by the name of 'Geeser'. SS-Obersturmbannführer Dr Paeffgen was previously head of Amt IV-D (PRO KV 2/170, Praetorius memorandum of 11 Oct. 1945).
47. *Sunday Dispatch*, 28 Sept. 1952, p. 9. Like O'Reilly, Kenny received no training in parachute techniques other than a quick briefing before the flight. When O'Reilly questioned the lack of airborne training, Peters is supposed to have replied that the odds of an injury increase with each successive jump and that if he only did it the one time, 'then the law of averages will be on your side'.

48. PRO KV 2/119, Kenny memorandum.
49. Ibid., undated O'Reilly memorandum.
50. In contrast, Günther Schütz said that he jumped from a height of 2,000 metres. In practice, most German airborne operations (Holland, Crete etc.) involved lower-altitude jumps than were standard in other armies. The military-issue RZ series German parachute was attached to the rear of the harness and did not have risers for precisely controlled landings. This meant that the parachutist stood a better chance of an exact landing when jumping from a lower altitude, with less time airborne to stray out of the drop zone. The ratio of injuries from such lower-level jumps is always correspondingly higher given the greater impact velocity, though the slightly larger chute somewhat compensated for this. Combat jumps were usually made at slightly over one hundred metres (*World War II German Military Studies*, Vol. 28, German Airborne Operations; Stephan, *Die Deutsche Keltologie und ihre Berliner Gelehrten bis 1945*, p. 181, transcript of a taped interview between Stephan and Schütz in 1958; and Edward, *German Airborne Troops*, pp. 23 and 55).
51. *Sunday Dispatch*, 19 Oct. 1952.
52. PRO KV 2/119, notes on the case of J.F. O'Reilly.
53. Carter states (*The Shamrock and the Swastika*, p. 139) that O'Reilly told LTC Joseph Guilfoyle that 'the German military boots he wore had belonged to a German soldier with whose widow he had formed an alliance'.
54. While testing the radio in January 1944, the Army operator monitored calls on the pre-set frequency from a German station identified as RGL. The German sender repeated the abbreviations QSA QSV QSY 416 GI. The technical report also noted that O'Reilly's radio receiver covered a narrow bandwidth, from 7941 kcs to 8137 kcs (day) and 3894 kcs to 4106 kcs (night). O'Reilly's transmitter/receiver is preserved at the Military Archives, Cathal Brugha Barracks, Dublin.
55. PRO KV 2/119, Kenny memorandum.
56. USNA, A.A. Abteilung Militär I, Abwehr Irland, v. Grote to Abwehr, 8 Feb. 1944 and response of Bentivegni on 23 Feb. 1944. The SD response is in A.A., Inland II Geheim, SD-Berichte und Meldungen zur Lage in und über Irland, Vol. I, Geiger to A.A., 25 Feb. 1944.
57. Dickel, *Die deutsche Aussenpolitik und die irische Frage*, pp. 210–11, citing A.A. Inland IIg – Waffen SS, Aufstellung englischer SS-Formation, 26 July 1944 and Bundesarchiv, Persönlicher Stab RFSS, NS 19/1481, Brandt to Klumm, 15 Jan. 1945.

CHAPTER 8

1. PRO KV 4/9, Liddell report, p. 94. Northern Ireland, being an integral member of the United Kingdom, was necessarily a belligerent.
2. William Joyce and John Amery, both British subjects, were hanged for collaboration with the enemy. At least two members of the British Free Corps were likewise sentenced to death, but had their sentences commuted to penal servitude for life.

3. Ibid., p. 73. Warnock's name is deleted from the Liddell report, but can be determined given a lack of anyone else holding a similar position in occupied Europe after 1940.

4. USNA, A.A. Büro USt-Sekr., Diplomatische Aufzeichnung 1942, Aufzeichnung [Hans] Dieckhoff, 11 Dec. 1942.

5. Bewley, *Memoirs of a Wild Goose*, p. 198.

6. Duggan, D.Litt. thesis, Appendix XVII, p. 386, memorandum of 23 Dec. 1942.

7. NAI, DFA SOF P. 17, Bryan to Walsh, 12 Dec. 1945. Despite his activities, or perhaps because of them, Seán MacBride (then Minister of External Affairs) authorized a diplomatic passport for Bewley in June 1951, though Bewley had not been in the diplomatic service for twelve years. The Department of External Affairs eventually reconsidered the matter, but Bewley continued pressing the point for another three years (Ibid., Warnock to External Affairs, 17 Dec. 1954 and Cremin to Warnock, 2 March 1955).

8. Bundesarchiv Potsdam, RSHA film No. 1581, undated card, P/38/1000; Roth, *Mr Bewley in Berlin*, p. 103.

9. Elborn, *Francis Stuart*, p. 124. Stuart was involved in translating material from German to English, although by his own admission, he did not speak very good German. In all likelihood, Stuart was correcting and improving texts that were already in English.

10. Miss Walsh also delivered copies of Irish newspapers to Stuart so he could stay relatively current on Irish affairs when he was broadcasting to Ireland. According to Stuart's 1992 interview with David O'Donoghue, he and Miss Walsh shared the same boarding house for a time. When interviewed by O'Donoghue, Walsh (from Youghal, Co. Cork) had the following comments to make about Jews in Germany: 'There was a lot of poverty, you know, really. The people were very poor and the Jews really had control, had everything. There is no doubt about it, they had. The poor Germans coming out of university had no hope of a job' (O'Donoghue, *Hitler's Irish Voices*, p. 111).

11. Stuart interview, 15 July 1999.

12. IMA G2/X/1722, *Irish Times*, 27 Aug. 1947.

13. In an interesting coincidence, if that is what it was, Hempel visited Iseult at Laragh Castle on 5 May, the same day Görtz landed in Ireland. Görtz arrived at Laragh on 9 May, after a 70-mile hike (IMA G2/X/1722, Garda surveillance report of 5 May 1940).

14. Given what is known of both Görtz and O'Mara, the title 'secretary' might have been used euphemistically. A more pertinent question might be why Görtz, as a junior officer in training with the Brandenburg Regiment, would qualify for one. According to Haller, Stuart and O'Mara were already together when Haller suggested to Görtz that he should meet them to better prepare for his mission.

15. In one of these documents, under the section for nationality, she describes herself as 'stateless – German' (*staatenlos – Deutsch*). Her date of birth is given as 2 July 1918 and she claims residency in Germany from 1936 (Bundesarchiv – Abteilung R, Berlin, File I 28044, Fragebogen betr. "Spende Künstlerdank", 13 March 1942).

16. PRO KV 2/119, notes on the case of J.F. O'Reilly, p. 3.

17. Ní Mheara-Vinard, *Cé Hí Seo Amuigh?*, p. 117. The title of her book may be translated into English a number of ways, from 'Who is that woman out there?' to 'Who is she on the outside?'

18. In a remarkably thorough search for the truth, David O'Donoghue contacted the living members of the Hamilton family and searched the available records. None of the Hamiltons had ever heard of her. MI5, which had access to the best sources of information available, was likewise unable to verify her claim.

19. Though his work is an invaluable source for personal accounts by IRA volunteers in the 1923–48 period, Uinseann MacEoin (*The IRA in the Twilight Years*) engages in a fawning and saccharine tribute to O'Mara. In addition to repeating the numerous historical inaccuracies advanced by O'Mara herself, he adds a few more – such as mistaking Abwehr II for 'Abwehr 11' and inventing a book by Kurt Haller that never existed (p. 928). He also manages to misspell the name Canaris as 'Canarias' (p. 930) and to totally misrepresent the facts in the Hermann Görtz affair (p. 926).

20. The book *Irische Freiheitskämpfer – Biographische Skizzen*, was published by R. Weiland in Berlin in 1940 (Dickel, *Die deutsche Aussenpolitik und die irische Frage*, p. 237).

21. When asked by this author to comment on her role in the Görtz mission, Ms O'Mara sent a terse reply: 'I must inform you that there is nothing more to add to my account of the brief encounter with Hermann Goertz, which you appear to have read. My opinions are the same and my admiration is lasting of this noblest of men I am happy to have known' (O'Mara to author, 9 Aug. 1999).

22. 'It was obviously a great relief to him when I offered my assistance. He proposed that I go ahead and prepare programmes and broadcasts' (Ní Mheara-Vinard, *Cé Hí Seo Amuigh?*, p. 193). She further opined that 'one could hope and trust in God that these programmes were listened to over there as a counter-attack against the lies which England no doubt was directing at Ireland to inveigle her to no purpose into the war' (Ibid., p. 194.) Her use of the pseudonym Róisín – a variant of her birth name Rosaleen – dates from her first talk on German radio. She has used it ever since.

23. Stephan, 'Die Vergessene Episode', pp. 131–2, interview with Kurt Haller. O'Mara was apparently working as an actress in 1942. On 12 March of that year, she was asking for a 500 RM grant from the theatre division of the Propaganda Ministry, as she was in serious financial difficulty from missing an existing theatre engagement. She had been sent to 'recover' at the health spa at Baden-Baden, by order of Propaganda Minister Joseph Goebbels. She got the grant (Bundesarchiv – Abteilung R, File I 28044, Frowein to Hilger, 12 March 1942).

24. O'Reilly, *Sunday Dispatch*, 20 June 1952, p. 2.

25. PRO KV 2/119, summary of O'Reilly contacts, p. 3. Despite her claims to the contrary (in her memoirs, she claimed to have married two Nazi officers), O'Mara indicated on her application to the Reichstheaterkammer in late 1944 that she was single (*ledig*), rather than married (*verheiratet*), divorced (*geschieden*) or widowed (*verwitwet*).

26. IMA G2/X/1164, Warnock report regarding Nora O'Mara, 15 July 1944. Mullally was her co-worker at the Irland-Redaktion.

27. Ibid.

28. Prionsias O'Drisceoil 'A monarchial republican', *Irish Times*, 13 Feb. 1993, p. 9. See also Eddie Doyle, 'Publisher of "pro-Nazi" book may get State grant,' *Sunday Business Post*, 3 Jan. 1993, p. 1.

29. Ibid. Certainly an irony, when one considers that some of the radio broadcasts for which Ms. O'Mara takes full credit are said to have actually been written by Susan Hilton, one of the other broadcasters at the Irland-Redaktion (O'Donoghue, *Hitler's Irish Voices*, p. 106).

30. Ms Ní Mheara-Vinard previously lived in Bernau, Germany. Ironically, the statements that she makes in her book concerning the Holocaust would be illegal under German law, with a penalty of up to three years' imprisonment.

31. PRO HO 45/25839, MI5 summary, 8 Feb. 1945.

32. Ibid., William Murphy statements to MI5, 19 Jan., 1, 2 and 6 Feb. 1945. Warnock was considered a soft touch for questionable passports and visas. Günther Schütz unsuccessfully approached him for one in 1941. MI5 alleged that Murphy's passport application was made to allow him to escape internment. However, the Dublin authorities considered anyone born in Ireland – North or South – to be an Irish citizen, since the 1937 Constitution laid claim to the whole island.

33. PRO HO 45/25839, Murphy statement, 19 Jan. and 1 Feb. 1945.

34. The old Drakestrasse legation had been destroyed by Allied bombing.

35. PRO HO 45/25839.

36. Ibid. Their earlier Abwehr contact, Hauptmann Steffens, was transferred to the Wiesbaden Ast.

37. Murphy was working with the 'New British Broadcasting Station' – a propaganda broadcast to England that pretended to be originating from inside the country. Büro Concordia was directed by Dr Erich Hetzler under the auspices of the Foreign Ministry.

38. Bundesarchiv – Abteilung R, Berlin, File 5622986, Henry Freeman. The Reichsschrifttumskammer was one of seven artistic/cultural associations organized under the Propaganda Ministry after 1 Nov. 1933.

39. Bundesarchiv – Abteilung R, Berlin. File 7161, John Freeman. According to Freeman's statement, about his activities in the First World War, 'Ich war dann im Dienst des Auswärtigen Amtes (Sonderabteilung d.h. Geheimabteilung)' (I was then in the service of the Foreign Office – Special Section, i.e. Secret Section).

40. Effectively, Haller was Veesenmayer's troubleshooter. He later accompanied Veesenmayer when the latter was appointed German Minister to Hungary in 1944.

41. Elborn, *Francs Stuart*, p. 134. Veesenmayer suggested a revised plan in August 1941, which envisaged transporting Ryan, Clissmann, and an RTO to Brandon Bay, County Kerry. It was ultimately abandoned.

42. IMA G2/X/0154, Irish in Germany. When I asked Francis Stuart about Mullally in my interview with him in July 1999, he noted that all the Berlitz people were 'very devious. All the Irish who had been teaching in the Berlitzwhen the war broke out, you see, they all made it home for Berlin, because that was where they took refuge. They were a dubious, as I said, a dubious sort of people.' Specifically speaking of Mullally, he described him as 'an absolute idiot, harmless if you like, but I don't know if this idiot was that harmless'.

43. O'Donoghue, *Hitler's Irish Voices*, p. 125.

44. PRO KV 2/119, summary of O'Reilly contacts, p. 3.

45. Francis Stuart interview, Dundrum, 17 Nov. 1989, courtesy of David O'Donoghue.

46. O'Donoghue, *Hitler's Irish Voices*, p. 212. Nora O'Mara claimed that Mullally taught her Irish (Ní Mheara-Vinard, *Cé Hí Seo Amuigh?*).

47. Francis Stuart interview, Dundrum, 24 Feb. 1990, courtesy of David O'Donoghue.

48. O'Donoghue, *Hitler's Irish Voices*, p. 166.

49. Reinhard Doerries, *Prelude to the Easter Rising: Sir Roger Casement in Imperial Germany* (London: Frank Cass, 2000), pp. 9–18.

50. The estimated number of prisoners interned varies. Haller put it between eighty and a hundred, Codd estimated the number to be about 125, Tim Ronan at 150, and Colonel McGrath later gave the figure as 180. All these estimates could be accurate, depending on when the particular individual was present.

51. Stephan, 'Die Vergessene Episode', p. 378, based on interview with Jupp Hoven.

52. Elborn, *Francis Stuart*, p. 135. Elborn dismisses the assertion in the Hayes confession that Ryan and Stuart were doing propaganda work in the camp. In a curious leap of logic, Elborn justifies this position by stating that 'Ryan and Stuart had visited a camp for Irish prisoners who indicated that they wished to join an Irish Guard. The plan came to nothing, and Ryan told Stuart he was sorry he had been there at all.'

53. Carter, *The Shamrock and the Swastika*, p. 124. Carter identifies the journalist as Lt. Bissell, which is phonetically close to the Lt. Birrell named by Sergeant Codd. According to Codd, Birrell, from County Clare, was most certainly Irish.

54. The late actor Denholm Elliot was among the internees at Stalag III B.

55. PRO KV 4/9, Liddell report, p. 48.

56. 'Irish Colonel's Story of Life in German Camps', *Irish Times*, 23 Oct. 1945. McGrath was a decorated officer from World War One and had been captured in 1939. He was later taken to Dachau, where he remained until freed when the camp was liberated. Cf. Carter, *The Shamrock and the Swastika*, pp. 127 and 135.

57. 'Back From the Camps', *Irish Times*, 14 June 1945.

58. 'Tim Ronan Remembers', *The Evening Echo*, 30 May 1979, p. 5.

59. IMA G2/4953, Garda Superintendent Dowd to G2.

60. Ibid., G2 report, 13 May 1944. Stalag III D at Genshagen was one of the recruitment/'holiday' camps for the British Free Corps, but O'Brien's name

does not appear on any of the existing documentation. Without exception, all BFC volunteers adopted an alias and the personnel records were later destroyed.

61. IMA G2/X/0154. Also listed as 'Irishmen in Germany who have come under special notice' (i.e. suspicion of collaboration with the Germans) were G.O. Johnson, Kevin McGann, Dominick O'Connor, Patrick Quinn, Timothy Ronan (Rosscarbery) and a John Sheehan (Kenmare, Co. Kerry) who was said to be 'working on submarines'. With the exception of Timothy Ronan, no details are available about the individuals and none were prosecuted after the war. Their names were circulated to embassies and customs officials in the event that they attempted to return to Ireland. Ronan returned to Rosscarbery and corresponded with David O'Donoghue in preparation for *Hitler's Irish Voices*: 'It is likely that Irish POWs were approached about propaganda work. To my knowledge, nobody took up the offer. I spent approximately two years in Friesack. During that time I was approached once to assist the Germans – they did not specify the type of work – I refused. Sometime afterwards, a number of us were transferred to a camp near the Polish border where we remained for approximately one and a half years. There were approximately 150 POWs in Friesack.' Tim Ronan died in 1996.

62. Haller himself described Codd as 'ein hochintelligenter, aber verschlossener und schwieriger Mann' (a highly intelligent, but reserved and difficult man) – Stephan, 'Die Vergessene Episode', p. 379, interview with Haller).

63. In his interviews with Carolle Carter, Father O'Shaughnessy said that Hoven, not Clissmann, made the initial approach.

64. IMA G2/4949, Appendix III, statement of Father O'Shaughnessy. Interviews with O'Shaughnessy, then living in California, formed the basis of Carolle Carter's chapter on Friesack in *The Shamrock and the Swastika*. Carter made several errors of fact, largely due to a lack of primary source material. Father O'Shaughnessy was not privy to any operational details of the missions (Thomas O'Shaughnessy, *Rest Your Head in Your Hand* [Dublin: Ward River Press, 1983], pp. 85–102). According to Carter (*The Shamrock and the Swastika*, p. 134), Codd had a homosexual relationship with Stringer while in Friesack and his later transfer to Dusseldorf occurred when he hit a policeman. She states, wrongly, that he was placed in a concentration camp after the decision to cancel his mission.

65. Elizabeth Clissmann also encountered Sergeant Codd during his adventures in Berlin. She remembered him as a 'drunk' and 'one of the worst kinds of people imaginable' (Telephone interview with Mrs Clissmann, 15 Feb. 1999.)

66. Stephan, 'Die Vergessene Episode', p. 379.

67. Codd was later told that Frank Richards/Mr Maloney/Frank Ryan was ill in Dresden and later that he 'died of a disease of the veins' (IMA G2/4949, Codd statement of July 1945, Appendix II).

68. Cushing had been given a false passport in the name of St John.

69. The Gestapo or *Geheime Staatspolizei* (Secret State Police) was another branch of the German security apparatus, the RSHA. Every Gestapo officer carried an embossed metal disc that gave unlimited powers of search and arrest. Cushing was sent to Sachsenhausen concentration camp where he was interned along with captured Russians Jakob Dzhugashvili and Vassily

Kokorin, Stalin's son and Molotov's nephew respectively. In a post-war article, Cushing stated that three other Irish were likewise interned there, and that he himself was then (1968) an employee of the British Ministry of Defence ('Stalins Sohn fühlte sich verstossen', *Der Spiegel*, 15 March 1968, p. 92). If accurate, it suggests that Cushing was an Allied plant.

70. Haller reported that he was able to free Brady (a.k.a. Metzger) from custody and that he later joined the SD. He also said that the other Irish veterans from Friesack were assigned to a *Gentleman-Abteilung* of a concentration camp, presumably Sachsenhausen. Their freedom at war's end was short-lived; regarded by the British as 'renegades', they were assigned to penal servitude in Malaysia from which only one returned (Stephan, 'Die Vergessene Episode', p. 382). Part of this information from Haller tallies with that reported by Codd, who stated that both Brady and Stringer were taken in by the SD and were last seen fighting the Russians on the Eberswalde sector near Berlin on 16 April 1945 (IMA G2/4949). In fact, Brady survived the war, was returned to the British by the Russians, court-martialled and sentenced to fifteen years ('Sentenced for Serving with Germans', *The Evening Post*, 21 Dec. 1946). While Irish reports indicated that Cushing was the informant, Haller suggested that the communal flat where the Irish stayed was under surveillance – possibly electronic – so the information could have been revealed in this manner.

71. IMA G2/4949 – Appendix IV, 'Notes on Cyphers taught to John Codd', prepared by Dr Richard Hayes. A summary of all the German ciphers encountered by G2 in the war can be found in the Richard Hayes Papers in the National Library of Ireland, MS 22,981–984. Dr Hayes also worked on the Japanese, Swedish, Italian and American codes, as well as the German diplomatic code.

72. IMA G2/4949, Codd's statement of July 1945. Otto Skorzeny (1908–1975) was Hitler's idea of the perfect SS man. At well over six and a half feet tall, and with a face crossed by duelling scars, Skorzeny led the team that successfully rescued Mussolini from his mountain prison at Gran Sasso in 1943. Hitler personally decorated Skorzeny with the Knight's Cross. Skorzeny later organized the sabotage/assassination squads that penetrated American lines during the Battle of the Bulge in 1944. After the war, Skorzeny periodically lived in Ireland, raising horses on a 170-acre farm, but died in Spain in 1975. Codd got his rank wrong; at this time, Skorzeny was an SS-Standartenführer (Colonel). The rank of SS-Hauptsturmbannführer did not exist.

73. Having a Gestapo officer with this name almost sounds like a bad joke. *Tod* is the German word for 'dead' as well as being a relatively common surname. SS concentration camp guards used the 'Totenkopf' (death's head) as one of their identifying insignia, as did the Wehrmacht Panzer units. The initial usage of this symbol dates back to the Prussians in the Napoleonic Wars.

74. In O'Reilly's serialized memoirs in the *Sunday Dispatch* (1952), he refers to this SS officer as 'Geisler' rather than Geise. I have used Codd's version in the section dealing with his narrative.

75. John O'Reilly, 'School Where the Pupils Were Crooks and Murderers!' *Sunday Dispatch*, 14 Sept. 1952, p. 5. O'Reilly went on to cite a description

of the students at the Lehnitz SS training school as 'for the most part, foreign criminals from occupied countries. Some were awaiting execution or were serving life sentences for civil crimes when they were freed by our [German] Security chiefs.'

76. Kahn, *Hitler's Spies*, p. 11. In this account, Codd is not referred to by name, but mention is made of a 'fake Irishman' assigned to the school.

77. Amery was hanged in December 1945 at Wandsworth Prison after his trial on charges of treason. For a time, Amery had been imprisoned in Italy along with former Irish Minister to Germany Charles Bewley.

78. IMA G2/4949. Codd also wrote a complaining letter to the *Standard* about the treatment of war refugees in Ireland. He described his circumstances and that he had been a POW, but conveniently forgot to mention the part about being in constant training for Nazi Germany's Intelligence services: 'An Irish DP Tells History', *The Standard*, 3 Nov. 1950.

79. Carter, *The Shamrock and the Swastika*, p. 131. O'Neill was trained to build a transmitter from scratch, obviating the need to supply him with one (USNA II, A.A., T-120, Reel 397, frame 302086, document of 19 Aug. 1942). She erroneously gives him the code name of 'Isebart'.

80. NLI MS 22,984, Richard Hayes papers, Hayes's report, p. 3.

81. PRO KV 2/173, Bryan to Liddell, 15 July 1946. Colonel Bryan requested that Lahousen be asked about O'Neill, Jupp Hoven, Fromme, Mahr, Mill-Arden and O'Donovan.

82. USNA II, A.A., T-120, Reel 89, frames 302088, 302091, 302092 and 302103, documents of 21 Aug. 1942, 3 Sept. 1942, 10 Dec. 1942 and 16 Dec. 1942.

83. IMA G2/X/0154.

84. Ibid., Dan Bryan to Dr Nolan, Department of External Affairs, 21 March 1946.

85. The individuals compiling the surveillance and situation reports in G2 were not above the occasional comment that probably reveals more about the reporter than the subject. In one instance, a woman was described as having 'eyes brown and closely set – she also knows how to use them ... features irregular and attractive ... some difficulty with 'th' ... can drink and make love' (IMA G2/X/0093, PM 301, 8 Feb. 1943).

86. This is also true for a lady named Shelia Ni Kearney – 'an Irishwoman in heart and soul' – who appeared on the Irland-Redaktion broadcast on July 4, 1943 at 7:15 pm.

87. IMA G2/X/0154.

88. The similarity of name and occupation is almost enough to suggest that this is the same John McCarthy, working on the SS *George Washington*, who made the advance arrangements for Sean Russell's return to occupied Europe in 1940. However, there is no documentary evidence of any connection.

89. PRO HO 45/25827, summary of Kenneth Landers. The BFC (also called the Legion of St George) personnel were recruited from the Marlag und Milag Bremen and other stalags, before being transferred to the Stalag III D 'holiday camp' at Genshagen.

90. Other Irish persons resident in Nazi Germany included Mrs Agnes Burke (Glengarriff), Dan Riordan (Cork), Denis Cremin (Dromore, Mallow), Timothy Crowley (Glengarriff) and M. Walsh (Kanturk).

91. IMA G2/3261, Joseph Andrews; NLI MS 22,984, Richard Hayes papers; G2/ 0154, merchant seamen (Irish Nationals).
92. PRO KV 2/119, undated summary.
93. IMA G2/0195, DMD summary, 4 March 1940 and John Regan, *The Irish Counter-Revolution, 1921–1936* (Dublin: Gill and Macmillan, 1978), p. 434, fn. 105.

CHAPTER 9

1. Jan van Loon interview, May 1999. Van Loon did the after-hours digging while Schütz kept watch. Their alarm signal was a string that connected between the adjoining cells, through the hole in the wall containing a heating pipe.
2. IMA G2/X/0203, Healy report, 2 Feb. 1942.
3. Interview with Jan van Loon, May 1999.
4. This is the actual date of the escape, though Schütz himself later said that it occurred on 28 February and this error has been repeated by other historians. Both the official file and even his wanted poster show the correct date, 15 February 1942. Curiously, the wanted poster used his alias, Hans Marschner.
5. Schütz, 'My Secret Mission to Ireland', *Sunday Press*, 14 June 1970. Almost simultaneously with the escape, one of the Mountjoy guards noticed that the latrine door was locked from the inside, though all the prisoners were asleep – or so he thought. He raised the alarm from inside the prison. Cf. Stephan, 'Die Vergessene Episode' p. 400.
6. Stephan, 'Die Vergessene Episode', pp. 401–3.
7. Mrs Brugha had five daughters, all of them active in illegal activity. Another daughter, Brenda, who worked at the National Bank on College Green, transmitted messages from Hermann Görtz (actually from Joseph Andrews, who was representing Görtz) and passed them on to radio operator Anthony Deery (IMA G2/3261, statement of Joseph Andrews, 3 Nov. 1943).
8. Ó Drisceoil, *Censorship in Ireland*, pp. 106–7.
9. IMA G2/X/0203, interview with Schütz, 1 May 1942. Mrs Brugha undoubtedly said this to boost the image of the IRA. The last agent radio link with Germany was shut down in March 1942, when Gardaí seized Anthony Deery and his transmitter. Neither German records nor personnel testify to the presence of another active transmitter. Görtz believed there was one, but did not realize that the 'transmitter' was actually G2 sending in messages to him in his own code. The legation transmitter was inactive after 1943 and was used only sparingly after 1942, at the polite request of the Irish government.
10. Ibid., interview with Schütz, 11 April 1946, Curragh Military Hospital. Schütz said that the boat was purchased from someone named Sutton in Wicklow and was scheduled to depart from Bray. He said that McNamee, Seán McCool and a 'Paul' were supposed to be his fellow passengers. Cf. Bell, *The Secret Army*, p. 221 on McGuinness's role
11. Carter, *The Shamrock and the Swastika*, p. 267, fn. 33, cites A.A. Reel 89, Frame 100778, document of 10 Sept. 1941 and Reel 397, frame 302012, Document of 6 Oct. 1941.

12. UCD Archives, Mulcahy papers, P7A220, Mulcahy to Boland, 8 June 1940.
13. NAI File S 12860.
14. IMA G2/X/0203. Dr Hayes successfully decoded the signal. Schütz later told G2 that the ten radios were supposed to be for 'inter-unit' activity in Northern Ireland, presumably requested by Mrs Brugha and/or the Belfast IRA. Cf. Schütz interview, 9 and 10 June 1942 by Commandant de Buitléar and Dr Hayes. 'Klingston' was presumably intended to be 'Kingston' – Caitlín Brugha's shirt company – or possibly 'Kingstown' (Dún Laoghaire), where Hempel had his house.
15. Carter, *The Shamrock and the Swastika*, p. 208, cites A.A. Reel 384, frames 301165, 301170, and 301179, documents of 2 April, 4 April, and 17 April 1942. The new cover address was to be Senõra Honor Herrero y Elosua, Bilboa, Espartero 36, España. The Abwehr also relayed some personal information: 'Ives had married, De Boer was okay, and Lilo was well and sent her love.' The fact that the Abwehr was thinking of dropping a replacement transmitter to Schütz raises the question of why they did not send one earlier to the IRA using the same means.
16. Stephan, 'Die Vergessene Episode', pp. 408–10. Though Schütz's statement to Enno Stephan would seem to support the idea that the detectives did not expect to find Schütz at Mrs Brugha's home, it is possible that Charles McGuinness, who had been arrested by this time, might have revealed Schütz's location to lessen his own sentence.
17. Bundesarchiv – Aachen Zentralnachweissstelle, Schütz file.
18. Van Loon interview, 20 May 1999. German radio generally started its news with the announcement of the situation in the armed forces. The opening line, 'Der Oberkommando der Wehrmacht gibt bekannt...' ('The High Command of the Armed Forces announces') was almost as famous as the voice of William Joyce and his trademark 'Germany Calling'. For obvious reasons, Joyce's talks were popular among the internees.
19. Ibid.
20. In their coded message back to Görtz, Irish Intelligence had to ask him to explain what he meant by a 'cholera belt' – apparently a device to keep the waist warm in cold conditions (IMA G2/1722, Part XII).
21. West, *MI5*, p. 416. Van Loon later lost his certificate, which he gave to the priest who instructed him in the Catholic faith. Van Loon also said (20 May 1999 interview) that he probably would have ended up in the Waffen-SS Division 'Nederland' (composed of Dutch volunteers) had they successfully escaped.
22. IMA G2/3748, letter from Col. F.H. Henry, Provost Martial, 24 June 1942.
23. Ibid., letter No. 112 (17 April 1944).
24. Ibid., letter of 25 Nov. 1945.
25. Van Loon interview, 20 May 1999. He was able to meet his family in Antwerp in 1960, but was unable to return to the Netherlands for his father's funeral. He was later given special permission by the Dutch Consul in Dublin to return for his sister's funeral.
26. As a Dutch national, van Loon was prohibited from joining the German Nazi Party, but had joined the Dutch version, the National Socialist Bewegung, before the German invasion in May 1940.

27. *Sunday Press*, 7 June 1970, p. 17.
28. IMA G2/X/0203, Hayes interview with Schütz, 29 May 1942.
29. When arrested, Weber-Drohl was in possession of the address of a Miss Mitchell, Kullmer Str. 31 vi, Berlin W 35 and the book *Diseases of Women* (IMA G2/1928 – Weber-Drohl arrest report, 13 Aug. 1942). The warrant for his arrest was signed on 6 August, but the arrest was not made until seven days later.
30. NAI A34, Summary of persons interned under the Emergency Powers Act, 27 Nov. 1946.
31. Ibid., Bryan to Provost Martial, 9 Nov. 1942.
32. Ibid., Bryan to Provost Martial, 8 Dec. 1942.
33. IMA G2/1722, Part XII, Görtz letter.
34. Ibid., Curragh Hospital report, Dec. 1943. Weber-Drohl's medical files are still held by the Irish Defence Forces Medical Corps, but privacy concerns prohibit their release (Telephone interview with Col. Monaghan, 21 April 2000).
35. Ibid., letter of 26 June 1944. This seems to have been another incident of the other inmates torturing Henry Obéd, but the investigation did not exclude the possibility that Weber-Drohl invented the event.
36. Ibid., Malloy report, 5 Dec. 1943.
37. Ibid., letter of 22 Nov. 1944. Hans Marschner was the cover name of Günther Schütz.
38. In another letter to his daughter, he states: 'I have served my earlier and young years in the French Foreign Legion in Africa.' (Ibid., letter of 21 Aug. 1944.) It is not known whether this is fact or fantasy, but if Weber-Drohl actually did serve in this unit, it is unusual that he would misspell the word 'Etranger' in his letter of November 1944.
39. Ibid., letters of 8 Nov. 1944 and Dec. 1944, both addressed to Minister David Gray at the US Legation. In his petition, Weber-Drohl mentions his daughter, Mrs Virginia Morris, a US citizen, who lived at 907 Laurel Avenue, Hollywood, California. Her husband, Robert Morris, worked for United Mechanical Labs in Hollywood. Virginia Morris was Weber-Drohl's illegitimate daughter.
40. IMA G2/1722, Part XII, undated, Weber-Drohl to Görtz.
41. Stephan, 'Die Vergessene Episode', p. 201.
42. IMA G2/2468, Simon to Elizabeth Simon, March 1941.
43. NAI DFA A34, appendix to memorandum concerning persons detained under the Emergency Powers (No. 20) Order.
44. IMA G2/2468, Walter Simon to Elizabeth Simon, March 1941. The Langenreihe address was unusual. Simon was ostensibly writing to a girlfriend, Karla Bramfeld at 87 Langenreihe, Hamburg. G2 noted that Pfaus had used 86 Langenreihe as a one-time address. The obvious suspicion was that it was a mail drop for the Abwehr. G2 noted that both Simon and Preetz were writing to the same address in the US, Hermann Kunekake, 272 Thomas Street, Hillside NJ. Simon also wrote to Preetz's accomplice, Joseph Donohue in Tuam. On 28 July 1941 Simon wrote a message to Dr Rantzau (an alias of Oberst Ritter at I-L Hamburg) care of Becker and Frank, Jungfernstieg 7/8, the Abwehr cover address given to Schütz: 'We are seven of us here including

one Indian. Three of us are of the same company.' (PRO KV 3/4, Curry history, p. 116.)

45. PRO KV 2/170, MI5 memo to Irish G2.
46. IMA G2/X/0703, Hayes to Bryan, 29 May 1942.
47. IMA G2/2468, Healy to Bryan, 10 Feb. 1942.
48. Ibid., book extract/outline in file.
49. Ibid., report of Captain J. Healy, 2 Feb. 1942.
50. Ibid., Power report, 6 Dec. 1942.
51. Carter, *The Shamrock and the Swastika*, p. 190.
52. IMA G2/1722, Notes on Görtz ciphers. Donohue can be excluded from this list as he was safely in Brixton Prison at the time and not picking up escape gear for anyone, including himself.
53. NAI DFA A34, undated G2 report.
54. Ibid., Obéd to Boland, 5 Feb. 1943.
55. Even many years after his release, and apparently unaware that G2 was feeding Görtz messages in his own code, Van Loon continues to believe that Obéd was an informer due to 'racial reasons'. Van Loon interview, 21 March 1999.
56. IMA G2/2468, Walter Simon to Elizabeth Simon, March 1941.
57. IMA G2/X/0203, Healy report, 2 Feb. 1942.
58. Görtz's identification of 'the traitor' varied. He occasionally accused Günther Schütz of being the informant, on one occasion threatening him with death. By far, Obéd was the easier target.
59. IMA G2/X/0345, letter of 27 March 1946.
60. Ibid., memorandum, 22 May 1942.
61. Austin Stack had been involved in the 1916 Casement affair, and was arrested after enquiring for him at the local police station. 'Not only reports that he had been tricked by police into coming to see them suggest that he was too clever by half: he had, in addition, carried the cut-out principle to such extraordinary lengths that once he was incommunicado none of his colleagues had any idea what to do next.' (Powell, *Our Gallant Allies*, p. 301). Mrs Stack was equally clumsy.
62. 'I volunteered for this work and asked for the assistance of two or three men with high University qualifications in science or mathematics. The help requested was not forthcoming and I was given instead three Lieutenants of clerical grade ability ... the work was then abandoned about June 1941 as there was not the slightest prospect of success [on the Legation codes] with the staff available.' (NLI, Ms 22,983, Richard Hayes papers, Hayes report, 2 Jan. 1946, p. 6.)
63. NLI, Ms 22,983, Richard Hayes papers.
64. NLI Ms 22,981. The Görtz keywords were Cathleen Ní Houlihan, Ellen Wiebke Rolf Ute, Gertrude Mathiessen, Departments of State and Amateur Theatricals.
65. IMA G2/1722, Part XII, summary of Görtz prison messages.
66. Ibid., Guilfoyle report, 11 Oct. 1944.
67. Ibid., Guilfoyle report of second interview with Lynch, 29 Oct. 1944.
68. Ibid., interview with Celena Heffernan (age 15), 28 Jan. 1943.
69. IMA G2/1722, part XII, Görtz prison messages, 26 Nov. 1943.

70. NLI Ms 22,982. This message had been burned by Görtz in his cell but was reconstituted by Dr Hayes at the Garda Technical Bureau at Kilmainham using the two-per-cent ferrocyanide solution and a few drops of hydrochloric acid.
71. NAI DFA A34, Görtz to Boland, 11 Aug. 1943.
72. Ibid., Guilfoyle to Boland, 3 July 1943.
73. IMA G2/3973, summary. Lundborg was almost certainly one of Nóinín Brugha's couriers between Dublin and Belfast. Many of her others were equally unsuccessful (Bell, *The Secret Army*, p. 221).
74. IMA G2/3364, memo of 20 Sept. 1944. Mrs Stack, a long-time supporter of Görtz, was arrested on 3 July 1943 when thirty-four Thompson machine guns were discovered at her home. De Valera made the decision not to prosecute her (NAI JUS P67/550).
75. IMA G2/1722, Major Joseph Guilfoyle report, 31 Aug. 1944. Görtz's original letter, complete with illustrations of his escape plan, is in the file at the Military Archives.
76. Original letter from Görtz, courtesy of Enno Stephan; Stephan, 'Die Vergessene Episode', p. 422. The Stephan material has been generously donated to the Irish Military Archives.
77. NAI DFA A34, 'Herr Hempel's Statement', 28 May 1947, drafted after Görtz's suicide.
78. Ibid., Görtz to Gerald Boland, 7 Sept. 1944.
79. PRO KV 4/9, Liddell report, pp. 103–4.
80. IMA G2/X/0203, Bryan to Boland, June 1946.
81. PRO CAB 78/22, Germans in Eire, Maffey to P.V. Emrys-Evans, Dominions Office, 31 May 1945.
82. Coogan, *Eamon de Valerai*, p. 614. Though he remained in Ireland at the end of the war, Hempel eventually returned home and died in Freiburg in 1972 (Duggan, *Neutral Ireland*, p. 250).
83. Ibid., p. 610. Cf. Keogh, *Jews in Twentieth Century Ireland*, pp. 173–92.
84. Keogh, ibid. de Valera received regular updates from Rabbi Isaac Herzog as well as access to the material in the British and American newspapers that was deemed too incendiary to Irish neutrality under the prevailing conditions of censorship. Cf. Ó Drisceoil, *Censorship in Ireland*, and O'Donoghue, *Hitler's Irish Voices*, p. 165.
85. Ibid., Boland to Bryan, 23 May 1946.
86. Coogan, *De Valera*, p. 548: 'The reason he gave [for the destruction], when the Battle of Britain was raging, was that Germany might use them after an invasion to justify her actions, as she had done with Holland. But why the destruction should have continued throughout the war, long after the threat from Germany had receded, must remain a matter of speculation.' Omissions in the files at the NAI are noticeable.
87. Ibid., G2 report, 29 May 1942.
88. IMA G2/X/0203, Dan Bryan to Gerald Boland, 28 May 1946. In the same correspondence, Bryan described Unland as 'a shrewd, cute and unscrupulous rogue' and Weber-Drohl as a 'hypocritical fraud'.
89. IMA G2/1722, Bryan to Gerald Boland, 28 May 1946.
90. Keogh, *Jews in Twentieth Century Ireland*, pp. 209–10.

91. NAI D/T S11007B/1, Department of Justice memorandum, 'Admission of One Hundred Jewish Children', 28 April 1948.
92. IMA G2/1722, Gerald Boland orders, 26 Aug. 1946.
93. UCD, MacEntee papers, Appendix II, p. 134.
94. Ibid., Görtz to Governor of Athlone, 6 Sept. 1946.
95. Ibid., Görtz letter of 19 Sept. 1946.
96. Ibid., Görtz to McDowell, Aug. 1946.
97. Ibid., G2 report, 5 Feb. 1946.
98. Degrelle was the wartime leader of the collaborationist Rexist movement in Belgium. He volunteered for service with the Waffen-SS, was promoted to SS-Sturmbannführer and received the Knight's Cross from Hitler. Degrelle was rumoured to be considering Ireland as a post-war refuge and he was favourably considered a 'political refugee' by Secretary of the Department of Justice, S.A. Roche, who had earlier sought to exclude Jewish immigration. Roche's view was opposed by the newly appointed Secretary of the Department of External Affairs, Frederick Boland. As it happened Degrelle never came to Ireland, preferring to remain in fascist Spain (PRO WO 204/1206 and Keogh, *Jews in Twentieth Century Ireland*, pp. 208–9).
99. IMA G2/3748, van Loon parole statement, 28 Oct. 1946.
100. Van Loon interview, 21 March 1999.
101. UCD, Ms P 67534, MacEntee papers, Appendix II.
102. Enno Stephan to author, 2 May 1999. Ritter remained active in intelligence work, though behind the scenes. He worked with the fledgling Bundesnachrichtendienst (BND), West Germany's intelligence service. Simon once told Stephan: 'That I have to die here so alone is the revenge of all the women I didn't marry.'
103. IMA G2/0265, deportation notice, 15 April 1947. Weber-Drohl's home of record was Gugelstrasse 129, Nürnberg. His daughters were Karoline and Augusta (MA G2/1928, Letter of 18 Sept. 1943).
104. Ibid., untitled newspaper cutting dated 18 April 1947.
105. Ibid., deportation notice, 15 April 1947.
106. Ibid., G2 file notation, 1 Sept. 1949. She was living at 6 Palmerston Park, Dublin.
107. Ibid. According to Mr van Loon, 'Paula', a German national, worked at the German Legation in Dublin, but he didn't know whether she and Tributh were ever actually married. Information on Tributh is from Gärtner telephone interview, 15 Dec. 1999.
108. Obéd's passport and a copy of his original letter to Nehru are kept at the Military Archives, Dublin. Obéd's family donated the documents when they visited Ireland.
109. Ibid.
110. UCD, MacEntee papers, Appendix II, p. 134.
111. 'My Secret Mission to Ireland', *The Daily Press*, 21 June 1970. Schütz added: 'Both Görtz and I were then told that the Allies had given a definite assurance that we were wanted in Germany for interrogation only ... a solemn undertaking was given that, when the interrogation was over, we would be released. ... Why didn't Görtz accept their word? Because he did not believe them. He felt that he was so important that he would be treated differently.'

112. NAI DFA A34, Gray to Clay, 12 May 1947.
113. *Irish Independent*, 17 April 1947.
114. NAI DFA A34, 'Herr Hempel's Statement', 28 May 1947, p. 1. This statement was taken during the coroner's inquest into Görtz's death.
115. Ibid., p. 3.
116. Ibid., pp. 7–8.
117. Stephan, 'Die Vergessene Episode', pp. 447–8.
118. NAI DFA A34, de Valera memorandum 'Re: Inquest on the late Dr Herman Goertz', 13 June 1947.
119. *Irish Times*, 24 May 1947, p. 1.
120. Kennedy, *Dr Hermann Görtz, A German Spy in South County Dublin*, p. 20.
121. Dr Alf MacLochlainn to author, 10 May 1999. After his release from Athlone, Görtz and Dr Richard Hayes met at Anne's Tea Shop in Nassau Street, where the code-breaker told the German what had actually happened. Dr MacLochlainn, who later worked with Dr Hayes in the National Library, was actually standing in the Passport Office when Görtz was carried past on his way to hospital.
122. Fisk, *In Time of War*, p. 376, Schütz interview, 11 April 1979.
123. IMA G2/1722, undated Görtz letter, possibly to Mrs Stuart.
124. Van Loon interview, 21 March 1999; and IMA G2/1722, Ellen Görtz to Department of External Affairs.
125. Van Loon telephone interview, 21 March 1999.
126. Elizabeth Clissmann interview, 15 Feb. 1999.
127. *Sunday Press*, 21 June 1970.
128. Michael Schütz interview, 20 Jan. 2000.
129. Stephan, 'Die Vergessene Episode', p. 444, interview with Günther Schütz, 1958.
130. Ibid.
131. Costello later became the Taoiseach in the inter-party government that cut the final ties with Britain to create the Republic of Ireland in 1949. He was also the barrister for Stephen Carroll Held.
132. *Irish Independent*, 17 April 1947, p. 1. Cf. NAI DFA A60.
133. *Evening Herald*, 25 Nov. 1947, p. 2.
134. Stephan to author, 1 Sept. 1999. Unland declined to be interviewed for this book.
135. Information courtesy of the Office of Births, Marriages, and Deaths, Dublin.
136. Van Loon interview, 21 March 1999.
137. IMA G2/X/1263, Kenny interview, 4 Jan. 1944.
138. Ibid., Kenny interview, 28 Dec. 1943.
139. IMA G2/X/1263, *Irish Times*, 20 May 1949.
140. IMA G2/3824, G2 report of 10 Jan. 1944, Florence O'Donoghue, G2 First Division to Bryan. Cf. file statement of Roddy Heron, 22 Feb. 1944.
141. USNA, CL-1566-BG, OWI file, 22 Jan. 1944.
142. Ibid., 10 Feb. 1944. Terrell was the frequent author of hilarious tongue-in-cheek reports from the US Legation. On 4 Nov. 1943 he reported: 'Mr de Valera has tossed out some strong hints that the government will continue censorship after the war. Dev still looks into his heart and knows what is best for the Irish people.' Terrell also added, in relation to the O'Reilly affair that 'parachutists won't have clean shirts this week due to a laundry strike'.

143. NLI Richard Hayes papers, Ms 22,982. Hayes to Bryan, 10 Feb. 1944.

144. Carter had O'Reilly 'slipping between the bars of the lavatory window' (*The Shamrock and the Swastika*, p. 139, fn 10) but she confused this with the escape of Schütz and van Loon in 1942. The escape point identified in the official investigation is the main window in O'Reilly's cell.

145. In the MI5 report on the escape, O'Reilly is said to have stopped in Drumcondra and borrowed money from relatives (PRO, KV 2/119, RUC to Liddell, 15 July 1944).

146. IMA G2/3824, G2 report, 9 July 1944. Cf. O'Reilly escape investigation report, same file.

147. *Daily Press*, 8 July 1944.

148. *Sunday Dispatch*, 11 Nov. 1952.

149. PRO, KV 2/119, Hughes to Liddell, 25 Jan. 1944. The MI5 file contains original G2 reports, passed to Liddell by the Irish.

150. IMA G2/3824, O'Reilly to Major Guilfoyle, 6 May 1944.

151. Letter from Dr Alf MacLochlainn, 10 May 1999.

152. O'Donoghue, *Hitler's Irish Voices*, p. 215, letter from Dr Alf MacLochlainn. Cf. NAI DFA/A 52 I.

153. Dr Hayes, by an ingenious combination of trial and error, developed three different systems for reconstituting burned messages. The above method was preferred for messages in pencil; for typed texts, he mounted the charred paper between glass and used infrared photography. (NLI Richard Hayes papers, Ms 22,984).

154. IMA G2/3824., Bryan to Carroll, 21 Sept. 1944. MacBride, as Minister for External Affairs from 1948 to 1951 – and Iseult Stuart's half-brother – played an important part in keeping Stuart out of Ireland, chiefly by refusing to renew his Irish passport. Stuart finally returned with his mistress (soon to become his second wife) in 1958, immediately after the death of Iseult Stuart (O'Donoghue, *Hitler's Irish Voices*, p. 166).

155. NLI Richard Hayes papers, Ms 22,982.

156. PRO, KV 2/119, report of 28 January 1944.

157. It was apparently standard practice to allow the prisoners to keep their money, even though much of this was obviously provided by the Germans to fund espionage activities. In the case of large amounts of cash (Schütz and Simon, for example), only parts of the funds were available during internment.

158. David O'Donoghue is perhaps the only historian to get this right. In every other instance, authors have seized on the idea that O'Reilly opened the 'Parachute Bar'. (O'Donoghue, Ph.D. thesis, p. 368, fn. 18.)

159. David M Kiely, *Bloody Women: Ireland's Female Killers* (Dublin: Gill & Macmillan, 1999), p. 205. By the time of her death (1956), the marriage had broken up. The couple first lived in Clifden, Galway, then moved to Dublin and finally County Wicklow. There were six children from the marriage. When O'Reilly left his wife to go off to Nigeria, the children were put into homes and Mrs O'Reilly moved to her sister's in Lancashire.

160. According to a newspaper story, O'Reilly was fined £3 on 27 March 1947 for possession of an unlicensed Webley revolver and 50 rounds of ammunition (IMA G2/3824).

161. The source for the story about O'Reilly in Cairo comes from Commandant Peter Young at the Irish Military Archives, Cathal Brugha Barracks, Dublin. This is not independently corroborated. Cf. O'Donoghue, *Hitler's Irish Voices*, p. 216 and O'Donoghue, Ph.D. thesis, p. 368.
162. O'Donoghue, *Hitler's Irish Voices*, p. 216. O'Reilly's brother Bernard is disinclined to discuss his brother's wartime activities (Ibid., p. 75).

CHAPTER 10

1. Kahn, *Hitler's Spies*, pp. 268–71 and PRO KV 2/103, summary.
2. This was a variant of the RSHA Amt VI (D) and was commanded by SS-Standartenführer Steimle (PRO KV 2/170, memorandum of 11 Nov. 1945, Praetorius interrogation report). A Major Kempf (Wehrmacht) directed Mil Amt B/I-Nord. SS-Standartenführer Otto Skorzeny was given headed the Mil Amt unit devoted to sabotage and special warfare operations.
3. PRO KV 2/103, summary. By this time, Germany had no active agents and any information coming out of Britain was manufactured by MI5's Double-Cross committee, which acted its part in concert with the greater deception scheme to disguise the Normandy landings.

CONCLUSION

1. PRO KV 4/8, 'Report on the operations of Camp 020 and Camp 020-R (B.I.E.) in connection with the interrogation of enemy agents during the war, 1939–1945', 27 Nov. 1945, p. 106.
2. This is to distinguish the permanent duty personnel at the Brandenburg Regiment (and later Division) from those who merely received special training there. Helmut Clissmann, who was attached to the unit, was sent on an abortive mission to Ireland in 1940, but never successfully reached the country.
3. PRO KV 4/9, p. 107.
4. NLI MS 22,983, Hayes report, 2 Jan. 1946. Hayes concluded that other than Görtz's cipher, the German encoding systems were rudimentary and unsophisticated.
5. IMA G2/0261, DMD summary, 5 April 1940. Minister Hempel at least had the capability for this mission. In March 1940, he visited Dixon and Hempenstall opticians and bought two thermometers and had two aneroid barometers repaired. He told the salesman that he already had a barograph. It is unlikely that Dr Hempel decided to take up meteorology as hobby. The FW-200 had an operational radius of slightly over 1,000 miles (Kenneth Munson, *Bombers 1939–1945* [London: Blandford Press, 1969], p. 83).
6. PRO KV 4/8, 'Report on the operations of Camp 020 and Camp 020-R (B.I.E.) in connection with the interrogation of enemy agents during the war, 1939–1945', p. 108.
7. Fisk, *In Time of War*, p. 77.
8. Though, as the 'Cambridge Five' proved, the security services were less adept at detecting Communist penetration of the British government.

9. In a post-war interview, de Buítléar stated that 'the chief of staff and his advisor Col. Dan Bryan really did not know their job and I do not think that they had the knowledge to carry out intelligence work'. De Buitléar simultaneously puffed his own credentials (Radio na Gaeltachta interview of de Buitléar by Pádraig Ó Catháin, courtesy of Éamon de Buitléar). His view of Bryan's ability and experience is not shared by anyone else who knew the two men (Interview with Mrs Jean Sheridan Healy, 5 Jan. 2000). Bryan related the incident with de Buitléar in his interview with Professor Eunan O'Halpin (Bryan interview, p. 30, courtesy of Professor Eunan O'Halpin).

10. Healy was fluent in German, Italian, Spanish, Irish, Greek and Latin. After the war, he returned to his position as a professor of modern languages at University College, Cork.

11. PRO DO 35/1230/WX132/1/124. The official number of Irish volunteers in the British forces was 42,665, though this number has been frequently enhanced by some historians.

Bibliography

ARCHIVAL SOURCES

National Archives of Ireland (NAI), Bishop Street, Dublin

Files

A20 – Annex	Frank Ryan – Berlin Legation file
A27	Parachutists (Lenihan)
A34	Hermann Görtz
A51	Miss M.P. Mains (restricted)
A52 I	O'Reilly/Kenny
A52 II	O'Reilly/Kenny
A60	Bryan–Liddell correspondence
A65	Rev. Oliver Kelly (restricted)
A66	Sidney Eyre Ievers (restricted)
A72	Francis Stuart
DFA SOF P. 14	MacWhite to External Affairs, 25 Aug. 1941
D/T S11007B/1	Jewish Refugees
202/664	Request for travel to Germany
235/65	Warnock to Boland re: *Reichsparteitag*
241/167	Proposal to recruit counter-espionage corps
S/12013	Obéd, Tributh, and Gärtner
S/12860	Charles McGuiness
S/13301	Hermann Görtz
S/13963	Hermann Görtz
JUS 8/842	German flag at Ballyheigue
JUS 8/888	'Aicein' – Irish youth fascist movement
JUS 8/893	Anti-British propaganda
JUS 8/905	Copy of 'Aiseiri'
JUS P67/550	IRA Activity

Irish Military Archives (IMA), Cathal Brugha Barracks, Dublin

G2/0077	Stephen Held	G2/0265	Unland/Preetz
G2/0089	Jupp Hoven	G2/0289	Dan Reeves
G2/0184	Charles Phillips	G2/0402	Johannesr
G2/0195	Thomas Gunning		Ernstberge
G2/0207	Walter Simon	G2/0421	Edeltrude
G2/0214	Francis and		Freidinger
	Iseult Stuart	G2/1722	Hermann Görtz
G2/0238	Kurt Hill	G2/1928	Weber-Drohl
G2/0246	Liam Walsh	G2/2016	Dr A. Cooney
G2/0257	Frank Ryan	G2/2029	Frank O'Connor
G2/0261	Werner Unland	G2/2146	Leon Mill-Arden
G2/2147	Séamus Hann	G2/X/0002	German classes
G2/2244	T. Kelly	G2/X/0058	IRA General file
G2/2278	Maude Gonne		1939–1943
	MacBride	G2/X/0093	Germans and IRA
G2/2457	Gerhard Günther	G2/X/0154	Irish in Germany
G2/2468	Walter Simon		(civilians)
G2/3010	Seán Russell	G2/X/0703	Günther Schütz
G2/3048	Stephen Hayes	G2/X/0265	German Activities
G2/3261	Joseph Andrews	G2/X/0345	Obéd, Tributh,
G2/3364	Helena Moloney		Gärtner
G2/3748	Jan van Loon	G2/X/0581	Pilots at Dublin
G2/3783	James O'Donovan		(McGuinness)
G2/3824	John O'Reilly	G2/X/0805	Joseph Lenihan
G2/3973	Henry Lundborg	G2/X/0947	Irish in Germany
G2/3997	Maisie O'Mahony		(POW)
G2/4430	Albert Arcari	G2/X/1091	Misc. enquiries
G2/4949	Sgt. Codd	G2/X/1164	Irish in Germany
	(Friesack Camp)		(suspect)
G2/4953	Patrick O'Brien		
G2/4961	Frank Stringer	G2/X/1263	John Kenny

National Library of Ireland (NLI), Dublin

MS 21,155	James O'Donovan papers
MS 22,983/81–4	Richard Hayes papers
MS 29,819	Frederick J. Allan Papers
McGarrity papers	

Trinity College, Dublin

MS 9308/613   Hauptmann Möllengarten letter

University College, Dublin

MacEntee Papers
Mulcahy Papers

Cork Archives Institute

Liam de Roíste papers
Liam Walsh papers
Seamus Fitzgerald papers

Bundesarchiv, Abteilung R, Berlin

Hermann Görtz – Nazi Party file
Wilhelm Preetz – Nazi Party file
Nora O'Mara – File I 28044
Johann Freeman – File 7161
Henry Freeman – File 5622986

Bundesarchiv, Zentralnachweisstelle, Aachen

Hermann Görtz – Personnel file
Günther Schütz – Personnel file

Bundesarchiv, Militärarchiv, Freiburg

Okw/Amt Ausland-Abwehr:
Aussenpolitische Übersichten, RW5/v. 350–6
Geheimakten über ND-Meldungen, RW5/v. 365–9
Kriegstagebuch der Abwehr II, RW5/v. 497

Reichswehrministerium:
Abt. Inland, Geheimakten über Grossbritannien u. Irland (1937–1939),
RW6/v. 91

OKW/Wehrwirtschafts und Rüstungsamt:
Irland (1938–44), WI/Ia, 2/11

Public Record Office (PRO), Kew Gardens, London

CJ 1/64	Anti-British activities in Ireland
CRIM 1/813	Görtz Criminal file
DO 35/894	UK–Eire Political and Constitutional Relations
DO 35/1230	Military Personal: Eire and Ulster's Contribution to the UK War effort 1943–1946
DO 121/86	Hermann Goertz
FO 371/24962	German propaganda in Italy – report on Charles Bewley
FO 940/49	Helmut Clissmann file
HO 45/25839	William Joseph Murphy
HW 19/3 – HW 19/10	ISOS: Abwehr hand cipher intercepts
HW 19/11 – HW 19/15	ISOS: Knox – Abwehr machine cipher intercepts
HW 19/85	ISOS: Knox – Abwehr machine cipher intercepts
KV 2/31	Karel Richter prosecution file
KV 2/45	Johannes Dronkers prosecution file
KV 2/85–8	Oberst Nikolaus Ritter file
KV 2/103	Herbert Wichmann interrogation file
KV 2/104	Heinz Jost interrogation file
KV 2/119	O'Reilly and Kenny
KV 2/167	Joachim Wilhelm Canaris
KV 2/170–1	Friedrich Karl Praetorius
KV 2/173	Erwin von Lahousen
KV 2/195	Albert Herman – pre-war commercial cover
KV 2/207–9	Hans Scharf – Breton liaison
KV 3/3	Canaris ISOS messages, May 1940–July 1943
KV 3/4–5	German Secret Service (Curry history)
KV 3/6	Notes on handbook – German Secret Service
KV 4/5	Masterman report on B1A (Double-Cross)
KV 4/6	B1 Inf collation of information on the Abwehr
KV 4/8	Report on Camp 020
KV 4/9	Liddell Report on B1H in Northern Ireland and Ireland
KV 4/13–15	A Digest of Ham, interrogations at Camp 020
KV 4/23	Report on B1C in connection with sabotage
WO 204/1206	Col. Constantine Canaris interrogation file
WO 208/4347	Erwin von Lahousen interrogation file

US National Archives II (USNA), College Park, Maryland

File CL-1566-BG	Correspondence between the US Legation Dublin and the Office of War Information, Washington
A3343-SSO-203-B	Veesenmayer SS officer file
A3343-RS-G406	Veesenmayer R u. RS file
OKM	German naval files
A.A.	Foreign Ministry files

Büro Staatssekretär: Irland, Vols. 1–3 (1939–44)
Büro Unterstaatssekretär: Diplomatische Aufzeichnungen, Vols. I–II (1942) Irland (Veesenmayer), 1941–2.

Dienstelle Ribbentrop:	SD 1936–43, Part I.
Inland II Geheim:	SD-Berichte u. Meldungen zur Lage in und über Irland, Vol. I. Waffen-SS England. Aufstellung einer englischen SS-Formation (1940–44)

OKW/WPr	Ministry of Propaganda files
RG Zentralkartei	NSDAP files
RG Ortsgruppe	NSDAP files
RG 0242–169A	Personal papers and photographs of Admiral Wilhelm Canaris
RG 165	Index to Military Intelligence files 1917–41
T-1022	Captured German Naval records

Unpublished material/theses

Dan Bryan Memoirs – Courtesy Professor Eunan O'Halpin.
LTC (ret.) John P. Duggan, 'Herr Hempel at the German Legation in Dublin, 1937–1945' (D.Litt. thesis, TCD, 1979).
Joseph G. Healy, Görtz Report of December 1944 – translation from coded original.
Michael Hill, IRA Radio Transmission Log, 1939–40.
Michael Mac Evilly – unpublished manuscript on Dr Andrew Cooney.
Oliver Murphy – unpublished manuscript on Stephen Hayes.
David O'Donoghue, 'Hitler's Irish Voices: The Story of German Radio's Irish Service, 1939–1945' (Ph.D. thesis, Dublin City University, 1995).
Mervyn O'Driscoll, 'Irish-German Diplomatic Relations, 1922–1939' (Ph.D. thesis, University College Cork, 1992).
Anthony G. Powell, 'Our Gallant Allies: A Tale of Ireland and Germany'.
Enno Stephan, 'Die Vergessene Episode: Deutsche Agenten im irischen Untergrundkampf'.
Enno Stephan, 'Die IRA im Spiegel der Weltpresse, 1936–1944'.

Newspapers and periodicals

An Cosantóir	Vol. IX, No. 1, January 1949; March 1975
Cork Examiner	2 Jun. 1945
Daily Telegraph	20 April 2000
Evening Echo	30 May 1979
Irish Independent	25 and 26 April 1949
Irish Press	1 Nov. 1940
Irish Sword	Vol. XIX, 1993
Irish Times	18 April 1947; 25 Aug.–10 Sep. 1947; 25 Nov. 1947; 6–17 July 1953; 3–4 June 1958; 13 Feb. 1993
Sunday Dispatch	June–Dec. 1952
Sunday Press	24 May–24 June 1970
Sunday Tribune	24 Jan. 1993
The Bell	Vol. XVII, Nos. 4 and 5, July and Aug. 1951
The Evening Herald	2 May 1947, 25 Nov. 1947
The Evening Mail	20 Oct. and 25 Sept. 1941
The People	18 Nov. 1967

Interviews

Ruiari Brugha – Dublin
Elizabeth Clissmann – Dublin
Morris Cogan – Bray, Co. Wicklow
John Duggan – Blackrock, Dublin
Douglas Gageby – Dublin
Dieter Gärtner – Swakopmund, Namibia
German Cultural Attaché – Booterstown, Co. Dublin
Jean Sheridan Healy – Cork
Commandant Victor Laing – Dublin
Col. (ret.) Joseph Latham – Dublin
Jan van Loon – Dublin
Hilda Mallie née Six – Dublin
David O'Donoghue – Bray, Co. Wicklow
Donal O'Donovan – Bray, Co. Wicklow
Brian O'Reilly – London
Mrs Timothy Ronan – Co. Cork
Michael Schütz – Dublin
Enno Stephan – Varel, Germany
Francis Stuart – Fanore, Co. Clare
Ion Stuart – Laragh, Co. Wicklow
Commandant Peter Young – Dublin

Published sources

Allen, Trevor, *The Storm Passed By: Ireland and the Battle of the Atlantic, 1940–41* (Dublin: Irish Academic Press, 1996).

Andrew, Christopher, *The Sword and the Shield The Mitrohkin Archive and the Secret History of the KGB* (New York: Basic Books, 1999).

Aronson, Schlomo, *Reinhard Heydrich und die Frühgeschichte von Gestapo und SD* (Stuttgart: Institut für Zeitgeschichte, 1971).

Baird, Jay W., *The Mythical World of Nazi War Propaganda, 1939–1945* (Minneapolis, MN: University of Minnesota Press, 1974).

Bell, J. Bowyer, *The Secret Army – The IRA 1916–1979* (Dublin: Poolbeg Press, 1989).

Bewley, Charles, *Memoirs of a Wild Goose* (Dublin: Lilliput Press, 1990).

Bower, Tom, *The Perfect English Spy* (London: William Heinemann, 1995).

Brammer, Uwe, *Spionageabwehr und Geheimer Meldedienst: Die Abwehrstelle X im Wehrkreis Hamburg 1935–1945* (Freiburg: Rombach Verlag, 1989).

Breitman, Richard, *Official Secrets* (London: Penguin Press, 1999).

Breuer, William B., *The Secret War with Germany* (Shrewsbury: Airlife Publishing, 1988).

Brown, Anthony Cave, *Bodyguard of Lies* (London: W.H. Allen, 1976).

Brown, Terence, *Ireland: A Social and Cultural History, 1922–1985* (London: Fontana Press, 1985).

Carroll, Joseph, 'US–Irish Relations, 1939–1945', *The Irish Sword*, Vol. XIX (1993).

Carroll, Joseph, *Ireland in the War Years, 1939–1945* (Newton Abbott: David & Charles, 1975).

Carter, Carolle J., *The Shamrock and The Swastika: German Espionage in Ireland in World War II* (Palo Alto, CA: Pacific Book Publishers, 1977).

Cass, Michael (ed.), *Intelligence and Military Operations* (London: Frank Cass, 1990).

Clausewitz, Carl von, *On War* (London: Everyman's Library, 1993).

Colvin, Ian, *Master Spy* (New York: McGraw-Hill, 1951).

Coogan, Tim Pat, *Eamon de Valera, The Man Who Was Ireland* (New York: Harper Perennial, 1995).

Coogan, Tim Pat, *The IRA: A History* (New York: Roberts Rinehart, 1994).

Cornwell, John, *Hitler's Pope: The Secret History of Pius XII* (London: Viking, 1999).

Cox, Colm, 'Militär Geographische Angaben über Irland', *An Cosantóir*, March 1975, pp. 80–94.

Cronin, Seán, *The McGarrity Papers* (Dublin: Anvil, 1972).

Cronin, Seán, *Frank Ryan, The Search for the Republic* (Dublin: Respol, 1980).

Cruickshank, C.G., *The German Occupation of the Channel Islands* (Oxford: Oxford University Press, 1975).

Deacon, Richard, *A History of the British Secret Service* (London: Frederick Muller, 1969).

Desarzens, Oliver, 'Nachrichtendienstliche Aspekte der "Weserübung" 1940', *Studien zur Militärgeschichte, Militärwissenschaft und Konfliktforschung* (Osnabrück), Vol. 34 (1988).

Dickel, Horst, *Die deutsche Außenpolitik und die irische Frage von 1932 bis 1944* (Wiesbaden: Franz Steiner Verlag, 1983).

Documents on German Foreign Policy, 1918–1945, Series D, Vols. X and XIII (London: His Majesty's Stationery Office, 1957).

Doerries, Reinhard R., *Prelude to the Easter Rising: Sir Roger Casement in Imperial Germany* (London: Frank Cass, 2000).

Doerries, Reinhard R., 'Tracing Kurt Jahnke: Aspects of the Study of German Intelligence', in George O. Kent (ed.), *Historians and Archivists* (Fairfax, VA: George Mason University, 1991).

Donnelly, Seán, *Elections '97* (Dublin: Brunswick Press, 1998).

Duggan, John, *Neutral Ireland and the Third Reich* (Dublin: Lilliput Press, 1989).

Duggan, John, 'The German Threat – Myth or Reality', *An Cosantóir*, September 1989.

Duggan, John, *A History of the Irish Army* (Dublin: Gill and Macmillan, 1991).

Duggan, John, 'Germany and Ireland in World War II', *The Irish Sword*, Vol. XIX, 1993.

Dwyer, T. Ryle, *Irish Neutrality and the USA, 1939–1947* (Dublin: Gill and Macmillan, 1977).

Dwyer, T. Ryle, *Guests of the State* (Dingle, Ireland: Brandon, 1994).

Edward, Roger, *German Airborne Troops* (New York: Doubleday, 1974).

Edwards, John Carter, *Berlin Calling* (New York: Praeger, 1991).

Elborn, Geoffrey, *Francis Stuart: A Life* (Dublin: Raven Arts Press, 1990).

Elsasser, *Germany and Ireland: 1000 Years of Shared History* (Dublin: Brookside, 1997).

Elting, John, *Swords Around a Throne* (London: Phoenix, 1997).

Farago, Ladislas, *The Game of the Foxes* (New York: David McKay, 1971).

Felstead, S. Theodore, *Germany and Her Spies* (London: Hutchinson & Co., 1940).

Fisk, Robert, *In Time of War, Ireland, Ulster and the Price of Neutrality 1939–1945* (London: Paladin Grafton Books, 1983).

Fleming, Peter, *Operation Sea Lion* (New York: Simon and Schuster, 1957).

Fleming, Peter, *Invasion 1940* (London: Hart-Davis, 1957).

Gehlen, Reinhard, *Der Dienst* (Mainz: Hase & Kohler Verlag, 1971).

Gellately, Robert, *The Gestapo and German Society* (Oxford: Clarendon Press, 1990).

Gellermann, Günther, *Moskau ruft Heeresgruppe Mitte* (Bonn: Bernard & Graefe Verlag, 1994).

Gellermann, Günther, *Tief in Hinterland des Gegners: Ausgewählte Unternehmen Deutscher Nachrichtendienste im Zweiten Weltkrieg* (Bonn: Bernard & Graefe Verlag, 1999).

Groehler, Otto and Moritz, Erhard, 'Zur Kaderauslese des faschistischen Geheimen Meldedienstes 1944/45', *Miltiärgeschichte*, 17 Jg. 1978.

Hilberg, Raul, *Die Vernichtung der europäischen Juden* (Frankfurt: Fischer-TB Verlag, 1999).

Hilton, Stanley E., *Hitler's Secret War in South America, 1939–1945* (Baton Rouge, LA: Louisiana State University Press, 1981).

Hinsley, F.H., and Simkins, C.A.G., *British Intelligence in the Second World War*, Vol. 4: Security and Counter Intelligence (London: H.M.S.O., 1990).

Hitler, Adolf, *Mein Kampf* (New York: Reynal and Hitchcock, 1939).

Irving, David, *Hitler's War* (London: Hodder & Stoughton, 1977).

Jahrbuch für Auswärtiges Politik (Berlin, 1940, 1941).

Johnson, David Alan, *Germany's Spies and Saboteurs* (Osceola, WI: MBI, 1998).

Jones, R.V., *Most Secret War* (London: Hamish Hamilton, 1978).

Kahn, David, *Hitler's Spies* (New York: Macmillan, 1978).

Kennedy, Brian, *Dr Hermann Goertz – A German Spy in South County Dublin*, Pub. No. 27, Foxrock Local History Club, 1989.

Keogh, Dermot, *Ireland and Europe 1919–1948* (Dublin: Gill and Macmillan, 1988).

Keogh, Dermot, 'Eamon de Valera and Hitler: An Analysis of the International Reaction Visit of the German Minister, May 1945', *Irish Studies in International Affairs*, Vol. 3, No. 1 (1989).

Keogh, Dermot, *Twentieth-Century Ireland: Nation and State* (Dublin: Gill and Macmillan, 1994).

Keogh, Dermot, *Jews in Twentieth Century Ireland: Refugees, Anti-Semitism and the Holocaust* (Cork: Cork University Press, 1999).

Kiely, David M., *Bloody Women: Ireland's Female Killers* (Dublin: Gill & Macmillan, 1999).

Kilbride-Jones, H.E., 'Adolf Mahr', *Archaeology Ireland*, Vol. 7, No. 3 (Autumn 1993), pp. 29–30.

Lee, J.J., *Ireland 1912–1985: Politics and Society* (Cambridge: Cambridge University Press, 1989).

Leuverkuehn, Paul, *Der geheime Nachrichtendienst der deutschen Wehrmacht im Kriege* (Frankfurt: Bernard and Graefe, 1957).

Liddell Hart, B.H. (ed.), *The Other Side of the Hill: Germany's Generals, Their Rise and Fall, With their own Account of Military Events, 1939–1945* (London: Cassell, 1948).

Liddell Hart, B.H., *History of the Second World War* (London: Cassell, 1970).

Littlejohn, David, *Foreign Legions of the Third Reich*, Vol. 1 (San Jose, CA: Bender Publishing, 1981).

Longford, Lord, and O'Neill, T.P., *Eamon de Valera* (London: Arrow Books, 1970).

Lucas, James, *Hitler's Enforcers* (London: Arms and Armour Press, 1996).

Lucas, James, *Kommando* (London: Arms and Armour Press, 1985).

MacEoin, Uinseann, *The IRA in the Twilight Years, 1923–1948* (Dublin: Argenta Publications, 1997).

McGarry, Fearghal, *Irish Politics and the Spanish Civil War* (Cork: Cork University Press, 1999).

McGuinness, Charles J., *Nomad* (London: Meuthuen & Company, 1934).

Manning, Maurice, *The Blueshirts* (London: Gill and Macmillan, 1970).

Manning, Maurice, *James Dillon, A Biography* (Dublin: Wolfhound Press, 1999).

Martienssen, A. *Hitler and His Admirals* (London: Secker and Warburg, 1948).

Masterman, *The Double-Cross System in the War of 1939 to 1945* (New Haven: Yale University Press, 1972).

Mollet, Ralph, *The German Occupation of Jersey, 1940–1945: Notes on the General Conditions, How the Population Fared* (St Helier: Société Jersiaise, 1954).

Molohan, Cathy, *Germany and Ireland 1945–1955: Two Nations' Friendship* (Dublin: Irish Academic Press, 1999).

Munson, Kenneth, *Bombers 1939–1945* (London: Blandford Press, 1969).

Murphy, J.A., *Ireland in the Twentieth Century* (Dublin: Gill and Macmillan, 1975).

Natterstad, J.H., *Francis Stuart* (London: Bucknell University Press, 1974).

Ní Mheara-Vinard, Róisín [Nora O'Mara], *Cé Hí Seo Amuigh?* (Dublin: Coiscéim, 1992).

Nowlan, Kevin B. and Williams, T. Desmond (eds), *Ireland in the War Years and After, 1939–57* (Dublin: Gill and Macmillan, 1969).

Ó Broin, Leon, *Just Like Yesterday, An Autobiography* (Dublin: Gill and Macmillan, 1985).

O'Callaghan, Sean, *The Jackboot in Ireland* (London: Allan Wingate Ltd., 1958).

O'Donoghue, David, *Hitler's Irish Voices: The Story of German Radio's Wartime Irish Service* (Belfast: Beyond the Pale, 1998).

Ó Drisceoil, Donal, *Censorship in Ireland, 1939–1945* (Cork: Cork University Press, 1996).

O'Duffy, Eoin, *Crusade in Spain* (Dublin: Browne and Nolan, 1938).

O'Halpin, Eunan, 'Aspects of Intelligence', *The Irish Sword*, Vol. XIX, Nos. 75 and 76 (1993–4), pp. 57–65.

O'Halpin, Eunan, *Defending Ireland* (Oxford: Oxford University Press, 1999).

O'Halpin, Eunan, 'Army, Politics and Society in Independent Ireland, 1923–1945', in T.G. Frasier and Keith Jeffery (eds), *Men, Women and War* (Dublin: Lilliput Press, 2000).

O'Halpin, Eunan, 'MI5's Irish Memories', in Brian Girvin and Geoff Roberts (eds) *Ireland in the Second World War* (London: Frank Cass, 2000).

O'Shaughnessy, Thomas, *Rest Your Head in Your Hand* (Dublin: Ward River Press, 1983).

Paine, Lauran, *The Abwehr: German Military Intelligence in World War Two* (New York: Stein and Day, 1984).

Phelan, Jim, *Ireland – Atlantic Gateway* (London: Stephen Austin & Sons, 1941).

Price, Alfred, *Luftwaffe Handbook 1939–1945* (New York: Scribner's Sons, 1977).

Quigley, Martin S., *A US Spy in Ireland* (Dublin: Marino Books, 1999).

Regan, John M., *The Irish Counter-Revolution, 1921–1936* (Dublin: Gill and Macmillan, 1999).

Roth, Andreas, *Mr Bewley in Berlin* (Dublin: Four Courts Press, 2000).

Saint Loup, *Les Hérétiques* (Paris: Presse de la Cité, 1965).

Share, Bernard, *The Emergency: Neutral Ireland, 1939–1945* (Dublin: Gill and Macmillan, 1978).

Schellenberg, Walter, *Memoiren* (Frankfurt: Verlag für Politik and Wirtschaft, 1959).

Showell, Jak P. Mallmann, *U-Boat Commanders and Crews, 1935–1945* (Wiltshire: Crowood Press, 1998).

Simpson, Christopher, *Blowback: America's Recruitment of Nazis and Its Effects on the Cold War* (London: Weidenfeld & Nicolson, 1988).

Singh, Simon, *The Code Book: The Science of Secrecy from Ancient Egypt to Quantum Cryptography* (London: Fourth Estate, 1999).

Smyllie, Robert M., 'Unneutral Neutral Éire', *Foreign Affairs*, Vol. 24, No. 2 (January 1946), pp. 316–26.

Spence, Richard, 'K.A. Jahnke and the German Sabotage Campaign in the United States and Mexico, 1914–1918', *The Historian*, 1998, pp. 89–112.

Stephan, Enno, *Geheimauftrag Irland* (Hamburg: Gerhard Stalling Verlag, 1961).

Stephan, Enno, *Spies in Ireland* (London: Macdonald, 1963).

Stephan, Enno, *Die Deutsche Keltologie und ihre Berliner Gelehrten bis 1945* (Berlin: Peter Lang, 1999).

Stuart, Francis, *Black List – Section H* (London: Penguin Books, 1996).

Sturm, Hubert, *Hakenkreuz und Kleeblatt: Irland, die Allierten und das Dritte Reich, 1933–1945* (Frankfurt a.M: Lang, 1984).

Sun Tzu, *The Art of War* (London: Hodder & Stoughton, 1981).

Taylor, James and Shaw, Warren (eds), *Penguin Dictionary of the Third Reich*, (London: Penguin, 1997).

The Trial of German Major War Criminals, Part I, 20 Nov.–1 Dec. 194 (London: His Majesty's Stationery Office, 1946).

Warlimont, Walter, *Inside Hitler's Headquarters 1939–1945* (Novaot, CA: Presidio Press, 1964).

Wighton, Charles, and Peis, Gunther, *They Spied on England* (London: Odhams, 1958).

West, Nigel, *MI5* (London: Triad Grafton, 1983).

West, Nigel, *Counterfeit Spies* (London: Triad Grafton, 1999).

World War II German Military Studies, Vol. 4, Part III; Vol. 5, Part III; and Vol. 8, Part IV (New York: Garland Publishing Inc., 1979).

Wykes, Alan, *Heydrich* (New York: Ballantine Books, 1973).

Young, Peter, 'The Way We Were', *An Cosantóir*, September 1989, pp. 33–8.

Zeutner, Christian, and Bedürftig, Friedrich (eds), *Encyclopedia of the Third Reich* (New York: Da Capo Press, 1997).

Index